Complete State Trials of the Tudor Era

Complete State Trials of the Tudor Era

James D. Taylor, Jr.

Algora Publishing
New York

Library of Congress Cataloging in Publication Control Number: —

Names: Taylor, James D., 1958- author.
Title: Complete state trials of the Tudor era / James D. Taylor Jr.
Description: New York: Algora Publishing, 2019.
Identifiers: LCCN 2018061742 (print) | LCCN 2019000592 (ebook) | ISBN 9781628943764 (pdf) | ISBN 9781628943764 (soft cover: alk. paper)
Subjects: LCSH: Trials (Political crimes and offenses)—England—History—16th century. | Trials (Political crimes and offenses)—England—History—16th century—Sources. | Great Britain—History—Tudors, 1485-1603—Sources. | LCGFT: Trial and arbitral proceedings.
Classification: LCC KD371.P6 (ebook) | LCC KD371.P6 .T39 2019 (print) | DDC 345.42/02323026409031—dc23
LC record available at https://lccn.loc.gov/2018061742

Printed in the United States

Dedicated to

Dr. Charlene H. Berry, DD, MBA
Madonna University

whose friendship, guidance and love of the arts was a constant inspiration
and will be greatly missed.

"No poet ever interpreted nature as freely as a lawyer interprets the truth."
—Jean Giraudoux, 1882-1944

Acknowledgements

I offer a special thank-you to the staff of the Harlan Hatcher Graduate Library, the Law Library and Angela Balla, Ph.D. of the Special Collections Library, all of the University of Michigan–Ann Arbor. In addition, I am grateful for the patience and assistance shown by the staff of the Purdy-Kresge Library and the Arthur Neef Law Library at Wayne State University, and the many people at the British Library who gave me their assistance and guidance.

Further appreciation goes to the staff of the Oxford University Archives, Bodleian Library, Oxford University; Marta Lomza, Archives Assistant at Oxford University Archives; Moritz College of Law–Ohio State University; John F. Schaefer Law Library–Michigan State University; and Halle Library–Eastern Michigan University.

Princeton University provided access to their collection of *A Full View of the Public Transactions in the Reign of Q. Elizabeth* in two volumes, London, 1740, and the University of Alberta gave access to their collection of *Miscellaneous State Papers from 1501 to 1726*, two volumes, London,1778. Both sets of papers were invaluable in producing the current work.

Table of Contents

Introduction

In a world that increasingly fosters the 'armchair researcher,' I must say that I remain 'old school' because I still frequent academic libraries, despite the steady progress in the digitalization of reference material. Not all works have been converted, and many of the most interesting ones still require human interaction. Indeed, many universities have decided that they cannot allow older works to be digitized because of the fragileness of the bindings and paper.

Working with archival material is a laborious process, but beyond that, separating fact from fiction is not as difficult as one may believe. It often does require a great deal of time to research a subject, an attribute lost in this age of 'instant information / instant gratification. Instant access to information has often resulted in misrepresented, diluted, and/or incorrectly interpreted facts, all too often without citing the sources used. Even the US President has found it necessary to emphasize the importance of 'fact checking,' as apparently that tiresome chore has gone out of fashion entirely. It is a shame that we have arrived at that point. I have even heard a student in a university class inform the professor that the facts she used in her report from Wikipedia were accurate 'because it said they were.'

> Where is the wisdom we have lost in knowledge?
> Where is the knowledge we have lost in information?
> — T.S. Eliot 1888–1965: *The Rock* (1934)

This work is not to be regarded as a primary study of Tudor law but as an attempt to include all known recorded state trials of the Tudor era. It is a platform where those who wish to do so can review the actual trial records of many familiar figures from that era; the actual trial records are too often omitted from their biographies.

Criminal trials were different from state trials, and they are outside the scope of this work. A fine work encompassing criminal trials is: *Criminal Trials in Scotland, from 1488 to 1624*, by Robert Pitcairn, esq., published in Edinburgh, 1833.

Many of the subjects in this book are familiar to those who are interested in Tudor history, through, most often, the rulers they served at the time. However, even though some of these individuals are the subject of their own biographies, including the events that led to their trial, the trial itself is too often not shared and rarely includes excerpts. I reviewed a recent publication in which the word 'Trial of' was included in the title, but only included short excerpts of that individual's actual trial. A well-known biographical author of recent times, known for embellishing a few facts and rather skillfully weaving them into a great story, totally excludes the trials of the individuals who were the subject of the writing.

The inducement for this book is rather two-fold: first, it is my opinion that the trials are an integral part of the individual's biographical story; second, some readers of my past publications have asked for additional information about the trials of those men and women best known to students of English Tudor history. Record keeping and trial transcripts became more frequent during the reign of Elizabeth I which is certainly a benefit.

Court trials and laws during the Tudor period were very different from those of today. In one example of many, by law if a condemned prisoner stood mute, or refused to plead, that person would be slowly pressed to death by weights placed on his chest. Furthermore, any woman convicted of counterfeiting gold or silver coin of the realm was sentenced to be drawn on a hurdle to the place of execution to be burned with fire until dead. At the time that King James I ascended the throne, thirty-one offences were punishable by death.

As will be seen in the following trials, it was very rare for those accused of a crime to have professional representation. Not all trials resulted in death, however, and though rare, it is fascinating to read how some individuals skillfully defended themselves, evading the sentence of death.

Through the evolution of trials from the times of Henry VII to Elizabeth, we can see that some refinements in laws did occur and, though the administration of justice did not become completely independent, it did improve. During this period, the decline of feudal powers and customs are noticed and attention to the forms of legal proceedings increased, though the royal prerogative became almost absolute. The sitting judges were often changed at the pleasure of the monarch and usually were inclined to favor that particular monarch. It was also common practice during this era that if a person was to suffer for political beliefs and or practices, the trial often fell under the process of treason. If a nobleman was to be humbled, it was by prosecution under an obscure or obsolete statute and if abated, it was by royal prerogative.

The following page is a sample of an original document I worked from for transcription. There is often a great deal of work involved in deciphering the text, content and archaic words used as can be seen in the example. This example is the opening of the trial for Sir Nicholas Throckmorton.

Holinshed, Raphael. *The First and Second Volumes of Chronicles, Comprising, The Description and History of England, Ireland and Scotland.* London England. 1587, pg. 1105.

Chapter 1: The Reign of Henry VII

Henry VII was born to Edmund Tudor and Margaret Beaufort on 28 January, 1457, in Pembroke, Wales, during the period of English history known as the "War of the Roses." He was a member of the House of Lancaster, who were feuding with the House of York.

In 1485, King Richard III was slain during the battle of Bosworth and Henry was proclaimed King. Soon after receiving recognition from Parliament, he married Elizabeth of York. This united the House of York with the House of Lancaster, bringing an end to the dynastic war.

Despite constant threats of being overthrown through plots and conspiracies, Henry rebuilt the royal finances by avoiding conflicts and wars, negotiating treaties of peace, and promoting trade and better relations — which in turn increased the wealth of the crown, the royal family and the kingdom. In 1503, he arranged a marriage of his daughter Margaret to James IV of Scotland, thus uniting the two countries. Furthermore, Henry arranged the marriage of his son Arthur to Catherine of Aragon in 1501, but unfortunately Arthur died suddenly and Catherine became a widow in 1502. Henry's daughter Mary eventually married Louis XII of France, but when he died, she married Charles Brandon, Duke of Suffolk.

King Henry VII made changes to his administration, including the creation of the committee of the Privy Council as an executive advisory board, and the court of the Star Chamber, thus increasing royal involvement in civil and criminal cases. Law and trade began to operate with reduced feudal constraints, and slowly a more centralized modern government evolved. Whether Henry was a great king is a topic of debate, but he certainly was successful. Unfortunately, he failed to secure general acceptance from his subjects because of the distance he maintained between them and the Crown.

Two accounts have survived of trials that occurred during the reign of King Henry VII. One is that of Sir William Stanley.There is no known actual court transcript, but there a very brief account that Mr. Bund shares in his collection of *State Trials*. Stanley was tried at Westminster, convicted, and on 16 February 1495, beheaded on Tower Hill. The second is that of Humphrey Stafford.

Humphrey Stafford

In 1486, King Henry VII received information that Lord Lovell, Humphrey Stafford and his brother Thomas Stafford had left their sanctuary in Colchester Abbey to form a rebellion against the King. Lovell was planning to raise troops in Yorkshire and the Stafford brothers would do the same in Worcestshire. The King quickly responded to the information by dispatching his uncle with a small army and possessed pardons for all who would renounce their rebellious action and return to their homes, except for Lovell. News of the approaching army caused the confederates to flee, leaving the three leaders without support or pardons. Given the quick response by King Henry, coupled with the fact that they were only minor nobles without enough wealth or outside support to fund a proper campaign, no one of importance stepped forward as a credible candidate to replace the King if he were to be deposed.

Lord Lovell escaped and eventually fled to Flanders. Humphrey and Thomas returned to their sanctuary. Thomas was eventually pardoned, but his brother Humphrey was not as fortunate.

> Humphrey Stafford being attained for treason took sanctuary at Colchester and fled from there to Worcestershire, where he raised an insurrection against the King. He then fled to Culham, in Oxfordshire, a sanctuary belonging to the Abbot of Abington, but was taken from there by force and sent to the Tower. Being brought by the constable of the Tower into the King's bench and asked what he had to say why he should not be sentenced to death, he urged that taking him from sanctuary by force was illegal, and asked for counsel to be assigned him to argue the point. This was done and the constable of the Tower not being an officer of the court of the King's bench, except to bring up the prisoner and take him back by virtue of a special writ, Stafford was during the argument committed to the custody of the Marshal of the King's bench, and when it was finished a special writ was issued to the constable of the Tower to receive him.
>
> It was argued on behalf of Stafford that Kenulph, King of the Mercians, in whose Kingdom Culham was, had given it and all its rights and privileges to the Abbey of Abington for ever; that his grant had been confirmed by Edwin, King of England, who had granted that Culham should be held free of all earthly services and that by virtue of these grants the Abbot of Abington and all his predecessors in title had always held Culham as a sanctuary, and that if any one had been taken out of sanctuary, he had always been restored.
>
> The court, after hearing this argument, directed a writ of *scire facias* to do to the abbot to prove his claim to the alleged sanctuary. The abbot appeared and pleaded the charter and letters patent, the charter of Kenulph, by an

inspeximus of Edward III, and the charter of Edwin sealed with the mark of the cross. None of the charters when produced contained an express grant of the privilege of sanctuary. Three points were then left to the court:

1. Could such a right as a protection of sanctuary in case of treason be claimed by prescription alone, no such right being expressly contained in the grant?

2. Was it necessary to produce a grant before the time of legal memory, and if so, to show its allowance within the time of legal memory?

3. Ought the judges to decide in accordance with the terms of the grants produced?

All the judges of both benches after hearing the argument were unanimously of opinion that such a right as claimed could not be prescribed for, but could only exist by express grant; for protection for treason was so great an infraction of the royal prerogative that it could not be prescribed for as other ordinary franchises could, but that it was like a grant of the goods of felons or outlaws for which the King's express grant must be shown. That there was nothing in the grant of Kenulph to show that the abbey was to be exempt from the jurisdiction of all the King's courts, it only gave the abbot jurisdiction to hold a court, and there was nothing in the pleadings to show that such a court had ever been held, nor that Stafford had been tried before the Abbot's court. So by consent of all the judges of England: "*Idem Humfridus adjudicatus fuit q'd iterum reducatur Turri London et abinde ponatur super quoddam herdillum et trahatur per medium civitatis London et sic usque Tiburnum et caput abscindatur et corpus ejus dividatur in quatuor partes et mittatur ad voluntatem Regis et Deus misereatur anime ejus &c.*"

From this case it appears that the judges were inclined to restrict the plea of sanctuary as far as possible, and only to allow it in cases where there was an expresses grant. It also shows that the sentence for treason was then practically the same as afterwards, and Tyburn was then the place of public execution. It is however to be observed that disemboweling did not from part of the sentence in this case. Mr. Pike, citing from the case of Andrew Harcla Earl of Carlisle in Edward II's reign, shows that it was then in use, and gives the following extract from the record as the reason for it. "The award of the court is that for your treason you be drawn, hanged and beheaded, that your heart, bowels, and entrails, whence came your traitorous thoughts be torn out and burnt to ashes, and that the ashes be scattered to the winds, that your body be cut into four quarters, and that one of them be hanged upon the Tower of Carlisle, another upon the Tower of Newcastle, a third upon the bridge of York, and the forth at Shewsbury, and that your head be set upon London Bridge for an example to others that they may never presume to be guilt of such treason as yours against their liege lord."

[Willis-Bund, J. W. *A Selection of Cases from the State Trials*, V-1. 42-44]

Chapter 2: The Reign of Henry VIII

What further can be said about who is undeniably the most famous of the Tudor Kings that has not already been covered in numerous editions throughout the centuries? The man himself, his lifestyle, his six wives and many of those who served during his reign are common sources for biographers. King Henry made several changes to legal definitions including nine acts which created new treasons. Four were directed to the object of asserting and maintaining the position taken by the King in opposition to the Pope, and the remaining five to maintaining the succession of the crown as it stood after the King's marriages. King Henry VIII changed the statue defining treason basically to suit his needs. Many changes had occurred to the statue during his reign and many offenders had been tried and convicted under the term just to please the King. Additions could be divided into four divisions and there are many articles to each division. I will attempt to only briefly describe the divisions.

The first was 26 Henry 8 c. 13 (1534) and was passed the following year after the King's divorce from Catherine of Aragon and the marriage with Anne Boleyn. The following four acts resulted:

> 1. Maliciously to wish, will, or desire by words or writing, or by any craft to imagine, invent, practice, or attempt any bodily harm to the King, Queen, or their heirs apparent; or
>
> 2. To deprive them, or any of them, of their dignity, title, name, or of their royal estates; or
>
> 3. Slanderously or maliciously to publish and pronounce by express writing or words, that the King or sovereign lord is an heretic, schismatic, tyrant, infidel, or usurper; or
>
> 4. Rebelliously detain or keep any of his ships, ammunition, or artillery and not to deliver them up when demanded.
>
> [Stephen, James. *A History of the Criminal Law of England.* 255-256]

The second, 28 Henry 8. c. 10 (1536) regarded the penalties of *praemunire* — asserting and maintaining the papal authority and obstinately refusing to take the oath of renunciation was defined as an act of high treason.

The third, 31 Henry 8. c. 8 (1539) provided that any proclamations by the king concerning religion were to be regarded as the same as acts of Parliament, and if any subjects traveled abroad in order to avoid the penalties enacted by those proclamations it was defined as an act of high treason.

The fourth, 35 Henry 8. c. 3. (1543) specified that the King's style was united and annexed to the imperial crown of England and it was regarded as an act of treason to imagine to deprive the king, queen, prince, or the heirs of the king's body, or any to whom the crown is or shall be limited, of any of their titles, styles, names, degrees, royal estate or regal power, annexed to the crown of England.

Though several early historians regard the reign of King Henry VIII as the most prolific period for trials of treason, chroniclers of the era have only recorded about fourteen. Of those fourteen, only half are recorded as trial transcripts. Not all the trials recorded during the reign of King Henry were for treason. It was also during this reign that 'poisoners' were, by act of Parliament, condemned to be boiled to death. This punishment was described as "not thrown into the vessel at once, but with a pulley or rope to be hanged under the armpits, and then let down into the oil by degrees; first the feet, and next the legs, and so to boil the flesh from their bones alive."

Catherine of Aragon

Catherine was born to Ferdinand of Aragon and Isabella of Castile on 16 December 1485 at Alcala de Henares, Spain. Before her fourth birthday, she was promised in marriage to Arthur, son of King Henry VII. She entered England in 1501 and married Arthur at the age of sixteen, but Arthur died of what was called 'the sweating sickness' soon after their marriage was consummated. She was then promised to Arthur's younger brother, Henry.

King Henry VII died in 1509 and the crown passed to his youngest and only living son Henry Prince of Wales. King Henry VIII married Catherine and their marriage appears to have been a happy one and she certainly tried to give Henry a son and heir. In their first nine years, she miscarried twice, delivered a stillborn daughter and two sons who died shortly after birth; the only surviving daughter was Mary, born in 1516.

King Henry was not unhappy about the birth of a princess, but he really wanted a son and heir to the throne when a young Englishwoman, Anne Boleyn, caused the King to re-evaluate the marriage to Catherine. What followed was, is, and will forever continue to be the source of biographies; novels and movies, but rarely the events within the court are shared. Much of the correspondence shared in the accounts by early historians is between King Henry and the Pope, but these are not retained here due to their length and relevance to the events of the court proceeding. Although there is no known transcript of the court proceeding of Catherine of Aragon, the following is primarily composed of early historical accounts from the period.

Public notice of a solemn hearing being given, the court was appointed to sit; the Queen choosing Archbishop Warham, and Nicholas West Bishop of Ely, doctors of the law, and John Fisher Bishop of Rochester, and Henry Standish Bishop of St. Asaph, doctors of divinity, her council, &c. according to the permission the King gave her in that behalf. The passages whereof, out of an ancient and authentic record in parchment, subscribed by the three notaries (used in this business, and remaining in the custody of that great antiquary, Sir Henry Spellman, Knight) I shall set down with as much particularity as the context of my history will suffer.

The place appointed for hearing and determining the cause was a great hall in Blackfryers in London, (commonly called the Parliament-Chamber.) The time; the 21st of May 1529. The judges, the two cardinals above-mentioned, whose commissions I have thought fit to set down at large.

Clement Bishop, servant of the servants of God, to our beloved sons Thomas Archbishop of York, Cardinal Sancta Cecilia, and Laurence Campejus Cardinal *Sancte Marie in Transtiberim*, our legates *de latere* from the Apostolical See to the Kingdom of England, health and apostolical benediction. The relation of very many persons of undoubted credit has reached our ears concerning the validity of that marriage which our beloved son in Christ Henry King of England, defender of the faith, and lord of Ireland, (a dispensation of the Apostolical See being first had) was known to have contracted and consummated with our dearly beloved daughter in Christ, Queen Katharine, from where in those parts a controversy has arisen which has so perplexed the minds of men, and held them in suspense and expectation, what justice and equity will determine in a case of so peculiar a nature and of so great moment, not yet tried in any public court of ecclesiastical judicature, that it is but necessary to proceed to some quick and speedy determination herein to avoid that danger which must unavoidably ensue upon deferring it. But since we, whom God has appointed servant of his servants, to administer to all men impartial justice in judgment and truth, are not able in our person to inquire into the truth of the fact, and examine this cause our selves considering likewise that the fact, concerning the right of which the present debate is, may with more certainty speed and expedition be inquired into and examined there than here; furthermore, being desirous that in that Kingdom which has always shown the greatest affection and obedience to the Apostolical See, all matter of dissention may be taken away, the bond of peace and love be strengthened and the blessed harmony of mutual charity, which has so many years continued, may still flourish and be conveyed down to posterity; and a decision may be made of the above-mentioned cause concerning the foresaid marriage, according to the rules of justice, judgment and truth, whereby this dispute may as it is most expedient it should obtain a firm, valid, certain and speedy conclusion and end. For these purposes, we do hereby give and grant a plenary authority, and most ample power and commission to your eminences in our own stead either both jointly or in case of unwillingness, or any other impediment, to either of you singly; that being subject to the authority and jurisdiction of no court or person whatever, nor liable to any appeal or question concerning your jurisdiction; you do hear and examine all and every thing which may relate to the validity or invalidity of the said marriage, or of any Apostolical dispensation whatever to be exhibited and produced before you and all other things, matters, circumstances, allegations and causes, which may anyways relate to and concern the said marriage and the said dispensation and that you do proceed judicially, without tumult or disturbance, summarily and plainly to examine all parties concerned and knowing in the case of the said marriage and of the validity of the said dispensation; and if it shall to you appear that any such Apostolical dispensations shall be sufficient, effectual and valid, or invalid, ineffectual, insufficient, surreptitious or repetitious, or on any account null and void, such you shall pronounce and declare finally that they are, and ought to be held; and in like manner concerning the said marriage, you shall if by either party required, define, determine, and finally sentence the same to be valid, just, lawful and firm, or on the other side unjust, invalid, and unlawful, and thereupon that it is and ought to be void and null and is therefore by you there declared invalid, unjust, unlawful, void and null, on either side pronouncing sentence, as shall appear most just according to the laws of reason and the dictates of your own consciences; and if it shall thus appear that the dispensation is invalid and the marriage null, that you do judicially, deliberately, summarily and clearly, as aforesaid, pronounce a sentence of divorce, and grant a faculty and license in the Lord to the foresaid King Henry and Queen Katherine to marry again. And we do hereby create and depute you jointly, or (if as above said any ways kindred) separately in our stead to execute, finish, fully and finally to determine all or any of the things contained in this commission in so ample a manner, that whatsoever we by our power and authority could have done in the premises, all that you are hereby enabled to do as fully and effectually. We do likewise of our own certain knowledge by our Apostolical authority and by the tenor of these presents, grant you power and authority to pronounce, sentence, and publish, if it shall to you seem convenient that the children by the first marriage as well as by the second are legitimate; and that you do confirm and establish the legitimacy of both sorts, either by censures and ecclesiastical punishments to be inflicted on the gainsayers or by way of decree and perpetual sanction, or by any other more valid and effectual method or form that can be thought of, or contrived to strengthen, and effectually support the same: any general councils, Apostolical canons, public ordinances or decrees whatsoever to the contrary notwithstanding. Given at Viterbo in the year of our Lord 1528, 6th of the Ides of June, in the fifth year of our Pontificat.

After the commission was read, our chronicles say the King was called and appeared personally in court, at whose feet the Queen prostrated herself demanding justice, right, and pity, &c. But now to come to the authentic record. I find the King and Queen were by Bishop Longland, the King's confessor, cited to appear upon 18th June next ensuing. The King (for observing his time,) gave Richard Sampson, Dean of his chapel, and John Bell, Doctor of the Decrees, a commission sealed in green wax and dated at Greenwich, 15th June; by which he constituted them his proctors, with authority to refuse or accept the court and judgment of the two cardinals, and if need were to appeal; allowing them also to substitute other proctors binding himself finally *sub hypotheca If obligatione bonorum*, to ratify what they should do. But the Queen using a shorter way, appeared in person protesting yet against the cardinals, as incompetent judges; requiring further that this her protestation might be recorded and so departed presently out of the court. This while the cardinals, who took into their commission John Longland Bishop of Lincoln; John Clark Bishop of Bath and Wells; John Islip Abbot of Westminster; and Doctor John Taylor Master of the Rolls; sent to the Queen's letters monitory; declaring if she appeared not, they would notwithstanding proceed to execute their commission; for which purpose the abovementioned Bishop of Bath and Wells was employed; but she refusing, is pronounced contumacious.

Certain articles were then put in by the legates against our King and Queen Katharine, the principal substance whereof was that Prince Arthur did marry and carnally know Queen Catharine, confirming also this marriage by cohabitation with her till his death. After which King Henry being his brother, did many the said Lady Catharine, *An. Dorn.* 1509, in *facie ecclesia*, and had children by her; which marriage yet being as well *Divino as Ecclesiastco* prohibited, and (unless it may be otherwise made good) to be reputed in its self *nullum omninu if invalidum*, had caused huge scandal both in the clergy and people of England and of many other places, insomuch that it has come to the Pope's ears, who taking notice hereof gave commission to those cardinals to hear and proceed in this business, according to the importance of it.

This being done, the Queen is cited a second time to appear; which she refusing, is pronounced again contumacious. This hindered not the court yet to proceed, and appoint Doctor Taylor, Archdeacon of Buckingham, to examine the witnesses; while themselves calling for the dispensations that were alleged in favor of this marriage, a certain bull and breve were exhibited

Against these dispensations, the following objections were used.

1. That the peace and unity between England and Spain was firm before the granting of the dispensation, which yet was alleged as a cause.

2. That the said dispensation as being grounded on this pretext, must be held surreptitious. Henry 8 being then not above 13 and consequently unable for marriage, which also if the Pope had known beforehand or that otherwise it had been represented to him, he would not have easily granted any such dispensation.

3. Because it was pretended that Henry 8 had desired the match only for maintaining peace between the two Kingdoms; whereas, (being then not above 13) he must be thought incapable of such thoughts.

4. That though this dispensation might once be thought to have his force and virtue, yet seeing the motive of granting it was grounded upon the above mentioned peace and that one of the said princes died before the solemnizing of the said marriage, the cause of the dispensation must be held void.

5. That supposing the objection of affinity were taken away by virtue of the said dispensation, yet the objection *de publica honestate* was not cleared.

6. That the breve above mentioned appears by the tenor of it to contain many falsehoods and suspicions and particularly that the stile, indicting as also many clauses and circumstances differ from the bull, so that it may be thought forged since the time of the questions moved concerning this matrimony; as by comparing them together may he manifestly gathered.

This also was urged by these reasons:

1. That in the register book of the breves at Rome, no such breve is found or any argument that such a breve was made.

2. That likewise neither in the chartophylacio, or paper-chamber of the King, no such breve is extant, nor other ways in the private treaties of the marriage, any mention is made thereof.

3. That in the date of the said breve, as it is exemplified, the year of our Lord is discrepant from the vulgar account; for whereas the stile of the court of Rome begins always from the nativity of our Lord this stems to be a year before Julius was made Pope.

All which objections were delivered to the King's Proctor that he might answer to them. Whereupon witnesses being summoned to appear July 12, Thomas Duke of Norfolk, Charles Duke of Suffolk, Thomas Marquis Dorset, George Earl of Shrewsbury, Thomas Viscount Rochfort, Robert Viscount Fitzwater, John Bishop of Carlisle, Sir David Owen, Sir John Hussey, Sir Richard Weston, Knights, with divers others presented themselves to be examined by the Archdeacon of Buckingham, above mentioned.

In the mean while, these two articles were added to the former, as serving to strengthen the objections above-mentioned.

1. That the year for Pope's breves begins Dec. 26, and the year for bulls the 25th of March.

2. That in all marriages contracted within the Kingdom of England, the form has been in words, *De prasenti, ego acripio te, &c.*

Businesses being thus ripe for examination of witnesses, the depositions of two ancient ladies who excused themselves by their infirmity from appearing in person, were publicly read.

1. The first being Mary Countess of Essex said little, but in general terms.

2. But Agnes the old Duchess of Norfolk, who was present at the marriage at St. Paul's in London, declared the age of Prince Arthur at the time of his said marriage to be about 15; and moreover did positively affirm that she saw Prince Arthur and the Lady Catharine alone in bed together, the next night after their marriage. Which therefore as also a following deposition of

the Viscounts Fitzwater may serve to answer Sander's tale, where he said a grave matron was put into the same bed with him to hinder the prince from knowing her carnally.

3. George Earl of Shrewsbury deposed the marriages was celebrated at St. Paul's, *Decimo septimo Henrici Septimi*, 1501, adding further that Prince Arthur was born at Winchester, *secundo Henrici Septimi;* and that he believed the prince knew his lady carnally, both as being able so to do as also because himself knew his wife being not sixteen.

4. William Warham Archbishop of Canterbury being examined, protests not to reveal any secrets of the Queen as being her sworn counselor. For the rest, as he answered warily to the questions propounded him concerning the validity of the match insomuch that he referred himself therein to the judges, who were to determine it; so yet he made no difficulty to confess that he approved it not at first; which also he declared not only in a contestation which he had with Richard Fox Bishop of Winchester who persuaded it, but in certain words to King Henry 7 himself, whom he told plainly that the marriage seemed to him neither honorable, nor well-pleasing to God. Adding further that because the said King Henry 7 appeared not much inclined to the marriage, that he the said deponent entreated him to persuade his son Prince Henry to protest that he would not take the Lady Catharine to wife, and that he should renew this protestation when he came to the crown; which also he the said deponent believeth was made. Notwithstanding that when the bull of dispensation was granted, that he the said deponent contradicted it no more; and that the murmuring of the people on that occasion was quieted till the King's conscience being troubled, revived it again.

5. Sir William Thomas, Knight, deposed Prince Arthur and the Lady Catharine lived five months partly about London and partly at Ludlow, in household together as man and wife and that he heard Sir William Wodal, who was at the prince's christening, pray that he was above 15 at the time of his marriage and the Lady Catharine elder.

6. Sir Anthony Poynes, Knight, deposed that Prince Arthur was above 15 at the time of his marriage.

7. Thomas Marquis Dorset, deposed he saw a register of the nativity of the King's children; by which he found the Prince Arthur born September 20, 1486, and that at the time of his marriage which was upon a Sunday, in November 1501, he was of a good and sanguine complexion and able as he supposed for that purpose.

8. Robert Viscount Fitzwater deposed the prince was then about 15, and Queen Catharine elder; and that the next day after being in bed together, (which he remembered after they entered to have been solemnly blessed) he waited at breakfast on Prince Arthur, where Maurice St. Johns did carve, and he the Lord Fitzwater gave drink at which time the said Maurice demanding of the prince how he had done that night? The prince answered, I have been in Spain this night.

9, 10, 11. Thomas Lord Darcy, William Lord Montejoy, and Henry Guideford, Knight of the Garter said little but by way of public report.

12. Charles Duke of Suffolk, deposed that he was in the Bishop of London's palace the morrow next following the day of marriage and that he waited there upon the prince at breakfast, confirming moreover in effect the words of Maurice St. John, before set down. Furthermore, he added that the Shrovetide following the marriage, (which was in November preceding) the said prince began to decay and grow feeble in body; which grew, as the said St. John related, by reason the said prince lay with the Lady Catharine.

13. David Owen, deposed that Prince Arthur was born at Winchester, *secundo Henrici Septimi;* which he knew, because he was at the christening.

14. Thomas Duke of Norfolk, Lord Treasurer of England, deposed that he being the day of the marriage in the Bishop of London's palace, and the morrow after at the prince's breakfast heard the prince's words to Maurice Saint John when he said he had been that night in the midst of Spain; by which words as also because Prince Arthur was a gentleman of a good complexion and nature and above 15, he believes that he carnally knew his lady; because himself also at the same age did carnally know and use and he believes this the rather, that he heard from credible persons that the said Prince Arthur did lie with the said Lady Catharine five or six nights afterwards.

15. Anthony Willoughby, Knight, deposed that being the morrow after the marriage in the prince's privy-chamber, the said prince spoke afore divers witnesses these words, 'Willoughby, give me a cup of ale, for I have been this night in the midst of Spain.' After which he said, 'Masters, it is a good pastime to have a wife;' which words he repeated also divers other times. Moreover, he heard say they lay at Ludlow together the Shrovetide next following.

16. Nicholas Bishop of Ely, said he could depose nothing concerning the *carnalis copula*, but that he doubted of it because the Queen often *sub testimonio conscienlia sua* said to this deponent that she was never carnally known of Prince Arthur, though otherwise he must confess them both to be *legitima atutis* at the time of their marriage. He doubted further whether the cardinals were competent judges, an appeal being made from them.

17. Rd. Sacheverel, Knight, deposed the people said commonly that it was unfit one brother should marry the other brother's wife.

18. Thomas Viscount Rochefort, deposed that he heard divers of Prince Arthur's followers confirm the words he used, of his having been in Spain the night of his marriage. Moreover, he heard say that King Henry 8 was persuaded by his confessor, about two years since, to abstain from the bed of the Lady Catharine, lest he should offend his conscience.

19, 20, 21, 22, 23. Sir Rd. Weston and Sir John Hussey, Knights, deposed the age of King Henry 8 was 38 upon the eve of the feast of Saint Peter and Saint Paul last; which Viscount Rochefort also confirmed saying the place of his birth was Greenwich and the year was 1491, and day the 28th of June;

which Robert Viscount Fitzwater confirmed also, adding that King Henry 7 died two days before the feast of Saint George, 20 years since; with whom David Owen, servant and counselor to King Henry 7 agreed, save only that he said it was three days before the feast.

24. Thomas Duke of Norfolk, deposed that Pedro de Ayala or Allen and Doctor de Puebla, ambassadors from Spain, were much in favor heretofore with Henry 7, and that Henry 7 died before the marriage betwixt his son Prince Henry and the Princess Catharine and Queen Isabel or Elizabeth her mother died also before that time.

25. Win. Warham, Archbishop of Canterbury and Counselor to Henry 7 and Henry 8, for 30 years last past, deposed that he conceived Henry 8 to be under 13 at the time of dispensation granted; because King Henry his father told him that he was *impubes* after that time. Whereupon this deponent replied to the King that any protestation he should then make, would be of no force and therefore be should make it again one or two days after his coming to *annos pubertatis.*

26, 27. Charles Duke of Suffolk and Thomas Marquis Dorset, examined again, said little but what was formerly set down.

28. Pedro Mates, *Utriusque Juris Doctor*, native of Barcelona in Spain, who had lived in the court of Rome 30 years in *exercitio causarum*, deposed that the date of years there is computed after three divers manners; so that judgments, contracts, and last wills, bear date from the nativity *25 Decembris; Litere Apostolicea sub plumbo 25 of March; Litera Apostolicae per Breve sub annulo piscatoris, cera rubeae impresso scribuntur simpliciter & absolute absque expressione ipsius Domini aut Navitatis, aut Incarnationis, sed solum Anno M. D. &c.* Yet so that he conceived it began always a *Nativitate, sciticel 25 Decembris*; neither does he know anything to the contrary, except the Pope's secretary alter the stile.

29. Nicolaus Rusticus of Lucca in Italy, said that *Annus Domini in Brevibus Apostolicus* is computed from the nativity of our Lord.

30, 31, 32, 33, 34, 35, 36. Thomas Viscount Rochefort, Henry Guilford, Knight, Thomas Marquis Dorset, Thomas Duke of Norfolk, William Falke *Notarius Publicus*, John Taverner and John Clamport, being examined, deposed that the forms of marriages are always in *verbis de praesenli*, in England.

37. The Lady Elizabeth, wife to Viscount Fitzwater, deposed that she saw the Lady Catharine and Prince Arthur in bed together, which was blest and that she left them alone together.

Hereupon the depositions were published, and the King's Proctor summoned to receive those acts and writings he delivered into the court; but he not appearing, is pronounced contumacious.

The commissioners yet proceeded to require the sight of the Archiva and record concerning this business; for which purpose Thomas Wriothesly and Thomas Tong King of Arms, had been employed, these men certified that Prince Arthur died in the castle of Ludlow the 2nd of April, 1502, and that his brother Henry was born the 28th of June, 1491, and that the marriage betwixt Prince Arthur and the Lady Catharine was the 14th of November, 1501. This being done, a deposition of Richard Fox, Bishop of Winchester taken by Doctor Woolman, April 5th and 6th, 1527, was read. The most substantial part whereof was that he conceived Doctor Puebla did first motion this match, and that more than one bull was impetrated for dispensing therewith whereof two remained in England, one or two were extant in Spain, but all of the same tenor and gotten without as King the consent of Henry 8. Furthermore, that he did not remember that Henry 8 when he came to age, did expressly consent to, or dissent from the intended marriage, yet that he believed that a protestation was made in the name of Henry 8 to this effect. That notwithstanding any contracts or tokens mutually sent, or cohabitation in the house of King Henry 7, he would not hold himself bound to ratify this act done in his nonage; and that this protestation is to be found *inter protocolla Magistri Ryden*, then clerk to the council, before whom it was made. As for the person by whom this protestation was made, *Coram Magistro Ryden Notario publico; credit quod vel ipsemet, vel Magister Thomas Ratha tunc Secretarius Domini Resis, & postea Episcopus Dunelm vel Mr. Doctor West tunc consiliarius ejusdem domini Regis & nunc Episcopus Eliene. Fecit eandem protestutionem nomine domini nostri Regis Henrici Octavi moderni; prasentibus tunc ibidem Comite de Surrey tunc Thesaurario Anglia & posiea Duce Norfolciae ac domino Doctore Peohebla, & coram stepe-dicta clarissima Domina Catharina. ut recolit, ac infra Aedes Episcopi Dunelm. Vuigariter nuncupat.* Duresme-place. Adding further, that our King was not present there, that he remembers. Furthermore, that upon conference had between Henry 7 and himself, he found it was the intention of that King that his son Henry should marry the said Lady Catharine, although he deferred the solemnization of this intended matrimony, by reason of some discord which was at that time between him and the King of Spain, for the calling back of the dowry. He added moreover that King Henry intended not (that he knew) to marry the mother of Charles 5, but his aunt Margaret, Duchess of Savoy.

This examination being complete and set down by Andrew Smith, notary, the said Doctor Woolman required him to subscribe his hand which was refused by the said bishop, both because he was blind of both eyes, as that be was not admitted to take any counsel or advice about it. But Doctor Woolman pressing him on the King's part, that he should subscribe his name, be at last assented out of the reverence he bore to the King and that he never contravened him in anything. Whereupon he subscribed his name April 8, the year above mentioned, being 1527. After which also another instrument of this tenor was produced.

King Henry's protestation against the match before its consummation.

In the name of God, amen. In the presence of you the reverend father in Christ, by the grace of God, and favor of the Apostolical See, Richard Lord Bishop of Winchester; I Henry, Prince of Wales, Duke of Cornwall, and Earl of Chester, do say, allege, and by this writing set forth; that although in my minority and being not as yet arrived to ripeness of age for giving my consent, I have *de facto* contracted a marriage with the most serene Lady Catharine, daughter of the King of Spain, which contract, although it be of itself invalid, imperfect and of no effect and force, by reason of my said minority; yet because this contract when I shall come to age and years of consent, may appear and seem valid and confirmed by tacit consent, mutual cohabitation, giving and receiving tokens and gifts or any other determinate way; for these causes, I the foresaid Henry Prince of Wales now nearly arrived to maturity of age and being just at years of consent, do hereby protest that by anything said or to be said, done, or to be done, I do not intend to ratify, confirm, or make valid the said pretended contract of marriage; but by these presents, being thereto moved neither by force, craft, nor entreaty, but voluntarily, freely, and without any compulsion whatever, I do renounce and disclaim the said contract; and do resolve and intend by the most powerful means in the most significant terms, and most effectual manner I can to renounce, disclaim, and dissent from the said pretended marriage contract, as the same is hereby renounced, disclaimed, and dissented from. And I further protest, that by any word, deed, action or behavior, said or done by myself or by any other in my name, or to be said, acted, done or performed by any person at any time, or in any manner whatsoever, I do not consent to the said marriage contract or receive the said Lady Catherine as my lawful spouse and wife; to all which premises, this my testimony is given, set forth and published by me, Henry Prince of Wales.

While these things passed thus in England, the Queen found means to inform the Lady Margaret, Regent of the Low-Countries, of the whole process who thereupon sends word of it to Charles and Ferdinand, entreating them to assist their aunt; which they accorded dispatching their orators to the Pope, whom also the Queen constituted her proctors in the court of Rome; giving them commission to tender to the Pope a copy of the bull, breve, and her declaration that she was never carnally known by Prince Arthur. Shortly after which, the said orators in the Queen's name, made a protestation against the two legates now in England (every page subscribed with Queen Catharine's own hand) entreating the Pope to evoke the cause, to annul the proceedings in England, to warn the King to desist his suit or at least to try it at Rome, &c. or otherwise that they would seek their remedies elsewhere. The Pope being thus pressed at Rome and having now concluded the treaty with the emperor at Barcelona, July 3rd, 1529, about three weeks before the cause was prorogued by Campejus, could no longer either with safety of his person or dignity, favor our King; so that what excuses so ever (in the frequent dispatches he made about this time) were given to our King, yet were they little more than compliment and evasion, till finally declaring himself more openly for the emperor, he signed an avocation of the cause to himself inhibiting further proceedings, under great penalties. And herein (as our agents did observe) the Pope's principal ministers did not a little concur that the benefit of deciding thereof might fall upon them. In vain therefore did our agents (being Sir Gregory Casalis and Dr. Bennet) both by representing the defection of our King from the Roman See and the mine of the Cardinal of York, labor to stay these proceedings. For the inhibition was brought into England about the beginning of September, the King then being in his progress; and because it was sent to the Queen to make her benefit of it, the King (by Stephen Gardiner now his secretary) sends to Wolsey to persuade the Queen to let this inhibition (or, as he calls it, a citatory letter) sleep, it containing matter prejudicial to his person and not to be published to his subjects and that it will be sufficient for the cessation of the process that the Pope by letter to Wolsey (July 19) has signified his avocation of the cause. Nevertheless, if the Queen will needs have the inhibition executed, then that it should be privately executed upon the two legates, (rather than be divulged in Flanders;) which it seems was done accordingly. Howbeit, shortly after the avocation was granted, the Pope conceiving that the censures and penalties mentioned in the inhibition would not be well taken by our King, dispatched a breve to him of August 20, which for the better satisfaction of the reader, I have thought fit to transcribe out of the original and insert here.

The Pope's breve to the King of England.

Most dearly beloved son in Christ, health, &c. A cause heretofore depending between your highness and our dearly beloved daughter in Christ, Catherine Queen of England, of and concerning your marriage contract; we, at the earnest request of your ambassadors, committed the said cause to be determined by our beloved sons, Thomas Lord Bishop and Cardinal Sanctae Cecilia, and Laurence Cardinal Sanctae Maria in *transtiberim* our *legats de latere* from the Apostolical See in which cause perhaps some process has been made; since which at the instance of our most dear son in Christ, Charles most Catholic King of Spain and elected emperor, and his most Catholic Queen, as well as for some other reasons us thereto moving, we ordered the said cause to be brought before our own selves and reserved the determination and decision thereof to ourselves, and the sacred college of our most venerable brethren their eminences the cardinals; on which account perhaps an inhibition has been given. Now whereas we have heard that this inhibition has been executed, and that therein are mentioned several censures and penalties; we whose intention it never was nor is to subject your highness's person who have so well deserved of us and of the Apostolical See, to any censures or penalties whatsoever; do hereby signify to your highness that those censures were inserted into the said inhibition by our judge or commissary without our knowledge, and contrary to our inclination which censures therefore and penalties so far as they may concern your own person, we do hereby rescind, declaring them to be null, of no power, efficacy or validity. As for the cause itself, we will that it be suspended till Christmas-day next ensuing and it is by these presents till then suspended. And herein we have done all that we could with a safe conscience in favor and affection to your highness that as we are assured that you have for conscience sake propounded your case, you may have time duly and carefully to consider an affair of so great moment and importance as this is and thereby settle it without the vexation and trouble which suits of law engender and produce, to the great comfort and quiet of your mind; wherein you shall never fail of our aid and assistance. In the mean time, we do exhort your majesty in the Lord, that for the sake of conscience, you would not leave the Queen, but till these things shall be determined, comfort and cherish her with the love and affection of a husband as we trust your highness of your great piety and goodness will do. Given at Rome Aug. 29, 1529, in the sixth year of our pontificat.

Sentence of divorce pronounced against Queen Catharine.

Queen Catharine was now at Ampthil in Bedfordshire; and because it concerned the King to acquaint her with the causes of this second marriage, he sent again some grave persons to prepare her thereto wishing her together to submit. But she persisting still, Cranmer, Archbishop of Canterbury, cited her to appear at Dunstable being six miles off. Where for deciding this business, he appointed a court to be held; and with him came the Bishops of London, Winchester, (being Stephen Gardiner) Bath, Lincoln, and many great clerks. Their first proceeding was a citation to our King to put away his wife Catharine, protesting otherwise that they would censure him. But the records which I have seen, mention only that Cranmer demanded and obtained leave of the King to determine the matter, since it caused much doubt among the common people and fears of great inconveniences in matter of succession. The court being now held and the Queen summoned 15 days together, without yet that she appeared, the archbishop having first pronounced her contumacious, proceeds to sentence, which also he caused to be publicly read in the chapel of our lady in the priory of Dunstable before two notaries, and then sent to the King, desiring further to know his mind concerning his second marriage, as soon as he had advised with his council.

The tenor of the sentence was this.

In the name of God, Amen. We, Thomas by divine permission Archbishop of Canterbury, primate of all England, and legate of the Apostolical See, in a certain cause of enquiry of and concerning the validity of the marriage contracted and consummated between the most potent and most illustrious prince, our sovereign Lord Henry 8, by the grace of God, King of England and France, defender of the faith, and Lord of Ireland, and the most serene Princess Catharine, daughter of his most Catholic majesty, Ferdinand King of Spain, &c. of glorious memory; we proceeding according to law and justice in the said cause, which has been brought judicially before us in virtue of our office, and which for some time has lain under examination, as it still is being not yet finally determined and decided, having first seen all the articles and pleas which have been exhibited and set forth of her part, together with the answers made thereto and given in on the part of the said most illustrious and powerful Prince Henry 8; having likewise seen, and diligently inspected the information's and depositions of many noblemen and other witnesses of unsuspected veracity exhibited in the said cause; having also seen, and in like manner carefully considered not only the censures and decrees of the most famous universities of almost the whole Christian world, but likewise the opinions and determinations both of the most eminent divines and civilians, as also the resolutions and conclusions of the clergy of both provinces of England in convocation assembled, and many other wholesome instructions and doctrines which have been given in and laid before us concerning the said marriage. Having farther seen, and with like diligence inspected all the treaties and leagues of peace and amity on this account, entered upon and concluded between Henry 7, of immortal fame, late King of England and the said Ferdinand of glorious memory, late King of Spain, having besides seen and most carefully weighed all and every of the acts, debates, letters, processes, instruments, writs, arguments, and all other things which have passed, and been transacted in the said cause at any time, in all which thus seen and inspected, our most exact care in examining and our most mature deliberation in weighing them, has by us been used reserving herein whatsoever of right ought to be by us reserved. Furthermore the said most illustrious and most powerful prince King Henry 8, in the aforementioned cause, by his proper proctor having appeared before us, but the said most serene Lady Catharine in contempt absenting herself, (whose absence may the divine presence always attend) by and with the advice of the most learned in the law, and of persons of most eminent skill in divinity, whom we have consulted in the premises, we have found it our duty to proceed to give our final decree and definitive sentence in the said cause, which accordingly we do in this manner. Because by acts, warrants, deductions, propositions, exhibitions, allegations, proofs and confessions, articles drawn up, answers of witnesses, depositions, information's, instruments, arguments, letters, writs, censures, determinations of professors, opinions, councils, assertions, affirmations, treaties and leagues of peace, processes and other matters in the said cause as is above-mentioned before us laid, had, done, exhibited, and respectively produced, as also from the same and sundry other reasons, causes and considerations, manifold arguments, and various kinds of proof of the greatest evidence, strength and validity, of which in the said cause we have fully and clearly informed ourselves, we find and with undeniable evidence and plainness, see that the marriage contracted and consummated as is aforesaid between the said most illustrious prince King Henry 8, and the most serene Lady Catharine, was and is null and invalid and that it was contracted and consummated contrary to the law of God. Therefore we Thomas, Archbishop, primate and legate aforesaid, having first called upon the name of Christ for direction herein, and having God altogether before our eyes, do pronounce sentence and declare for the nullity and invalidity of the said marriage, decreeing that the said pretended marriage always was, and still is null and invalid, that it was contracted and consummated contrary to the will and law of God, that it is of no force or obligation, but that it always wanted, and still wants the strength and sanction of law, and therefore we sentence, decree and declare, that it is not lawful for the said most illustrious and powerful Prince Henry 8, and the said most serene Lady Catharine to remain in the said pretended marriage; and we do separate and divorce from each other the said most illustrious and most powerful King Henry 8, and the said most illustrious Lady Catharine, in as much as they contracted and consummated the said pretended marriage *de facto* and not *de jure*, and that they so separated and divorced, are absolutely free from all marriage bond, with regard to the foresaid pretended marriage, we do pronounce, decree and declare by this our definitive sentence and final decree, which we now give and by the tenor of these presents publish. May 23, 1533.

The King hereupon (according to the decree of the last Parliament) commands strictly Catharine should no more be called Queen, but princess dowager, and widow of Prince Arthur.

The sentence was to this effect.

That Pope Clement the seventh with the consent of his other brethren the cardinals assembled together in the consistory, sitting there in the throne of justice calling upon the name of Christ, and having God only before his eyes, does pronounce, define, and declare in the cause and causes between his dear daughter Catharine Queen of England appealing to the see apostolate, and his beloved son Henry the 8th, King of England, concerning the validity and invalidity of the matrimony heretofore contracted between them, and yet depending in the consistory court of the said Pope Clement; that the said matrimony always has and still does stand firm and canonical, and that the issue proceeding or which shall proceed of the same, stands and shall stand lawful and legitimate; and that the aforesaid Henry, King of England, is and shall be bound and obstruct to the matrimonial society and cohabitation with the said Lady Catharine his lawful wife and Queen, to hold and maintain her with such love and princely honor as becomes a loving husband and his Kingly honor to do. Also that the said Henry King of England, if he shall refuse so to perform and accomplish all and singular the premises, in all effectual manner is to be condemned and compelled hereto by all remedies of the law, and enforced, according as we do condemn, compel, and enforce him so to do, providing, that all molestations and refusals whatsoever made by the said King Henry against the said Queen Catharine, upon the invalidity of the said marriage, to have been and be judged unlawful and unjust; and the said King from henceforth for ever to hold his peace, and not to be heard in any court hereafter to speak touching the invalidity of the said matrimony like as we also do here will and charge him to hold his peace, and do put him to perpetual silence herein; willing moreover and adjudging the said King Henry to be condemned and presently here we do condemn him in the expenses on the said Queen Catharine's behalf here in our court, expended and employed in traversing the aforesaid cause, the valuation of which expenses we reserve to ourselves to be limited and taxed, as we shall judge meet hereafter. We do so pronounce, I, at Rome in our Apostolical palace publicly in our consistory, 25th March 1534. Blosius.

The King's marriage, with Catharine made void by act of Parliament.

In the year 1534, 23 Hen. 8, upon the suit of Parliament to the King for the establishing of the succession to the crown (the uncertainty whereof has caused heretofore great division and bloodshed in this realm) it was enacted that the King's marriage with the Lady Catharine, wife and carnally known to his brother Prince Arthur (as was lawfully proved before Thomas, Archbishop of Canterbury) as contrary to God's law, shall be held void and she styled no more Queen, but dowager to Prince Arthur, and the matrimony with Queen Anne shall be taken for firm and good; and the issue thence procreate be accounted lawful; the inheritance of the crown to belong to the same, in manner following, viz. First to the eldest son begotten by the King on Queen Anne, and to the heirs of the said son lawfully begotten, and for default of such heir then to the second son, &c. and if Queen Anne decease without issue male, then the crown to descend to the son and heir of the King's body lawfully begotten and the heirs of the said son lawfully begotten, and for a default of such issue to the second son in like manner, &c. And for default of sons, that then the crown shall belong to the issue female of the King by Queen Anne; and first to the first begotten the Princess Elizabeth, and to the heirs of her body lawfully begotten. And for default of such issue then to the second daughter in like sort, &c. And for default of all such issue, to the right heirs of the King's highness. It was ordained that this act shall be proclaimed before May next throughout the Kingdom. And all persons of age shall swear to accept and maintain the same. They who refuse the oath standing guilty of misprision of high treason; and they who speak or write against the marriage or succession here established wished to be adjudged traitors.

Two bishops sent to acquaint Queen Catharine with this act.

The Pope having proceeded in those rigorous terms with our King, (as is formerly mentioned) and for more authorizing his sentence, made the emperor executor thereof, hoped now to have his revenge, but he was deceived. For though the emperor did gladly accept this overture for his aunt Queen Catharine's sake, and the hope he had to dispose of the Princess Mary, as *inheritrix* of the crown, yet as he had deeper designs in aspiring to the conquest of Italy and indeed to an universal monarchy, he was no less glad of the occasion to take off our King from the Pope howsoever each side prepared for war. The emperor's intention was to give the Princess Mary to some one who upon her title might pretend to the crown, whom therefore he promised to second. Our King and Francis not ignorant of the Emperor's designs, agreed on the other side partly to join with the Duke of Gueldres for invading the adjoining territories to France, and partly to renew the ancient claim to Navarre and assail the emperor in those quarters. Yet neither did that of the emperor take effect because there was no means to recover the person of the princess Mary. Nor this of our King's because Francis employing his thoughts wholly on the affairs of Italy did not think fit to comply openly with one against whom the Pope had fulminated. Howbeit, our King for defense of his authority and second marriage, neglected not to obtain from the Parliament a confirmation thereof and of the succession in that line, sending also to Queen Catharine at Bugden near Huntingdon in sequence thereof, Edward Lee, Archbishop of York, and Cuthbert Tonstall, Bishop of Duresme, to signify to her that he took it ill that she still claimed the title of Queen, &c. the passages of which negotiation I have thought fit to transcribe out of the original record as containing many material points concerning the whole frame of the business.

Their letter to the King was this:

Please it your highness to understand that this day we repaired to the princess dowager, and there I, the Archbishop of York, for an introduction to declare to her the effect of our commission, said to her;

1. That your highness had often sent to her divers of your council, and amongst them me, one, to declare to her the invalidity of the marriage between your highness and her;

2. That carnal knowledge which is the great key of the matter, is sufficiently proved in the raw as also some that were of the council do avow;

3. That upon proof so sufficiently made of carnal knowledge; divorce was made between your highness and her;

4. That upon divorce made by lawful sentence, she was admonished to leave the name of a Queen and not to account or call herself hereafter your highness wife;

5. How that after your highness was discharged of the marriage made with her, you contracted new marriage with your dearest wife Queen Anne;

6. That for so much as thanked be God, fair issue is already sprung of this marriage, and more likely to follow by God's grace that the whole body of your realm gathered together in Parliament has for the establishment of this issue, by your dearest wife Queen Anne, and the succession coming of this marriage, made acts and ordinances against all them that would in word or in deed withstand them and that for these purposes, we were sent to her grace, to the intent she might understand the true purpose of these acts with the pains; lest by ignorance she should fall in any of them, and so I declared the act. Which thing being thus declared to her, she being therewith in great choler and agony, and always interrupting our words to the aforesaid points, made these answers following.

To the first, that she took the matrimony between your highness and her for good, and so always would account herself to be your highness's lawful wife in which opinion she said she would continually, till death, persist.

To the second, she utterly denied that ever carnal knowledge was had between her and Prince Arthur and that she would never confess the contrary and with loud voice when mention was made of that point, she said they lied falsely that so said.

To the third, she answered that she is not bound to stand to that divorce made by my Lord of Canterbury, whom she called a shadow and that although he had given sentence against her, yet the Pope had given sentence with her, whom she took for Christ's vicar, and therefore would always obey him his faithful daughter.

To the fourth, she answered that she would never leave the name of a Queen and she would always take herself for your highness wife.

To the fifth, she said that this marriage made after her appeal, which she made by your highness leave and consent, is of no value.

To the sixth, she answered that she is not bound to the acts of the Parliament, for so much as she is your highness's wife and not subject to your highness, and also because these acts were made by your highness subjects in your favor, your highness being party in this matter; with divers other unseeming words.

To which her answer, I the Bishop of Duresme replying, forasmuch as she had said in her communication that both I and the residue of her council had always showed to her that her matter is just and good; I said that all the question whereupon we were consulted at such time as the legates were here, depended only upon the validity of the bull and breve, albeit I said that since that time divers other questions had risen and been debated by many universities, the chief of Christendom of which one was Bononia, the Pope's own town; and by them concluded that after the decease of the brother, who had had carnal knowledge with his wife, the brother living might not marry the said wife by any dispensation of the Pope because it was forbidden by the law of God. And forasmuch as the Pope (albeit the said conclusions, have been by learned men sent from your highness, declared to him) never made answer to maintain lawfully his power to the contrary, but rather in confirmation of the opinions of the said universities, said at Marseilles, that if your grace would send a proxy there, he would give the sentence for your highness against her, because that he knew that your cause was good and just, which his saying was accordingly also to an *Epistle Decretal* sent here by the Legate Campejus, whereof the effect was that if marriage and carnal knowledge were had betwixt prince Arthur and her, the legates should pronounce for the divorce according whereto proofs were brought in before the legates and also since before the convocations of this realm and the Bishop of Canterbury, and by them allowed and approved as sufficient and lawful whereby does plainly appear that the sentence given by the Pope to the contrary was not viable because it pronounced the dispensation, (which he had no power to grant, seeing it was against the law of God) to be good; therefore I had now changed my former opinion and exhorted her to do the semblable, and forbear to usurp any more the name of a Queen; specially for that the sentence she stuck so greatly to was given after your grace's appeal to the council general and intimate to the Pope, so that it could not be viable. And that if she should so do, she might thereby attain much quietness for herself and her friends, and that she being conformable so to do, I doubted not but your highness would suffer her to have about her such persons as should be to her pleasure and entreat her as your graces most dearest sister with all liberty and pleasure with divers other things which by her much interlacing I was forced to answer to. The specialties whereof, and of her obstinacy that she will in no wise be for any peril of her life or goods relinquish the name of a Queen, we do remit for tediousness to the wisdoms and discretions of my Lord of Chester, Mr. Almoner, and Mr. Redell, who like as they have very substantially, wisely, and effectually ordered themselves in the execution of the premises, so we doubt not, but that they will sincerely report the circumstances of the same to your highness whom we beseech almighty God long to preserve in much honor to his pleasure, and your hearts desire. At Huntington, the 21 day of May. By your highness most humble subjects, servants and chaplains, Edovard Ebor, Cuthbert Duresme.

Queen Catharine, or (as the King commanded her to be called) the Princess Dowager, finding now no assistance but spiritual from the Pope, nor reparation procured by the emperor but uncertain and slow, and for the rest grieving at the prosperity and fruitfulness of Queen Anne (now with child again, whereof yet she miscarried) fell into her last sickness at Kimbolton in Huntingdonshire in the 50th year of her age and the three and thirtieth since her coming into England; during which time, though comforted by the King and Eustachio Chapuys, doctor of both laws and ambassador resident from Charles, she fell so desperately ill as finding death now coming, she caused a maid attending on her to write to the King to this effect:

My most dear lord King and husband; the hour of my death now approaching, I cannot choose but, out of the love I bear you, advise you of your soul's health which you ought to prefer before all considerations of the world or flesh whatsoever. For which yet you have cast me into many calamities and yourself into many troubles. But I forgive you all; and pray God to do so likewise. For the rest I commend to you Mary our daughter, beseeching you to be a good father to her, as I have heretofore desired. I must entreat you also to respect my maids and give them in marriage, which is not much they being but three; and to all my other servants, a year's pay besides their due, lest otherwise they should be unprovided for. Lastly, I make this vow that mine eyes desire you above all things. Farewell. Besides which letter she dictated another to Eustachius, desiring him to procure that the emperor might put our King in mind of her request when otherwise he forgot it; and soon afterwards she died.

[*Cobbett's Complete Collection of State Trials. V1.* 299-367]

Thomas Wolsey

Thomas Wolsey was born circa 1474, in Ipswich, Sussex, England to a father often believed to have been a butcher. Nevertheless, his father was able to provide a good education for him and Thomas later attended Magdalen College, Oxford and ordained about 1498 then served as chaplain to King Henry VII.

Thomas Wolsey began to rise in power with the ascension of Henry VIII to the throne. In 1513, the King appointed him the Dean of York and the following year he was created Archbishop of York and Bishop of Lincoln. In 1514 the Pope appointed him as a cardinal and very shortly after, King Henry VIII appointed him Lord Chancellor. Wolsey is credited with contributing a great deal to the reformation of the English legal system resulting in a modernized and efficient system. With the reduction in power of the church, courts were replaced by the power of the Star Chamber. For approximately fourteen years, his authority was unchallenged. He served in several capacities including diplomatic assignments addressing state business and earned a considerable amount of control of England's foreign policy.

Cardinal Wolsey certainly benefited from the King's generosity and displayed his wealth by constantly adding to his homes in Whitehall and Hampton Court. He also founded Cardinal College at Oxford (now Christ's Church), but early historians point out that his contemptuousness was a major contributing factor to his declining popularity. This also increased when King Henry VIII requested Cardinal Wolsey to use his influence with the Pope to help him gain an annulment of his marriage with Catherine of Aragon, allowing the King to remarry. However, Wolsey was unable to fulfill the King's request and very quickly fell from the King's favor. In September 1529, Wolsey was dismissed as chancellor and by October he no longer held the position as Bishop of Winchester. His deteriorating power was exasperated by the influential Boleyn family and King Henry ordered his arrest.

Proceedings against Thomas Wolsey, Cardinal and Archbishop of York, upon a praemunire, and for other offences: 20 Hen. VIII. A.D. 1529.

Cardinal Wolsey being now divested of his late power (wherein he had the glory, in some sort to have been superior to his King) and for the rest being left alone, and exposed not only to a general hatred, but to the private machinations of the present and future Queen, became sensible of his ill estate; though yet he did not believe himself so near his overthrow as it appeared afterwards. But what could he hope for when such puissant enemies did procure his destruction? Therefore though he received some advices from Rome which might argue an ear rather than a power for his conservation, yet in effect what secret intelligence so ever passed between the Pope and him, came to the emperor first and after to Queen Catharine, who cunningly caused it to be whispered into the King's ears by some more indirect ways than it could possibly be imagined to proceed from her. Likewise Mistress Anne Boleyn having learned from some of the King's wisest and gravest counselor's diver's malformations of the cardinal was so far from disguising them, that she even misinterpreted his better actions. Edmund Campion adds to these reasons that Sir Francis Bryan being in Rome, did by the means of a familiar one who kept the Pope's papers obtain a letter of the cardinal's which wrought his ruin in this manner having first showed her the cardinal's hand-writing and then corrupted her, this courtesan so dexterously performed the rest, as upon pretence of visiting her servant in his study, she conveyed away this letter and gave it Bryan who failed not immediately to send it to our King. Which relation of Campion, though I will not contradict, yet I suppose to be the more improbable that I find by original dispatches Bryan was come from Rome before any argument of the King's disfavor to the cardinal appeared. Howsoever the way the King took to overthrow him was merely legal, though approaching to *Summum Jus*, after most men's opinion. In the carriage whereof yet that secrecy was used that the cardinal did not or perchance out of greatness of mind, would not take notice of what was intended against him. So that though the bill or indictment was put in (at the beginning of Michaelmas term) yet did he ride that day to the Chancery with his accustomed pomp. Of which our King being advertised, thought fit to forbid him the place; as thinking it indecent, that a man who was upon terms of conviction should administer that high charge. Therefore the Dukes of Norfolk and Suffolk were sent the 18th of October to require the great seal of him. But the cardinal instead of rendering it disputed their authority alleging the place of Lord Chancellor was by the King's letters patents given him during life. The two dukes hereupon returned to court bringing the next day the King's letters to the cardinal, who having read them, delivered immediately the great seal; in sequence thereof, also submitting himself to the King who commanded him to leave York-Place and simply to depart to Asher, a country-house near Hampton-Court belonging to the Bishop of Winchester. He charged his officers also to inventory and bring forth his goods. Whereupon much brave furniture made into hangings, besides whole pieces of rich stuffs were set upon divers tables in his house; the variety and number whereof may he imagined, when (as Cavendish has it) of fine Holland cloth alone there were a thousand pieces. Besides the walls of his gallery on the one side were hanged with rich suits of cloth of gold, cloth of silver, cloth of tissue, and cloth of bodkin; on the other side was placed the most glorious suit of copes that had been seen in England. In a chamber near to the gallery was a great cupboard of plate of massy gold and in a chamber adjoining, vast quantity of other plate. All which the cardinal commanded Sir William Gaseogne (his treasurer) to deliver to the King, when he was required.

The bill against the cardinal.

In the mean while the bill against the cardinal proceeded, the most substantial plans whereof being extracted out of the original record I have thought fit to present to the reader. The ground upon which Christopher Hales, the King's attorney, prosecuted the cardinal was a statute of 16 Richard 2 in which is enacted that whereas the commons of the realm ought of right, and were wont of old time to sue in the King's court to recover their presentments to churches, prebends, and other benefices of holy church to which they had right to present, and when judgment shall be given in the said court upon such a plea and presentment, the archbishops, bishops, and other spiritual persons which have institutions of such benefices within their jurisdictions, lie bound, and have made execution of such judgments by the King's commandments of all the time aforesaid without interruption, and also be bound of right to make execution of many other the King's commandments of which right the crown of England has been peaceably seized, as well now as in the time of all his progenitors. And whereas the Bishop of Rome (for so he is termed in the act) had made divers processes and censures of excommunication upon certain bishops in England because they have made execution of such commandments, and also because he has ordained and purposed to translate some prelates of the realm, some out of the realm and some from one bishopric to another within the said realm without the King's assent and knowledge, and without the assent of the prelates, which so shall be translated; which prelates be much profitable and necessary to our lord the King and to all his realm; which translations if they should be suffered the statutes of the realm should be defeated and made void and his said liege sages of his council, without his assent and against his will, carried away and gotten out of his realm and the substance and treasure of the realm shall be carried away and so the realm destitute as well of counsel as of substance to the final destruction of the same realm; and so the crown of England which has been so free at all times, that it has been in no earthly subjection, but immediately subject to God in all things touching the legality of the same crown, and to none other, should he submitted to the Pope; and the laws and statutes of the said realm by him defeated and avoided at his will, in perpetual destruction of the sovereignty of the King our lord, his crown, his regality and of all his realm, &c. Therefore the King by the assent of his lords and at the request of the commons, has ordained and established that if any purchase or pursue, or cause to be purchased or pursued in the court of Rome, or elsewhere, any translations, processes, and sentences of excommunication, bulls, instruments, or other things whatsoever, which touch the King, against him, his crown, and regality or realm, and they which bring within the realm, or them receive, or make thereof notification, or any other execution whatsoever within the same realm or without; that they, their notaries, procurators, maintainers, abettors, factors and counselors, shall be put out of the King's protection, and their lands and tenements, goods and chattels, forfeit to the King, and that they be attached by their bodies if they may be found, and brought before the King and his council there to answer to the cases aforesaid, or that process be made against them by a writ of *Praemunire facias*, in manner as it is ordained in other statutes of provisors, and other which do sue in any other court, in derogation of the regality of our lord the King.

Upon which statute it was alleged that Thomas, *legatus de latere*, Cardinal, Archbishop of York and Primate of England, being not ignorant of the premises, had obtained certain bulls from Clement 7, by which he exercised jurisdiction and authority legatine, to the deprivation of the King's power established in his courts of justice; which said bulls he caused to be publicly read in Westminster, (Aug. 28, 1523) assuming to himself thereupon the dignity and jurisdiction of *Legatus de Latere*, which he has exercised from the said 28th of August to this day, to the prejudice of the right of both secular and ecclesiastical persons, and that by color thereof, he had given away the church of Stoke-Guildford in the county of Surrey to one James Gorton who also enjoyed it accordingly. All which was to the contempt of the King and his crown and contrary to the aforesaid statutes of 16 Rd. 2. Moreover that by color of the said authority he had caused the last wills and testaments of many to be exhibited and proved in his court and their goods and chattels to be administered by such as he appointed. Also, that under color of the said authority, he had made divers visitations out of his dioceses and drawn divers pensions from abbeys, to the contempt of the King and his laws.

The proofs of which particulars, though evident and notorious, were not yet urged to his conviction, until through the King's special permission (by writ of October 28.) John Scuse and Christopher Genney appeared in court as his attorneys; where for all other answers, they protested in the said cardinal's name that the said cardinal did not know the impetration of the said bulls to have been to the contempt and prejudice of the King or that it was against any statute of provisors heretofore made. As for the particulars wherewith he was charged by master attorney, he confessed them all true in the manner and form alleged and so submit himself to the King. Whereupon the court gave sentence that he was out of the King's protection, and his lands, goods, and chattels forfeit, and that this person might be seized on.

The cardinal is condemned in the Star Chamber.

Not contented herewith yet, another proof of the same kind was by the King's attorney produced against the cardinal, namely that contrary to the right of the true patron, he had by the same authority, given away the parish church of Galby in Leicestershire, and dioceses of Lincoln to one John Allen, doctor of both laws, and placed him in it. And thus fell the cardinal, together with all his vast possessions, into the King's hands. But the King did not think it enough that he had particularly advantaged himself of the cardinal's punishment unless he made some use thereof to the general, so he called a council of the nobles to sit in the Star-Chamber who having sufficiently condemned him, he afterwards remitted him to the Parliament which began November 3, 1529. Wherein the King also did wisely, since by interesting the public in his condemnation, he both declined the censure of those who thought the late proceedings to have been of the severest and endeared his people by putting the power of punishing him into their hands. Therefore they took it as an entire satisfaction for all they had hitherto suffered; and by applauding of the King, made him know how thankfully they took this favor. And thus did the King return to that former good opinion he had of his subjects.

Articles preferred against the cardinal in Parliament.

Hereupon, certain articles against the cardinal were preferred in Parliament. The original whereof found among our records, I have thought fit to transcribe; and the rather for that our vulgar chronicles misreport them.

Constrained by necessity of our fidelity and conscience, complain and show to your royal majesty, we your graces humble, true, faithful, and obedient subjects, that the Lord Cardinal of York, lately your graces chancellor, presuming to take upon him the authority of the Pope's legal *de latere*, has by divers and many sundry ways and fashions committed notable, high, and grievous offences, misusing, altering, and subverting the order of your graces laws, and otherwise contrary to your high honor, prerogative, crown, estate, and dignity royal, to the inestimable damage of your graces subjects of every degree and consequently to the great hindrance, diminution, and decay of the universal wealth of this your graces realm as is it touched summarily and particularly in certain articles here following; which be but a few in comparison of all his enormities, excesses, and transgressions committed against your graces laws. That is to say;

1. First, where your grace and your noble progenitors within this your realm of England, being Kings of England, have been so free that they have had in all the world no other sovereign, but immediate subject to almighty God in all things, touching the regality of your crown of England and the

same pre-eminence, prerogative, jurisdiction, lawful and peaceable possession, your grace and your noble progenitors have had, used, and enjoyed without interruption, or business therefore, by the space of 200 years and more; whereby your grace may prescribe against the Pope's holiness that he should not, nor ought to send or make any legate to execute any authority legatine, contrary to your graces prerogative within this your realm. Now the Lord Cardinal of York being your subject, and natural liege born, has of his high, orgullous, and insatiable mind, for his own singular advancement and profit in derogation and to the great blemish and hurt of your said royal jurisdiction and prerogative, and the large continuance of the possession of the same, obtained authority legatine by reason whereof he has not only hurt your said prescription, but also by the said authority legatine has spoiled and taken away from many houses of religion in this your realm, much substance of their goods; and also has usurped upon all your ordinaries within this your realm much part of their jurisdiction, in derogation of your prerogative, and to the great hurt of your said ordinaries, prelates, and religious.

2. Also, the said lord cardinal, being your ambassador in France, made a treaty with the French King for the Pope, your majesty not knowing any part thereof, nor named in the same; and binding the said French King to abide his order and award if any controversy or doubt should arise upon the same betwixt the said Pope and the French King.

3. Also, the said lord cardinal, being your ambassador in France, sent a commission to Sir Gregory de Casalis under your great seal in your graces name to conclude a treaty of amity with the Duke of Ferrara, without any command or warrant of your highness, nor your said highness advertised or made privy to the same.

4. Also, the said lord cardinal, of his presumptuous mind in divers and many of his letters and instructions sent out of this realm to outward parties, had joined himself with your grace as in saying and writing in his said letters and instructions; 'The King and I.' And, 'I would ye should do thus. The King and I give to you our hearty thanks.' Whereby it is apparent that he used himself more like a fellow to your highness, than like a subject.

5. Also, where it has ever been accustomed within this your realm, that when noblemen do swear their household servants, the first part of their oath has been that they should be true liegemen to the King and his heirs Kings of England; the same lord cardinal caused his servants to be only sworn to him, as if there had been no sovereign above him.

6. And also, whereas your grace is our sovereign lord and head in whom stands all the surety and wealth of this realm, the same lord cardinal knowing himself to have the foul and contagious disease of the great pox, broken out upon him in divers places of his body, came daily to your grace groaning in your ear and blowing upon your most noble grace with his perilous and infective breath, to the marvelous danger of your highness if God of his infinite goodness had not better provided for your highness. And

when he was once healed of them, he made your grace to believe that his disease was an impostume in his head and of none other thing.

7. Also, the said lord cardinal, by his authority legatine, has given by prevention, the benefices of divers persons as well spiritual as temporal; contrary to your crown and dignity and your laws and estates therefore provided; by reason whereof he is in danger to your grace of forfeiture of lands and goods, and his body at your pleasure.

8. Also, the said lord cardinal, taking upon him otherwise than a true counselor ought to do, has used to have all ambassadors to come first to him alone and so hearing their charges and intents it is to be thought he has instructed them after his pleasure and purpose, before that they came to your presence; contrary to your high commandment by your graces mouth to him given, and also to other persons sent to him by your grace.

9. Also, the said lord cardinal has practiced so, that all manner of letters sent from beyond the sea to your highness have come first to his hands contrary to your high commandment by your own mouth, and also by others sent to him by your grace; by reason whereof your highness, nor any of your council had knowledge of no matters, but such as it pleased him to show them; whereby your highness and your council have been compelled of very force to follow his devices, which oftentimes were set forth by him under such crafty and covert means, that your highness and your council have oftentimes been abused. Insomuch, that when your council have found, and put divers doubts and things which have afterwards ensued, he to abuse them used these words; 'I will lay my head that no such thing shall happen.'

10. Also, the said lord cardinal has practiced that no manner of person having charge to make espial of things done beyond the sea, should at their return come first to your grace, nor to any other of your council, but only to himself and in case they did the contrary, he punished them for so doing.

11. Also, the said lord cardinal has granted license under your great seal for carrying out of grain and other victual, after the restraint has been made thereof, for his own lucre, and singular advantage of him and his servants, for to send thither as he bare secret favor, without your graces warrant or knowledge thereof.

12. Also, the said lord cardinal used many years together, not only to write to all your ambassadors resident with other princes in his own name all advertisements concerning your graces affairs, being in their charge; and in the same his letters wrote many things of his own mind without your graces pleasure being known, concealing divers things which had been necessary for them to know; but also caused them to write their advertisements to him and of the same letters he used to conceal for the compassing of his purposes many things both from all your other counselors, and from yourself also.

13. Also, where good hospitality has been used to be kept in houses and places of religion of this realm and many poor people thereby relieved, the said hospitality and relief is now decayed and not used; and it is commonly reported that the occasion thereof is, because the said lord cardinal has

taken such impositions of the rulers of the said houses as well for his favor in making of abbots, and priors, as for his visitation, by his authority legatine and yet, nevertheless, takes yearly of such religious houses, such yearly and continual charges, as they be not able to keep hospitality as they used to do; which is a great cause that there be so many vagabonds, beggars and thieves.

14. Also, where the said lord cardinal said before the suppression of such houses as he has suppressed that the possessions of them should be set to farm among your lay-subjects, after such reasonable yearly rent as they should well thereupon live, and keep good hospitality; and now the domain possessions of the said houses, since the suppression of them has been surveyed, metered and measured by the acre, and be now set above the value of the old rent; and also such as were farmers by covent-seal, and copy-holders be put out and moved of their farms, or else compelled to pay new fines contrary to all equity and conscience.

15. Also, the said lord cardinal sitting among the lords and other of your most honorable council, used himself that if any man would show his mind according to his duty contrary to the opinion of the said cardinal, he would so take him up with his accustom words, that they were better to hold their peace than to speak, so that he would hear no man speak, but one or two great personages so that he would have nil the words himself and consumed much time with a fair tale.

16. Also, the said lord cardinal by his ambition and pride, has hindered and undone many of your poor subjects for want of dispatch of matters; for he would no man should meddle but himself. Insomuch, that it has been affirmed by many wise men that ten of the most wise and most expert men in England, were not sufficient in convenient time to order the matters that he would retain to himself and many times he deferred the ending of matters, because that tutors should attend and wait upon him, whereof he had no small pleasure that his house might be replenished with tutors.

17. Also, the said lord cardinal by his authority legatine, has used, if any spiritual man having any riches or substance, deceased, he has taken their goods as his own; by reason whereof their wills be not performed and one mean he had to put them in fear that were made executors, to refuse to meddle.

18. Also, the said lord cardinal constrained all ordinaries in England yearly to compound with him, or else he will usurp half or the whole of their jurisdiction by prevention, not for good order of the dioceses, but to extort treasure; for there is never a poor arch-deacon in England, but that he paid yearly to him a portion of his living.

19. Also, the said lord cardinal had not only by his untrue suggestion to the Pope, shamefully slandered many good religious houses and good virtuous men dwelling in them, but also suppressed by reason thereof above 30 houses of religion; and where by authority of his bull, he should not suppress any house that had more men of religion in number above the number of 6 or 7, he had suppressed divers houses that had above the number and

thereupon has caused divers offices to be found by verdict, untruly that the religious persons, so suppressed, had voluntarily forsaken their said house, which was untrue and so had caused open perjury to be committed to the high displeasure of almighty God.

20. Also, the said lord cardinal has examined divers and many matters in the chancery after judgment thereof given at the common law in subversion of your laws; and made some persons restore again to the other partly condemned, that they had in execution by virtue of the judgment in the common law.

21. Also, the said lord cardinal has granted many injunctions by writ, and the parties never called thereto, nor bill put in against them. And by reason thereof, divers of your subjects have been put from their lawful possession of their lands and tenements. And by such means, he has brought the more party of the tutors of this your realm before himself, whereby he and divers of his servants have gotten much riches and your subjects suffered great wrongs.

22. Also, the said lord cardinal, to augment his great riches has caused divers pardons granted by the Pope to be suspended, which could not be revived till that the said lord cardinal were rewarded and also have a yearly pension of the said pardon.

23. Also, the said lord cardinal not regarding your laws nor justice of his extort power, has put out divers and many farmers of his lands and also patents of the Archbishop of York and Bishop of Winchester, and of the Abbey of St. Albans, which had good and sufficient grant thereof by your laws.

24. Also, the same lord cardinal at many times when any houses of religion have been void, he has sent his officers thither and with crafty persuasions has induced them to compromise their election in him. And that before he named or confirmed any of them, he and his servants received so much great goods of them that in manner it has been to the undoing of the house.

25. Also, by his authority legatine, the same lord cardinal has visited the most part of the religious houses and colleges in this your realm, has taken of them the twenty-fifth part of their livelihood, to the great extortion of your subjects and derogation of your laws and prerogative; and no law to bear him so to do.

26. Also, when matters have been near at judgment by process at your common law, the same lord cardinal has not only given and sent injunctions to the parties, but also sent for your judges and expressly by threats commanding them to defer the judgment, to the evident subversion of your laws, if the judges would so have ceased.

27. Also, whereas neither the Bishop of York, nor Winchester, nor the Abbey of St. Albans, nor the profit of his legation, nor the benefit of the chancery, nor his great pension out of France, nor his wards, and other inordinate taking could not suffice him, he has made his son Winter to spend

2700£ by the year, which he took to his own use and gave him not past 200£ yearly to live upon.

28. Also, where the said lord cardinal did first sue to your grace to have your assent to be *legate de latere*, he promised and solemnly protested before your majesty and before the lords both spiritual and temporal, that he would nothing do or attempt by virtue of his legacy, that should be contrary to your gracious prerogative or regality, or to the damage or prejudice of the jurisdiction of any ordinary and that by his legacy no man should be hurt or offended and upon that condition, and no other, he was admitted by your grace to be legate within this your realm which condition he has broken, as is well known to all your subjects. And when that he made this promise, he was busy in his suit at Rome to visit all the clergy of England, both exempt and not exempt.

29. Also, upon the suit of the said lord cardinal at Rome, to have his authority legatine, he made untrue surmise to the Pope's holiness against the clergy of your realm, which was that the regular persons of the said clergy had given themselves in *reprobum sensum;* which words St. Paul writing to the Romans applied to abominable sin; which slander to your church of England, shall forever remain in the register at Rome against the clergy of this your realm.

30. Also, the said lord cardinal had the more part of the goods of Dr. Smith, late Bishop of London, Bishop Savage of York, Mr. Dalby, Archdeacon of Richmond, Mr. Tornyers, Dr. Rothal, late Bishop of Durham, and of Dr. Fox, late Bishop of Winchester, contrary to their wills and your laws and justice.

31. Also, at the Oyer and Terminer at York, proclamation was made that every man should put in their bills for extortion of ordinaries and when divers bills were put in against the officers of the said lord cardinal of extortion for taking 12*d* of the pound for probation of testaments, whereof divers bills were found before justice Fitz-Herbert and other commissioners, the same lord cardinal removed the same indictments into the chancery by Certiorari and rebuked the same Fitz-Herbert for the same cause.

32. Also, the said lord cardinal has busied and endeavored himself by crafty and untrue tales to make dissension and debate amongst your nobles of your realm, which is ready to be proved.

33. Also, the said lord cardinal's officers have divers times compelled your subjects to serve him with carts for carriages. And also his servants have taken both corn and cattle, fish, and all other victuals at your graces price or under, as though it had been for your grace, which is contrary to the laws.

34. Also, the said lord cardinal has misused himself in your most honorable court in keeping of as great estate there in your absence, as your grace would have done if you had been there present in your own person.

35. Also, his servants, by virtue of your commission under your broad seal by him to them given, has taken cattle and all other victual, at as low price as your purveyors have done for your grace by your prerogative, against the laws of your realm.

36. Also, where it has been accustomed that your purveyors for your honorable household have had yearly out of your town and liberty of St. Albans 300 or 400 quarters of wheat, truth it is, that since the lord cardinal had the room of abbot there, your said purveyors could not be suffered by him and his officers to take any wheat within the said town or liberties.

37. Also he has divers times given injunction to your servants that have been for causes before him in the Star Chamber, that they nor other for them should make labor by any manner of way directly or indirectly to your grace to obtain your gracious favor or pardon which was a presumptuous intent for any subject.

38. Also, the said lord cardinal did call before him Sir John Stanley, Knight, which had taken a farm by covent-seal of the Abbot and Covent of Chester, and afterwards by his power and might, contrary to right, committed the said Sir John Stanley to the prison of Fleet by the space of one year until such time as he compelled the said Sir John to release his covent seal to one Leghe of Adlington, which married one Lark's daughter, which woman the said lord cardinal kept and had with her two children. Whereupon the said Sir John Stanley upon displeasure taken in his heart, made himself monk in Westminster, and there died.

39. Also, on a time your grace being at St. Albans according to the ancient custom used within your verge, your clerk of the market doing his office, did present to your officers of your most honorable household the prices of all manner of victual within the precinct of the verge; and it was commanded by your said officers to set up the said prices both on the gates of your honorable household and also in the market-place within the town of St. Albans as of ancient custom it has been used; and the lord cardinal hearing the same, presumptuously and not like a subject, caused the aforesaid prices which were sealed with your graces seal, customarily used for the same to be taken off and pulled down in the said market-place where they were set up and in the same place set up his own prices sealed with his seal, and would, if it had not been letted in semblable manner used your seal standing upon your graces gates; and also would of his presumptuous mind, have openly set in the stocks within your said town your clerk of your market. By which presumption and usurpation your grace may perceive, that in his heart he has reputed himself to be equal with your royal majesty.

40. Also, the said lord cardinal, of his further pompous and presumptuous mind, has enterprise to join and imprint the cardinal's hat under your arms in your coin of groats made at your city of York, which like deed has not been seen to have been done by any subject within your realm before this time.

41. Also, where one Sir Edward Jones, Clerk, Parson of Crowley in the county of Buckingham in the 18th year of your most noble reign, let his said parsonage with all titles and other profits of the same to one Win. Johnson by indentures for certain years within which years the dean of the said Cardinal's College in Oxford pretended title to a certain portion of titles within the said parsonage, supposing the said portion to belong to the

parsonage of Chichley which was appropriated to the priory of Tykeford, lately suppressed, where of truth the parsons of Crowley have been peaceably possessed of the said portion time out of mind whereupon a subpoena was directed to the said Johnson to appear before the said lord cardinal at Hampton-Court; where without any bill, the said lord cardinal committed him to the Fleet, where he remained by the space of twelve weeks because he would not depart with the said portion; and at the last, upon a recognizance made, that he should appear before the said lord cardinal where so ever he was commanded, he was delivered out of the Fleet. Howbeit, as yet the said portion is so kept from him, that he dare not deal with it.

42. Also, where one Martin Docowra had a lease of the manor of Balsul in the county of Warwick for term of certain years, an injunction came to him out of the Chancery, by writ, upon pain of 1000£ that he should avoid the possession of the same manor and suffer Sir George Throckmorton, Knt. to take the profits of the same manor to the time the matter depending in the chancery between the Lord of St. Johns and the said Docowra were discus; and yet the said Docowra never made answer in the chancery, never was called into the chancery for that matter. And now of late he has received the like injunction, upon pain of 2000£ contrary to the course of the common law.

43. Also, whereas in the Parliament chamber and in the open Parliament, communication and devices were had and moved, wherein mention was by an incident made of matters touching heresies, and erroneous sects. It was spoken and reported by one bishop there being present and confirmed by a good number of the same bishops in presence of all the lords spiritual and temporal then assembled, and two of the said bishops were minded and desired to repair to the university of Cambridge, for examination, reformation, and correction of such errors as then seemed, and were reported to reign amongst the students and scholars of the same, as well touching the Lutheran sect and opinions as otherwise; the lord cardinal informed of the good minds and intents of the said two bishops in that behalf, expressly inhibited and commanded them in no wise so to do. By means whereof the same errors (as they affirmed) crept more abroad, and took greater place saying furthermore that it was not in their defaults that the said heresies were not punished, but in the said lord cardinal and that it was no reason any blame or lack should be erected to them for his offence. Whereby it evidently appears that the said lord cardinal, besides all other his heinous offences, has been the impeacher and disturber of due and direct correction of heresies; being highly to the danger and peril of the whole body and good Christian people of this your realm.

44. Finally, forasmuch as by the aforesaid articles is evidently declared to your most royal majesty that the lord cardinal by his outrageous pride has greatly shadowed a long season your graces honor, which is most highly to be regarded and by his insatiable avarice and ravenous appetite to have riches and treasure without measure, has so grievously oppressed your poor subjects with so manifold crafts of bribery and extortion that the common-

wealth of this your graces realm is thereby greatly decayed and impoverished and also by his cruelty, iniquity, affection and partiality, has subverted the due course and order of your graces laws to the undoing of a great number of your loving people; please it your most royal majesty therefore of your excellent goodness towards the weal of this your realm and subjects of the same, to set such order and direction upon the said lord cardinal, as may be to the terrible example of others to beware so to offend your grace and your laws hereafter and that he be so provided for, that he never have any power, jurisdiction, or authority, hereafter to trouble, vex, and impoverish the commonwealth of this your realm, as he has done heretofore to the great hurt and damage of every man almost high and low. Which for your grace so doing, will daily pray as their duty is to almighty God, for the prosperous estate of your most royal majesty long to endure in honor and good health to the pleasure of God, and your hearts most desire.

Subscribed the 1st day of December, the 21st year of the reign of our sovereign Lord King Henry 8. T. More T. Norfolk, Char. Suffolk, Tho. Dorset, H. Exeter, G. Shrewsbury, It. Fitzwater, Jo. Oxenford, H. Northumland, T. Dairy, T. Rochford, W. Mountjoy, Wm. Sandys, Win. Fitz-William, Henry Guideford, Anthony Fitz-Herbert, John Fitz-James.

These articles being agreed to by the whole house were presented to the King by the lords and then sent down to the lower house where Thomas Cromwell (obtaining the place of a burgess) so wittily defended the cardinal his master that no treason could be laid to his charge. Yet could not the resisting of this brunt, nor even the gracious messages received frequently from the King, cheer up the cardinal. For as he found the Pope had now a long while neglected to give the King any satisfaction, which certainly was the only way to procure the cardinal's restitution, and that, for the rest, no evident sign of the King's relenting appeared, so being not able to support any longer his many afflictions, he fell dangerously sick. The news whereof being brought to the King's ears, moved so much compassion as not only he, but by his entreaty mistress Anne Bolen, whom the cardinal had ill vain importuned to intercede for him, also sent him several tokens; whereof one was a ruby wherein the King's image was curiously engraved, a gift heretofore of the cardinal's together with a gracious message delivered by Dr. Butts, his physician; that his highness was not angry with him in his heart, which he should know shortly. Whereupon the cardinal recovered his health, for the King so confirming his promises, sealed his pardon, Feb. 12, and three days after by letters patents, restored him to the Archbishop of York. Moreover, he sent him money, plate, rich hangings, and furniture for his house and chapel, in that quantity as the cardinal was for the present much recovered hoping also that since he had resigned his house called York House, but afterward by the King styled the manor of Westminster now Whitehall, that his punishment ended there and himself now upon terms of regaining the King's favor. The confidence whereof also made him to be a humble suppliant to the King, that for his health's sake, he might have leave to remove to Richmond house, the use of which he had received in exchange from the King for that his sumptuous palace which he built and called by the name of Hampton-court.

The cardinal sent to his Bishop of York.

And now Cardinal Wolsey, it seems, had tried his utmost skill for recovering of the King's favor; whereof also some hope was given him in his being permitted to remove to Richmond. But as his enemies suspected he would make use of this nearness to obtain access to the King, so they labored instantly to send him to the north. Wherein they prevailed at length, obtaining further that the revenues of the Bishop of Winchester and Abbey of Saint Albans, as also some other places of his, forfeited by the *praemunire* might be applied in part to the King's servants; a pension only out of Winchester, being reserved to the cardinal. The revenues also of his two colleges were torn and divided which grieved him more than any other affliction insomuch, that he wrote to the King, humbly, as on his knees with weeping eyes that the college of Oxford might stand and importuned Cromwell to this purpose, since they are in a manner, said he, *Opera munuam tuarum.* But Cromwell returned him no comfort herein, saying the King was determined to dissolve them though whether he meant to restore them again and found them in his own name, he knew not; but wishes him to be content, &c. howsoever, in the traffic of these and other lands, as well as negotiating his masters business, Cromwell showed that dexterity which at last won him much credit both with the King and his principal counselors. And now the cardinal being commanded to York, had no excuse for retarding his journey, but want of means which also he signified to the King; who thereupon sent him a thousand pounds with which and a train reduced now to about 160 persons, he set forth giving by the way much arms and not a few other arguments of devotion which also made him gracious with the people, who resorted from all places adjoining to him. And thus with slow and unwilling removes, he came to Cawood castle near York about the end of September 1530, where he prepared according to the ancient custom, to be installed with much ceremony about a month after; all access to the choir being till then forbidden. But whether the solemnity of this action was thought by our King to be unreasonable, and unbecoming one in disgrace; or that otherwise the cardinal had cast forth some discontented words which were related again to the King; here certainly began his final ruin. Which, as his enemies (at this distance) did with more boldness and advantage procure, so had he less means to repair himself. Insomuch that without being able to discover or prevent their machinations, he was forced to surfer all that could be either truly or almost falsely surmised against him. Neither had he other hope, but that the punishments he had already endured might be accepted as an entire satisfaction for all his offences.

The cardinal is arrested in York of high treason.

And now his salvation grew near when the Earl of Northumberland Warden of the Marches, with one Sir Walter Welsh gentleman of the King's privy chamber, came by the King's command to Cawood to arrest the cardinal, wherein he used that diligence and secrecies that he had placed his guards in the hall before any escaped to advertise the cardinal thereof. Neither did he at the earls coming up stairs, receive him in other terms than those of a guest till entering into a private chamber together, the earl in a low and troubled voice arrested him of high treason. The dismayed and pensive cardinal stayed a while before he answered, but at last recovering his spirits, demanded the sight of the earl's commission protesting that otherwise he would not obey; urging further that he was a member of the College of Cardinals at Rome, and so except from all princes jurisdiction. But while the earl replied that he might not show his commission, Sir Walter Welsh who had now arrested Dr. Augustine the cardinals physician, comes in and confirms what the earl had said. The cardinal believing, by this time that they were in good earnest yields to Sir Walter Welsh as the King's servant and not to the earl; to whom he said he would not submit himself, before he was better satisfied of his authority. Which whether he did out of stubbornness to the earl, who had been heretofore educated in his house, or out of despite to mistress Anne Bolen, who (he might conceive) had put this affront upon him in finding means to employ her ancient suitor to take revenge in both their names, does not appear to me by my author. Howsoever he protested he was no way faulty in his allegiance. Dr. Augustine whose offence yet does not appear to me, was dispatched to London in the posture of a traitor, his legs tied to his horse. But the cardinal had some respite; though yet commanded to prepare for his journey; which he began at length in that deliberate manner that if he removed slowly before from the King, he moved now more slowly to him. Insomuch that had not the Earl of Shrewsbury, to whom being the steward of the King's household, the Earl of Northumberland was commanded to deliver him till the King's further pleasure were known, told him that the King commanded he should be used kindly as one whom he highly favored; it is probable that the afflicted cardinal would have fallen under the burthen of his own grief. Furthermore, the earl assured him on the King's part, that though his highness could do no less than put him to his trial, yet that it was more for the satisfying of some persons than out of mistrust of his traitorous doings.

The cardinal's last speech, and death.

And thus at Sheffield castle, he staid a fortnight when a wind-colic, which ended in a dysentery, took him. In which state, Sir Win. Kingston Captain of the King's Guard and Constable of the Tower, attended with 24 yeomen of the guard (all of them formerly servants to the cardinal) did find him. So that notwithstanding the many encouragements of the earl, seconded by Sir Win. Kingston (who on his knees saluted him) the cardinal remained still sick and comfortless. Neither did it avail him that Sir Win. Kingston (on the King's part) gave him many gracious words, adding furthermore that he should make no more haste than stood with his health and convenience. For the cardinal became still more and more dejected. Notwithstanding as he considered that delay would but argue guiltiness, so he proceeded in his journey the best he could till he came to Leicester abbey where a fever, complicated with his former disease, seizing on him, he languished not without manifest signs of his end. Being thus upon his bed, Sir William Kingston came again to comfort him, but the cardinal finding now that death would discharge him of all trials, but that before God, spoke to this effect:

Had I served God as diligently as I have done the King, he would not have given me over in my gray hairs; but this is my just reward. Notwithstanding, I pray ye commend me most humbly to the King, desiring him to call to remembrance all matters that have past between us, and specially about Queen Catharine and then shall his grace know whether I have offended him. He is a prince of royal courage but rather than he will want or miss any part of his will or pleasure, he will endamage the loss of one half of his realm. For, I assure you, I have often kneeled before him, sometimes the space of three hours to persuade him from his will and appetite, but could never dissuade him from it. Therefore Master Kingston, I warn you, if ever you be of his council (as for your wisdom you are meet) that ye be well assured and advised what you put in his head, for you shall never put it out again.

After which words as Cavendish has them, he began an exhortation to take heed of the Lutherans by the example of those of Bohemia, lest they should likewise subvert the secular power. But as in the prosecuting of this discourse his speech failed him, so did his breath presently after insomuch that he died and was buried there in the Abbey Church, Nov. 30, before day. And not where he had begun a monument for himself, long since, wherein as appears by our records he had not omitted his own image which one Benedetto, a statuary of Florence, took in hand 1524 and continued till 1529 receiving for so much as was already done 4250 ducats. The design whereof was so glorious that it exceeded far that of Henry 7. Nevertheless, I find the cardinal when this was finished did purpose to make a tomb for Henry 8, but dying in this manner, King Henry made use of so much as he found fit, and called it his. Thus did the tomb of the cardinal partake the same fortune with his college as being assumed by the King; both which yet remain still imperfect. The news of the cardinal's death being brought to our King, did so much afflict him that he wished it had cost him twenty thousand pounds upon condition he had lived. Howbeit he omitted not to enquire of about one thousand and five hundred pounds which the cardinal had lately got without that the King could imagine how. So that, till it appeared he borrowed it of diver's persons, he might perchance suspect it to be the remainder of some of his ancient acquisitions.

And thus concluded that great cardinal. A man in whom ability of arts and industry were equally eminent, though for being employed wholly in ambitious ways they became dangerous instruments of power in active and mutable limes. By these arts yet he found means to govern not only the chief affair of this Kingdom, but of Europe; there being no potentate, which in his turn did not seek to him and as this procured him divers pensions, so when he acquainted the King therewith, his manner was so cunningly to disoblige that prince who did see him last, as he made way thereby oftentimes to receive as much on the other side. But not of secular princes alone but even of the Pope and clergy of Rome he was no little courted; of which therefore he made especial use while he drew them to second him on most occasions.

His birth being otherwise so obscure and mean, as no man had ever stood so single for which reason also, his chief endeavor was not to displease any great person which yet could not secure him against the divers pretences of that time. For as all things passed through his hands, so they who failed in their suits generally hated him, all which though it did but exasperate his ill nature, yet this good resistance followed, that it made him take the more care to be just; whereof also he obtained the reputation in his public hearing of causes. For as he loved no body, so his reason carried him. And thus he was a useful minister of his King in all points where there was no question of disserving the Roman Church; of which (at what price so ever) I find he was a zealous servant; as hoping thereby to aspire to the papacy, whereof (as the factious times then were) he seemed more capable than any, had he not so immoderately affected it. Whereby also it was not hard to judge of his inclinations. That prince, who was ablest to help him to this dignity, being ever preferred by him, which therefore was the ordinary bait by which the emperor and French King one after the other, did catch him. And, upon these terms, be doubted not to convey vast treasures out of this Kingdom, especially to Rome where he had not a few cardinals at his devotion. By whose help, though he could not obtain that supreme dignity he so passionately desired, yet he prevailed himself so much of their favor, as he got a kind of absolute power in spiritual matters at home. Wherewith again he so served the King's turn as it made him think the less of using his own authority. One error seemed common to both which was that such a multiplicity of offices and places were invested in him. For as it drew much envy upon the cardinal in particular, so it derogated no little from the regal authority while one man alone seemed to exhaust all. Since it becomes princes to do like good husbandmen when they sow their grounds, which is to scatter, and not to throw all in one place. He was no great dissembler, for so qualified a person; as ordering his businesses for the most part so cautiously as he got more by keeping his word than by breaking it. As for his learning, (which was far from exact) it consisted chiefly in the subtleties of the Thomas's, wherewith the King and himself did more often weary than satisfy each other. His style in missives was rather copious than eloquent, yet ever tending to the point. Briefly, if it be true (as Polydore observes) that no man ever did rise with fewer virtues, it is as true that few that ever fell from so high a pines had lesser crimes objected against him though yet Polydore (for being at his first coming into England committed to prison by him, as we have said) may be suspected as a partial author. So that in all probability he might have subsisted longer, when either his pride and immense wealth had not made him obnoxious, and suspected to the King, or that other than women had opposed him who as they are vigilant and close enemies, so for the most part they carry their businesses in that manner, they leave fewer advantages against themselves, than men do. In conclusion, as I cannot assent to those who thought him happy for enjoying the untimely compassion of the people a little before his end, so I cannot but account it a principal felicity that during his favor with the King, all things succeeded better than afterwards though yet it may be doubted whether the impressions he gave did not occasion divers irregularities which were observed to follow.

[Howell, Thomas. A Complete Collection of State Trials. V-1. 368-386]

Thomas More

Thomas More was born to John More, a successful lawyer, and Agnes Graunger in London, February 1477. John More was able to send Thomas to one of London's best schools-St. Anthony's at Threadneedle Street. His father's influence earned Thomas a position as household page to John Morton, Archbishop of Canterbury, who is perhaps best remembered as the creator of a very successful tax policy for King Henry VII. It was Thomas's connection to John Morton that secured his entrance to Oxford were he studied for two years before returning to study as a student of law under the guidance of his father.

Thomas quickly earned the respect of many in court and had a bright career in law, but he was torn between a life of civil service and a monastic calling. He moved into the Carthusian monastery to participate in the monks' way of life while continuing to pursue his legal career for three years. Soon after departing the monastery, he married the daughter of a farmer-Jane Colt. History records that it was both a happy and prosperous marriage as she gave him three daughters and a son before Jane died in 1511.

Thomas More was successful as an under-sheriff and a representative for London in Parliament were he proved himself an impartial judge and a capable administrator. Early scholars share the opinion that his first and potentially scandalous act was remarrying in less than a month after the Jane died to Alice Middleton, although history records that it also was a happy marriage.

Thomas More became involved with King Henry VIII and Cardinal Wolsey about the same time as the King began to seek an annulment in his marriage with Catherine of Aragon. In 1515, Thomas accompanied Cardinal Wolsey as part of a delegation to revise a treaty and began work on his *Utopia.* He also began writing his *History of King Richard III* and through those works, he was hailed as 'one of the foremost humanist thinkers'. Furthermore, he earned a place, though one not completely embraced by Thomas Wolsey, into the King's service. Thomas was appointed as a member of the Privy Council and accompanied the cardinal on a diplomatic assignment. He impressed Wolsey so much that Thomas was knighted upon their return and was to serve as the King's personal secretary and advisor and in 1513, he was elected speaker of the House of Commons.

In 1527, Thomas found himself amidst the events surrounding an annulment the King was seeking with his marriage with Catherine. Thomas did not share the same opinion as the King and became convinced that he needed to leave royal service augmented by the death of Cardinal Wolsey. When the King forced the clergy to acknowledge him as supreme head of their church,

Thomas attempted to resign his post and this action began the declination of the King's favor. The King eventually accepted Thomas's resignation and their relationship was never the same. As Thomas Cromwell quickly became a powerful and influential advisor to the King, Thomas More's opinion became detrimental. Cromwell believed that Thomas More should accept the King as the supreme head of the church or die. Thomas More brought it to fruition when he refused to attend the coronation of the new Queen. His name appeared on a bill of attainder and he appeared before the Privy Council in February 1534, and though defended himself with great skill; it was his popularity that saved him, at least for the moment.

The following month, the act of succession was passed and sealed his fate. Thomas could recognize the new Queen but he would not recognize the King as the supreme head of the church. This resulted in his arrest and imprisonment in the Tower of London in April 1534. In July 1535, he was indicted on high treason.

The trial of Sir Thomas More, Knight, Lord Chancellor of England, for high treason in denying the King's supremacy: 26 Henry VIII.

A bill being preferred in Parliament, Nov. 1534, to attaint Elizabeth Barton and several others of high-treason. Bishop Fisher and Sir Thomas More were also brought into it for misprision of treason for the refusing of the oath of succession says my Lord Herbert. The same author avows the bill did so pass; but Sir Thomas's great-grandson in his life, shows the contrary and that notwithstanding the Archbishop of Canterbury, the Lord Chancellor, Duke of Norfolk, and Secretary Cromwell, by the King's command, went to him and pressed him to a compliance, yet the chancellor influenced the King so far that the matter of misprision was dropped. Sir Thomas was also examined at other times by the Lord Chancellor, Dukes of Norfolk and Suffolk, Mr. Secretary, and others of the Privy Council, who pressed him with all the arguments they could think of to own the King's supremacy in direct and open terms, or plainly to deny it; but he being loath to aggravate the King's displeasure, would say no more than that the statute was like a two-edged sword, for if he spoke against it, it should he the cause of the death of his body; and if hc assented to it, he should purchase the death of his soul. Those examinations being over, Richard Rich, newly made solicitor general, and afterwards Lord Rich with Sir Richard Southwell and Mr. Palmer, Secretary Cromwell's man, were sent by the King to take away his books. Rich, pretending friendship to him and protesting he had no commission to talk with him about the former affair of the supremacy, he put a case to him thus if it were enacted by Parliament that Richard Rich should be King, and that it should be treason in any body to deny it, what offence it were to contravene that act? Sir Thomas More answered that he should offend if he said so, because he was bound by the act; but that this was *cusus levis*. Whereupon Sir Thomas said he would propose a higher case suppose it were enacted by Parliament, *Quod Deus non sit Deus*, and that it were treason to contravene whether it were not an offence to say it according to the said act? Rich replied, yea; but said withal, I will propose a middle case because this is too high. The King, you know, is constituted supreme head of the church upon earth; why should not you Master More, accept him for such? As you would me if I were made King by the aforesaid supposition. More answered the case was not the same, because, said he, a Parliament can make a King and depose him and that every Parliament man may give his consent thereto, but that a subject cannot be bound so in the case of supremacy. *Quia consersum ab co ad Parliamentum preabere non potest* (so, says my Lord Herbert, it is in my copy if it be not mistaken) *& quanquam Rex sic acceptus sit in Anglia, plurimae tamen Partes exterae idem non affirmant.*

Sir Thomas, having continued a prisoner in the Tower somewhat more than a twelvemonth for he was committed about the middle of April 1534, and was brought to his trial on the 7th of May, 1535, he went into the court leaning on his staff, because he was much weakened by his imprisonment, but appeared with a cheerful and composed countenance. The persons constituted to try him, were, Sir Thomas Audley, Lord Chancellor, Thomas Duke of Norfolk, Sir John Fitz-James, Lord Chief Justice, Sir John Baldwin, Sir Richard Leicester, Sir John Port, Sir John Spelman, Sir Walter Luke, Sir Anthony Fitz-Herbert.

The indictment was very long, but where to procure a copy of it, I could never learn; it is said in general it contained all the crimes that could be laid to the charge of any notorious malefactor; and Sir Thomas professed it was so long, that he could scarce renumber the third part of what was objected therein against him. It was read aloud by the attorney-general; and Sir Thomas's mortal sin seemed plainly to be his refusing the oath of succession, already mentioned. To prove this, his double examination in the Tower was alleged against him. The first before Secretary Cromwell, Thomas Beade, John Tregonnel, &c. to whom he professed he had given over all thoughts of titles either to Popes or princes, though the whole world should be given him, he being fully determined only to serve God. The second time before the Lord Chancellor, the Duke of Suffolk, Earl of Wiltshire, and others before whom he compared that oath to a two-edged sword, as before observed.

Presently after the indictment was read, the Lord Chancellor and the Duke of Norfolk spoke to him to this effect; you see now how grievously you have offended his majesty; yet he is so very merciful that if you will lay aside your obstinacy and change your opinion, we hope you may obtain pardon and favor in his sight. But Sir Thomas stoutly replied, most noble lords I have great reason to return thanks to your honors for this your great civility, but I beseech almighty God that I may continue in the mind I am in, through his grace, to death. Then having intimation given that he might say what he thought fit in his own defense, he began thus. When I consider the length of my accusation and what heinous matters are laid to my charge, I am struck with fear, lest my memory and understanding which are both impaired, together with my bodily health through a long indisposition contracted by my imprisonment, should now fail me so far as to make me incapable of making such ready answers in my defense, as otherwise I might have done.

The court being sensible of his weakness, ordered a chair to be brought in wherein he might seat himself which he did accordingly and then went on thus: this my indictment, if I mistake not, consists of four principal heads, each of which I purpose, God willing to answer in order. As to the first crime objected against me that I have been an enemy out of stubbornness of mind to the King's second marriage; I confess, I always told his majesty my opinion according to the dictates of my conscience which I neither ever would, nor ought to have concealed. For which I am so far from thinking myself guilty of high treason, that on the contrary, being required to give my opinion by so great a prince in an affair of so much importance upon which the peace of the Kingdom depended; I should have basely flattered him, and my own conscience had not I spoke the truth as I thought then indeed I might justly have been esteemed a most wicked subject, and a perfidious traitor to God. If I have offended the King herein; if it can be an offence to tell one's mind freely when his sovereign puts the question to him; I suppose I have been sufficiently punished already for the fault by the great afflictions I have endured by the loss of my estate, and my tedious imprisonment which has continued already near fifteen months. The second charge against me is that I have violated the act made in the last Parliament that is, being a prisoner, and twice examined, I would not out of a malignant, perfidious, obstinate and traitorous mind, tell them my opinion whether the King was supreme head of the church or not; but confessed then that I had nothing to do with that act, as to the justice or injustice of it because I had no benefice in the church, yet then I protested that I had never said nor done anything against it; neither can any one word or action of mine be alleged, or produced to make me culpable. Nay, this I own was then my answer to their honors that I would think of nothing else hereafter, but of the bitter passion of our blessed savior and of my exit out of this miserable world. I wish no body any harm and if this does not keep me alive, I desire not to live; by all which I know, I would not transgress any law or become guilty of any treasonable crime, for this statute, nor no other law in the world can punish any man for his silence, seeing they can do no more than punish words or deeds; 'tis God only that is the judge of the secrets of our hearts.

The Attorney General (Christopher Hales.) Sir Thomas, though we have not one word or deed of yours to object against you, yet we have your silence which is an evident sign of the malice of your heart because no dutiful subject, being lawfully asked this question, will refuse to answer it.

Sir Thomas More. Sir, my silence is no sign of any malice in my heart which the King himself must own by my conduct upon divers occasions; neither does it convince any man of the breach of the law; for it is a maxim amongst the civilians and canonists, *Qui tacet consentire videtur*, he that holds his peace, seems to give his consent. And as to what you say that no good subject will refuse to give a direct answer; I do really think it to be the duty of every good subject, except to be such a subject as will be a bad Christian, rather to obey God than man; to be more cautious to offend his conscience than of anything else in the whole world; especially if his conscience be not the occasion of some sedition and great injury to his prince and country for I do here sincerely protest that I never revealed it to any man alive. I come now to the third principal article in my indictment, by which I am accused of malicious attempts, traitorous endeavors, and perfidious practices against that statute, as the words therein do allege, because I wrote, while in the Tower, divers packets of letters to Bishop Fisher; whereby I exhorted him to violate the same law, and encouraged him in the like obstinacy. I do insist that these letters be introduced and read in court, by which I may be either acquitted or convinced of a lie; but because you say the bishop burnt them all, I will here tell you the whole truth of the matter. Some of my letters related only to our private affairs, as about our old friendship and acquaintance. One of them was in answer to his, wherein he desired me to let him know what answers I made upon my examinations concerning the oath of supremacy; and what I wrote to him upon it was this, that I had already settled my conscience, and let him satisfy his according to his own mind. God is my witness, and as I hope he will save my soul, I gave him no other answer; and this I presume is no breach of the laws. As to the principal crime objected against me, that I should say upon my examination in the Tower, that this law was like a two-edged sword; for in consenting to it, I should endanger my soul, and in rejecting it should lose my life, 'tis evidently concluded, as you say, from this answer because Fisher made the like that he was in the same conspiracy. To this I reply that my answer there was conditional, if there were both danger either in allowing or disallowing that act; and therefore like a two-edged sword it seemed a hard thing it should he put upon me, who had never hitherto contradicted it either in word or deed. These were my words; what the bishop answered I know not if his answer was like mine, it did not proceed from any conspiracy of ours, but from the similitude of our learning and understanding. To conclude, I do sincerely avouch that I never spoke a word against this law to any man living, though perhaps the King's majesty has been told the contrary.

There was little or no reply made to this full answer by Mr. Attorney or any body else; the word malice was what was principally insisted on, and in the mouths of the whole court though for proof of it no body could produce either words or actions, nevertheless to set the best gloss that could be upon the matter, Mr. Rich was called to give evidence in open court upon oath which he immediately did affirming what we have already related concerning a conference between him and Sir Thomas in the Tower. To which Sir Thomas made answer if I were a man, my lords, that had no regard to my oath, I had had no occasion to be here at this time as is well known to everybody as a criminal; and if this oath, Mr. Rich, which you have taken be true, then I pray I may never see God's face, which were it otherwise, is an imprecation I would not be guilty of to gain the whole world.

More having recited in the face of the court all the discourse they had together in the Tower as it truly and sincerely was, he added in good faith, Mr. Rich, I am more concerned for your perjury than my own danger; and I must tell you that neither myself, nor any body else to my knowledge, ever took you to be a man of such reputation, that I or any other would have anything to do with you in a matter of importance. You know that I have been acquainted with your manner of life and conversation a long time, even from your youth to the present juncture, for we lived in the same parish; and you very well know, I am sorry I am forced to speak it, you always lay under the odium of a very lying tongue of a great gamester, and of no good name and character either there or in the temple where you were educated. Can it therefore seem likely to your lordships that I should in so weighty an affair as this, act so unadvisedly as to trust Mr. Rich, a man I had always so mean an opinion of in reference to his truth and honesty, so very much before my sovereign lord the King, to whom I am so deeply indebted for his manifold favors, or any of his noble and grave counselors that I should only impart to Mr. Rich the secrets of my conscience in respect to the King's supremacy the particular subject, and only point about which I have been so long pressed to explain myself? Which I never did, nor never would reveal when the act was once made, either to the King himself, or any of his privy-counselors as is well known to your honors who have been sent upon no other account at several times by his majesty to me in the Tower. I refer it to your judgments, my lords, whether this can seem credible to any of your lordships. But supposing what Mr. Rich has swore should be true, seeing the words were spoke in familiar and private conversation and that there was nothing at all asserted, but only cases put without any offensive circumstances; it cannot in justice be said that they were spoke maliciously, and where there is no malice, there is no offence. Besides my lord, I cannot think so many reverend bishops, so many honorable personages, and so many virtuous and learned men of whom the Parliament consisted in the enacting of that law, ever meant to have any man punished with death in whom no malice could be found, taking the word *Mulitia* for *Mulerolentia;* for if *Mulitia* be taken in a general signification for any crime, there is no man can be free wherefore this word maliciously is so far significant in this statute, as the word forcible is in that of forcible entry; for in that case if any enter peaceably and puts his adversary out forcibly it is no offence; but if he enters forcibly, he shall be punished by that statute. Besides, all the unspeakable goodness of his majesty towards me who has been so many ways my singular good and gracious lord, who has so dearly loved and trusted me, even from my first entrance into his royal service, vouchsafing to honor me with the dignity of being one of his Privy Council, and has most generously promoted me to offices of great reputation and honor and lastly to that of Lord High Chancellor, which honor he never did to any layman before the same being the highest dignity in this famous Kingdom, and next to the King's royal person, so far beyond my merits and qualifications; honoring and exalting me by his incomparable benignity for these twenty years and upwards, heaping continual favors upon me; and now at last at my own humble request giving me liberty to dedicate the remainder of my life to the service of God for the better saving of my soul has been pleased to discharge and free me from that weighty dignity; before which he had still heaped more and more honors upon me. I say all this his majesty's bounty, so long and so plentifully conferred upon me, is enough in my opinion to invalidate the scandalous accusation so injuriously surmised and urged by this man against me.

This touched the reputation of Mr. Rich to the very quick, and was a slur that could not be effaced without the utmost difficulty; and the only way to do it was if possible to produce substantial and creditable witnesses to attest the contrary and therefore he caused Sir Rd. Southwell and Mr. Palmer, who were in the same room with Sir Thomas and Mr. Rich when they conferred together, to so sworn as to the words that passed between them. Whereupon Mr. Palmer deposed that he was so busy in thrusting Sir Thomas's books into a sack, that he took no notice of their talk. And Sir R. Southwell likewise swore that because his business was only to lake care of conveying his books away, he gave no ear to their discourse.

Sir Thomas having urged other reasons in his own defense to the discrediting of Mr. Rich's evidence; the judge proceeded to give the charge to the jury. Whether Sir Thomas had challenged any of the panel when they were returned to serve, does not appear; but the twelve persons on whose verdict his life now depended were these: Sir Thomas Palmer, Kt. Sir Tho. Peirt, Knt. George Lovell, Esq. Tho. Burbage, Esq. Geoffry Chamber, Edw. Stockmore, Jasper Leake, Wm. Browne, Tho. Billington, John Parnel, Rd. Bellame, George Stoakes, gents.

Now the jury having withdrawn, scarce were out a quarter of an hour before they returned with their verdict by which they found the prisoner guilty; upon which the Lord Chancellor as chief in the commission for this trial, immediately began to proceed to judgment which Sir Thomas observing, he said to him, my lord when I was concerned in the law, the practice in such cases was to ask the prisoner before sentence, whether he had anything to offer why judgment should not be pronounced against him. The Lord Chancellor here upon stopping his sentence wherein he had already proceeded in part, asked Sir Thomas what he was able to say to the contrary? Who presently made answer in these words: I or as much as, my lords, this indictment is grounded upon an act of Parliament directly repugnant to the laws of God and his holy church, the supreme government of which or of any part thereof, no temporal person may by any law presume to take upon him being what of right belongs to the see of Rome which by special prerogative was granted by the mouth of our savior Christ himself to St. Peter and the bishops of Rome his successors only, whilst he lived and was personally present here on earth, it is therefore amongst Catholic Christians, insufficient in law, to charge any Christian to obey it. And in order to the proof of his assertion, he declared among other things that whereas this Kingdom alone being but one member, and a small part of the church, was not to make a particular law disagreeing with the general law of Christ's universal Catholic Church, no more than the city of London being but one member in respect to the whole from there drawn on a hurdle through the city of London being but one member in respect to the whole Kingdom, might enact a law against an act of Parliament to be binding to the whole realm; so he showed farther that law was even contrary to the laws and statutes of the Kingdom, yet un-repealed as might evidently be seen by Magna Charta, wherein are these words; *Ecclesia Anglicana libera sit, & habeat omnia jura Integra, & libertates suas illicsas:* and it is contrary also to that sacred oath which the King's majesty himself, and every other Christian prince always take with great solemnity at their coronations. So great was Sir Thomas's zeal, that be further alleged that it was worse in the Kingdom of England to refuse obedience to the see of Rome, than for any child to do to his natural parent for as St. Paul said to the Corinthians, have regenerated you my children in Christ so might that worthy Pope of Rome, St. Gregory the Great say of us Englishmen you are my children because I have given you everlasting salvation for by St. Augustine and his followers his immediate messengers, England first received the Christian faith which is a far higher and better inheritance than any carnal father can leave to his children for a son is only by generation, we are by regeneration made the spiritual children of Christ and the Pope.

Here the Lord Chancellor took him up, and said that seeing all the bishops, universities, and the most learned men in the Kingdom had agreed to that act, it was much wondered that he alone should so stiffly stickle and so vehemently argue there against it. His answer was that if the number of bishops and universities were so material as his lordship seemed to make it, then, my lord, I see no reason why that thing should make any change in my conscience for I doubt not, but of the learned and virtuous men now alive, I do not speak only of this realm, but of all Christendom, there are ten to one of my mind in this matter; but if I should take notice of those learned doctors and virtuous fathers that are already dead, many of whom are saints in heaven, I am sure there are far more who all the while they lived thought in his case as I do now. And therefore my lord, I do not think myself bound to conform my conscience to the counsel of one Kingdom against the general consent of all Christendom.

Here it seems the Lord Chancellor not willing to take the whole load of his condemnation upon himself, asked in open court the advice of Sir John Fits-James, the Lord Chief Justice of England, whether the indictment was valid or no? Who wisely answered thus: my lords, all by St. Gillian (for that was always his oath) I must needs confess that if the act of Parliament be not unlawful, then the indictment is not in my conscience invalid. Some have wrote that the Lord Chancellor should hereupon say *Quid adhuc desideramus testimonium, reus est mortis,* and then presently proceeded to give sentence to this effect that he should be carried back to the Tower of London by the help of William Kingston, sheriff, and from there drawn on a hurdle through the city of London to Tyburn, there to be hanged till he should be half dead; that then he should be cut down alive, his privy parts cut off, his belly ripped, his bowels burnt, his four quarters set up over four gates of the city, and his head upon London Bridge.

This was the judgment pronounced upon this great man who had deserved so well both of the King and Kingdom and for which Paulus Jovius calls King Henry 8, another Phalaris. This severe sentence was afterwards by the King's pardon changed to beheading because he had borne the greatest office in the Kingdom; of which mercy of the King's word being brought to Sir Thomas be merrily said, God forbid the King should use anymore such mercy to any of my friends, and God bless all my posterity from such pardons. When he had received sentence of death, he spoke thus with a resolute and sedate aspect: Well, seeing I am condemned, God knows how justly, I will freely speak for the disburdening my conscience what I think of this law. When I perceived it was the King's pleasure to list out from whence the Pope's authority was derived, I confess I studied seven years together to find out the truth of it and I could not meet with the works of any one doctor approved by the church that avouch a layman was, or ever could be the head of the church.

Chancellor. Would you be esteemed wiser, or to have a sincerer conscience than all the bishops, learned doctors, nobility and commons of this realm?

More. I am able to produce against one bishop which you can produce on your side, a hundred holy and Catholic bishops for my opinion; and against one realm the consent of Christendom for a thousand years.

Norfolk. Sir Thomas, you show your obstinate and malicious mind.

More. Noble sir, it is no malice or obstinacy that makes me say this, but the just necessity of the cause obliges me to it for the discharge of my conscience; and I call God to witness that nothing but this has excited me to it.

After this the judges kindly offering him their favorable audience if he had anything else to say; he answered most mildly and charitably, I have no more to say, but that as the blessed apostle St. Paul as we read in the acts of the apostles was present, and consenting to the protomartyr Stephen, keeping their clothes that stoned him to death, and yet they are both now holy saints in heaven and there shall continue friends to eternity; so I verily trust and shall therefore heartily pray that albeit your lordships have been on earth my judges to condemnation, yet that we may hereafter meet joyfully together in heaven to our everlasting salvation and God preserve you, especially my sovereign lord the King, and grant him faithful counselors.

Sir Thomas, after his condemnation was conducted from the bar to the Tower, an axe being carried before him with the edge towards him.

Sir Thomas More having remained a prisoner in the Tower about a week after his sentence, on the 6th of July early in the morning his old friend Sir Thomas Pope came to him with a message from the King and council to acquaint him that his execution was appointed to be before nine that morning. Whereupon Sir Thomas said he thanked him heartily for his good news. I have been, says he, much obliged to his majesty for the benefits and honors he has most bountifully conferred upon me; yet I am more bound to his grace I do assure you for confining me in this place where I have had convenient place and opportunity to put me in mind of my last end. I am most of all bound to him that his majesty is pleased to rid me out of the miseries of this wretched world. Then Sir Thomas Pope acquainted him it was the King's pleasure he should not use many words at the place of execution. Sir, said he, you do well to acquaint me with the King's pleasure; for I had otherwise designed to have made a speech to the people; but it matters not, and I am ready to conform myself to his highness's pleasure. And I beseech you sir, you would become a suitor to his majesty that my daughter Margaret may attend my funeral. To which Pope replied, that the King was willing his wife and children and other friends should be present. Sir Thomas Pope being about to take his leave, could not refrain from tears. Whereupon Sir Thomas More said let not your spirits be cast down, for I hope we shall see one another in a better place where we shall be free to live and love in eternal bliss. And to divert Pope's grief, he took up his urinal and shook it, saying merrily I see no danger but that this man may live longer, if the King pleases.

About nine he was brought out of the Tower; his beard was long, his face pale and thin and carrying a red cross in his hand, he often lift up his eyes to heaven; a woman meeting with him with a cup of wine, he refused it saying Christ at his passion drank no wine but gall and vinegar. Another woman came crying and demanded some papers she said she had left in his hands when he was Lord Chancellor, to whom he said, good woman have patience but for an hour and the King will rid me of the care I have for those papers and every thing else. Another woman followed him, crying, he had done her much wrong when he was Lord Chancellor, to whom he said I very well remember the cause and if I were to decide it now, I should make the same decree.

When he came to the scaffold, it seemed ready to fall; whereupon he said merrily to the lieutenant, pray sir, see me safe up; and as to my coming down, let me shift for myself. Being about to speak to the people, he was interrupted by the sheriff and thereupon he only desired the people to pray for him and bear witness he died in the faith of the Catholic Church, a faithful servant both to God and the King. Then kneeling, he repeated the Miserere Psalm with much devotion; and rising up, the executioner asked him forgiveness. He kissed him, and said pluck up thy spirits man, and be not afraid to do the office; my neck is very short, take heed therefore thou strike not awry for saving thy honesty. Laying his head upon the block, he bid the executioner stay till he had put his beard aside for that had committed no treason. Thus he suffered with much cheerfulness; his head was taken off at one blow and was placed upon London-Bridge where having continued for some months and being about to be thrown into the Thames to make room for others, his daughter Margaret bought it, enclosed it in a leaden box, and kept it for a reliquary.

It is said when news of his death was brought to the King who was at that time playing at tables, Anne Boleyn looking on, he cast his eye upon her and said, thou art the cause of this man's death and presently leaving his play he betook himself to his chamber and thereupon, fell into a fit of melancholy. More's great grandson in his life, relates that money was miraculously supplied for the purchase of his winding sheet and that one of his teeth preserved as a relic was miraculously converted into two.

[*Cobbett's Complete Collection of State Trials. V-1.* 386-452]

The Charterhouse Monks

The Charterhouse Monks were of the monastery of the Carthusian order in central London that refused to acknowledge King Henry VIII as the supreme head of the church. Later historians place them into different groups determined by the dates of their executions from the first, to the last group executed in 1540, with eighteen in all.

The following trial is slightly different from those trials in this book as it represents the prosecution in Henry's reign for treason in denying the King's rule under the statute 26 Henry VIII., c.2, and treason in connection with religion. It deserves notice as showing the horrible laws which were placed on the statute book.

> The first prosecution under the act of 26 Henry VIII., c.2 for treason in denying the King to be supreme head of the church seem to have been those directed against Carthusian monks. Unfortunately for this order, some of their number had been mixed up with the nun of Kent. When the commissioners had been appointed to administer the oath under the statute 25 Henry VIII., c.22, they attended at the charter house and required the prior to take the oath. He refused, alleging that he knew nothing of such matters and could not meddle with them; and as he refused to give other answer, was sent with Father Humphry, another of their number to the Tower. There they remained for a month, and then took oath with reservations. They do not seem to have been further troubled until April 1535, when the government gave the order notice that their submission was required, and that they must admit the King to be the supreme head of the church.
>
> John Haughton Prior of Charter House, Augustine Webster Prior of Axholme; Robert Laurence Prior of Bellville, went to Cromwell and begged to be excused from submission to the act of supremacy. Cromwell, instead of granting their request, sent them to the Tower, and Richard Reynolds, a monk of Syon who and also refused submission, was soon sent there also. On 26 April 1535, they were brought before a committee of the Privy Council. The act of supremacy was placed before them; they were required to tender their submission; they refused and were sent back to the Tower. Two days afterwards they were brought to trial at Westminster on a charge of treason for that the 'treacherously machinating and desiring to deprive the King our sovereign lord of the title of supreme head of the church of England, did openly declare and say that the King of sovereign lord is not supreme head on earth of the church of England.' they all pleaded not guilty. A wrangle seems to have taken place between the prisoners and the judges as to the legality of the statute, a point with which the court had obviously nothing to do. They were taken back to the Tower, and the next morning again brought to the bar and put on their trial. Under the law as it stood, only one result was possible. They were convicted and sentenced. Two other priests, Hall and Robert Fearon, were put on their trial at the same time. Their treason was different. A conversation of theirs at Syon had been overheard in which they had said the King was a tyrant, heretic, robber, and

adulterer; that they hoped he would die such a death as King John and King Richard III died; that they looked forward to the time when those in Ireland and Wales should invade England; that they were assured that three parts in four of England were against the King; that they should never live merrily till the King and the rules were plucked by the plates and brought to the pot; and that it would never be well with the church till that was done. Not only was this conversation overheard, but a letter in the same tone from Hall to Frearon, of the 10th March 1535, had fallen into the hands of the government. They were indicated not only under the 26 Henry VIII c. 12, which made calling the King a schismatic, heretic, or usurper, treason but also under the 25 Edward III for compassing and imagining the King's death and conspiring to levy war against the King. They at first pleaded not guilty, but after some evidence was given, withdrew their plea and threw themselves on the mercy of the court; a verdict of guilty was given. They were sentenced to die. Fearon was pardoned; why, does not appear. On the 4th May the four Carthusians and Hall were hung at Tyburn, when for the first time in English history ecclesiastics were hung in the habits as ecclesiastics, not having been previously degraded. It seems that the sentence was carried out in all its details, and Haughton's arm was hung up over the archway of the Charter House.

In the next Trinity term, about six weeks afterwards, three more of the Charter House monks, Humphry Middlemore, William Exmew and Sebastian Newdigate were indicated for treason for having said on the 25th May, 1535, that they neither could nor would consent to be obedient to the King's highness as true, lawful, and obedient subjects and take him to be supreme head on earth of the church of England. They pleaded not guilty; were tried, convicted, sentenced, and executed. It is stated that after their condemnation they asked to be allowed to receive the sacrament, but the court refused it saying that is could be only allowed in such cases by the special order of the King.

Of the rest of the Carthusian monks, two; John Rochester and James Wolver were hanged for treason at York in May, 1535; ten more were imprisoned in Newgate on the charge of treason, nine died of prison fever and the tenth was hung in the beginning of August. Of the rest, some were sent to different religious houses in various parts of the country, some escaped abroad.

The case of Forrest, the Prior of the Observants at Greenwich who had been confessor to Queen Katharine, came next. It was said that he had, as confessor, told his penitents that he had denied the Bishop of Rome in his outward, but not in his inner man, and had encouraged them to resist taking the oath of allegiance. It appears he wavered for some time between rebellion and conformity, not having courage for the one and having some scruples as to the other. On being arrested and charged with treason, he admitted his offence and was pardoned. Afterwards he again declared his loyalty to the Pope. He stated that that blessed man St. Thomas of Canterbury suffered death for the rights of the church, for there was a great man, meaning thereby King Henry

VII, which, because St. Thomas of Canterbury would not grant him such things as he asked, contrary to the liberties of the church, first banished him out of this realm and at his return he was slain at his own church for the rights of Holy Church, as many holy fathers have suffered now of late, as that holy father the Bishop of Rochester, and he doubted not that their souls be now in heaven. He said and believed that he ought to have a double obedience; first to the King's highness by the law of God, and they, second to the Bishop of Rome by his rule and profession. He confessed that he used and practiced to induce men in confession to hold and stick to the old fashion of belief that was used in the realm of long time past.

With their opinions he was clearly guilty of treason as the law then stood, but the government determined not to prosecute him for treason, but for hearsay. Again at first he seemed inclined to abjure his religious views, but as he declined to sign an abjuration of this opinion, he was convicted by an ecclesiastical court of heresy and delivered over by them to secular arm. He was brought to Smithfield. Latimer was to preach the sermon or, as he said, 'play the fool, after his customable manner.' The sermon made no effect on Forrest. Over the stake a gallows was placed from which swung a cradle of chains. In this Forrest was placed. There had been in North Wales, at Llandderfil, an image of a great Welsh saint known as Dderfil Gadern, which was said by the Welsh to have power to save any one who offered anything to it out of hell. The Welsh were very much attached to it and offered to pay a large sum if they might keep it; but this Cromwell refused. It was sent to London by Cromwell's orders, cut up into pieces, and served as the fuel for the fire over which the unfortunate Forrest was in the presence of the lord mayor, the Dukes of Norfolk and Suffolk, Lord Southampton, Cromwell, slowly roasted to death for treason and heresy.

In the same year George Crofts Chancellor of the Cathedral of Chichester, was tried and convicted for treason for saying 'that the King was not, but the Pope was, supreme head of the church.'

John Collins was also indicted, tried, and convicted for saying that 'the King would hang in hell one day for plucking down the abbeys.'

Other instances might be given. It is however needless to multiply the list of these unhappy persons. But trial by indictment was not the only mode by which persons were executed for treason. The number was swelled by the attainder of persons found guilty by act of Parliament without being heard in their defense. This list of those who suffered for treason might easily be swelled, but enough has been stated to show that the law of treason under Henry VIII was administered with such severity that English history may be vainly searched to find any parallel.

[Willis-Bund, J. W. A Selection of cases from the State Trials. 104-108]

Anne Boleyn

The attractive young woman who was the twinkle in the eye of King Henry VIII certainly has provided a wonderful source for biographies. Historians speculate as to her birth date, but place it between 1500 and 1508. She was born into an important family and her father served as a member of the Privy Council and a diplomat. They spent about 6 to 7 years at the French court and it was through this interaction that Anne grew to love and appreciate French cultural activities.

Anne was to wed James Butler through a pre-arraigned marriage by her father which was a politically advantageous union, though it did not occur because Anne preferred Lord James Percy. She was sent to her father's homeland in Ireland and in 1522 she returned to England to later serve as Queen Catherine's lady-in-waiting. Many historians perpetuate a story that Anne had an affair with Sir Thomas Wyatt the Elder, but there is no evidence to support that, furthermore, Thomas was a happily married man.

Regardless of any possible affairs that Anne may or may not have had, she caught the eye of King Henry VIII, who was unhappy with his current marriage. In January 1533, the King wed Anne in a small and private ceremony. It was believed that Anne was pregnant with Elizabeth at the time. Though stories of Anne's past relationships are plentiful, the King's passion for her in the beginning can be read in the seventeen love letters that currently reside in the Vatican Library. Some people despised her, while others praised her, and though she had friends at court, she had as many, if not more, enemies. Anne played a large role in the downfall of Cardinal Wolsey and was known to have plotted against Catherine of Aragon and her daughter Mary. Furthermore, history has recorded her sharp tongue and rather arrogant nature towards others, sometimes including the King. Anne was reputed to have had a sixth finger or thumb and a very large mole on her back. Some have gone as far to indicate that she had a third breast.

By the time that Catherine of Aragon died in 1536, Anne had fallen out of favor with the King as she had yet to produce him a male heir. History records that Anne was pregnant again and on the day of Catherine's funeral, Anne found one of her maids of honor, Jane Seymour, sitting on the King's knee, became hysterical and had a miscarriage. A Spanish ambassador wrote to his King, 'she miscarried her savior,' for it was reported to have been a boy.

Thomas Cromwell framed a 'device' for the King that would allow him to dispose of Anne, thus launching an investigation which would result in her being charged with treason. In April 1536, Mark Smeaton, who was a friend and a musician to Anne, was arrested and — possibly through torture — he revealed information that could be used against the Queen. Sir Henry Norris was arrested, then the Queen's brother Lord Rochford and Sir Francis Weston were arrested and placed in the Tower.

On 2 May 1536, Queen Anne was arrested and informed of the numerous charges against her that included adultery, incest and plotting to murder the King.

The case of Queen Anne Boleyn is remarkable as being one of the very few examples of a prosecution for treason under the second section of the statute 25 Edward III. The details of the trial and the evidence against the Queen and those who were accused with her are wanting, but enough remains to show what the proceedings were.

In April, 1536, certain of the Privy Council were engaged in collecting evidence with regard to the Queen. Whether the King had determined on a divorce and was collecting evidence for it, is doubtful. Such at least is the impression, to which a perusal of Chapuy's letters as given by Mr. Froude would lead. The result of the evidence was the discovery of the Queen's love affair with the Earl of Northumberland. How far this went it is difficult to say. Some said only to an engagement; some to an actual marriage. Northumberland, when examined, denied that the affair had any existence; but other witnesses were forthcoming who were ready to prove it. One thing led to another and the inquiry into the Queen's conduct gave rise to such grave charges that on the 24th April, 1536, Parliament was ordered to assemble at once. A commission was appointed to investigate these charges and the result of their deliberation was that on the 26th April, Sir William Brereton was arrested on a charge of treason and sent to the Tower. On the 30th, Mark Smeton, a musician was arrested on a like charge and sent to the Tower. On the next day, the 1st May, the celebrated tournament at Greenwich (at which the Queen's brother, Lord Rochford and Sir Henry Norris took part) was held. At the tournament the King suddenly left Greenwich and did not return. The Queen remained there on the 2nd May. A Privy Council presided over by the Queen's uncle the Duke of Norfolk, was held at Greenwich before which the Queen was summoned to appear. Being examined, she declared herself innocent of the charges. Either on that or the previous day to further arrests, those of Sir Henry Norris and Sir Francis Weston were made. After the Queen's examination Smeton, Norris, and Weston were examined by the council. Smeton confessed to actual intercourse with the Queen. Norris, on being pressed by the council, did the same; but both he and Smeton afterwards retracted their confession saying they were deceived into making it. Weston denied the charge. In the afternoon the three and the Queen were sent to the Tower. The same afternoon the Queen's brother Lord Rochford was arrested, charged with the same offense and sent to the Tower. Smeton was put into irons. The Queen in the Tower had some conversation with several persons as to the charges against her and some communications on the subject, it would seem passed between her and the King, but as the inferences from these conversations and correspondence are dubious, and as they could not be evidence one way or the other, it is needless, looking at the case from a legal as opposed to a moral point of view, to refer to them.

Indictments against all the prisoners were found by a grand jury of Middlesex and a grand jury of Kent, the offence having been committed, as was alleged, in both counties at Hampton Court and at Greenwich, and a special commission was appointed to try Smeton, Norris, Weaton and Brereton. The commissioners were the Chancellor Sir Thomas Audley, the Duke of Norfolk, (the uncle of the Queen and Lord Rochford), the Duke of Suffolk, the Earl of Wiltshire (The Queen's father), the Earls of Oxford, Westmorland and Sussex, Lord Sandys, Thomas Cromwell, the Lord High Admiral (Sir William Fitzwilliam), the Lord Treasurer (Sir William Paulet), and nine judges, Sir John Fitzjames, Sir John Baldwin, Sir Richard Lister, Sir John Porte, Sir John Spelman, Sir Walter Luke, Sir Anthony Fitzerbert, Sir Thomas Englefield, and Sir William Shelly.

On Friday, the 12th May, Sir Henry Norris, Sir William Brereton, Sir Francis Weston, and Mark Smeton, were arraigned before the commissioners at Westminster upon two indictments which were in substance as follows:

1. That the Lady Anne, Queen of England, having been the wife of the King for the space of three years and more, she, the said Lady Anne contemning the marriage so solemnized between her and the King and bearing malice in her heart against the King, and following her frail and carnal lust, did falsely and traitorously procure by means of indecent language, gifts, and other acts, divers of the King's daily and familiar servants to be her adulterers and concubines, so that several of the King's servants by the said Queen's most vile provocation and invitation, became given and inclined to the said Queen.

2. That the said Queen on the 6th day of October, 1533 at Westminster, by words &c, procured and incited Henry Norris, a gentleman of the King's privy chamber to have illicit intercourse with her, and that the said act was committed at Westminster on the 12th October 1533.

3. That the said Queen on the 2nd of November, 1535, by the means therein mentioned, procured and incited George Boleyn, Knight, Lord Rochford, her own natural brother, to have illicit intercourse with her and that such intercourse took place at Westminster on the 5th of November, 1535, against the commands of Almighty God and all laws human and divine.

4. That the said Queen on the 3rd day of December, 1533, as therein stated, procured and incited William Brereton of the gentlemen of the King's privy chamber, to have illicit intercourse with her and that such intercourse took place at Hampton Court on the 25th December 1533.

5. That the said Queen on the 8th of May, 1534, procured and incited by the means therein stated, Francis Weston, one of the gentlemen of the King's privy chamber, to have illicit intercourse with her and that such intercourse took place at Westminster on the 20th of May, 1534.

6. That the said Queen on the 12 day of April, 1534, by the means therein mentioned, procured and incited Mark Smeton, one of the grometers of

the King's chamber, to have illicit intercourse with her and that such illicit intercourse took place at Westminster on the 26th day of April, 1534.

7. Moreover, the said George Lord Rochford, Henry Norris, William Brereton, Francis Weston, and Mark Smeton, being thus inflamed by carnal love of the Queen, and having become very jealous of each other, did, in order to secure her affection, satisfy her inordinate desires; and that the said Queen was equally jealous of the said Lord Rochford and the other before mentioned traitors and would not allow them to show any familiarity with any other woman without her exceeding displeasure and indignation, and that she on the 27th day of November, 1535, and on divers other days, gave them gifts and great rewards to inveigle them to her will.

8. Furthermore, that the said Queen and other the said traitors jointly and severally on the 31st day of October, 1535, and at divers other times before and after, compassed and imagined the King's death; and that the said Queen had frequently promised to marry some one of the said traitors whenever the said King should depart this life affirming that she never would love the King in her heart.

9. Furthermore, that the said King, having within a short time before become acquainted with the before mentioned crimes, vices, and treason, had been so grieved that certain harm and danger had happened to his royal body.

Smeton pleaded guilty to the illicit intercourse and admitted that it had taken place three times. Weston, Norris, and Brereton pleaded not guilty.

What evidence against them was we do not know. Norris's confession seems to have been read against him and he urged in extenuation that Sir William Fitzwilliam had deceived him into making it. We know nothing of the evidence against Weston and Brereton; but whatever it was, the jury convicted them all of treason and the usual sentence in such cases was passed on them.

The Queen and Lord Rochford were to be tried before the court of the Lord High Steward. The Duke of Norfolk was appointed Lord High Steward and the lords summoned to act on the trial were the Duke of Suffolk, the Marquis of Exeter, the Earl of Northumberland, (the Queen's old lover), the Earls of Arundel, Oxford, Westmoreland, Derby, Worcester, Rutland, Sussex, and Huntington; Lords Audley, Delawarr, Montague, Morley, Dacre, Cobham, Maltravers, Powis, Mounteagle, Clinton, Sandys, Windsor, Wentworth, Burgh, and Mourdant.

On the 15th of May, the Lord High Steward's court composed of these noblemen, sat in the Tower and the Queen was brought before them.

The indictment against her alleged that she had procured her brother, Norris, Smeton, Weston, and Brereton to have illicit intercourse with her, which they had often done; that she had told them that the King had never had her heart and told each of them by themselves that she loved them better that any person whatsoever, the first part of the indictment being based on the 25 Edward III, the last part being held to be treason under statute 25

Henry VIII, c. 22, as slander of the issue which was begotten between the King and her. It is a curious example of the irony of history that the statute which was passed for the protection of the Queen and her children was then made the means of her destruction. When the indictment was read, the Queen held up her hands and pleaded not guilty. She was allowed to be seated and the trial proceeded.

We have no account of the evidence against her except that Smeton's confession was read. Witnesses, it seems, were examined in court, but the substance of the testimony is not known. The Queen, it is said, having an excellent quick wit and being a ready speaker, did so answer to all objections that had the peers given in the verdict according to the expectation of the assembly, she would have been acquitted. All the details known of the trial are from the record, which is as follows:

Before the Lord High Steward at the Tower, Queen of England comes in under the custody of Sir William Kingston, Constable of the Tower, and is brought to the bar; being arraigned of the before mentioned treasons, she pleads not guilty and puts herself upon her peers. Whereupon the Duke of Suffolk, the Marquis of Exeter, and others before the mentioned earls and barons, peers of the said Queen, being charged by the said Lord High Steward to say the truth and afterwards being examined severally by the Lord High Steward for the lowest peer to the highest, each of them severally said that she is guilty.

Judgment; that the Queen be taken by the said constable back to the King's prison within the Tower and then as the King shall command be brought to the Green within the said Tower, and there burned or beheaded, as shall please the King.

This sentence, it appears, was of doubtful legality. The punishment by the law of England for a woman attainted of treason was burning. The judges held that the court had no power to pass a sentence in the alternative; their duty was to pronounce the sentence the law prescribed; if it was to be altered it was not for them to do it. A disjunctive sentence was something wholly unknown to the law.

Lord Rochford's trial followed the Queen's. He too pleaded not guilty. What the evidence against him was not known, but he also was convicted and sentenced to die.

There was little delay between the sentence and the execution. On the 17th of May, Lord Rochford, Norris, Weston, Smeton and Brereton were executed. Smeton was hanged, the others were beheaded. Why this difference, except that Smeton had confessed of that he was of a lower social rank, is not easy to see. "In a manner" says a contemporary who had good opportunities of knowing, "all confessed but Mr. Norris, who said almost nothing at all." Chapuy's states that to enhance the Queen's misery and grief, she was made to see the execution from the window of the Tower.

While this scene was going on Tower Hill, so far as it could be done in law, the innocence of these criminals was being asserted at Westminster.

Cranmer had been sent to the Queen after the trial as her confessor and the Queen then stated, or was alleged to have stated to him that previous to her marriage with the King something had taken place which rendered that marriage invalid.

On the 17th May, she was taken to Lambeth and the archbishop sitting in his court received the Queen's confession "of certain just, true and lawful impediments unknown at the making of the said acts, by which it plainly appeared that the said marriage was never good nor consonant to law." What those impediments were is not known. Rumors there are in plenty, facts there are none. Lord Northumberland was examined as to the alleged marriage or contract and denied it in person on oath before the archbishop and in a letter to Cromwell. On the Queen's part it was alleged, "*que le Roy n'estoit habille en cas de soy...avec femme et qu'il n'avoit ny vertu ny puissance.*" (That the King was not dressed in case of being with wife, and that he had neither virtue nor power.) Another story was that the Queen's sister Mary Boleyn had been the King's mistress before his marriage with Anne. Whatever was the real story the sentence was pronounced that the King's marriage with Anne had been void *ab initio*.

[Willis-Bund, J. W. *A Selection of Cases from the State Trials. V-1.* 86-92]

Though Mr. Bund provides a wonderful account of the trial not found in Cobbett's or Howell's collection of state trials, both end with Anne's execution occurring without expanding on the subject. Mr. Friedman, (*Anne Boleyn, a Chapter of English History*) of all the biographies I reviewed, provides more detail of the events after her sentence to the execution with more detail and has a place here.

Her hopes of life had not lasted long, for Kingston had soon undeceived her. After the sitting at Lambeth her execution was fixed for the morning of the 18th, and she was told of it. She slept little that night; her almoner was in attendance, and from two o'clock onwards she remained in prayer with him. In the morning she sent for Kingston, and asked him to be present when she was to receive the sacrament and to assert her innocence of the crimes laid to her charge. Shortly afterwards the communion was celebrated, and both before and after receiving the host she declared on the salvation of her soul that she had never been unfaithful to the King. After this she patiently waited; but as time passed on she became restless and asked her attendants when she was to die. They answered that she would not be executed before noon. In reality, the execution was not to take place until the following day.

The explanation of this change of plan is not perfectly clear. It seems that Anne, faithful to her French education, considered it more honorable to die by the stroke of a sword than to have her head hacked off with an axe. The hangman of Calais, the only subject of Henry who knew how to behead with a sword, had, therefore, been sent for, and he may not have arrived at the expected time. It is more probable, however, that the delay was due to a different cause.

The government now regretted that so many people had been allowed to hear the incredible accusations against Anne and her brother, and their able and eloquent defense. Many strangers [foreigners] had been present at the trials; and it was feared that after their return to their homes they would give a very unfavorable account of the King's proceedings. On Thursday morning, therefore, Cromwell wrote to Kingston that all foreigners were to be expelled from the Tower. In reporting that this order had been obeyed, Kingston expressed the opinion that if the exact time was not made public there would probably be few spectators; and it is not unlikely that the government decided to postpone the execution in the hope that this suggestion would prove to be right.

When Anne's attendants told her that she would not die before noon, she sent for Kingston and complained to him of the delay. She had hoped, she said, to be past her pain. The constable tried to console her; it was no pain, he said it was so quickly done. Anne spoke of the executioner's skill and of the smallness of her neck; and then, the long waiting having unstrung her nerves, she had another attack of hysterical laughter by which the constable was sorely puzzled. "I have seen many men and also women executed," he wrote, "and that they have been in great sorrow; and to my knowledge this lady has much joy and pleasure in death." The rest of the day Anne spent partly in praying, partly in chatting with her attendants on her past life and on her future fame. Those ingenious persons, she said, who had forged so infamous a name for the late Queen would have no trouble in finding one for her. They would call her Queen Lackhead. And therewith came another burst of hysterical laughter. There was but one thing which preyed on her mind, her behavior to the Princess Mary. She repeatedly spoke of it, saying that she had been brought to this end by divine judgment for being the cause of Mary's ill-treatment and for having tried to bring about her death. Of the common story that Anne, kneeling, asked Lady Kingston to beg Mary to pardon her, I have found no trace; and it may be dismissed as an embellishment of later writers.

In this way the time went on. During the night Anne seems to have taken scarcely any rest, her nerves being too excited for sleep. She continued to talk to her ladies, and conversed and prayed with her almoner. As the morning of Friday, the 19th of May approached, Kingston informed her that she would shortly be executed, and he handed her a purse with twenty pounds which she was to distribute, according to custom, as alms before her death. A little before nine he returned and announced that the moment had come.

During the night a platform had been erected in the courtyard of the Tower. It rose but a few feet above the ground, for it had been deemed inexpedient to raise a high scaffold which might be seen from afar. In the courtyard the Lord Chancellor, the Dukes of Suffolk and of Richmond, Sir Thomas Cromwell and others of the council were assembled to witness Anne's death. The lord mayor, with some aldermen and representatives of the crafts of the city, attended by order; and as their coming had attracted attention, they had been followed by a considerable number of people. But strict watch had been kept at the gates and although Englishmen had been freely admitted, all foreigners had been excluded.

Anne now appeared, led by Kingston and followed by the four ladies. She wore a dressing gown of grey damask, which she had chosen because it was low round the neck and would not interfere with the executioner's work. For the same reason she had tied up her hair in a knot over which she wore the customary head dress. In this guise she was handed over by Kingston to the sheriffs who led her up to the platform.

Permission was granted to her to address the crowd, and she did so in few words and very simply. She had not come to preach, she said, but to die. She asked those who were present to pray for the King, who was a right gentle prince and had treated her as well as possible. She said that she accused nobody on account of her death, for she had been sentenced according to the law of the country. So she was ready to die, and asked the forgiveness of all whom she might have wronged. Having said these words, she herself took off her head dress which she handed to one of the ladies. Then she once more asked the bystanders to pray to God for her.

During the whole time that she had been on the scaffold, she had been nervously looking round towards the place where the executioner stood leaning on his heavy sword. Now she knelt down, and one of her attendants bound a handkerchief round her eyes. After this the ladies also knelt down, silently praying, while she repeated the words: "Oh God, have pity on my soul." The executioner stepped quickly forward and took his aim; the heavy two handled blade flew hissing through the air, and Anne's head rolled in the dust.

Head and trunk were taken up by the ladies, wrapped in a sheet, laid in a plain coffin, and carried to the Tower chapel. Here they were buried with little ceremony. No inscription, except a few letters was put upon Anne's grave and the exact spot was soon forgotten. It was discovered only a few years ago.

[Friedman, *Anne Boleyn, A Chapter of English History*, V-2. 290-296]

Thomas Cromwell

Thomas Cromwell was born circa 1485 in Putney, London to a father often described as a jack-of-all-trades. Records show that he worked as a blacksmith; fuller and more frequent are the records that mention him as a brewer and tavern owner. It is through the latter his name appears numerous times in court rolls for having committed various misdemeanors.

History recorded colorful accounts of Thomas Cromwell's life from boyhood to early adulthood. He ran away from home at about 16 and gained passage on a ship for the Low Countries then to France in which a story recounts he had joined the French army as a soldier's servant against England. He is later found in a battle of Garigliano near Naples, Italy where the Spanish defeated the French army. While in Italy, Cromwell met a member of the prominent banking Frescobaldi family and he proved to be a loyal, intelligent and fast learning servant who later conducted transactions for the family and also began to study law.

Upon returning to England he married the widow Elizabeth Wykys. In 1517 he was approached to help secure an audience with the Pope to procure necessary funds for a church in Lincolnshire. To gain favor with the Pope, Cromwell utilized the Pope's love for sweetmeats and was successful in his mission and returned to England earning a reputation as a 'fixer.' Coupled with that accomplishment and his knowledge of Italy, he also gained recognition from Cardinal Wolsey and found himself involved in the cardinal's 'legacy project' which was a fabulous tomb in which he employed many skilled Italian sculptors. It was through his time with Cardinal Wolsey that Cromwell earned a position as a member of Parliament in 1523.

Cromwell's life took a sharp turn for the worse when his wife and two daughters died of the 'sweating sickness,' leaving his son Gregory to help him through his dark period. Returning to court shortly after, Cromwell found himself involved in the turmoil when the King sought an annulment from Catherine of Aragon. By that point the King lost faith in Cardinal Wolsey and when Wolsey was arrested, Cromwell remained loyal to him although an early account mentions that he wrote his will fearing the worst.

Cromwell was successful in maintaining the fine line defining his loyalty to the King while still maintaining a clear conscience. The King eventually divorced Catherine and married Anne Boleyn, but she suffered a miscarriage of a boy and thus the King turned his attention to Jane Seymour. Cromwell was instrumental in 'getting rid' of Anne and she was tried and convicted of treason, allowing the King to marry Jane. Jane died in 1537 after giving birth to the male heir that the King had so longed for, Edward VI.

Thomas Cromwell began to assist in the search for a suitable wife for the King and suggested Anne of Cleves. He commissioned Hans Holbein to paint a portrait of her for the King to see. The King was rather disappointed with her appearance, but Cromwell managed to persuade the King to proceed with the marriage. It was a catastrophe by contemporary standards and for an annulment to be granted, King Henry VIII was required to testify in court about his failings in the bedroom. The King was furious with Cromwell and his enemies seized the opportunity to remove him from court and charged him with treason.

Proceedings against Thomas Cromwell, Earl of Essex for treason: 33 Hen. VIII. A.D. 1541.

That beauty and attraction which should take the King's eye in Anne of Cleve, not appearing, nor that conversation which should please his ear; and her brother besides excusing himself in the performance of some articles of the treaty, he did more willingly think of a divorce; for which purpose, the pre-contract with the Duke of Lorain's son was chiefly pretended. For though Olesleger, Chancellor of Cleves, had according to his promise, 26 Feb. 1510, procured an instrument in writing out of the records of Düsseldorf, dated Feb. 15, 1535, testifying the Sponsalia heretofore made by the parents between the Duke of Lorain's son and the Lady Anne, should not take effect. Yet this it seems either was not showed, or did not satisfy our King. Howsoever it was not deposited in *archivis liegiis*, but found among Cromwell's papers after his apprehension. And now although all scruples seemed the more considerable in that so many doubts had been already cast concerning the Kings former marriages, yet the King determined at what price so ever to separate himself from Anne of Cleve, and together to ruin Cromwell. For though he had not long before made him Knight of the Garter, Earl of Essex and High Chamberlain of England, yet as he was odious by reason of his low birth to all the nobility, and hated particularly by Stephen Gardiner and the Roman Catholics for having operated so much in the dissolution of abbes; and that the reformers themselves found he could not protect them from burning; and lastly, that besides a subsidy that the clergy gave of 4s. in the pound, he had gotten in the present Parliament, not without much relocation, one tenth, and one fifteen parts of all laymen's goods; he was universally hated which our King considering, and having besides divers article brought against him, he now judged him no longer necessary therefore he gave way to nil his enemies accusations; which could not but be material it being impossible that any man, who meddled so much in great and public affairs, should not in divers kinds so mistake, forget, and err as to incur the note of a criminal, when severe inquisition were made against him. And now the King caused Cromwell to be arrested at the council-table by the Duke of Norfolk, when he least suspected it to which Cromwell obeyed, though judging his perdition more certain, that the duke was uncle to the Lady Catharine Howard, whom the King began now to affect. The news whereof and his commitment to the Tower being divulged, the people with many acclamations witnessed their joy; so impatient are they usually of the good fortune of favorites arising from mean place, and insolent over the ill whereof the King being informed, proceeded more overtly, both in his Parliament business, and the divorce; and the rather that all former faults being now imputed to Cromwell, every body began to hope of a better age. But Cromwell (if we may believe some of our authors) foresaw his fall two years before, and therefore provided for his family; neither did the late honors give him much comfort or security when he thought they were conferred only to make him the greater sacrifice.

Crimes and accusations brought against the Lord Cromwell.

After this he was attainted by Parliament; in the which attainder, divers and sundry crimes, surmises, objections, and accusations were brought against him, but chiefly and above all other he was charged and accused of heresy, for that he was a supporter of them (whom they recounted for heretics) as Barns, Clark, and many other, whom he by his authority and letters written to sheriffs and justices in divers shires rescued and discharged out of prison. Also that he did divulgate and disperse abroad among the King's subjects great numbers of books containing, as they said, manifest matter of much heresy, diffidence, and disbelief. Item, that he caused to be translated into our English tongue books comprising matter expressly against the sacrament of the altar, and that after the translation thereof, he commended and maintained the same for good and Christian doctrine. Over and besides all this, they brought in certain witnesses, what they were, the attainder expresses not, which most especially pressed or rather oppressed him with heinous words spoken against the King in the Church of St. Peter the Poor in the month of March in the thirtieth year of the King's reign. Which words, if they be true, as the attainder does purport, three things says Fox, I have here much to marvel at. First, if his adversaries had so sure hold and matter against him, then what should move them to make such hasty speed, in all post haste to have him dispatched and rid out of the way and in no case could abide him to come to his purgation? Which, if he might have done, it is not otherwise to be thought, but he would easily have cleared himself thereof. Secondly; this I marvel that if the words had been so heinous against the King as his enemies did pretend, why then did those witnesses which heard those words in St. Peter's Church in the thirtieth year of the King's reign, conceal the said words of such treason so long, the space almost of two years, and now uttered the same in the two and thirtieth year of the ling's reign in the month of July. Thirdly, here is again to be marveled, if the King had known or believed these words to be true, and that Cromwell had indeed been such a traitor to his person, why then did the King so shortly after lament his death, wishing to have his Cromwell alive again? What prince will wish the life of him whom he suspected undoubtedly to be a traitor to his life and person? Whereby it may appear what judgment the King had of Cromwell in himself, howsoever the Parliament by sinister information was otherwise incensed to judge upon him.

The proceedings against him were thought rigorous, but so few pitied him that all was easily passed over, nevertheless, I find by an original that Cranmer wrote to the King in his behalf boldly considering the times; 'for though,' as is in his letter, he heard yesterday in his grace's council, that he is a traitor; yet, he said, who cannot be sorrowful and amazed that he should be a traitor against your majesty? He that was so advanced by your majesty, he whose surety was only by your majesty, he who loved your majesty, as I ever thought no less than God; he who studied always to set forward whatsoever was your majesty's will and pleasure; be that cared for no man's displeasure to serve your majesty; he that was such a servant, in my judgment, in wisdom, diligence, faithfulness, and experience, as no prince in this realm ever had; he that was so vigilant to preserve your majesty from all treasons, that few could be so secretly conceived, but he detected the same in the beginning? If the noble princes of memory, King John, Henry 2, and Richard 2, had had such a counselor about them, I suppose they should never have been so traitorously abandoned and overthrown as those good princes were. After which, he says again, I loved him as my friend, for so I took him to be, but I chiefly loved him for the love which I thought I saw him bear ever towards your grace singularly above all others, but now, if he be a traitor, I am sorry that ever I loved him, or trusted him, and I am very glad that his treason is discovered in time; but yet again I am very sorrowful; for who shall your grace trust hereafter, if you might not trust him? Alas! I bewail and lament your grace's chance herein, I want not whom your grace may trust. But I pray God continually night and day to send such a counselor in his place, whom your grace may trust, and who for all his qualities can and will serve your grace like to him and that will have so much solicitude and care to preserve your grace from all dangers as I ever thought he had. All which as being a character of Cromwell in Cranmer's opinion, I have faithfully copied out of the original. Not yet that I will pretend excuses for him, whom the laws have condemned; but that his punishment may serve as a caution for those that serve severe princes to procure sufficient warrant for all that they do. The crimes objected to Cromwell seeming to be chiefly an usurpation of power to set at liberty certain persons not capable of it and granting certain licenses, and making certain commissions in high affairs, without the King's knowledge for which, though Cromwell in his discretion might have found due motives; yet as he proceeded not warily therein, he fell into the danger of the law. Furthermore, he was accused for being a heretic and favoring them as for his speaking certain high presumptuous words concerning the King, and sundry of the nobility, many thought it proceeded rather out of mistaking and rashness, than any ill intention.

Cromwell thus unheard and almost un-pitied, being condemned while he was in the Tower, omitted not yet to write to the King. Amongst the rest of the commissioners which came to him, one there was whom the Lord Cromwell desired to carry for him a letter to the King, which when he refused saying that he would carry no letter to the King from a traitor; then the Lord Cromwell desired him at least to do from him a message to the King. To that the other was contented, and granted, so that it were not against his allegiance. Then the Lord Cromwell taking witness of the other lords what he had promised; you shall commend me, said he, to the King, and tell him by that he has so well tried and thoroughly proved you as I have done, he shall find you as false a man as ever came about him. Besides this, he wrote also a letter from the Tower to the King, whereof when none does take the carriage upon him, Sir Ralf Sadler, (whom he also had preferred to the King before, being ever trusty and faithful to him) went to the King to understand his pleasure, whether he would permit him to bring the letter or not, which when the King had granted, the said Master Sadler, as he was required, presented the letter to the King, which he commanded thrice to be read to him, insomuch as the King seemed to be moved therewith.

The Lord Cromwell brought to the scaffold.

Notwithstanding by reason of the act of Parliament afore passed, the worthy and noble Lord Cromwell oppressed by his enemies and condemned in the Tower, and not coming to his answer, the 28th of July 1541 was brought to the scaffold on Tower-Hill where he said these words following:

I am come hither to die and not to purge myself, as some think peradventure that I will. For if I should so do, I were a very wretch and a miser. I am by the law condemned to die, and thank my lord God that has appointed me this death for mine offence. For since the time that I have had years of discretion, I have lived a sinner, and offended my lord God, for the which I ask him heartily forgiveness. And it is not unknown to many of you, that I have been a great traveler in this world, and being but of a base degree was called to high estate, and since the time I came thereto I have offended my prince, for the which I ask him heartily forgiveness and beseech you all to pray to God with me, that be will forgive me. And now I pray you that be here to bear me record, I die in the Catholic faith, not doubting in any article of my faith nor doubting in any sacrament of the church. Many have slandered me and reported that I have been a bearer of such as have maintained evil opinions, which is untrue. But I confess, that like as God by his holy spirit doth instruct us in the truth, so the devil is ready to seduce us, and I have been seduced; but hear me witness that I die in the Catholic faith of the holy church and I heartily desire you to pray for the King's grace, that he may long live with you in health and prosperity; and that after him his son, Prince Edward that goodly imp, may long reign over you. And once again I desire you to pray for me that so long as life remains in this flesh, I waver nothing in my faith.

And so making his prayer, kneeling on his knees he spoke these words, the effect whereof here follows:

A prayer that the Lord Cromwell said at the hour of his death.

O Lord Jesus, which art the only health of all men living and the everlasting life of them which die in thee; I wretched sinner do submit myself wholly to thy most blessed will, and being sure that the thing cannot perish which is committed to thy mercy, willingly now I leave this frail and wicked flesh in sure hope that thou wilt in better wise restore it to me again at the last day in the resurrection of the just. I beseech thee most merciful Lord Jesus Christ, that thou wilt by thy grace make strong my soul against all temptations, and defend me with the buckler of thy mercy against all the assaults of the Devil. I see and acknowledge that there is in myself no hope of salvation, but all my confidence, hope and trust is in thy most merciful goodness. I have no merits nor good works which I may allege before thee. Of sins and evil works (alas) I see a great heap; but yet through thy mercy I trust to be in the number of them to whom thou wilt not impute their sins; but will take and accept me for righteous and just, and to be the inheritor of everlasting life. Thou merciful lord was born for my sake, thou did suffer both hunger and thirst for my sake; thou didst teach, pray, and fast for my sake, all thy holy actions and works thou wrought for my sake; thou suffered most grievous pains and torments for my sake, finally, thou gave thy most precious body and thy blood to be shed on the cross for my sake. Now most merciful savior, let all these things profit me, that thou freely hast done for me, which hast given thyself also for me. Let thy blood cleanse and wash away the spots and foulness of my sins. Let thy righteousness bide and cover my unrighteousness. Let the merits of thy passion and blood-shedding be satisfaction for my sins. Give me lord thy grace, that the faith of my salvation in thy blood waver not in me, but may ever be firm and constant. That the hope of thy mercy and life everlasting never decay in me, that love wax not cold in me. Finally, that the weakness of my flesh be not overcome with the fear of death. Grant me merciful savior, that when death has shut up the eyes of my body, yet the eyes of my soul may still behold and look upon thee, and when death has taken away the use of my tongue, yet my heart may cry and say to thee, Lord into thy hands I commend my soul, Lord Jesus receive my spirit. Amen.

And thus his prayer being made after he had godly and lovingly exhorted them that were about him on the scaffold, he quietly committed his soul into the hands of God, and so patiently suffered the stroke of the axe by a ragged and butcherly miser, which very ungodly performed his office.

To this end came Cromwell, who from being but a blacksmiths son, found means to travel into divers foreign countries to learn their languages, and to see the wars, (being a soldier of Bourbon at the sacking of Rome;) when returning, he was received into the Cardinal Wolsey's service to whom he so approved himself by his fidelity and diligence that the King after his fall voluntarily took him for his servant; in which place he became a special instrument for dissolving the abbeys, and other religious houses, and keeping down the clergy; whom in regard of their oath to the Pope, he usually termed the King's half subjects. And for expelling the monks, he said it was no more than a restoring them to the first institution of being lay and laboring persons. Neither did it move him, that so much strictness and austerity of life was enjoined them in their several orders since he said they might keep it in any condition. But as these reasons again were not admitted by divers learned and able persons, so he got him many enemies, who at last procured his fall; but not before he had obtained successively the dignities of Master of the Rolls, Baron, Lord Privy-Seal, Vicegerent to the King in spiritualities, Knight of the Garter, Earl of Essex, Great Chamberlain of England, &c. He was noted in the exercise of his places of judicature to have used much moderation; and in his greatest pomp, to have taken notice and been thankful to mean persons of his old acquaintance, and therein had a virtue which his master the cardinal wanted as for his other descriptions, I leave them to be taken out of Cranmer's letter formerly mentioned, with some deduction; for it seems written to the King in more than ordinary favor of his ancient service.

At the same time with Cromwell, Walter Lord Hungerford suffered. The crimes objected to him were for taking into his house as chaplain one William Bird who had called the King heretic, &c. That he had procured certain persons to conjure, to know how long the King should live; also, that he had used the sin of buggery.

Rapin observes that the care Cromwell took when he came to die, to say nothing which might offend the King, proved to the advantage of his son Gregory who was that very year created a peer by the title of Lord Cromwell.

Shortly after this followed the countess of Salisbury's execution, who had with Cromwell been excepted from the general act of pardon, which, whether occasioned by the late rebellion, (as being thought of Cardinal

Pool's instigation) or that she gave some new offence, is uncertain the old lady being brought to the scaffold, set up in the Tower, was commanded to lay her head on the block; but she (as a person of great quality assured me) refused; saying, 'So should traitors do, and I am none.' Neither did it serve that the executioner told her it was the fashion; so turning her gray head every way, she bid him, if he would have her head, to get it as he could. So that he was constrained to fetch it off slovenly.

She was daughter of George Duke of Clarence, brother of Edward the 4th. She had four sons, Cardinal Pole was the youngest. The eldest was Henry Lord Montacute, from a daughter of whom the present Earl of Moira is descended.

[Cobbett's, *Complete Collection of State Trials, V-1.* 434-440]

Catherine Howard

Catherine Howard was born circa 1520 in Lambeth, London. She was the tenth child of Edmund Howard and Joyce Culpepper. She was a niece of the Duke of Norfolk and first cousin of Anne Boleyn. Catherine spent a portion of her childhood in the household of the Duchess of Norfolk and spent most of that time at Lambeth and Horsham.

History mentions several romantic interludes Catherine had while in her late teens, most notably was with her music teacher, Henry Mannox. Another was with Francis Dareham, whom she wanted to marry after he returned to England from Ireland, but the Duchess of Norfolk found out and quickly sent her to serve as a lady-in-waiting for the King's new wife, Anne of Cleves. In all likelyhood, it was at that point she had caught the eye of the King and it has been suggested that her uncle, the Duke of Norfolk, instructed Catherine to respond to the King's attentions, motivated by a chance to increase his favor with the King and to seize on the opportunity to discredit a rival, Thomas Cromwell.

The King accumulated many extra pounds of weight as a result of less activity, perhaps in part from an ulcerated leg which caused difficulty while walking. The King did in fact shower the young Catherine with gifts and within a few weeks after the King successfully annulled his marriage with Anne, he married Catherine on 28 July 1540. The King was 49 and Catherine was 19. The King's young bride did raise his spirits and referred to her as 'his rose without a thorn' and the 'very jewel of womanhood.'

Rumors began to circulate within a year of her infidelity with a distant relation, Thomas Culpepper. It would be, perhaps, not hard to understand why Catherine sought someone closer to her age over a grumpy, obese man, but she may not have contemplated the ramifications of any flirtations noticed while in court. This was augmented by her appointment of an admirer as her personal secretary.

History records an account when the Queen and Culpepper accompanied the King to York on the Northern Progress preceding what is commonly known as the 'Pilgrimage of Grace'. At that point, Thomas Cranmer learned of Catherine's indiscretions and immediately reported it to the King who refused, at first, to believe. Shortly after, Culpepper and Dareham were arrested and as some accounts suggest, tortured into admitting their guilt. Catherine's musician friend, Mannox, also testified against her. There was enough evidence to place Catherine in the Tower and she was stripped of her title as Queen.

Proceedings against Queen Catharine Howard for incontinency: 33 Henry VIII. A.D. 1542.

But our King encountered a greater vexation; for the Queen was supposed to offend in incontinency; some particulars whereof being extant in our records, I have thought fit, says Lord Herbert, to transcribe rather than to make other narration; the family of which she came being so noble and illustrious and the honor of her sex (which is tender) being concerned therein. The letter sent from divers of the council to William Paget, our ambassador then in France, was this:

After our hearty commendations by these our letters, we be commanded to signify to you a most miserable case, which came lately to revelation, to the intent that if you shall hear the same spoken of, you may declare the truth as follows, where the King's majesty upon the sentence given of the invalidity of the pretended matrimony between his highness and the Lady Anne of Cleve, was earnestly and humbly solicited by his council and the nobles of this realm, to frame his most noble heart to the love and favor of some noble personage to be joined with him in lawful matrimony, by whom his majesty might have some more store of fruit, and succession to the comfort of this realm; it pleased his highness upon a notable appearance of honor, cleanness and maidenly behavior, to bend his affection towards mistress Catharine Howard, daughter to the late Lord Edmond Howard, brother to me the Duke of Norfolk, insomuch as his highness was finally contented to honor her with his marriage, thinking now in his old days, after sundry troubles of mind, which have happened to him by marriages, to have obtained such a jewel for womanhood, and very perfect love towards him as should not only have been to his quietness, but also brought forth the desired fruit of marriage like as the whole realm thought the semblable, and in respect of the virtue and good behavior which she showed outwardly, did her all honor accordingly. But this joy is turned into extreme sorrow; for when the King's majesty receiving his maker on Allhallows day last past, then gave him most humble and hearty thanks for the good life he led and trusted to lead with her, and also desired the Bishop of Lincoln, his ghostly father, to make like prayer and give like thanks with him; on all-souls day being at mass, the Archbishop of Canterbury having a little before heard that the same mistress Catharine Howard was not indeed a woman of that pureness and cleanness that she was esteemed; but a woman who before she was joined with the King's majesty, had lived most corruptly and sensually; for the discharge of his duty opened the same most sorrowfully to his majesty and how it was brought to his knowledge, which was in this form following. While the King's majesty was in his progress, one John Lossels came to the said Archbishop of Canterbury and declared to him that he had been with a sister of his married in Sussex, which sometimes had been servant with the old Duchess of Norfolk, who did also bring up the said mistress Catharine, and being with his said sister, chanced to fall in communication with her of the Queen, wherein he advised her (because she was of the Queen's old acquaintance) to sue to be her woman; whereto his sister answered that she would not so do; but she was very sorry for the Queen; why, quote Lossels? Marry, quote she, for she is light both in living and condition, how so, quote Lossels? Marry, quote she, there is one Francis Derrliani, who was servant also in my Lady of Norfolk's house which has lien in bed with her in his doublet and hose between the sheets an hundred nights. And there has been such puffing and blowing between them, that once in the house a maid which lay in the house with her, said to me, she would lie no longer with her, because she knew not what matrimony meant. And further she said to turn, that one Mannock, sometimes also servant to the said duchess, knew a privy mark of her body. When the said Lossels had declared this to the said Archbishop of Canterbury, he considering the weight and importance of the matter, being marvelously perplexed therewith, consulted in the same with the Lord Chancellor of England and the Earl of Hertford, whom the King's majesty going in his progress left to reside at London to order his affairs in those parts; who having weighed the matter and deeply pondered the gravity thereof, wherewith they were greatly troubled and un-quieted, resolved finally that the said archbishop should reveal the same to the King's majesty; which because the matter was such, as he has sorrowfully lamented, and also could not find in his heart to express the same to the King's majesty by word of mouth, he declared the information thereof to his holiness in writing. When the King's majesty had read this information thus delivered to him, his grace being much perplexed therewith, yet nevertheless so tenderly loved the woman and had conceived such a constant opinion of her honesty, that he supposed it rather to be a forged matter, than of truth. Whereupon it pleased him secretly to call to him the Lord Privy Seal, the Lord Admiral Sir Anthony Brown, and Sir Thomas Wriothesley; to whom he opened the case, saying he could not believe it to be true and yet seeing the information was made, he could not be satisfied till the certainty thereof was known; but he would not in any wise, that in the inquisition any spark of scandal should rise towards her. Whereupon it was by his majesty resolved that the Lord Privy Seal should go straight to London where the said Lossels that gave the information was secretly kept, and with all dexterity to examine and try whether he would stand to his saying who being so examined, answered that his sister so told him, and that he had declared it for the discharge of his duty and for none other respect; adding that he knew what danger was in it; nevertheless, he had rather die in declaration of the truth, as it came to him, seeing it touched the King's majesty so nearly, than live with the concealment of the same which asseveration being thus made by the said Lossels, the King's majesty being informed thereof, sent the Lord Privy-Seal into Sussex to examine the woman, making a pretence to the woman's husband of hunting, and to her for receiving of hunters; and sent the said Thomas Wriothesley to London at the same instant, both to examine Mannock, and also to take the said Derrham upon a pretence of piracy, because he had been before in Ireland and had been noted before with that offence; making these pretences to the intent no spark of suspicion should rise of these examinations. The said Lord Privy Seal found the woman in her examination constant in her former sayings and Sir Thomas Wriothesley found by the confession of Mannock, that he had commonly used to feel the secrets and other parts of her body, ere ever Derrham was so familiar with her; and Derrham confessed that he had known her carnally many times, both in his doublet and his hose between the sheets, and in naked bed, alleging such witnesses of three sundry women one after another, that had lien in the same bed with them when he did the acts, that the matter seemed most apparent. But what inward sorrow the King's majesty took when he perceived the information true, as it was the most woeful thing that ever came to our hearts, to see it; so it were too tedious to write it to you. But his heart was so pierced with pensiveness, that long it was before his majesty could speak and utter the sorrow of his heart to us and finally with plenty of tears (which was strange in his courage) opened the same. Which done, she was spoken withal in it by the Archbishop of Canterbury, the Lord Chancellor, the Duke of Norfolk, the Lord Great Chamberlain of England, and the Bishop of Winchester; to whom at the first she constantly denied it; but the matter being so declared to her, that she perceived it to be wholly disclosed, the same night she disclosed the whole to the Archbishop of Canterbury, who took the confession of the same in writing subscribed with her hand then were the rest of the number being eight or nine men and women which knew of their doings, examined, who all agreed in one tale.

Now may you see what was done before the marriage; God knows what has been done since, but she had already gotten this Derrham into her service and trained him upon occasions as sending of errands, and writing of letters when her secretary was out of the way to come often into her privy chamber. And she had gotten also into her privy chamber to be one of her clamberers, one of the women which had before lien in the bed with her and Derrham, what this pretended is easy to be conjectured. Thus much we know for the beginning; whereof we thought meet to advertise you to the intent afore specified and what shall further succeed and follow of this matter, we shall not fail to advertise you thereof accordingly. You shall also receive herein enclosed a packet of letters directed to Sir Henry Knevet, his graces ambassador with the emperor, which his highness's pleasure is you shall see conveyed to him by the next post. Thus fare you right heartily well. From the King's palace at Westminster the 12th of November. Your loving friends, [Other names would have appeared here but have been defaced in the original document] Thomas Audeley, Chancellor; K. Hertford, William Southampton, Robert Sussex, Stephen Winton, Anthony Wingfield.

Besides the persons specified in this letter, one Thomas Culpepper (being of the same name with the Queen's mother) was indicted for the same fault (as our histories have it,) which he and Derrham at their arraignment confessing, Culpepper had his head cut off and Derrham was hanged and quartered. But it rested not here; for the Lord William Howard (the Queen's uncle, newly returned from as ambassador in France) and his wife, and the old Duchess of Norfolk, and divers of the Queen's and the said duchess's kindred and servants, and a butter wife, were indicted of misprision of treason (as concealing this fact,) and condemned to perpetual prison; though yet by the King's favor some of them at length were released. The King yet not satisfied thus for more authorizing his proceeding, referred the business to the Parliament sitting the 16th of January, 1511. On the 21st of the same month a bill was brought into the house and read a first time for the attainder on the charge of high treason of Catherine Howard, late Queen of England, and Jane Lady Rochford, with others. And in the same bill was contained the attainders on misprision of treason of Agnes Howard Duchess of Norfolk, William Howard, &c. On the 28th, the Lord Chancellor declared to the rest of the peers, how much it concerned all their honors, not to proceed to give too hasty a judgment on the bill for the attainder of the Queen and others, which had yet been only once read amongst them. For that they were to remember that a Queen was no mean or private person, but an illustrious and public one. Therefore, her cause was to be judged with that sincerity that there should I be neither room for suspicion of some latent I quarrel, or that she should not have liberty to clear herself, if perchance, by reason or council she was able to do it, from the crime laid to her charge. For this purpose he thought it I but reasonable, that some principal persons, as well of the lords as commons, should be deputed to go to the Queen partly to tell her the cause of their coming, mid partly in order to help her womanish fears, by advising and admonishing her to have presence of mind enough to say anything to make her cause better. He knew for certain that it was but just that a princess should be judged by equal laws with themselves; and he could assure them that the clearing herself in this manner would be highly acceptable to her most loving husband. But that some answer ought to be had from her and to report the truth of it to his majesty, his advice was that they should choose the Archbishop of Canterbury; Charles Duke of Suffolk, Grand Master of the Household; William Earl of Southampton, Lord Privy Seal; with the Bishop of Westminster; if the King's council approved of this, day after day, to repair to the Queen to treat of this matter, according as their own prudence might think it necessary. And in the mean time, the sentence concerning the bill against her majesty was ordered to be suspended. On the 30th of January, the chancellor declared to the lords openly that the Privy Council, on mature deliberation, disliked the message that was to be sent to the Queen; nevertheless, in the mean time they had thought of another way, less faulty, to be put to the King, or rather to be altogether demanded of him. 1st. That his majesty would condescend according to his usual wisdom in council to weigh by an equal balance the mutability of all human affairs; that nature is weak and corrupt; none made free from accidents; and that no man can be happy in every thing. 2nd. That the whole state of the Kingdom depends on his majesty's resolution to divert his mind from all trouble and solicitude. Next, that the attainder of Thomas Culpepper and Francis Derrham, with the King's assent, should be continued by authority of Parliament, also the attainder on misprision against Lord William Howard. And that the Parliament might have leave to proceed to give judgment and to finish the Queen's cause; that the event of that business may be no longer in doubt. 3rd. That when all these things are completed in a just Parliamentary method without any loss of time, that then his majesty would condescend to give his royal assent to them; not by being present and speaking openly as the custom has been in other Parliaments, but absent by his letters patent under the great seal of England, and signed by his own hand. That the remembrance of this late and sorrowful story and wicked facts, if repeated before him, may not renew his grief and endanger his majesty's health. Lastly, they were to beseech his majesty that if by chance, by speaking freely on the Queen, they should offend against the statutes then in being out of his great clemency, be would pardon all and every of them for it. And to propound all these mutters to his majesty, the Archbishop of Canterbury, Charles Duke of Suffolk, with the Earl of Southampton, were deputed for that purpose. January 31, the Lord Chancellor declared to the house that their message and request of yesterday had been delivered to his majesty by the lords commissioners; and that the King had denied no part of their petition, but had orderly granted every part of it. That he had returned them thanks for their loving admonition in regard to his health; which he said he took care of, not so much for the sake of his own body, as that of the whole republic. Nay, his majesty declared further to them than they durst ask of him, as in the case of desiring liberty of speech, &c. For he told them he granted yet more in giving leave for each man to speak his mind freely and not incur the penalty which the laws had fixed on those who took the liberty to talk on the incontinency of Queens; especially when the said person did not do it out of malice or ill will, but out of zeal for his service.

On the 11th of February, the Lord Chancellor produced two statutes which had passed both lords and commons; one concerning the attainder of the Queen, and the other about the method of proceeding against lunatics, who before their insanity had confessed themselves guilty of high treason. Each statute signed with the King's own hand, and together with his majesty's assent to them under the broad seal and signed also which was annexed to the said statutes. This the chancellor held forth in both hands, that both lords and commons, who were called for that purpose, might apparently see it, and that the statutes might from thence have the full force and authority of a law. Which, when done, the Duke of Suffolk, Grand Master of the King's household, delivered himself in a very serious discourse, to this effect, he told the houses, that he and his fellow-deputies, appointed to wait upon the Queen, had been with her; and that she had openly confessed and acknowledged to them the great crime she had been guilty of against the most high God and a kind prince, and lastly against the whole English nation. That she begged them all to implore his majesty not to impute her crime alone to her whole kindred and family. But that his majesty howsoever unworthy she might be and undeserving, would yet extend his unbounded mercy and his singular beneficence to all her brothers that they might not suffer for her faults. Lastly, to beseech his majesty that it would please him to bestow some of her clothes on those maid-servants who had been with her from the time of her marriage, since she had now nothing else left to recompense them as they deserved. The Earl of Southampton, Lord Privy Seal, next stood up in the house, and in near the same words, confirmed what the duke had said, adding; [Here the journal book again breaks off abruptly, and we are only told that the chancellor prorogued the Parliament to the Tuesday following.] This last *hiatus in manuscripto*, along with the former, makes it seem evident that they were not done by neglect of the clerks, but by design; and that it was a trick of state to prevent posterity from being acquainted with some matters, not consistent with the respect they then paid to their grand monarch.

And so the Queen and Lady Jane Rochford (wife to the late Lord Rochford, and noted to be a particular instrument in the death of Queen Anne) were brought to the Tower, and after confession of their faults, had their heads cut off. An act also passed, declaring that it shall be lawful for any of the King's subjects, if themselves do perfectly know, or by vehement presumption do perceive any will, act or condition of lightness of body in her which shall be the Queen of this realm to disclose the same to the King, or some of his council; but they shall not openly blow it abroad, or whisper it until it be divulged by the King or his council. If the King, or any of his successors shall marry a woman which was before incontinent, if she conceal the same, it shall be high-treason, &c. But this act was repealed 1 Edward VI. 12. and 1 Mary 1.

[Howell, Thomas. *A Complete Collection of State Trials. V-1.* 445-452]

Chapter 3: The Reign of Edward VI

Edward VI was born on 12 October, 1537 in Greenwich to Henry VIII and Jane Seymour who died of what is believed to be a fever shortly after his birth. Edward spent most of his first six years under the care of women. After six, his education included the classical studies in Latin, Greek and French, lessons in music, fencing and other gentlemanly pursuits. He also studied history and its lessons and geography centering on the ports and havens in Scotland, England and France. He believed a King should know such strategic information. Though history mentions that Edward was serious and studious, he displayed a rather violent temper-he tore a living falcon apart during a fit. Unlike his father, he had little interest in sporting events such as jousting, but instead preferred intellectual pursuits and was known to have prepared himself with great discipline to rule.

Edward succeeded his father as King of England in 1547, but because he was a minor, a council oversaw his actions and a 'protector' was elected to oversee the young King's decisions. Most factions sought to control the young monarch's naive mind, showing early signs of the Tudor obstinacy.

King Edward VI had a brief reign cut short by illness. Much of what history knows is learned from a diary he kept until close to death. He found several close and trusted individuals had deceived and violated not only his trust, but the trust that his father had hoped would guide his son through his younger years on the throne. Edward recorded an apparent cold-blooded indifference towards the executions of his uncles as nothing more than royal business.

Edward's health declined after a bout of small pox in April 1552, and early the following year it was clear that the King was dying of tuberculosis. The over-ambitious Duke of Northumberland devised a plan to further his position in court. He manipulated the dying Edward to alter his father's will to exclude the Princess Mary and Elizabeth from succession in favor of Lady Jane Grey. The Duke's son would wed Jane Grey and the Duke would be the father of the

King of England. The Duke was successful in pushing the new 'device' through Parliament by various tactics before Edward's death on 6 July, 1553.

An example of the changes Edward VI made to the legal system following the death of his father was:

> If any man or woman able to work should refuse labor, and remain idle for three days, he or she should be branded on the breast with the letter V, and adjudged the slave, for two years, of any one who should inform against such idler. If the slave ran away, he or she when recaptured was to be branded on the cheek with the letter S, and to become a slave for life, and running away for the second time was punishable by death.
>
> [Trumbull, *The True-Blue Laws of Connecticut and New Haven*, pg. 13-14]

Thomas Seymour

Thomas Seymour was born circa 1508 in Wiltshire, a county in Southwest England. Upon the birth of Edward VI, both Thomas and his older brother Edward saw their positions in court increase. This would grow stronger when Thomas married King Henry VIII's sixth wife, Catherine, after the death of the King. Thomas moved into Chelsea manor in London with his wife and her step-daughter Elizabeth and many stories survive regarding his relationship with Elizabeth including his tickling her, slapping her playfully on her behind as she lay in her bed and visiting her in her bedchamber in his night clothes. Those actions caused concern and eventually Elizabeth was sent to live with Anthony Denny when Catherine was pregnant in 1548 and gave birth to a daughter, but died soon after leaving her fortune to Thomas.

Despite his new wealth and position, Thomas was jealous of his brother's position as Protector to King Edward VI. Thomas began various means to manipulate the young King to his favor which included giving Edward spending money and history records that the King became accustomed to those allowances. Thomas tried to get a bill through Parliament granting him the position as the King's personal governor, but the King would not sign it given that he was reluctant to go behind the back of the Protector. Frustrated by his inability to gain influence over Edward, Thomas began to plan other means to remove his brother from his appointment.

During 1547, when the Protector was absent from court on a campaign in Scotland, Thomas began to voice his disapproval of how his brother handled his duties as Protector. Thomas gained the attention of several nobles who advised him to accept things as the late King willed, but he would not accept that and entered into negotiations with pirates on the western coasts for support in case of a rebellion; a duty as Lord High Admiral, he had taken an oath to prevent.

By 1548, the regency council set up by the late King Henry VIII was aware of Thomas's posturing. His brother held a council meeting that would allow Thomas to explain his actions, but he did not appear. During the night of

16 January 1549, Thomas was caught breaking into the King's apartments at Hampton Court. He woke one of the King's pet spaniels and shot it as it barked. He was arrested the following morning.

Being caught outside the King's bedchamber with a loaded weapon was easily considered a capital crime. On 18 January, the council questioned everyone associated with Thomas, including Princess Elizabeth. On 22 February, the council officially accused him of thirty-three charges of treason. Following is the record of his trial.

> Proceedings in Parliament against Sir Thomas Seymour, Knight, Lord Seymour of Sudley, Lord High Admiral of England, uncle to the King and brother to the Lord Protector, for high treason: 2 & 3 Edward VI. A.D. 1549.
>
> About the year 1547, Sir Thomas Seymour the Protector's brother, was brought to such a share of his fortunes, that he was made a baron and Lord Admiral. But this not satisfying his ambition, he endeavored to have linked himself into a nearer relation with the crown by marrying the King's sister, the Lady Elizabeth. But finding he could not compass that, he made his addresses to Catherine Parr, the Queen dowager, and they were married privately. Being by this match possessed of great wealth, he studied to engage all about the King to be his friends. His design was that since he was the King's uncle as well as his brother, he ought to have a proportioned share with him in the government. About Easter that year he first set about that design; and corrupted some about the King who should bring him sometimes privately through the gallery to the Queen dowager's lodgings; and he desired they would let him know when the King had occasion for money, they should not trouble the treasury, for he would furnish him. Thus he gained ground with the King.
>
> When the Protector was that year in Scotland, the admiral began to act more openly, and was for making a party for himself of which Paget charged him in plain terms, yet all was ineffectual; for the admiral was resolved to go on and either get himself advanced higher, or perish in the attempt. During the session, the admiral got the King to write with his own hand a message to the house of commons for making him governor of his person, and he intended to have gone with it to the house, and had a party there, by whose interest he was confident to have carried his business he dealt also with many of the lords and counselors to assist him in it. When this was known, before he had gone with it to the house, some were sent in his brother's name to see if they could prevail with him to go no further; he refused to hearken to them, and said that if he were crossed in his attempt, he would make this the 'blackest Parliament' that ever was in England. Upon that he was sent for by order from the council, but refused to come; then they threatened him severely, and told him the King's writing was nothing in law, but that he who had procured it was punishable for doing an act of such a nature, &c. so they resolved to have him sent to the Tower. But at last he submitted himself to the Protector and council; and his brother and he seemed to be perfectly reconciled. (A) Though it was visible he only put off his projects till a fitter, conjuncture, and was on all occasions infusing into the

King a dislike of every thing that was done, persuading him to assume the government himself, and bribing his servants.

Thus he continued contriving and plotting for some time; the Protector had often been told of these things and warned him of the danger into which he would throw himself. But his restless ambition seeming incurable, he was on the 19th of January sent to the Tower. (B) And now many things broke out against him, particularly a conspiracy of his with Sir William Sharington, Vice Treasurer of the Mint at Bristol, who was to have furnished him with 10,000£ and had already coined about 12,000£ false money. (C) And had clipped a great deal more to the value of 40,000£ in all; for which he was attainted by a process at common law, and that was confirmed in Parliament. (D) Fowler also, that waited in the privy-chamber, with others, were sent to the Tower; many complaints being brought against him, the Lord Russell, the Earl of Southampton and Secretary Petre were ordered to receive their examinations.

The Protector finding he could not persuade him to submit, on the 22d of February a report was made to the council of all the information's against him; consisting not only of the particulars before-mentioned, but of many foul misdemeanors in the discharge of the admiralty, several pirates being concerned with him, &c. The whole charge against him, consisting of 33 articles, is as follows, viz.

Articles of high treason and other misdemeanors against the King's majesty and his crown, objected to Sir Thomas Seymour, Knight. Lord Seymour of Sudley, and High Admiral of England;

1. Whereas the Duke of Somerset was made governor of the King's majesty's person, and Protector of all his realms, and dominions, and subjects, to the which you yourself did agree, and gave your consent in writing; it is objected and laid to your charge, that this notwithstanding you have attempted and gone about, by indirect means, to undo this order and to get into your hands the government of the King's majesty, to the great danger of his highness's person, and the subversion of the state of the realm.

2. That by corrupting with gifts, and fair promises, divers of the privy chamber, you went about to allure his highness to condescend and agree to the same your most heinous and perilous purposes, to the great danger of his highness's person, and of the subversion of the stare of the realm.

3. That you wrote a letter with your own hand, which letter the King's majesty should have subscribed, or written again after that copy, to the Parliament house; and that you delivered the same to his highness for that intent with the which so written by his highness, or subscribed, you have determined to have come into the commons house yourself; and there with your suitors and adherents before prepared, to have made a broil, or tumult, or uproar, to the great danger of the King's majesty's person, and subversion of the state of this realm.

4. That you yourself spoke to divers of the council, and labored with divers of the nobility of the realm to stick and adhere to you for the alter-

ation of the state, and order of the realm and to attain your other purposes, to the danger of the King's majesty's person, now in his tender years, mid subversion of the state of the realm.

5. That you did say openly and plainly, you would make the blackest Parliament that ever was in England.

6. That being sent for by the authority to answer to such things as were thought meet to be reformed in you, you refused to come to a very evil example of disobedience and danger thereby of the subversion of the state of the realm.

7. That since the last sessions of this Parliament, notwithstanding much clemency showed to you, you have still continued in your former mischievous purposes; and continually, by yourself and others, studied and labored to put into the King's majesty's head and mind, a disliking of the government of the realm, and of the Lord Protector's doings to the danger of his person and the great peril of the realm.

8. That the King's majesty being of those tender years, and us yet by age unable to direct his own things, you have gone about to instill into his grace's head, and as much as lies in you, persuaded him to take upon himself the government and managing of his own affairs to the danger of his highness's person, and great peril of the whole realm.

9. That you had fully intended and appointed to have taken the King's majesty's person into your own hands and custody, to the danger of his subjects, and peril of the realm.

10. That you have corrupted with money, certain of the privy chamber to persuade the King's majesty to have a credit towards you; and so to insinuate you to his grace, that when he lacked anything, he should have it of you and none other body to the intent he should dislike his ordering, and that you might the better when you saw time, use the King's highness for an instrument to this purpose to the danger of his royal person, and subversion of the state of the realm.

11. That you promised the marriage of the King's majesty at your will and pleasure.

12. That you have labored and gone about to combine and confederate yourself with some persons; and especially moved those noblemen whom you thought not to lie contented to depart into their countries and make themselves strong; and otherwise to allure them to serve your purpose by gentle promises and offers, to have a party and faction in readiness to all your purposes to the danger of the King's majesty's person, and peril of the state of the realm.

13. That you have parted, as it were, in your imagination and intent, the realm, to set noblemen to countervail such other noblemen as you thought would let your devilish purposes, and so labored to be strong to all your devices; to the great danger of the King's majesty's person and great peril of the stale of the realm.

14. That you had advised certain men to entertain and win the favor and good-wills of the head yeomen and ringleaders of certain countries to the intent that they might bring the multitude and commons when you should think meet, to the furtherance of your purposes.

15. That you have not only studied and imagined how to have the rule of a number of men in your hands, but that you have attempted to get, also gotten, divers stewardships of noblemen's lands, and their manors, to make your party stronger for your purposes aforesaid to the danger of the King's majesty's person and great peril of the state of the realm.

16. That you have retained young gentlemen and hired yeomen, to a great multitude, and far above such number as is permitted by the laws and statutes of the realm, or were otherwise necessary or convenient for your service, place, or estate, to the fortifying of yourself towards all your evil intents and purposes; to the great danger of the King's majesty and peril of the state of the realm.

17. That you had so travailed in that matter, that you had made yourself able to make of your own men out of your lands and rules and other your adherents, ten thousand men, besides your friends to the advancement of all your intents and purposes; to the danger of the King's majesty's person and the great peril of the state of the realm.

18. That you had conferred, cast, and weighed so much money as would lend the said ten thousand men for a month; and that you knew how and where to have the same sum; and that you had given warning to have and prepare the said mass of money in a readiness; to the danger of the King's majesty's person and great peril to the state of the realm.

19. That you have not only before you married the Queen, attempted and gone about to marry the King's majesty's sister, the Lady Elizabeth, second inheritor in remainder to the crown, but also being then let by the Lord Protector and others of the council since that time, both in the life of the Queen, continued your old labor and love; and alter her death, by secret and crafty means practiced to achieve the said purpose of marrying the said Lady Elizabeth; to the danger of the King's majesty's person and peril of the state of the same.

20. That you married the late Queen so soon after the late King's death, that if she had conceived straight after, it should have been a great doubt whether the child born should have been accounted the late King's or yours; whereupon a marvelous danger and peril might, and was like to have ensued to the King's majesty's succession and quiet of the realm.

21. That you first married the Queen privately, and did dissemble and keep close the same; insomuch that a good space after you had married her, you made labor to the King's majesty and obtained a letter of his majesty's hand to move and require the said Queen to marry with you; and likewise procured the Lord Protector to speak to the Queen to bear you her favor towards marriage by which coloring, not only your evil and dissembling

nature may be known, but also it is to be feared that at this present you did intend to use the same practice in the marriage of the Lady Elizabeth's grace.

22. That you not only, so much as lay in you, did stop and let all such things as either by Parliament or otherwise, should tend to the advancement of the King's majesty's affairs, but did withdraw yourself from the King's majesty's service; and being moved and spoken to, for your own honor and for the ability that was in you to serve and aid the King's majesty's affairs, and the Lord Protector's, you would always draw back and feign excuses and declare plainly that you would not do it. Wherefore, upon the discourse of all these foresaid things, and of divers others, it must needs be intended that all these preparations of men and money, the attempts and secret practices of the said marriage; the abusing and persuading of the King's majesty to dislike the government, state, and order of the realm that now is and to take the government into his own hands and to credit you; was to none other end and purpose but after a title gotten to the crown, and your party made strong both by sea and land, with furniture of men and money sufficient to have aspired to the dignity royal by some heinous enterprise against the King's majesty's person; to the subversion of the whole state of the realm.

23. That you not only had gotten into your hands the strong and dangerous isles of Sicily, bought of divers men; but that so much as lay in your power, you travailed also to have Londay, and under pretence to have victualled the ships therewith, not only went about, but also moved the Lord Protector and whole council that you might by public authority, have that which by private fraud and falsehood and confederating with Sharington, you had gotten that is the mint at Bristol, to be yours wholly, and only to serve your purposes, casting, as may appear, that if these traitorous purposes had no good success, yet you might thither convey a good mass of money; where being aided with ships and conspiring at all evil events with pirates, you might at all times have a sure and safe refuge, if anything for your demerits should have been attempted against you.

24. That having knowledge that Sir William Sharington, Knight, had committed treason and otherwise wonderfully defrauded and deceived the King's majesty, nevertheless you both by yourself and by seeking counsel for him, and by all means you could, did aid, assist, and bear him, contrary to your allegiance and duty to the King's majesty, and the good laws and orders of the realm.

25. That where you owed to Sir Win. Sharington, Knight, a great sum of money, yet to abet, bear, and cloak the great falsehood of the said Sharington, and to defraud the King's majesty, you were not afraid to say and affirm before the Lord Protector and the council, that the same Sharington did owe to you a great sum of money, viz. 3800£ and to conspire with him in that falsehood and take a bill of that feigned debt into your custody.

26. That you by yourself and ministers, have not only extorted and bribed great sums of money of all such ships as should go into island, but also as should go any other where in merchandise, contrary to the liberty of this

realm and to the great discouragement and destruction of the navy of the same, to the great danger of the King's majesty and the state of the realm.

27. That where divers merchants, as well strangers as Englishmen, have had their goods piratously robbed and taken, you have had their goods in your hands and custody, daily seen in your house and distributed among your servants and friends, without any restitution to the parties so injured and spoiled; so that thereby foreign princes have in a manner been weary of the King's majesty's amity, and by their ambassadors divers times complained; to the great slander of the King's majesty and danger of the state of the realm.

28. That where certain men have taken certain pirates, you have not only taken from the takers of the said pirates, all the goods and ships so taken without any reward, but have cast the said takers, for their good service done to the King's majesty into prison and there detained them a great time; some eight weeks, some more, some less, to the discouraging of such as truly should serve the King's majesty against his pirates and enemies.

29. That divers of the head pirates being brought to you, you have let the same pirates go again free to the seas and taken away from the takers of them not only all their commodity and profit, but from the true owners of the ships and goods, all such as ever came into the pirates hands as though you were authorized to be the chief pirate and to have had all the advantages they could bring to you.

30. That where order has been taken by Lord Protector and the whole council that certain goods, piratically taken upon the seas, and otherwise known not to be wreck nor forfeited, should be restored to the true owners and letters thereupon written by the Lord Protector and the council; to the which letters, you yourself among the other, did set to your hand yet you, this notwithstanding have given commandment to your officers that no such letters should be obeyed; and written your private letters to the contrary commanding the said goods not to be restored, but kept to your own use and profit contrary to your own hand before in the council-chamber written; and contrary to your duty and allegiance, and to the perilous example of others, and great slander and danger of the realm.

31. That where certain strangers, which were friends and allies to the King's majesty, had their ships with wind and weather broken, and yet came un-wrecked to the shore; when the Lord Protector and the council had written for the restitution of the said goods and to the country to aid and save so much of the goods as might, you yourself subscribing and consenting thereto yet this notwithstanding, you have not only given contrary commandment to your officers, but as a pirate have written letters to some of your friends to help that as much of these goods as they could, should be conveyed away secretly by night farther off upon hope that if the said goods were assured, the owners would make no further labor for them and then you might have enjoyed them, contrary to justice and your honor and to the great slander of this realm.

32. That you have not only disclosed the King's majesty's secret council, but also where you yourself among the rest, have consented and agreed to certain things for the advancement of the King's affairs, you have spoken and labored against the same.

33. That your deputy steward, and other your ministers of the Holt in the county of Denbigh, have now against Christmas last past at the said Holt, made such provision of wheat, malt, beefs, and other such things as be necessary for the sustenance of a great number of men; making also by all the means possible, a great mass of money; insomuch that all the country does greatly marvel at it, and the more, because your servants have spread rumors abroad that the King's majesty was dead; whereupon the country is in a great maze, doubt and expectation, looking for some broil and would have been more if at this present, by your apprehension, it had not been stayed.

These articles (as entered in the council books) were so manifestly proved not only by witnesses, but by letters under his own hand, that it did not seem possible to deny them; yet he had been sent to and examined by some of the council, but refused to make a direct answer to them or to sign those answers that he had made. So it was ordered that the next day, all the Privy Council, except the Archbishop of Canterbury, and Sir John Baker, speaker of the house of commons, who was engaged to attend in the house, should go to the Tower, and examine him. On the 23d, the Lord Chancellor with the other counselors went to him and read the articles of his charge, and earnestly desired him to make plain answers to them, excusing himself where he could and submitting himself in other things; and that he would show no obstinacy of mind. He answered them that he expected an open trial and his accusers to be brought face to face. All the counselors endeavored to persuade him to be more tractable, but to no purpose. At last the Lord Chancellor required him on his allegiance, to make his answer. He desired they would leave the articles with him and he would consider of them, otherwise he would make no answer to them. But the counselors resolved not to leave them with him on those terms. On the 24th of February, it was resolved in council that the whole board should after dinner acquaint the King with the state of that affair, and desire to know of him whether he would have the law to take place? And since the thing had been before the Parliament, whether he would leave it to their determination? When the counselors waited on him, the Lord Chancellor opened the matter to the King and delivered his opinion for leaving it to the Parliament; then every counselor by himself spoke his mind all to the same purpose. Last of all the Protector spoke. He protested this was a most sorrowful business of him that he had used all the means in his power to keep it from coming to this extremity. But were it son or brother, he must prefer his majesty's safety to them, for he weighed his allegiance more than his blood; and that therefore he was not against the request that the other lords had made, and said if he himself were guilty of such offences, he should not think he were worthy of life, and the rather because he was of all men the most bound to his majesty; and therefore he could not refuse justice. The King answered them in these words: "We perceive that there are great things objected and laid to my

Lord Admiral my uncle, and they tend to treason and we perceive that you require but justice to be done. We think it reasonable, and we will, that you proceed according to your request". However, the lords resolved that some of both houses should be sent to the admiral before the bill should be put in against him, to see what he could or would say; so my Lord Chancellor, the Earl of Shrewsbury, Warwick, and Southampton, and Sir John Baker, Sir Thomas Cheney, and Sir Anthony Denny, were sent to him. He was long obstinate, but after much persuasion was brought to give an answer to the first three articles, viz.

The Lord Admirals answer to three of the articles.

To the first, he said that about Easter Tide was twelvemonths, he said to Fowler, as he supposed it was that if he might have the King in his custody, as Mr. Page had, he would be glad; and that he thought a man might bring him through the gallery to his chamber, and so to his house, but this he said he spoke merrily, meaning no hurt. And that in the mean time after he heard, and upon that, sought out certain precedents that there was in England at one time, one Protector, and another regent of France, and the Duke of Exeter, and the Bishop of Winchester, governors of the King's person upon that he had thought to have made suit to the Parliament house for that purpose, and he had the names of all the lords and totted them whom he thought he might have to his purpose to labor them. But afterwards communing with Mr. Comptroller at Ely-Place, being put in remembrance by him of his assenting and agreeing with his own hand that the Lord Protector should be governor of the King's person, he was ashamed of his doings, and left off that suit and labor.

To the second, he said he gave money to two or three of them which were about the King. To Mr. Cheek, he said he gave at Christmas-Tide was twelvemonths when the Queen was at Enfield, 40£ whereof to himself 20£ the other for the King to bestow where it pleased his grace amongst his servants. Mr. Cheek was very loath to take it, howbeit he would needs press that upon him; and to him he gave no more at no time, as he remembered, since the King's majesty was crowned. To the grooms of the chamber he has at New Years Tides given money, he does not well remember what. To Fowler, he said he gave money for the King, since the beginning of this Parliament now last at London, 20£. And divers times, he said the King has sent to him for money and he had sent it. And what time Mr. Latimer preached before the King, the King sent to him to know what he should give Mr. Latimer; and he sent to him by Fowler, 40£ with this word that 20£ was a good reward for Mr. Latimer, and the other he might bestow amongst his servants. Whether he had given Fowler any money for himself, he does not remember.

To the third, he said it is true he drew such a bill indeed himself, and proffered it to the King, or else to Mr. Cheek, he cannot well tell; and before that he said he caused the King to be moved by Mr. Fowler whether he could be contented that he should have the governance of him as Mr. Stanhope had. He knows not what answer he had but upon that he drew the said bill to that effect, that his majesty was content; but what answer he had to the bill, he cannot tell, Mr. Cheek can tell.

Then he on a sudden stop short and bade them be content, for he would go no further and no entreaties would work on him, either to answer the rest or to set his hands to the answers he had made. On February the 25th was read in the house of lords the first time the bill for attainder of the Lord Admiral. February 26, read the second time. February 27, read the third time; and concluded with the common assent of all the peers. The same day, being Wednesday, the bill was sent down to the commons; when it was thought good by them to send down certain members of the house to declare to the commons the manner after which the lords had proceeded in that matter; and further to declare to them, that in case they were minded to proceed in like sort, certain noblemen who had given evidence against the said Lord Admiral should be sent to them to declare by mouth and presence such matters, as by their writing should in the mean time appear to them. The Master of the Rolls, Sir James Hales, and Sergeant Molineux, were the persons sent by the lords. March the 2nd, they were sent again to the lower house with the like commission in effect as they were sent the Wednesday before. Answer was made that they would consult together, and thereupon they would with speed send up their resolution. But no haste having been made therein by them of the neither house, the lords having sat so long, as it was thought the time now far spent, they concluded to depart; desiring the Lord Protector, that it would please him to receive such answer as should be sent touching that purpose, and to make report thereof at their next assembly which should be the next Monday. March the 5th, the bill was brought from the commons for the attainder of the Lord Sudley. Thus it is related in the journal of the house of lords.

By the journal of the house of commons it appears that this bill was read there the last day of February the first time; March the 1st read again; and March 2nd the Master of the Rolls, Sergeant Molineux, Sergeant Hales, and the King's Solicitor, were sent from the lords to know the pleasure of this house, if it should be resolved there to pass upon the attainder of the admiral in such order as it passed in the higher house. Whereupon it was ordered that advertisement thereof be sent to the lords by some of that house that it was resolved, that the evidence should be heard orderly as it was before the lords and also to require that the lords who affirmed that evidence, might come hither and declare it *viva voce*. And this to be delivered to the Lord Protector by Mr. Speaker and other the King's Privy Council of the house. March the 4th, the Master of the Rolls, &c. declared the King's pleasure to be that the admiral's presence was not necessary in this court; and therefore not to be there. And further declared that if the house would require to have the lords to come and to satisfy the house for the evidence against the admiral, the lords would come. Then it was ordered that master comptroller and others of the King's Privy Council, should hear the lords; and require that if it were judged necessary to have the lords come down, that upon any further suit they might come down to the house. And the bill for the attainder of high-treason of Sir Thomas Seymour, Lord Sudley, was read the third time. Thus far the journal of the house of commons. On the 5th of March the royal assent was given to the bill, which here follows:

An act for the attainder of Sir Thomas Seymour, Knight. Lord Seymour of Sudley, High Admiral of' England.

In their most humble wise beseeching your most excellent majesty, the lords spiritual and temporal, and the commons in this present Parliament assembled; that where Sir Thomas Seymour, Lord Seymour of Sudley, High-Admiral of England, not having God before his eyes, nor regarding the duty which by nature, benefits, and allegiance he ought to your highness, nor being content with his honorable state and condition, whereto your majesty has called and indued him with; but replenished and filled with the most dangerous, insatiable, and fearful vice of ambition, and greediness of rule, authority, and dominion, did in the first year of your most noble and victorious reign, determine and resolve with himself to take into his hands your most noble person, and the same either by violence, stealth, or other undue means, to have in his possession, with the order, rule, and government of your majesty's realms, dominions, and affairs, which were before that time, as well by your royal-assent as by the consent and liberate advice of all your nobles and council whereof he the said Lord-Admiral was one, otherwise ordered, decreed, and determined; by the means whereof and by the most prudent foresight and direction of your grace's dearest uncle the Duke of Somerset, governor of your majesty's most royal person and Protector of your highness's realms, dominions and subjects, being the said admiral disappointed of his malicious enterprise. The same admiral continuing nevertheless his great ambition and most detestable, malicious, and traitorous purposes, thinking by tumult and violence openly to achieve that thing which by slight he could not secretly compass, travailed with your majesty, being yet for your tender years not able to conceive his falsehood, by crafty, subtle, and traitorous means and persuasions, having also prepared about your grace, by corruption, sundry persons to be instruments to help forward all his naughty traitorous purposes, to have caused your grace at his contemplation, to have written a bill or letter of your majesty's own hand, to your high court of Parliament, desiring the same thereby to be good to the said Lord Seymour in such suits and matters as he should open and declare to them; which bill or letter the said Lord Admiral thought and determined not only in his own person to have brought into the nether house of your said court of Parliament, but also to have likewise opened the same in the higher house, having in both the same houses labored, stirred, and moved a number of persons to take part and join with him in such things as he would set forth and enterprise, whereby he thought to breed such a tumult, uproar, and sedition, as well in the said court, as in the whole realm, as by the troubling of the whole state and body of this your realm, he might the more fancily and easily bring to pass his most fearful, devilish, and naughty purpose for the more sure and certain compassing whereof, like as he feared not to say to certain noblemen and others, that he would make the blackest Parliament that ever was seen here in England, so most traitorously, for the further accomplishment of his lewd enterprise he retained a great number of men and prepared a great furniture of weapons and habiliments of war ready for the execution of the said traitorous attempts. And to color and cloak his said mischievous purposes, did by all such ways and means as he could possibly devise and imagine, practice as it were, for his entry towards the same to seek and attain the government of your most noble person, and thereby to have gotten into his hands the order of your realms and dominions, whereto he aspired in such sort as he did even then travail expressly with the most part of your highnesses most honorable council to help him to the said government, doing likewise all he could in the Parliament by himself, his servants and ministers, not only to hinder and let all things there proponed which touched the honor, surety, and benefit of your majesty and the realm; but also spreading abroad slanders touching your majesty's person your dearest uncle the said Lord Protector and the whole state of your council, over vile, dangerous, and unmeet to be here recited which things being by the goodness of God revealed as your said uncle the Lord Protector could not chase but heartily lament the said Lord Admiral's evil, malicious, and corrupt disposition, chiefly in respect of the apparent and irrecoverable danger which was like by the same, presently to have ensued to your majesty and to your realms and dominions. And secondly, for that he was by proximity of blood so nearly joiner to him. So hoping that by good advertisements and counsels, he might yet recover and save him, and by the grace of God cause him to cast away his naughty, vile and ambitious disposition and to have had a better consideration hereafter to his duty, both to God and to your majesty, whereto he was most bounden; the said Lord Protector labored with the whole council and otherwise to reconcile and reform him, which presently must else have perished in his folly and outrage. And albeit the said Lord Protector had then perfect knowledge of the attempts and misbehaviors of the said admiral before rehearsed; and that the said admiral had then said that he would not come at the said Lord Protector and council, although they sent for him and that he would not be committed to any ward for his doings by the best of them, whereby it appeared that he thought his party strong enough to resist your majesty's power and ordinary authority; yet the said Lord Protector not ceasing with all clemency to follow his godly and charitable purpose, did not only use all the good means he could devise by the persuasions of certain of your grace's council and otherwise to frame him to the amendment of his evils and so to bring him to the better remembrance of his duty; but also considering that if the matter should have grown to extremity, being so near, and so much bound to your majesty, being new come to your Kingdom, your subjects not altogether left in the best concord for matters of religion, great slander, tumult, and danger might have ensued thereby as well here at home in your realm, as from some outward parts with whom you were in the war, and in some secret enmity ready to enter the wars, thought it with the advice of your whole council most meet and surest for your majesty to pass his evil-doings over in silence, and in somewhat the more in respect of the better stay for the time of your present estate, to bridle him with your liberality, and therefore to give to him lands to the yearly value of 800£, trusting thereby and by such other good means as were used towards him, to encourage and move him to leave for ever that ambition, and seditious mind, and to live in such order as might have pleased God, and served your majesty, and your public weal. But all this notwithstanding, the Devil who had before planted that vile and evil need so deeply in his heart, that the root of the same could not be clearly pulled out, but caused his ambition eftsoons to spring and show itself more rankly than it had done before for it plainly appears that he tarried not long in his dissembled good mood and promise, but began afresh to imagine, compass and devise for the satisfying of his traitorous desire to make a party, faction, and confederation, whereof he would be the head and did not only get as many rules and offices into his hands of all men, as he could possibly attain and retained many gentlemen and yeomen into his service, making a full account and reckoning which he declared secretly to some of his familiars, that he was thereby able of his own ruled tenants and servant, to make ten thousand men for the obtaining of his said purpose; for whose wages he had also devised after 10,000£ by the month, out of your majesty's mint at Bristol which he had obtained with all your treasure in the same, by the menus and consent of Sir W. Sharington, Knight, Vice-Treasurer there to be at his commandment, which Sir William now stands attainted of treason; and also had put your grace's castle of the Holt, whereof he had the keeping, even now of late in a readiness and there caused to be prepared a great furniture of wheat, malt, beefs, and a great mass of money for the feeding and entertainment of a number of men which money he caused to be levied mid taxed half the year before the same was due; bruiting also for the better achieving of his purpose and to amaze therewith the more the people that your majesty (whom God long preserve to us) should be dead; but also he labored sundry of your nobles, and other your grace's subjects to join with him devising with divers of them, how and by what policy, ways, and means they should make themselves strong in their countries for that purpose and how they should win to them the head yeomen, and ringleaders of the common people; declaring how he meant to have matched, and set one nobleman against another nobleman as he thought he could never compass and win to assent to this faction and false conspiracy, promising to divers of them sundry benefits; yea, taking so much upon him, for the accomplishment of his said traitorous intent and purpose as he spared not to promise your most excellent person in marriage to a nobleman's daughter of this your realm. And yet not contented herewith for the further advancement of his most naughty and traitorous purpose, did traitorously and unnaturally practice even with your highness's own person, to make your most excellent majesty (for your tender years unable to understand his false and traitorous purposes) an instrument towards the undoing and destruction of your highness, and the subversion of the whole state of this your grace's realm pursuing your majesty, as much us in him did lie, not only to take upon you now in your young and tender age, the rule and order of yourself, unending and meaning by the color thereof, to take in his hands your most royal person the rules and orders of all the affairs of your realms and dominions; being already by the said Lord

Protector, with the advice of your grace's most honorable council, as well prudently and politically governed as valiantly and nobly defended against our outward enemies, to the increase of your immortal fame and honor; but also to receive and engender a hatred in your most noble heart, both against your dearest uncle the said Lord Protector, and all your true and faithful councilors to the which his devilish persuasions and assaults, God gave your highness, even at this age, to the treat rejoice of all us your faithful subjects and servants, a special grace to resist above common reason and all expectation, and most graciously without any advice or counsel to refuse and deny his evil advertisements and persuasions. And further, the said admiral did most falsely and traitorously corrupt sundry of your highness's privy-chamber with many gifts, and otherwise to the intent they should move and procure your majesty to write sundry letters at his or their devices, and to put into your grace's head a special and singular favor, affection, and trust towards him, and a disposition to follow whatsoever he would have wrought towards all others, that he might the rather have compassed his most traitorous purpose which must needs have tended to your majesty's destruction (which God forbid) and to the utter ruin of all us, your highness's most loving, faithful, and obedient subjects.

For most gracious sovereign lord, besides all this, it is most evident and apparent that as immediately after the King your father's death of most noble memory, he bare a special love and favor to your grace's sister the Lady Elizabeth, second person in the remainder of the state of succession to the crown of this realm after your majesty, and the heirs of your body whom the living God long preserve to us with the increase of much fruit; and would then of his great presumption and traitorous determination have married her, if he could by any means have brought to pass the same, but that he was stayed by the said Lord Protector and other of your grace's council; so he did not only continue in his said determination towards her, in the Queen his late wife's time, but also by divers secret and crafty means and practices, continually sought by achieving of the same since the Queen's death, as by sundry ways is confessed and appears. Insomuch as the same being perceived by your said dearest uncle, and some others beside of your council and other personages of reputation; and the said admiral by them earnestly advised to beware of it, and to forbear his pretense purpose, specially for that it could not be but dangerous to your grace's person, he has not been afraid to defend his naughty doings and purposes in it and to ask why he should not continue his suit towards the said Lady Elizabeth with sundry other words declaring his full intent and determinations to it; and neglecting all good advices, reasons, and admonitions made, given or alleged, contrary to his purpose, he has secretly and earnestly followed it in such sort, as if sundry other his mischievous devices and practices had not appeared and come to knowledge, it is evident that he would have done what he could secretly to have married her, as he did the late Queen, whom it may appear he married first, and after sued to your majesty, and the Lord Protector, and your council, for his preferment to it whom nevertheless it has been credibly declared, he helped to her end to haste forwards his other purpose. But what this marriage of your said sister with his prepared forces and confederacies should mean, and what the getting of the rule and order of your majesty's mint at Bristol into his hands with ten thousand men, which besides all his friends and divers retainers, he accounted himself furnished of and able to make all times within his own rules, and of his own servants and tenants should tend to, for the wages and entertainments of whom he had prepared, as is aforesaid, considering that the said admiral at all times, when occasion of the service of your majesty was necessary or requisite, went always back and refused to take it upon him, whether it were by sea or land, as your graces council both know and divers times have lamented, and in that case traveled with him (in vain) to bring him to it, whereby no good mind or will of him toward your majesty's safety or assurance can appear. And upon all these sinister ways and means, what his corrupt and subtle attempts of getting your most noble person into his hands by color whereof he might have wrought what he would, and whatsoever his ambitious intent could have devised with his preparation of victuals and money, and other his said doings at your grace's castle of the Holt and in the parts thereabouts, would have wrought in the end, especially in this tender age of your highness, and whilst your majesty is in the government of a Protector, it is fearful to consider and think upon and cannot otherwise be taken, but to be indeed more than a manifest declaration of a traitorous aspiring to your crown of this realm and to be King of the same, and an open deed and act and a false and traitorous compass and imagination to depose and deprive your majesty from your royal estate and title of your realms, and to compass and imagine the death of your most noble person, and most traitorously to take away and destroy all things which should have sounded to the let and impediment of his most traitorous and ambitious enterprise. And further, gracious sovereign lord, to declare the traitorous disposition of his nature and how little he cared to offend your grace's law and how he did yet less regard his truth and duty towards your grace, where Sir Win. Sharington, Knight, late of London, the tenth day of July, in the first year of your grace's reign, has in the county and city of Bristol, falsely and traitorously forged and counterfeited certain of your grace's coin, and further embezzled and purloined from your majesty untruly and falsely at the least, the sum of 40,000£ for part whereof the same Sir W. Sharington upon his own confession is attainted of treason according to your grace's laws; to which said traitorous acts the said Lord Admiral did not only abet and procure the said Sir W. Sharington, laboring him he should get as much money from time to time into his hands for his purpose as he could, so that he might ever have a good mass in a readiness; but also since the time of the said treasons and traitorous acts, so done by the said Sir W. Sharington, the said Lord Admiral having perfect knowledge thereof, as well by the declaration of the most part of your highness's council, as by some of his own counsel learned, has traitorously comforted, aided, assisted, and maintained the same Sir W. Sharington in his said traitorous acts and faults against your grace's law and statutes of this realm; taking the patent, indentures, books and reckonings of the same Sir W. Sharington of his own authority into his custody, and affirming both to sundry of your grace's council, and to divers of your subjects, that the said Sharington had wrong to be committed; devising all the ways he could possible, contrary to his duty and allegiance, traitorously to bear him in his evil and traitorous doings and to deliver him, if he by any means might have come by him. And for a further proof to induce that the said admiral did maintain and comfort the same Sharington, where the said admiral owed to the said Sharington 2,800£, the said Sharington upon a mistrust which he had before his apprehension, that he should for his fault and proceedings come one day to his trial and examination, communicating the same with the said Lord Admiral, and the said admiral agreed and promised not only to aid and maintain and bear him to the uttermost of his power as indeed he did both as is aforesaid and in consulting with learned men for him, and otherwise, but also for his more assured aid, being indebted to the said Sharington the sum of 2,000£ untruly conspired with the said Sharington upon a bill, whereby it appeared that the said Sharington should owe to him the sum of 2,000£ with interest, so as the said admiral might help and relieve him with that 2,000£ with the interest at your majesty's hand, as a debt to himself; and also with 2,800£ which the said admiral owed indeed to the said Sharington, amounting in the whole to 5,600£ which bill most untruly and to the maintenance and favor of the said Sharington, the said Lord Admiral affirmed before the said Lord Protector, and your highness's council, to be a true bill and the same 2,800£ with the interest to he his just debt, and so was taken, until the said Sharington himself confessed and affirmed the truth, whereby the coven and falsehood plainly appeared to the contrary. Finally, most gracious sovereign lord, it were too much and over tedious to molest and trouble your excellent majesty, either with the remembrance of his evil doings in his office of the admiralty, wherein he has so manifestly recited, maintained, aided and comforted sundry pirates, and taken to his own use the goods piratously taken against your laws, and expressly against the orders determined by the Lord Protector and the whole council, whereto his own hand has been for the restitution of them; whereby he has moved almost all princes Christian to conceive a grudge and displeasure, and by open wars to seek remedies at their own hands to the great trouble and danger of your majesty, your realms and dominions, and to the great charge, lots and disquiet of your most loving and faithful subjects, and to the peril of breaking of the leagues and treaties of amity between your majesty and other foreign princes as their ambassadors here have plainly declared, and as present experience teaches; or to express his innumerable untruths, falsehoods, and deceitful practices, discovering and opening of your majesty's counsels, refusal to serve your highness as he has been commanded, oppression mid manifest extortion of your majesty's subjects, using island and other voyages by the sea; and his determination or revenge towards all men with whom he was offended, which his own letters and other testimonies do declare against him; with a full resolution to have put the whole of his intent, shortly in experience and execution (if God had not prevented it), to the destruction of your most royal person and the subversion and alteration of the whole estate of your realms and dominions. Wherefore considering as well that he is a member so unnatural, unkind and corrupt, and such a heinous offender of your majesty and your laws, as he cannot, nor may conveniently be suffered to remain in the body of your grace's commonwealth, but to the extreme danger of your highness, being head and of all the good members of the same, and is too pernicious and dangerous an example, that such a person so much bound and so forgetful of it, so mercifully heretofore entreated and by sundry and great benefits allured and called, and so cruelly and ingrate continuing in his false and traitorous intents and purposes against your highness, and the whole estate of your realm should remain amongst us. It may therefore please your excellent majesty that it may be enacted with your highness's assent, the lord spiritual and temporal, and the commons in this present Parliament assembled, and by authority of the same, that the said Sir Thomas Seymour, Knight, Lord Seymour of Sudley, High Admiral of England, for the said traitorous offences and deeds, shall be by the authority of this present Parliament adjudged and attainted of treason and that the same Sir Thomas Seymour, Knight Lord Seymour of Sudley, High Admiral of England, shall have, suffer, and sustain such pains of death as in cases of high treason have been used and accustomed. And also, that the said Lord Seymour of Sudley shall forfeit and lose to your majesty and your heirs all such castles, manors, lands, tenements, leases, meadows, pastures, woods, waters, rents, reversions, services, offices, fees, annuities, and all other hereditaments, goods, chattels and debts whatsoever, the same Lord Seymour had enjoyed or was seized or possessed of at the seventeenth day of January, in the second year of your grace's reign, or at any time since. And that all such castles, manors, lands, tenements, meadows, leases, pastures, woods, waters, rents, reversions, services, offices, fees, annuities, and other hereditaments, to be by authority of this present act adjudged, vested, and deemed in the actual and real possession of your highness from the said 17th of January, without any office or inquisition to be thereof had or found. Saving to all and every person and persons, and bodies politick and corporate, and to their heirs, assigns, and successors, and to every of them (other than the said Lord Seymour of Sudley and his heirs) all such rights, titles, interests, uses, possessions, reversions, remainders, entries, conditions, leases, foes, offices, rents-services, rents-charges, rents-seek, annuities, commons, and all other commodities, profits, and hereditaments whatsoever, they or any of them had, might, or ought to have had if this present act had never been had or made. Furthermore, the King's majesty is pleased that it be enacted that all person and persons, bodies politick and corporate, and their executors and administrators, shall be well and truly contented and paid upon their humble suit and petition hereafter to be made to his highness of all such debts, which either by specialty, or by any other just and true contract, the said Lord Admiral did owe to them or any of them, at any time before the said 17th day of January, in the said second year of his majesty's reign.

On the 10th of March, the council resolved to press the King that justice might be done on the admiral and since the case was so heavy and lamentable to the Protector (so it is in the council-book) though it was also sorrowful to them all, they resolved to proceed in it, so that neither the King, nor he, should be further troubled with it; after dinner they went to the King, the Protector being with them. The King said he had well observed their proceeding, and thanked them for their great care of his safety, and commanded them to proceed in it without further molesting him or the Protector; and ended, 'I pray you, my lords, do so.' Upon this they ordered the Bishop of Ely to go to the admiral and to instruct him in the things that related to another life, and to prepare him to take patiently his execution; and on the 17th of March, he having made report to them of his attendance on the admiral, the council signed a warrant for his execution, viz.

The warrant for the admiral's execution.

This day, the 17th of March, the Lord Chancellor and the rest of the King's council meeting in his highness's palace of Westminster, heard the report of the Bishop of Ely, who by the said lords and others of the council was sent to instruct and comfort the Lord Admiral; after the hearing whereof, consulting and deliberating with themselves of the time most convenient for the execution of the said Lord Admiral, now attainted and condemned by the Parliament, they did condescend and agree that the said Lord Admiral should be executed the Wednesday next following between the hours of nine and twelve in the forenoon the same day upon Tower-Hill. His body and head to be buried within the Tower; the King's writ (as in such cases as heretofore has been accustomed) being first directed and sent forth for that purpose and effect. Whereupon calling to the council-chamber the Bishop of Ely, they willed him to declare this their determination to the said Lord Admiral; and to instruct and teach him the best he could to the quiet and patient suffering of justice, and to prepare himself to almighty God. (Signed) K. Somerset, T. Cantuarien. R. Rich, Cancel. W. St. John, J. Russell, J. Warwick, F. Shrewsbury, Thomas Southampton, Wm. Paget, Anthony Wingfield, Wm. Petre, A. Denny, Edward North, It. Sadler.

The said bishop after he had been with the Lord Admiral, repairing again to the court, made report to Mr. comptroller and secretary Smith of the Lord Admiral's requests, the which were that he required Mr. Latimer to come to him the day of execution to be deferred, certain of his servants to be with him, his daughter to be with my Lady Duchess of Suffolk to be brought up and such like. Touching which requests the said lords and the rest of the council declared their minds to Mr. Secretary Smith, willing him to write their answer in a letter to the Lieutenant of the Tower, who should show in all those requests their resolute answer to the said Lord Admiral which was done accordingly.

On the 20th of March he was brought to the scaffold.

Hugh Latimer's sermon on the death of the Lord Admiral.

And in the fourth sermon of Master Hugh Latimer which he preached before the

King within his graces palace at Westminster, the 29th day of March, is the following account of the Lord Admiral:

I know more of my Lord Admiral's death since that time, then I did know before. O say they, the man died very boldly, he would not have done so had he not been in a just quarrel. This is no good argument my friends. A man seems not to fear death, therefore his cause is good. This is a deceivable argument. He went to his death boldly, ergo, he stands in a just quarrel. If I should have said all that I knew, your ears would have worked to have heard it and now God has brought more to light. And as touching the King of his death, whether he be saved or no, I refer that to God only. What God can do, I can not tell. I will not deny but that he may in the twinkling of an eye save a man, and turn his heart. What he did, I cannot tell. And when a man has two strokes with an axe, who can tell that between two strokes he does repent. It is very hard to judge; well, I will not go so live to work, but this I will say if they ask me what I think of his death, that he died very dangerously, irksomely, horribly. The man being in the Tower, wrote certain papers which I saw myself. They were two little ones, one to my Lady Mary's grace, and another to my Lady Elizabeth's grace, tendering to his end that they should conspire against my Lord Protector's grace. Surely so seditious as could be. Now what a kind of death was this, that when he was ready to lay his head upon the block, he turns me to the lieutenant's servant and says bid my servant speed the thing that he wants of well the word was over-heard. His servant confessed these two papers and they were found in a shoe of his. They were so sown between the souls of a velvet shoe. He made his yoke so craftily, and with such workmanship, as the like has not been seen. I was prisoner in the Tower myself, and I could never invent to make yoke so. It is a wonder to hear of his subtleties. He made his pen of the aglet of a point that he plucked from his hose, and thus wrote these letters so seditious as you have heard, enforcing many matters against my Lord Protector's grace and so fourth. God had left him to himself, he had clean forsaken him. What would he have done if he had lived still if that went about this genre, when he laid his head on the block at the end of his life. Charity (they say) works but godly, not after this sorely. Well, he is gone, he knows his fate by this, he is either in joy or in pain. There is no repentance after this life, but if he dies in the state of damnation, he shall rise in the same. Yea, though he has a whole mockery to sing for him, he shall have his final sentence when he dies. And that servant of his that confessed and uttered his word, was an honest man. He died honestly in it. God put it in his heart. And as for the other, whether he be saved or no, I leave it to God. But surely, he was a wicked man, the realm is well rid of him. It has a treasure, that he is gone, he knows his fare by this. A terrible example surely and to be noted of every man; now before he should die, I heard say he had commendations to the King and spoke many words of his majesty. All is the King, the King. Yea, Bona verba. These were fair words, 'the King, the King.' It has been the cast of all traitors to pretend nothing against the King's person, they never pretend the matter to the King, but to other. Subjects may not resist any magistrates, nor ought to do nothing contrary to the King's laws. And therefore these words, 'the King,' and so fourth are of small effect. I have heard much wickedness of this man, and I have thought oft, Jesu, what will worth, what will be the end of this man? Among others (that went to execution) I heard of a wanton woman, a naughty liar, a whore, a vain body and was led from Newgate to the place of execution, for a certain robbery that she had committed, and she had a wicked communication by the way. This woman, I say, as she went by the way, had wanton and folic she talk, as this that if good fellow's had kept touch with her, she had not been at this time in that case; and amongst at other talk, she said that such a one and named this man had her maidenhead first; and hearing this of him at that time, I looked ever what would be his end, what would become of him. He was a man the farthest from the fear of God that ever I knew or heard of in England. First he was author of all this woman's whoredome. For if he had not had her maidenhead, she might have been married, and become an honest woman; whereas now being naught with him, she fell afterward by that occasion to other and they that were naught with her fell to robbery, and she followed; and thus was the author of all this. This gear came bi-sequels, peradventure this may seem to be a light matter, but surely it is a great matter and he, by unrepentance fell from evil to worse and from worse to worst of all, till at the length he was made a spectacle to all the world. I have heard say, he was of the opinion that he believed not the immortality of the soul, that he was not right in the matter. And it might well appear by the taking of his death. But you well say what you slander, you break charity. Nay, it is charity that I do, we can have no better use of him now than to warn others to beware by him. Christ said, 'Remember Lot's wife!' she was a woman that would not be content with her good state, but wrestled with God's calling; and she was for that cause turned into a salt stone, &c. Thus may this man be an example to us. Let us all subjects judge well of our magistrates in such matters, and be content with their doings and look not to be of the counsel. And thus took I occasion to speak of him, and to profit you thereby, and I beseech you so to take it, he may be a good warning to us and this is the best use that wee can have of him now.

In his fifth sermon he said, "You will say this, the Parliament house are wiser than I am; you might leave them to the defense of themselves although the men of the Parliament house can defend themselves, yet have I spoken this of a good zeal, and a good ground of the admiral's writing. I have not fained, nor lied one jolt. I will now leave the honorable counsel to answer for themselves. He confessed one fact, he would have had the governance of the King's majesty, and not you why? He said, he would not in his minority have him brought up like a ward. I am sure he has been brought up so godly, with such school-masters, as never King was in England, &c."

And in his seventh sermon he said thus: "I have heard say when that good Queen (meaning Queen Catherine) that is gone, had ordained in her house daily prayer both before none and after none, the admiral gets him out of the way like a mole digging in the earth. He shall be Lot's wife to me as long as I live. He was a covetous man, a horrible covetous man; I would there were no more in England he was an ambitious man; I would there were no more in England he was a seditious man, a condemner of commune prayer, I would there were no more in England he is gone, I would he had left none behind him. Remember you, my lords, that you pray in your houses, to the better mortification of your flesh."

[Cobbett's Complete Collection of State Trials. VI. 484-508]

Edward Seymour

Edward Seymour, brother of Thomas Seymour, was born circa 1505 in Wiltshire England. Early historians believe that he received an education at Oxford University and Cambridge University. At the age of eighteen he married Katherine Fillol, and together they had two sons. In 1523, he served with Charles Brandon, 1st Duke of Suffolk in a campaign in France and was knighted by the Duke at Roze in November 1523. Four years later, he accompanied Cardinal Wolsey to France and over the span of a few years received several rather generous land grants.

Edward grew in favor with King Henry VIII and in 1531 was appointed an esquire to the King. The following year he accompanied the King and Anne Boleyn to Boulogne to meet with Francois I. In October 1535, the King visited Edward at his manor at Elvetham in Hampshire. A year later he was created Viscount Beauchamp of Hache in Somerset and he was promoted to Earl of Hertford after the birth of Edward VI.

Edward Seymour continued to rise in power and in 1541 was appointed Warden of the Scottish marches and shortly after, Lord High Admiral. In March 1544, he received the appointment of Lieutenant-General of the North. In May, he landed at Leith to capture and pillage Edinburgh 'to teach the Scots a lesson' because they had disregarded the treaty of marriage between Prince Edward and the young Mary Queen of Scots.

In July 1544, he received the appointment as Lieutenant of the Realm and in August he was present with the King during the surrender of Boulogne. In January 1545, he was placed in command at Boulogne. Edward spent a short time in the North again to avenge a Scottish victory at Ancrum Moor. Afterward, he returned to Boulogne to relieve Henry Howard, Earl of Surrey, who had an unsuccessful campaign. Shortly after, Edward was engaged in a peace treaty with France.

Edward remained in attendance with King Henry VIII until his death and continued serving when his son Edward VI ascended the throne. Given the new King was a minor, his father set in place a council of regency composed of sixteen nobles to assist the young King in governing his new realm. Several individuals were considered to serve the King as Protector and Edward Seymour rose above the others and became the Lord Protector to Edward VI. It was not long before Somerset began to institute changes to the Church of England. His views were based on the Protestant religion and his reformation included bold measures of political and promoted agricultural interests. In 1547, legislation was passed that eliminated the treasons and felonies created under Henry VIII and from that point two witnesses were required for proof of treason instead of one.

In 1548, his brother Thomas shot the King's barking dog outside his bedchamber and was arrested, tried and convicted of treason and it appears that Somerset was instrumental in his brother's execution. Shortly after, rebellions and small riots were held in Cornwall and quickly spread to outlining counties over the following months. Though some were upset over Somerset's religious reformations, the majority were angry with farmers switching from crops to raising sheep because it was considerably more profitable. The farmers began enclosing pastures, resulting in villagers tearing down the hedges that had once separated the lands. Somerset persuaded the King to show compassion by pardoning those involved hoping to win the acclaim of the common people, but it provoked them to further demonstration. In July 1549, rebellion broke out in Norfolk with attacks on local pasture enclosures including those put up by Robert Kett. Kett was nominated as the spokesperson and composed a list of demands, formed a governing council then sent their demands to the King. Somerset responded by telling the rebels to abandon their protests and to return to their homes with full pardons, although he would use force if required.

The rebels rejected those demands on 21 July and decided to enter Norwich, but were refused entry to the city and Kett's army, armed with various weapons, overtook the city. The King immediately responded by dispatching approximately 1400 men who failed to regain the city. In August 1549, Somerset dispatched John Dudley, later Duke of Northumberland, with 1200 troops and eventually seized Norwich after several days of fighting. An estimate of 3000 of Kett's army was slaughtered and Kett captured the following day.

Somerset was criticized for how he handled those involved in the rebellion. It was well noted that the way he dealt with the uprising had fueled the motives for the rebellion and he betrayed the governing calls. His reluctance to assume military leadership instead of delegating John Dudley only exacerbated matters. Furthermore, his popularity with the 'commoners' caused many to believe he could be a potential revolutionary and quickly led his opponents to demand his removal as Lord Protector. On 14 January 1550, Parliament confirmed his dispositions as Lord Protector and also deprived him of all other positions and sent to the Tower. The following is an account of the trial.

Proceedings in Parliament against Edward, Duke of Somerset, Lord Protector, for misdemeanors and high treason: 3 Edw. VI. A.D. 1550.

The Duke of Somerset having taken the part of the common people against the nobility in the business of enclosures, made himself many enemies. He had also given great grounds of jealousy by entertaining foreign troops in the King's service; and the noble palace he was raising in the Strand out of the ruins of some bishops houses and churches, drew as public an envy on him as anything he had done and his acting by his own authority without asking the advice of the council, and often against it, was assuming a regal power and seemed not to be endured by those who thought they were in all points his equals. Thus, all September there were great heats between the lords and him. The King was then at Hampton Court where the Protector also was with some of his retinue and servants about him, which increased the jealousies for it was given out, he intended to carry away the King. On the 6th of October some of the council met and sent to the lord mayor and aldermen of London to obey no letters from the Protector, and wrote to the nobility to inform them how they were proceeding. The Protector hearing of these things, removed the King to Windsor in all haste and armed such as he could gather for his preservation whereupon several letters passed between the council at London, and those at Windsor and at last a proclamation was published against the Protector to the following effect:

1. That the Protector by his malicious and evil government, was the occasion of all the sedition that of late happened within the realm.

2. The loss of the King's pieces in France.

3. That he was ambitious and sought his own glory, as appeared by building of sumptuous and costly houses in the time of the King's wars.

4. That he esteemed nothing the grave counsel of the councilors.

5. That he sowed division between the nobles, the gentlemen, and the commons.

6. That the nobles assembled themselves together at London, for none other purpose but to have caused the Protector to have lived within limits, and to have put such order for the surety of the King's majesty as appertained whatsoever the Protector's doings were, which they said were unnatural, ingrate, and traitorous.

7. That the Protector slandered the council to the King, and did what in him lay to cause variance between the King and the nobles.

8. That he was a great traitor and therefore the lords desired the city and commons to aid them to take him from the King.

This was signed by the Lord Rich, Lord Chancellor; the Lord St. John, President of the Council; the Marquis of Northampton; the Earl of Warwick, Great Chamberlain; and most of the council. On the 12th of October the whole council went to Windsor, and coming to the King, they protested that all they had done was only out of zeal and affection to his person and service. The King received them very kindly and thanked them for their care of him. On the 13th they sat in council, and sent for those who were ordered to be kept in their chambers, only Cecil (afterwards the famous Lord Burleigh) was let go; and in the end, the Lord Protector was commanded from the King's presence and committed to ward in a Tower within the castle of Windsor, called Beauchamp Tower and the next day, being the 14th, they brought from there the Protector and conveyed him to the Tower of London. Some time after, the lords resorted to the Tower and there charged the Protector with the following articles of misdemeanor and high treason.

Articles objected to the Duke of Somerset.

1. That he took upon him the office of Protector, upon express condition that he should do nothing in the King's affairs but by assent of the late King's executors, or the greatest part of them.

2. That contrary to this condition, be did hinder justice and subvert laws of his own authority as well by letters as by other command.

3. That he caused divers persons, arrested and imprisoned for treason, murder, man-slaughter, and felony, to be discharged against the laws and statutes of the realm.

4. That he appointed lieutenants for armies and other officers for the weighty affairs of the King under his own writing and seal.

5. That he communed with ambassadors of other realms alone of the weighty matters of the realm.

6. That he would taunt and reprove divers of the King's most honorable councilors, for declaring their advice in the King's weighty affairs against his opinion; sometimes telling them that they were not worthy to sit in council; and sometimes that he need not to open weighty matters to them; and that if they were not agreeable to his opinion, he would discharge them.

7. That against law he held a court of request in his own house; and did enforce divers to answer there for their freehold and goods and did determine of the same.

8. That being no officer without the advice of the council or most part of them, he did dispose offices of the King's gift for money; grant leases and wards, and presentations of benefices pertaining to the King; gave bishoprics and made sales of the King's lands.

9. That he commanded alchemy and multiplication to be practiced, thereby to abase the King's coin.

10. That divers times he openly said that the nobility and gentry were the only cause of death; whereupon the people rose to reform matters of themselves.

11. That against the mind of the whole council, he caused proclamation to be made concerning enclosures; whereupon the people made divers insurrections and destroyed many of the King's subjects.

12. That he sent forth a commission with articles annexed concerning enclosures, commons, highways, cottages, and such like matters, giving the commissioners authority to hear and determine those causes, whereby the laws and statutes of the realm were subverted and much rebellion raised.

13. That he suffered rebels to assemble and lie armed in camp against the nobility and gentry of the realm without speedy repressing of them.

14. That he did comfort and encourage divers' rebels by giving them money and by promising them fees, rewards, and services.

15. That he caused a proclamation to be made against law and in favor of the rebels that none of them should be vexed or sued by any for their offences in their rebellion.

16. That in time of rebellion, he said, that he liked well the actions of the rebels; and that the avarice of gentlemen gave occasion for the people to rise; and that it was better for them to die than to perish for want.

17. That he said the lords of the Parliament were loath to reform enclosures and other things therefore the people had a good cause to reform them themselves.

18. That after declaration of the defaults of bullion and the pieces there by such as did survey them, he would never amend the same.

19. That he would not suffer the King's pieces of Newhaven, and Blackness, to be furnished with men and provision; albeit he was advertised of the defaults and advised thereto by the King's council; whereby the French King was emboldened to attempt upon them.

20. That he would neither give authority, nor suffer noblemen and gentlemen to suppress rebels in time convenient; but wrote to them to speak the rebels fair and use them gently.

21. That upon the 5th of October the present year at Hampton-Court, for defense of his own private causes, he procured seditious bills to be written in counterfeit hands and secretly to be dispersed into divers parts of the realm; beginning thus: 'Good people' intending thereby to raise the King's subjects to rebellion and open war.

22. That the King's Privy Council did consult at London to come to him and move him to reform his government; but he hearing of their assembly, declared by his letters in divers places that they were high traitors to the King.

23. That he declined untruly as well to the King as to the other young lords attending his person that the lords at London intended to destroy the King and desired the King never to forget, but to revenge it; and he desired the young lords to put the King in remembrance thereof; with intent to make sedition and discord between the King and his nobles.

24. That at divers times and places, he said, 'the lords of the council at London intended to kill me; but if I die, the King shall die and if they famish me, they shall famish him.'

25. That of his own head he removed the King so suddenly from Hampton-Court to Windsor without any provisions there made, that he was thereby not only in great fear, but cast thereby into a dangerous disease.

26. That by his letters he caused the King's people to assemble in great numbers in amour after the manner of war to his aid and defense.

27. That he caused his servants and friends at Hampton-Court and Windsor to be appareled in the King's amour when the King's servants and guards went unarmed.

28. That he caused at Windsor his own person in the night-time to be guarded in harness by many persons leaving the King's majesty's person

unguarded; and would not suffer his own guard and servants to be next the King's person, but appointed his servants and friends to keep the gates.

29. That he intended to fly to Jersey or Wales and laid post-horse and men and a boat to that purpose.

After he had read and considered the above articles he sent the underwritten submission to the lords.

Edward Duke of Somerset's first submission.

I Edward, Duke of Somerset, have read and considered these said 29 articles before specified and do acknowledge my said offences, faults, and crimes done and contained in the same and most humble prostrate on my knees, do fully and wholly submit myself to the most abundant mercy and clemency of the King's majesty for the moderation of my side offences; having my full trust and confidence that his majesty, with the advice of his highness most honorable counsel, will consider my offences, faults, words and proceedings, that if any of my side offences be by his clemency pardoned, remitted, or otherwise discharged, that I may enjoy the benefit thereof, although the same become unknowns and farther, I do most humbly beseech all my lords and other his majesties most honorable counsel, not only to be means to his majesty to take away and consider my offences to have proceeded more of ignorance, negligence, folly, willfulness and for lack of good consideration than of any cankered or malicious heart, evil intent or thought tending to any treason to his majesty or realm but that it may please his majesty by the charitable advise of their good lordships to have pity upon me, my wife and children, and to take some merciful way with me not according to the extremity of his laws, but alter his great goodness and clemency, whereto whatsoever it shall be, I do most humbly with all my heart submit myself. Written with mine own hand the 23rd day of December in the 3rd year of our sovereign King Edward the sixth.

However, on the 2nd of January, a bill was put in against the Duke of Somerset of the articles before-mentioned with the above confession. This he was prevailed with to do upon assurance given that he should be gently dealt with, if he would truly confess and submit himself to the King's mercy. But some of the lords said they did not know whether that confession was not drawn from him by force and that it might be an ill precedent to pass acts upon such papers without examining the party, whether he had subscribed them freely and uncompelled whereupon a committee was appointed of four temporal lords and four spiritual who were sent to examine him concerning it. The day following the Bishop of Coventry and Litchfield made the report that he thanked them for their kind message, but that he had freely subscribed the confession that lay before them. He made it on his knees before the King and council, and signed it and he protested his offences had flowed from rashness and indiscretion rather than malice; and that he had no treasonable design against the King or his realm. So both houses soon passed the bill against him, and he was fined by an act of Parliament entitled, "An act touching the fine and ransom of the Duke of Somerset" that is, for the punishment of his late misdemeanors, whereby he was fined 2000£ a year of land and lost all his goods and offices. Upon this he sent another submission.

The second submission of Edward Duke of' Somerset, prisoner in the Tower.

I am most fearful and full of heaviness my very good lords, to understand that my last letter was no better accepted at your lordships hands, to whom I am bound during my life, for your most gentle and merciful dealing with me, that it pleased your goodness to bring my case to a fine. I trust your lordships never think that ever I did, or would intend to stand against the King's majesty and your lordship's goodness, or that I would go about to justify my cause seeing his majesty and your lordship's offer of clemency, mercy, and pardon. Although the fine be to me importable, yet I do commit myself wholly to his highness and your lordships mercies; I pray only the moderation of it and did covet to declare to your goodness my inability to bear it and yet referred all to his majesty and your wisdom, goodness, and discretion. And I most humbly desire your lordships not to think that I was about to contend with your lordships when I did speak of my conscience, I might ere in that I thought I did for the best as I do acknowledge and confess that neither I am the wisest man in the world, nor yet if I were, I should not escape without a most singular grace, but many times I should offend, but I leave all that and most humbly, simply, wholly, and lowly, I submit myself to the King's majesty and to your good lordships; appealing from the rigor and extremity of his majesty's laws, to his majesty's great mercy and clemency; praying your goodness to be means to his majesty, not to be offended with me, nor to exclude his majesty's mercy and benignity from me, for my rudeness and lack of discretion but to accept my good mind as one that fain would do that were well. And when I cannot or have not done that things I ought to do, I would gladly amend, and am ready at all times without condition to do and suffer willingly that thing that your honors will appoint me, accepting what clemency or mercy so ever I obtain to be of his majesty's and your goodness. Most humbly on my knees praying his majestic and your good lordships to pardon my offences and to order me for them, as to his most high merciful clemency shall appear convenient. And finally flying from extremity of justice, desire mercy, as you be and are called most merciful counselors, not imputing my writings and doings hitherto as of stoutness or stubbornness, but only for lack of discretion and wisdom. For the which once again I require pardon and favor to be showed, and if it pleased your good lordships to hear me, I trust you should find me lowly to your honors and so conformable to your lordships orders that I trust to make amends and obtain pardon for my former folly. And thus I most humbly commit your good lordships to almighty God, to whom I shall always pray that you may long continue in honor. From the Tower, the 2d of February.

He came out of the Tower on the 6th of February giving bond of 10,000£ for his good behavior, but limited that he should stay at the King's house at Sheen, or his own at Sion and should not go four miles from them, nor come to the King or council, unless he was called; and when he knew that the

King was to come within four miles of these houses, he was to withdraw from them.

On the 16th he had his pardon and carried himself so well that on the 18th of April following, he went by invitation to court, to the King's majesty at Greenwich where he was honorably received by the King and his council and dined with the King and was sworn of the Privy Council and the King of his special favor, and at the humble petition of the council by patent dated June the 4th, gave him back almost all his estate that was forfeited.

Proceedings against Edward Duke of Somerset, for high treason and felony, at Westminster: 5 Edward VI. A.D. 1551.

The Duke of Somerset had such access to the King and such freedoms with him (notwithstanding the late judgment against him), that the Earl of Warwick had a mind to get rid of him. The duke seemed also in April this year to have got the King again in his power and dealt with the Lord Strange to persuade the King to marry his daughter Jane; and that he would advertise him of all that passed about the King. The Earl of Warwick had got himself created Duke of Northumberland; and for several of his friends he procured a creation of new honors. The new Duke of Northumberland could no longer bear such a rival in greatness as the Duke of Somerset was, who was the only person that he thought could take the King out of his hands so a design being laid to destroy him, he was apprehended on the 17th of October, and sent to the Tower and with him the Lord Gray, Sir Ralph Vane, Sir Thomas Palmer, Sir Thomas Arundel were also taken, and some of his followers, Hammond, Newdigate and two of the Seymour's, and were sent to prison. The day after, the Duchess of Somerset was also sent to the Tower with one Crane and his wife, and two of her chamber-women, after these, Sir Thomas Holdcroft, Sir Miles Patridge, Sir Michael Stanhope, Wingfield, Bannister, and Vaughan were all made prisoners.

But Sir Thomas Palmer though imprisoned with him as an accomplice, was the person that ruined him. The evidence against the duke was chiefly Sir Thomas Palmer's information; who being brought by the Duke of Northumberland privately to the King related the whole conspiracy.

Sir Thomas Palmer's examination.

He declared, that upon St. George's-Day last, before the Duke of Somerset being upon a journey towards the north in case Sir William Herbert, Master of the Horse, had not assured him that he should receive no harm, would have raised the people and that he had sent the Lord Gray before to know who would be his friends also that the Duke of Northumberland, the Marquis of Northampton, the Earl of Pembroke and other lords, should be invited to a banquet; and if they came with a bare company, to be set upon by the way; if strongly, their heads should have been cut off at the place of their feasting. He declared further that Sir Ralph Vane had 2000 men in readiness, that Sir Thomas Arundel had assured the Tower, that Partridge should raise London and take the great seal; that Seymour and Hammond would wait upon him and that all the horse of the gendarmerie should be slain.

The Earl of Rutland did affirm that he had made a party for getting himself declared Protector in the next Parliament.

The above-mentioned particulars were told the King with such circumstances that he was induced to believe them and resolved to leave him to the law.

Sir Thomas Palmer's second examination.

That the gendarmerie, upon the muster-day, should be assaulted by 2,000 men under Sir Ralph Vane and by a hundred horses of the Duke of Somerset's, besides his friends, which should stand by and besides the idle people which were thought inclinable to take his part. That this done, he would run through the city and proclaim 'Liberty, liberty,' to raise the apprentices, &c. And in case his attempt did not succeed, he would go to the Isle of Wight or to Poole.

Crane's examination.

He confessed all that Palmer had said to which he added, that the Lord Paget's house was the place where the nobility being invited to a banquet should have lost their heads and that the Earl of Arundel was made acquainted with the conspiracy by Sir Michael Stanhope who was a messenger between them and that the thing had been done, but that the greatness of the enterprise caused delays and some diversity of advice. And further, that the Duke of Somerset once feigning himself sick, went to London to see what friends he could procure.

Hammond's examination.

He confessed that the Duke of Somerset's chamber at Greenwich had been strongly guarded in the night by many armed men.

All these were sworn before the council and the greatest part of the nobility, that their confessions were true; and they did say that what was sworn was without any kind of compulsion, force, or envy, or displeasure, but as favorable to the duke as they could swear to with safe consciences.

Lord Strange's examination.

He voluntarily informed how the duke desired him to move the King to take to wife his third daughter the Lady Jane; and that he would be his spy about the King to advertise him when any of the council spoke privately with him and to acquaint him what they said.

Hereupon the Lord Chancellor openly declared in the Star Chamber these accusations against the Duke of Somerset; and on the 22nd of October with much show and ceremony, were all the crafts and corporations of London commanded to repair to their halls, and there it was showed them that the Duke of Somerset would have taken the Tower, seized on the broad-seal and have destroyed the city and then to have gone to the Isle of Wight. After this declaration, they were charged each corporation to ward every gate in

London and to have a walking watch through the city. Towards the latter end of November a letter was sent to the Lord Chancellor to cause a sufficient commission to he made and sealed with the great seal of England of Oyer and Terminer, to the Lord Marquis of Winchester, that he may thereby be the King's seneschal, *hac unica vice tantum*, for the bearing and determining of the treasons and felonies of the Duke of Somerset, giving the date of the said commission the 28th of November; and the 1st of December was ordered for his trial.

December 1. The Duke of Somerset came to his trial at Westminster-Hall. The Lord Treasurer sat as High Steward of England under the cloth of state on a bench between two posts, three degrees high. All the lords to the number of twenty-seven, *viz.* Dukes; Suffolk, Northumberland. Marquis; Northampton. Earls; Derby, Bedford, Huntington, Hutiand, Bath, Sussex, Worcester, Pembroke. Viscount; Hereford. Barons; Burgaveny, Audley, Wharton, Evers, Latimer, Borough, Zouch, Stafford, Wentworth, Darcy, Sturton, Windsor, Cromwell, Cobham, Bray. These sat a degree under, and heard the matter debated.

The crimes laid against him were cast into five several indictments as King Edward VI has it in his journal; but the record mentions only three, whether indictments or articles, is not so clear.

1. That he had designed to have seized on the King's person and so have governed all affairs.

2. That he with 100 others, intended to have imprisoned the Earl of Warwick, afterwards Duke of Northumberland.

3. That he had designed to have raised an insurrection in the city of London. But the indictment which here follows is only for designing to seize on and imprison the Duke of Northumberland. London.

"Inquisitio capt' fuit apud Guihald Civitat London die Sabbathi, videlicet vicesimo primo die Novembris, anno regni domini Edwardi nuper Regis Anglie sexti, quinto, coram Richurdo Dobbes tunc Majore Civitat' London, ac aliis Justiciariis, & Commissioniariis per sacramentum duodecim, &c. qui dixerunt super sacramentum suutn, quod Edwardus dux Somers' nuper de Sion in Comitat' Middlesex' Deum pre oculis suis non habens, sed instigatione Diabolica seduct' &: debit', legiantie sue miniine ponderans, apud Holborne, in paroclia sancta Andree infra civit' London, vicesimo die Aprilis anno regni dicti nuper Regis Edwardi sexti quinto supradicto, & diversis diebus & vicibus antea & postea false, malitiose, & proditorie, per aperture factum circumivit, compassavit, & immaginavit, cum diversis aliis personis predictuin nuper Regem Edwardum sextum de statu suo Regali deponere & deprivare, necnou ex injuria sua propria Persona Regalem ipsius nuper Regnis natural' & supremi domini absq; authoritate altqua sibi per ipsium nuper Regein dat', sive concessa in solam gubernationem predicti nuper Ducis habere & retinere, ac ad voluntatem ejusdem nuper Ducis regere & tractare, ac etiam omnia & singula dominia, negotia, authoritatesque Regias hujus regni Anglie ad libit' ipsius nuper Dueis, ordiuare & uti, adtunc & ibidem arrogant, false, malitiose, & proditorie compassavit & imaginavit: Et ulterius juratores predicti presentabant, quod idem nuper Dux Somers ad suam proditoriam intentionent perimplend, & profic end, ex inalitia sua precogitat seipsum simul cum

Michaele Stanhope nuper de Bedington in Comitat Sur Milit, Milone Patriche nuper de London, Milit, Thom Hoicroft nuper de London, Milit, Francisco Newdigate nuper de London generos, ac cum diversis aliis personis ad numerum centum personarum Jurator predictis ignot in forcibili modo ex eorum propriis authoritatibus ad intentionem capiend & imprisonund prenobilem Johannem nuper Ducem Northuberl adtunc Comitem Warr, unum de Privat Concilio dicti nuper Regis tunc existen adtunc & ibidem illicite, false, malitiose, & proditorie assemblaverunt, ipsisque modo & forma predictis, illicite, voluntaries & malitiose assemblat, ad perimplend & exequend falsam & proditoriam intentionem suam predictam, false, voluntarie, malitiose, & proditorie, adtunc & ibidem per spatium duarum horarum & amplius insimul continuaverunt & remanserunt, contra legiantiam suam debitam,& contra pacem dicti nuper Regis coronam & dignitatem suas, ac contra formam diversorum satutorum in hujusmodi casa nuper edit & provis. Et ulterius Juratores predicti pretentabant, quod predictus Edwardus nuper Dux Somers Deuni pre oculis suis non habens, sed instigatione Diabolica seduct vicesimo die Maii, anno regni dicti nuper Regis Edwardi sexti quinto supradicto, & diversis aliis diebus & vicibus antea, & postea apud Holborne, in predicta parochia sancti Andree infra Civitat London, & apud diversa alia loca, infra Civitat London predictam felonice, ut felo dicti nuper Regis per aperta verba & facta procuravit, movit & instigavit complurim subdit dicti nuper Regis ad insurgend & apertam rebellionem & insurrectionem infra hoc regnum Anglie movend, contra ipsum nuper Regem, & adtunc & ibidem felonice ad capiend & imprisonand predictum prenobil Johannem nuper Ducem Northumberland, tunc Comit Warwic de Privat' Concilio dicti nuper Regis adtunc existen' contra pacem ipsius nuper Regis coronam & dignitatem suas, ac contra formam statuti in hujusmodi causa editi & provis. Et postea scilicet die Martis primo die Decembris, anno quinto supradicto, coram Willielmo Marchione Wynton, Thesaurar Anglie, necnon Seneschallo Anglie, hac vice apud Westmonasterium ven preadictus Edwardus nuper Dux Somers, sub custod Johunnis Gage prenobil ordinis Garterii Milit, Constubular dicti Turr London, in cujus custod preantea ex causa predicta, & aliis certis de causis commissus fuit ad barr apud Westmonasterium predictam duct in propria persona sua qui committebatur prefat Constabular, &c. Et statim de omnibus & singulis seperalibus proditionibus, & feloniis predictis sibi superius imposit allocat qualit se voluisset inde acquietari, dixit quod ipse in nullo fuit calpabil. Et inde de bono & mulo pon se super pares suos, &c. Super quo Henric. Dux Sutfole, Johannes Dux Northumberland, & ceteri Comit & Barones, predict Edwardi nuper Ducis Somers pares instant super eorum fidelitatibus & legianc dicto nuper Regi debit per prefat Seneschal Anglie de veritate inde dicend onerati; Et postea per eundem Seneschal ab inferior pare, usque ad supremum parem illorum seperatim publice examinati quilibet eorum seperatini dixerunt, quod predictus Edwardus nuper Dux Somers de seperalibus proditionibus predictis libi seperatim in forma predicta superius imposit in nullo fuit inde culpabil. Et ulterius quilibet eorum seperatum dixerunt, quod predictus Edwardus nuper Dux Somers de feloniis predictis sibi seperatim in forma predicta superius imposit fuit culpabil modo et forma, prout per seperalia indictamenta inde superius supponebatur, super quo instant servien dicti nuper Regis ad legem, ac ipsius nuper Regis Attorn juxta debit legis formam pet versus eundem Edwardum nuper Ducem Somers judicium, & executionem super seperalibus felouiis predictis pro dicto nuper Rege habend, &c.

Et super hoc visis per Curiam predictam ad tunc intellectis omnibus & singulis premissis, consideratum fuit quod predictus Edwardus nuper Dux Somers quoad seperales proditones predictus sibi seperatim in forma predicta superius imposit, & quamlibet eorum iret inde quiet. Et quoad seperalis felonias predict, eidem nuper Duci Somers in forma predicta superius imposit unde invent fuit culpabil, ulterius consideratum fuit, quod idem Edwardus nuper Dux Somers suspenderetur, &c.

Then were read the depositions of Palmer, Crane, Hammond, &c. and the King's counsel opened the indictment and urged strongly Palmer's voluntary examination (as they called it) with Crane's and the other examinations.

The Duke of Somerset being, it seems, little acquainted with laws did not desire counsel to plead or assist him in point of law, but only answered to matters of fact, he desired no advantage might be taken against him for any idle or angry word that might at any time have fallen from him; he protested he never intended to have raised the northern parts, but had only upon some reports sent to Sir William Herbert to be his friend; that he had never determined to have killed the Duke of Northumberland or any other person, but had only talked of it without any intention of doing it. That for the design of destroying the gendarmerie, it was ridiculous to think that he with a small troop could destroy so strong a body consisting of 900 men; in which though he had succeeded, it could have signified nothing. That he never designed to raise any stirs in London, but had always looked upon it as a place where he was most safe. That his having men about him at Greenwich was with no ill design, since when he could have done mischief with them, he had not done it but upon his attachment rendered himself a prisoner without any resistance. He objected also many things against the witnesses and desired they might be brought face to face. He particularly spoke against Sir Thomas Palmer, the chief witness. But the witnesses were not brought, only their examinations before mentioned read. Upon this the King's counsel replied and avouched the law to be to assemble men with intent to kill the Duke of Northumberland, was treason by a statute of the 3rd and 4th of Edward VI made against unlawful assemblies, which enacts, 'That if twelve persons should have assembled together to have killed any privy counselor, and upon proclamation they have not dispersed themselves, it was treason or, if such twelve had been by any malicious artifice brought together for any riot and being warned, did not disperse themselves, it was felony without benefit of clergy or sanctuary.' That to raise London or the north parts of the realm, was treason. That to have men about him to resist his attachment, was felony. That to assault the lords and to devise their deaths, was felony. These things were urged against him by the counsel (as is their usual way of pleading) with much bitterness. Then the peers withdrew to debate the matter. The proofs about his design of raising the north or the city, or of killing the gendarmes, did not satisfy them, (for all these had been without question treasonable) so they only held to that point, 'of conspiring to imprison the Duke of Northumberland.' The Duke of Suffolk was of opinion that no contention among private subjects should be on any account screwed up to be treason. The Duke of Northumberland said he would never consent that any practice against him should be reputed treason. Several of the lords said they held it unfit that the Duke of Northumberland, the Marquis of Northampton and the Earl of Pembroke should be on the trial; because the prisoner was chiefly charged with practices intended against them. But answer was made that a peer of the realm might not be challenged. So after great difference of opinion, they all acquitted him of treason. But the greater number found him guilty of felony and judgment was given that he should be hanged.

Then the Duke of Northumberland addressed himself to the duke, and told him that now since by the law he was condemned to die as he had saved him formerly, so he would not now be wanting to serve him, how little so ever he expected it from him, he desired him therefore to fly to the King's mercy in which he promised him he would faithfully serve him. The Duke of Somerset then thanked the lords for their favor, and asked pardon of the Duke of Northumberland, Northampton, and Pembroke for his ill intentions against them; and made suit for his life and for his wife and children and from thence be was carried to the Tower where he remained till January 22, when his petition for life having been rejected, he was brought to the scaffold about eight o'clock in the morning.

Account of the duke's execution.

Touching which execution a few words here would be bestowed in describing the wonderful order and manner thereof, according as it has faithfully been suggested to us upon the credit of a certain noble personage who not only was there present at the deed doing, but also in manner next to him upon the scaffold, beholding the order of all things with his eyes and with his pen also reporting the same in order and manner as here follows:

In the year of our Lord 1552, the 22nd day of January, the noble Duke of Somerset, uncle to King Edward, was brought out of the Tower of London and delivered to the sheriffs of the city and compassed round about with a great number of armed men, both of the guard and others, he was brought to the scaffold on Tower-Hill; where as be nothing changing neither voice nor countenance, but in a manner with the same gesture which he commonly used at home, kneeling down upon both his knees and lifting up his hands, commended himself to God. After that he had ended a few short prayers, standing up again, and turning himself toward the east-side of the scaffold, nothing at all abashed (as it seemed to me standing about the midst of the scaffold, and diligently marking all things), neither with the sight of the axe, neither yet of the hangman, or of present death; but with the like alacrity and cheerfulness of mind and countenance as before times he was accustomed to hear the causes and supplications of others, and especially the poor, lie uttered these words to the people:

"Dearly beloved friends; I am brought here to suffer death, albeit that I never of

offended against the King, neither by word nor deed and have been always as faithful and true to this realm as any man hath been. But forasmuch as I am by a law condemned to die, I do acknowledge myself as well as others to be subject thereto. Wherefore to testify my obedience which I owe to the laws, I am come here to suffer death; whereto I willingly offer myself with most hearty thanks to God, that has given me this time of repentance who might through sudden death have taken away my life, that neither I should have acknowledged him nor myself. Moreover, dearly beloved friends, there is yet somewhat that I must put you in mind of as touching Christian religion; which, so long as I was in authority, I always diligently set forth and furthered to my power. Neither I repent me of my doings, but rejoice therein, since that now the state of Christian religion comes most near to the form and order of the primitive church. Which thing I esteem as a great benefit given of God both to you and me most heartily exhorting you all, that this which is most purely set forth to you, you will with like thankfulness accept and embrace and set out the same in your living. Which thing if you do not without doubt greater mischief and calamity will follow."

When he had spoken these words, suddenly there was a terrible noise heard whereupon there came a great fear on all men. This noise was as it had been the noise of some great storm or tempest which to some seemed to he heard from above; like as if a great deal of gunpowder being enclosed in an armory, and having caught fire, had violently broken out. But to some again, it seemed as though it had been a great multitude of horsemen running together, or coming upon them. Such a noise then was in the ears of all men, albeit they saw nothing. Whereby it happened, that all the people being amazed without an evident cause without any violence or stroke stricken, or any man seen, they ran away some into the ditches and puddles and some into the houses thereabout; other some being afraid with the horror and noise, fell down groveling to the ground with their pole-axes and halberds; and most of them cried out, 'Jesus save us, Jesus save us!' Those which tarried still in their places for fear knew not where they were. And I myself which was there present among the rest, being also afraid in this hurly-burly, stood still altogether amazed, looking when any man would knock me on the head. In the mean time, whilst these things were thus in doing, the people by chance spied one Sir Anthony Brown riding to the scaffold, which was the occasion of a new noise; for when they saw him coming, they conjectured that which was not true, but notwithstanding which they all wished for, that the King by that messenger had sent his uncle pardon; and therefore with great rejoicing, and casting up their caps, they cried out, 'Pardon, pardon is come: God save the King!' Thus this good duke, although he was destitute of all man's help, yet he saw before his departure in how great love and favor he was with all men. And truly I do not think that in so great slaughter of dukes as has been in England within these few years, there were so many weeping eyes at one time; and not without cause for all men did see in the decay of this duke, the public ruin of all England, except such as indeed did perceive nothing. But now to return from whence we have strayed, the duke in the mean time standing still in the same place, modestly, and with a grave countenance made a sign to the people with his hand, that they would keep themselves quiet. Which thing being done, and silence obtained, he spoke to them in this manner:

"Dearly beloved friends, there is no such matter here in hand as you vainly hope or believe. It seems thus good to almighty God whose ordinance it is meet and necessary that we all be obedient to. Wherefore I pray you all to be quiet and to be contented with my death; which I am most wiling to suffer and let us now join in prayer to the Lord for the preservation of the King's majesty, to whom hitherto I have always showed myself a most faithful and true subject. I have always been most diligent about his majesty in his affairs both at home and abroad, and no less diligent in seeking the common commodity of the whole realm. At which words all the people cried out and said, "It was not true." Then the duke proceeding, said, "To whose majesty I wish continual health with all felicity and all prosperous success." Whereto the people again cried out, 'Amen.' "Moreover, I do wish to all his counselors the grace and favor of God, whereby they may rule in all things uprightly with justice. To whom I exhort you all in the Lord to show yourselves obedient as it is your bounden duty under the pain of condemnation and also most profitable for the preservation and safeguard of the King's majesty. Moreover, for so in such as heretofore I have had oftentimes affairs with divers men, and hard it is to please every man, therefore if there be any that has been offended and injured by me, I must humbly require and ask him forgiveness; but especially almighty God, whom throughout all my life I have most grievously offended and all other whatsoever they be that have offended me, I do with my whole heart forgive them. Now I once again require you, dearly beloved in the Lord, that you will keep yourselves quiet and still, lest through your tumult you might trouble me. For albeit the spirit be willing and ready, the flesh is frail and wavering; and through your quietness, I shall be much more quieter. Moreover, I desire you all to hear me witness, that I die here in the faith of Jesus Christ; desiring you to help me with your prayers, that I may persevere constant in the same to my life's end."

After this, he turning himself again about like a meek lamb, kneeled down upon his knees. Then Dr. Cox, who was there present to counsel and advertise him delivered a certain scroll into his hand, wherein was contained a brief confession to God; which being read, he stood up again upon his feet without any trouble of mind, (as it appeared) and first had the sheriffs farewell, then the lieutenant of the Tower and others, taking them all by the hands which were upon the scaffold with him. Then, he gave the hangman certain money. Which done, he put off his gown and kneeling down again in the straw, untied his shirt-strings. After that the hangman coming to him, turned down his collar round about his neck and all other things which did let or hinder him. Then lifting up his eyes to heaven where his only hope remained, and covering his face with his own handkerchief, he laid himself down along showing no manner or token of trouble or fear, neither did his countenance change, but that before his eyes were covered there began to appear a red color in the midst of his cheeks. Thus this most meek and gentle duke lying along, and looking for the stroke; because his doublet covered his neck, he was commanded to rise up and put it off; and then laying himself down again upon the block and calling thrice upon the name of Jesus, saying, 'Lord Jesus, save me!' As he was the third time repeating the same, even as the name of Jesus was in uttering in a moment he was bereft both of head and life.

[Howell, *A Complete Collection of State Trials*-V.1. 509-526]

Stephen Gardiner

Stephen Gardiner's date of birth is a topic of controversy among historians, but it is believed to have occurred circa 1490. He was born to John Gardiner, a cloth merchant who tried to provide a good education for his son. Gardiner attended Cambridge where he studied at Trinity Hall during the years 1525 to 1549. He specialized in Greek studies and later canon and civil law receiving a degree of doctor of civil law in 1520 and of canon law the following year.

His knowledge of law attracted the attention of Cardinal Wolsey. He served as his secretary, meeting King Henry VIII for the first time in 1525 for the signing of a treaty between the King and Frances I of France. Two years later, Gardiner and Sir Thomas More served as commissioners in arranging a treaty to obtain support for an army against the Holy Roman Emperor, Charles V. In 1529, Gardiner accompanied Wolsey to France in an attempt to gain the French King's support for King Henry VIII's great matter or 'secret matter' regarding his divorce from Catherine of Aragon. The following year, Gardiner was dispatched to Italy with Edward Foxe to secure a Decretal commission from the Pope that would allow Wolsey power to rule on the validity of King Henry's marriage to Catherine of Arragon without appeal to Rome. The Pope refused to grant the Decretal commission and instead, granted a general commission thus allowing Wolsey to try the case in England with a papal legate.

In 1529, Gardiner received the appointment as Archdeacon of Norfolk. He resigned that post in 1531 after receiving the appointment as Bishop of Winchester after securing a decision from Cambridge on the unlawfulness of a man marrying his dead brother's wife. In May 1533, Gardiner assisted the Archbishop of Canterbury, Cranmer, in pronouncing the marriage between the King and Catherine of Aragon null and void. Two years later, he was asked to vindicate the King's new title "Supreme Head of the Church of England." That was accomplished by composing his treaties '*De Vera obedientia*' in which he debated that rulers, not the Pope, were entitled to supremacy in their respective countries' churches.

Through the following consecutive years, Gardiner spent the majority of his time on diplomatic assignments. In 1539 he assisted in the preparations of 'The Six Articles' in which the reaffirmation of traditional Catholic doctrine on transubstantiation, clerical celibacy, the withholding of the cup from the laity at communion and private masses. In 1534, Gardiner was involved in the Prebendaries' Plot against Cranmer with this nephew Germain Gardiner. Though the plot failed when the King gave his support to Cranmer, Gardiner survived, but his nephew was executed for treason. Three years later, Gardiner and Chancellor Wriothesly attempted to turn King Henry VIII against his sixth wife Catherine Parr, but that failed. Gardiner remained a major figure until the death of the King. Upon the ascension of Edward VI to the throne, Gardiner was forthright in his opposition to the new Reformists. He maintained his Catholic beliefs even as Somerset became the King's Protector and was eventually placed in the Tower because of his unchanging beliefs. He remained there until his trial in 1551.

Proceedings against Stephen Gardiner, Bishop of Winchester, for opposing the reformation of religion and disobeying the King's orders and injunctions respecting the same: 5 Edw. VI A.D. 1551.

First we will set before the reader the copy of a certain writ or evidence against the said bishop, wherein as in a brief sum, generally is described the whole order and manner of his disordered demeanor, copied out of the public records in manner as follows:

The writ or evidence touching the order and manner of the misdemeanor of Winchester with declaration of the faults wherewith he was justly charged.

Whereas the King's majesty, by the advice of the Lord Protector and the rest of his highness's Privy Council, thinking requisite for sundry urgent considerations to have a general visitation throughout the whole realm, did about ten months past address forth commissioners and by the advice of sundry bishops and other the best learned men of the realm, appointed certain orders or injunctions to be generally observed; which being such as in some part touched the reformation of many abuses and in other parts concerned the good governance and quiet of the realm, were (as reason would) of all men of all sorts obediently received and reverently observed and executed, saving only of the Bishop of Winchester, who as well by conference with other as by open protestation and letters also showed such a willful disobedience therein, as if it had not been quickly espied, might have bred much un-quietness and trouble upon the knowledge thereof he being sent for, and his lewd proceedings laid to his charge in the presence of the whole council, so used himself, (as well in denying to receive the said orders and injunctions, as otherwise) as he was thought worthy most sharp punishment and yet considering the place he had been in, he was only sequestered to the fleet (prison), where after he had remained a certain time, as much at his ease as if he had been at his own house upon his promise of conformity he was both set at liberty again and also licensed to repair to and remain in his diocese at his pleasure. Where when he was forgetting his duty and what promise he had made, he began forthwith to set forth such matters, as bred again more strife, variance, and contention in that one small city and shire, than was almost in the whole realm after. Besides that, the Lord Protector's grace and the council were informed that to withstand such as he thought to have been sent from their grace and lordships into those parts, he had caused all his servants to be secretly armed and harnessed, and moreover when such preachers as being men of godly life and learning, were sent into that diocese by his grace and lordships to preach the word of God, had appointed to preach, the bishop, to disappoint and disgrace them and to hinder his majesty's proceedings, did occupy the pulpit himself not fearing in his sermon to warn the people to beware of such new preachers, and to embrace none other doctrine but that which he had taught them, (than the which words none could have been spoken more perilous and seditious.)

Whereupon, being eftsoons sent for and their grace and lordships objecting to him many particular matters, wherewith they had just cause to charge him, they did in the end upon his second promise leave him at liberty, only willing him to remain at his house at London because they thought it most meet to sequester him from his diocese for a time; and being come to his house, he began afresh to ruffle and meddle in matters wherein he had neither commission nor authority; part whereof touched the King's majesty. Whereof being yet once again admonished by his grace and their lordships, he did not only promise to conform himself in all things like a good subject, but also because he understood that he was diversely reported of, and many were also offended with him, he offered to declare to the world his conformity and promised in an open sermon so to open his mind in sundry articles agreed upon that such as had been offended, should have no more cause to he offended but well satisfied in all things. Declaring further that as his own conscience was well satisfied and liked well the King's proceedings within this realm, so would he utter his conscience abroad to the satisfaction and good quiet of others. And yet all this notwithstanding at the day appointed, he did not only most arrogantly and disobediently, and that in the presence of his majesty, their grace and lordships, and of such an audience as the like whereof has not lightly been seen, speak of certain matters contrary to an express commandment given to him on his majesty's behalf, both by mouth and by letters, but also in the rest of the articles whereto he had agreed before, used such a matter of utterance as was very like even there presently to have stirred a great tumult and in certain great matters touching the policy of the realm, handled himself so colorable as therein be showed himself an open great offender and a very seditious man for so much as these his proceedings were of such sort as being suffered to escape unpunished, might breed innumerable inconveniences and that the clemencies showed to him afore by their grace and lordships, did work in him no good effect, but rather a pride and boldness to demean himself more and more disobediently against his majesty's and his grace's proceedings, it was determined by their grace and lordships that he should be committed to the Tower and be conveyed there by Sir Anthony Wingfield, and that at the time of his committing, Sir Ralph Sadler and William Hunnings, Clerk of the Council, should seal up the doors of such places in his house as they should think meet; all which was done accordingly. By this evidence above mentioned, first here is of the reader to be noted how lewdly and disobediently the said Stephen Gardiner misused himself in the King's general visitation in denying to receive such orders and injunctions as for the which he justly deserved much more severe punishment, albeit the King with his uncle the Lord Protector, more gently proceeding with him, were contented only to make him taste the fleet. In the which house, as his durance was not long, so his entreating and ordering was very easy. Out of the which fleet, divers and sundry letters he wrote to the Lord Protector and other of the council, certain also to the Archbishop of Canterbury and some to Master Ridley Bishop of London; the particulars were too long here to rehearse, considering how this book is overcharged as you see already; and especially seeing the same to be notified in our first edition sufficiently, as is aforesaid.

Articles and positions ministered and objected, each of them jointly and severally to the Bishop of Winchester and contained in a letter from the Lord Protector to the said bishop as follows:

Article 1. *Imprimis*, that the King's majesty justly and rightfully is, and by the laws of God ought to be supreme head in earth of the Church of England, and also of Ireland, and so is by the clergy of this realm in their convocation, and by act of Parliament justly and according to the laws of God recognized.

Winchester. This first article the bishop granted.

Art. 2. Item, that his majesty as supreme head of the said churches has full power and authority to make and set forth laws, injunctions, and ordinances for and concerning religion and orders of the said churches, for the increase of virtue, and repressing of all errors, heresies, and other enormities, and abuses.

Winchester. To this second article he answered affirmatively.

Art. 3. Item, that all and every his grace's subjects are bound by the law of God to obey all his majesty's said laws, injunctions, and proceedings concerning religion and orders in the said church.

Winchester. To the third article the said bishop answered affirmatively and granted it.

Art. 4. Item, that you Steven Bishop of Winchester have sworn obedience to his majesty as supreme head of this Church of England, and also of Ireland.

Winchester. To the fourth article, the said bishop answered affirmatively and granted it.

Art. 5. Item, that all and every his grace's subjects that disobey any his majesty's said laws, injunctions, ordinances, and proceedings already set forth and published, or hereafter to be set forth and published, ought worthily to be punished according to his ecclesiastical law used within this his realm.

Winchester. To this fifth article the said bishop answered affirmatively and granted it.

Art. 5. Item, that you the said bishop as well in the King's majesty's late visitation within your diocese as at sundry times have been complained upon, and sundry information's made against you for your doings, sayings, and preaching's against sundry injunctions, orders, and other proceedings of his majesty, set forth for reformation of errors, superstitions, and other abuses of religion.

Winchester. This article touched other men's acts who or how they have complained or informed, I cannot thoroughly tell. For at the time of the King's majesty's visitation I was in the fleet, and the morrow alter Twelfth Day, I was delivered at Hampton-Court, my Lord of Somerset and my Lord of Canterbury then being in council with many other counselors and was delivered by these words: The King's majesty has granted a general pardon and by the benefit thereof I was discharged whereto I answered that I was learned never to refuse the King's majesty's pardon, and in strength as that was; and I would and did humbly thank his majesty therefore and then they began with me in an article of learning touching justification, whereto they willed me to say my mind; adding therewith that because other learned had agreed to a form delivered to me, I should not think I could alter it which I received of them, and promised the Thursday after to repair to my Lord of Somerset's house at Sheen with my mind written; which I did, and at that day seven-night following, appearing before him and other of the council, was committed to my house for prisoner, because I refused to subscribe to the form of words and sentences that other had agreed to us they said. In which time of imprisonment in my house, the Bishop of Rochester then being sent to me, and after Master Smith, and then Master Cecil, to which Master Cecil, when I had by learning resolved my mind in the matter, I delivered it, and he delivering it to my lord's grace, wrote me in his name thanks for it; and it was within the time of Lent, ere I was discharged of that trouble, and so went to Winchester as a man clearly out of all travel or business. And within 14 days after that, or thereabouts, began other travel with me upon a request made by my Lord of Somerset to surrender a college in Cambridge, and divers letters were written between his grace and me in it. Wherein I might perceive the secretary with his pen took occasion to prick me more than I trusted my lord's grace himself would have done. And by this trouble was I deduced to an end. Then shortly after I received letters to come to the council, and by reason I alleged my disease, I was respited by other letters and three days before Whitsuntide received your other letters to come by which it might seem to me that it was not of all believed that I was diseased. And therefore with all expedition, when I could not ride, I came in an horse litter and according to my duty presented myself to my lords of the council, who all then entertained me secretly among them before the matters were objected to me, as if I had been in the same place with them that I was in our late sovereign lord's days. Afterwards my Lord of Somerset's grace charged me with these matters following, and in this form having the articles written in a paper. First, with disobedience that I came not at his sending for. Whereto I answered that I had his letters of license to stay till I might come conveniently. And upon these last letters I came incontinently in a horse litter. Then it was objected that I bare palms and crept to the cross. Whereto I answered that they were misinformed, and I trusted they would not think I do deny it, if I had done it, because ceremonies had such circumstances as I might easily be reproved if it were otherwise. Then it was objected, that at Easter I had a solemn sepulcher in the church, and such other ceremonies. I answered that I had even as many as the King's majesty's proclamations commanded me; declaring plainly that I thought it not expedient to make any alteration, wherein to offend the King's majesty's proclamation; adding how he that followed as he is commanded is very obedient. It was then objected to me that I went about to deface two of the King's majesty's chaplains sent down to be canons of the Church of Winchester. Whereto I answered declaring the fact truly as it was, which I am your able to justify. After this matter thus oft objected and answered, I was commanded to go apart and being called in again, my Lord of Somerset's grace, looking upon a bill of articles, said I had preached how the apostles went from the presence of the council, which matter I denied, adding that it was not my fashion of preaching, so to play in iteration of words. After that, it was objected to me for preaching of the sacrament, to say the body of Christ was really present being a fault to use the word 'really', not comprised in the scripture, whereto I answered that I did not use the word 'really', which needed not. For as I once heard my Lord of Canterbury reason against one Lambert in the presence of the King's majesty that dead is; the words of the scripture, this is my body that shall be betrayed for you, do plainly and lively express the very presence, and so did I set it forth to the people in my diocese. And this is the effect of all that was said against me at my being at the council, as I can remember. To whom I declared how much I esteemed obedience and told them I had taught in my diocese how the whole life of a Christian man consisted in suffering properly; and therefore we may not do our own will, but the will of God and among men we must either suffer the rulers will or their power; their will to order us, and their power to punish us. Alter declaration whereof, my Lord of Somerset said you must tarry in the town. Whereto I answered I would be contented at their commandment or pleasure to tarry; but seeing I was no offender, I desired them I might not tarry as an offender and for declaration thereof that I might have some house in the country about London to remove to for a shift. In devising whereof I stuck much to borrow Asshar. My Lord of Somerset said if he had any, in faith he would lend me one. And in the end my Lord of Somerset desired me to write what my mind was in ceremonies, and to send it to him and with that departed. Thus I have truly opened after what sort I have been complained on, that has certainly come to my knowledge; truth it is that one Philpot in Westminster, whom I accounted altered in his wits as I have heard, devised tales of me, the specialties whereof I never was called to answer to. Players and minstrels also railed on me, and others made ballads and rhymes of me, but never man had just cause to complain of any my sayings, doings, or preaching's, or to my knowledge did otherwise than afore. And if any man shall put me in remembrance of any other complaint that might in my absence be made of me, if I have heard it, I will grant so. But well assured I am, I was never complained on, and called to make answer to the complaint, but this one time in all my whole life by any man of any degree. Once the Lord Cromwell, God pardon his soul and forgive him, caused one day and a half to be spent in a mutter between Sir Francis Brian and me, which was ended, and I declared an honest man, which the King's majesty that dead is, God pardon his soul, set forth with his familiarity to me incontinently. And this is all the trouble that I have had in my life, saving the sending to the fleet, being occasioned by my own letter to the council upon a zeal that I had which they allowed not. And finally, this sending of me to the Tower; which was without calling me before the council to hear what I could say. I am loath to be forsworn, and therefore I account all the complaints in my whole life made against me whereto I have been made privy.

Art. 7. Item, that after and upon occasion of those and many other complaints and information's, you have been sundry times admonished, commanded and enjoined to conform yourself as to your duty appertained.

Winchester. To this seventh article I answer; I was never called afore the council by way of outward complaint and information, but only once in all my whole life, which was at my last coming to London. Whereto I answered as afore, and have told the form and process of speech to serve for furniture of answer to this mid that article for other than I have before written I remember not to have done or suffered by the hither powers in all my whole life, till my coming into the Tower without that I have had any by admonitions as a man faulty or negligent at any time that I remember not for the observation of anything already made or set forth by the King's majesty, that now is, but have kept and caused to be kept to my power the King's majesty's acts, statutes, injunctions, and proclamations inviolably, having for that purpose such a chancellor as in orders and ordinances has been always himself diligent and precise, for that time I might have knowledge of his doings.

Art. 8. Item, that after the premises and for that those former admonitions and commandments notwithstanding, you did yet still show yourself not conformable and for that also others by your example were much animated, and thereby occasion of much un-quietness ministered among the people, you were called before the King's majesty's council in the month of June in the second year of his majesty's reign, and by them on his majesty's behalf commanded to preach a sermon before his majesty, and therein to declare the justness and godliness of his majesty's father in his proceedings upon certain matters partly mentioned in certain articles to you delivered in writing, and partly otherwise declared to you. The effect whereof was touching the usurped power and authority of the Bishop of Rome that the same was justly and godly taken away in this realm and other the King's majesty's dominions; touching the just suppressing and taking away of monasteries and religious houses of pilgrimages, reliques, shrines and images. The superstitious going about of St. Nicholas Bishop, St. Edmund, St. Katharine, St. Clement, and such like; and just taking away of chantries, abbeys and colleges, hallowing of candles, water, ashes, palm, holy bread, beads, creeping to the cross, and such like. Also, touching the setting forth of the King's majesty's authority in his young years to be as great as if his highness were of many more years. That auricular confession is indifferent and of no necessity by the law of God; and touching the procession and common prayer in English.

Winchester. This article being of so many parts as it is, some true, some otherwise, must be answered by division of it into divers members, to divide the one from the other, granting that which is true, denying that which is otherwise, and opening that which is ambiguous, avoiding that which is captious; so as according to my oath, I may open directly and plainly the truth with sincerity of conscience. The motion of reaching was made to me in mine own house by Master Cecil upon the Duke of Somerset's behalf after I had been before the council as I have before said; from which council I departed as before is rehearsed as no offender; and therefore when master Cecil spoke to me of preaching before the King's majesty with request to write my sermon before, I denied that manner of preaching because I said it was to preach like an offender, and I was none, but departed from the council otherwise as I have before showed. And the said Master Cecil did not say to me that I was moved to preach because I was not conformable; for I had at that time no manner of variance with the council, but was in all conformity with them for anything that I know as I will answer afore God. As for evil example to any man I could none give for I never offended law, statute, or proclamation in this realm. I did never any act to the impairing of due obedience to the King's majesty in all my whole life; but by observation of them and letting innovations have done as much as in me lay to maintain obedience. After Master Cecil had spoken to me of preaching and delivered two papers containing die matters whereupon I should entreat because I refused to give my sermon in writing which was to me like an offender, or to read those papers of another man's device as the conception and sincere manner of uttering of mine own conscience which me thought then since, and yet a marvelous unreasonable matter touching both my conscience and honesty, I was then set to the Duke of Somerset's grace's chamber and came in at a back door to himself alone saving he took to him as witness he said the lord now of Wiltshire, then great master; and after many words, he showed me certain articles subscribed by lawyers what a bishop might command and what the King might command and what pain to the disobeyer. To whom I said plainly and truly how those lawyers subscription could not serve in this case to command me to utter to the people, for mine own devise in words that which is not indeed so; and if I might speak with these lawyers, I said his grace should soon perceive them to agree with me. My lord said I, should speak with no man and I should do as I was bidden, or do worse, and had me advise me till dinner was done. And then was I conveyed by the lord great master to his chamber and there left alone to dine as was indeed honorably prepared. But I took myself to be in the nature of a prisoner and a restrained man. And about two of the clock at afternoon came to me Master Thomas Smith, then secretary, to whom I complained of the unreasonableness of the matter and showed him certain particularities; who said it was not meant so precisely, but to speak of the matters. To whom I said I was content to speak of the matters and then if I speak not according to the truth of them, there should be enough to bear witness to my condemnation, and if I speak the truth, then they had their desire. And I said further I thought I might with my conscience say so as men ought and should be content and satisfied. And further, if I thought that in my manner of the uttering of those matters, I should offend the council, I had rather deny to speak of the thing and begin the contention secretly with them, than to begin with pulpit and so bring myself in further trouble than needed; and therefore if they would have me preach, I would preach as of myself and of these matters so as I thought they should be content. Whereupon I was brought up to my Lord of Somerset's chamber, and there the matter ended thus, that my Lord of Somerset said he would require no writing of me, but remit it to me, so I spoke of the matters in the papers delivered me by Master Cecil. I told him I would speak of them, saving for children's toys, of going about of Saint Nicholas, and Saint Clement. If that be now gone, quote I, and forgotten, if I be too busy in rehearsal of them, they will say I cumber their heads with ceremonies and thus they will defame me. When ceremonies were plenty, they will say I did nothing but preach on them and now they be gone, I babble of them still. I said I would teach the chief points, adding that I would speak of other matters also and with that being put to my liberty to choose the day, departed; and otherwise I was not spoken with concerning preaching, saving after Master Cecil came to me, whereof I shall speak anon. And concerning the matters to be spoken of, all such things as be here rehearsed be named in the papers delivered to me although not altogether after this sort; saving the setting forth of the King's majesty's authority in his minority, whereof there is no word in those papers, now was there ever any promise made of me to speak of it. Truth it is, that after I had signified the day when I would preach, Master Cecil came to me, making the chief message to know the day when I would preach to whom I had sent word before that it should be St. Peter's day, because me thought the Gospel served well for that purpose, and in process of communication he told me that he liked gaily well a word that I had said in another communication, how a King was as much a King at one year of age as at an hundred years of age, and if I touched it, he thought it would be well taken. I told him again, every man knew that, and then opened of myself the matter further. And at his next repair to me, which was the Monday before I preached, the said Master Cecil brought me papers of the King's majesty's hand, showing me how the King's highness used to note every notable sentence, and specially if it touched a King; and therefore (quote he) if you speak of a King, you must join counsel with all. Whereto I made no answer, but shifted to other matter without making him any promise, or denial, because I would neither bind myself, nor trouble myself to discuss that matter. For albeit it is godly and wisely done of every prince to use counsel; yet, speaking of a King's power by scripture, I cannot by express scripture limit the King's power by counsel. And hearing blindly by report some secret matter that I will not speak of here, I thought not to meddle with it at all in the pulpit and yet to the effect to have our sovereign lord now obeyed, of which mind I was ever, I pointed to our sovereign lord there in presence and said he was only to be obeyed and I would have but one King and other words to that purpose. But for any promise to be made by me, I utterly deny it. And tell plainly the cause why I spoke not otherwise of it. There was also in the papers delivered to me occasion given me to speak of the Mass, because of Masses satisfactory, as some understand them. And also there was occasion to speak of the sacrament of the altar because of the proclamation passed of the same which to be true, I shall justify by the said papers.

Art. 9. Item, that you receiving the same; and promising to declare the same in a sermon by you made before his majesty for that purpose on the feast of St. Peter in the said second year of his reign, did then and there contemptuously and disobediently omit to declare and set forth many of the said matters, and of divers other of the said articles you spoke and uttered your mind in such doubtful sort, as the justness and godliness of his majesty's father's and his proceedings was not set forth according to die commandment given to you and your own promise, to the great offence of the hearers and manifest contempt of his majesty, and dangerous example of others.

Winchester. Touching that promise I answer as before; and as touching omission of that I should have spoken of by contempt or disobedience, I answer by my oath; I did not omit anything (if I did omit it) by contempt or disobedience; for I ever minded to satisfy the promise, to speak of all matters in those papers according to my former declaration. And if I did per case omit anything, whereof I can make now no assurance, it being two years and an half past since I preached; but if I did omit anything, he who knew my travel in the matter would not marvel being troubled with a letter sent from the Duke of Somerset, whereof I shall speak after. So as from four of the clock on Thursday till I had done my sermon on the Friday, I did neither drink, eat, nor sleep, so careful was I to pass over the travel of preaching without all slander of the truth and with satisfaction of my promise and discharge of my duty to God and the King's most excellent majesty. Wherein, whether anything were omitted or not, I could have answered more precisely than I can now, if according to my most instant suit and the suit of my servants, the matter had been heard while it was in fresh memory. But because omission may be by infirmity of nature, in which oblivion is a pain of our original sin in which case it is no mortal offence, if a man being put in remembrance will purge it; I therefore, according to the true testimony of mine own conscience, dare the more boldly deny all contempt and disobedience, having for my declaration a general sentence spoken in my sermon that I agreed with the upper part in their laws, orders and commandments, or such like words and found fault only in the lower part. By which sentence it appeared, how I allowed in the whole that was past hitherto and only dissented from the doings of them that attempt innovations of I heir own presumption. And furthermore I say that that saying [omission] here objected to me, if it were true as I know it not to be, may happen two ways; one way by infirmity of nature, another way of purpose. Charity of a Christian man permits not to determine the worst of that which is doubtful and ambiguous to both parties as touching doubtfulness objected, I take God to record, I minded to speak simply and to be on the King's majesty's side only and not to go invisible in the world with ambiguities, esteeming him, &c. The worst man of all is he that will make himself a lock of words and speech which is known not to be my fashion, nor do I think this life worth that dissimulation and how can that be a doubtful speech in him, that professed to agree with the King's laws, injunctions and statutes, which I did expressly? There be that call in doubt whatsoever served not their appetite.

It is not in the speaker to satisfy the hearer that will doubt where doubt is not. The sum of my teaching was that all visible things be ordered to serve us, which we may in convenient service use. And when we serve them, that is an abuse, and may then at the ruler's pleasure, unless scripture appoints a special use of them be corrected in that use or taken away for reformation. And this is a plain teaching that has no doubt in it, but a yea and nay on both sides without a mean to make a doubt, and if any that doubted comes to me, I will resolve him the doubt as I can. And if I promised to speak plainly, or am commanded to speak plainly, and cannot, then is my fault to promise only in the nature of folly and ignorance, whereto I resort, not for a shift, whereof indeed I profess the knowledge, but to show how sometime to my hindrance I am noted learned that can speak plainly and yet speak doubtfully other whiles am rejected as one that understands not the matter at all. As touching contempt, there can be none manifest that proceeded of a privy promise; if I had broken it, I intended not, but intended to take it as appears by my general sentence to agree with the superiors, and only find fault in the inferior subjects, who daily transgress the King's majesty's proclamations and other, whereof I spoke then.

Article 10th. Item, that you being also commanded on his majesty's behalf, for avoiding of tumult and for other great considerations, inhibited to treat of any matter in controversy concerning the Mass and of the communion, then commonly called the sacrament of the altar, did contrary to the said commandment and inhibition, declare divers your judgments and opinions in the same in the manifest contempt of his highness's said inhibition to the great offence of the hearers, and disturbance of common quiet and unity of the realm.

Winchester. To the tenth article the said bishop answered that the Wednesday at afternoon, next before the Friday when I preached, M. Cecil came to me and having in all his other accesses spoken no word thereof did then utter and advise me from the Duke of Somerset that I should not speak of the sacrament or of the Mass, whereby he said I should avoid trouble. And when he saw me not to take it well, I mean, quote he, doubtful matters. I asked him what? He said transubstantiation. I told him he knows not what transubstantiation meant. I will preach, quote I, the very presence of Christ's most precious body and blood in the sacrament which is the Catholic faith, and no doubtful matter, he yet in controversy saving that certain unlearned speak of it they want not what. And among the matters, quote I, whereof I have promised to speak, I must by special words speak of the sacrament and of the Mass also. And when I shall so speak of them, I will not forbear to utter my faith and true belief therein which I think necessary for the King's majesty to know; and therefore if I wish to be hanged when I came down, I would speak it. Which plain zeal of my conscience grounded upon God's commandment to do his message truly, I would not hide, but utter so, as my lord should if he would not have it spoken of, not let me to come there as he might have done whereas else, if I had had a deceitful purpose, I might have accepted the advice, and without any color of trouble have refused to follow it as a thing grounded upon wealth only, as it was then uttered. With this my answer M. Cecil departed, and upon the Thursday which was the next day following, and the evening before I preached between three and four at afternoon, I received a letter signed with the hand of the Duke of Somerset, the copy whereof I am ready to exhibit, and took it then and esteemed it so now to contain no effectual inhibition whereto I might by God's law, or the King's majesty's laws, with discharge of my conscience and duty obey, although the said letters had been as they were not in such terms framed as had precisely forbidden me, as they did not, but only uttered to speak of matters in controversy of the sacrament which indeed I did not, but only uttered a truth to my conscience most certainly persuaded of the most holy sacrament necessary to be known to the King's majesty, and to be uttered by me admitted to that place of preaching from whence God commanded his truth to be uttered, which in this nature of truth, the undue estimation and use whereof Saint Paul threatened with temporal death, may in no wise be omitted. So as I was and am persuaded the right estimation of the sacrament to be to acknowledge the very presence of the same most precious body and blood present in the sacrament to feed us, that was given to redeem us. If I showed not my sovereign lord the truth thereof, I for my part suffer him wittingly to fall into that extreme danger of body which Saint Paul threatened, whose person I am bound by nature, by special oaths and by God's laws, to preserve to my power, as I will do, and must do by all ways and means. And if the King's majesty does vouchsafe to teach his people not to obey his commandment where God commanded the contrary, I might not take my Lord of Somerset's letter for an inhibition to hold my peace when God bid me to speak, as he does when the wolf comes and not to hide myself in silence, which is the most shameful running away of all. I have much mutter to allege against the letter why I should not credit it, written in his name alone against a common letter, as I took it, written by him and the council and published in print the first day of the said month which maintains my preaching of the sacrament and Mass according to the proclamation and injunctions, the violation of which public letters, had been a disorder and contempt, whereas I neither offended in the one, nor the other. And as for tumult, none could reasonably be feared of anything spoken agreeable to the King's majesty's laws, as there did follow none, nor the people, nor any man did offer my person any wrong, or make tumult against me notwithstanding, players, jesters, rhymers, ballad-makers, did signify me to be of the true Catholic faith, which I according to my duty declared to the King's majesty, from whom I may hide no truth that I think expedient for him to know. And as the name of God cannot be used of any creature against God, no more can the King's name be used of any subject against his highness. Wherefore seeing the abuse of this holy sacrament has in it a danger assured by scripture of body and soul; whosoever is persuaded in the Catholic faith as I am, finds himself so burdened to utter that to his majesty as no worldly loss can let him to do his duty in that behalf, and much less my lord's private letters written without other of the council's hands.

Art. 11. Item, that after the premises, *viz.* in the month of May or June or one of them, in the third year of his highness reign, his majesty sent eftsoons to you to know your conformity towards his said reformations, and specially touching the book of common prayer, then lately set forth by his majesty whereto you at the same time refused to show yourself conformable.

Winchester. To the 11th article for answer and declaration thereof, he said the next day at afternoon after he had preached, when he looked for no such matter, came to his house the right worshipful Sir Anthony Wingfield, and Sir Kate Sadler, Knights, accompanied with a great number of the guard, and used themselves for their part according to their worships, and (I doubt not) as they were appointed and Sir Rafe Sadler began thus with me; my lord, said he, you preached yesterday obedience, but you did not obey yourself and went forth with his message very soberly, as he can, and discreetly. I asked him wherein I obeyed not. He said, touching my Lord of Somerset's letter. Master Sadler, quote I, I pray you say to say lord's grace, I would he never made mention of that letter for the love I bear him. And yet, quote I, I have not broken that letter, and I was minded, quote I, to have written to my lord upon the receipt of it, and lo, quote I, you may see how I began and showed him (because we were then in my study) the beginning of my letter and reasoned with him for the declaration of myself, and told him therewith I will not spend, quote I, many words with you, for I cannot alter this determination. And yet in good faith, quote I, my manner to you and this declaration may have this effect, that I be gently handled in the prison and for that purpose I pray you make suit on my behalf. Master Wingfield laid his hand on my shoulder and arrested me in the King's name for disobedience. I asked him whither I should? They said to the Tower. Finally I desired them that I might bespoken with shortly and heard what I could say for myself and prayed them to be suitors in it, and so they said they would. After that I was once in the Tower until it was within six days of one whole year, I could hear no manner, word, message, comfort, or relief, saving once when I was sick and me thought some extremity towards me, my chaplain had leave to leave to me once, and then denied again, being answered that my fever was but a tertian, which my said chaplain told me when he came to me at the Easter following and there being with me from the morning till night on Easter any departed, and for no suit could I ever have him since. To master lieutenant I made divers suits to provoke the Duke of Somerset's grace to hear me and if I might have the liberty of an Englishman, I would plainly declare I had neither offended law, statute, act, proclamation, nor his own letter neither; but all would not help, and I shall report me to Mr. Lieutenant whether in all this time I maligned, grudged, or used any unseemly words, ever demanding justice, and to be heard according to justice. When I had been thus in the Tower one whole year within six days or seven, as I remember, came to the Tower the Lord Chancellor of England, now being the Lord Treasurer, and Master Secretary Peter, who calling me to them, as I remember, entered thus; they said they had brought with them a book passed by the Parliament which they would I should look on and say my mind to it, and upon my conformity in it, my Lord of Somerset would be suitor to the King's majesty for mercy to be ministered to me. Whereto I answered that I trusted if I might be heard, the King's majesty's justice would relieve me, which I had long sued for and could not be heard. And to sue for mercy, quote I, when I have not in my conscience offended and also to sue out of this place, where asking of mercy implied a further suspicion than I would be for all the world touched in, were not expedient; and therefore, quote I, not guilty is and has been continually allowed a good plea for a prisoner. Then my lord said, why quote he, were you not commanded to preach of the King's authority in his young age, and did not? I told him I was not commanded. Is not, quote he, that article in the papers you had delivered you? I assured him no. And after communication of the King's majesty's authority wherein was no disagreement, then my Lord Chancellor said I had disobeyed my lord's graced letter I told him I thought not, and if the matter came to judgment it should appear. And then I said to him, my lord, how many open injunctions under seal and in open court have been broken in this realm? The punishment whereof has not been handled after this sort, and yet I would stand in defense that I have not broken his letter, weighing the words of his letter, wherein I reasoned with Master Secretary Peter what a controversy was, and some part what I could say further. But whatsoever I can say, quote I, you must judge it and for the passion of God do it, and then let me sue for mercy when the nature of the offence is known, if I will have it. But when I am, quote I, declared an offender, I will with humility of suffering make amends to the King's majesty, so far as I am able; for I should never offend him and much less in his young age. My Lord Chancellor then showed me the beginning of the act for common prayer, how dangerous it was to break the order of it. I told him that it was true and therefore if I came abroad, I would be well aware of it. But it is, quote I, after in the act, how no man should be troubled for this act, unless he were first indicted, and therefore (quote I) I may not be kept in prison for this act. Ah (quote he) I perceive you know the law well enough. I told him my chaplain had brought it to me the afternoon before. Then they required me to look on the book and to say my mind in it; I answered that I thought not meet to yield myself a scholar to go to school in prison, and then slander myself as though I redeemed my faults with my conscience. As touching the law which I know, I will honor it like a subject, and if I keep it not, will willingly suffer the pain of it. And what more conformity I should show, I cannot tell; for mine offences be past if there be any. If I have not suffered enough, I will suffer more, if upon examination I be found faulty and as for this new law, if I keep it not, punish me likewise. Then my Lord Chancellor asked me whether I would not desire the King's majesty to be my good lord. At which words I said alas my lord, quote I, do you think that I have so forgotten myself? My duty, quote I, requires so, and I will on my knees desire him to be my good lord and my Lord Protector also, quote I: that is well said, quote my Lord Chancellor. And what will he say further? quote my Lord Chancellor, in good faith, quote I, this, that I thought when I had preached, that I had not offended at all, and think so still and had it not been for the article of the supremacy, I would have rather fained myself sick than be occasion of this that has followed; but going to the pulpit, I must needs say as I said. Well, quote my Lord Chancellor; let us go to our purpose again. You will, quote he, desire the King's majesty to be your good lord, and the Lord Protector also, and you say you thought not to have offended. All this I will say, quote I; and you will (quote my Lord Chancellor) submit yourself to be ordered by my Lord Protector. Nay, quote I, by the law for my Lord Protector, quote I, has scourged me over sore this year to put my matter in his hands now. And in the latter point I varied with my Lord Chancellor when I would not refer my order to my Lord Protector, but to the law; and staying at this point they were content to grant me of their gentleness to make their suit to procure me to be heard, and to obtain me liberty to go in the gallery and that I should hear of one of them within two days following. I desired them to remember that I refused not the book by way of contempt, nor in any evil manner, but that I was loath to yield myself a scholar in the Tower and to be seen to redeem my faults, if I had any, with my conscience. My body, I said, should serve my conscience, but not contrary wise. And this is the truth, upon my conscience and oath that was done and said at their coming. There was more said to the purposes aforesaid. And I bind not myself to the precise form of words, but to the substance of the matter and fashion of the entreating. So near as I can remember I have truly discharged my oath. But I heard no more of my matter in one whole year after almost within fourteen days, notwithstanding two letters written by me to the council of most humble request to be heard according to justice. And then at the end of two years almost, came to me the Duke of Somerset with other of the council; which matter because it is left out here, I shall not touch, but prepare it in a matter apart for declaration of my behavior at all times.

Art. 12. Item, that after that, &c. the ninth day of July, in the fourth year of his majesty's reign, his highness sent to you his grace's letters, with a certain submission and articles whereto his grace willed and commanded you to subscribe. To which submission you contemptuously refused to subscribe.

Winchester. To the twelfth article, for answer thereto, he granted that about the time mentioned in this article, the Lord Treasurer, the Earl of Warwick Lord Great Master, Sir William Herbert, and Master Secretary Peter came to the Tower and called me before them and delivered to me the King's majesty's letters, which I have to shown and received them at the hands of the Lord Treasurer upon my knees, kissed them as my duty was, and still upon my knees read them, whereas they gently required me to take more case and go apart with them and consider them which after that I had thoroughly read, I much lamented that I should be commanded to say of myself as was there written and to say otherwise of myself than my conscience will suffer me, and here I trust my deeds will not condemn me, there to condemn myself with my tongue. I should sooner (quote I to them) by commandment, I think if you would bid me tumble myself desperately into the Thames. My Lord of Warwick seeing me in that agony, said what say you my lord, quote he, to the other articles? I answered that I was loath to disobey where I might obey, and not wrest my conscience, destroying the comfort of it, as to say untruly of myself. Well, quote my Lord of Warwick, will you subscribe to the other articles? I told him I would. But then, quote I, the article that touched me must he put out. I was answered, that needs not, for I might write on the outside what I would say to it. And then my Lord of Warwick entertained me very gently and would needs whiles I should write, have me sit down by him; and when he saw me make somewhat strange so to do, he pulled me nearer him and said we had ere this sat together and trusted we should do so again. And then having pen and ink given me, I wrote as I remember on the article that touched me these words; I cannot with my conscience say this of myself; or such like words. And there followed an article of the King's majesty's primacy, and I began to write on the side of that and had made an I onward, as may appear by the articles, and they would not have me to do so; but write only my name after their articles which I did. Whereat because they showed themselves pleased and content, I was bold to tell them merrily that by this means I had placed my subscription above them all; and thereupon it pleased them to entertain me much to my comfort. And I was bold to recount to them merry tales of my misery in prison which they seemed content to hear; and then I told them also (desiring them not to discontent with that I should say) when I remember each of them alone, I could not think otherwise but they were my good lords and yet when they meet together I feel no remedy at their hands. I looked (quote I) when my Lord of Somerset was here, to go out within two days and made my farewell feast in the Tower and all; since which time there is a month past, or thereabout; and I agree with them and now agree with you, and I may fortune to be forgotten. My Lord Treasurer said nay I should hear from them the next day; and so by their special commandment I came out of the chamber after them, that they might be seen depart as my good lords; and so was done. By which process appears how there was in me no contempt as is said in this article, but such a subscription made as they were content to suffer me to make which I took in my conscience for a whole satisfaction of the King's majesty's letters which I desire may he deemed accordingly. And one thing was said to me further, that other would have put in many more articles, but they would have no more but those.

Art. 13. Item, that you having eftsoons certain of the King's majesty's honorable council sent to you the 12th of July in the said 4th year with the said submission and being on his majesty's behalf required and commanded to consider again and better the said commission and to subscribe the same, stood in justification of yourself and would in no wise subscribe thereto.

Winchester. To the 13th article he said the next day after the being in the Tower of the said Lord Treasurer, the Earl of Warwick, and other, came to me Sir William Herbert and Master Secretary Peter, to devise with me how to make some acknowledging of my fault (as they said) because the other form liked me not. Whereto I said, I knew myself innocent and to enter with you to entreat of a devise to impair my innocence in any the least point either by words or writings, it can have no policy in it. For although I did more esteem liberty of body than the defamation of myself, yet, quote I, when I had so done with you, I were not so assured by you to come out. For when I were by my own pen once made a naughty man, then were I not the more sure to come out, but had locked myself the more surer in; and a small pleasure were it to me to have my body at liberty by your procurement and to have my conscience in perpetual prison by mine own act. Many more words there were and persuasions on their parts; which caused me to require of them for the passion of God that my matter might take an end by justice; and so they departed, there being no contempt or faction of disobedience showed on my behalf, but only allegation for my defense of my innocence in the best manner I could devise as I trust they will testify.

Art. 14. Item, that after all this, *viz.* the 14th day of July in the said 4th year, the King's majesty sent you again to you certain of his majesty's honorable council with another submission and divers other articles willing and commanding you to subscribe your name thereto. Which to do you utterly refused.

Winchester. To the 14th article he said that on the Monday in the morning following came the Bishop of London, Sir William Herbert, Master Secretary Peter, and another whom I know not, who brought with them a paper with certain articles written in it, which they required me to subscribe. Whereupon I most instantly required that my matter might be tried by justice, which although it were more grievous, yet it has a commodity with it, that it ended certainly the matter. And I could never yet come to my assured stay, and therefore refused to meddle with any more articles or to trouble myself with the reading of them; and yet they desired me so instantly to read them that I was content and did read, and to show my perfect obedient mind, offered incontinently upon my delivery out of prison to make answer to them all such as I would abide by and suffer pain for if I have deserved it. I would indeed gladly have been in hand with my Lord of London; but he said he came not to dispute and said it was the hand of God that I was thus in prison because I had so troubled other men in my time. Finally, my request was that they should in this form make my answer to my lords of the council as follows, that I most humbly thank them of their good will to deliver me by the way of mercy, but because in respect of mine own innocent conscience I had rather have justice, I desired them seeing both was in the King's majesty's hands, that I might have it; which if it happen to me more grievous, I will impute it to myself and evermore thank them for their good will; and so departed I with them as I trust they will testify, and no misbehavior or misdemeanor to have been used on my behalf.

Art. 15. Item, that after all this videlicet, the 19th day of July in the said 4th year, you being personally called before the King's majesty's Privy Council, and having the said submission and articles openly and distinctly read to you and required to subscribe the same, refused for unjust considerations by you alleged to subscribe the same.

Winchester. To the 15th article I grant that upon a Saturday at afternoon, even at such time of the day as they were at evensong in the chapel at the court, I was brought here and at my coming the lords of the council said they were all my judges by special commission, and intended to proceed thus with me that I should subscribe certain articles which were then read, and I must directly make answer whether I would subscribe them or no. I answered on my knees in this wise for the passion of God, my lords, he my good lords and not me be tried by justice, whether I be faulty or no; and as for these articles as soon as you deliver me to my liberty, I would make answer to them whether I would subscribe them or no. Then they having further to say, I answered these articles were of divers sorts; some be laws which I may not qualify; some be no laws, but learning and fact which may have divers understandings and a subscription to them without telling what I mean, were over dangerous. And therefore I offered for the more declaration of my obedience to all their requests, that if they would deliver me the articles into the prison with me, I would shortly make them particular answer and suffer the pains of the law, that by my answer I might incur into. Whereupon I was commanded to go apart and they sent to me the Lord Treasurer and Master Secretary Peter who communed with me of a mean way and that liked not the lords. And then I was called forth again, and my absolute subscription required again and I again made offer to answer particularly, for I could not with my conscience subscribe them as they were absolutely. And these my considerations I trust to be just; seeing no man for any commandments ought to offend his conscience as I must have done in that case.

Art. 16. Item, that for your sundry and manifold contempt's and disobediences in this behalf used, the fruits of your bishopric were then by special commission of his majesty justly and lawfully sequestered.

Winchester. To the 16th article, I deny contempt's and disobedience of parts, and say that my doings cannot so be termed because it is taught in this realm for a doctrine of obedience that if a King command that which is contrary to the commandment of God, the subject may not do as he is commanded but humbly stand to his conscience, which is my ease, who could not with my conscience do as I was required. And as touching the fact of decree, there was indeed a decree read having words so placed and framed as though I were such an offender, which matter I deny. And in that decree was mention made of administration of fruits; but whether the former words were of the present tense, or else to be sequestered, I cannot precisely tell, but do refer that to the tenor of the decree.

Art. 17. Item, that after this you had intimation and peremptory monition with communication that you should within three months next following the said intimation, reconcile and submit yourself under pain of deprivation.

Winchester. To the 17th article I answer that in the same decree of sequestration at the same time read, I kneeling from the beginning of the decree to the latter end, I remember there was an intimation and three months spoken of and expressed also how at every month's end I should have pen and ink offered to write if I would yet subscribe, and as I understand it was upon the pain of proceeding further. And I do not remember that I heard the word deprivation, but therein I refer me to the acts of the sentence; which when it was read, I desired it might be testified what mine offer was to answer all those articles particularly even remaining in prison. And this done, I made suit for some of my servants abroad to resort to me to the Tower, partly for my comfort, partly for my necessary business, which could not be obtained.

And yet to provoke it, I said to my Lord of Warwick how for agreeing with my Lord of Somerset I had some commodity, and for agreeing with him had nothing, and therefore would needs by intercession press him that I might by this means have some of my servants resorting to me. He answered very gently. And then one said I should within two or three days have somebody come to me. And then I was dismissed with commandment to the lieutenant to let me have the same liberty I had, but no more.

Art. 18. Item, that the said three months are now thoroughly expired and run.

Winchester. To the 18th article he said there is almost six months passed in time and number of days, but not one month past to the effect of the law, nor ten days neither, because I have been so kept in prison, that I could not seek for remedy in form above said, nor was there at every month after the form of the sentence offered me pen, ink, and liberty given me to consult and deliberate with other learned men and friends what were best to do, or to send to them. And furthermore, the very eighth day after the decree given, I protested before my servants whom I had only commodity to use as witnesses of the nullity of the decree for the evident and apparent matter in it; but if it were any ill law, I appended to the King's majesty because my request was not admitted to have the copy of the articles to answer them particularly and because it is excessive correction to sequester my fruits and keep me in prison. With other cases to be deduced where I might have opportunity. Which appellation I protested to imitate as soon as I could come to any presence meet therefore, as I did in this assembly at my last repair desiring therewith the benefit *restitutionis in integrum*, because of my imprisonment; and therefore do answer this matter with protestation of that appeal and utterly deny all manner of contempt.

Art. 19. Item, that you hitherto, according to the said intimation and monition, have not submitted, reconciled, nor reformed yourself, but contemptuously yet still remain in your first disobedience.

Winchester. To the 19th article I say that I have been all this while in prison so kept, as no man could have access to council with me, nor any means to write or send to any man, having made continual suit to master lieutenant and master marshal, under whose custody I am here to make suit in my name to the lords of the council, that I might come to hearing, or else be bailed upon surety, which I could not obtain and so have remained under the benefit of my said appeal to the King's majesty, made as I might for the time which I eftsoons desire I may have liberty to prosecute. And whereas answering to these articles for declaration of the integrity of my conscience, I use in the same places general words; I protest I mean not by those words to set forth myself otherwise more arrogantly then as my direct intent (which excludes malice) and purpose moves me to say and as my conscience bears witness to me at this time, and therefore will say therein with St. Paul, *Nihil mihi consciui sum, sed non in hoc justificatus sum*. Wherefore if any especially be objected to me, wherein, by ignorance or oversight and negligence any offence of mine may appear against the King's majesty's laws, statutes and injunctions, I shall desire and protest that it be not prejudicial to mine answer (for this present, *cedrio*, as lawyers in civil matters use that term) to be true, that is to say such as without any alteration in my conscience presently I may of myself say in affirmation or denial, as afore is answered. And whereas I spoke of commandment to be made to me against God's law, I protest not to touch my sovereign lord's honor therein which my duty is by all means to preserve, but that the commandment given resolves to be against God's law on my part in the obedience to be given, because I may not answer or say otherwise but *est, est; non, non*. So as my words and heart may agree together, or else I should offend God's law, which my sovereign, if he knew my conscience would not command me.

After these things thus passed certain of the council by the King's appointment, had sundry days and times access to him in the Tower to persuade with him, which were these, the Duke of Somerset, the Lord Treasurer, the Lord Privy Seal, the Lord Great Chamberlain, and Mr. Secretary Peter. Who repairing to him the 10th day of June, anno 1550, he desired of them to see the King's book of proceedings; upon the light whereof he would make a full answer seeming to be willing in all things to conform himself thereto; and promising that in case anything offended his conscience, he would open it to none but to the council. Whereupon it was agreed the book should be sent him to see his answer that his case might be resolved upon and that for the mean time he should have the liberty of the gallery and garden in the Tower when the Duke of Norfolk were absent. The King then was lying at Greenwich at which time the lieutenant of the Tower was appointed to deliver the King's book to the Bishop of Winchester. Who, within three days after which was the 13th of June, made declaration again to the council that the bishop having perused it, said to him he could make no direct answer unless he were at liberty and so being he would say his conscience. Whereupon the lords and other that had been with him the other day, were appointed to go to him again to receive a direct answer that the council thereupon might determine further order for him. The answer of the bishop being received through the report of the lords which had been with him, declaration was made again the 8th day of July, 1550, that his answers were ever doubtful, refusing while he were in prison to make any direct answer. Wherefore it was determined that he should be directly examined whether he would sincerely conform himself to the King's majesty's proceedings or not. For which purpose it was agreed that particular articles should be drawn to see whether he would subscribe them or not, and a letter also directed to him from the King's highness with the which the Lord Treasurer, the Lord Great Master, the Master of the Horse, and Master Secretary Peter, should repair to him.

Sentence definitive against Stephen Gardiner Bishop of Winchester:

In the name of God, amen. By authority of a commission by the high and mighty prince our most gracious sovereign Lord Edward the 6th, by the grace of God King of England, France, and Ireland, defender of the faith and of the Church of England and also of Ireland, in earth the supreme head, the tenor whereof hereafter ensues; Edward the Sixth, &c. We Thomas by the sufferance of God, Archbishop of Canterbury, Primate of all England, and metropolitan, with the right reverend fathers in God, Nicholas Bishop of London, Thomas Bishop of Ely, and Henry Bishop of Lincoln, Sir William Peter Knight, one of our said sovereign lord's two principal secretaries, Sir James Hales Knight, one of our said sovereign lord's justices of his common pleas, Griffith Leison and John Oliver, doctors in the civil law, Rich, Goodrick and John Gosnold, Esq. Delegates and judges assigned and appointed, rightfully and lawfully proceeding according to the form and tenor of the said commission for the hearing, examination, debating, and final determination of the causes and matters in the said commission mentioned and contained and upon the contents of the same, and certain articles objected of office against you Stephen Bishop of Winchester, as more plainly and fully is mentioned and declared in the said commission and articles all which we repute and take here to be expressed; and after sundry judicial assemblies, examinations and debating; of the said cause and matters with all incidents, emergent, and circumstances to the same or any of them belonging, and the same also being by us oft heard, seen, null well understood and with good and mature examination and deliberation debated, considered, and fully weighed and pondered, observing all such order and other things as by the laws, equity, and the said commission ought or needed herein to be observed in the presence of you Stephen Bishop of Winchester, do proceed to the giving of our final judgment and sentence definitive in this manner following. Forasmuch as by the acts enacted, exhibits, and allegations proposed, deduced, and alleged, and by sufficient proofs with your own confession in the causes aforesaid had and made, we do evidently find and perceive that you Stephen Bishop of Winchester have not only transgressed the commandments mentioned in the same, but also have of long time notwithstanding many admonitions and commandments given to you to the contrary, remained a person much grudging, speaking, and repugnant against the godly reformations of abuses in religion set forth by the King's highness's authority within this his realm; and forasmuch as we do also find you a notable, open, and contemptuous disobeyer of sundry godly and just commandments given to you by our said sovereign lord and by his authority in divers great and weighty causes touching and concerning his princely office and the state and common quietness of this realm and forasmuch as you have and yet do contemptuously refuse to recognize your notorious negligence's, and misbehaviors, contempts and disobediences, remaining still after a great number of several admonitions, always more and more indurate, incorrigible, and without all hope of amendment, contrary both to your oath, sworn obedience, promise, and also your bounden duty of allegiance; and for that great slander and offence of the people arise in many parts of the realm through your willful doings, sayings, and preaching, contrary to the common order of the realm and for sundry other great causes by the acts, exhibits, your own confession and proofs of this process more fully appearing; considering withal that nothing effectually has been on your behalf alleged, proposed, and proved, nor by any other means appears which does or may impair or take away the proofs made against you upon the said matters and other the premises therefore we Thomas Archbishop of Canterbury, Primate of all England and metropolitan, judge delegate aforesaid, having God before our eyes with express consent and assent of Nicholas Bishop of London, Thomas Bishop of Ely, Henry Bishop of Lincoln, Sir Wm. Peter Knight, Sir James Hales Knight, Griffeth Leison and John Oliver, doctors of the civil law, Rd. Goodrick and John Gosnold, esquires, judges, and colleagues with us in the matters aforesaid and with the counsel of divers learned men in the laws with whom we have conferred in and upon the premises, do judge and determine you Stephen Bishop of Winchester, to be deprived and removed from the Bishopric of Winchester, and from all the rites, authority, emoluments, commodities, and other appurtenances to the said bishopric in any wise belonging, whatsoever they be, and by these presents we do deprive and remove you from your said bishopric and all rites and other commodities aforesaid; and further pronounce and declare the said Bishopric of Winchester to all effects and purposes to be void by this our sentence definitive, which we give, pronounce, and declare, in these writings.

This sentence definitive being given, the said Bishop of Winchester under his former protestations, dissented from the giving and reading thereof and from the same, as unjust and of no efficacy or effect in law; and in that the same contains excessive punishment and for other causes expressed in his appellation aforesaid, he did then and there *apud acta,* immediately after the pronouncing of the sentence, by word of mouth appeal to the King's royal majesty first, secondly, and thirdly, instantly, more instantly, most instantly, and asked apostles, or letters dismissorials to be given and granted to him and also under protestation not to recede from the former appellation, asked a copy of the said sentence the judges declaring that they would first know the King's pleasure and his counsel therein. Upon the reading and giving of which sentence the promoters willed William Say and Thomas Argall to make a public instrument and the witnesses then and there present to bear testimony thereto, &c.

[Howell, *A Complete Collection of State Trials.* V-1. 551-632]

When Mary I ascended the throne in 1553, she released all Catholic prisoners and Gardiner was returned all his possessions and positions and made Lord Chancellor in August 1553, then became, once again, a major figure in the new regime and continued to promote the Catholic religion until his death, of natural causes, on 12 November 1555.

Chapter 4: The Reign of Mary I

Mary I or Mary Tudor was born 8 February, 1516 to King Henry VIII and Catherine of Aragon. Mary was tutored by her mother and leading scholars at the time were she excelled in music and languages. Later, Henry's marriage to Catherine of Aragon was declared null also declaring Mary's claim to the throne illegitimate. Mary was further pushed aside with Henry's separation from Rome and declared himself supreme head of the Church of England.

King Edward VI died on 6 July, 1553, at Greenwich Palace after an illness believed to be consumption (tuberculosis). Before his death, John Dudley, Duke of Northumberland, convinced the dying King that Mary and Elizabeth should be eliminated from the succession and replaced with the Lady Jane Grey; and then after securing the King's signature, he used various tactics to get the 'device' through Parliament.

This author recognizes Lady Jane Grey's reign. Though it was only for nine days, she did nevertheless reign as Queen of England. Queen Jane did not hold a trial, or at least none is known at this time, and the prisoners in the Tower remained there, including Stephen Gardiner. Mary took the throne from her and placed Jane and her husband in the Tower for what many believed would be a short period.

With any possible threats to her throne locked in the Tower, Queen Mary began considering a husband. When no suitable candidate was found within her realm, she settled for Philip of Spain, also a Catholic. That was not a popular decision within the kingdom as many felt that bringing in a foreigner could have dire consequences. Dissension soon turned to rebellion and Sir Thomas Wyatt the Younger led a sizable army that was finally stopped within a mile of where Mary sought refuge. Hundreds of executions followed Wyatt's rebellion and earned Mary the moniker 'Bloody Mary'.

Those executions included the Lady Jane and her husband because of her father's involvement in Wyatt's rebellion and Mary would not take the chance that Jane could reclaim the throne. An account has survived history of the horrible events that occurred the day of Jane's execution:

> Thus this black Monday began, with the execution of this most noble and virtuous lady and her husband. On the same day, for a terrifying sight, were many new pairs of gallows set up in London. As at every gate one, two pair in Cheapside, one in Fleet street, one in Smithfield, one in Holborne, one at Leadenhall, one at St. Magnus, one at Billingsgate, one at Pepper Alley Gate, one at St. George's, one in Barnsby Street, one on Tower Hill, one at Charring Cross, and one at Hide Park Corner. These gallows remained standing until Wednesday when men were hanged on every gibbet, and some quartered also. In Cheapside six; at Aldgate one, hanged and quartered; at Leadenhall three; at Bishopgate one, and was quartered; at Moorgate one, and he was quartered; at Ludgate one and he was quartered; at Billingsgate three hanged; at St. Magnus three hanged; at Tower Hill three hanged; at Holborne three hanged; at Fleet street three hanged; at Paul's Churchyard four; at Pepper Alley Corner three; at Barnaby Street three; at St. George's three; at Charring Cross four; whereof two belonged to the court; at Hide Park Corner three, one of them named Pollard, a water bearer. Those three were hanged in chains. But seven were quartered, and their bodies and heads set upon the gates of London. [Strype, *Historical Memorials*, XX]

Dissension within the Kingdom diminished and Mary and Philip were wed in July 1554. In early 1555, Mary acted on restoring the Catholic faith and medieval heresy laws were restored by Parliament and about 270 people perished for their Protestant beliefs. Into 1556 the trials and burning continued including Thomas Cranmer. Mary had survived a couple false pregnancies and Philip had been away more than with her. Philip returned long enough for England to declare war with France in mid-1557 and led forces into France to capture St. Quentin, but France struck back and retook Calais.

Early 1558, Mary again thought she was pregnant and in March she drafted her will with an inclusion which alluded to her being with child. But it was not to be and she became very ill and revised her will in October indicating her half-sister Elizabeth would succeed her. Mary died 17 November 1558 without child.

Following are trials held during the reign of Queen Mary I.

John Dudley, Duke of Northumberland

John Dudley was born the eldest of the three sons to Edmund Dudley and his second wife, Elizabeth Grey circa 1504. In 1510, his father Edmund was executed for high treason. In 1512, John became the ward of Sir Edward Guildford where he resided. During that time he was restored 'In name and blood' from the dishonor his father brought to the family. Early historians believe that at about age 15, John accompanied his guardian to the Pale of Calais where he remained for several years.

John Dudley participated in diplomatic assignments with Cardinal Wolsey in 1521 and 1527 and was knighted by Charles Brandon during his first military experience in France in 1523. The following year he became a Knight of the Body. In 1525, he married Sir Edward Guildford's daughter Jane and together they had thirteen children.

In 1532, John Dudley was with King Henry VIII in Calais during their meeting with Francis I. He was also present during the christening of Princess Elizabeth and Prince Edward. In 1536, he led one of the small forces against the Pilgrimage of Grace and the following year he was appointed Vice-Admiral of the English navy. In 1543 he received the appointment of Lord Admiral, a Knight of the Garter and a member of the Privy Council. In 1544, he provided vessels to Edward Seymour for a campaign against Scotland and he joined the land campaign that destroyed Edinburgh earning the appointment as Governor of Boulogne that year.

Lord Admiral Dudley was responsible for making the English navy the most efficient in Europe and he was successful in several campaigns including the Battle of the Solent in 1545. Upon the succession of Edward VI, John Dudley was elevated to Earl of Warwick and passed his post as Lord Admiral to the new protector's brother, Thomas Seymour. Dudley soon proved himself a worthy solider against the Scottish in the battle of Pinkey, leading his forces towards an English victory. Following that campaign, Dudley led the forces against Robert Kett and crushed the rebellion, ultimately becoming responsible for about three-hundred executions.

Dudley turned his attention to manipulating young King Edward's political education. Under his influence, when the King was about age 14 he started signing documents without the council countersigning them and conducted meetings with members of his own choosing, including Dudley. Despite his reputation as a power-hungry individual, Dudley made changes in policies concerning the needy including abolishing the 'act for the punishment of vagabonds.' In 1550 and 1552 Dudley pushed the bill 'poor law' through Parliament which provided weekly parish-based collections for those in need. In October 1551, John Dudley was again elevated, this time to Duke of Northumberland.

In February 1553, King Edward VI fell ill and although he did recover, those close to him began to make plans should he die. Soon thereafter he fell ill again and was unable to recover, prompting him to draft his 'device for the succession.' In it he made changes, including a provision that Lady Jane Grey would succeed him instead of Mary or Elizabeth. Having changed the order of succession, Dudley's son Guildford married Lady Jane and when she took her place on the throne, he would become the father of the King of England. Dudley supervised as unsettled council members discussed the King's revised will and used intimidating tactics to influence those who did not support it. King Edward died on 6 July, 1553, and Jane was placed on the throne, although Mary vehemently voiced her opinion that she was the rightful heir.

After nine days, Mary took the throne from Jane and placed her and her husband in the Tower. Dudley was seen throwing his cap into the air proclaiming Mary Queen, but he was quickly arrested by the Earl of Arundel. On 25 July, Dudley was escorted to the Tower as many lined the streets shouting 'death to the traitor.' Rocks, filth from the gutters and a dead cat were hurled at the duke as he held his head down. His trial was held on 18 August, 1553, in Westminster Hall.

> The trials of John Dudley Duke of Northumberland, William Parr Marquis of Northampton, for high treason in the court of the Lord High Steward at Westminster, 18th August, 1 Mary, A.D. 1553; and also of Sir John Gates, Sir Henry Gates, Sir Andrew Dudley, and Sir Thomas Palmer, at Westminster for the same crime the day following.
>
> Thomas Duke of Norfolk sitting as High Steward of England, on the 18th day of August were brought before him John Dudley Duke of Northumberland, William Parr Marquise of Northampton, and the Earl of Warwick, son to the Duke of Northumberland. The Duke of Northumberland, at his coming to the bar used great reverence towards the judges, and protesting his faith and obedience to the Queen's majesty whom he confessed grievously to have offended, he said; that he meant not to speak anything in defense of himself; but would first understand the opinion of the court in two points.
>
> 1. Whether a man doing an act by the authority of the prince and counsel, and by a warrant of the great seal of England and doing nothing without the same, may be charged for treason for anything which he might do by warrant thereof?
>
> 2. Whether any such persons as were equally culpable in that crime and those by whose letters and commandments he was directed in all his doings, might be his judges, or pass upon his trial at his death?
>
> Whereto was answered that as concerning the first, the great seal which he laid for his warrant was not the seal of the lawful Queen of the realm, nor passed by authority, but the seal of an usurper and therefore would be no warrant for him.
>
> And to the second, it was alleged that if any were as deeply to be touched as himself in that case, yet as long as no attainder were of record against them, they were nevertheless persons able in the law to pass upon any trial and not to be challenged therefore, but at the princes pleasure.
>
> After which answer, the Duke using few words declared his earnest repentance in the case, (for he saw, that to stand upon uttering any reasonable matter would little prevail) and moved the Duke of Norfolk to be a means to the Queen for mercy, and without further answer confessed the indictment; by whose example also the other prisoners arraigned with him did likewise confess the indictment produced against them, and thereupon had judgment.

The judgment being pronounced, he craved favor of such a death as was executed on noblemen and not the other; he beseeching also that a favorable regard might be had of his children in respect of their age and that he might be permitted to confer with some learned divine for the settling of his conscience; and lastly, that her majesty would be pleased to send to him four of her counsel for the discovery of some things which might concerns the state.

The Marquise of Northampton pleaded to his indictment that after the beginning of these tumults he had forborne the execution of any public office; and that all the while he intent to hunting and other sports, did not partake in the conspiracy; but it being manifest that he was party with the Duke of Northumberland, sentence passed on him likewise.

The Earl of Warwick, finding that the judges in so great a cause, admitted no excuse of age, with great resolution heard his condemnation pronounced against him, caring only this favor; that whereas the goods of those who are condemned for treason are totally confiscated; yet her majesty would be pleased that out of them his debts might be paid. After this they were all returned again to the Tower.

On the 18th of August, the Duke of Norfolk sitting as Lord High Steward, those concerned in the rebellion were tried at Westminster; where the Duke of Northumberland with his eldest son the Earl of Warwick, and the Marquis of Northampton, were found guilty of high treason. The account of that day's proceedings and of the day following, I shall here transcribe from Thuanus, a writer of great fame; because though I do not entirely approve all he has set down, I think he keeps very near to truth and the reader, perhaps, will not be ill entertained with the variety of opinions upon this matter.

The Duke of Northumberland, says he, alleged that he did nothing but by order of the council, yet this would not excuse him; so that he was condemned as a traitor. When the sentence was pronounced, he begged that it might be mitigated as to the manner of his death, and that his children in regard to their tender years, might find mercy; and that he might have the liberty of speaking with some learned divine (for the settling of his conscience). And lastly, that her majesty would be pleased to send to him four of her Privy Council to whom he had some things to communicate, relating to the public. Then came on the trial of the Marquis of Northampton, who pretended that he had not any hand in the rebellion, nor was engaged in any party, but having no public post, had spent all the time in his usual diversion of hunting and other sports. However, it appeared that he was engaged on Northumberland's side, and therefore he was likewise condemned. Afterwards, the Earl of Warwick, Northumberland's eldest son, when the plea of his youth would not be admitted in excuse of so great a crime, received his sentence of death with a wonderful constancy; and only prayed her majesty that out of his estate confiscated, his debts might be discharged. These were presently sent back to the Tower. The next day, Sir Andrew Dudley, Northumberland's brother, and Sir John Gates, who was supposed the first author of setting up Lady Jane with his brother Henry Gates, and Sir Thomas Palmer, were condemned. The 22d of August they were brought out to execution, having two days before received the sacrament in prison. Northumberland, by the persuasion of Heath, afterwards Archbishop of York, made a speech to the people in which he confessed his crime and repentance and advised all who were present to adhere to the ancient religion of their forefathers, and rejecting the new opinions as the source of all the evils that had befallen them for 30 years past to drive the preachers of them as trumpeters of sedition out of the Kingdom, if they would approve themselves innocent before God and the public. He declared that in his heart he had always been for the old religion, and appealed for the truth of this to his intimate friend the Bishop of Worcester, but he had temporized out of ambition for which he now was a sincere penitent; and lastly, that he willingly submitted to his death which he owned he had deserved. Having said this, he recommended himself to God and desiring the prayers of the spectators, prepared to receive the stroke; and immediately the executioner performed his office. Northumberland's exhortations variously affected the minds of the people who were amazed to hear him speak against that religion which he had professed for above 30 years; and on the account of which chiefly he had advised King Edward to exclude his sisters. Most have written, that being a cunning man and fond of life, he did this in hopes of a pardon; and that when he looked round him and saw he was deceived, he repented of it. He was charged upon no trivial conjectures with having poisoned the late King. But nothing of this was mentioned at his trial; because his judges undertook not the examination into King Edward's death, but only the business of the rebellion against Queen Mary. Gates too and Palmer underwent the same punishment.

[*Cobbett's Complete Collection of State Trials, Vol. 1.* 765-768]

John Dudley, Duke of Northumberland was executed before 10,000 people and had confessed his guild on 22 August 1553.

James Hales

James Hales was born to John Hales and Isabel near Canterbury, but the date is not known nor of his early life. James was a member of Gray's Inn (professional association for barristers and judges) and records mention his serving as an autumn reader in 1533, double Lent reader in 1537 and triple Lent reader in 1540. A reader was a person literally elected to read and would take his place in a reading of a particular topic or ask to give a lecture.

James was appointed to receive Lady Anne of Cleves when she arrived at Dover in 1539. He was appointed sergeant-at-law in Trinity in 1540 and four years later received the appointment as King's sergeant and also served as counsel to Archbishop Cranmer. Upon the coronation of Edward VI, he was created a knight of the Bath and in 1549 was a member of a commission for detecting and abolishing heresy and the following year appointed a judge of the common pleas.

James Hales was a member of the committee to try Bishop Gardiner in December 1550 and remained during the sentencing passed in February 1551. During the next preceding couple years, he served on several committees and commissions. In 1553, Hales was required to affix his official seal to King Edward VI's 'device' that removed Mary and Elizabeth from succession, but refused. Hales was one of the few that did not succumb to the Duke of Northumberland's intimidating tactics. On the accession of Mary, he maintained his strict adherence to the law by charging the judges at the assizes in Kent that the laws established during the reigns of Edward IV and Henry VIII against nonconformists should remain in effect and not relaxed in favor of Roman Catholics.

That action did not place him in a good light with the new Catholic Queen, but nevertheless she renewed his patent of justice of the common pleas. When he appeared in Westminster Hall to take his oath, Lord Chancellor Gardiner refused to administer it because of his conduct at the assizes in Kent and was placed in the King's Bench prison.

> Proceedings against Sir James Hales, Justice of the Court of Common Pleas, for his conduct at the Assizes in Kent:
>
> Mr. Fox introduces this short but interesting procedure thus:
>
> The first day of October 1553, Queen Mary was crowned at Westminster, and the 10th of the same month of October then following began the Parliament with a solemn Mass of the Holy Ghost after the popish manner celebrated with great pomp in the palace of Westminster. Mass being done, the Queen accompanied with the estates of the realm, was brought into the Parliament house there according to the manner to enter and begin the consultation at which consultation or Parliament were repealed all statutes made in the time of King Henry the 8th for *praemunire*, and statutes made in King Edward the 6th's time for administration of common prayer and the sacrament in the English tongue. And such as would stick to the laws made in King Edward's time till others should be established, some of them were marked and some presently apprehended. Among whom Sir James Hales, a Knight of Kent, and Justice of the Common Pleas, was one; who notwithstanding he had ventured his life in Queen Mary's cause in that he would not subscribe to the un-inheriting of her by the King's will, yet for that he did at a quarter sessions give charge upon the statutes made in the time of King Henry the 8th and Edward the 6th, for the supremacy and religion, he was imprisoned in the Marshalsea, Counter, and Fleet, and so cruelly handled and put in fear by talk that the warden of the fleet used to have in his hearing of such torments as were in preparing for heretics, (or for what other cause God knows; that he sought to rid himself out of this life by wounding himself with a knife; and afterward was contented to say as they willed him whereupon he was discharged, but after that he never rested till he had drowned himself in a river, half a mile from hit house in Kent.

The communication between the Lord Chancellor (Stephen Gardiner Bishop of Winchester) and Judge Hales, being there among other judges, to take his oath in Westminster Hall, Oct. 6, 1553.

Master Hales. You shall understand that like as the Queen's highness has heretofore conceived good opinion of you, especially for that you stood both faithfully and lawfully in her cause of just succession, refusing to set your hand to the book among others that were against her grace in that behalf, so now through your own late deserts against certain her highness's doings, you stand not well in her grace's favor and therefore before you take any oath, it shall be necessary for you to make your purgation,

Hales. I pray you my lord, what is the cause?

Chancellor. Information is given that you have indicted certain priests in Kent for saying Mass.

Hales. My lord, it is not so, I indicted none; but indeed certain indictments of like matter were brought before me at the last assizes there Holden and I gave order therein as the law required. For I have professed the law against which in cases of justice I will never, God willing, proceed, nor in any wise dissemble, but with the same show forth my conscience, and if it were to do again, I would do no less than I did.

Chancellor. Yea, Master Hales, your conscience is known well enough, I know you lack no conscience.

Hales. My lord, you may do well to search your own conscience; for mine is better known to myself than to you and to be plain, I did as well use justice in your said Mass case by my conscience, as by law, wherein I am fully bent to stand in trial to the uttermost that can be objected. And if I have therein done any injury or wrong, let me be judged by the law; for I will seek no better defense, considering chiefly that it is my profession.

Chancellor. Why Master Hales, although you had the rigor of the law on your side, yet you might have had regard to the Queen's highness present doings in that case. And further, although you seem to be more than precise in the law, yet I think you would be very loath to yield to the extremity of such advantage as might be gathered against your proceedings in the law as you have sometime taken upon you in place of justice, and if it were well tried, I believe you should not be well able to stand honestly thereto.

Hales. My lord, I am not so perfect, but I may err for lack of knowledge. But both in conscience and such knowledge of the law as God has given me, I will do nothing but I will maintain it and abide in it and if my goods and all that I have be not able to counterpoise the case, my body shall he ready to serve the turn; for they be all at the Queen's highness pleasure.

Chancellor. Ah sir, you be very quick and stout in your answers. But as it should seem that which you did was more of a will favoring the opinion of your religion against the service now used than for any occasion or zeal of justice, seeing the Queen's highness does set it forth as yet, wishing all her faithful subjects to embrace it accordingly and where you offer both body and goods in your trial, there is no such matter required at your hands, and yet you shall not have your own will neither.

Hales. My lord, I seek not willful will not to show myself as I am bound in love to God and obedience to the Queen's majesty in whose cause willingly for justice sake, all other respects set apart, I did of late, as your lordship knows, adventure as much as I had. And as for my religion, I trust it be such as pleased God, wherein I am ready to adventure as well my life as my substance, if I be called thereto. And so in lack of mine own power and will, the Lord's will be fulfilled.

Chancellor. Seeing you be at this point Master Hales, I will presently make an end with you. The Queen's highness shall be informed of your opinion and declaration. And as her grace shall thereupon determine, you shall have knowledge. Until such time as you may depart as you came, without your oath for as it appears, you are scarce worthy the place appointed.

Hales. I thank your lordship and as for my vocation being both a burden and a charge more than ever I desired to take upon me; when so ever it shall please the Queen's highness to ease me thereof, I shall most humbly with due contestations obey the same; and so he departed from the bar.

Not many days after this communication, or colloquy in Westminster-Hall which was Oct. 6, 1553, Master Hales at the commandment of the bishop was committed to the King's bench where he remained constant until Lent, then was he removed to the counter in Bread Street, and afterward from thence was carried to the Fleet. What afterwards befell him has been before related.

[*Cobbett's Complete Collection of State Trials, Vol. 1.* 715-716]

To expand slightly on his death: during his imprisonment he was visited by a few colleagues that also served on the bench and became so distraught over their comments that he attempted to commit suicide by opening his veins with a small knife. He recovered from that then released in April 1554, and drowned himself in a stream at Thanington, near Canterbury on 4 August 1554.

Lady Jane Grey

Jane Grey was born to Henry Grey and Lady Francis Brandon in circa 1537 at Bradgate in Leicestershire. Her father's status would have provided a foundation for a comprehensive education including studies in Greek, Latin and French. Her pursuits are best noted by an account of a principle tutor of hers upon arrival at her house to find her parents out hunting while Jane was in her chamber reading *Pheado* in Greek. When asked why she was not with her parents she replied "I wisse (think) all their sport in the park is but a shadow to that pleasure that I find in Plato. Alas, good folk, they never felt what true pleasure means."

Lady Jane's early life appears to be content and studious as shown by the high regard she earned from several prominent religious figures of the time, but, unbeknownst to her, that would change. King Edward VI had several bouts of illnesses but was unable to overcome one in particular and felt that he would not live long. The Duke of Northumberland took advantage of the situation and manipulating the terminally ill King to alter the order of succession by placing Lady Jane on the throne instead of Mary and or Elizabeth, then to wed his son to Jane, thus the Duke would be the father of the King of England.

The reluctant and obstinate Jane married Guildford Dudley in May, 1553 and Jane assumed that she would resume a life of quiet contemplation and study. Following the death of Edward VI, Mary was notified of his death and to show allegiance to Queen Jane-she refused. Jane was summoned to Syon house where the Duke of Northumberland informed her that she was now Queen of England. One can only guess at the emotions that a girl of about 15 would feel upon receiving such information, but she undertook what was placed before her.

Mary would not allow her rightful claim to remain unchallenged and nine days later, Mary took the throne from Jane and placed her and Guildford in the Tower for what should have been a short period. When Mary announced her choice for husband was Philip of Spain, Thomas Wyatt the Younger set out to remove her from the throne with the assistance from Henry Grey, Jane's father.

Wyatt's attempt failed, though he did come within a mile of where Mary was, and everyone involved was imprisoned. There are accounts that so many were imprisoned that churches where utilized to house the overflow of prisoners. Hundreds were executed for their participation in Wyatt's rebellion and because Jane's father had participated in the rebellion, her fate was clear. Though there is no known surviving trial manuscript, history has recorded the following account of Lady Jane Grey's trial:

> The compilers of the Biographia Britannica, who have taken great pains in collecting and arranging from the several historians of the time, the particulars relating to this most excellent person, conclude their account of her in these words:
>
> Lady Jane and her husband the Lord Guilford Dudley, remaining still in confinement, were on the 3rd of November 1553 carried from the lower to Guildhall, and with Archbishop Cranmer and others arraigned and convicted of high-treason before Judge Morgan, who pronounced on them sentence of death, the remembrance of which afterwards affected him so far, that he died raving. From this time the unfortunate Lady Jane and her no less unhappy husband, lived in the very shadow of death, and yet not without some gleams of comfort. For in the month of December, the Marquis of Northampton, who in the same cause had fallen into the like circumstances, was pardoned and discharged; and at the same time the strictness of their confinement mitigated by permission granted to take the air in the Queen's garden and other little indulgences that would however have been so many acts of cruelty, if the Queen had then intended what she afterwards thought fit to inflict. But this, by the consent of our best historians, is allowed to be altogether improbable; and that there are good reasons to

believe the Queen would have spared Lady Jane, since she had already pardoned her father who was much more guilty, and that she would have extended her mercy to Lord Guilford Dudley as well as to his cider brothers. However, in the first Parliament of her reign, an act was passed for establishing the validity of such private contracts as were dated during Jane's nine days administration, with a proviso, that all public nets, grants of lands, or the like, if any such there were, should be void. Another act likewise passed for continuing the attainders of Northumberland, Canterbury, and the rest, who had been convicted of high treason, which perhaps was thought necessary to confirm the opinion of the judges who had over-ruled their plea; that what they did was in obedience to the supreme authority then subsisting, but whatever hopes Lady Jane and her husband might entertain, whatever ease they might enjoy, were quickly taken away by an unhappy event, which it was impossible for them to foresee, and in which it is not so much as pretended that either of them had the least hand. There was a great spirit raised in the nation against the Queen's marriage with Philip of Spain; and upon this a general insurrection was concerted, which, if it had been executed with any degree of that prudence shown in the planning of it, or rather if the providence of God had not interposed, could scarce have failed of succeeding; Sir Thomas Wyatt of Kent, a man of a great estate and a greater influence, managed those who were afraid under color of this marriage, the Kingdom would be delivered up to a foreign prince and his partisans. Sir Peter Carew, in Cornwall, dealt with such as were desirous of seeing the Princess Elizabeth upon the throne, and in the arms of Courtenay, whom the Queen had lately restored to the title of Devonshire, and the Duke of Suffolk, to whom danger had in vain preached discretion, and who could not learn loyalty even from mercy, made use of that great interest which his large estates gave him though he held them by the Queen's favor, to mislead her subjects from their duty and to take up arms against her person. What the real view of this design was even time has not discovered; but by rashness, and mis-intelligence of those at the head of it, all miscarried. The Duke of Suffolk with his brothers Lord John and Lord Thomas Grey, were in arms and with a body of three hundred horse presented themselves before the city of Coventry, in which they had a strong party; but the Queen having sent down the Earl of Huntingdon, he secured that place, and Suffolk finding his design abortive, and his people dropping away, retired with as many as he could keep about him to a house of his in Leicestershire, where, having distributed what money he had to those who were the companions of his fortune, he advised them to shift for themselves, trusting to the promises of one Underwood his park-keeper who undertook to conceal and who is suspected to have betrayed him to the Earl of Huntingdon, by whom himself and his brother Lord John being apprehended, were carried to Coventry and after some stay there, sent to London under a guard where they did not arrive until the 10th of February and were then committed to the Tower, out of which the duke never came but to his trial and to his death. This weak and ill managed business gave the ministers an opportunity of persuading the Queen, that her safety could be no otherwise provided for, than by putting Lady Jane and her husband to death to which, a learned prelate assures us, the Queen was not wrought without much difficulty; and it is very remarkable that Sanders makes the very same observation, so that the truth of it can hardly be called in question. The news of tint, fatal resolution made no great impression upon this excellent lady; the bitterness of death was passed, she had expected it long and was so well prepared to meet her fate, that she was very little discomposed. But the Queen's charity hurt her more than her justice. The day first fixed for her death was Friday February the 9th, and she had in some measure taken leave of the world, by writing a letter to her unhappy father who she heard was more disturbed with the thoughts of his being the author of her death, than with the apprehension of his own. In this serene frame of mind, Dr. Feckenham, Abbot of Westminster, came to her from the Queen who was very desirous she should follow her father in-law's example and be reconciled to the Church of Rome. He was indeed a very fit instrument (if any had been fit) for this purpose; for he had an acute wit, a very plausible manner of speaking, and a great tenderness in his nature. Lady Jane received him with much civility, and behaved towards him with so much calmness and sweetness of temper that he could not help being overcome with her distress; so that either mistaking or pretending to mistake her meaning, he procured a respite of her execution until the 12th. Yet he did not gain anything upon her in regard to the design upon which he was sent; on the contrary, though she heard him patiently, yet she answered all his arguments with such strength, such clearness, and such a steadiness of mind as showed plainly that religion had been her principal care, and that the hopes of being happy in a future state from acting according to the dictates of her conscience in this, had fortified her not only against the fears of death, but against all doubts or apprehensions whatever. On the Sunday evening, which was the last she was to spend in this world, she wrote a letter in the Greek tongue, as some say on the blank leaves at the end of a Testament in the same language, which she bequeathed as a legacy to her sister the Lady Catherine; which piece of hers, if we had no other left, would be sufficient to render her memory immortal, and therefore the substance of it in English. The fatal morning being come, the Lord Guilford earnestly desired the officers that he might take his last farewell of her. Which though they willingly permitted, yet upon notice she advised the contrary, assuring him that such a meeting would rather add to his afflictions than increase that quiet wherewith they had possessed their souls for the stroke of death; that he demanded a lenitive which would put fire into the wound and that it was to be feared her presence would rather weaken than strengthen him; that he ought to take courage from his reason and derive constancy from his own heart; that if his soul were not firm and settled, she could not settle it by her eyes nor confirm it by her words; that he should do well to remit this interview to the other world; that their indeed friendships were happy and unions indissoluble, and that theirs would be eternal if their souls carried nothing with them of terrestrial, which might hinder them from rejoicing. All she could do was to give him a farewell out of a window as he passed toward the place of his dissolution, which he suffered on the scaffold on Tower-Hill with much Christian meekness. His dead body being laid in a car and his head wrapped up in a linen cloth, were carried to the chapel within the Tower in the way to which, they were to pass under the window of the Lady Jane; which sad spectacle she likewise beheld, but of her own accord and not either by accident, or as some without any color of truth have insinuated by design and with a view to increase the weight of her afflictions. About an hour after the death of her husband, she was led out by the lieutenant to the scaffold that was prepared upon the green over against the White Tower. It is said that the court had once taken a resolution to have her beheaded on the same scaffold with her husband; but considering how much they were both pitied and how generally Lady Jane was beloved, it was determined to prevent any commotions that this execution should be performed within the Tower. She was attended to and upon the scaffold by Feckenham, but she was observed not to give much heed to his discourses, keeping her eyes steadily fixed on a book of prayers which she had in her hand, after some short recollection she saluted those who were present with a countenance perfectly composed; then taking leave of Dr. Feckenham, she said, "God will abundantly requite you, good sir, for your humanity to me, though your discourses gave me more uneasiness than all the terrors of my approaching death." She next addressed herself to the spectators in a plain and short speech. Then kneeling down she said the Miserere in English, after which she stood up and gave her women, Mrs. Elizabeth Tilney and Mrs. Helen, her gloves and her handkerchief; and to the Lieutenant of the Tower, whom Heylin calls Sir John Gage, but Holinshed, Bridges, her prayer-book. When she untied her gown, the executioner offered to assist her, but she desired him to let her alone; and turning to her women, they undressed and gave her a handkerchief to bind about her eyes. The executioner kneeling desired her pardon; to which she answered "most willingly." He desiring her to stand upon the straw, which bringing her within sight of the block, she said I pray dispatch me quickly; adding presently after, will you take it off before I lay me down? the executioner said No madam: upon this, the handkerchief being bound close over her eyes, she began to feel for the block, to which she was guided by one of the spectators; when she felt it, she stretched herself forward and said, lord into thy hands I commend my spirit, and immediately, at one stroke her head was divided from her body.

Her fate was universally deplored, even by those who were best affected to Queen Mary; and as she is allowed to have been a princess of great piety, it must certainly have given her much disquiet to begin her reign with such an unusual effusion of blood; and in the present case of her near relation, one formerly honored with her friendship and favor, who had indeed usurped, but without desiring or enjoying the royal diadem which she assumed by the constraint of an ambitious father and an imperious mother; and which, at the first motion, she cheerfully and willingly resigned. This made her exceedingly lamented at home and abroad, the fame of her learning and virtue having reached over Europe, so as to excite many commendations, and some express panegyrics in different nations and in different languages.

But whereas, some of our own writers seem to doubt whether she was with child or not at the time of her decease, and foreigners have improved this into a direct assertion, that she was five months gone, it seems to be improbable since there were at that time so many busy and inquisitive people that if the fact had been true it must have been known and would have been perpetually repeated in those pieces that were every day sent abroad in order to exasperate the tuition against the Queen and her ministers. On the twenty-first of the same month, the father of Queen Jane, Henry Grey Duke of Suffolk, lost his head upon Tower-Hill: neither was the jealousy excited by King Edward's appointment and their nearness in blood to the royal line, so fully extinguished by the blood of so many victims, but that it revived in the succeeding reign and proved a new source of disquiet to the sad remains of this unhappy family. We have treated this article the more largely, because hitherto, excepting Heylin, none of our historians have represented the public and private life of this admirable person with any tolerable degree of distinctness; but have been content to hurry over her short possession of the crown as if it had been an ordinary insurrection and to speak of her death in general terms of compassion with an exaggeration of some and a suppression of other circumstances, so as to put it out of the power of the reader to form a just notion of the whole transaction.

[*Cobbett's Collection of State Trials*, V-1. 732-735]

Henry Grey

The date of Henry Grey's birth was a matter of controversy, but evidence I reviewed indicates it to be circa 1500. His father Thomas was able to provide a comprehensive education including studies in Latin and French taught by tutors King Henry VIII also used for his children. Inconstancies exist about Henry's first marriage to Catherine in about 1530. In early March 1533, Henry married Frances Brandon. It is not clear about the fate of Catherine. Frances was eldest daughter of Charles Brandon and Mary Tudor, daughter of King Henry VII. On 19 May 1533, Henry carried the scepter during the procession of Queen Anne from the Tower of London to Westminster Abbey.

Henry and Frances were blessed with three girls, Jane, Catherine and Mary. Following the death of Henry VIII and the accession of Edward, Henry Grey became a member of the Knights of the Garter. Several nobles greeted the new King at the Tower of London including Henry Grey who held a prominent position during the procession to Westminster for the coronation.

On 2 February 1550, Henry Grey received the appointment of chief justice and justice in Eyre of the Royal forests south of Trent, a position his father held in 1523. In July 1550, Henry Grey and the Marquis of Northampton escorted French ambassadors to court and participated in various activities including sporting matches. In February 1551, Henry was appointed warden of the marches against Scotland and served in that capacity until early June when a treaty between Scotland and England was concluded. As a result of his service, Henry was elevated to Duke of Suffolk in October 1551.

The Duke of Suffolk spent the next couple years in close association with the Duke of Northumberland during the illness of Edward VI while Northumberland executed his plans. Following the death of Edward, the two became the most powerful individuals in the Kingdom.

Jane was proclaimed Queen, but Mary would not concede. Suffolk and Northumberland attempted to send forces to apprehend Mary, but Queen Jane would not allow her father to leave her alone with Northumberland and sent Northumberland instead. He received information that Mary was proclaimed Queen on 20 July, and orders were sent to arrest him. Suffolk was with his daughter at the time and is perhaps the reason his life was spared as his signature appears on the letter to Northumberland. Careful of preventing further instances, Suffolk and his daughter were placed in the Tower and he was eventually released about the end of July 1553. On 22 August, 1553, the Duke of Northumberland was executed on Tower Hill. Suffolk continued to remain quiet for most of the remaining year, but at some point late 1553, he was approached by either Thomas Wyatt or an associate with a plan to restore his daughter to the throne. Most certainly he was very apprehensive because he knew he was closely watched and valued his freedom. In mid-December, the council learned that the brother of the Duke of Suffolk was involved in the unrest within the realm and the possibility of a rebellion.

During the week of January 1554, Peter Carew approached Suffolk hoping for his support. Late January, Suffolk and his brothers attempted to gain support in the north counties and would join Wyatt's forces marching to London, but with each town they entered, they found no support. They returned to his home where they split up; Suffolk was discovered hiding in a hollowed-out tree. His brother was discovered in a bale of hay while his other brother was later captured when he returned to claim his hat that he forgot.

The Duke of Suffolk was placed in the Tower until his trial on 17 February, 1554 at Westminster.

> Arraignment and execution of Henry Grey Duke of Suffolk. 1: I Mary, A.D. 1553. As to the Duke of Suffolk, there is in the Cottonian collection a brief MS. account of him in the following words:
>
> Henry Fitzallan Lord Maltravers and Lord Steward of her majesty's household and Lord High Steward of England at the arraignment of Henry Lord Grey Duke of Suffolk, father of the Lady Jane, married to Guilford Dudley:
>
> This Henry Duke of Suffolk being condemned by his peers for combining in rebellion with Wyatt against the Queen and her proceedings with Spain had sentence of death pronounced against him, which he suffered the 23rd of February upon the Tower-Hill, where he most Christianly made profession of his faith with great repentance of his fact. This duke's facility too by practices had occasioned the troubles wherewith this realm had for some

years been distracted, and his rash ingratitude, the Queen having once pardoned him beyond expectation, had diverted the current of the Queen's clemency towards his daughter the Lady Jane, whose life, it was generally conceived, she would have pardoned but her father's mis-counseled rashness hastened her death.

Upon Saturday, being the 17th of February, the Duke of Suffolk was arraigned at Westminster and the same day condemned to die by his peers, the Earl of Arundel was chief judge for this day. Upon the Sunday following, which was the 18th day of the said month, sessions was kept in London which has not before been kept upon the Sunday. Upon the Monday, the 19th of February Lord Cobham's three sons, and four other men were arraigned at Westminster of which sons the youngest was condemned, whose name was Thomas, and the other two came not at the bar, and the other four were condemned. Upon the Tuesday, being the 20th of February, the Lord John Gray was arraigned at Westminster and there condemned the same day, and other three men whereof one was named Nailer. Upon Wednesday, the 21st of Feb. the Lord Thomas Grey, and Sir James Croft were brought through London to the Tower with a number of horsemen. Upon the Thursday, being the 22nd of February, Sir Nicholas Throckmorton was committed to the Tower.

Upon the Friday, being the 23d of February 1554, the Duke of Suffolk was beheaded at the Tower Hill, the order of whose death here follows:

The godly end and death of the Duke of Suffolk beheaded at Tower-Hill, February 23rd 1554.

On Friday the 23rd of February 1554, about nine of the clock in the forenoon, the Lord Henry Grey, Duke of Suffolk, was brought forth of the Tower of London to the scaffold on the Tower-Hill with a great company, &c. and in his coming thither, there accompanied him Doctor Weston as his ghostly father, notwithstanding as it should seem against the will of the said duke. For when the duke went up to the scaffold, the said Weston being on the left hand, pleased to go up with him. The duke with his hand, put him down again off the stairs and Weston, taking hold of the duke, forced him down likewise. And as they ascended the second time, the duke again put him down. Then Weston said that it was the Queen's pleasure he should so do. Wherewith the duke casting his hands abroad, ascended up the scaffold and paused a pretty while after. And then he said "Masters, I have offended the Queen, and her laws, and thereby am justly condemned to die, and am willing to die, desiring all men to be obedient and I pray God that this my death may be an example to all men, beseeching you all to bear me witness that I die in the faith of Christ, trusting to be saved by his blood only, and by no other trumpery, the which died for me and for all them that truly repent and steadfastly trust in him. And I do repent, desiring you all to pray to God for me; and that when you see my breath depart from me, you will pray to God that he may receive my soul." And then he desired all men to forgive him saying that the Queen had forgiven him.

Then Mr. Weston declared with aloud voice that the Queen's majesty had forgiven him. With that divers of the standers by said with meekly good and audible voice. Such forgiveness God send thee, meaning Dr. Weston. Then the duke kneeled down upon his knees and said the psalm Miserere met Deus to the end, holding up his hands and looking up to heaven. And when he had ended the Psalm, he said, *In manus tuas Domiue commendo spiritual tneitm, &c.* Then he arose and stood up, and delivered his cap and his scarf to the executioner.

Then the said executioner kneeled down and asked the duke forgiveness. And the duke said God forgive thee, and I do and when thou doest thine office, I pray thee do it well and bring me out of this world quickly, and God have mercy to thee. Then stood there a man and said, my lord how shall I do for the money that you do owe me? And the duke said alas good fellow, I pray thee trouble me not now, but go thy way to my officers. Then he knit a kerchief about his face and kneeled down and said, "Our Father which art in heaven, &c." to the end. And then he said, Christ have mercy upon me, and laid down his head on the block and the executioner took the axe and at the first chop stroke off his head, and held it up to the people, &c.

The same day a number of prisoners had their pardon and came through the city with their halters about their necks. There were in number about 200.

[*Cobbett's Complete Collection of State Trials. V1.* 762-764]

Thomas Wyatt the Younger

No records are known of his exact date of his birth, but a record survives describing him as 'twenty-one years and upwards' in the '*inquisito post mortem*' of his father in 1543. Thomas was born to Thomas Wyatt the Elder who co-introduced the sonnet into English literature, and Elizabeth daughter of Thomas Brooke, Lord Cobham.

Because of his father's position in court, Thomas would have received a good education and most certainly included in Latin and French and undoubtedly would have been exposed to the literary and musical world. It has been suggested that because Thomas accompanied his father on an ambassadorial assignment as a boy when his father was captured outside Rome and threatened by the Inquisition in January 1527, he developed a strong contempt toward the Spanish that he carried into his adult years.

During 1536, Thomas Wyatt the Elder informed the King that he must turn his duties as the current resident ambassador to the Emperor Charles V of Spain to his son due to failing health. In March 1537, he wrote his son giving advice as he had received information about his marriage to Jane, daughter of Sir William Hawte. Late 1542, shortly after his father died, Thomas Wyatt the Younger was pardoned for robbery. The following year, he was arrested for eating meat during Lent and for breaking out glass windows in homes of several prominent citizens and churches injuring one person by shooting stones with a cross bow. Thomas was sent to the Tower and remained there until 3 May, released by the King's desire.

During his imprisonment he had time to reflect on his errors and following his release, he joined the King's army for a period of 120 days to defend the Emperor's Low Countries against the French King. He had distinguished himself as a worthy military commander in that campaign and subsequent campaigns during the reign of Henry VIII.

During the reign of Edward VI, Thomas held several positions including sheriff in the county of Kent and served under the Protector Somerset during the Battle of Pinkey where ten thousand Scots lost their lives. Thomas served with the Earl of Arundel to capture the traitorous Duke of Northumberland on 24 July, 1553 after the accession of Mary to the throne.

Thomas was quiet until Mary announced her choice for a husband in late 1553. Several confederates including Peter Carew and Thomas Wyatt the Younger met to discuss a plan to remove Mary from the throne that was prematurely launched by Carew in early January 1554. Carew relied on support from Sir Nicholas Throckmorton and Edward Courtenay who did not arrive. Late January 1554, Wyatt received information that Carew launched the campaign and Mary quickly reacted by dispatching a herald and trumpeter to confront Wyatt allowing him the opportunity to disclose his intent. Furthermore, a summons was dispatched to Elizabeth ordering her to appear before the Queen because she was suspected as a motivating influence behind the rebellion.

Wyatt's army was augmented by a legion of about five-hundred deserters of the Queen's army. With the increase in forces, Wyatt set out for London, but found all the bridges across the Thames removed to prevent their crossing. Eventually, Wyatt and his army crossed the Thames River and proceeded toward London through the rainy, cold and miserable weather. When he finally arrived, he encountered the Queen's army and artillery and a battle ensued causing Thomas's forces to fragment. Thomas arrived at the Temple Bar gate with less than a hundred men to find no support and eventually surrendered to a knight passing by on horse back then placed in the Tower as a prisoner instead of a victor.

The following account of the trial of Thomas Wyatt the Younger is taken from the account recorded in Raphael Holinshed's 1586 chronicles, though Mr. Holinshed did not include a date. Several early historians have indicated that Holinshed's account is the most accurate; a comparison with the complete record found in *Cobbett's Complete Collection of State Trials*, London 1809, found only minor differences.

Wyatt was brought from the Tower to Westminster where he stood trial on the charge of treason before the Earl of Sussex, Sir Edward Hastings and Sir Thomas Cornwallis acting as judges with a group of Wyatt's peers present. Wyatt was charged with leading a large force of armed men with ensigns displayed at Brainford where they openly declared war against the forces of the Queen with the intent to remove her from the throne.

The council asked Wyatt whether he was guilty or not. Wyatt responded by asking if he might ask a question before he answered the question and the council allowed him to do so. Wyatt asked if he confessed and pleaded guilty, would the court not be prejudicial to him and by his confession not be permitted to speak further on the matter.

The court answered: Master Wyatt, you shall have both leave and leisure to say what you can.

Wyatt: Then my lords, I must confess myself guilty, and in the end the truth of my case must enforce me. I must acknowledge this to be a just plague for my sins, which most grievously I therefore have committed against God who suffered me thus brutishly and beastly to fall into this horrible offense of the law. Wherefore all you lords and gentlemen, with other here present, note well my words, lo here and see in me the same end which all other commonly had, which have attempted the like enterprise from the beginning.

For peruse the chronicles through and you shall see that never rebellion attempted by subjects against their prince and country, from the beginning did ever prosper, or had ever better success except the case of King Henry the Fourth: who although he became a prince, yet in his act was but a rebel, for so must I call him and though he prevailed for a time, yet was it not long but that his heirs were deprived and those that had right again restored to the Kingdom and crown, and the usurpation so sharply revenged afterward in his blood, as it well appeared that the long delay of God's vengeance was supplied with more grievous plagues in the third and forth generation.

For the love of God all you gentlemen that be here present, remember and be taught as well by examples past, as also by this my present infelicity and most wretched case. Oh most miserable, mischievous, brutish and beastly susieus imaginations of mine! I was persuaded that by the marriage of the prince of Spain, the second person of this realm, and next heir to the crown, should have been in danger; and that I being a free borne man, should with my country have been brought into the bondage and servitude of aliens and strangers. Which brutish beastly opinion when seemed to my reason, and wrought in me such effects, that it led me headlong into the practice of this detestable crime of treason.

But now being better persuaded, and understanding the great commodity and honor which the realm should receive by this marriage; I should stand firm and fast in this opinion, that if it should please the Queen to be merciful to me, there is no subject in this land that should more truly and faithfully serve her highness than I shall; nor no sooner die at her graces feet in defense of her quarrel.

I served her highness against the Duke of Northumberland as my Lord of Arundel can witness. My grandfather served most truly her graces grandfather, and for his sake was set upon the rack in the Tower. My father also served King Henry the Eight to his good contention, and I also served him and King Edward his son. And in witness of my blood spent in his service, I carry a name. I allege not all this to set forth my service by way of merit, which I confess by duty, but to declare to the whole world that by abusing my wits in pursuing my misadvised opinion, I have not only overthrown my house and defaced all the well doing of me and my ancestors (if ever there were any) but also have been the cause of my own death and destruction. Neither do I allege this to justify myself in any point, neither for an excuse of mine offense but most humbly submit myself to the Queen's majesty's mercy and pity, desiring you my Lord of Sussex, and you Master Hastings, with all the rest of this honorable bench, to be means to the Queen's highness for her mercy, which is the greatest treasure that may be given to any prince from God, such a virtue as God has appropriate to himself, which if her highness vouchsafe to extend to me, she shall bestow it on him who shall be most glad to serve truly, and not refuse to die in her quarrel. For I protest before the judge of all judges, I never meant hurt against her highness person.

The Queen's Attorney said, Master Wyatt you have great cause to be sorry and repent for you fault, whereby you have not only undone yourself and your house, but also a number of other gentlemen, who being true men might have served their prince and country yet if you had gone no further, it might have been borne withal the better.

But being not so contented to stay yourself, you have so procured the Duke of Suffolk (a man soon trained to your purpose) and his two brethren also by means whereof without the Queen's greater mercy, you have overthrown that noble house. And yet not so stayed, your attempt has reached as far as in you lay to the second person of the realm, in whom next to the Queen's highness rests all our hope and comfort, whereby her honor is brought in question and what danger will follow, and to what end it will come God knows of all this you are the author.

Wyatt replied, as I will not in anything justify myself, so I beseech you, I being in this wretched estate, not to overcharge me, nor to make me seem to be that I am not. I am loath to touch any person by name; but that I have written I have written.

The judge said, Master Wyatt, master attorney has well moved you to repent your offenses, and we for our parts with you the same.

Sir Edward Hastings then addressed Wyatt, Master Wyatt, do you remember when I and Master Cornwallis were sent to you from the Queen's highness to demand the cause of your enterprise, and what you required? Were not these your demands, that the Queen's grace should go to the Tower, and there remain and you to have the rule of the Tower and her person with the treasure in keeping, and such of her council as you would require to be delivered into your hands, saying that you would be trusted and not trust?

Wyatt then confessed that all that Hastings had stated was true and then he addressed the Queen's solicitor, Your presumption was over great, and you attempt in this case has purchased you perpetual infamy, and shall be called Wyatt's rebellions as Wat Tyler's was called Wat Tyler's rebellion.

Then the Attorney addressed Wyatt, Master Wyatt, were you not privy to a devise whereby the Queen should have been murdered in a place where she should walk? I do not burden you to confess this, for thus much I must say on your behalf, that you disliked that devise?

Wyatt responded that devise was the devise of William Thomas, whom ever after I abhorred for that cause.

A member of the court then held a letter up for the members of the court to see. It was the letter that Wyatt, while in Southwark, had written to the Duke of Suffolk requesting that he should meet him at Kingston Bridge and from there accompany him to London. At first, Wyatt did not seem to remember any such letter, but when he was shown the letter; he confessed that he did write it.

A member of the court then asked several questions of Wyatt one being why he refused that Queen's pardon when it was offered to him.

Wyatt responded my lords, I confess my fault and offense to be most vile and heinous, for the which first I ask God's mercy, without the which I cannot challenge anything such is my offense already committed. And therefore I beseech you to trouble me with no more questions, for I have delivered all things to her grace in writing. And finally here I must confess that of all the voyages wherein I have served, this was the most desperate and painful forney that ever I made. And where you asked why I received not the Queen's pardon when it was offered to me; Oh unhappy man! What shall I say? When I was entered into this devilish and desperate adventure, there was no way but wade through with that I had taken in hand; for I had thought that other had been as far forward as myself, which I found far otherwise. So that being bent to keep promise with all my confederates, none kept promise with me; for I like a mole went through thick and thin with this determination, that if I should come to any treaty, I should seem to betray all my friends.

But whereto should I spend any more words? I yield myself wholly to the Queen's mercy, knowing will that it is only in her power to make me (as I have deserved) an open example to the world with Wat Tyler; or else to make me participant of that pity which she has extended in as great crimes as mine; most humbly beseeching you all to be means for me to her highness for mercy, which is my last and only refuge. The will of God be done on me."

[Holinshed. *The First and Second Volumes of Chronicles.* 1103, 1104]

Thomas Wyatt the Younger was executed on Tower Hill 11 April, 1554.

Sir Nicholas Throckmorton

The trial of Nicholas Throckmorton is unique for a couple reasons; it is perhaps the most comprehensive trial transcript from the Tudor era and the skill in which Nicholas displayed in his own defense resulted in a full acquittal. Furthermore, the jury was severly punished for their verdict.

The date of birth for Nicholas Throckmorton is 1513 at Coughton, Warwickshire. Nicholas was the forth son of George Throckmorton and Anne Katherine Vaux. At the time of his birth, both his father and grandfather were serving as captains on supply ships for the royal navy. In early 1530, Nicholas entered the service of Henry Fitzroy, the Duke of Richmond (King Henry VIII's bastard son) and accompanied him to France. Nicholas served as a captain of the King's army against Scotland in October 1543 and he was involved in the battle of Pinkey in September 1547 against the Scots, this is when he met Thomas Wyatt the Younger. As a result of his service, Edward VI knighted Nicholas in 1551. He then served as under-treasurer of the royal mint until January 1552.

Sir Nicholas Throckmorton learned of the death of King Edward and of Lady Jane's ascension before many others through his brother who was in the service of the Duke of Northumberland. Nicholas informed Mary and she immediately dispatched a letter stating her rightful claim to the throne. Soon after Mary's announcement of her proposed marriage with Philip of Spain, rumors surfaced about Nicholas's frequent visits to the Princess Elizabeth. Several early historians indicate that Nicholas was one of the primary conspirators in Thomas Wyatt's rebellion. Wyatt's rebellion failed and no records mention Nicholas until his name appears as a prisoner in the Tower with others awaiting arraignment and execution.

On 17 April, 1554, Sir Nicholas Throckmorton appeared before the bar at Guildhall, London on the charge of high treason. The oldest known trial copy was first printed in *The First and Second volumes of Chronicles* collected by Raphael Holinshed in 1586. That transcript was compared with the version in *Cobbett's Complete Collection of State Trials, London 1809* and with that in *The Lives and Criminal Trials of Celebrated Men, Philadelphia, 1839* and many differences were found with reference to the Holinshed version. A solitary record mentioned that the trial began at 7:00 A.M. and lasted to almost 5:00 P.M. It is Holinshed's copy that follows.

> The order of the arraignment of Nicholas Throckmorton Knight, in the Guildhall of London the seventeenth day of April (Tuesday) 1554, expressed in a dialog for the better understanding of every mans part.
>
> The names of the commissioners. Sir Thomas White, Knight, Lord Mayor of London, the Earl of Shrewsbury, the Earl of Derby, Sir Thomas Bromley, Knight, Lord Chief Justice of England, Sir Nicholas Hare, Knight, Master of the Rolls, Sir Francis Englefield, Knight, Master of the Court of Wards and Liberties, Sir Richard Southwell, Knight, one of the Privy Council, Sir Edward Waldegrave, Knight, one of the Privy Council, Sir Roger Cholmley, Knight, Sir William Portman, Knight, one of the Justices of the King's Bench, Sir Edward Sanders, Knight, one of the Justices of the Common Pleas; Master Stanford and Master Dyer Sergeants, Master Edward Griffin,

Attorney General, Master Sendall and Peter Tichbourne, Clerks of the Crown.

First after proclamation made and the commission read, the Lieutenant of the Tower, Master Thomas Bridges, brought the prisoner to the bar; then silence was commanded and Sendall said to the prisoner as follows:

Sendall. Nicholas Throckmorton Knight hold up thy hand, thou art before this time indicted of high treason, and that thou then and there didst falsely and traitorously and conspire and imagine the death of the Queens majesty, and falsely and traitorously did levy war against the Queen with her realm and also thou was adherent to the Queen's enemies within her realm, giving to them aid and comfort, and also falsely and traitorously did conspire and intend to depose and deprive the Queen of her royal estate and so finally dethrone her, and also thou did falsely and traitorously devise and conclude to take violently the Tower of London, of all which treasons and every of them in manner, form art thou guilty or not guilty?

Throckmorton. May it please you my lords and masters, which be authorized by the Queens commission to be judges this day to give me leave to speak a few words, which do both concern you and me, before I answer to the indictment, and not altogether impertinent to the matter, and then plead to the indictment.

Bromley. No, the order is not so, you must first plead whether you be guilty or no.

Throckmorton. If that be your order and law, judge accordingly to it.

Hare. You must first answer to the matter where with you are charged, and then you may talk at your pleasure.

Throckmorton. But things spoken out of place, were as good not spoken.

Bromley. These be but delays to spend time, therefore answer as the law will you.

Throckmorton. My lords I pray you make not too much hast with me, neither think not long for your dinner, for my case requires leisure, and you have well dined when you have done justice truly. Christ said, blessed are they that hunger and thirst for righteousness.

Bromley. I can forbear my dinner as well as you, and care as little as you peradventure.

Shrewsbury. Come you hither to check us Throckmorton; we will not be so used, no no, I for mine own part have forborne my breakfast, dinner, and supper to serve the Queen.

Throckmorton. Yea my good lord I know it right well, I meant not to touch your lordship, for your service and pains is evidently known to all men.

Southwell. Master Throckmorton, this talk need not, we know what we have to do, and you would teach us our duties, you hurt your matter: go to, go to.

Throckmorton. Master Southwell, you mistake me, I meant not to teach you, nor none of you, but to remember you of that I trust you all be well instructed in; and so I satisfy myself, with I shall not speak, thinking you all know what you have to do, or ought to know so I will answer to the indictment, and do plead not guilty to the whole, and to every part thereof.

Sendall. How wilt thou be tried?

Throckmorton. Shall I be tried as I would, or as I should?

Bromley. You shall be tried as the law will, and therefore you must say by God and by the country.

Throckmorton. Is that your law for me? It is not as I would, but with you will have it so. I am pleased with it and do desire to be tried by faithful just men, which more fear God that the world.

Then the entire was called. The names of the jurors. Lucar, Low, Young, Whetston, Martin, Painter, Bestwick, Banks, Barscarfeld, Calthrop, Knightley, Cater.

What time the attorney went forthwith to Master Cholmley, and showed him the sheriff's return, who being acquainted with the citizens, knowing the corruptions and dexterities of them in such cases, noted certain to be challenged for the Queen (a rare case) and the same men being known to be sufficient and indifferent, that no exceptions were to be taken to them, but only for their upright honesties notwithstanding the attorney prompting Sergeant Dyer, the said sergeant challenged one Bacon, and an other citizen peremptorily for the Queen. Then the prisoner demanded the cause of the challenge; the sergeant answered; we need not to show you the cause of the challenge for the Queen. Then the inquest was furnished with other honest men, that is to say, Whetston and Lucar, so the prisoner used these words:

Throckmorton. I trust you have not provided for me this day, as in times past I knew an other gentleman occupying this woeful place was provided for. It chanced one of the justices upon jealousy of the prisoners acquittal, for the goodness of his cause, said to an other of his companions a justice, when the jury did appear. I like not this jury for our purpose, they seem to be too pitiful and to charitable to condemn the prisoner. No no, said the other judge, I warrant you, they be picked fellows for the nonce, he shall drink of the same cup his fellows have done. I was then a looker on of the pageant as others be now here, but now woe is me, I am a player in that woeful tragedy. Well, for these and such other like the black ox has of late trodden on some of their feet but my trust is, I shall not be so used. Whilst this talk was, Cholmley consulted with the attorney about the jury, which the prisoner espied and then said as here ensues; Ah, ah, Master Cholmley, will this foul packing never be lest?

Cholmley. Why, what do I, I pray you Mr. Throckmorton? I did nothing, I am sure you do pick quarrels to me.

Throckmorton. Well, Master Cholmley if you do well, it is better for you, God help you.

The jury then was sworn and proclamation made that whosoever would give evidence against Sir Nicholas Throckmorton Knight, should come in and be heard for the prisoner stood upon his deliverance, whereupon Sergeant Stanford presented himself to speak.

Throckmorton. And it may please you master sergeant and the others my masters of the Queen's learned counsel, like as I was minded to have said a few words to the commissioners, if I might have had leave for their better remembrance of their duties in this place of justice, and concerning direct indifference to be used towards me this day, so by your patience I do think good to say some what to you, and to the rest of the Queen's learned counsel appointed to give evidence against me. And albeit you and the rest by order be appointed to give evidence against me and entertained to set forth the depositions and matter against me; yet I pray you remember I am not alienate from you, but that I am your Christian brother; neither you so charged, but you ought to consider equity; nor yet so privileged, but that you have a duty of God appointed you how you shall do your office; which if you exceed, will be grievously required at your hands. It is lawful for you to use your gifts which I know God has largely given you as your learning art and eloquence, so as thereby you do not seduce the minds of the simple and unlearned jury, to credit matters otherwise than they be.

Master Sergeant. I know how by persuasions, enforcements, presumptions, applying, implying, inferring, conjecturing, deducing of arguments, wresting and exceeding the law. The circumstances, the depositions and confessions that unlearned men may be enchanted to think and judge those that be things indifferent, of at the worst but oversights to be great treasons; such power orators have and such ignorance the unlearned have. Almighty God by the mouth of his prophet does conclude such advocates be cursed, speaking these words: Cursed be he that does his office craftily, corruptly, and maliciously. And consider also, that my blood shall be required at your hands and punished in you and yours, to the third and fourth generation. Notwithstanding, you and the justices excuse always such erroneous doings when they be after called in question by the verdict of the twelve men, but I assure you the purgation serves you as it did Pilate, and you wash your hands of the bloodshed, as Pilate did of Christ's, and now to your matter.

Stanford. And it please you my lords, I doubt not to prove evidently and manifestly that Throckmorton is worthy and rightly indicted and arraigned of these treasons and that he was a principal deviser, procurer, and contriver of the late rebellion; and that Wyatt was but his minister. Now say you Throckmorton, did not you send Winter to Wyatt into Kent, and did devise that the Tower of London should be taken with other instructions concerning Wyatt's rebellion.

Throckmorton. May it please you that I shall answer particularly to the matters objected against me in as much as my memory is not good, and the same much decayed since my grievous disquietness. I confess I did say to Winter that Wyatt was desirous to speak with him, as I understand.

Stanford. Yea sir and you devised together of the taking of the Tower of London, and of the other great treasons.

Throckmorton. No, I did not so, prove it.

Stanford. Yes sir, you met with Winter sundry times as shall appear, and sundry places.

Throckmorton. That granted prove no such matter as is supposed in the indictment.

Stanford read Winters confession which was of this effect that Throckmorton met with Winter one day in the Tower Street and told him that Sir Thomas Wyatt was desirous to speak with him and Winter demanded where Wyatt was, Throckmorton answered at his house in Kent, not far from Gillingham, as I heard say where the ships lie, then they parted at that time, and shortly after, Throckmorton met with Winter to whom Winter said; Master Wyatt does much as daily he hears thereof, does see daily divers of them arrive here, scattered like soldiers; and therefore he thinks good the Tower of London should be taken by a flight, before the prince came, least that piece be delivered to the Spaniards. How say you Throckmorton to it? Throckmorton answered; I dislike it for diverse respects. Even so do I, said Winter. At another time Throckmorton met me the said Winter in Paul's when he had sent one to my house to seek me before and he said to me you are admiral of the fleet that now goes into Spain.

I answered Yea. Throckmorton said when will your ships be ready? I said within ten days. Throckmorton said, I understand you are appointed to conduct and carried the Lord Privy Seal into Spain and considering the danger of the Frenchmen, which you say arm them to the sea apace, me think it well done, you put my said lord and his train on land in the west country to avoid all dangers. Throckmorton said also that Wyatt changed his purpose for taking the Tower of London. I said I was glad of it, as for the Frenchmen, I care not much for them. I will so handle the matter, that the Queens ships shall be (I warrant you) in safeguard. Another time I met with Master Throckmorton when I came from the emperors ambassadors to whom I declared that the emperor had sent me a fair chain and showed it to Throckmorton, who said; for this chain you have sold your country. I said it is neither French King nor emperor that can make me sell my country, but I will be a true Englishman. Then they parted. This is the sum of the talk between Throckmorton and Winter.

Stanford. Now my masters of the jury, you have heard my saying confirmed with Winter's confession. Now say you Throckmorton, can you deny this. If you will, you shall have Winter say it to your face.

Throckmorton. My lords, shall it please you that I shall answer.

Bromley. Yea, say your mind.

Throckmorton. I may truly deny some part of this confession, but because there is nothing material greatly, I suppose the whole be true and what is herein deposed, sufficient to bring me within the compass of the indictment.

Stanford. It appears that you were of counsel with Wyatt in as much as you sent Winter down to him, who uttered to him diverse traitorous devises.

Throckmorton. This is but conjectural, yet with you will construe it so maliciously, I will recount how I sent Winter to Wyatt and then I pray you of the jury judge better than master sergeant do. I met by chance a servant of Master Wyatt who demanded of me from Winter, and showed me that his master should gladly speak with him and so without any further declaration, desired me if I met Winter to tell him Master Wyatt's mind, and where he was. Thus much for the sending down of Winter.

Attorney. Yea sir, but now say you to the taking of the Tower of London, which is treason.

Throckmorton. I answer, though Wyatt thought meet to attempt so dangerous an enterprise, and that Winter informed me of it, you cannot pretend Wyatt's devise to be mine and to bring me within the compass of treason. For what manner of reasoning or proof is this? Wyatt would have taken the Tower, ergo, Throckmorton is a traitor? Winter does make my purgation in his own confession, even now read as it was by Master Sergeant, though I say nothing for Winter does avow there that I did much dislike it. And because you shall the better understand that I did always not allow these Master Wyatt's devises, I had there words to Winter when he informed me of it; I think Master Wyatt would no Englishman hurt and this enterprise cannot be done without the hurt and slaughter of both parties. For I know him that has the charge of the peace, and his brother, both men of good service, the one had in charge a peace of great importance, Bulloingne I mean, which was stoutly assailed and notwithstanding he made a good account of it for him time the like I am sure he will do by this his charge. Moreover, to account the taking of the Tower is very dangerous by the law. These were my words to Winter. And besides, it is very unlike that I of all men would confederate in such a matter against the Lieutenant of the Tower whose daughter my brother has married and his house and mine allied together by marriage sundry times within these few years.

Hare. But how say you to this that Wyatt and you had conference together sundry times at Warner's house and in other places?

Throckmorton. This is a very general charge to have conference, but why was it not as lawful for me to confer with Wyatt as with you, or any other man? I then knew no more by Wyatt than by any other. And to prove to talk with Wyatt was lawful and indifferent, the last die that I did talk with Wyatt, I saw my Lord of Arundel, with other noble men and gentlemen, talk with him familiarly in the chamber of presence.

Hare. But they did not conspire nor talk of any stir against the Spaniards as you did pretend and meant it against the Queen, for you, Crofts, Rogers, and Warner did oftentimes devise in Warner's house about your traitorous purposes, or else what did you so often there?

Throckmorton. I confess I did dislike the Queens marriage with Spain, and also the coming of the Spaniards here, and then me thought I had reason to do so for I did learn the reasons of my disliking of you Master Hare, Master Southwell, and other in the Parliament House, there I did see the whole consent of the realm against it; and I a hearer, but no speaker, did learn my disliking of those matters, confirmed by many sundry reasons amongst you but as concerning any stir or uproar against the Spaniards, I never made any, neither procured any to be made and for my much resort to Master Wyatt, but to show my friendship to my very good lord the Marquise of Northampton, who was lodged there when he was enlarged.

Stanford. Did not you Throckmorton tell Winter that Wyatt had changed his mind for the taking of the Tower, whereby it appeared evidently that you knew of his doings?

Throckmorton. Truly I did not tell him so. But I care not greatly to give you that weapon to play you withal, now let us see what you can make of it.

Stanford. Yea sir, that proves that you were privy to Wyatt's mind in all his devised and treasons and that there was sending between you and Wyatt from time to time.

Throckmorton. What master sergeant does this prove against me, that I knew Wyatt did repent him of an evil devised enterprise? Is it to know Wyatt's repentance sin? No, it is but a venial sin, if it be any it is not deadly. But where is the messenger of message that Wyatt sent to me touching his alteration, and yet it was lawful enough for me to hear from Wyatt at that time as from any other man, for any act that I knew he had done.

Dyer. And it may please you my lords and you my masters of the jury, to prove that Throckmorton is a principal doer in this rebellion, there is yet many other things to be declared among other, there is Croft's confession, who said that he and you and your accomplices did many times devise to all his determinations, and you showed him that you would go into the west country with the Earl of Devon, to Sir Peter Carew, accompanied with others.

Throckmorton. Master Crofts is yet living and is here this day, how happens it he is not brought face to face to justify this matter, neither has been of all this time? Will you know the truth? Either he said not so, or he will not abide by it, but honestly has reformed himself. And as for knowing his devises, I was so well acquainted with them, that I can name none of them, nor you neither as matter known to me.

Attorney. But why did you advise Winter to land my Lord Privy Seal in the west country?

Throckmorton. He that told you that my mind was to land him there, does partly tell you a reason why I said so, if you would remember as well the one as the other but because you are so forgetful, I will recite wherefore. In communication between Winter and me as he declared to me that the Spaniards provided to bring their prince hither so the Frenchmen prepared to interrupt his arrival for they began to arm to the sea, and had already certain ships on the west coast (as he heard). Into who, I said, that peradventure not only the Queens ships under his charge might be in jeopardy, but also my Lord Privy Seal and all his train; the Frenchmen being well prepared to meet with them and therefore for all events it were good you should put my said lord in the west country in case you espy any jeopardy. But what does this prove to the treasons if I were not able to give convenient reasons to my talk?

Stanford. Merry sir, now comes the proof of your treasons, you shall hear what Cuthbert Vaughan said against you.

Vaughan's confession was read by Stanford. Then Sergeant Stanford did read Vaughan's confessions tending to this effect. That Vaughan coming out of Kent, met with Throckmorton at Master Warner's house, who after had had done commendations from Wyatt to him, desired to know where Crofts was. Throckmorton answered. Either at Arundel house where he lodged or in Paul's. Then Vaughan desired to know how things went at London, saying; Master Wyatt and we of Kent do much dislike the marriage with Spain, and the coming of the Spaniards for diverse respects: howbeit, if other countries dislike them as Kent does, they shall be but hardly welcome, and so they parted. Shortly after Throckmorton met with Vaughan in Paul's to whom Throckmorton declared with sundry circumstances, that the Western men were in a readiness to come forwards and that Sir Peter Carew had sent to him even now and that he had in order a good band of horsemen, and an other of footmen.

Then Vaughan demanded what the Earl of Devonshire would do. Throckmorton answered, he will marvel, for he will not go hence and yet Sir Peter Carew would meet him with a band, both of horsemen and footmen, by the way at Andover for his safeguard and also he should have been well accompanied from hence with other gentlemen, yet all this will not move him to depart hence. Moreover, the said earl has (as is said) discovered all the whole matter to the chancellor, or else it is come out by his tailor, about the trimming of a shirt on mail and the making of a cloak. At another time, Vaughan said Throckmorton showed him that he had sent a post to Sir Peter Carew to come forward with as much speed as might be and to bring his force with him. And also Throckmorton advised Vaughan to will Master Wyatt to come forward with his power for now was the time in as much as the Londoners would take his part if the matter were presented to them. Vaughan said also that Throckmorton and Warner should have ridden with the said earl westward. Moreover the said Vaughan deposed that Throckmorton showed him in talk of the Earl of Pembroke that the said earl would not fight against them, though he would not take their parts. Also Vaughan said that Throckmorton showed him that he would ride down into Berkshire to Sir Francis Englefield's, house, there to meet his eldest brother to move him to take his part. And this was the sum of Cuthbert Vaughan's confession.

Stanford. Now say you? Does not here appear evident matter to prove you a principal, who not only gave order to Sir Peter Carew and his adherents for their rebellious acts in the west country, but also procured Wyatt to make his rebellion, appointing him and the others also when they should attempt their enterprise, and how they should order their doings from time to time. Besides all this evident matter, you were specially appointed to go away with the Earl of Devon as one that would direct all things and give order to all men. And therefore Throckmorton with this matter is so manifest and the evidence so apparent, I would advise you to confess your fault and submit yourself to the Queen's mercy.

Bromley. How say you, will you confess the matter and it will be best for you?

Throckmorton. No, I will never accuse myself unjustly, but in as much as I am come hither to be tried, I pray ye let me have the law favorably.

Attorney. It is apparent that you lay at London as a factor, to give intelligence as well to them in the west, as to Wyatt in Kent.

Throckmorton. How prove you that, or who does accuse me but this condemned man?

Attorney. Why will you deny this matter? You shall have Vaughan justify his whole confession here before your face.

Throckmorton. It shall not need, I know his unshamefastness, he has avowed some of the untrue talk before this time to my face, and it is not otherwise like, considering the price, but he will do the same again.

Attorney. My lord and masters, you shall have Vaughan to justify this here before you all and confirm it with a book oath.

Throckmorton. He that has said and lied will not being in this case strike to swear and lie.

Then was Cuthbert Vaughan brought into the open court.

Sendall. How say you Cuthbert Vaughan, is this your own confession and will you abide by all that is here written?

Vaughan. Let me see it and I will tell you.

Then his confession was showed him.

Attorney. Because you of the jury the better may credit him, I pray you my lords let Vaughan be sworn.

Then was Vaughn sworn on a book to say nothing but the truth.

Vaughan. It may please you my lords and masters, I could have been will content to have chose seven years imprisonment, though I had been a free man in the law, rather than I would this day have given evidence against Sir Nicholas Throckmorton; against whom I bear no displeasure but with I must needs confess my knowledge, I must confess all that is there written is true. How say you Master Throckmorton, was there any displeasure between you and me, to move me to say aught against you?

Throckmorton. None that I know, how say you Vaughn, what acquaintance was there between you and me and what letters of credit or token did you bring me from Wyatt or any other to move me to trust you?

Vaughan. As for acquaintance, I knew you as I did other gentlemen and as for letters, I brought you none other but commendations from Master Wyatt, as I did to diverse other of his acquaintance at London.

Throckmorton. You might as well forge the commendations as the rest but if you have done with Vaughan my lords, I pray you give me leave to answer.

Bromley. Speak and be short.

Throckmorton. I speak generally to all that be here present, but specially to you of my jury, touching the credit of Vaughn's depositions against me, a condemned man, and after to matter and note I pray you the circumstance, as somewhat material to induce the better. First I pray you remember the small similarity between Vaughan and me as he has avowed before you, and moreover to procure credit at my hand, brought neither letter nor token from Wyatt nor from any other to me, which he also has confessed here and I will suppose Vaughan to be in as good condition as any other man here, that is to say, an uncondemned man; yet I refer it to your good judgment, whether it were like that I knowing only Vaughan's person from another man, and having none other acquaintance with him, would so frankly discover my mind to him in so dangerous a matter. How like (I say) is this, when diverse of these gentlemen now in captivity, being my very familiars, could not depose any such matter against me, and nevertheless upon their examinations have said what they could and though I be no wise man, I am not so rash as to utter to an unknown man (for so I may call him in comparison) a matter so dangerous for me to speak, and him to hear. But because my truth and his falsehood shall the better appear to you, I will declare his inconstancy in uttering this his evidence. And for my better credit, it may please you Master Southwell, I take you to witness when Vaughan first insinuated this his unjust accusation against me before the Lord Paget, the Lord Chamberlain, you Master Southwell, and other, he referred the confirmation of this his surmised matter to a letter sent from him to Sir Thomas Wyatt, which letter does neither appear, not any testimony of the said Master Wyatt against me touching the matter; for I doubt not Sir Thomas Wyatt has been examined of me, and has said what he could directly or indirectly. Also Vaughan said that young Edward Wyatt could confirm this matter as one that knew this pretended discourse betwixt Vaughan and me, and there upon I made suit that Edward Wyatt might either be brought face to face to me, or otherwise be examined.

Southwell. Master Throckmorton you mistake your matter, for Vaughan said that Edward Wyatt did know some part of the matter and also was privy of the letter that Vaughan sent Sir Thomas Wyatt.

Throckmorton. Yea sir, that was Vaughan last shift when I charged him before the master of the horse and you with his former allegations touching his witness, whom when he espied would not do so lewdly as he though, then he appears neither his first nor his last tale to be true. For you know Master Bridges, and so does my lord your brother that I desired twice or thrice Edward Wyatt should be examined and I am sure, and most assured he has been willed to say what he could and here is nothing deposed by him against me, either touching any letter of other conference. Or where is Vaughan's letter sent by Sir Thomas Wyatt concerning my talk? But now I will speak of Vaughan's present estate in that he is a condemned man, whose testimony is nothing worth by any law. And because false witness is mentioned in the gospel, treating of accusation, hear I pray you what St. Jerome said expounding that place. It is demanded while Croft's accusers be called false witness, which did report Christ's words not as he spoke them. They be false witness, said St. Jerome, which do add, alter, wrest, double, or do speak for hope to avoid death, or for malice easily gather he cannot speak truly of me, or in the case of another mans life, where he has hope of his own by accusation. Thus much speak St. Jerome of false witness. By the evil law there be many exceptions to taken against such testimonies but because we be not governed by that law, neither have I my trial by it, it shall be superfluous to trouble you there with, and therefore you shall hear what your own law does say. There was a statue made in my late sovereign lord and master his time, touching accusation and there be the words.

Be it enacted that no person nor persons shall be indicted, arraigned, condemned, or convicted for any offense of treason, petit treason, misprision of treason, for which the same offender shall suffer any pains of death, imprisonment, loss or forfeiture of his goods, lands, and unless the same offender be accused by two sufficient and lawful witnesses of shall willingly without violence confess the same. And also in the sixth year of his reign, it is thus ratified as ensued.

That no person nor persons shall be indicted, arraigned, condemned, convicted or attainted of the treasons or offenses aforesaid, or for any other treasons that now be, or hereafter shall be; unless the same offender or offenders be thereof accused (if they be then living) shall be brought in person before the said party accused and avow and maintain that they have to say against the said party to prove him guilty of the treason or offense contained in the bill of indictment laid against the party arraigned, unless the said party arraigned shall be willing without violence to confess the same. Here note (I pray you) that our law does require two lawful and sufficient accusers to be bought face to face, and Vaughan is but one, and the same most unlawful and insufficient. For who can be more unlawful and insufficient than a condemned man, and such one as knows to accuse me is the mean to save his own life? Remember (I pray you) how long and how many times Vaughn's execution has been respited and how often he has been conjured to accuse (which by Gods grace he withstood until the last hour) what time perceiving there was no way to live, but to speak against me or some other (his former grace being taken away) did redeem his life most unjustly and shamefully, as you see.

Hare. Why should he accuse you more than any other, seeing there was no displeasure between you, if the matter had not been true?

Throckmorton. Because he must either speak of some man or suffer death, and then he did rather choose to hurt him whom he least knew and so loved least than any other well known to him whom he loved most. But to you of the jury I speak specially, and therefore I pray you not what I say. In a matter of less weight than trial of life and land, a man may by the law take exceptions to such as he impaneled to try the controversies between the parties, as for example. A man may challenge that the sheriff is his enemy and therefore has made a partial return; or because one of the jury is the sheriff my adversaries servant and also in case my adversaries villain or bondman be impaneled, I may lawfully challenge him because the adversarial part has the use of his body for servile office much more I may of right take exception to Vaughan's testimony, my life and all that I have depending thereupon, and the same Vaughan being more bound to the Queen's highness my adversary (that woe is me therefore) but so the law does here so term her majesty, than any villain is to his lord for her highness has not only power over his body, lands and goods, but over his life also.

Stanford. Yea, the exception are to be taken against the jury in that case, but not against the witness or accuser and therefore your argument serves little for you.

Throckmorton. That is not so, for the use of the jury and the witness and the effect of their doings does serve me to my purpose, as the law shall discuss. And thus I make my comparison. By the civil law the judge does give sentence upon the depositions of the witness and by your law the judge does give judgment upon the verdict of the jury; so as the effect is both one to finish the matter, trial in law as well by the depositions of the witness, as by the juries verdict though they vary in form and circumstance and so Vaughan's testimony being credited, may be the material cause on my condemnation as the jury to be induced by his depositions to speak their verdict, and so finally there upon the judge to give sentence. Therefore I may use the same expectations against the jury, or any of them, as the principal mean that shall occasion my condemnation.

Bromley. Why do you deny that every part of Vaughan's tale is untrue?

Attorney. You may see he will deny all, and say there was no such communication between them.

Throckmorton. I confess some part of Vaughan confession to be true, as the name, the places, the time, and some part of the matter.

Attorney. So you of the jury may perceive the prisoner does confess some thing to be true.

Throckmorton. As touching my sending to Sir Peter Carew, of his sending to me, or concerning my advise to Master Wyatt to stir or to repair hither, or touching the Earl of Devonshire parting hence, and my going with him, and also concerning the matter of the Earl of Pembroke, I do avow and say that Vaughan has said untruly.

Southwell. As for my Lord of Pembroke, you need not excuse the matter, for he has showed himself clear in these matters like a noble man and that we all know.

Hare. Why what was the talk betwixt Vaughan and you so long in Paul's, if these were not so, and what meant you oft meetings?

Throckmorton. As for our meetings, they were of no act purpose, but by chance, and yet no oftener than twice. But since you would know what communication passed between us in Paul's church, I will declare. We talked of the incommodities of the marriage of the Queen with the Prince of Spain and how grievous the Spaniards would be to us here. Vaughan said, "that it should be very dangerous for any man, that truly professed the gospel to live here, such was the Spaniards cruelty, and especially against Christian men". Whereto I answered, "it was the plague of God justly come upon us and now almighty God dealt with us as he did with the Israelites, taking from them for their unthankfulness their godly Kings, and did send tyrants to reign over them. Even so he handled us Englishmen, which had a most godly and virtuous prince to reign over us, my late sovereign lord and Master King Edward, under whom we might both falsely and lawfully profess Gods word, which with our lewd doings, demeanor, and living, we handled so irreverently that to whip us for our faults he would send so stranger, yea such very tyrants to exercise great tyranny over us and did take away the virtuous and faithful King from amongst us for every man of every estate did color his naughty affections with a pretense of religion, and made the gospel a stalking horse to bring their evil desires to effect". This was the sum of our talk in Paul's somewhat more dilated.

Stanford. That it may appear yet more evidently how Throckmorton was a principal doer and counselor in this matter, you shall hear his own confession of his own handwriting.

The clerk began to read, Throckmorton desired master Stanford to read it and the jury well to mark it. Then Master Stanford did read the prisoners own confession to this effect that Throckmorton had conference with Wyatt, Carew, Crofts, Rogers, and Warner, as well of the Queen's marriage with the Prince of Spain, as also of religion, and did particularly confer with every the forenamed of the matters aforesaid. Moreover, with Sir Thomas Wyatt the prisoner talked of the brute that the Western men should much dislike the coming of the Spaniards into the realm, being reported also that they intended to interrupt their arrival here. And also that it was said that they were in consolation about the same at Exeter. Wyatt also did say that Sir Peter Carew could not bring the same matter to good effect, not that there was any man so need to bring it to good effect as the Earl of Devonshire, and specially in the west parts insomuch as they drew not all by one line.

Then Throckmorton asked now the Kentish men were affected to Spaniards? Wyatt said; "The people like them evil enough, and that appeared now at the coming of the Count of Egmount, for they were ready to stir against him and his train, supposing it had been the prince." "But" said Wyatt, "Sir Robert Southwell, Master Baker and Master Noile, and their affinity, which be in good credit in some places of the shire, will for other malicious respects hinder the liberty of their country". Then Throckmorton should say; "Though I know there has been an unkindness between Master

Southwell and you for a money matter, wherein I traveled to make you friends, I doubt not, but in so honest a matter as there is, he will for the safeguard of his country join with you and so you may be sure of the Lord Abergavenny and his force." Then Wyatt said, "It is for another matter than for money that we disagree, wherein he has handled me and others very doubly and unneighborly, howbeit, he can do no other, neither to me, nor to any other man and therefore I forgive him.

Item, with Sir Peter Carew, Throckmorton had conference touching the impeachment of the landing of the said prince, and touching provision of amour and munitions as ensued, that is to say, that Sir Peter Carew told Throckmorton that he trusted his countrymen would be true Englishmen and would not agree to let the Spaniards to govern them.

Item, the said Sir Peter Carew said the matter importing the French King, as it did, he thought the French King would work to hinder the Spaniards coming hither, with whom the said Sir Peter did think good to practice for amour, munitions, and money.

Then Throckmorton did advise him to beware that he brought any Frenchmen into the realm forcibly, inasmuch as he could as evil abide the Frenchmen after that sort as the Spaniards. And also Throckmorton thought the French King unable to give aid to us by means of the great consumption in their own wars. Master Carew said; as touching the bringing in of the Frenchmen, he meant it not, for he loved neither party, but to serve his own country and to help his country from bondage declaring further to Throckmorton that he had a small bark of his own to work his practice by and so he said that shortly he intended to depart to his own country to understand the devotion of his countrymen.

Item, Throckmorton did say he would for his part hinder the coming in of the Spaniards as much as he could by persuasion.

Item, to Sir Edward Warner, he had and did become his own estate, and the tyranny of the time extended upon diverse honest persons for religion and wished it were lawful for all of each religion to live safely according to their conscience; for the law will be intolerable and the clergies discipline now may rather be resembled to the Turks tyranny than to the teaching of Christian religion.

This was the sum of the matter which was read in the foresaid confession, as matters most grievous against the prisoner.

Then Throckmorton said, since Master Sergeant you have read and gathered the place (as you think) that makes most against me, I pray you take the pains and read further that hereafter whatsoever become of me, my words be not perverted and abused to the hurt of some others, and especially against the great personages of whom I have been sundry times (as appears by my answers) examined, for I perceive the net was not cast only for little fishes, but for the great ones.

Stanford. It shall be but loss of time and we have other things to charge you withal, and this that you desire does make nothing for you.

Dyer. And for the better confirmation of all the treasons objected against the prisoner and therein to prove him guilty, you for the jury shall hear the Duke of Suffolk's depositions against him, who was a prisoner, amounting to this effect that the Lord Thomas Grey did inform the said duke that Sir Nicholas Throckmorton was privy to the whole devises against the Spaniards and was one that should go into the west country with the Earl of Devonshire.

Throckmorton. But what does the principal author of this matter say against me, I mean the Lord Thomas Grey who is yet living? Why be not his depositions brought against me, for so it ought to be if he can say anything? Will you know the truth? Neither the Lord Thomas Grey has said, can say, or will say anything against me, notwithstanding the duke his brothers confession and accusation, who has affirmed many other things besides the truth. I speak not without certain knowledge for the Lord Thomas Grey being my prison-fellow for a small time, informed me that the duke his brother had misreported him in many things, amongst others in matters touching me, which he had declared to you Master Southwell, and other the examiners not long ago. I am sure if the Lord Thomas could, or would have said anything, it should have been here now. And as to the duke's confession, it is not material for he does refer to the matter to the Lord Thomas report who has made my purgation.

The Attorney. And it please you my lords, and you my masters of the jury, besides these matters touching Wyatt's rebellion, Sir Peter Carew's treasons and confederating with the Duke of Suffolk, and besides the prisoners conspiracy with the Earl of Devonshire, with Crofts, Rogers, Warner and sundry others in sundry places, it shall manifestly appear to you that Throckmorton did conspire the Queen's majesties death with William Thomas, Sir Nicholas Arnold, and other traitors intending the same, which is the greatest matter of all others and most to be abhorred. And for proof hereof, you shall hear what Arnold said.

Then was Sir Nicholas Arnold's confession read saying that Throckmorton showed to him, riding between Hinam and Crossland in Gloucestershire, that John Fitzwilliams was very much displease with William Thomas.

Attorney. William Thomas devised that John Fitzwilliams should kill the Queen, and Throckmorton knew of it, as appears by Arnold's confession.

Throckmorton. First I deny that I said any such thing to Master Arnold, and though he be an honest man, he may either forget himself or devise means how to unburden himself of so weighty a matter as this is; for he is charged with the matter as principal. Which I did perceive when he charged me with his tale, and therefore I do blame him the less, that he seeks how to discharge himself using me as a witness, if he could so transfer the devise to William Thomas. But truly I never spoke any such words to him. And for my better declaration, I did see John Fitzwilliams here even now, who can testify that he never showed me of any displeasure between them, and as I know nothing of the displeasure between them, so I know nothing of the cause. I pray you my lords let him be called to depose in this matter what he can.

Then John Fitzwilliams drew to the bar and presented himself to depose his knowledge in the matter in open court.

The Attorney. I pray you my lords suffer him not to be sworn, neither to speak, we have nothing to do with him.

Throckmorton. Why should he not be suffered to tell the truth? And why be ye not so well contented to hear truth for me as untruth against me?

Hare. Who called you hither Fitzwilliams, or commanded you to speak? You are a very busy officer.

Throckmorton. I called him and do humbly desire that he may speak and be heard as will as Vaughan; or else I am not indifferently used, especially seeing Master Attorney does so press this matter against me.

Southwell. Go your ways Fitzwilliams, the court has nothing to do with you peradventure you would not be so ready in a good cause.

Then John Fitzwilliams departed the court and was not suffered to speak.

Throckmorton. Since this gentleman's declaration may not be admitted, I trust you of the jury can perceive it was not for anything he had to say against me, but contrariwise that it was feared he would speak for me. And now to Master Arnold's depositions against me, I say I did not tell him any such words, so as if it were material, there is but his yea and my nay. But because the words be not sore strained against me, I pray you Master Attorney why might not I have told Master Arnold that John Fitzwilliams was angry with William Thomas and yet know no cause of the anger? It might be understood to disagree oftentimes. Who does confess that I know anything of William Thomas's devise touching the Queen's death? I will answer, no man for Master Arnold does mention no word of that matter, but of the displeasures between them. And to speak that does neither prove treason. Is here all the evidence against me that you have to bring me within the compassed of the indictment?

Stanford. Me think the matters confessed by others against you, together with your own confession, will weigh shrewdly. But how say you to the rising in Kent and Wyatt's attempt against the Queen's royal person at her palace.

Bromley. Why do you not read Wyatt's accusation to him, which does make him partner to his treasons?

Southwell. Wyatt has grievously accused you and in many things that others have confirmed.

Throckmorton. Whatsoever Wyatt has said of me in hope of his life, he unsaid it at his death. For since I came into this hall, I heard one say (but I know him not) that Wyatt upon the scaffold did not only purge my Lady Elizabeth her grace, and the Earl of Devonshire, but also all the gentlemen in the Tower saying they were all ignorant of the stir and commotion. In which number I take myself.

Hare. Not withstanding he said all that he had written and confessed to the council, was true.

Throckmorton. Nay sir, by your patience, Master Wyatt said not so, that was Master Doctors addition.

Southwell. It appears you have had good intelligence.

Throckmorton. Almighty God provided that revelation for me this day since I came hither for I have been in close prison these eight and fifty days where I heard nothing but what the birds told me, which did fly over my head. And now to you of my jury I speak specially whom I desire to mark attentively what shall be said. I have been indicted, as it appears, and now am arraigned of compassing the Queen majesties death, of levying war against the Queen, of taking the Tower of London, of deposing and depriving the Queen of her royal estate, and finally to destroy her and of adherence to the Queen's enemies. Of all which treasons, to prove me guilty, the Queen's learned counsel has given in evidence these points material; that is to say for the compassing or imagining the Queen's death; and the destruction of her royal person, Sir Nicholas Arnold's depositions, which is, that I should say to the said Sir Nicholas in Gloucestershire, that Master John Fitzwilliams was angry with William Thomas.

Whereto I have answered, as you have heard, both denying the matter and for the proof on my side, do take exceptions prove nothing concerning the Queen's death. For levying of war against the Queen, there is alleged my conference with Sir Thomas Wyatt, Sir James Crofts, Sir Edward Rogers, Sir Edward Warner. Against the marriage with Spain and the coming of the Spaniards hither, which talk I do not deny in sort as I spoke it, and meant it and notwithstanding the malicious gathering this day of my conference, proves yet no levying of war. There is also alleged for proof of the same article, Sir James Croft's confession, which (as you remember) implied no such thing, but general talk against the marriage with Spain. And of my departing westward with the Earl of Devon, which the said James does not avow, and therefore I pray you consider it as not spoken. There is also for proof of the said article, the Duke of Suffolk's confession with whom I never had conference; and therefore he avouched the tale of his brothers mouth who has made my purgation in those matters; and yet if the matter were proved, they be not greatly material in law.

There is also alleged for the further proof of the same article and for deposing and depriving the Queen of her royal estate and for my adhering to the Queens enemies, Cuthbert Vaughan's confession, whose testimony I have sufficiently disproved by sundry authorities and circumstances and principally by your own law which does require two lawful and sufficient witnesses to be brought face to face. Also for the taking of the Tower of London, there is alleged Winter's depositions which uttered my disliking, when he uttered to me Sir Thomas Wyatt's resolution and devise for attempting of the said peace. And last of all, to enforce these matters, mine own confession is ingreeved against me, wherein there does appear neither treason, neither concealment of treason, neither whispering of treason, nor procurement of treason.

And forasmuch as I am come hither to be tried by the law, though my innocence of all these points material objected, be apparent to acquit me, where to I do principally clean yet I will for your better credit and satisfactions, show you evidently that if you would believe all the depositions laid against me, which I trust you will not do, I ought not to be attainted of the treason comprised within my indictment, considering the statute of repeals the last Parliament of all treasons other than such as be declared in the five and twentieth year of King Edward the Third, both which statutes, I pray you my lords may be read here to the inquest.

Bromley. No sir, there shall be no books brought at your desire, we do all know the law sufficiently without book.

Throckmorton. Do you bring me hither to try me by the law and will not show me the law? What is your knowledge of the law to these men's satisfactions which have my trial in hand? I pray you my lords and my lords all let the statutes be read, as will for the Queen as for me.

Stanford. My Lord Chief Justice can show the law, and will, if the jury do doubt of any point.

Throckmorton. You know it were indifferent that I should know and hear the law whereby I am adjudged, and for as much as the stature is in English, men of meaner learning than the justices can understand it, or else how should we know when he offend?

Hare. You know not what belongs to your case and therefore we must teach you it appertained not to us to provide books for you, neither sit we here to be taught of you, you should have taken better heed to the law before you had come hither.

Throckmorton. Because I am ignorant, I would learn, and therefore I have more need to see the law and partly as well for the instructions of the jury as for my own satisfaction which me think were for the honor of this presence. And now if it please you my Lord Chief Justice, I do direct my speech specially to you. What time it please the Queen's majesty to call you to this honorable office, I did learn of a great personage of her highness Privy Counsel, that amongst other good instructions, her majesty charged and enjoined you to minister the law and justice indifferently without respect of persons. And not withstanding the old error amongst you which did not admit any witness to speak, or any other matter to be heard in the favor of the adversary, her majesty being party; her highnesses pleasure was that whatsoever could be brought in favor of the subject, should be admitted to be heard. And moreover that you specially and likewise all other justices should not persuade themselves to sit in judgment otherwise for her highness, than for her subject. Therefore this manner of indifferent proceeding being principally enjoined by Gods commandment, which I had thought partly to have remembered you and others here in commission, in the beginning, if I might have had leave; and the same also being commanded you by the Queens own mouth, me think you ought of right to suffer me to have the statutes read openly and also to reject nothing that could be spoken in my defense; and in thus doing, you shall show yourselves worthy ministers, and fit for so worthy a mistress.

Bromley. You mistake the matter; the Queen spoke those words to Master Morgan Chief Justice of the Common Pleas, but you have no cause to complain, for you have been suffered to talk at your pleasure.

Hare. What would you do with the statute book? The jury does not require it, they have heard the evidence and they must upon their conscience try whether you be guilty or no, so as the book needs not; if they will not credit the evidence so apparent, then they know what they have to do.

Cholmley. You ought not to have any books read here at your appointment, for where does arise any doubt in the law, the judges sit here to inform the court and now you do but spend time.

The Attorney. I pray you my Lord Chief Justice repeat the evidence for the Queen, and give the jury their charge, for the prisoner will keep you here all day.

Bromley. How say you? Have you any more to say for yourself?

Throckmorton. You seem to give and offer me the law, but in very deed I have only the form and image of the law, nevertheless, with I cannot be suffered to have the statutes read openly in the book, I will by your patience guess at them as I may, and I pray you to help me if I mistake, for it is long since I did see them. The statute of repeal made the last Parliament has these words be it enacted by the Queen that from henceforth none act, deed, of offense, being by act of Parliament or statute made treason, petit treason, of misprision of treason, by words, writing, printing, ciphering, deeds, or otherwise whatsoever, shall be taken, had deemed, or adjudged treason, petit treason but only such as be declared of expressed to be treason, in or by an act of Parliament made in the five and twentieth year of Edward the Third touching and concerning treasons and the declaration of treason and none other.

Here may you see this statute does refer all the offenses aforesaid to the statute of the five and twentieth year of Edward the Third, which statute has these words touching and concerning the treasons that I am indicted and arraigned of, that is to say whosoever does compass of imagine the death of the King or levy war against the King in his realm, or being adherent to the Kings enemies within this realm, or elsewhere, and be therefore probably attainted by open deed by people of their condition; shall be judged a traitor. Now I pray you of my jury which have my life in trial, note well what things at this day be treasons and how these treasons must be tried and discerned; that is to say, by open deed, which the laws does at some time term. And now I ask notwithstanding my indictment, which is but matter alleged, where dooly appear the open deed of any compassing of imagining the Queen's death? Or where does appear any open deed of being adherent to the Queen's enemies, giving to them aid and comfort? Or where does appear any open deed of taking the Tower of London?

Bromley. Why do not you of the Queen's learned counsel answer him? Me think, Throckmorton, you need not have the statutes, for you have them meetly perfectly.

Stanford. You are deceived to conclude all treasons in the statute of the five and twentieth year of Edward the Third, for that statute is but a declaration of certain treasons which were treason before at the common law. Even so there did remain divers other treasons at this day at the common law which be expressed by that statue as the judges can declare. Nevertheless, there is matter so lucent alleged and proved against you, to bring you within the compass of the same statute.

Throckmorton. I pray you express those matters that bring me within the compass of the statute of Edward the Third. For the words be these and be thereof attainted by open deed by people of like condition.

Bromley. Throckmorton you deceive yourself and mistake these words; by people of their condition. For thereby the law does understand the discovering of your treasons. As for example, Wyatt and the other rebels attainted for their great treasons, already declare you to be his and their adherent in as mind as diverse and sundry times you had conference with him and them about the treason, so as Wyatt is now one of your condition, who (as all the words knows) has committed an open traitorous fact.

Throckmorton. By your leave my lord, this is a very strange and singular understanding. For I suppose the meaning of the law-makers did understand these words but people of their condition; for the state and condition of those persons which should be on the inquest to try the party arraigned, guilty or not guilty, and nothing to the betraying of the offense by another mans act, as you say. For what have I to do with Wyatt's acts, that was not nigh him by one hundred miles?

The Attorney. Will you take upon you to still better of the law than the judges? I doubt not but you of the jury will credit as it becomes you.

Cholmley. Concerning the true understanding of these words. By people of their condition, my Lord Chief Justice here has declared the truth, for Wyatt was one of your condition, that is to say, of your conspiracy.

Hare. You do not deny, Throckmorton, that there has been conference and sending between Wyatt and you and he and Winter does confess the same with others, so as it is plain; Wyatt may be called one of your condition.

Throckmorton. Well, seeing you my judges rule the understanding of there words in the statute by people of your condition, thus strangely against me, I will not stand longer upon them. But where does appear in me an open deed whereto the treason is specially referred?

Bromley. If three of four do talk, devise, and conspire together of a traitorous act to be done, and afterwards one of them does commit treason, as

Wyatt did, then the law does repute them and every of them as their acts, so as Wyatt's acts do imply and argue of your open deed and so the law does term it and take it.

Throckmorton. These be marvelous expositions and wonderful implications that another man's act whereof I was not privy should be accounted mine for Wyatt did purge me that I knew nothing of his stir.

Hare. Yea sir, but you were a principal procurer and contriver of Wyatt's rebellion, though you were not with him when he made the stir. And as my Lord Hare has said, the law always does procure treason or any other man to commit treason, of a traitorous act, as you did Wyatt and others for so the overt act of those which did it by your procurement shall in this case be accounted your open deed. We have a common case in the law, if one by procurement should seize you of your land, the law holds us both wrong doers and gives remedy as well against the one as the other.

Throckmorton. For Gods sake apply not such constructions against me, and though my present estate does not move you, yet it were well you should consider your office and think what measure you give to others, you yourselves I say shall assuredly receive the same again. The state of mortal life is such that men know full little what hangs over them. I put on within these XIJ months such a mind that I most woeful right was as unlike to stand here as some of you that sit there. As to your case last recited whereby you would conclude; I have remembered and learned of you Master Hare, and you Master Stanford in the Parliament house, where you did sit to make laws to expound and explain the ambiguities and doubts of law sincerely and that without affections. There I say I learned of you and others my master of the law, this difference between such cases as you remembered one even now, and the statute whereby I am to be tried. There is a maxim of principle in the law which ought not to be violated, that no penal statute may, ought, or should be conferred, expounded, extended, or wrested, otherwise than the simple words and nude letter of the same statute does warrant and signify. And amongst diverse good and notable reasons by you there in the Parliament house debated (Master Sergeant Stanford) I noted this one while the said maxim ought so be inviolable. You said considering the private affections many times both of princes and ministers within this realm, for that they were men and would and could err, it should be no security, but very dangerous to the subject to refer the construction and extending of penal statutes to any judges equity (as you termed it) which might either by fear of the higher powers be seduced or by ignorance and folly abused and that is an answer by procurement.

Bromley. Notwithstanding the principal (as you allege it) and the preciseness of your sticking to the bare words of the statute, it does appear and remain of record in our learning that diverse cases have been adjudged treason without the express words of the statute as the Queen's learned counsel there can declare.

The Attorney. It does appear the prisoner did not only entice or procure Wyatt, Carew, Rogers, and others to commit their traitorous act and there does his open facts appear, which Vaughan's confession does witness, but also he did mind shortly after to affect at himself with those traitors for he minded to have departed with the Earl of Devonshire westward.

Throckmorton. My innocence concerning these matters I trust sufficiently appears by my former answers, notwithstanding the condemned man's unjust accusation. But because the true understanding of the statute is in question, I say procurement and specially by words only is without the compass of it and that I do learn and prove by the principle which I learned of Master Stanford.

Stanford. Master Throckmorton, you and I may not agree this day in the understanding of the law, for I am for the Queen and you are for yourself, the judges must determine the matter.

Bromley. He that does procure another man to commit a felony or a murder, I am sure you know well enough the law does adjudge the procurer there a felon or a murderer; and in case of treason it has been always so taken and reputed.

Throckmorton. I do and must cling to my innocence, for procured no man to commit treason but yet for my learning I desire to hear some case so ruled when the law was as it is now. I do confess it, that at such time there were statutes provided for the procurer, counselor, aide, abettor, and such like, as there were in King Henry the Eights time; you might lawfully make this cruel construction and bring the procurer within the compass of the law. But these statutes being repealed, you ought not now so to do and as to the principal procurer in felony and murder, it is not like as in treason; for the principal and accessories in felony and murder be trialable and punishable by the common law and so in those cases the judges may use their equity, extending the determination of the fault as they think good, but in treason it is otherwise the same being limited by statute, which I say and avow is restrained from any judges construction by the maxim that I recited.

Stanford. Your lordships do know a case in Richard the Thirds time where the procurer, to counterfeit false money, was judged a traitor and the law was as it is now.

Hare. Master Sergeant does remember you Throckmorton of an experience before our time that the law has been so taken and yet the procurer was not expressed in the statute, but the law has been always so taken.

Throckmorton. I never studied the law, whereof I do much repent me, yet I remember while penal statutes were talked of in the Parliament house, you the learned men of the house remembered some cases contrary to this last spoken of. And if I misreport them, I pray you help me. In the like case you speak of concerning the procurer to counterfeit false money at one time the procurer was judged a felon, and at another time neither felon nor traitor so as some of your predecessors adjudged the procurer no traitor in the same case, but leaned to their principal though some other extend their constructions too large. And here is two cases with me, for one against me.

Bromley. Because you reply upon the principal, I will remember where one taking the Great Seal of England from one writing and putting it to another, was adjudged a traitor in Henry the Fourths time, and yet his act was not within the express words of the statute of Edward to Third. There be diverse other such like cases that may be alleged and need were.

Throckmorton. I pray you my Lord Chief Justice call to your good remembrance, that in the self same case of the seal, justice Spellman, a grave and well learned man since that time, would not condemn the offender but did reprove that former judgment by you last remembered as erroneous.

Stanford. If I had thought you had been so well furnished in book cases, I would have been better provided for you.

Throckmorton. I have nothing but I learned of you specially Master Sergeant, and of others my masters of the law in the Parliament house and therefore I may say with the prophet (*salutem ex ininicis nostris*).

Southwell. You have a very good memory.

The Attorney. If the prisoner may avoid his treasons after this manner, the Queen's surety shall be in great jeopardy. For Jack Cade and the blacksmith, and diverse other traitors, sometime alleging the law for them, sometime they meant no harm to the King, but against his counsel, as Wyatt, the Duke of Suffolk and these did against the Spaniards when there was no Spaniards within the realm. The duke and his brethren did mistake the law, as you do, yet at length did confess their ignorance, and submitted themselves and so were you best to do.

Throckmorton. As to Cade and the blacksmith, I am not so well acquainted with their treasons as you be but I have read in the chronicle they were in the field with a force against the prince, whereby a manifest act did appear. As to the Duke of Suffolk's doings, they appertain not to me. And though you would compare my speech and talk against the Spaniards to the duke's acts who assembled a force in armies, it is evident they differ much. I am sorry to aggrieve any other man's doings, but it serves me for a peace of my defense and therefore I wish that no man should gather evil of it. God forbid that words and acts be thus confounded.

The Attorney. Sir William Stanley used this shift that the prisoner uses now; he said he did not levy war against King Henry the Seventh, but said to the Duke of Buckingham that is a good quarrel he would aid him with five hundred men; and nevertheless Stanley was for those words attained, who (as all the world knows) had before that time served the King very faithfully and truly.

Throckmorton. I pay you Master Attorney do not conclude against me by blind contraries. Whether you allege Stanley's case truly or no. I know not. But admit it be as you say, what does there prove against me? I promised no aid to Master Wyatt nor to any other. The Duke of Buckingham levied war against the King, with whom Stanley was confederate so to do as you say.

The Attorney. I pray you my lords that be the Queens commissioners, suffer not the prisoner to use the Queen's learned counsel thus, I was never interrupted thus in my life, nor I never knew any thus suffered to talk as this prisoner is suffered; some of us will come no more at the bar and we be thus handled.

Bromley. Throckmorton you must suffer the Queen's learned counsel to speak or else we must take order with you, you have had keeve to talk at your pleasure.

Hare. It is proved that you did talk with Wyatt against the coming of the Spaniards and devised to interrupt their arrival and you promised to do what you could against them where upon Wyatt being incorporated by you, did levy a force, and attempted war against the Queen's royal person.

Throckmorton. It was no treason nor procurement of treason to talk against the coming hither of the Spaniards, neither was it treason for me to say I would hinder their coming hither as much as I could (understanding me rightly as I mean it) yea though you would extend it to the worst, it was but words, it was not treason at this day as the law stands. And as for Wyatt's doing, they touch me nothing; for at his death when it was not time to report untruly, he purged me.

Bromley. By sundry cases remembered here by the Queen's learned counsel (as you have heard) that procurement which did appear none otherwise but by words and those you would make nothing, has been of long time and by sundry will learned men in the laws adjudged treason. And therefore, your procurement being so evident as it is, we may lawfully say it was treason because Wyatt performed a traitorous act.

Throckmorton. As to the said alleged fore precedents against me, I have recited as many for me, and I would you my Lord Chief Justice should incline your misjudgments rather after the example of your honorable predecessors justice Markham, and others which did ensure corrupt judgments, judging directly and sincerely after the law and the principles in the same than after such men as swerving from the truth, the maxim, and the law, did judge corruptly, maliciously, and affectionately.

Bromley. Justice Markham had reason to warrant his doings for it did appear a merchant of London was arraigned and slanderously accused of treason for compassing and imagining the Kings death, he did say he would make his son heir of the crown and the merchant meant it of a house in Cheapside at the sign of the crown, but your case is not so.

Throckmorton. My case does differ I grant, but specially because I have not such a judge, yet there is an other cause to restrain these your strange and extraordinary constructions that is to say, a provide in the latter end of the statute of Edward the Third having these words. Provided always if any other case of supposed treason shall chance hereafter to come in supposed treason shall chance hereafter to come in question of trial before any justice, other than is in the said statute expressed, that then the justice shall forbear to adjudge the said case until it be showed to the Parliament to try whether it should be treason or felony. Here you are restrained by express words to adjudge any case that is not manifest mentioned before, and until it be showed to the Parliament.

Postman. That provision is understood of cases that may come in trail which has been in use, but the law has always taken the procurer to be a principal offender.

Sanders. The law always in cases of treason does account all principals and no accessories as in other offenses, and therefore a man offending in treason either by covert act or procurement whereupon an open deed has insured, as in this case, is adjudged by the law a principal traitor.

Throckmorton. You adjudge (me think) procurement very hardly, besides the principal, and besides the good proviso and besides the good example of you best and most godly learned predecessors, the judges of the realm as I have partly declares, and notwithstanding this grievous racking and extending of this word procurement, I am not in the danger of it, for it does appear by no disposition that I procured neither one or other to attempt any act.

Stanford. The jury have to try whether it be so or not, let it weigh as it will.

Hare. I know no mean so apparent to try procurement as by words and that mean is probable enough against you, as well by your own confession, as by other men's depositions.

Throckmorton. To talk of the Queen's marriage with the prince of Spain and also the coming hither of the Spaniards, is not to procure treason to be done for then the whole Parliament House, I mean the common house did procure treason. But with you will make no difference between words and acts, I pray you remember a statute made in my late sovereign lord and masters time, King Edward the First, which apparently expressed the difference. These be the words: Whosoever does compass of imagine to depose the King of his royal estate by poem preaching, express words or sayings, shall for the first offense loose and forfeit to the King all his and their goods and cattle and also shall suffer imprisonment of their bodies at the Kings will and pleasure.

Whosoever and for the second offence shall loose and forfeit to the King the whole issues and profits of all his or their lands, tenements and other hereditariness, benefices, prebends, and other spiritual promotions. Whosoever and for the third offense shall for term of life or lives of such offender or offenders, and shall also forfeit to the Kings majesty all his or their goods and cattle and suffer during his or their lives perpetual imprisonment of his or their bodies. But whosoever and by writing, ciphering, or act and shall for the first offense be adjudged a traitor and suffer the pains of death. Here you may perceive how the whole realm and all your judgments has before this understood words and acts diversely and apparently. And therefore the judgments of the Parliament did assign diversity of punishments, because they would not confound the true understanding of words and deeds, appointed for compassing and imagining by word, imprisonments and for compassing and imagining by open deed, pains of death.

Bromley. It is agreed by the whole bench that the procurer and the adherent be deemed always traitors when as a traitorous act was committed by any one of the same conspiracy and there is apparent proof of your adhering to Wyatt, both by your own confession and other ways.

Throckmorton. Adhering and procuring be not all one, for the statute of Edward the Third does speak of adhering, but not of procuring; and yet adhering ought not to be further extended than to the Queen's enemies within her realm for so the statute does limit the understanding. And Wyatt was not the Queen's enemy, for he was not so reputed when I talked with him last, and our speech implied no enemy, neither tended to any treason, or procuring of treason and therefore I pray you of the jury note though I argue the law, I allege my innocence as the best part of my defense.

Hare. Your adhering to the Queen's enemy within the realm is evidently proved for Wyatt was the Queen's enemy within the realm as the whole realm knows it and he has confessed it both at his arraignment and at his death.

Throckmorton. By your leave, neither Wyatt at his arraignment nor at this death, did confess that he was the Queen's enemy when I talked last with him; neither was he reputed not taken in fourteen days after until he assembled a force in arms, what time I was at your house Master Englefield, where I learned the first intelligence of Wyatt's stir. And I ask you who does depose that there passed any manner of advertisement between Wyatt and me after he had discovered his doings and showed himself an enemy? I had been so disposed, who did let me that I did not repair to Wyatt or to send to him, or to the Duke of Suffolk either who was in my own country, and thither I might have gone and conveyed myself with him, unsuspected for my departing homewards.

Englefield. It is true that you were there at my house accompanied with others your brethren, and to my knowledge, ignorant of these matters.

Bromley. Throckmorton, you confessed you talked with Wyatt and others against the coming of the Spaniards and of the taking of the Tower of London whereupon Wyatt levied a force of men against the Spaniards he said, and so you say all but in deed it was against the Queen which he confessed at length therefore Wyatt's acts do prove you counselor, and procurer, howsoever you would avoid the matter.

Throckmorton. Me think you would conclude against me with a misshapen argument in logic and you will give me leave, I will make an other.

Stanford. The judges sit not here to make disputations, but to declare the law, which has been sufficiently done, if you would consider it.

Hare. You have heard reason and the law, if you ill conceive it.

Throckmorton. Oh merciful God, oh eternal Father, which sees all things, what manner of proceedings are these? To what purpose serves the statute of repeal the last Parliament where I heard some of you here present, and diverse other of the Queen's learned counsel, grievously inveigh against the cruel and bloody laws of King Henry the Eight and against some laws made in my late sovereign lord and master's time, King Edward the First. Some termed them Dracos laws which were written in blood, some said they were more intolerable than any laws that Dionysius or any other tyrant made. In conclusion, as many men so many bitter terms and names those laws had.

And moreover, the preface of the same statute does recite that for words only, many great personages and others of good behavior have been most cruelly cast away by these former sanguinolent thirsty laws with many other suggestions for the repeal of the same. And now let us put on indifferent eyes, and thoroughly consider with ourselves as you the judges handle the constructions of the statute of Edward the Third with your equity and extensions, whether we be not in much worse case now than we were when those cruel laws yoked us. These laws albeit they were grievous and captious, yet they had the very property of a law after Saint Paul's description. For these laws did admonish us and discover our sins plainly to us, and when a man is warned, he is half armed.

These laws as they be handled, be very baits to catch us and only prepared for the same, and no laws for at the first sight they ascertain us we be delivered from our old bondage and by the late repeal the last Parliament, we live in more security. But when it pleases the higher powers to call any man's life and sayings in question, then there be constructions, interpretations, and extensions reserved to the justices and judges equate that the party trialable, as I am now, shall find himself in much worse case than before when those cruel laws stood in force. Thus our amendment is from Gods blessing into the warm sun. But I require you honest men which are to try my life, consider their opinions of my life, judges be rather agreeable so the time than to the truth for their judgments be repugnant to their own principle, repugnant to their godly and best learned predecessors opinions, repugnant I say to the provision in the statute of repeal made in the last Parliament.

The Attorney. Master Throckmorton quiet yourself and it shall be the better for you.

Throckmorton. Master Attorney, I am not so unquiet as you be, and yet our cases are not alike but because I am so tedious to you and have long troubled this presence, it may please my Lord Chief Justice to repeat the evidence wherewith I am charged, and my answers to all the objections, if there be no other matter to lay against me.

Then the chief justice remembered particularly all the depositions and evidences given against the prisoner and either for want of good memory, or good will, the prisoners answers were in part not recited whereupon the prisoner craved indifference and did help the judges old memory with his own recital.

Sendall. My masters of the jury, you have to inquire whether Sir Nicholas Throckmorton Knight, here prisoner at the bar, be guilty of these treasons or any of them, whereof he has been indicted and this day arraigned, yea or no. And if you find him guilty, you shall inquire what lands, tenements, goods, and cattle he had at the day of his treasons committed of anytime since and whether he fled for the treasons or no, if you find him not guilty.

Throckmorton. Have you said what is to be said?

Sendall. Yea for this time.

Throckmorton. Then I pray you give me leave to speak a few words to the jury. The weight and gravity of my cause has greatly occasioned me to trouble you here long with any prolix oration you perceive not withstanding this day great contention between the judges and Queen's learned counsel on the one party, and me the poor and woeful prisoner on the other party. The trial of our whole controversy, the trial of my innocence, the trial of my life, lands, and goods, and the destruction of my posterity forever, does rest in your good judgments. And albeit many this day have greatly inveighed against me, the final determination thereof is transferred only to you. How grievous and horrible the shedding of innocents blood is in the fight of almighty God, I trust you do remember. Therefore take heed (I say) for Christ's sake, do not defile your consciences with such heinous and notable crimes. They by grievously and terribly punished as in this world and vale of misery upon the children's children to the third and forth generation, and in the world to come with everlasting fire and damnation. Lift up your minds to God, and care not too much for the world, look not back to the fleshpots of Egypt which will allure you from heavenly respects to worldly security, and can thereof neither make you any surety. Believe I pray you, the Queen and her magistrates be more delighted with favorable equity than with rash cruelty. And in that you be all citizens, I will take my leave of you with St. Paul's farewell to the Ephesians, citizens also you be, whom he took to record that he was pure from shedding any blood, a special token and doctrine left for your instruction that every of you may wash his hands of innocents bloodshed when you shall take your leave of this wretched world. The Holy Ghost be among you.

Sendall. Come hither sergeant, take the jury with you and suffer no man to come at them, but to be ordered as the law appoints until they be agreed upon their verdict.

Throckmorton. It may please you my lords and masters which be commissioners, to give order that no person have access or conference with the jury, neither that any of the Queen's learned counsel be suffered to repair them, or to talk with any of them, until they present themselves here in open court to publish their verdict.

Upon the prisoners suit on this behalf, the bench gave order that two sergeants were sworn to suffer no man to repair to the jury until they were agreed according to order. Whereupon then the prisoner was by commandment of the bench withdrawn from the bar and the court adjourned until three of the clock at afternoon, at which hour the commissioners returned to the Guildhall and there did tarry until the jury were agreed upon the verdict. And about five of the clock, their agreement being advertised to the commissioners, the said prisoner Sir Nicholas Throckmorton was again brought to the bar where also the jury did repair; and being demanded whether they were agreed upon their verdict answered universally with one voice, yea. Then it was asked who should speak for them, they answered Whetston the foreman.

Sendall. Nicholas Throckmorton Knight, hold up thy hand.

Throckmorton. Then the prisoner did so upon the summons.

Sendall. You that be of the jury, look upon the prisoner.

Jury. The jury did as they were enjoined.

Sendall. How say you, is Master Throckmorton Knight there prisoner at the bar, guilty of the treasons whereof he has been indicted and arraigned in manner and form, yea or no?

Whetston. No.

Sendall. How say you, did he flee upon them?

Whetston. No, we find no such thing.

Throckmorton. I had forgotten to answer that question before, but you have found according to truth and for the better warranty of your doings understand that I came to London and so to the Queen's counsel unbrought when I understood they demanded for me and yet I was almost an hundred miles hence, where if I had not presumed upon my truth, I could have withdrawn myself from catching.

Bromley. How say you the rest of you, is Whetston's verdict all your verdicts?

Jury. The whole inquest answered, yea.

Bromley. Remember yourselves better, have you considered substantially the whole evidence in sort as it was declared and recited; the matter does touch the Queen's highness and yourselves also, take good heed what you do.

Whetston. My lord, we have thoroughly considered the evidence laid against the prisoner and his answers to all these matters, and accordingly we have found him not guilty agreeable to all our consciences.

Bromley. If you have done well, it is the better for you.

Throckmorton. It is better to be tried, than to live suspected. Blessed be the Lord God of Israel, for he has visited and redeemed his people and has raised up a mighty salvation for us in the house of his servant David. And it may please you my Lord Chief Justice, forasmuch as I have been indicted and arraigned of sundry treasons, and have according to law put my trial to God and my country, that is to say to these honest men which have found me not guilty, I humbly beseech you to give me such benefit, acquittal and judgment, as the law in this case does appoint.

When the prisoner had said these words the commissioners consulted together.

Throckmorton. May it please you my Lord Chief Justice to pronounce sentence for my discharge?

Bromley. Whereas you do ask the benefit that the law in such case does appoint, I will give it you; to wit that where you have been here this day before the Queen's commissioners and justices arraigned of the said treasons, whereto you have pleaded not guilty, and have for trial therein put yourself on God and your country and they have found you not guilty, the court does award that you be clearly discharged paying your fees. Notwithstanding Master Lieutenant take him with you again, for there are other matters to charge him withal.

Throckmorton. It may please you my lords and masters of the Queen's highness Privy Counsel to be on my behalf humble suitors to her majesty, that like as the law this day (God be praised) has purged me of the treasons wherewith I was most dangerously charged so it might please her excellent majesty to purge me in her private judgment, and both forgive and forget my over rash boldness that I used in talk of her highness's marriage with the prince of Spain, matter too far above my capacity, and I very unable to consider the gravity thereof, a matter impertinent for me a private person to talk of which did appertain to her highness Privy Counsel to have in deliberation. And if it shall please her highness of her bountiful liberality to remit my former oversights, I shall think myself happy for trial of the danger that I have this day escaped, and may thereby admonish me to eschew things above my reach and also to instruct me to deal with matters agreeable to my vocation. And God save the Queen's majesty and grant the same long to reign over us. And the same Lord be praised for you the magistrates, before whom I have had my trial this day indifferently by the law and you have proceeded with me accordingly and the grace of God be amongst you now and ever.

There was no answer made by any of the bench to the prisoners suit, but the attorney did speak these words.

The Attorney. And it please you my lords, forasmuch as it seems these men of the jury which have strangely acquitted the prisoner of his treasons whereof he was indicted, will forthwith depart the court. I pray you for the Queen, that they, and every of them may be bound in recognizance of five hundred pounds a piece to answer to such matters as they shall be charged with in the Queen's behalf, whosoever they shall be charged or called.

Whetston. I pray you my lords be good to us and let us not be molested for discharging our consciences truly. We be poor merchantmen and have great charge upon our hands, and our livings do depend upon our travels, therefore it may please you to appoint us a certain day for our appearance, for perhaps some of us may be in foreign parts about our business.

Thus much for Sir Nicholas Throckmorton's arraignment, wherein is to be considered that the repealing of certain statute in the last Parliament was the chief matter he had to allege for his advantage whereas the repealing of the same statutes was meant notwithstanding for an other purpose (as before you have partly heard) which statutes of the effect of the chief branched of them have been since that time again revived as by the books of the statutes it may better appear, to the which I refer the reader.

[Holinshed, *The First and Second volumes of Chronicles*. Pg. 1104-1117]

There is no real comparison of Sir Nicholas's trial with those of modern times. The court and council employed tactics one would not see in a court today, such as literally baiting Sir Nicholas with questions and accusations to confess his guilt from the beginning to end of the trial. The skill that Sir Nicholas displayed is evidence of his talents and his boldness gave him unusual advantages in his altercations with the judges and council. A man of lesser abilities would not have been able to defend himself, and that is the reason why this trial is so well remembered in history. He was completely acquitted of the charge of high treason; unheard of at that time of turbulent Tudor history, especially with the hundreds of executions of those involved in Wyatt's Rebellion.

Unquestionably, Sir Nicholas was in communications with the rebels; he had promised to accompany Edward Courtenay into the west, had numerous conversations with Thomas Wyatt and actually invited the pursuit of his armed followers and his close friend and patroness the Princess Elizabeth was supposed to have encouraged the rebellion.

An early historian suggested that the conscience of the jury probably found less difficulty in the facts against Sir Nicholas than in the guilt attached to them. The verdict was perhaps a rebuke in response to the mass executions administered by the Crown, and it was reported by the ambassador Simon Renard to the emperor that the verdict was an insult to the Crown and that Mary was ill for three days as a result. Renard mentions that a crowd greeted Sir Nicholas after the trial; they threw up their caps and shouted. The Queen ordered that the jurors be punished and they were arrested then imprisoned for almost eight months.

It appears that Sir Nicholas remained in the Tower following his trial and nothing was heard from him until 14 July 1554. Then, in a letter to Sir William Petre (council member), Dr. Wotton mentioned that he had not yet received word on what the Queen wanted to do with Sir Nicholas and that Nicholas has yet to receive mercy from her. Furthermore, Sir Nicholas was in such bad need of money that he had requested to serve her majesty in 'these wars' and had promised not to serve with the rebels but to be employed by the Gascons (those who lived in an area of southwest France).

On 18 January 1555, a couple of records suggest that Sir Nicholas Throckmorton was finally released after paying a fine. There were several others released from the Tower that day also and Henry Machyn mentions in his diary that 'and after there was a great shooting of guns'. It was also about this time that Sir Nicholas's jury finally gained their freedom after to be released upon payment of a fine of £2000 each.

Shortly after his release, Nicholas fled to France, mostly because of his Protestant views. His name came up in another English rebellion but he was in Paris at the time. Many recent historians indicate that he was executed on 28 April, 1556, but I am happy to say that he lived for many additional years.

Following the death of Mary, Nicholas slowly became a trusted and valuable member of Elizabeth's court and many pieces of correspondence survive giving insight to the high esteem Queen Elizabeth had of him and his ambassadorial duties. Nicholas Throckmorton died 12 February 1571.

Thomas Cranmer

Thomas Cranmer was born in 1489 at Aslaction, now Aslockton near Nottingham England, to Thomas and Agnes who were, even by the standards of that time, poor and possessed little land. Thomas and his younger brother joined the church where he excelled in his studies and in 1510 was awarded a fellowship at Jesus College, Cambridge. Love apparently outweighed studies because in 1515 he married Joan, niece of the landlady of Dolphin Tavern. This resulted in his expulsion from Cambridge because they required that fellows remain celibate. Nevertheless, he lectured at Magdalene College, a constituent College of Oxford. In 1519 Joan died during childbirth and he regained his fellowship at Oxford and is remembered as a devote student in unorthodox philosophy. In 1523, he earned a doctorate of divinity and was ordained that same year.

In August 1523, Cranmer left Cambridge for the safety of Essex during another outbreak of the bubonic plague. While staying with a student of his, two counselors of King Henry VIII also sought refuge at the same house and it was not long before they discussed the King's desire to divorce Catherine of Aragon. Cranmer pointed out that the Queen's previous marriage was probably illegal and that if Oxford and Cambridge agreed, a petition could be sent to Rome. In 1530, Cranmer composed the *Collectanea Satis Copiosa* (large enough collection) allowing the King to break from Rome.

On 30 March, 1530, he received the appointment of Archbishop of Canterbury following the death of William Warham. In 1532, he was appointed ambassador to Charles V and married a German woman Margurete. Margurete accompanied Thomas on his appointment, but he attempted to keep her presence concealed because the marriage was clearly a violation of clerical celibacy.

Cranmer was successful in securing a declaration that the King's marriage with Catherine was null and void and his marriage with Anne Boleyn was legal. In September, Anne gave birth to Elizabeth and Thomas was godfather.

During the reign of Henry VIII, Cranmer was successful in implementing many changes in the reformation of the Church of England. A significant amount of emphasis was placed on the 'middle way' between Catholic and Protestant beliefs. Clergy could marry and religious orders were dissolved.

Cranmer ordered that a copy of the English bible be on display in all churches. Cranmer is credited for contributing the first two editions of the Book of Common Prayer in 1549.

During the dissolution of monasteries during the King's remaining years, Cranmer was awarded grants for various former church properties such as the Cluniac Nunnery at Arthington Priory. Only about ten nuns resided there at the time of the dissolution and so it became a farmland with a private dwelling.

Following the death of King Henry VIII, Cranmer was indispensable as an advisor to Edward VI who was raised with Protestant views. Thomas Cranmer had many accomplishments to that point, but following the death of Edward VI, Mary was quick to restore the Catholic religion and began the process of counter-reformation which included the imprisonment of Cranmer as a heretic. Removed from office and based primarily on a pamphlet he published condemning Mass, he was excommunicated and confined in Oxford Prison where he remained until his trial in 1556.

> The New Year opened to Cranmer and his fellow prisoners with no alleviation of their melancholy state. Nearly nine months had passed when the condemnation, which Weston had pronounced upon them, was considered necessary to be repeated by commissioners, who should derive their authority from Rome. When Weston was their judge that authority had not been received in England nor by any law then in force was his sentence justifiable. By the legate, therefore a commission was issued to examine, absolve, or degrade, or deliver to the secular arm, Latimer and Ridley. In regard to Cranmer, another was sent by the Pope himself. To Brookes, Bishop of Gloucester, on this occasion the delegate of the Cardinal de Puteo who was the principal commissioner, named by the pontiff for the sake of form and to the civilians Martin and Story who were the royal proctors, was deputed the cognizance of the crimes alleged against the Archbishop. On the 9th of September they opened their commission in the Church of St. Mary at Oxford, and settled other preliminaries as to the proceeding. It was not till the 12th that all things were ready for the renovated trial. Brookes then was seated on a lofty scaffold, erected over the high altar; beneath him were the proctors, with other civilians; and around them a numerous auditory. From his prison, guarded, Cranmer then was introduced. His dress was that of a black gown with his doctor's hood over it. His head was as yet covered. Nor, when he saw the papal representative on his throne, did he "vail his bonnet," but stood silent till the charge against him was proclaimed, which was, "Thomas, Archbishop of Canterbury, appear here, and make answer to that which shall be laid to thy charge; that is to say, for blasphemy, incontinency, and heresy; and make answer here to the Bishop of Gloucester, representing the Pope's person."
>
> Being now brought nearer to the scaffold and observing the regal proctors, to them as the representatives of the sovereign, he respectfully bowed and pulled off his cap. To Brookes he still refused this tribute; when the mitered commissioner, resenting the slight, told him it might beseem him well considering the authority that was represented not to withhold from

him the same courteous acknowledgment. The archbishop answered that once he had taken a solemn oath never to consort to the readmission into the realm of England of the papal authority; that still he would keep that oath; and that, therefore, no sign or token which might argue his consent to receiving the same would he give. Not for any contempt of the commissioner's person, he continued, did he thus act; for if his commission had been regal like that of the proctors, instead of papal, he would not have failed immediately to respect it.

Brookes then addressed him in a long speech, no less distinguished by absurdity than by abuse in which he reminded him of the charges proclaimed against him; urged him to repent of his apostasy; bade him consider in his own case the tender mercies of the Queen, pretending that yet she spared him under the hope of amendment; and condescended to be the first of those treacherous advisers, who, in order to make him "unsay what he had said," resorted to the artifices by which the poor archbishop was afterwards overcome; saying, "As for the loss of your estimation, it is ten to one that when you were Archbishop of Canterbury and metropolitan of England—it is ten to one, I say, that you shall be as well still, yea, and rather better."

The proctor Martin followed the delegate in an oration, condensing the insolence of the latter into a smaller compass after which he exhibited the instrument that empowered him and Story to act as the royal proctors, as well as the articles of accusation against the prisoner. His oration being ended, the archbishop said, "Shall I now make my answer," Martin replied, "As you think good no man shall hinder you."

The archbishop then kneeling down, said first the Lord's prayer: then, rising up, recited the articles of the creed; and afterwards thus declared his protestation against the proceedings.

Cranmer. This I do profess as touching my faith, and make my protestation, which I desire you to note. I will never consent that the Bishop of Rome shall have any jurisdiction within this realm.

Story. Take a note thereof.

Martin. Mark, Dr. Cranmer, how you answer for yourself. You refuse and deny him, by whose laws you do remain in life, being otherwise attainted of high treason, and but a dead man by the laws of this realm.

Cranmer. I protest before God I was no traitor; but, indeed, I confessed more at my arraignment than was true.

Martin. That is not to be reasoned at this present. You know you were condemned for a traitor, *and resjudicata pro veritate acaipitur.* But proceed to your matter.

Cranmer. My lord, addressing the Bishop of Gloucester, you have very learnedly and eloquently in your oration put me in remembrance of many things touching myself, wherein I do not mean to spend the time in answering of them. I acknowledge God's goodness to me in all his gifts, and thank him as heartily for this state wherein I find myself now as ever I did for the time of my prosperity; and it is not the loss of my promotions that grieves me. The greatest grief I have at this time and one of the greatest that ever I had in all my life, is to see the King and Queen's majesties by their proctors here to become my accusers, and that in their own realm and country before a foreign power. If I have transgressed the laws of the land, their majesties have sufficient authority and power, both from God and by the ordinance of this realm, to punish me, whereto I both have been, and at all time shall be content to submit myself.

Alas, what has the Pope to do in England whose jurisdiction is so far different from the jurisdiction of this realm, that it is impossible to be true to the one and true to the other. The laws also are so diverse that whosoever swears to both, must needs incur perjury to the one; which, as oft as I remember, even for the love that I bear to her grace, I cannot but be heartily sorry to think upon it, how that her highness the day of her coronation at which time she took a solemn oath to observe all the laws and liberties of this realm of England; at the same time, also took an oath to the Bishop of Rome, and promised to maintain that see. The state of England being so repugnant to the supremacy of the Pope, it is impossible but she must needs be forsworn to the one; wherein, if her grace had been faithfully advertised by her council, then surely she would never have done it.

The laws of this realm are that the King of England is the supreme and sole governor of all his countries and dominions, and that he holds his crown and scepter of himself by the ancient laws, customs, and descents of the Kings of the realm, and of none other. The Pope says that all emperors and Kings hold their crowns and regalities of him, and that he may depose them when he list; which is high treason for any man to affirm or think, being born within the King's dominions.

The laws of England are, that all bishops and priests offending in cases of felony or treason, are to be judged and tried by the laws and customs of the realm. The Pope's laws are, that the secular power cannot judge the spiritual power and that they are not under their jurisdiction; which robs the King of the one part of his people.

The laws also of England are, that whosoever hinders the execution or proceeding of the laws of England for any other foreign laws, ecclesiastical or temporal, incurred the danger of a praemunire. The Pope's laws are, that whosoever hinders the proceedings or executions of his laws for any other laws of any other King or country, both the prince himself, his council, all his officers, scribes, clerks, and whosoever give consent or aid to the making or executing of any such laws, stand accursed. A heavy case, if his curse were anything worth, that the King and Queen cannot use their own laws, but they and all theirs must stand accursed.

And as for the matter of heresy and schism, wherewith I am charged, I protest and call God to witness that I know none that I have maintained. But if that were a heresy to deny the Pope's authority, and the religion which the see of Rome has published to the world these latter years, then all the ancient fathers of the primitive church, the apostles, and Christ himself, taught heresy; and I desire all present to bear me witness that I take the traditions and religion of that usurping prelate to be most erroneous, false, and against the doctrine of the whole scripture; which oftentimes I have well proved by writing, and the author of the same to be very antichrist, so often preached of by the apostles and prophets in whom did most evidently concur all signs and tokens whereby he was pointed out to the world to be known.

The archbishop then exposed other arrogant pretensions of the pontiff, not without alluding to his own unjustly condemned opinion as to the doctrine of the sacrament of the altar; for if it can be proved said he, by any doctor above a thousand years after Christ, that Christ's body is there really, I will give over. My book was made seven years ago, and no man has brought any authors against it. He concluded this uninterrupted defense by expressing his hope, that the King and Queen, if they were rightly informed, would do well. This observation awakened the zeal of Martin.

Martin. As you understand then, if they maintain the supremacy of Rome, they cannot maintain England too?

Cranmer. I desire you to declare to the King and Queen what I have said, and how their oaths do stand with the realm and the Pope. St. Gregory said, he that takes upon him to be head of the universal church is worse than the antichrist. If any man can show me that it is not against God's word to hold his stirrup when he takes his horse, or kiss his feet, as Kings do, then I will kiss his feet also. And you, for your part my lord, are perjured; for now you sit judge for the Pope, and yet you did receive your bishopric of the King. You have taken an oath to be adversary to the realm; for the Pope's laws are contrary to the laws of the realm.

Bishop of Gloucester. You were the cause that I did forsake the Pope, and did swear that he ought not to be supreme head and gave it to King Henry the Eighth, that he ought to be it and this you made me to do.

Cranmer. To this I answer, you report me ill and say not the truth; and I will prove it here before you all. The truth is that my predecessor, Archbishop Warham, gave the supremacy to King Henry the Eighth, and said that he ought to have it before the Bishop of Rome and that God's word would bear him. And upon the same was there sent to both universities, Oxford and Cambridge, to know what the word of God would do touching the supremacy; and it was reasoned upon, and argued, at length. So at the last both universities agreed, and set to their seals, and sent it to King Henry, that he ought to be supreme head and not the Pope. You were then doctor of divinity, and your consent was thereto, as your hand does appear. Therefore you misreport me that I was the cause of your falling away from the Pope; but it was yourself. All this was in Bishop Warham's time, and whilst he was alive; so that it was three quarters of a year after, ere I had the Archbishopric of Canterbury in my hands, and before I might do anything. So that here you have reported of me that which you cannot prove; which is evil done.

The self-convicted judge could only meanly reply: We come to examine you; and you, methinks, examine us.

After Story had next interposed an oration in behalf of the papal supremacy, Martin again addressed the archbishop; whose words, together with the replies to them, Foxe resolved not to overpass, although the Romish reporter employed to note them had been extremely partial, omitting nothing that might promote the object of the accuser, but much that was favorable to that of the accused. Such as the dialogue was, even thus unfairly described, it is too important not to be copied. The Proctor Martin opens it.

Master Cranmer, you have told here a long, glorious tale, pretending some matter of consequence in appearance, but in verity you have no conscience at all. You say that you have sworn once to King Henry the Eighth against the Pope's jurisdiction, and therefore you may never forswear the same; and so you make a great matter of conscience in the breach of the said oath. Here will I ask you a question or two. What if you made an oath to a harlot to live with her in continual adultery, ought you to keep it?

Cranmer. I think not.

Martin. What if you did swear never to lend a poor man one penny, ought you to keep it?

Cranmer. I think not.

Martin. Herod did swear whatsoever his harlot asked of him he would give her, and he gave her John Baptist's head. Did he well in keeping his oath?

Cranmer. I think not.

Martin. Jephthah, one of the judges of Israel, did swear to God that if he would give him victory over his enemies, he would offer to God the first soul that came forth of his house. It happened that his own daughter came first; and he slew her to save his oath. Did he well?.

Cranmer. I think not.

Martin. So said St. Ambrose, *De Officiis*: It is a miserable necessity which is paid with parricide. Then, Master Cranmer, you can no less confess by the premises, but that you ought not to have conscience of every oath, but if it be just, lawful, and advisedly taken.

Cranmer. So was that oath.

Martin. That is not so. For, first, it was unjust; for it tended to the taking away of another man's right. It was not lawful; for the laws of God and the church are against it. Besides it was not voluntary; for every man and woman were compelled to take it.

Cranmer. It pleases you to say so.

Martin. Let all the world be judge. But sir, you that pretend to have such a conscience to break an oath, I pray you did you never swear and break the same?

Cranmer. I remember not.

Martin. I will help your memory. Did you never swear obedience to the see of Rome?

Cranmer. Indeed I did once swear to the same.

Martin. Yea, that you did twice as appears by records and writings here ready to be shown.

Cranmer. But, I remember I saved all by protestation that I made by the counsel of the best-learned men I could get at that time.

Martin. Hearken, good people, what this man said. He made a protestation, one day to keep never a whit of that which he would swear the next day. Was this the part of a Christian man? If a Christian man would bargain with a Turk, and before he makes his bargain, solemnly before witness reads in his paper that he holds secretly in his hand, or peradventure protested before one or two, that he minds not to perform whatsoever he shall promise to the Turk; I say if a Christian man would serve a Turk in this manner, that the Christian man were worse than the Turk. What would you then say to this man, that made a solemn oath and promise to God and his church, and made protestation before quite contrary?

Cranmer. That which I did, I did by the best-learned men's advice I could get at that time.

Martin. I protest before all the learned men here, that there is no learning will save your perjury herein. For there be two rules of the civil law against you (which he produced, and then turning to the audience said) But will you have the truth of the matter? King Henry even then meant the lamentable change, which after you see came to pass; and to further his pitiful proceedings, from the divorcement of his most lawful wife to the detestable departing from the blessed unity of Christ's church, this man made the foresaid protestation; and, on the other side, he let not to make two solemn oaths quite contrary, and why? For otherwise, by the laws and canons of this realm, he could not aspire to the Archbishopric of Canterbury.

Cranmer. I protest before you all, there was never man came more unwilling to a bishopric, than I did to that. Insomuch that when King Henry did send for me in post that I should come over, I prolonged my journey by seven weeks at the least, thinking that he would be forgetful of me in the meantime.

Martin. You declare well by the way that the King took you to be a man of good conscience, who could not find within all his realm any men that would set forth his strange attempts, but was enforced to send for you in post to come out of Germany. What may we conjecture hereby, but that there was a compact between you, being then Queen Anne (Boleyn's) chaplain, and the King, give me the Archbishopric of Canterbury and I will give you license to live in adultery?

Cranmer. You say not true.

Martin. Let your protestation, joined with the rest of your talk, give judgment. *Hinc prima mali labes.* Of that your execrable perjury, and his colored and too shamefully suffered adultery, came heresy and all mischief to this realm. And thus have I spoken as touching the conscience you make for breaking your heretical oath to the King. But to break your former oath, made at two sundry times both to God and his church, you have no conscience at all. And now to answer another part of your oration, wherein you bring in God's word that you have it on your side, and no man else, and that the Pope has devised a new scripture contrary to the scriptures of God; you play herein as the Pharisees did, which cried always, *Verbum Domini, Verbum Domini,* (the word of the Lord, the word of the Lord,) when they meant nothing so. This betters not your cause, because you say you have God's word for you; for so Basilides and Photinus the heretics said that they had God's word to maintain their heresy. So Nestorius, so Macedonius, so Pelagius, and briefly all the heretics that ever were, pretended that they had God's word for them; yea, and so the Devil being the father of heresies, alleged God's word for himself, saying, *Scriptum est*, (It is written.) So said he to Christ, *Mitte te deorsum*, (Cast thyself downward,) which you applied most falsely against the Pope. But if you mark the Devil's language well it agreed with your proceedings most truly. For *Mitte te deorsum*, (Cast thyself downward,) said he, and so taught you to cast all things downward; down with the sacrament, down with the Mass, down with the altars, down with the arms of Christ, and up with a lion and a dog; down with the abbeys, down with chantries, down with hospitals and colleges, down with fasting and prayer, yea, down with all that good and Godly is. All your proceeding, and preaching's, tended to no other but to fulfill the Devil's request, *Mitte te deorsum*. And therefore tell us not that you have God's word. I would here ask but one question of you: Whether God's word be contrary to itself, or no I for you Master Cranmer, have taught in this high sacrament of the altar three contrary doctrines, and yet you pretend in every one *Verbum Domini*.

Cranmer. Nay, I taught but two contrary doctrines in the same.

Martin. What doctrine taught you when you condemned Lambert the sacrament in the King's presence in Whitehall?

Cranmer. I maintained then the Papists' doctrine.

Martin. That is to say the Catholic and universal doctrine of Christ's church. And how, when King Henry died ? Did you not translate Justus Jonas' book?

Cranmer. I did so.

Martin. Then there you defended another doctrine touching the sacrament by the same token that you sent to Lynne your printer, that whereas in the first print there was an affirmative, that is to say, Christ's body really in the sacrament you sent then to your printer to put in a not, whereby it came miraculously to pass that Christ's body was clean conveyed out of the sacrament.

Cranmer. I remember there were two printers of my said book, but where the same not was put in I cannot tell.

Martin. Then from a Lutheran you became a Zuinglian, which is the vilest heresy of all in the mystery of the sacrament; and for the same heresy you did help to burn Lambert the sacrament, which you now call the Catholic faith and God's word.

Cranmer. I grant that then I believed otherwise than I do now; and so I did until my Lord of London, Dr. Ridley, did confer with me and by sundry persuasions and authorities of doctors drew me quite from my opinion.

Martin. Now sir, as touching the last part of your oration, you denied that the Pope's holiness was the supreme head of the Church of Christ.

Cranmer. I did so.

Martin. Who, say you then, is supreme head?

Cranmer. Christ.

Martin. But whom has Christ left here on earth his vicar and head of his church?

Cranmer. Nobody.

Martin. Ah, why told you not King Henry this when you made him supreme head, and now nobody is? This is treason against his own person, as you then made him.

Cranmer. I mean not but every King in his own realm and dominion is supreme head; and so was he supreme head of the Church of Christ in England.

Martin. Is this always true? And was it ever so in Christ's church?

Cranmer. It was.

Martin. Then what say you by Nero? He was the mightiest prince of the earth after Christ was ascended. Was he head of Christ's church?

Cranmer. Nero was Peter's head.

Martin. I ask whether Nero was head of the church or no? If he were not, it is false that you said before that all princes be, and ever were, heads of the church within their realms.

Cranmer. Nay, it is true. For Nero was head of the church, that is in worldly respect of the temporal bodies of men of whom the Church consists; for so he beheaded Peter and the apostles. And the Turk too is head of the church in Turkey.

Martin. Then he that beheaded the heads of the church and crucified the apostles, was head of Christ's Church; and he, that was never member of the church is head of the church by your new-found understanding of God's word.

The impatience of the archbishop's adversaries, vexed as they must have been by some of his replies, now appears to have immediately demanded from him an answer to the formal interrogatories articulated against him. By the Romish reporter, as Foxe has copied them, these questions together with the answers to them, were preserved as they were delivered in our own language. The official account of them to the Cardinal de Puteo is in Latin; agreeing, in substance, with what the martyrologist has printed. The articles are in number sixteen:

I. First it was objected that he, being yet free, and before he entered into holy orders married one Joan, surnamed Black, or Brown, dwelling at the sign of the Dolphin in Cambridge.

Answer. Whereto he answered that whether she was called Black or Brown, he knew not, but that he married there one Joan, that he granted.

II. That after the death of the foresaid wife he entered into holy orders, and after that was made archbishop by the Pope.

Answer. He received, he said, a certain bull of the Pope which he delivered to the King, and was [made] archbishop by him.

III. That he, being in holy orders, married another woman as his second wife, named Anne, and so was twice married.

Answer. This he granted.

IV. In the time of King Henry he kept the said wife secretly and had children by her.

Answer. This he also granted; affirming that it was better for him to have his own, than to do like other priests, holding and keeping other men's wives.

V. In the time of King Edward he brought out the said wife openly, affirming and professing publicly the same to be his wife.

Answer. He denied not but so he did, and lawfully might do the same, forasmuch as the laws of the realm did so permit him.

VI. That he shamed not openly to glory himself to have had his wife in secret many years.

Answer. And though he did so, he said there was no cause why he should be ashamed thereof.

VII. That falling afterwards into the deep bottom of errors, he did fly and accuse the authority of the church; did hold and follow the heresy concerning the sacrament of the altar; and also did compile, and cause so be set abroad, divers books.

Answer. When the names of the books were recited to him, he denied not such books of which he was the true author. As touching the treatise of Peter Martyr upon the sacrament, he denied that he ever saw it before it was abroad, yet did approve and well like of the same. As for the Catechism, the book of articles, with the other book against Winchester, he granted the same to be his doings.

VIII. That he compelled many against their wills to subscribe to the same articles.

Answer. He exhorted, he said, such as were willing to subscribe; but against their wills he compelled none.

IX. Forasmuch as he surcease not to perpetrate enormous and inordinate crimes, he was therefore cast into the Tower, and from thence was brought to Oxford at what time it was commonly thought that the Parliament there should be held.

Answer. To this he said that he knew no such enormous and inordinate crimes that ever he committed.

X. That in the said city of Oxford he did openly maintain his heresy, and there was convicted upon the same.

Answer. He defended, he said there the cause of the sacrament; but to be convicted in the same, that he denied.

XI. When he persevered still in the same, he was by the public censure of the university pronounced a heretic, and his books to be heretical.

Answer. That he was so denounced, he denied not; but that he was a heretic, or his books heretical, that he denied.

XII. That he was, and is, notoriously infamed with the note of schism, as [one] who not only himself receded from the Catholic Church and see of Rome, but also moved the King and subjects of the realm to the same.

Answer. As touching the receding, that he well granted; but that receding or departing, said he, was only from the see of Rome and had in it no matter of any schism.

XIII. That he had been twice sworn to the Pope; (and Dr. Martin then brought out the instrument of the public notary, wherein was contained his protestation, made when he should be consecrated asking if he had anything else protested.)

Answer. Whereto he answered, that he did nothing but by the laws of the realm.

XIV. That he did not only offend in the premises, but also in taking upon him the authority of the see of Rome, in that without leave or license from the said see he consecrated bishops and priests.

Answer. He granted that he did execute such things as were wont to be referred to the Pope, at what time it was permitted to him by the public laws and determination of the realm.

XV. That when the whole realm had subscribed to the authority of the Pope, he only still persisted in his error.

Answer. That he did not admit the Pope's authority, he confessed to be true, but that he erred in the same that he denied.

XVI. That all and singular the premises are true.

Answer. That likewise, he granted, excepting those things whereto he had now answered.

The Proctor Martin had procured eight witnesses to maintain the truth of these articles. But before their depositions were given, other questions appear to have been urged which drew from the archbishop a repetition of his unwillingness to accept the see of Canterbury, and when the King had overruled it, of his determination not to receive the honor from the pontiff's hand; of his having made the protestation, which the King's civilians had recommended against the papal authority, and of having caused that public act to be enrolled in his archiepiscopal register.

The witnesses were then examined, a perfectly useless formality. The contradictions in some of their depositions the archbishop forbore to censure, and the session closed. Nor was it re-opened till after the sentence against him was received from Rome. The provisions of the canon law, Dr. Lingard says, were scrupulously observed; Cranmer underwent two examinations, and was then served as a matter of form with a citation to answer before the pontiff in the course of eighty days he owed this distinction to his dignity of archbishop, and to his ordination, which had been performed according to the ancient pontifical. The reader will be at no loss to appreciate the distinction, and this narrative of the scrupulous bestowal of it when he perceives that notwithstanding the archbishop professed his readiness to go to Rome, it had been resolved that he should never more behold any other city than that in which he was confined.

On the subject of this citation to Rome, Cranmer immediately addressed a long letter to the Queen, in which he thus describes the Pope:

And thus he sits in the temple of God, as if he were a god, and named himself God's vicar, and yet he dispensed against God. If this be not to play antichrist's part, I cannot tell what is antichrist, which is no more to say but Christ's enemy and adversary, who shall sit in the temple of God advancing himself above all other, yet by hypocrisy and feigned religion shall subvert the true religion of Christ, and under pretence and color of Christian religion shall work against Christ, and therefore has the name of antichrist. Now if any man lift himself higher than the Pope has done, who lifts himself above all the world; or can be more adversary to Christ, than to dispense against God's laws, and where Christ has given any commandment, to command directly the contrary, that man must needs be taken for antichrist. But until the time that such a person may be found, men may easily conjecture where to find antichrist.

Wherefore, seeing the Pope thus (to overthrow both God's laws and man's laws) takes upon him to make emperors and Kings to be vassals and subjects to him and specially the crown of this realm with the laws and customs of the same; I see no mean how I may consent to admit his usurped power within this realm, contrary to mine oath, mine obedience to God's law, mine allegiance and duty to your majesty, and my love and affection to this realm.

Another letter, of which a fragment only remains, has a special bearing on this point of the archbishop's case, for it intrepidly requests of her majesty to ponder well the terms of her oath to the Pope, and to consider whether they could be reconciled with the language of her oath to the Kingdom, taken on the day of her coronation. It therefore repeats, as it were, to her majesty's face, what he had publicly intimated in his examination before Brookes; namely that she must needs be forsworn either to the Bishop of Rome or to the state of England. It concludes by protesting, that if her majesty would permit him, he would appear at Rome in person, conformably to the canonical citation, trusting that God would enable him to defend the truth there as honestly as he had defended it in his own country.

These two papers, observes Mr. Le Bas, were addressed by Cranmer when he was under sentence of death, to one who had notoriously closed the gates of mercy against him. He must have known that he was regarded by the Queen as the instrument of her sainted mother's degradation, as a conspirator against her own title to the crown of England as an apostate from the doctrine of the Catholic church, and as a traitor to the apostolic authority of its head. He must, in short, have been conscious that he was in the very jaws of destruction. And yet, in this fatal extremity, he suffers not one syllable of deprecation to escape him. Unwilling as he had been to die under the imputation of treason, he was well content to suffer for the truth of God; and accordingly, presents to his exasperated and implacable sovereign a firm but respectful vindication of the principles which she abhorred. And this, too, he did at a time when the fires of persecution were blazing throughout the land, and when his two most honored associates were in readiness to be offered up. These letters, therefore, are invaluable as monuments of his hitherto immovable fidelity to the cause of the reformation.

The office of answering these addresses was consigned by her majesty to Cardinal Pole. His performance, in obedience to the mandate, is dated November the 6th; and on one account, it is quite as interesting as the letters to which it replies; for it proves beyond all possibility of contradiction, that up to that period likewise, the fortitude of Cranmer remained wholly unshaken. It speaks of him throughout as an incurably blind and pertinacious heretic; charges him with covetousness and ambition, with deliberate malice, abject ignorance, and gross perjury; and declares that if he is not plucked out of the lion's mouth, he must inevitably be undone both in body and in soul. Language like this could only be addressed to one whose courage had, to that hour, withstood every assault. It would, therefore, be most injurious to doubt that if Cranmer had been called to suffer at the same time with Latimer and Ridley, and before his powers of resistance had been undermined by temptation and artifice, he would then, like them, have poured out his soul to death with the heroism of a Christian martyr.

A report of the last proceedings against the archbishop had been dispatched to Rome immediately on their termination. On the 29th of November, the eighty days appointed for his appearance had elapsed. On the 4th of December, at the instance of the Cardinal de Puteo, he was sentenced to excommunication and deprived of the archbishopric; and on the 11th of the same month, the administration of the see of Canterbury was conferred on Cardinal Pole. The final executor letter of the Pope was dated on the 14th of December. In faithful conformity with the canonical fiction adverted to above, this document affirms that having been cited to Rome, he took no care to appear; and by this neglect had incurred the guilt of contumacy. It then proceeded to declare (much in the same spirit of fiction), that he, Pope Paul IVth, sitting in the throne of justice and having before his eyes God alone who is the righteous Lord, and judges the world in righteousness, did make his definitive sentence, decreeing the said Thomas Cranmer guilty of the crimes of heresy and of other enormities and unmindful of his soul's health, and of the doctrines of the fathers, and traditions and usages of the Church, more especially in the matter of the Sacrament of our Lord's body and blood, respecting which he had introduced the perversions of those arch-heretics, Berengarius, Wycliffe, and Luther. For these causes, he, the Pope, declared him excommunicated and commanded the Bishops of London and Ely (Bonner and Thirlby) first to degrade him from his archbishopric, and then to deliver him to the secular arm.

It was not till the 14th of February that this pontifical mandate was carried into execution. On that day the archbishop was summoned to appear before the two papal delegates in St. Mary's church. When he was brought into their presence, their commission was recited to him, in which it was specified that all things had been indifferently examined on both parts, and counsel heard, as well on the behalf of their majesties who were the accusers, as also on the behalf of the accused; so that he wanted nothing which was needful to his defense. Here was another fictitious statement of such enormous impudence that it extorted an indignant exclamation from Cranmer, who, although he was a most accomplished canonist, appears to have been quite unable to comprehend the canonical scruples which dictated these insulting and mendacious formalities. It was notorious, he said, that he had been so closely imprisoned that it would have been utterly impossible for him to employ an advocate, even if his cause had been finally adjudged in his own country. How then, was he to produce witnesses or appoint counsel to represent him at Rome? God, he added, must needs punish this open and shameless lying.

[*The Life of Thomas Cramer*, 207-224]

Thomas Cranmer was sentenced to death by being burnt at the stake. He remained a prisoner until March 21, 1556, the day his sentence was to be carried out. At about 9 in the morning, he was escorted by several members of the council from the prison of Bocardo to St. Mary's church. The day was described as a 'foul and rainy day' and Cranmer was also accompanied by two friars who left him at the church where he was expected to recant.

But when he came to the place where the holy bishops and martyrs of God, Hugh Latimer and Nicholas Ridley, were burnt before him for the confession of the truth, kneeling down, he prayed to God; and not long tarrying in his prayers, putting off his garments to his shirt, he prepared himself to death. His shirt was made long, down to his feet. His feet were bare; likewise his head, when both his caps were off, was so bare that one hair could not be seen upon it. His beard was long and thick, covering his face with marvelous gravity. Such a countenance of gravity moved the hearts both of his friends and of his enemies.

Then the Spanish Friars, John and Richard, of whom mention was made before, began to exhort him and play their parts with him afresh, but with vain and lost labor. Cranmer, with steadfast purpose abiding in the profession of his doctrine, gave his hand to certain old men, and others that stood by bidding them farewell.

And when he had thought to have done so likewise to Ely, the said Ely drew back his hand and refused, saying it was not lawful to salute heretics, and specially such a one as falsely returned to the opinions that he had forsworn. And if he had known before that he would have done so, he would never have used his company so familiarly and chide those sergeants and citizens which had not refused to give him their hands. This Ely was a priest lately made and student in divinity, being then one of the fellows of Brasenose.

Then was an iron chain tied about Cranmer, whom when they perceived to be more steadfast than that he could be moved from his sentence, they commanded the fire to be set to him.

And when the wood was kindled and the fire began to burn near him stretching out his arm, he put his right hand into the flame, which he held so steadfast and immovable (saving that once with the same hand he wiped his face), that all men might see his hand burned before his body was touched. His body did so abide the burning of the flame with such constancy and steadfastness, that standing always in one place without moving his body, he seemed to move no more than the stake to which he was bound; his eyes were lifted up into heaven, and oftentimes he repeated "this unworthy right hand", so long as his voice would suffer him; and using often the words of Stephen, "Lord Jesus, receive my spirit", in the greatness of the flame he gave up the ghost.

[*The Life of Thomas Cramer*, 244-247]

Chapter 5: The Reign of Elizabeth I

Queen Elizabeth I is one of England's most famous rulers and is often credited with bringing England out of the dark ages. Although her life has been written about extensively, the following trials offer a fresh insight into her reign.

James, Earl of Bothwell

James Hepburn, 4th Earl of Bothwell, Duke of Orkney and Shetland, was born circa 1536 to Patrick 3rd Earl of Bothwell and Agnes, daughter of Henry, Lord Sinclair. In 1556, he succeeded his father's titles, lands and hereditary offices including Lord High Admiral of Scotland. In 1560, he was sent on a mission to France and detoured into Denmark where he either married, or possibly seduced, Anne daughter of Christopher Thorren. He later deserted her and returned to Scotland.

Having gained favor of Mary Stuart, she appointed him as a member of her Privy Council, but he was soon implicated in riots and partisan disorders and was ordered to leave Edinburgh. After the plot to seize Queen Elizabeth, he was imprisoned in Edinburgh castle, but managed to escape. He was later captured and placed in the Tower of London. He gained his freedom and fled to France, having eluded capture by the Queen several times.

In 1556, he was united by 'handfasting' to Janet Betoun of Cranstoun Riddell. Despite everything that he had been involved in, he became one of Mary's chief advisers. She required a protector, but her husband, the 'feeble Darnley' could not fulfill her requirements and the Earl of Bothwell caught her eye for many reasons. Mary took refuge with him at Dunbar and presented him with several estates including a castle making him the most powerful noble in Southern Scotland.

He accompanied Mary on the night of 9 February, 1567, in which a violent explosion claimed the life of Darnley. Suspicions about the earl's involvement in the death of Mary's husband led to an investigation by Darnley's father and gained enough evidence to arrest Bothwell and place him on trial.

The trial of James Earl Bothwell for the murder of Henry Lord Darnley, husband to Mary Queen of Scots, at the senate-house of Edinburgh, April 12. 1567. The 9th of Elizabeth.

At the justice court of our sovereign Lady the Queen, held and begun in the senate-house of Edinburgh, the 12th Day of April, 1567 by the noble and potent Lord Archibald Earl of Argyle, Lord Campbell, and Lord Justice General for our sovereign lady in all the parts of her realm, where there's a convention and lawful assembly of judges.

In this court appeared personally in judgment Mr. John Spence of Conde, and Robert Crichton of Choc, advocates for our sovereign lady, and in her name; and there the said Mr. John Spence produced letters from our said sovereign lady, executed and indorsed with the summons: the tenor of which letters, endorsements, and summons hereafter follows.

The commission of Mary Queen of Scots, to try James Earl Bothwell, for the murder of her husband Henry Lord Darnley.

Mary, by the grace of God, Queen of Scotland. To our beloved Masters William Purves, William Lawson, Gawin Ramsey messengers, ours sheriffs in that part conjunctly and severally constitute, greeting. Whereas it has been most humbly remonstrated to us by our beloved and faithful counselors, Mr. John Spence of Conde, and Robert Crichton of Choc, our advocates, that they are informed that our well beloved cousin and counselor Matthew Earl of Lennox, father of our most dear spouse, has asserted that James Earl Bothwell, Lord Hallis and Creighton, Sec. and some others, were the contrivers of the traitorous, cruel, detestable, and abominable murder of his highness, committed the 9th day of February last past, in the dead of the night, in his palace, for the time being in our city of Edinburgh near the church in the fields, willfully and with premeditated felony; and have declared their suspicion of the said earl and others as having committed the said crime and horrid murder. And having therefore resolved that the truth of it should be tried in a course of justice, with all possible diligence and brevity, we have by advice of the lords of our Privy Council, and also at the humble request and petition of the said Earl Bothwell made to us, and in our presence, offering to submit himself to a fair trial of what he is charged with according to the laws of the land, ordered a court of justice to meet in the senate-house of Edinburgh on the 12th of April next ensuing, in order to do justice upon the said earl and others for committing the said cruel and abominable crime and offence, as is more at large set forth in an act inserted in the registers of our said Privy Council. Therefore it is our pleasure, and we enjoin and command you most expressly, that incontinent these our letters seen, you proceed and in our name and authority, summon the said Matthew Earl of Lennox at his own house to appear together with all others of our subjects, having and pretending to have interest in this cause by public proclamation made at the Mercat Crosses of our towns of Edinburgh, Dumbarton, Glasgow, Lanark, and other places necessary to the end that they may appear before our judges, or their deputies, in our senate house at Edinburgh, on the said 12th day of April, next ensuing, and join with us in the prosecution of this cause, by giving them a summons. And in case that they don't appear, we order that our judges, or their deputies, shall proceed and give sentence the same day according to the laws and customs of our realm without any further delay or prolongation; and that you summon every one of them to appear the same day under the penalty of a fine of 40£ Sterling, for which they shall answer before us as for their own act and deed and for this end, we give to every one of you conjunctly and severally our full power by these our letters, to the intent that you may deliver and execute them duly, and indorse them to him who shall be the bearer thereof. Given under our seal at Edinburgh the 27th day of March, and of our reign the 25th, in the year 1567. Signed accordingly by advice of the Queen's council,

Mary.

What was indorsed on the back of the said commission.

The 19th day of March, 1567. I William Purves messenger and sheriff constitute for that part, according to the command of the letters of our sovereign lady, and in her name and authority, have summoned Matthew Earl of Lennox, and all others of her majesty's subjects, having and pretending to have interest in what is within specified by public proclamation, made at the Mercat Cross of the city of Edinburgh, in order to appear before the judges or their deputies in the senate-house at Edinburgh, the 12th day of April next ensuing, and to prosecute and join with our said sovereign lady in the cause herein set forth with the summons as it is mentioned in the said commission; a copy of which I have affixed to the cross of the said Mercat, in presence of John Anderson and David Land, and many others. And in further testimony of this my execution and endorsement, I have hereto set my seal.

Signed, William Purves.

Another summons. The last day of March but one, the first and second days of April, in the year above mentioned, I Gawin Ramsey, messenger, and one of the sheriffs constitute for that part, went according to the command contained in the letters of our sovereign lady, and in her name and authority summoned the said Matthew Earl of Lennox, particularly at his houses in Glasgow and Dumbarton. And whereas I sought him, but could not find him in person, nor her majesty's other subjects, pretending to have interest in the prosecution of the cause herein set forth, I made a proclamation at the Mercat Crosses of the towns of Glasgow, Dumbarton, and Lanark, in order to make them appear before the judge or his deputy at the said senate-house of Edinburgh on the said 12th day of April next ensuing, and to join in the prosecution with the Queen our said sovereign lady, in the action within mentioned with the summons, as it is there declared and according to the form and tenor of her letters, of which I have set up a copy on each of the said crosses in those markets. I have done and executed the above before the witnesses that follow, *viz.* George Herbesoun, Nicholas Andrew, Robert Letteric, Messenger; William Smollet, John Hamilton, James Bannatine, Robert Hamilton, and many others. And in further testimony hereof, I have signed these presents with my sign manual. Gawin Ramsey, Messenger.

Another summons:

The first day of April, 1567. I William Lawson, messenger, and sheriff constitute for that part, went according to the command signified in the commission of our sovereign lady to the Mercat Cross of Perth, and there by public proclamation made according to law, I summoned Matthew Earl of Lennox and all other subjects of our said sovereign lady, having and pretending to have interests in order to prosecute James Earl Bothwell, Lord of Hallis and Creighton, &c. and others, for the cruel murder committed on the King and have affixed a copy on the said cross, according to the form and tenor of these presents. And this in presence of the witnesses hereafter named *viz.* James Marshal, Alexander Borthwith, and John Anderson, Messengers, and many others. And in further testimony of this my execution and endorsement, I have signed these presents with my sign manual. Signed accordingly, William Lawson, Messenger, with my own hand.

The indictment. You James Earl Bothwell, Lord of Hallis, Creighton, &c. are indicted on account of the cruel and horrid murder of the most excellent, most high and most mighty prince the King, the late most dear spouse of the Queen's majesty, our sovereign lady, committed in the dead of the night at his house near the church of the fields in this city, as he was taking his rest, by treasonably setting fire to a great quantity of gunpowder in the said house, by the violence whereof the whole house was blown up into the air and the King himself by you killed traitorously and cruelly, willfully, and by premeditated felony. And this you did the 9th day of February last past, in the dead of the night as aforesaid, as is notorious, and you cannot deny.

Upon the producing of which letters, so executed, indorsed, and published, the said advocate demanded an act and instrument in the court, and required that the judge should proceed according to the form of them.

These letters being read in judgment with the endorsements, the judge, by virtue thereof, ordered the said James Earl Bothwell to be called as defendant of the one part, and Matthew Earl of Lennox, and all other subjects of our said sovereign reign lady, pretending to prosecute this matter, as plaintiffs on the other part; that they might appear in court, and exhibit their complaints and defenses, according to the laws of the realm.

And immediately appeared in judgment the said James Earl Bothwell, and entered the court in person; after which he chose Master David Bothwick of Lutchill, and Mr. Edmund Hay for his advocates, who appearing also in judgment, were admitted by the judge for that effect.

Appeared also Mr. Henry Kinloch, calling himself proctor for his Master Andrew Lord Errol, Constable of Scotland, and alleged that the constable of the realm had at all times been owned to be the only judge competent of men of that quality when accused of having committed murder and bloodshed near the prince's chamber, and four miles round; and therefore his said master being at present constable of this realm, ought to be judge to James Earl Bothwell, and others his accomplices, summoned to appear this day and to be charged with the above mentioned act of the cruel murder of Henry King of Scotland. And in case that Archibald Earl of Argyle, as justice-general of this realm, proceed and take cognizance of this fact, the said Mr. Henry Proctor above mentioned, protested solemnly that this trial should not be prejudicial to the said constable, his office, right, tide, profit, jurisdiction, and possession, in any manner whatever; but that he might exercise his said jurisdiction in all such causes for time to come according to the seizing of his office, and take cognizance of them as his predecessors had been used to do in the like case. This he would make appear by the possession which his predecessors had of it at all times and otherwise; and he required that this protestation should be registered in the acts, and affirmed that the jurisdiction of the present judge ought not to be allowed in this case.

The judge having no regard to this protestation, did by advice of his assessor, decree that he would take cognizance of the fact notwithstanding, since nothing had been produced by the said Mr. Henry to verify the contents of what he had alleged and protested of all which the Earl Bothwell demanded an act and instrument.

The said Matthew Earl of Lennox, and other subjects of our sovereign lady, having and pretending to have interest in this prosecution, being called several times to appear and to join with the said advocates in prosecuting the said action, there appeared Robert Cunningham who called himself servant to the said Matthew Earl of Lennox and exhibited a writing, signed with his own hand in full court, as being authorized thereto, and made a protestation and requisition of the whole, agreeable to the said writing of which the tenor follows.

The protestation of the Earl of Lennox.

My lords, I am come hither, being sent by my master my Lord of Lennox, to declare the cause why he is this day absent, having full power from him for that effect, as the truth is. The cause then of his absence is the shortness of the time allowed him, and that he is hindered to have his friends and servants, who ought to accompany him for his honor, and the safety of his person, considering the strength of the opposite party, and that he has no assistance from any of his friends, but must stand by himself: therefore his lordship has commanded me to require another competent day according to the importance of this cause, that he may be here present; but if you will proceed now, I protest that I may without offence to any person, make use of the authority committed to me by my said lord and master, of which I demand an act.

Item, I protest that if those who assist in this judgment and inquest upon the persons accused, do undertake to acquit them of the King's murder, that it shall be held as a voluntary error and not of ignorance; since is notoriously known who they are that have murdered the King, as my said lord and master affirms; of which protestation I require an act thus signed, Robert Cunningham, of the production of which writing and protestation the said Robert demanded an act and instrument.

The judge considering the writing and protestation produced by the said Robert Cunningham, and having regard to the letters sent to our sovereign lady by Matthew Earl of Lennox, also produced and read in judgment, the tenor of which is hereafter inserted; by which letters and writing the said Earl of Lennox requires that a brief and summary trial may be made of this cause and having also regard to the act, and the order thereupon taken by the lords of the Privy Council, and other such things; and to what the advocates insist upon as to the same fact, requiring that justice may be done to the said Earl Bothwell; and taking notice likewise of the request and demand which he has made that the whole may be thoroughly examined; the judge, by the advice of the lords and barons his assistants, found that they ought to proceed to the decision of the said cause the same day according to the laws of the realm, notwithstanding the writing and protestation produced by the said Robert Cunningham, and that in the mean time he shall be admitted to join with and assist the said advocates for the final trial of the said cause, if he thinks good.

Copies of the letters sent to the Queen by the Earl of Lennox.

Madam, I return most humble thanks to your majesty for the gracious and consolatory letters which I received the 24th of this present month; by which I perceive that is your majesty's pleasure to put off the trial of this late execrable fact, till the Parliament meets. May it please your majesty to consider that though I be assured that your highness must needs think the time long till the truth of this fact be found out, and the authors of it punished according to their demerits; yet I most humbly beg pardon of your majesty for troubling and importuning you so often as I am forced to do, the affair being such as touches me so near; and therefore most humbly request that your majesty would take in good part my advice as follows: It is, that it is too long to wait for the meeting of the Parliament; besides, this is not an affair of that sort which uses to be treated of in Parliament, but being such, and of so great importance, it is evident to every one it ought rather to be inquired into with all diligence that the authors may suffer an exemplary punishment. I know that your majesty is much more able to judge of it than I; but being informed that certain placards or writings have been affixed to the gate of the senate-house of Edinburgh, which answered to your majesty's first and second proclamation, and named some persons as authors of the said cruel murder, I most humbly request of your majesty, for the honor of God, and for that of your majesty and your realm, and for the welfare and peace of it, that you would be pleased not only to cause those who are named in the said placards to be apprehended and put in safe custody, but likewise to assemble your nobility with all possible diligence, and then to summon by proclamation the authors of the said placards to appear for the ends therein mentioned; and if they appear not, your majesty may by the advice of your nobility and council, set at liberty those who are therein named. Your majesty will do an honorable act in bringing this matter to this issue, that according as the matter shall appear to your majesty, you may punish and chastise the authors of this cruel fact; or if the said placards shall be found false and of no validity, those who are charged may be acquitted and set at liberty according to your majesty's good pleasure. Madam, I pray God almighty to take your majesty into his protection and safeguard, and to preserve you in health and happy prosperity. From Houston the 26th of February.

A second letter from the Earl of Lennox.

Madam, I beseech your majesty to attend to what follows: your highness in your last letters acquainted me that if there were any names in the placards, which were set up at the door of the senate-house of Edinburgh, of such persons as I thought worthy of condemnation, for the murder of the King your majesty's husband, you would, according to my advice, make it your business to bring them to trial according to the laws of this realm, and as the nature of the crime required. May it therefore please your majesty to know that from the time I received your said letters, I always expected that some of those bloody murderers would be made openly known to you; but since I perceive they are not, I cannot find in my heart to conceal them from you any longer. Your majesty therefore has here the names of those whom I greatly suspect, *viz.* The Earl of Bothwell, Sir James Balfour, and Gilbert Balfour his brother; Master David Chamers; Black Master John Spence; the Sieur Francifcus Bajlian, John de Bourdeaux, and Joseph, the brother of Davy Rizio: whom I most humbly beseech your majesty according to my former petition, not only to cause to be apprehended and committed to safe custody, but also with all diligence to assemble your nobility and council, and then to take such advice about the fact of the persons above-mentioned, as they may be duly examined. And as I hope, so I make no doubt, but that by proceeding in this manner, the spirit of God will assist toward bringing it to a good conclusion. Herein your majesty will do an act holy and honorable for yourself, who are a party, and highly satisfy those who stand in any relation to the deceased, whom you loved so dearly. And not doubting that your majesty will give proper orders for the whole, according to the importance of the matter (as I most humbly beseech you to do) I shall pray to almighty God to take you into his protection and to give you long life and health with grace, that your reign may be both long and prosperous. Houston, March 17.

The names of the judges or jury deputed for the absolution of the Earl of Bothwell.

Andrew Earl of Roth's, George Earl of Caithness, Gilbert Earl of Cassils, Lord John Hamilton, Commentator of Arbroth, son to the duke, James Lord Ross, Robert Lord Semple, John Maxwell Lord Harris, Lawrence Lord Oliphant, John Master of Forbes, John Gourdon of Lochinvar, Robert Lord Boyde, James Cockburn of Lanton, John Sommerville of Cumbusnethan, Moubray of Barnbougal, and Ogilbye of Boyne.

The above named being chosen, admitted, and sworn to give sentence according to custom, and the Earl of Bothwell being accused by indictment of the crime above declared, and submitting and referring himself to the sentence of the said judges, they went out of the senate-house to another place, and after having long disputed together upon all the articles of the said accusation, they did each of them, one after another, declare the said James Earl of Bothwell quit and absolved of the whole and every part of the murder of the King, and in general of whatever depended on the said accusation.

Afterwards the said George Earl of Caithness, chancellor or president at the said trial (i.e. foreman of the jury) as well in his own name as that of the other judges, demanded an act to the end that as well the advocates, as the said Robert Cunningham, having a proxy from the Earl of Lennox, and all others whomsoever, might be debarred hereafter from producing any other writing or proofs whatsoever, in order to support the said indictment, and that the judges might not be induced to give any other opinion than they had done before; the rather because no body had proved the truth of the accusation, nor so much as any part of it, and that no accuser appeared but the above-mentioned, who were presented in order to carry on the trial and therefore the judges having regard to the same, declared him free as far as they could have any knowledge of the fact, with a protestation that this might not be afterwards imputed to them as a fault. Which act and protestation, when the said Earl of Caithness president and some of the judges above-mentioned, returned to the court in the senate-house and before the pronouncing of the aforesaid sentence, was at the request of the said Earl of Caithness, read publicly and in full court and he demanded an act and instrument of it, protesting as above.

Extracted from the registers of the acts of our sovereign lady's court of justice, by me John Bellenden of Auchnoule, Knight, and clerk general of the said court, under my sign manual. Signed, John Bellenden, Clerk of the Court.

Note, that at the same time protestation was made by George Earl of Caithness, Chancellor of the said Assize, that the said dictate or indictment was not in this point true, *viz.* alleging the murder to be committed the 9th day of February, for that indeed the murder was committed the next day, being the 10th day in the morning at two hours after midnight, which in law was and ought to be truly accounted the 10th day; and so the acquittal that way, but caviling defended.

The proclamations and placards in answer to them mentioned in the trial, and others that happened after, were as follows.

Incontinent after the murder of the King, the 10th of February, 1566, a proclamation was issued, setting forth that whoever would discover the murderers should have 2000£ Sterling. This proclamation was answered by a placard fixed on the door of the senate-house of Edinburgh on the 16th day of February in form as follows:

Whereas public notice has been given that whosoever will discover the murderers of the King, should have 2000£ Sterling; I who have made inquiry by those who committed the act it self, affirm that the authors of the said murder are the Earl of Bothwell, Sir James Balfout, the Curate Flisk, Master David Chamber's and Black Master John Spens, who above all was the principal author of this murder and the Queen, who consented to it at the persuasion of the said Earl of Bothwell, by the witchcraft of the Lady Buccleugh.

Upon this, another proclamation was issued the same day requiring the person who had set up the placard to appear, own, and subscribe it in person that he might have the sum promised by the former proclamation and more if he deserved it, as the Queen and her council should think fit.

To this the following answer was given and set up at the same place the day following.

Forasmuch as a proclamation has been issued since I set up my former, requiring that I should come to subscribe and own it; for answer I do likewise require, that the money may be consigned into the hands of some man of substance, and I will appear next Sunday, and four others with me and then I will subscribe and maintain what I have said. Moreover, I require that the Sieur Francis Bastein, and Joseph the Queen's goldsmith, may be apprehended; and I will declare what each of them and their accomplices did in particular.

To this no answer was returned.

Though the Earl of Bothwell was acquitted as above-mentioned, yet knowing that the world did still esteem him guilty, he did, in order to clear himself further, set up a paper in the market-place bearing that albeit he had been acquitted by law, yet to make his innocence the more manifest, he was ready to try the same by single combat with any man of honorable birth and reputation who would accuse him of the King's murder.

To which answer was made by another placard, set up immediately after in the same place, that forasmuch as the said Earl of Bothwell had caused a placard to be set up, signed with his own hand, whereby he challenged any man of quality and of a fair reputation who would and dared to say that he was guilty of the death of the King, adding that he who said it, or went about to import that charge, should be forced to eat his words: a gentleman of honor and good renown accepted his offer, and said he would prove by the law of arms that he was the principal author of that horrid murder, of which the judges had rashly acquitted him for fear of death after so much enquiry had been made into it. And whereas the King of France and the Queen of England required by their ambassadors that the said murder might be punished, he also entreats their majesties to insist with the Queen, his sovereign lady, that by her consent a time and place may be appointed in their countries to combat the earl, according to the law of arms in their presence, or in that of their deputies; at which time and place he promises and swears on the word of a gentleman, to be present and do his duty provided their majesties will by proclamation, grant safe conduct to him and his company to pass and re-pass through their dominions without any molestation. He refers it to the judgment of the readers and hearers what just cause he has to desire this of the King of France and the Queen of England, and by this he advertises the rest of the murderers to prepare themselves; for he will give each of them the like challenge and publish their names in writing, that they may be known to every body.

To this Bothwell made no reply.

Some time afterwards, Bothwell was constrained to fly the Kingdom and went first to the Orcades and then to the isles of Shetland, where being reduced to extreme want, he turned pirate: but being in danger of being taken, he went to Denmark; where, not being able to give a good account of himself, he was taken into custody, and afterwards being known by some merchants, he was clap up close prisoner; and after a loathsome imprisonment for ten years, that and other miseries made him distracted and thus he came to a most ignominious death, suitable to his vile and wicked course of life.

[Emlyn, Sollom. *A Complete Collection of State Trials-V-6.* 78-82]

Following the trial, Mary announced her intention to marry Bothwell as soon as Bothwell's divorce from his wife was decreed by civil court, based upon his adultery with a maidservant. Following the ceremony, he was created Duke of Orkney and Shetland. His rise to power was short lived and soon nobles from both religions united to induce his destruction. Meanwhile, troops loyal to Mary were deserting and Bothwell deserted Mary for Norway.

In 1568, he was removed to Sweden and corresponded with Mary, though he was unable to restore himself in her favor. Mary demanded a divorce that was granted in 1570. Bothwell was later placed in the castle of Dragsholm or Adelersbourg in Zealand where the close and solitary confinement in addition to the lack of hope of his release, proved too taxing on his health and he became insane and died in April 1578, and buried in the church of Faareveille. In 1858, his supposed coffin was opened and a portrait was taken of the head and body, now in the museum of the Society of Antiquaries in Scotland.

Thomas Howard, Duke of Norfolk

Thomas Howard, 4th Duke of Norfolk, was born circa 1536 in Kenninghall, Norfolk England to Henry Howard, Earl of Surrey who was executed for his alleged treasonous activities in 1547. Thomas was restored to his father's titles in 1553 and succeeded the title of duke the following year after the death of his grandfather. In 1556, he married Mary Fitzalan, but she died after childbirth. The following year, he married Margaret Audley. In 1559 Norfolk joined the Knights of the Garter. Queen Elizabeth utilized him to command English forces in Scotland as Lieutenant-General of the North.

In 1567, Margaret died and Thomas married Elizabeth Leyburne, but she only lived a few months after the marriage ceremony. Some historians suggest that he began to seek the hand of Mary Stuart in marriage.

Thomas was in charge of the commissioners investigating the murder of Mary's husband, Henry Lord Darnley and a certain amount of political and religious posturing occurred during the conference. One of the key ingredients of the conference was the Casket Letters. The Casket Letters were eight letters and poems written in French, alleged by the Earl of Morton to be written by Queen Mary of Scots to the Earl of Bothwell. The validity of the letters was questionable and did not prove to be sufficient evidence for prosecution. Many theories exist about the letters and they have and will provide fuel for historians to debate regarding their authenticity. The original letters have disappeared, but copies remain.

Mary saw the marriage to Norfolk as a means of extricating herself from prison. Norfolk began to correspond with Mary as soon as the conference concluded, and they exchanged several gifts. He had apparently proposed to her, and though they never met, they were secretly betrothed. When Elizabeth received that information, she presented many opportunities for him to disclose his desire to marry Mary, but he denied everything.

He was implicated in planning a rebellion, but it had failed due to the overall lack of support. In 1569, one of his initial supporters gathered a large faction to free Mary. When information arrived at London, Norfolk was arrested for treason and placed in the Tower. He admitted to Elizabeth his consideration to marry Mary, but had always intended to seek her approval. Following his release, he continued to exchange correspondence and gifts with Mary. Mary and Norfolk used the Italian banker Ridolfi to pass correspondence between them all the while acting as a double agent reporting the contents of their letters, although no incriminating evidence was discovered. Norfolk sought aid from the Duke of Alva in the form of military support for a religious rebellion in England, but no evidence was presented of Mary's involvement.

A warrant for the arrest of Norfolk was issued on the charge of treason and was arrested at his London home and returned to the Tower. During his trial, efforts were made to incriminate Mary, but none were brought forward. Norfolk was executed on Tower Hill on 2 June, 1572.

Following is the full recorded trial often omitted from biographies possibly due to its length. Because of many attempts to shorten the transcript to fit into some biographies, I discovered many errors in the form of omissions and incorrect quotes utilized by some modern sources.

> The trial of Thomas Howard, Duke of Norfolk, before the Lords Westminster for high-treason, January 16. 1571. 14 Elizabeth.
>
> First of all, there was prepared in Westminster-Hall a large scaffold, about a foot distant from the chancery court and to the same scaffold a long passage, about six foot broad and high built all the way as far as to the all the common pleas bar. In the middle, on the south side of the scaffold, was erected a chair, somewhat higher than the rest, with a cloth of state for the Lord High Steward of England, who for that day was George Earl of Shrewsbury. On both sides of the Lord High Steward sat the lords in this order: on the right hand of the Lord High Steward; Reynold Earl of Kent, Thomas Earl of Sussex, Ambrose of Warwick, Earl of Pembroke, Robert Earl of Leicester,

Lord Clinton, Lord High Admiral of England, William Lord Burleigh, James Lord Mountjoy, Lord Wentworth, Lewis Lord Mordant, Lord Chandois, Oliver Lord St. John of Bletshoe. On the left hand; Earl of Worcester, Earl of Huntingdon, Francis Earl of Bedford, Edward Earl of Hertford, Viscount Hereford, William Lord Howard of Essingham, Lord Grey of Wilton, Lord Sandes, Lord Burgh, Lord St. John, Lord Rich, Lord North, Thomas Lord Buckhurst, Lord De La Were.

On both sides of the Lord High Steward, on a lower form at the lord's feet, sat the judges, *viz.* on the right hand; Sir Robert Catlin, Lord Chief Justice of England; Sir James Dyer, Lord Chief Justice of the Common Pleas; Sir Edward Saunders, Lord Chief Baron of the Exchequer.

On the left hand, the rest of the judges sat according to their order.

At the feet of the Lord High Steward, directly before him, in a hollow place cut in the scaffold for that purpose, sat Mr. Miles Sands Clerk of the Crown with his secondary. Next, beneath the justices in the same row, sat at the right hand, *viz.* on the east-side, Sir Francis Knowles, with three of the Queen's household, and Sir Walter Mildmay, Chancellor of the Exchequer with several others of the Queen's Privy Council. On the left side, on the west part of the scaffold in the same degree, sat next the judges, Dr. Wilson, Master of the Requests, and several other persons of note.

On the north part of the scaffold, directly before the bar where the prisoner came, sat Mr. Nicholas Barham the Queen's Sergeant, Mr. Gilbert Gerard the Queen's Attorney-General, Mr. Thomas Bromley Solicitor-General, and Mr. Thomas Wilbraham the Queen's Attorney of the Court of Wards. On the right hand, by permission, sat Mr. William Fleetwood Recorder of London; and on their left hands were Mr. Thomas Norton, who wrote down this trial upon the scaffold as also garter King at arms, two gentlemen ushers, and two sergeants at arms.

The Lord High Steward being set in his chair, and all the lords and others set in their places with a great number of people in the hall, the hall being kept by the Knight Marshal and the Warden of the Fleet and their servants with tipstaffs; about half an hour past eight in the morning, the Lord High Steward stood up at his chair bare-headed, and Mr. Norris the gentleman usher holding the white rod before him, Littleton the sergeant at arms made proclamation as follows:

My lord's grace, the Queen's majesty's commissioner, High-Steward of England, commanded every man to keep silence on pain of imprisonment, and to hear the Queen's majesty's commission read. Which then was read by the Clerk of the Crown.

Then the said Lord High Steward sat down again in his chair, and the gentleman-usher delivered him the white rod, which he held in his hand a great while; and after the indictment read, redelivered it to the gentleman-usher, who held it up before him all the time of the arraignment. Then Littleton the sergeant again made order, and proclaimed thus: Thomas Edwards, Sergeant at Arms, return thy precept; which being put in immediately, he delivered to the Clerk of the Crown the names of the peers summoned for the trial.

Then Littleton the sergeant again made order, and proclaimed thus: all earls, viscounts, and barons, summoned to appear this day, every one answer to your names on pain of future peril. Then were all the lords called in order by their names of Baptism, and surnames of dignity, beginning at the ancientness; and every one severally, as he was called, stood and signified their appearance.

Their order of ancientry as they were called was thus: Reynold Earl of Kent, William Earl of Worcester, Thomas Earl of Sussex, Henry Earl of Huntingdon, Ambrose Earl of Warwick, Francis Earl of Bedford, Earl of Pembroke, Edward Earl of Hertford, Robert Earl of Leicester, Walter Viscount Hereford, Lord Clinton, William Lord Howard of Essingham, William Lord Burleigh, Lord Grey of Wilton, James Lord Mountjoy, Lord Sandes, Lord Wentworth, Lord Burgh, Lewis Lord Mordant, Lord St. John, Robert Lord Rich, Lord North, Lord Chandois, Oliver Lord St. John of Bletshoe, Thomas Lord Buckburst, Lord De La Ware.

Then the sergeant again made order and proclaimed thus: Robert Catlin Knight, Chief Justice of England, return thy certiorari and thy precept; which was immediately delivered to the Clerk of Crown and read. The sergeant again made order and proclaimed thus: Lieutenant of the Tower of London, return thy *habeas corpus*, and bring forth thy prisoner Thomas Duke of Norfolk.

Then was the duke brought upon the long half pace to the bar, Sir Owen Hopton Lieutenant of the Tower leading him by the right hand, and Sir Peter Garow by the left, and so he was placed at the bar, they still holding him by the arms, the chamberlain of the tower with the axe of the tower standing with the edge towards Sir Peter while behind the duke stood Mr. Henry Skipwith, who after the duke's imprisonment, was appointed to attend on him in the Tower.

Then the duke with a haughty look, and oft biting his lip, surveyed the lords on each side of him. In the mean time the Lieutenant of the Tower delivered in his return; then the sergeant made order and proclamation of silence, while the Clerk of the Crown said to the duke thus: Thomas Duke of Norfolk, late of Remming-Hall in the county of Norfolk, hold up thy hand: which the duke did very lustily. Then the Clerk of the Crown read the indictment, the tenor whereof is thus:

Middlesex.

The jury present and say in behalf of our lady the Queen, that Thomas Duke of Norfolk, late of Remming-Hall in the county of Norfolk, as a false traitor against the most illustrious and Christian princess Elizabeth Queen of England, France, and Ireland, defender of the faith, &c. and his sovereign lady, not having the fear of God in his heart, nor weighing his due allegiance, but seduced by the instigation of the Devil, contrary to that cordial affection and bounden duty that true and faithful subjects of our said lady the

Queen do bear, and of right ought to bear towards our said lady the Queen; and intending to cut off and destroy the said Queen Elizabeth, the 22nd day of September in the 11th year of the reign of our said sovereign Lady Queen Elizabeth, and divers other days and times before and after at the charter-house in the county of Middlesex, has falsely, maliciously, and traitorously conspired, imagined and gone about, not only to deprive, depose, and cast out the said Queen, his sovereign lady from her royal dignity, title, power, and government of her Kingdom of England; but, also to bring about and compass the death and final destruction of our said sovereign lady the Queen, and to make and raise sedition in the said Kingdom of England, and to spread a miserable civil war amongst the subjects of our said lady the Queen, and to procure and make an insurrection rebellion against our said lady the Queen, his supreme and natural lady, and so to make public war within the realm of England, contrary to your said lady the Queen, and the government of her said Kingdom, and to endeavor a change and alteration of the sincere worship of God, well and religiously established in the said Kingdom; and also totally to subvert and destroy the whole constitution of the said state, so happily instituted and ordained in all its parts; with divers aliens and foreigners, not the subjects of our said lady the Queen, hostilely to invade the said Kingdom of England, and to make cruel war against our said lady the Queen and her dominions.

And for the compassing and bringing to pass all the said wicked and notorious treasons, imaginations, and intentions proposed as aforesaid, he the said Thomas Duke of Norfolk, well and truly knew and understood that Mary late Queen of Scots had laid claim and pretended a title and interest to the present possession and dignity of the imperial crown of this Kingdom of England; well and truly knowing and understanding that the aforesaid Mary, late Queen of Scots, had falsely, wickedly, and unjustly said and affirmed that our aforesaid lady, Queen Elizabeth, had no right and title to the crown of this realm of England. And also well and truly knowing and understanding that the aforesaid Mary, late Queen of Scots, had falsely, wickedly, and unjustly usurped the sale, title, and regal name of this Kingdom of England; and that she, the aforesaid Mary, late Queen of Scots, had impaled and joined the arms of the Kingdom of England with the arms of the Kingdom of Scotland, as well in her seals and plate, as other things, without any difference and distinction. And furthermore, well and truly knowing and understanding that the said Mary, late Queen of Scots, had not revoked or renounced her wicked and unjust claims and usurpations aforesaid the 23rd day of September, in the 11th year of our said lady, now Queen of England, and divers other days and places before and after the said time at the charter-house aforesaid, in the County of Middlesex aforesaid, falsely, subtlety and traitorously sought and endeavored without the assent, consent, or agreement of the aforesaid our Lady Queen Elizabeth, his supreme and sovereign lady, to be joined in marriage with the aforesaid Mary, late Queen of Scots. And for this reason and cause, he the said duke aforesaid, the 23rd day of September in the 11th year aforesaid, and divers other days and places before and after, at charter-house aforesaid, in the county of Middlesex aforesaid, falsely, subtlety and traitorously writ divers letters to the aforesaid Mary, late Queen of Scots; and as well as letters, sent several pledges of tokens to the aforesaid Mary, late Queen of Scots, the 23rd day of September aforesaid in the year aforesaid, and divers other days and times before and after. And also on the said 23rd day of September, in the 11th year of the reign of the said Queen Elizabeth, and divers other days and places before and after at charter-house aforesaid, in the county of Middlesex aforesaid, falsely, subtlety, and traitorously gave to, and accommodated the said Mary, late Queen of Scots with divers sums of money; which the said Mary, late Queen of Scots, falsely and traitorously had and received of him the said Thomas Duke of Norfolk, the 23rd day of September aforesaid, in the year aforesaid, at charter-house aforesaid, in the county of Middlesex aforesaid notwithstanding the aforesaid duke had been distinctly and especially forbid and prohibited by the aforesaid lady Queen Elizabeth, upon his allegiance, that he should upon no account whatsoever hold correspondence, or treat with the aforesaid Mary late Queen of Scots, concerning marriage with her the said Mary late Queen of Scots; and notwithstanding the aforesaid duke, by divers letters and instruments writ with his own hand to the said Lady Queen Elizabeth, his supreme sovereign lady, publicly denied and renounced the aforesaid marriage, protesting that he the said duke was never engaged, or had proceeded in the said marriage.

And also the said jurors upon their corporal oaths, further present and say, that Thomas Earl of Northumberland, late of Topcliffe in the county of York, and Anne his wife; Charles Earl of Westmoreland, late of Branspeth in the county of Durham; Richard Norton, late of Norton Comers in the county of York; Thomas Markenfield, late of Markenfield in the said county, esq.; together with several other false traitors, rebels, and public enemies of our said Lady Queen Elizabeth, not having the fear of God before their eyes, nor considering their due allegiance, but seduced by the instigation of the Devil, imagined, devised, and conspired to deprive and depose the said Lady Queen Elizabeth from her royal dignity, tide, and power of her Kingdom of England; and also to bring about and compass the death and final destruction of the said Lady Queen Elizabeth with the intention and design to complete and fulfill all their traitorous conspiracies and devices on the 16th day of November, in the 11th year of the reign of the said Queen, at Rippon in the said county of York; by their own consent and appointment, they did falsely and traitorously meet and assemble themselves together with a great multitude of people, to the number of four thousand men and more, ready armed and prepared for open war against their said Queen Elizabeth, their supreme and sovereign lady, at Rippon aforesaid, the 16th Day of November aforesaid, in the year aforesaid, falsely and traitorously they were ready prepared and armed to execute all and singular the treasons and conspiracies aforesaid, of the said Thomas Earl of Northumberland and Anne his wife, Charles Earl of Westmoreland, Richard Norton, and Thomas Markenfield, with many others of the said false traitors and rebels aforesaid, by due form of law legally indicted, and afterwards upon that legally outlawed and attainted, as they now stand upon record in her said majesty's court of Queen's bench.

And after the perpetration and commission of the aforesaid wicked treasons, in manner aforesaid by them committed, the aforesaid Thomas Earl of Northumberland, and Anne his wife; Charles Earl of Westmoreland, Richard Norton, and Thomas Markenfield; with many other false traitors and rebels aforesaid, the 20th day of December in the 12th year of the reign of our said sovereign lady the Queen, for those treasons fled out of this Kingdom into the Kingdom of Scotland; and there resided, and were received, aided and assisted by several noblemen and other great men of the said Kingdom of Scotland, *viz.* by James Duke of Chastelleroy, the Earl of Huntley, Mr. Harris, Mr. Hume, and, Mr. Firmberst, and other Scots, then subjects of the said Kingdom of Scotland, detained from our said Lady Queen Elizabeth in and towards which noblemen and other great men of the aforesaid Kingdom of Scotland, the said Lady Queen Elizabeth afterwards proclaimed, and caused war to be made upon the said rebels as public enemies to her Kingdom of England by Thomas Earl of Sussex her majesty's lord lieutenant and lieutenant-general of the north, with a powerful and strong army to oppose the enemy. Upon which account, Charles Earl of Westmoreland, Anne wife of Thomas Earl of Northumberland, Richard Norton, and Thomas Markenfield, fled from the aforesaid Kingdom of Scotland and transported themselves to Antwerp in Brabant where they resided. And there the same Charles Earl of Westmoreland, Anne wife of the said Thomas Earl of Northumberland, Richard Norton, and Thomas Markenfield, contrary to their due allegiance staid in manifest contempt of the said Queen and her laws. Yet the aforesaid Thomas Duke of Norfolk, not ignorant of the premises, but well and truly knowing all and singular the transactions in manner and form aforesaid; the 6th day of August, in the 12th year of the reign of the said Queen Elizabeth, at charter-house aforesaid, in the county of Middlesex aforesaid, and divers other days and places afore and after, falsely and traitorously took care and caused to be sent; delivered and distributed, several sums of money to aid, assist, and support Charles Earl of Westmoreland, and Anne wife of Thomas Earl of Northumberland.

And further, that the said Thomas Duke of Norfolk, the 16th day of July in the 13th year of the reign of Lady Elizabeth Queen of England at charter-house aforesaid, in the county of Middlesex aforesaid, and divers other days and places afore and after, falsely and traitorously adhered to, aided and assisted James Duke of Chastelleroy, Earl of Huntley, Mr. Harris, Mr. Hume, Mr. Burleigh, and Mr. Firmberst, public enemies to our said Lady Elizabeth, then Queen of England.

And further, the jurors aforesaid upon their oaths, present and say, that *pius Quitus*, sometime Bishop of Ross, was and is known to be a deadly and public enemy to our said Lady Queen Elizabeth and her Kingdom of England, that the said Thomas Duke of Norfolk well and truly knowing and understanding this, the 13th day of March, in the 13th year of the reign of the said Lady Queen Elizabeth, at charter house aforesaid, in the county of

Middlesex aforesaid, and divers other days and places afore and after, with intention to produce the said traitorous effects, falsely, subtly, and traitorously conferred, consulted, advised, and procured one Robert Ridolph, a foreign merchant beyond the seas and out of the Kingdom of England to send to the aforesaid Bishop of Ross, to Philip King of Spain and to the Duke of Alva, to obtain of the aforesaid Bishop of Ross certain sums of money, towards the rallying and maintaining of an army to invade this Kingdom of England; and to make war in the said Kingdom against the aforesaid Lady Elizabeth Queen of England, &c. And that the said King of Spain, by the mediation of the said Duke of Alva did send into this Kingdom of England a certain army of Germans to invade and make open and cruel war against the said Lady Queen Elizabeth and also that the same Thomas Duke of Norfolk, the same 10th day of March in the said 13th year of the reign of the said Lady Queen Elizabeth aforesaid, and divers other days and places afore and after, at charter-house aforesaid in the count of Middlesex aforesaid, falsely, wickedly and traitorously conspired, consented, and agreed with the aforesaid Robert Ridolph to advance; stir up and raise within this Kingdom of England the forces and power that he the aforesaid Thomas Duke of Norfolk and his confederates were by any means capable of raising or engaging others to raise within this Kingdom of England, to join with the aforesaid army and with other subjects of this Kingdom of England whom the same Duke of Norfolk could gather together and join with the said army by the said King of Spain in order to make open war against our said Lady Queen Elizabeth within this her Kingdom of England and to take away and free Mary, late Queen of Scots, out of the custody and possession of our said Lady Elizabeth, Queen of England and at the same time to deprive, depose, and eject the most illustrious and Christian Princess Queen Elizabeth her royal dignity, title; power, preeminence, and government of this Kingdom of England and at the same time, him the said Thomas Duke of Norfolk, to join himself in marriage with the aforesaid Mary, late Queen of Scots.

And further, the jurors upon their oaths present and say, that the aforesaid Robert Ridolph had writ and composed three distinct and separate letters of credit in the name of the aforesaid Thomas Duke of Norfolk for him the said Robert Ridolph, in his false, and wicked and treasonous messages aforesaid, *viz.* one of those letters to the aforesaid Duke of Alva, another to the aforesaid Bishop of Ross and a third to the aforesaid Phillip King of Spain that afterwards the same Thomas Duke of Norfolk falsely and traitorously intending, willing, and desiring success and effect from the aforesaid false and traitorous messages by the aforesaid Robert Ridolph, as appeared by his sending one William Baker gent. one of the servants of the said Thomas Duke of Norfolk, the 20th day of March, in the 13th year of the reign of the Queen, at charter-house aforesaid, in the county of Middlesex aforesaid, falsely and traitorously sent to Guerrawe Despeis ambassador of the said Philip King of Spain declare, show, and affirm to the aforesaid ambassador of the aforesaid Philip King of Spain, that he the said Thomas Duke of Norfolk had affirmed and would affirm the aforesaid credential letters to the aforesaid Duke of Alva, the Bishop of Ross, and Philip King of Spain, composed and writ in his name, were as valid to all intents and purposes as if he the said Thomas Duke of Norfolk had writ them with his own hand.

And further; the said jurors upon their oaths present and say, that the aforesaid Robert Ridolph, the 24th Day of March, in the 13th year of the reign of the said Lady Elizabeth Queen of England aforesaid, at Dover in the county of Kent, took his journey to several parts beyond the seas, in order to execute, perfect, and complete the said treasonable messages with the consent and agreement of the aforesaid Thomas Duke of Norfolk. And afterwards the aforesaid Robert Ridolph conveyed, declared and communicated the said wicked and traitorous messages in foreign countries and parts beyond the sea, as well to the aforesaid Duke of Alva, as to the aforesaid Bishop of Ross. And that the aforesaid Robert Ridolph, amongst his many other false and traitorous messages, conveyed one letter in unusual characters called ciphers, which the aforesaid Duke of Alva caused to be writ and sent to Thomas Duke of Norfolk; which very letter, as declared to be writ and sent, he the said Duke of Norfolk, the eighteenth day of April, in the thirteenth year of the reign of the said Queen Elizabeth aforesaid, at charter-house aforesaid, in the county of Middlesex aforesaid, falsely and traitorously received and had; and then and there gave and delivered to the aforesaid William Baker his servant several written pages in known letters, commonly to be deciphered. And the said papers in common and known ciphers or characters he the said duke afterwards, on the 25th day of April, in the 13th year of the reign of the said Queen Elizabeth, at charter-house aforesaid, in the county of Middlesex aforesaid, falsely and traitorously received, inspected, and read over the said papers, and then and there falsely and traitorously retained and kept them. By which letters of the said Robert Ridolph to him the said Thomas Duke of Norfolk, amongst other things, are signified, and he makes known what a kind audience and reception he the said Robert met with from the aforesaid Duke of Alva in his wicked and traitorous messages aforesaid. And that the said Duke of Alva required and willed the friends and abettors of the said confederacy to be ready when so ever a foreign power should be sent into this Kingdom of England.

And furthermore, the same jurors upon their oaths present and say, that the said Thomas Duke of Norfolk, the 16th day of June, in the 13th year of the reign of the said Lady Queen Elizabeth, at charter-house aforesaid, in the county of Middlesex aforesaid, falsely and traitorously received a letter directed to him the said duke, from *pius quintus* Bishop of Ross, by which the said Bishop of Ross promised to the said Duke of Norfolk, aid, help, and assistance towards executing the said wicked and traitorous designs of the aforesaid Mary, late Queen of Scots, contrary to their due allegiance and the peace of our sovereign Lady Elizabeth, now Queen of England, her crown and dignity, and in manifest contempt of the laws of this Kingdom, as well as the worst and most pernicious example of all other delinquents in the like case, and contrary to the form of several statutes in this case made and provided.

After the reading of the indictment, the Clerk of the Crown said to the duke; how say's thou Thomas Duke of Norfolk, art thou guilty of these treasons whereof thou art indicted in manner and form as thou art thereof indicted, yea or no?

Thereupon the duke began, and said to this effect:

May it please your grace, and you the rest of my lords here, the hearing of this indictment gives me occasion to enter into the making of a suit, which I meant not to have done before my coming hither. I beseech you, if the law will permit it, that I may have counsel allowed me for the answering of this indictment.

The Lord Chief Justice answered, that in case of high-treason he cannot have counsel allowed and that he was to answer to his own fact only, which himself best knew, and might without counsel sufficiently answer.

Duke. That you may understand that I speak it not without some ground, these be the causes that move me to make this suit. I was told before I came here, that I was indicted upon the statute of the 25th of Edward III. I have had very short warning to provide to answer so great a matter; I have not had fourteen hours in all, both day and night, and now I neither hear the same statute alleged, and yet I am put at once to the whole herd of laws, not knowing which particularity to answer to. The indictment contains sundry points and matters to touch me by circumstance and so to draw me into matter of treason, which are not treasons themselves therefore with reverence and humble submission I am led to think I may have counsel. And this I show, that you may think I move not this suit without any ground. I am hardly handled; I have had short warning, and no books; neither book of statutes, nor so much as the brevity of statutes. I am brought to fight without a weapon: yet I remember one case in law, I think it is in the first year of King Henry VII. It is the case of one Humphrey Stafford, which was indicted of high-treason and had counsel allowed him. If the precedent in his case be such, as it may extend to me, I require it at your hands that I may have it allowed. I show you my ground why I crave it, I refer me to your opinions therein.

Then Sir James Dyer, Lord Chief Justice of the Common-Pleas, said; my lord, that case of Humphrey Stafford in primo of Henry VII. was about pleading of sanctuary, for that he was taken out of sanctuary at Culneham, which belonged to the Abbot of Abingdon: so the question was whether he should be allowed sanctuary in that case, and with that form of pleading, which was matter of law in which case he had counsel, and not upon the point or fact of high-treason; but only for the allowance of sanctuary, and whether it might be allowed being claimed by prescription, and without showing any former allowances in err, and such like matters, but all our books do forbid allowing of counsel in the point of treason; but only it is to be answered guilty, or not guilty.

Duke. Humphrey Stafford's case was high-treason and he had counsel. I must submit myself to your opinions: I beseech you, weigh what case I stand in. I stand here before you for my life, lands and goods, my children and my posterity, and that which I esteem most of all, for my honesty; I forbear to speak of my honor. I am unlearned if I ask anything, and not in such words as I ought, I beseech you bear with me and let me have that favor that the law allows me. If the law does not allow me counsel, I must submit me to your opinions. I beseech you, consider of me; my blood will ask vengeance if I be unjustly condemned. I honor your learning's and your gravities. I beseech you, have consideration of me and grant me what the law will permit me. I am now to make another suit to you, my lords the judges. I beseech you, tell me if my indictment be perfect and sufficient in law; and whether in whole, or in the parts, and in which parts that I may know to what I should answer.

Lord Chief Justice Catlin. The Lord Chief Justice said, for the sufficiency of your indictment, it has been well debated and considered by us all; and we have all, with one assent, resolved and so do certify you that if the causes in the indictment expressed be true in fact, the indictment is wholly and in every part sufficient.

Duke. Be all the points treasons?

Lord Chief Justice Catlin. All be treasons, if the truth of the case be so in fact.

Duke. I will tell you what moves me to ask you this. I have heard of the case of the Lord Scroope; it was in the time or Henry the IVth (the judges said Henry the Vth) he confessed the indictment, and yet traversed that the points thereof were no treasons.

Lord Chief Justice Catlin. My lord, he had his judgment for treason upon that indictment, and was executed.

Then the Clerk of the Crown said again, How says thou Thomas Duke of Norfolk, art thou guilty of the treasons whereof thou art here indicted in manner and form as thou art indicted, yea, or no?

The Duke answered, not guilty.

The Clerk said, by whom wilt thou be tried?

The Duke said, by God and my peers.

Then the Duke spoke to the lords, and said thus: now I am not to use a short speech, which I meant before to have used, but that the reading of the indictment have driven me to other occasions. Although these heinous treasons and outrageous faults objected against me, do much abash me; yet I conceive no small comfort to think under how gracious a Queen and sovereign lady I live, which well appears by her most gracious proceeding with me according to the course of law. Her majesty seeks not my blood, but gives me the trial which the laws admit, and in the most favorable manner that I can require; for which I am most bounden to her majesty. Now I am to make two suits: the one to your grace, my Lord High Steward, that as your place requires to do justice, so it may please you to extend to me your lawful favor that I may have justice and that may not be overlaid in speeches: my memory was never good, it is now much worse than it was; fore troubles, fore cares, closeness in prison, evil rest, have much decayed my memory; so as I pray God that this day it fail me not, and another time I will forgive it. I beseech this of you my Lord High Steward. The second request, I thought to make to you my lords, my peers. I think myself happy to have my trial in such a company. A much greater matter, if I could have greater, I durst put it into your hands, and (a very few accepted) even into every one of your hands singly; that opinion I have of you. I know religion bears a stroke among you, which I hope so rules your consciences, that for no respect you will swerve from justice; you will not bring a worm into your own consciences; you will not burden your souls with condemning me wrongfully; you will not do what God's law and right allows not, this above all things comforts me, next to her majesty's most gracious favor of my lawful trial. If I had not made a full account to have this for the way of my lawful purgation, I needed not to have been here at this time, neither for matters passed two years ago, nor for that whereof I am charged at this present. I have chosen, my peers, I have chosen rather to come here to be tried by you than with needless and cowardly running away, to have left a gap open for my enemies slanderously to lay to my charge in my absence what they could maliciously invent. I have this day (though I am sorry for any cause to come in this case before you) even the day that I could wish to be tried by such peers. I will not enter into particularities, and discourse my whole cause at large, but answer from point to point as I shall be charged; for my memory was never good, and it is now worse than ever it was. Yet one request more I beseech of you, my peers, which I with favor may ask, and you with justice may grant, unhappy man that I am, though I have to this indictment pleaded not guilty of the treasons therein objected against me, nor of no treasons; yet I confess, as I have with all humility, and with tears confessed, and as some of you, my lords, here present can witness, that I have neglected my duty to the Queen's most excellent majesty in cases inferior to treason, and that be no parts of treason. I have laid them at her majesty's feet and poured them forth before her in confession, so far as my conscience will suffer me to declare. Let, I beseech you, neither my confession already made of inferior faults, that be not in compass of treason; nor, if I shall now in mine answers confess them again, if they be objected against me; lead you to judge the worse of me in the greater case. Let each fault have his own pine; I beseech you, remember the differences and degrees of offences, and not to mix my smaller faults with this great cause, let these mean crimes rest at her majesty's feet where I with all humility have laid them. Thus I beseech you all, have consideration of me.

Then spoke the Queen's Sergeant, Mr. Banham, and said to this effect: it has appeared to your grace and your lordships all that the Duke of Norfolk is by this indictment charged with three principal points of high treason: the first is that forgetting his allegiance and duty to his sovereign lady the Queen, he has traitorously imagined, devised and practiced to deprive and depose the Queen's majesty of and from the crown of this realm, and her royal style, name and dignity, and to bring her to death and destruction; and so to alter the whole state of government of this realm. The second point is that he has traitorously relieved and comforted the English rebels that levied war against her majesty within her realm, and which since fled into Scotland, and from thence beyond the sea. The third point is that he has traitorously given relief and maintenance to the Duke of Chastelleroy, the Earl of Huntley, the Lord Harris, the Lord Hume, and other Scots, the Queen's majesty's public enemies, scourers and detainees of the said rebels. To prove these great treasons, there is in this indictment set forth to you good and sufficient matter; first, to prove that the Duke of Norfolk sought, imagined, compassed and practiced to deprive and depose the Queen's majesty of her royal crown, estate and dignity, and consequently to bring her to death and destruction, are alleged two matters: the first is that the duke knowing the Scottish Queen falsely and unjustly to claim and pretend title, to have and enjoy the present possession of the crown of England; and that she untruly usurped the name and style of this realm; and that she gave and quartered the arms of England without difference; and that she continued in that fact and usurped claim without renunciation thereof, and without acknowledging her error to the Queen's majesty, though she has been thereto required: he, I say, knowing all this, yet without the Queen's majesty's assent, against her majesty's special and express commandment upon his allegiance and against his own promise and protestation upon his faith, has nevertheless secretly sought and practiced to join himself with the said Scottish Queen in marriage and to advance and maintain her laid false and pretended title to the present possession of the crown of this realm, which cannot be without purpose to depose and deprive the Queen's majesty and consequently to bring her to death and destruction. The second is that the Duke of Norfolk has conspired and practiced to procure strangers to enter into this realm, and invade the same, and to make open war against her majesty within her own realm; and so forcibly to work her deposing, deprivation, death and destruction hereupon the said duke has pleaded not guilty, and for his trial has put himself upon his peers; yours therefore is the trial. And now sought evidence to prove him guilty of the treasons contained in the laid indictment, it may please your lordships to hear such a matter as I shall for the Queen bring forth against him.

Duke. I am occasioned by the speech of Mr. Sergeant, to gather what I shall find in the rest of them; a meaning with circumstance to draw me into treason, with eloquence to overlay me, and to exasperate matters extremely against me, and to enforce things that be not treasons indeed. I beseech you my masters, for God's sake do your duty, remember equity, consider conscience, and what I am: I am no stranger; I am a Christian man, and an English man. You may do your duties to the Queen sufficiently, and yet deal conscionably with me, and heap not, unconscionably, circumstances to cloy my memory. Go directly to the indictment, it is no praise or glory for you to overlay me. I am unlearned, unable to speak, and worst of all to speak for myself; I have neither good utterance, as the world well knows, nor understanding, for God's sake do not overlay me with superfluous matter. One thing I had forgotten, I know a man suspected is half condemned. Now as it happened in my last trouble, so at this time there want not to put abroad to the world, and heap up things which I never thought; a great number of such there be as I see many here at this present. They have published that

I took an oath of things which afterwards proved contrary; blame me not that I mistrust the worse, because I have found the worst. But to take away scruple from you, true it is, that I took an oath, but not generally, but to special points. And now when I take an oath to points, to draw me to the whole and to take *Pars fro Toto,* is great injury. To prove that I took that oath to parts, and not to the whole, I refused to set my hand without expressing of the point, for my hand, my oath, and my heart shall go all together. And for further proof that my oath was but to special points, I can name good witnesses to whom I did presently within three hours after my oath taken, specially report the three points that I made mine oath to. This I say, to take from you the scruple of such matter as I have been charged with, and which perhaps you have heard of me to my discredit.

Then said Mr. Sergeant Banham, I have yet given no evidence, and for that oath you are not once yet charged withal. I have done nothing yet, but recited the matters contained in the indictment, now will I bring forth matter for the Queen in evidence, and will prove the things in the indictment to be true. There are alleged three great treasons, as I have before said; the first only I will deal with, that is, to prove that the Duke of Norfolk imagined, compassed and conspired, to deprive and depose the Queen's majesty, our sovereign lady, of her crown and royal estate and dignity and I will use the second matter but for inducement of the first by showing how the Scottish Queen falsely and unjustly claimed the present possession of the crown of this realm; and that he knowing that the Scottish Queen so unjustly claimed the said crown, that she quartered the arms of England that she usurped the style and royal name; that she has not acknowledged her error, nor renounced her untrue and unjust claim and usurpation, though she has been required thereto; and whereto himself has been privy and has dealt in treaty as a chief commissioner for the Queen's majesty for that purpose, this matter, I say, I will set out; how he knowing all this, yet without the assent of the Queen's majesty, against her highness's express commandment upon his allegiance against his own faith and promise to the contrary, practiced to join himself in marriage with the said Queen of Scots: and I mean to join thereto an intent of his to advance and maintain that unjust title of the Scottish Queen. If then this attempting to join himself in marriage with the Scottish Queen shall be proved to you, and that he knew of her unjust claim and pretence of tide and that thereby he joined himself to advance and maintain the said title, this must needs tend to a purpose and imagining to depose and deprive the Queen's majesty, and thereupon consequently to bring her to death and destruction, which is high-treason within the compass of the statute of 25 of King Edward III. For whoso shall imagine and go about to maintain a title to the present possession of the Queen's crown, and to join himself in marriage with her that so claims without doubt he means to aspire to the crown himself; and so meaning, it plainly follows that he cannot suffer her majesty to reign, and his jealousy cannot suffer her to live where he desire to reign. Now will I show you the manner of his procuring to match himself in marriage with the Scottish Queen and first the beginning thereof, first of all, to prove how secretly he dealt to that end by suits and means before he was a commissioner, to examine causes between the Scottish Queen and the young King her son, and other the lords of Scotland. Before that time there were secret suits and practices between them by motions, by messages, by letters and tokens, and pleaded so far forth, as that the Scottish Queen took it, that she was assured of his good will. For when commission was directed to him and to the Earl of Sussex, and to Sir Ralph Sadler, counselors of the Duchy of Lancaster, the Scottish Queen had reposed full affiance in the Duke of Norfolk to have at his hands favorable hearing; and so she reported, and so indeed it followed. And where you speak of an oath, and seem so loath to be disproved and would so feign have it taken that your oath, hand, and heart go all together; there was an oath specially appointed for the commissioners, that they should deal in that matter between the Scottish Queen and her son and nobility, directly, sincerely, and uprightly, and to weigh all things that should be objected or answered on either part indifferently without all partiality. Then after this oath taken, the duke being the first named commissioner, this oath notwithstanding, dealt indirectly, deceived the Queen's majesty's trust, and demeaned him partially against his said oath wherein he committed willful perjury, besides that, without regard of his oath of a sworn counselor to the Queen's majesty of her Privy Council, he disclosed her majesty's secrets and fell to practicing for matching himself with the Scottish Queen in marriage. Now shall I prove his knowledge at the same time, that the Scottish Queen pretended title to the present possession of the crown of this realm.

Duke. Then the duke asked if all the treasons contained in his indictment were upon the statute of King Edward III and it was answered by Mr. Sergeant and Mr. Attorney-General, that they were grounded upon the same statute only. Then the duke began thus: here the matters that Mr. Sergeant has proved against me stand in two points; by which he charges me with imagining the deprivation and death of the Queen's majesty and with indirect and untrue dealing in the Scottish Queen's cause; and therein he burdened me with perjury. The Scottish cause has divers pleas, and therefore bear with me, I pray you, if I cast back again to rehearse my doing therein, for my memory is not good. As for my dealing therein, God is my witness that I have done uprightly.

Sergeant. Then Mr. Sergeant urged him to confess if he had knowledge that the Scottish Queen pretended title to the present possession of the crown of England; offering, if the duke would deny it, to make proof of it.

Duke. The duke said, I will make mine own confession; I pray you to teach me not how to answer or confess, because it is the first ground that you build upon against me and because I know not whether my peers do all know it or no, I will make a short declaration of my doings in that matter with the Scottish Queen.

Sergeant. First we pray your grace (speaking to the Lord High Steward) that he may directly answer whether he knew that the Scottish Queen so claimed or no; if he say no, we will prove it.

Duke. Then being ruled over by the Lord High Steward that he should answer directly to that question, he answered, that indeed he knew that she had so claimed, but with circumstance.

Sergeant. Say plainly, did you know it or no? For if you say nay, we can prove it.

Duke. You handle me hardly, you would so trap me by circumstance and infer upon me that she was the Queen's enemy, and so make me a traitor. I will answer directly to the whole matter of my dealing with her.

Sergeant. Answer to the parts as they fall out. Did you know that she claimed the present possession of the crown? That she usurped the arms and royal style of this realm and that she made no renunciation of that usurped pretence? If you say you knew it not, we will prove every part of it.

Duke. I did not know it in such sort as is alleged, I know that renunciation of that claim was offered, and upon certain causes respite.

Sergeant. It is well known, and yourself then knew it, that the Scottish Queen claimed the present possession of the crown of England, quartered the arms of England with the arms of Scotland, and usurped the style of this realm; and that there was a French power sent to prosecute it by invading this land by the way of Scotland: yourself was made the Queen's majesty's lieutenant, and levied an army to expulse them. Afterward the Queen's majesty sent her ambassadors which met with the French Lords and Scottish Queen's commissioners at Edinburgh, and agreed upon a treaty of peace; in which one special article was that the Scottish Queen should acknowledge her error, and should renounce her pretended claim to the present possession of the crown of this realm. It was not done, nor yet is done. My Lord of Norfolk was at this treaty and when this last commission went out when the commissioners sat at York about the matter between the Scottish Queen, her son, and the nobility of Scotland, wherein were commissioners the Duke of Norfolk, the Earl of Sussex, and Mr. Chancellor of the Duchy; one special instruction was for the Scottish Queen's recognition of her unjust claim, and to require that she should ratify the former treaty of peace. The duke knows well it was not done.

Duke. What is this to me? I need not enter to defend her doings, I like them not. It is not my case, but that you make it my case; else I would not meddle with it, answer it who would for me. Indeed I have heard that being covert baron then married to the French King, in her husband's life she made claim to the crown of England, and quartered the arms of England with the arms of Scotland. I have heard also that Sir Nicholas Throckmorton made complaint thereof and moved for redress, and thereupon it was laid down. I have heard that she has been requested to make renunciation of that claim when the peace was concluded, when Montmorency came over, and time was taken for it. After this there grew amity between the Queen's majesty and the Scottish Queen; the Queen took her for her friend, sent ambassadors to her, and christened her child; all this excluded enmity. And when my Lord of Bedford was there, and moved her for ratifying of the treaty, and for the renunciation, she refused not, but said she would send to show causes why she did it not presently. And then it was refused not absolutely, but upon certain words, and the treating thereof committed to my Lord Burleigh and Mr. Wotton. As for our commission at York, it took no end; the matter was brought up hither, and here was sat upon at Westminster in the Parliament-Chamber. And this is my understanding, that she claimed the crown and I have not otherwise known it.

Sergeant. Thus have you confessed far enough. That you knew that she did pretend title to the present possession of the crown; that she quartered the arms, and usurped the royal style of this realm.

Duke. It was in her husband's time, when she was covert-baron.

Sergeant. You knew also, how since her husband's time, she has not renounced that claim; and you had in special instruction to require it when you were commissioner.

Duke. A full renunciation was offered when the Lord Burleigh was with her, and our commission was ended, and the matter brought up hither.

Sergeant. But what was the cause why it took no end by your commission? Yourself was the cause that the commission broke up, because you dealt indirectly; you set out your own affection and partiality and behaved yourself partially, without regard to the Queen's majesty's special commandment, without regard of your oath, then specially taken for that commission, or of your oath as a counselor: you uttered your partiality, you disclosed to the other side forehand the Queen's secrets: you devised with the one side, and gave them counsel how to deal for stay of the matter: you did prevaricate the Queen's intention; and when you were by your commission to examine the Scottish Queen's adulteries and her murdering of her husband, you practiced with those that were dealers for the Scottish Queen, and you told them by way of advice, that if these matters went forwards to hearing, the Earl of Murray and his side, would disclose all the foul matter that they could, both by her letters and other evidences to her dishonor; and that the Queen's majesty had some such counselors about her, as if these things were once produced, she would cause them to be published, that all foreign princes should understand them, to the Scottish Queen's great infamy, and to move foreign princes to proceed no further suing for her. And this was the cause of the breach and dissolution of your commission.

Duke. You said you would prove that I knew of the Scottish Queen's claiming the present possession of the crown.

Sergeant. Yourself have confessed it; for you know there was yet no renunciation made, and you were special commissioner for that purpose; and though your commission took no effect, yet by that, that the requiring of the renunciation was matter of your instructions and the same not done, it is plain that you knew sufficiently of her former unjust claiming of the present possession of the crown and now will we by good evidence prove your partial and indirect dealing in that commission. Here I will produce matter of your own conference at York with Ledington and the Bishop of Ross, and how yourself told them that you understood at Lithe that rigorous matter would be set out by the Earl of Murray and the rest of that side against the Scottish Queen, touching her whoredom and the murder of her husband. You gave advice to stay the Earl of Murray from so doing; you told the Scottish Queen's ministers how the Queen of England had some counselors that could cause her to publish all those matters to the Scottish Queen's infamy; you practiced with them to devise to qualify the matter; you told the way that you thought best to do it; you advised them to deal with the Earl of Murray, that the matter might be compounded, or else so to handle it, that it might take no end.

Duke. Here the duke took advantage of that Mr. Sergeant had said that the duke understood at Lyth; for the duke then protested that at that time he had never been at Lyth. Whereupon the Lord Burleigh dissolved that knot and said on the duke's behalf to Mr. sergeant.

Burleigh. You were best proceed with your evidence, you may mistake my Lord Norfolk had not then been at Lyth, otherwise than he and I were there once secretly in a morning. The cause of this error rose thus: in one Scottish paper produced for that matter, was contained, how the duke understood at Lyth, which in Scotch is as much as at length; which Mr. Sergeant, in perusing the matters for evidence delivered to him, took for Lyth, as the Clerk of the Crown also afterwards did in reading the same paper.

Then was produced an examination of the Bishop of Ross taken at the Tower, Nov. 5, 1571 as follows:

The Scottish Queen told the Bishop of Ross that the conference at York was to make the Earl of Murray and other her disobedient subjects, to answer before the Queen's majesty of England's commissioners, for their unnatural and unjust proceedings against her; and that after their offences acknowledged for the Queen of England's pleasure, they should be remitted and received into favor again, and so all matters compounded.

The bishop's answer to this was that he was sorry she had agreed to any conference wherein they should be accused, for he was assured in that case they would utter all that they could for their defenses, although it were for her dishonor, and of the whole realm: for they would be loath to confess openly that they were evil subjects and she a good princess, and therefore he wished that the matter might be treated by way of Concord, before any entry to accusations and to that end he counseled her to travel with her friends at court to York. To this she replied, that there was no such danger in the matter as I supposed; for she trusted I would find the judges favorable, principally the Duke of Norfolk, who was first in commission; and doubted not but the Earl of Sussex would be ruled by him as his tender friend, and Sir Ralph Sadler would not gain stand their advice; and that Liggons had been at Bolton, by whose message, told by him to the Lord Scroope, he understood of the duke's good will towards her, and the bruit was also spread abroad of a marriage between the duke and her; and besides that she had many good friends in the country that did favor her, and seek to her, such as the Earl of Northumberland and his lady, by whom she had many intelligences and messages; the Norton's, Markenfield and others, who would all be with the duke at York, and would persuade him to favor her case. In the mean time, before our passage to York, Robert Melvin came to Bolton with letters sent by Ledington from Fauly Castle to the Queen my mistress, to advertise her that the Earl of Murray was wholly bent to utter all that he could against her, and to that effect had carried with him all the letters which he had to produce against her, for proof of the murder, whereof he had recovered the copies, and had caused his wife to write them, which he sent to the Queen; and that he had not come into England in the Earl of Murray's company, unless it had been to do her service, and to travel for mitigation of those rigors intended; desiring to be certified by Robert Melvin, that she wished to stay those rigorous accusations, and because he was well acquainted with the Duke of Norfolk, desired him to travel with the duke in his favor, and that he would confer with the Bishop of Ross, by whom he should understand his whole mind particularly from time to time. After this, Robert Melvin at York did bring me to Ledington's lodging where we talked almost a whole night, where he told, that he had conferred with, the duke, who seemed to bear great good-will to the Queen my mistress, and had willed him to counsel the Earl of Murray, and others, to abstain from uttering any dishonest matter against the Queen, but to grant to some compositions amongst themselves, so that Ledington said, it appeared to him that the duke had some intention to marry with the Queen, as the bruit was; and that he did verily believe, that if it were followed, the marriage would take effect, which would be most of all other things for the Queen's honor and weal and willed me to speak with the duke secretly alone, without the commissioners, and Ledington should advertise the duke to appoint the time convenient, as he did one day in the morning by seven of the clock, before the meeting of the commissioners. I talked with the duke alone in a gallery, where he uttered to me that he bore good will to the Queen my mistress, and that he had talked with the earl this was Murray length and had seen the letters which they had to produce against the Queen my mistress, and other defenses, whereby there would such matter be proved against her, that would dishonor her for ever; and if it were once published, the Queen's majesty of England would get counsel by such as loved not the Queen my mistress, to publish the same to the world, and to send ambassadors to all other princes to make the same known to them; so that they would make no further suit for her delivery, and perhaps greater rigor might ensue to her person therefore he advised me to confer with Ledington; and that betwixt him and me, we might find some means to stay the rigor intended; and promised all that he could do, to that effect, by Ledington's advertisement, he would do. I replied, that Ledington would have her to ratify the demission made at Locblevin for a time, for he had assured her it could hurt her no more, being kept prisoner in England, than that which was done in Locblevin, for so should she stay the uttering of any matter against her, and within six months she should be restored to her country with honor; and so might revoke all done by her.

To this the duke: What if that were done, to be quit of the present infamy and slander, and let him work out the rest? I told him, we were come to that conference for to make an agreement, and not to answer to accusations and therefore wished him to further the agreement amongst us. He answered that their commission was only to hear the differences amongst us; and if I would propound anything, he would like well of it, and should advertise the Queen's majesty, his mistress, thereof, and get her answer. In this conference, the duke did often times insinuate the good will that he did bear to the Queen my mistress, but spoke nothing to me particularly of the marriage at that time; but referred all to Ledington. Upon this I did confer with Ledington diver's times, by whose advice I rode to Bolton to speak with my mistress, in the time of my conference and during my remaining there, the conference was broken up, and the whole commissioners for our part, came to Bolton. And so my Lord Harris and I were sent to London. In the mean time, Robert Melvin came to Bolton to the Queen, with messages of Ledington's, of such conference as he had with the duke at the hunting in the fields, where I believe Ledington did well encourage the duke to attempt the marriage, as he told me afterwards; declaring her properties, and the honor and commodities that might ensue to them both thereby; and that the duke did give good ear thereto, wishing to the Queen to follow that course. In the mean time, the duke had Liggons, and others, going between them and the Lady Scroope, who did entertain the matter between them. After this, the duke coming to Hampton-Court, Ledington made the mean with the duke, to cause him to send Liggons to deal with me upon this behalf, and to give me some favorable advertisement of the weal for our cause. And likewise the duke caused the Lord Lumley sometimes to speak with me, to advise me what was best to be done, and especially when the Spanish ambassador had spoken to me of the marriage of one of the house of Austria; the duke, by my Lord Lumley, counseled me to open the matter to the Queen's majesty, by my Lord of Arundel, which might be an occasion to move her to like better of the match with him, than with any foreigner. And then he sent me word by Liggons, that the Queen's majesty was informed of such a like bruit of his marriage with the Queen of Scots; but he had satisfied her well enough, and so still did follow the matter, and did treat thereupon with the Earl of Murray and Ledington at Hampton-Court: by whose advice Robert Melvin was sent to the Queen, my mistress at Rippon, to move the matter upon the Earl of Murray's behalf, with a full determination, that the Earl of Murray liked of it, which message I heard afterward that Murray alleged he did send it, for fear of some enterprise against him at Northallerton, in his return to Scotland. And so after this manner the matter had been entertained betwixt the Queen and the duke from time to time, as is at length declared in the former Examinations.

Sergeant. The effect of all, is the duke's partial and untrue dealing; for that before the Bishop of Ross's going to York, the Scottish Queen declared to the Bishop of Ross that she doubted not of the favor of the Duke of Norfolk; for she told him that my Lady Scroope had by motions and means assured her of his good will, and me doubted not of my Lord of Sussex's, for the great friendship and tender love he bare to the duke; and she made account that Mr. Sadler would be friendly, for that he alone would not stand to them both. It appears also, for further proof of his partial dealing, that though he were sworn, both as a counselor to the Queen's majesty, and also specially for the matter of this commission; yet he indirectly, secretly, and underhand, dealt with Ledington, and told him how that the Earl of Murray and his side intended to utter sharp matter against the Scottish Queen. The duke gave his advice how to stay it, and so dealt partially and against the Queen's majesty's special trust and commandment, and against his own oath and promise. Next after that in conference had with the Duke of Norfolk on the Scottish Queen's part, the duke declared his good will that he bare to the Scottish Queen, he showed how that if the same matter of evidence against her, were once uttered by the Earl of Murray, some of the Queen's majesty's counselors of England would procure her majesty to publish them. He advised that the matter should be compounded with the Earl of Murray; and that he should not stick, being here in England, and not at her own liberty, for the present time to be content to ratify the demission of the crown of Scotland, which she made at Locblevin; and so she might be restored into her own country, and then she might undo all again at her pleasure and upon pretence of constraint and fear, as well revoke that which she should do in England, as she before revoked that which she had done at Locblevin in Scotland. Also the duke at that time was privy to the device, that Ledington accompanied the Earl of Murray only to understand his secrets, and to betray him and that Ledington stole away the letters and kept them one night, and caused his wife to write them out. Howbeit, the same were but copies translated out of French into Scotch; which, when Ledington's wife had written out, he caused them to be sent to the Scottish Queen. She labored to translate them again into French as near as she could to the originals wherein she wrote them; but that was not possible to do, but there was some variance in the phrase; by which variance, as God would, the subtlety of that practice came to light.

Duke. What if all this be true? What is this to the matter? Any dealing of mine with the Scottish Queen by my sister Scroope's means, I utterly deny. As for Ledington and the Bishop of Ross, what their speeches were to me, I care not; I am to answer but for mine own speeches.

Sergeant. The Bishop of Ross accuses you of your own speeches, and this he does, being examined freely and without any compulsion.

Duke. He is a Scot.

Sergeant. A Scot is a Christian man.

Duke. At my being at York in commission, Ledington broke with me himself to have the matter compounded between the Scottish Queen and the Earl of Murray. I told him that our commission was only to hear indifferently what should be alleged on both parts, and thereof truly to make report. What hurt is this? The Bishop of Ross afterwards sent for me, that he might speak with me when we met, he moved me for the compounding of the matter, as Ledington had done. I told him, that our commission was but to hear and report, as I had told Ledington before; and therefore if they would fall to compounding, I willed them to devise the means themselves, and to make offers; and thereupon we would advertise the Queen's majesty thereof, as we would of all the matters alleged. If it be otherwise, and as you say, let my letters be looked on, and see if they contain any such matter. If the Bishop of Ross, for fear or for malice, have said untruly; if being a Scot, he care not how many English men, by his false testimony, he bring to destruction; I beseech you let not that hurt me.

Sergeant. You made the first motion of compounding the matter to Ledington yourself; and another time to the Bishop of Ross, you offered to further it all that you could.

Duke. I never saw the Bishop of Ross before I came to York; and would I think you, deal so dangerously with a Scot that I never saw before? Also, I did by my letters signify to the Queen's majesty our proceeding, and my disliking of the Scottish Queen's part, let that letter be seen; which letter was written after my talk with Ledington. I wrote it when I went from York, and I never saw the Bishop of Ross afterward, till I came to London.

Sergeant. The writing of your letters to the Queen's majesty, wherein you advertised against the Scottish Queen, and though the same were written after your conference with Ledington and the Bishop of Ross, is no proof but that you dealt partially for the Scottish Queen; for those letters were written by others as well as yourself, namely by my Lord of Sussex, and Mr. Chancellor of the Duchy, and you could not otherwise do, but so signify, notwithstanding your partial secret dealing; for else you should have too openly betrayed your intention.

Duke. When Ledington moved me of the marriage of the Scottish Queen, I utterly refused it.

Sergeant. That is not so. And for proof, as well of your partial dealing in the commission as for the marriage, there shall be brought forth sufficient evidence.

Here was alleged how a letter had been written to the Earl of Murray requiring to be advertised by him of so much as he knew concerning the doings of the Duke of Norfolk, both for the matter of the commission, and the practice of his marriage with the Scottish Queen. And the Earl Murray's answer to the same letter was produced, and read as follows. Note, that the beginning and ending of this letter was not read; but so much only as pertained to the matter, *viz.*

In York, at the meeting of all the commissioners, I found very honorable and neutral dealing with the duke and others her highness's commissioners in the beginning of the cause, as in the making of the oaths to proceed sincerely, *&c.* During which time I only entered into general speech, sticking at our just defense in the matters that were objected against us by the said Queen's commissioners; looking certainly for none other thing but a summary cognition in the causes of controversy, with a small declaratory to have followed. Upon a certain day, the Lord Ledington's secretary rid with the duke to Caoecod; what purpose they held, I cannot say, but that night, Ledington returning and entering in conference with me upon the state of our action, I was advised by him to pass to the duke, and to require familiar conference; by the which I might have some seeing to what issue our matters would tend. According to which advice, having gotten time and place convenient in the gallery of the house where the duke was lodged; after renewing of our first acquaintance made at Berwick the time before the siege of Lyth, and some speeches passed betwixt us, he began to say to me how he in England had favor and credit, and I in Scotland good will and friendship of many. It was thought there could be none more fit instruments to travel for the continuance of the amity betwixt the two realms, than we two. And from that discourse upon the state of both, and how I was entered in that action tending so far to the Queen's dishonor, I was willed by him to consider how matters stood in this isle, what honor I had received of the Queen and what inconveniences her defamation in the matters laid to her charge, might breed to her posterity, whose respect was not little to the crown of England. There was but one babe, the Hamilton's, my un-friend, had the next respect; and if I should, the issue of her body would be the more affectionate to me and mine, than any other that could attain to that room and so it should be meekest that she affirmed her dismissing made in Locblevin, and we to abstract the letters of her hand writ, that she should not be defamed in England. My reply to that was how the matter had passed in Parliament, and the letters seen to many; so that the abstracting of the same, could not then serve her to any purpose: and yet should we in that doing bring the ignominy upon us, affirming it could not be sure for us that way to proceed, seeing the Queen's majesty of England was not made privy to the matter as she behooved to be, in respect we were purposely come into England for that end and for the justifying of the grounds of our cause. The duke's answer was, he would take in hand to handle matters well enough at the court. After this, at the occasion of certain articles that were required to be resolved in, before we entered directly in the declaration of the very ground of our action, we came up to the court; where some new commissioners were adjoined to the former and the hearing of the matter ordained to be in the Parliament-House at Westminster. In presence of which commissioners for the said Queen and partly through the sharp rebuking of the Queen's majesty of England's commissioners, we uttered the grounds of the action, and produced such evidences, letters, and probations as we had, which might move the Queen's majesty to think well of our cause. Whereupon expecting her highness's declaration and seeing no likelihood of the same to be suddenly given, but daily motions made to come to an accord with the said Queen, our matters at home in Scotland in the mean season standing in hazard and danger; we were put to the uttermost point of our wit to imagine whereto the matters would tend for albeit we had left nothing undone for the justification of our cause, it appeared yet no end, but continual motions made to come to some accord with the Queen, and restore her to whole or half reign. I had no other answer to give them, but that I could neither do against conscience nor honor in that matter. Not withstanding, seeing this my plain answer wrought no end or dispatch to us, and that I was informed that the duke began to dislike of me, and to speak of me as that I had reported of the said Queen irreverently, calling her whore and murderer; I was advised to pass to him and to give him good words, and to purge myself of the things objected to me; that I should not upon the hidden enter in his evil grace, nor have him to our enemy, considering his greatness, it being therewithal whispered and showed to me, that if I departed, he standing discontented and not satisfied, I might peradventure find such trouble in my way, as my throat might be cut before I came to Berwick. And therefore since it might well enough appear that he aspired to her marriage, I should not put him in utter despair that my good will cannot be had therein. So, few days before my departing, I came to the park at Hampton-Court where the duke and I met together; and there I declared that it was come to my ears how some misreport should be made of me to him, as that I should speak irreverently and rashly of the said Queen, my sovereign's mother, such words as before expressed, that he might perceive my affection to be so alienated from her, as I could not love her, nor be content of her preferment. Howbeit, he might persuade himself of the contrary; for as she once was the creature in the earth that I loved best, having that honor to be so near to me and having received such advancement and honor by her, I was not so unnatural ever to wish her body harm, or to speak of her as was untruly reported of me, howsoever the truth were in itself. And as the preservation of her son, now my sovereign, had moved me to enter in this cause and that her own pressing was the occasion of that which was uttered to her infamy; so when so ever God shall move her heart to repent of her by past behavior and life, and after her known repentance, that she should be separate from that ungodly and unlawful marriage that she was entered in, and then after were joined with such a godly and honorable personage, as were affectionate to the true religion, and whom we might trust, I could find in my heart to love her, and to show her as great pleasure, favor, and good will as ever I did in my life. And in case; he should be that personage, there was none whom I should better like of the Queen's majesty of England being made privy to the matter, and she allowing thereof; which being done, I should labor in all things that I could to her honor and pleasure, that were not prejudicial to the King my sovereign's estate, and prayed him not to think otherwise of me, for my affection was rather buried and hid within me, waiting until God should direct her to know herself, than utterly alienate and abstracted from her. Which he seemed to accept in very good part, saying, Earl of Murray, thou knows of me that thing whereto I will make none in England nor Scotland privy, and thou hast Norfolk's life in thy hands. So departing, I came to my lodging, &c.

Thus have I plainly declared how I have been dealt withal for this marriage, and how just necessity moved me not to rebut directly that which the duke appeared so bent to. And for my threatening to assent to the same, I have expressed the manner. The persons that laid the terror before me, were of mine own company, and the duke since has spoken that it was his writing which saved my life at that time. In conclusion, I pray you persuade her majesty that she let no speeches, nor any other thing passed and objected to my prejudice, move her majesty to alter her favor towards me, or anyways to doubt of my assured constancy towards her highness: for in anything that may tend to her honor and surety, I will, while I live, bestow myself and all that will do for me, notwithstanding any hazard or danger; as proof shall declare when her majesty finds time to employ me.

Sergeant. Thus appears it that the Duke of Norfolk first traveled with Ledington for stay and compounding the matter, and afterward likewise with the Bishop of Ross, and at both times first moved it of himself: so now the Earl of Murray also by his letters does testify that in conference with him, it came first of the duke to move the stay of the contention, and to what end the duke did it, namely, for that he aspired to the marriage of the Scottish Queen, and therein made account of her respect to the crown of England; and that without the Queen's majesty's assent or knowledge. Now shall you also see, for further proof thereof, the Bishop of Ross's letter to the Scottish Queen, for the Bishop of Ross went from York to Bolton as you have before heard in his examination. On the way, before he came to Bolton to the Scottish Queen from his lodging he wrote a letter to her, which letter was lost by his servant; but as good hap was, he reserved a copy thereof, and negligently left it behind him in his lodging at Newcastle where the Earl of Murray half a year after being lodged in the same chamber, found it and sent it to the Queen's majesty's council, and here it is all written with the bishop's own hand, as himself, being examined thereof, has confessed. Here he set out the conference between the Duke of Norfolk and Ledington, and himself. He showed the Duke of Norfolk's advice to the Scottish Queen for a letter by her to be written to the Queen's majesty; and also he opened the duke's advice, how to work for the Scottish Queen, with disclosing the Queen's majesty's secrets.

Here was the said letter produced, and read as follows:

Copy of the letter sent from York by the Bishop of Ross to the Queen-mother, to the Queen our sovereign lady, then remaining at Bolton.

Please your majesty, I conferred at great length with Ledington one great part of the night; who assured me he had reasoned with the Duke of Norfolk this Saturday, as yesterday on the fields who the day he rode to Cawood determined to him, that it was the Queen's majesty determinate purpose not to end your cause at this time, but to hold the same suspense; and did what was in her power to cause us the English Queen's commissioners pursued extremely to the effect the Lord Regent of Scotland and his adherents might utter all that they could to your dishonor; to the effect, as was supposed, to cause you come in disdain with the whole subjects of this realm, that you may be the more unable to attempt anything to her disadvantage; and to this effect is all her intention. And when they have produced all they can against you, the Queen will not appoint the matter instantly, but transport you up in the country, and reserve you there till she thinks time to show you favor; which is not able to be hastily, because of your uncles in France, and the fear she has of yourself to be her un-friend. And therefore their counsel is that you write a writing to the Queen, meaning that you are informed concerning your subjects which have offended you, this in effect; that your majesty hearing the estate of your affairs, as they proceed in York, was informed that her majesty was informed of you, that you could not godly remit your subjects in such sort, as they might credit you hereafter, which was one great cause of the stay of this controversy to be ended. And therefore persuading her grace effectively to trust any who made such narration; but like as you had rendered you in her hands, as most tender you of any living, so prayed her grace to take no opinion of you: but you would use her counsel in all your affairs, and would prefer her friendship to all others, as well uncles as others, and assure her to keep that tiling you would promise to your subjects by her advice. And if her grace discredit you, you would be glad to satisfy her in that point, to be removed within her realm in secret and quiet manner, where her grace pleased to the time her grace were fully satisfied, and all occasion of discredit removed from her; so that in the mean time your realm were held in quietness and your true subjects restored and maintained in your own estate, and such other things tending to this effect and affirms that they believe that this may be occasion to cause her credit you better, that you offer safer, and may I come that within two or three months she may become better minded toward your grace; for now while she is not well minded, and will not show you any pleasure, for the causes aforesaid.

Duke. Here be many things and many parts very hard for me to remember; and here be produced three witnesses against me, Ledington, the Bishop of Ross, and the Earl of Murray. Hereto I will answer as my memory will serve me: Ledington, because he and I were acquainted at Lyth, came to me and practiced to search at my hands, and to feel how the Queen's majesty was satisfied. I told him, that till I heard what the Queen's majesty would resolve, I could tell him nothing, and so time spent away. And in the mean season, upon a Saturday, I being at dinner with the Lord of Sussex, Ledington came in; and after dinner talking with me, he broke more earnestly for me with the Scottish Queen and for a marriage between her and me which I utterly refused as by my letters from York to the Queen's majesty it may appear; wherein I signified my opinion of the Scottish Queen, or else she must be maintained by the Queen of England. I said to him again, that the Queen's majesty sought the quietness of that realm; but for any advice of restoring the Scottish Queen into her country, I could not see how it might be considered and so I advised him to submit the whole matter to the Queen's majesty's judgment. Otherwise he and I never talked. Of those other doings between Ledington and the Scottish Queen, I know nothing. The Bishop of Ross shortly after said to me, and entreated to have my help for compounding of the matter, as you know well he can speak fair. I told him I could do nothing without my fellows and only in such manner as was prescribed by our commission. I told him also that we were but to hear and certify; and for the matter of compounding, they were best to make offers themselves; for we were but to receive such devices as they should cause, and to give advertisement of the same. To what end should I need to utter the matters of the Earl of Murray's part to the other side, when Ledington himself was present and privy to all? I spoke not with the Bishop of Ross, but at that time only. And as for that advice, to avoid the discovering of those rigorous matters by the earl and the publishing thereof to the Queen's majesty, to the Scottish Queen's infamy; I never disclosed any such secrets, nor gave any such advice. Only I did advise the Bishop of Ross that he and that side should hold themselves contented with the Queen's majesty's dealing, and with the determination taken at Hampton-Court, which was such as might content them, and such as my Lord Burleigh then disliked. As for the Earl Murray, he began with me, and not I with him, he came to me at Cawood and prayed me to tell him what end would come of the matter. I said I knew not; for it must come from the Queen's majesty: we knew not of the differing of the commission at that time, or till such time as Mr. Sadler was sent for. How could I tell him, and knew it not my felt? I never yielded to the marriage between the Scottish Queen and me. I cannot gather such matter of looks alone, I never dealt more therein, but only that Ledington broke it. Have I not answered all these matters? If I have or put me in anything I have omitted, and I will answer it.

Sergeant. Your answer is but only denial; Ledington and the rest write otherwise that you made the first motion to them and therefore Ledington, by practice between you and him, sent the Earl of Murray to you under pretence of searching to learn the state of their own cause to be moved by you for the marriage; upon your answer, it is but yea and nay between you. If you meant directly, then needed you not to have dealt so secretly in conference with Ledington, without the rest of the commissioners, and besides Ledington's conference with you, both the Bishop of Ross and the Earl of Murray affirm your practicing with them to the same intent which is sufficient proof against your own bare denial.

Duke. The Earl of Murray sought my life, the other are not of credit; yet all these prove not that I dealt in the matter of the marriage with the Scottish Queen, in any respect of her claim to the crown of England. Is the Bishop of Ross, or any other, can say otherwise; let them be brought before me face to face. I have often so desired it, but I could not obtain it.

Sergeant. The Bishop of Ross confessed it; this is his own hand; and here you shall have, by witnesses, proved the duke's assent to the marriage with the Scottish Queen and to practice the furtherance thereof, you shall see how that afterwards he was privy to a device that the Earl of Murray should have been murdered at Northallerton in his way homeward by the Norton's, Markenfield, and other rebels; and afterwards being satisfied at the Earl of Murray's hand, a letter was written to stay that device containing also a device of compounding the matter, and how the Earl of Murray had assented to the marriage.

Here was contained the Bishop of Ross's confession in article the ninth; wherein appears:

That the Earl of Murray should have been murdered by the way going home into Scotland; and that the Bishop of Ross wrote to the Scottish Queen that the Duke of Norfolk advised her to stay that murder because the Earl of Murray had yielded his good will to the marriage as follows:

Out of the Bishop of Ross's examination, taken the 6th of November, 1571.

To the 9th he said, that the Earl of Murray was in fear to have been murdered by the way in his return to Scotland; whereupon this examinee, by the duke's advice, did write to the Queen of Scots that the attempt might be staid, for that Murray had yielded to the duke to be favorable; and the murder should have been executed about Northallerton by the Norton's, Markenfield, and others, as this examinee was advertised by the Scottish Queen's servants that came from Bolton.

Sergeant. Thus it appears that the duke so far assented to the marriage, that rather than it should not have taken effect, he was contented that the Earl of Murray should have been murdered.

Duke. The unkindness between the Earl of Murray and me was not about this matter of his mistress the Scottish Queen, but for another cause; it was because the Earl of Murray had reported that I sought the marriage of the Scottish Queen. I charged him therewith by message, he excused himself thereof, and laid it upon the Earl of Moreton and the Bishop of Orkney; and for the device of murdering him, I was never privy to it. And where the article faith that I heard it by the Scottish Queen's servants that came from Bolton, it is not true. I never heard of it till Whitsuntide after when John Wood came and then I heard it not but by the Bishop of Ross, neither did I hear that it should have been done by the Norton's, but by my brother of Westmoreland being hunting when the Earl of Murray espying a great company on the hill side, imagined that he should have been slain.

Sergeant. You shall also understand that the duke himself wrote to the Earl of Murray, wherein is plainly declared his practice and assent to the marriage which very letter we have not, but the copy thereof under the regent's own hand, which the regent sent to the Queen's majesty, whereby the matter most plainly appears.

My good lord,

I have received your courteous letter, whereby I do not only perceive you well affected for the advancement of your common weal, and the uniting of this island, but also your good mind towards me; which two points I cannot but note to your special commendation, and my great comfort. As you shall prove me industrious to assist you with all my power in the one, so shall you not find me ungrateful in the other, but really to requite you to my uttermost for your friendship so frankly offered; the rather I shall have occasion to employ myself for the just reward of your deserts, the sooner I shall think myself in nature, friendship, and conscience discharged of my obligation. In the mean time, good my lord, assure yourself that you have not only purchased a faithful friend, but also a natural brother who is not, nor will not be less careful for your weal and surety than his own honor and credit; whereof I am fully persuaded you doubt not and therefore in that point I need not to be over tedious, but briefly to return to that you desire to be satisfied of, which is for my marriage with all sincerity with your sister; wherein I must deal plainly with your lordship, as my only friend, that I have so far proceeded herein, as I, with conscience, can neither revoke that that I have done, nor never do mean, while I do live to go back from this that is done, nor with honor proceed further until such time as you there shall remove such stumbling blocks as be impeachment to our more apparent proceeding which when by me it shall be finished upon mine honor the rest shall follow to your contentment and comfort. Wherefore my earnest request at this present to my good lord, is that you will proceed herein with such expedition, as the enemies of this good purpose which will be no small number against the uniting of this land into one Kingdom in time coming, and the maintenance of God's true religion, may not have opportunity, through the delay given them to hinder our intended determination against the which I am of opinion, there will be no practices by foreign princes omitted. This I hope will be sufficient to resolve you my lord of your desire touching the marriage; referring myself wholly for your more ample instruction and satisfaction in all points to my Lord Boyd, who has commission both by the Queen of Scotland, your sister, and also by me to resolve you of all doubts, whom I wish you to credit as myself. You shall not want the furtherance in this enterprise of the most part of the noblemen of this realm; whose faithful friendship in this case, and all other my actions, I have to my contentment sufficiently proved. Thus being persuaded that your lordship's endeavor is for the maintenance of God's glory and the advancement of the common weal of this island, I have adventured to impart my secret determination, as to one whom I make account to be assured of, and to whom I wish long life and prosperous health, to his heart's desire. So with my hearty commendations at this present without further molestation, I am from my house in London, July 1, my good lord, your faithful and most assured friend.

I have heard you have been in the north, the Queen of your conferences with Ledington and Scotland, and doubt not but you have satisfied the request I made for the Bishop of Ross and have caused his servants to be obeyed of his benefices; and what is left undone, I pray you cause it to be effectually furthered. He has the Queen of Scots letter directed to you for that effect; but trusting that my request shall make him to be obeyed, ere the other come to your hands wherein you shall do me singular pleasure.

Norfolk.

Duke. All these are letters and answered two years ago when Mr. Sadler and Mr. Attorney were sent to examine me upon interrogatories. Indeed I must confess my folly; it is an ill cook that cannot lick his own fingers. The Bishop of Ross wrote the letter and he licked his own fingers. The Earl of Murray wrote to me very humbly, and that he was at my commandment with such like words. I having no leisure to write answer to him drew articles to give him thanks but that the noblemen liked of that marriage, and that I wished no man's friendship more than his in it, the Bishop of Ross added of his own, and put it in cipher in this form, which cipher I had not then.

Sergeant. This is the very copy of your own letter.

Duke. See my answer made in my first troubles, two years past.

Sergeant. The Queen's majesty understanding the duke's intention to marry with the Scottish Queen, the duke himself, by way of prevention complained to her majesty of the rumor that was spread against him, that he sought the Scottish Queen's marriage and prayed it might be examined. In which her complaint, as I have heard her majesty herself declare it, and some here of my lords have likewise heard it, he said among other things, to what end should I seek to marry her, being so wicked a woman, such a notorious adulteress and murderer? I love to sleep upon a safe pillow: I account myself to your majesty's good favor, as good a prince at home in my bowling alley at Norwich as she is, though she were in the middle of her Kingdom. The revenues of the crown of Scotland (all the ordinary charges deducted) about the necessary affairs of the realm, are not comparable to mine own that I enjoy by your goodness, as I have heard of the chief officers of that realm; considering also that her Kingdom is not in her hand, but possessed by another; if I should leek to match with her, knowing as I do know that she pretends a title to the present possession of your crown, your majesty might justly charge me with seeking your own crown from your head. This the duke spoke to the Queen's majesty in his excuse when the same went of his marriage with the Scottish Queen, when yet beside that time, he had dealt earnestly in it.

Duke. I may not nor will not stand against her majesty's testimony, I must give place to it; but hereof I was examined two years ago, and then I declared, as I now do, that at that time I intended not the marriage. And true it is that I have at sundry times, some at one time, and some at another, used some of those kinds of speeches; but at that time I dealt not with that marriage, nor minded it.

Sergeant. Your own confession is otherwise; for yourself have since confessed that you concealed from the Queen your conferences with Ledington and Rome about the marriage, both the conferences had at York and at Hampton-Court.

Duke. I never consented to the marriage at those times of their conferences, and so I might well use their speeches.

Then was produced his own examination the 6th of November, 1571 and it was read, and he confessed his concealment of those speeches and conferences before used about the marriage and that it had indeed been moved, but not concluded on. He remembered that the Queen charged him straightly not to proceed in that marriage; but he remembered not that she charged him upon his allegiance.

The Duke of Norfolk, the 6th of November, 1571.

To the first and second, he said that he remembered that at Hampton-Court, upon a report made by Robert Melvin, so declared by Woolcock, that this examinant had gone about a matter of marriage with the Scottish Queen for himself, wherein he took himself to be much wronged, and desired to have the matter examined; for that he had not dealt in that matter, and does not remember what the Queen's to him at that time at which for himself, that he intended no such thing, nor meant any such thing; and yet he confessed that he did not declare to the Queen's majesty at that time, of any speech that had been used to him by Ledington at York, and the Earl of Murray at Hampton-Court, touching the said marriage. Being at Titchfield the Queen's majesty called him to her gallery asking of him whether he had dealt any while for the marriage of the Queen of Scots, as it was reported. Whereto he answered, he thought her majesty had heard by others. But she willed him to declare the truth, because she had rather hear it of himself and so he declared that he had received letters from her that the matter had been moved and written to her; but he had not made any conclusion in that matter with her. Whereupon her majesty showing herself to dislike thereof, commanded and charged him that he should not deal any further therein with the Queen of Scots, nor any other person in that matter but that he was charged upon his allegiance, he does not certainly remember; but that he was straightly commanded, he does well remember.

At length he confessed that he was charged upon his allegiance.

Sergeant. At Titchfield the Queen's majesty expressly commanded the Duke of Norfolk upon his allegiance, as himself has now confessed, not to proceed in that marriage with the Scottish Queen. Now, if we prove that this commandment notwithstanding, and against his own promise, he afterward still proceeded and that much more earnestly than before, and yet nevertheless that he had all the while conceived an evil opinion against the Scottish Queen and upon the sight of her letters, and other evidences, showed he thought her plainly guilty of abominable whoredom, of the murder of her husband and signified it by letters, and declared the same his opinion to Bannister and also that he made no account of her Kingdom of Scotland, which she had not in possession, or if she would have it, yet he counted it not comparable to his own dukedom. He (I say) so doing, and so conceiving and so declaring, and yet still more and more prosecuting the marriage, cannot be said to have prosecuted it, in respect of her person but of some other thing (forsooth the crown of England) which he hoped to attain under her pretended title. You never saw her, you could not then be carried with love of her person; you conceived ill opinion of her, so could you not be led with love of her conditions; the same of her good qualities and virtuous conditions you never heard much of except it were by herself, or the Bishop of Ross, or some of her ministers; her Kingdom of Scotland you esteemed not, both because she had it not in possession, but it was in possession of her son, by her own demise ratified by Parliament, and for that it was not of so good value as your own possessions were.

To what end then pursued you the marriage? To no other end surely, but to advance and maintain the false and pretended title to the present possession of the crown of England; and for the attaining thereof, to practice the deprivation, death and destruction of the Queen's majesty. If further, we shall plainly prove that after your departing from the court, you meant not only to prosecute the marriage, but also to prosecute it with force against the Queen in her own realm; then it must needs be with intent of her majesty's deprivation and destruction and so high-treason, within compass of the statute of 25 of Edward the Third. For whoso shall take upon him to prosecute and maintain a title to the crown by force against the Queen, and within her own realm, must needs make account that the Queen must and will resist that force; if then that force may overcome the prince's force, what is the likelihood then to ensue? There must needs follow deprivation of the Queen, and thereupon her death and destruction; for the jealousy of a usurper by force can in no wise suffer a rightful prince to live. Now to prove your intention to pursue the marriage with force against the Queen. In your journey towards London, you entered into conference and device between another and you for taking the Tower of London with all the Queen's ordnance, ammunition and treasure therein, and to have kept the Tower by force against the Queen and so to have brought the marriage to pass by force, whether the Queen would or no. But it took not effect for the Queen's majesty having understanding thereof before, provided for enforcing the place with new supply; and Mr. Pelham, Lieutenant of the Ordnance, was for that purpose, put in with sufficient power. Afterward being at your own house, the Charter-House, the Queen's majesty understanding of these attempts, sent for you; whereto you make a feigned excuse of doubt of sickness and that you had taken physick, so that for four or five days you could not journey; promising after those four or five days, to wait on her majesty, according to your duty. And immediately after this excuse sent, without tarrying four or five days, or any more days, the same night, you by and by stole away into Norfolk, and there intended to have levied force; but that the Queen's majesty and her council suspecting your purpose, had secretly sent into those parts before, and taken order for impeaching of your intention. If this then be proved true, that you still prosecuted the marriage without liking of her person, without estimation of her possessions, with only respect to her false title to the crown of England, and with force; and since it cannot be pursued with force against the Queen, nor force levied against her majesty without purpose to suppress her majesty's force, and to depose her from her crown and dignity; and he that so seeks to depose her must needs be thought that he will not suffer her to live. All these matters considered, the seeking of this marriage in this form, must needs be high-treason within compass of the statute of 25 of Edward the Third.

Here was produced the duke's own letter, and the other commissioners from York to the Queen's majesty; wherein is signified the great abomination of the Scottish Queen, appearing in her own letters, and the certainty of the truth of those letters, both by offer of oath of those that exhibited them, and by discourses of some matters there which could not be written but by herself, being known to none other. The commissioner's letter is as follows.

Afterwards they showed to us a horrible and long letter of her own hand (as they say) containing foul matter and abominable to be either thought of, or to be written by a princess with divers fond ballads of her own hand; which letters, ballads, and other writings before specified, were closed in a little coffer of silver and gilt, heretofore given to her by Bothwell. The said letters and ballads did discover such inordinate and filthy love between her and Bothwell, her loathsomeness and abhorring of her husband that was murdered, and the conspiracy of his death in such sort as every good and godly man cannot but detest and abhor the same. And those men here do constantly affirm the said letters and other writings which they produce of her own hand, to be her own hand indeed, and do offer to swear and to take their oath thereupon; as indeed the matter contained in them being such as could hardly be invented or devised by any other than by herself; for that the discourse of some things which were unknown to any other than to herself and Bothwell, does the rather persuade us to believe that they be indeed of her own hand-writing. And as it is hard to counterfeit so many and so long letters; so the matters of them, and the manner how these men came by them is such, as it seemed that God, in whose sight the murder and blood of the innocent is abominable, would not permit the same to be hid or concealed. In a paper herein enclosed, we have noted to your majesty the chief and principal points of their letters, written (as they say) with her own hand to the intent it may please your majesty to consider of them and so to judge whether the same be sufficient to convince her of the detestable crime of the murder of her husband; which in our opinion and consciences, if the said letters be written with her own hand (as we believe they be) is very hard to be avoided.

Duke. This makes for me, for this proves that I so much disliking her, and signifying by my letter so much against her, dealt not on that side when I was at York, where this letter was written.

Sergeant. There were others joined with you in the letter, so that you could not otherwise write, however you otherwise dealt, but this makes much against you, for it proved you had an evil opinion of her, and so could not seek the marriage in respect of her person, but only in respect of her false title; and that not to the Kingdom of Scotland, which she had not, and which you despised, but to the crown of England. Now you shall, to the same end, hear your own report against her to Bannister.

Duke. Bannister was shrewdly cramped when he told that tale. I beseech you let me have him brought face to face.

Sergeant. No more than you were.

Then was read Bannister's confession, in October, 12 Elizabeth.

Sergeant. This shows that you had an evil opinion of her, and so no affection to the person; therefore you're seeking of that marriage was for another respect; and therefore Ledington, Ross, and you practiced the matter at York.

Duke. They broke it to me. What is this to me? Did I consent?

Sergeant. You consented.

Duke. No.

Sergeant. They say plainly that you practiced to withdraw the things that might charge her.

Wilbraham. You have said, that the Bishop of Ross has accused you of malice; but you answer nothing to that which the Bishop of Ross wrote to his mistress the Scottish Queen, in secrecy, wherein could be no malice.

Duke. Ledington broke it to me, and the Earl of Murray broke it to me. I pray you, let them be brought face to face to me. I have often relinquished it, and the law I trust is so.

Sergeant. The law was so for a time, in some cases of treason, but since the law has been found too hard and dangerous for the prince and it has been repealed. You intended to have proceeded with the marriage by force, and for proof thereof you have heard of the device for taking of the Tower. Now to prove further your purpose to pursue your enterprise by force, let be read the confession of the Bishop of Ross to the second article.

The Bishop of Ross's confession the 3rd of November, 1571.

To the second article. The duke being after conferred with by the Bishop of Ross from his mistress, to know what he would do in the matter of the marriage, if the Queen would not assent, said he knew she would, though not at the first because most of the council and noblemen thought it meet; and that he had known the minds of most of the noblemen. And after when the Queen was offended with him coming from Southampton, he told the Bishop he would depart into his own country, and so was resolved by the Earls of Arundel and Pembroke who would do the like; and there would take purpose, by the advice of his countrymen and friends, and do that was likeliest for the advancement of the cause. The Bishop said the Queen's majesty would by force fetch him out of his country. He answered that no nobleman in England would accept that charge at her commandment; for he knew their mind, specially for those in the north who would assist. And if that he might once have that open quarrel against her, that she would first pursue him, he would have friends enough to assist him and that the Scottish Queen should be lately enough provided for; for that was the principal mark he shot at, and would do what he could to have her in his hands. And the Earls of Arundel and Pembroke had promised to do as he did; and they in the north had promised the like. Item, Liggons told the Bishop that the duke was resolved to go through with the matter by force if the Queen would not assent to it. At this time common messages past between the Scottish Queen and the duke, and them of the north.

Duke. All is false, saving that the Bishop of Ross once spoke with me; and then understanding him to be a suspected man, I desired him to forbear to come to me; nevertheless, by his great earnestness and importunity that I would but once admit him to come to me, at length he came, and then he moved me for certain money of the Scottish Queen's, about 2000£ remaining in my keeping, one letter he brought me, and no more letters till after my first trouble. As for my going into Norfolk, I can bring good witness that I meant not to go into Norfolk, four hours before I went, and that I spoke not with him in two days before. It is of good ground that I have prayed to have the Bishop of Ross brought to me in private examination face to face, whereby I might have put him in remembrance of truth; but I have not had him face to face, nor have been suffered to bring forth witnesses, proofs, and arguments, as might have made for my purgation. As for sending of letters to my Lord of Northumberland, or my brother of Westmoreland, all is false;

I never received letters from them in all my time. If ever I sent to them, or received from them any letters in three quarters of a year before, let me never be credited.

Sergeant. You shall have proofs that the Bishop of Rose has said it. You stand much upon your own credit now therefore to your credit I will say somewhat against your oath specially taken, when you were appointed commission for the matter at York; and against your oath of a counselor to the Queen's majesty, you dealt indirectly and partially; you deceived the Queen's majesty's trust, and disclosed her secrets.

Duke. I deny it.

Sergeant. It is well proved that at Hampton-Court, being examined of the matter by the Queen's majesty, you dissembled it being examined of money lent by you to the Scottish Queen; you denied it being charged upon your allegiance, you promised not to proceed further in the matter. Notwithstanding that express commandment of her majesty; yet against your duty, against your promise and faith, you still proceeded.

Duke. I confess this was mine error; but I have already made humble petition to my peers not to compound my faults together, nor to mingle my inferior offences with this great cause.

Sergeant. Since the commandment given to you at Titchfield not to proceed in dealing with the Scottish Queen in any wise, you have continually dealt with her; you have lent her money; you have maintained Liggons, your man and your solicitor continually to advertise you from the Bishop of Glasgow, and the Pope's Nuncio; and you have advertised him from hence. He has had money of you, and you have received letters from him four times in coffers.

Duke. Liggons is not my solicitor.

Sergeant. He is your solicitor, and so yourself have expounded him; for where the Scottish Queen in her letters, speaks of your solicitor being asked whom she meant thereby, you have answered, Liggons.

Duke. At the first indeed she so called him; but solicitor is no name of use. He has not been so since my first trouble; and so for her calling, it is no matter, she once called me Legista.

Sergeant. He is your solicitor; for she so takes him, and yourself do so expound it.

Then was read his own confession of money lent 2000£ and received, the duke confessed this receiving and lending of money.

Then was read the Bishop of Ross's confession, concerning money sent by Barthwick and of money delivered to Francis Bishop.

Duke. This I deny not.

Sergeant. Francis Bishop was a traitor.

Duke. I knew him not.

Sergeant. Now for the matter of taking the Tower.

Duke. I deny it.

Sergeant. Was it not mentioned to you in the way when you came from Titchfield, by one that came to you and moved you a device between you and another for taking the Tower?

Duke. I have confessed that such a motion was made to me, but I never assented to it.

Sergeant. You concealed it: and to what end should you have taken the Tower, but to have kept it against the Queen by force? But you say you liked not the motion, you asked advice of it.

Duke. Indeed I told one of it. Owen met me by the way from Titchfield, and told me how we were all in danger; and said that some of our friends thought it was best to take the Tower. I refused to do it, and said take the Tower that were a proper device indeed! And thence I went to my Lord of Pembroke and there dined; and then I told my Lord of Pembroke of that device; whereto he answered, we are well and safe enough: let them that be faulty take the Tower, if they will. And to what end should I have taken the Tower?

Sergeant. To maintain by force that which you had practiced against the Queen's majesty's commandment, which was the marriage with the Scottish Queen.

Duke. I had not then dealt with it.

Sergeant. It is well proved that you had; and afterward at your house at Charter-House, you received letters, messages, and tokens from the Scottish Queen; you received from her a brooch with a hand cutting down a vine, and this poesy upon it, *Virescit vulnere Virtus.* But my lord, do green vines grow when they be cut? And a green vine it was.

Wilbraham. My lord, you still say you dealt not at this time or that time against her majesty's commandment; I pray you at what time, since her majesty's commandment upon your allegiance, did you forbear to deal with the Scottish Queen?

Sergeant. Beside this you have given advice as a counselor to the Scottish Queen, against the Queen's majesty: namely, when in treaty between the Queen's majesty and her, there were three articles propounded on the Queen's majesty's part; the one for the delivery of her son into the Queen's majesty's custody; the other for delivering the English rebels that were fled into Scotland; the third for delivering of certain holds in Scotland into English men's possession: he gave advice herein as a counselor against the Queen his sovereign lady. The articles were expressly sent to the duke to have his advice before that the Scottish Queen would resolve of any answer; and she respited her answer to be made according to his direction. He gave advice, that she should in no wise deliver her son, for it was against her own safety, not knowing whether she delivered him into her friends hands or no. As for the rebels, she should in no wise deliver them, for it were against her honor, and as for the holds, she should not deliver any; for it were against the safety of her friends in Scotland.

Duke. For advising not to deliver the rebels, I deny that ever I gave any such advice. As for delivery of her son, I advised her no otherwise but thus, that I wished her to bestow him there, where she might have sure friends.

Sergeant. Thus, contrary to your oath, allegiance, and fidelity, and against the credit that you would fain be thought of, you became by your own confession, a counselor to a foreign prince against your own sovereign lady.

Burleigh. My lord, did you ever desire to have any proofs or witnesses produced for your part to prove anything that might make for you I and were you denied?

Duke. I have divers times prayed that if anything were denied to be true which I said, I might be driven to my proof of it.

Burleigh. I ask it, because I have not heard it reported to her majesty that you made any such request to have any special witnesses examined, or proofs heard, on your part.

Here was produced and read the confession of Hickford to the 3rd article.

Duke. I advised her, touching her son, that she should first be well assured that he should be bestowed among her friends. For her castles, I advised her, that she should in any wise take heed that they might not after come into the hands of her enemies; for so if she delivered Edinburgh Castle, she should not be safe in Holyrood-House.

Sergeant. How stands this with the duty and oath of a counselor to give advice to a foreign prince against the Queen's majesty?

Duke. I excuse it not, herein I confess my error; I beseech you call not these my inferior faults which I have confessed, among the greater wherewith I am charged.

Sergeant. Thus appears how he has given advice against the Queen to the Scottish Queen. Now it shall be further proved to you that where the Scottish Queen is here in custody as the Queen's prisoner, he has also been privy to devices for conveying her away.

Here was produced the confession of Barker, October 5. 1571. Article 13.

Duke. This is not true, saving that indeed advice was broken to me of conveying her away at a window, at a gallery's end in one of my Lord of Shrewsbury's houses of the which window the Bishop of Ross had taken a measure; but this device was overthrown at such time as it was told me. As for that which Barker has here confessed, it is utterly false.

Sergeant. Now shall you hear the duke's own confession.

Here was read the duke's examination, 13 October.

Sergeant. Besides this, the duke being in prison in the Tower, made a submission to the Queen's majesty, confessed his error in dealing with the Scottish Queen and promised upon his faith and allegiance, never to deal with that marriage, nor with any other matter touching the Scottish Queen.

Duke. I confess I did so.

Sergeant. Before his subscribing his said submission, he first made the Scottish Queen privy to it, and sent her a double of it.

Duke. I sent it to the Bishop of Ross.

Sergeant. All is one.

Duke. I confess it.

Sergeant. What should move my Lord of Norfolk now so earnestly still to pursue this marriage? You see he liked not the person, she was not of good fame, he so signified to the Queen, he so reported to Bannister. The Kingdom of Scotland he esteemed not, and also it was out of her possession in the hands of the King her son, by her own dismission ratified by Parliament. Forsooth he had an old blind prophecy lying by him: in *exalt at ione Lunæ Leo fuccumbet, & Leo cum Leone conjungetur, catuli eorum regnabunt;* which belike is thus to be expounded at the exaltation of the moon (which was the rising of the Earl of Northumberland, that gives the moon) the lion (which is the Queen's majesty) shall be overthrown; then shall the lion be joined with a lion (which is the Duke of Norfolk with the Scottish Queen, for they both bear lions in their arms) and their whelps shall reign, (that is, their posterity shall have the Kingdom.)

Duke. I do not remember any such prophecy.

Sergeant. It was in your own keeping.

Duke. What should I do with it?

Sergeant. Such blind prophecies have oft deceived noblemen.

Duke. This is nothing to the purpose; I kept it not to any such end.

Sergeant. You uttered it to your servant Hickford.

Here was produced and read Hickford's testimony.

Duke. A toy! You see I call it a foolish prophecy.

Sergeant. Where had you it?

Duke. I remember it not.

Sergeant. Hitherto have you heard the evidence to prove the duke's imagination, compassing, and conspiracy, to deprive the Queen's majesty of the crown and her royal estate, and so to bring her highness to death and destruction. For proving this his intent, you have heard those matters proved, his practice to join himself in marriage with the Scottish Queen, whom he then well knew falsely to claim and pretend title to the present possession of the crown of England: also his prosecuting the same marriage without the Queen's majesty's knowledge against her highness's express commandment upon his allegiance against his faith, promise, and submission; yea, and to pursue that with force, and to use the advice and strength of his friends, to maintain the same force against the Queen; his hearkening to blind prophecies, money by him lent to the Scottish Queen and against the Queen his sovereign lady. It then was his purpose so were to pursue it with force, it must needs follow that the same must be of intent, imagination, and compassing, to deprive and depose the Queen's majesty from her crown, royal estate, and dignity, and to advance and maintain that false and usurped title of the Scottish Queen to the present possession of the crown of England and so consequently for maintenance of his imagination and purpose, to compass the Queen's majesty's death and destruction. Now shall you further hear proof of his own words, declaring the same intent to pursue the marriage by force, and rather to lose his life than to give it over.

Cavendish's deposition.

That at his several journeys to the places of the Queen of Scots abode, the duke procured him to labor the cause of his marriage with her with all diligence. Item, that her majesty being at Southampton, Richard Candish, a certain night walking in his chamber, and persuading him by all means to labor for the Queen's favor concerning that marriage the duke affirmed that before he lost that marriage he would lose his life: and said moreover that if ever he handled thing wisely or cunningly, I would say it was die matter of that marriage, if I knew it from the beginning. Item, that the Monday at night, after the duke's departure from Southampton, Richard Candish being at Hayward-House with him in the company of the Lord Lumley, the duke and the said Lord Lumley talking secretly together, suddenly the duke broke out into this speech: Candish, quote he, is able to accuse me of no distal practices. Whereat the Lord Lumley, as it were wondering can he not indeed, quote he? No indeed, quote the duke; and turning to Candish, said, Candish I in this case defy thee, say thy worst. To which Candish answered, besides the practice of this marriage, I truly can accuse you of none. Item, the duke at another time in the said house asked Candish if God take away the Queen's majesty, whether be could assure him or his brother Candish, and procure his said brother to promise to him Sir Robert Ningfield? Item, at his jail being at Remming-Hall among many others talking, he had this speech; Candish (quote he) nothing will undo us but the rising of the northern lords. To whom I answered, God forbid that any such thing should be, for it will undo us all; whereat he replying, said fear they will rise.

Duke. The duke looking upon Cavendish with a scornful and smiling countenance, said, thou are an honest man! That which he said of the talk between him and me at Southampton is utterly false: at that time you were most earnest on my part and came to me as for succor, for that as you laid your cousin Christina's was fallen out with you. When we rode to my Lord of Pembroke's, you came to me and told me my Lord Burleigh finds me well, I will ride with him and find his humor, and I will face that fellow thoroughly; so from Salisbury you said you would ride to Leicester and so home with my Lord Burleigh, and you doubted not to bring me such word from him as should satisfy me. You told me how my Lord of Leicester was firm and Sir Nicholas Throckmorton my sure friend, and that they would both join to deal with the Queen for me; and how Sir Nicholas Throckmorton lent me word that he doubted not the Queen would take order to my contention at her next coming to a said house. Then came you to London, and though I had no great liking of you, yet because you were loath to lie at Arundel's, and were somewhat ill at ease, I let you lie in my house. I never made great account of you; my Lord of Leicester made us first acquainted, your brother you know was not my friend, I then took you as I now find you. While you could hold on, you showed your letters that you did write on my behalf; then you came to me and said you had need, and borrowed money of me; I had none at that time, but I sent it you by Bowes. I was warned by divers of my friends to take heed of you; you dealt with Dier and with Strange very maliciously. As for the speech at Remming-Hall, that you speak of me, it is untrue; I dealt not with you there about any such matter; I left you at London, I looked not for you; when you came, I was glad to be rid of you, you said you were going to Norwich and I was glad you were going, and willed you to look at my house at Norwich and tell me how you liked it: out of the north I heard nothing in six weeks before. You suddenly slipped away from me, and then came I up to London ward; you are an honest man indeed, it is all false that he has said.

Then Cavendish began to report and justify what he had said, and to put the duke in remembrance when the duke gave him reproachful words of discredit.

Sergeant. He is sworn, there needs no more proving; you sent Havers to the Earl of Westmoreland.

Then was alleged the examination of one Haveling touching Havers, whom the duke sent to the Earl of Northumberland with this message, that if the two earls should rise, he were undone.

Duke. This may be seen of two years old, and by me fully declared and answered.

Then was read the confession of Havers.

Then was alleged a letter of the Scottish Queen's in cipher to the duke containing that the Lord of Shrewsbury had told her that the Earl of Northumberland was delivered to the Earl of Sussex; for which she was very sorrowful three days together, for fear of cumbering of friends if he were taken.

Sergeant. What friends was she so careful for, that she wrote to the duke, unless she thought it should light upon the duke himself?

Duke. That letter never came to my hands.

Sergeant. It was found in the bag which you willed to be burned.

Then the said letter was read.

Duke. All this is nothing to me.

Sergeant. This proves in you a practice to the rebellion; for all her sorrow of the yielding of the Earl of Northumberland was for fear he should betray and cumber her friends.

Duke. That touches not me; for I am sure the Earl of Northumberland has been sought for me, and yet he cannot accuse me.

Sergeant. Had it not concerned you, it had not been written to you.

Duke. Some letters never came to my hands: sometimes they came to the Bishop of Ross, sometimes to Bannister, sometimes not all deciphered; as Strange and Bowes and other that have been messengers for me can tell.

Here Mr. Attorney began to prosecute the second part and spoke first to this effect.

Attorney. Now you have heard enough of the first matter. In this indictment are contained three principal treasons whereof the first is imagining and conspiring the deprivation, death, and destruction of the Queen's majesty: for proof hereof, it has been truly said that to imagine, compass, or procure the deposing or death of the prince, is high-treason by the statute of 25 Edward III and at the common law; for the statute is but a declaration what was treason at common law: which imagination, when it appears by overt fact, must needs be judged treason; for overt fact is but a showing of a man's mind, which when a man by outward speech or deed has uttered, it must needs be judged that so was his meaning; which must be gathered by such means as it may be made to appear. For no traitor is so bold to say expressly he will depose or kill the King; but often it has been seen that they go about indirectly, and by means that tend to that end: and therefore he that goes about to stir the people to rebellion, or to levy war within the realm, to assail or withstand the prince by force, is taken to seek the death of the prince. Now therefore to prove that the Duke of Norfolk has imagined and compassed the deposing and death of the Queen's majesty, this has been showed you: first, by secret and indirect means he sought to join himself in marriage with the Scottish Queen, who pretended title to the Queen's crown. This he did without the Queen's majesty's private, against her highness's express commandment upon his allegiance, against his own promise and submission. First, being at York, a commissioner appointed by the Queen, contrary to his oath and charge, he dealt indirectly and partially, and played an untrue part with the Queen; he secretly practiced for the marriage. This being objected against him, he has denied it: you have heard it testified by three witnesses, the Earl of Murray, Ledington and the Bishop of Ross. So it appears that all that practice and indirect dealing was to this end, to compass the deprivation and death of the Queen's majesty; for he well knew that the Scottish Queen made title to the present possession of the crown of England; that she denied the Queen's majesty to be lawful Queen of this realm; that she usurped the royal style, that she quartered the arms of England without any difference: all this he knew, he was of the Queen's majesty's Privy Council at the same time, he knew that she made no renunciation of her unjust claim, though it were required of her. It was also one article in the commission where he himself was commissioner, to require the recognition of her error, and of the Queen's majesty's present right: he knew well it was not done. It the Scottish Queen claimed such present title, then was she no friend to the Queen's majesty, but a seeker of her highness's overthrow and destruction and yet the Duke of Norfolk knowing this, practiced to compass this marriage. Wherefore, I pray you, sought he that marriage? Yea, and sought it as he meant to achieve it with force. It was not in respect of her person, for he knew her not; it could not be for any good report of her virtuous conditions, for he had an evil opinion of her: he did by his writing certify against her, he declared to Bannister that he thought very ill of her. It was not for her title to the Kingdom of Scotland, for neither was she possessed of it, neither did he esteem it though she had it. Wherefore sought he her then? Surely in respect of that unjust claim and title that she pretended to the present possession of the crown of England; which title cannot be maintained without evident purpose to depose the Queen's majesty and to bring her to death and destruction which is plain treason by the statute of 25 Edward III for no more can England bear two Queens, than the world can bear two suns. And how should we have maintained it but with force? And how could that have been without depriving of the Queen's majesty from the royal estate? And how could that have been done without compassing her highness's death and destruction? For the jealousy of an usurper cannot suffer the just prince to live. This your honors are to search and consider, and to your judgments we refer it. Now my Lord of Norfolk's chief and only answer is but his bare denial, which is no sufficient answer; specially since he himself has fallen into so great discredit by doing against his word, his hand, and his oath. He promised, being commanded upon his allegiance, never to deal in that matter; he promised by his submission under his own hand, utterly to forsake it and to deal no more with the Scottish Queen for that marriage, nor any other matter: he promised by oath specially taken when he was commissioner for hearing the matter at York to do therein directly and indifferently without partiality. All these oaths and promises he has broken, beside the oath of a counselor which he has also broken in disclosing the Queen's secrets and in secret practicing against her express commandment. Now also, since he was last apprehended and committed, he has denied certain things which he has afterward, being constrained with strength of proof, confessed; yea, he has denied those things upon his oath which he has afterward granted to be true: so is he not to be believed upon his word if his own word discredit him, how great so ever he be in degree.

Duke. Upon the statute of 25 Edward III he inferred that it is treason to imagine or compass the deprivation and death of the Queen's majesty, as the Lord forbid, and I pray God I may sooner be buried in the earth, than I should leak or attempt anything to the destruction of her majesty's person. There is a maxim in law, that penal statutes must be construed strictly, and no penal statute ought to be extended further than the very words: now in all that my accusers have deposed or said against me, how false so ever it be, there is not one of them that say I went about any hurt to her majesty's person or that I levied or practiced to levy any power against her, or to do any of those things that are contained for treasons within the words of the statute. Is the Bishop of Ross a sufficient witness against me? There be points enough in the law to prove him no sufficient witness: he is a stranger and a Scot; a stranger can be no sufficient witness, much less a Scot: for whereas when there is peace between the Queen's majesty and a foreign realm, the people of that foreign realm may freely come and traffic in this realm; yet though there be a peace between England and Scotland, if a Scot come into England without a passport, he may be a lawful prisoner. Again, I cannot tell what he may for fear. Bratlon said, that witnesses must be *Liberi Homines*, free men, full age, honest, and of good report: the Bishop of Ross is none such. So is nothing proved of any overt fact against me, neither am I accused by any but the Bishop of Ross, who can be no sufficient witness against me. What care I what Hamlin says? It touches me not. As for Havers, I never sent him with any such message: indeed I asked him what company he found with my brother of Westmoreland. He told me he found none but my brother Westmoreland. But as for my Lord of Northumberland, I sent not to him. If I might have brought forth my proofs, I could have brought forth proofs of good fame that I sent no such message; I could have proved it by confessions, and not by hearsay. So is only the Bishop of Ross witness against me, and what he is, all you perceive. I never heard of the rebellion till Sir Henry Neville told me of it. If I had had such a mind when I was in Norfolk, I needed not to have come hither; I could have made a shift well enough. If I had intended any such rebellion or treason, I would not have put my Lord of Northumberland in trust withal, nor yet my brother of Westmoreland, nor would have come hither to put my head in the halter in the Tower: but being as I was in such place where I might have shifted, I would have kept me from coming here well enough. If fear had moved me, and that I doubted of mine own case, I could easily have avoided. So, I say to prove me guilty of treason, you must show some overt fact that I have done against her majesty's person: and to the witnesses, I think I have said sufficiently. As touching my dealing with the Scottish Queen, so far as I dealt without compass of treason, this I say for my meaner faults, inferior to treason, I have with all repentance and humility submitted myself to the Queen's majesty, I beseech you confound not those with this case: but in my dealing with her about marriage, I pray you draw it not to such intention, to advance her title against the Queen; because, though she once made such claim, yet considering what amity has since been between the Queen and her to make her now an enemy, is hard; and surely to marry her, though I treated of it, I never minded, nor intended, where it's said I was privy to the device of her taking away, I utterly deny it. If I had been so I would not have been against her, nor would have certified against her; I ever advised her to submit herself to the Queen's majesty: but when no overt fact of treason can be proved against me, to bring me in thus by arguments and circumstances, I think it very hard. If I should have stolen her away, I could not do it alone: was I so destitute of friends, that I could not make any man privy to it? And who is there that accuses me of it, that may spend five marks a year? Now since nothing is proved against me by any witness sufficient, I beseech you consider favorably of me indeed my brother of Westmoreland sent me his man with recommendations; and I sent him, by his man, a ring which my sister had sent me before; and also Havers with this message, commend me to my brother of Westmoreland and tell him that I am well, mine innocence shall deliver me: but nothing touching any rising at all. If ever I were privy to that rebellion, then condemn me of all the treasons that you lay against me.

Attorney. My lord and I are now at issue upon this point; I affirm it with proofs, and his lordship barely denies it. If his intent were to compass the marriage, knowing her to pretend title to the present possession of the crown; then must this grow to an imagining to depose the Queen, and then it is treason. An overt fact is a declaration of the mind; letters, tokens, speeches, messages, and such like, be overt facts. Now if you had married her, you must have maintained her pretended title which you could not have done without manifest purpose and compassing to depose the Queen and to bring her to death, which is high-treason. Now beside, there is one other fact which I will give you in evidence; which most evidently proves the Duke of Norfolk's imagination and compassing to depose and destroy the Queen. It is well known that Pius V, the Bishop of Rome, is the Queen's majesty's notorious enemy, he has been so published; he has so showed himself in his proceedings; he has showed it in his bulls, they have been brought into this realm, and some have suffered for them. The Duke of Norfolk knowing it to be so, has practiced with his factor, has sent to the Pope for aid and force against the Queen, he conferred with one Rudolph a merchant stranger to go over sea to the Duke of Alva, and to the Pope, in the name of the Scottish Queen and the Duke of Norfolk to procure power to invade this realm, for the advancement of the Scottish Queen's false title to the crown of this realm of England; and in the mean time, the duke promised to move her friends to levy such power as they were able to assist the strangers when they came in. If this be proved to you, then is it flat treason. To use force against her majesty in her own realm, must needs be done with intent to depose her, which force she must needs resist; which if she be not able to do, then follows her death and destruction. My lords, here goes still all to one manner of purpose, his own bare denial, and allowing of no sufficient witness; but here God himself shall be witness this is a matter opened by God himself. It was known that a treason was in hand; many searches were made to understand it, no man could by any travel find it out, till God himself opened it; so as the saying is fulfilled, what is done in secret shall be made open. The treasons my lords of the council knew of; it appeared in April last that such a treason was; but whom it touches was not known to them, no not to him that opened it. So as God has opened it to affirm these mean men to be of credit. The treason being known to the Privy Council half a year together, yet could they not understand the party, till God disclosed it by marvelous chance. In August last, there was six hundred pounds of money prepared to be sent with letters into Scotland since nothing is proved against me by any witness to the Queen's enemies, for their relief and maintenance, and by the Duke of Norfolk's appointment to be conveyed to his man Bannister and so into Scotland. This money was delivered to one Browne of Shrewsbury, by one of the Duke's servants, one Hickford; who said to Browne, here is 50£. I pray you help that it be conveyed to Mr. Bannister dwelling near Shrewsbury. Browne having received the money, though the bulk was somewhat like the proportion of 50£ in silver, yet die weight, by reason it was gold, made him suspect it: whereupon he went to one of the Queen's Privy Council and disclosed his suspicion, that so he might learn what he carried. This bag being opened, there was found 600£ in gold and certain letters withal to the Queen's enemies, and to Bannister: whereupon the duke's man that sent the money was apprehended; and then by God's good providence, was it found that this treason touched the Duke of Norfolk under the name and cipher of Quarante 40, and another nobleman was signified by the cipher of 3 Trente. Then fell out new matters: certain of the duke's servants examined, whether they knew of any cipher used to any man by the name Quarante, they confessed that Quarante was the Duke of Norfolk; they were kept in several places, the bishop also a prisoner in a place several from them all, and yet they all agreed in one. So God's work has enforced their credit by their agreement, being severally kept. Thus came it to light by God's own work. Now see what the cause was, the great treason was contained in letters written in cipher to one signified by the number Quarante; this Quarante was for the duke, and so the duke confessed. What cause had they to suspect him? Letters from Rudolph made mention of great treason and of provision of men from beyond the seas to invade this realm, according to his order and request, who was meant by Quarante. If then we shall prove to you that Rudolph had this message and commission from the Scottish Queen and the Duke of Norfolk to treat with the Pope, King Philip, and the Duke of Alva for the bringing in of ten thousand men to invade England, and to make war against the Queen in her own realm; there must needs be compassing to depose the Queen and to bring her to death, and so high treason: for he that will levy force to invade or make war in a prince's realm and that in maintenance of a title to the present enjoying of the crown, does what he can to depose the prince, and consequently also does what he can to destroy the prince. Now to prove that the Duke of Norfolk dealt in this manner, sent this message and practiced to bring in this force of strangers, and to levy war against the Queen within the realm, it shall be good first to show what manner of man this Rudolph was: he was one that lived divers years here in this realm, a notable traitor and enemy to the Queen and realm of England and of long time the Pope's factor. In the duke's first trouble, this Rudolph was suspected of such practices, and therefore by the council committed to the custody of Mr. Walsingham till October was twelve month; and for that no evident matter appeared, he was delivered again in the November following: so soon as he was delivered, he by and by opened to the Bishop of Ross that he was factor for the Pope; he showed him his commission and sundry letters written to him by Pope's Nuncio in France about matters of the practice a long time. This Rudolph was well known to the Scottish Queen, the Pope himself and his Nuncio recommending him to the Scottish Queen: the duke was made privy of it and made him privy to his dealings, and kept it secret from the Queen and her council. When the bull was brought over, that Felton died for, this Rudolph had six copies of it and dispersed them; whereof he gave one to the Bishop of Ross, one other to the Spanish ambassador, and the third to the French ambassador, and the rest we know not what he did with them. Now the duke knowing him to be such a one, he was a fit man to deal with. That he was such a one, and that the duke well knew it and sent him in message to the Duke of Alva, and to the Pope, you shall see plainly proved. Then what his message was, you shall see also disclosed, and how things hidden will by God's providence, come to light. The letters were written in cipher, and deciphered, and the cipher hid in the tiles and found by chance; so as it may appear God's own work to open these treasons.

Here the duke took exception to his saying that the cipher was found in the tiles; and said it was not the cipher that was found there, but the alphabet: so the duke always in his speech called the letters or matter written in strange characters, the cipher; and the paper of the characters themselves he called the alphabet, which Mr. Attorney usually called the cipher.

Then was read the Bishop of Ross's confession the 3rd of November to the 5th article. Also Ross's confession and 7 article, litera 6. Also his confession the last of October, Article 23.

All this the duke denied, and said I never saw any letters from the Pope, but one, which I will speak of anon.

Then was read the Bishop of Ross to the 6th, 7th, and 8th, making mention of a packet wherein was one letter to the duke by the title of Quarante.

Then was read the Bishop of Ross's confession, 26th of October, Fo. 2. concerning Andrew Beton's coming.

Attorney. The duke had these deciphered, and read them.

Then was read Barker's confession, 6th of November, Article 3.

Attorney. Thus plainly appeared that the duke was privy to these messages to the Pope and conference with his factor: now it rested to understand what followed of this course begun with Rudolph die Pope's factor; what messages were sent what practices devised; and what ensued. Upon this letter, the Scottish Queen wrote a letter to the Bishop of Ross, wherein she wrote back a discourse of her estate and device, what she thought best to be done referring all to the direction of the Duke of Norfolk. Here is the letter itself to be seen.

This letter came to the Bishop of Ross; he sent it over to the duke with a letter from the Scottish Queen to the duke. This letter was deciphered and found hidden in the duke's house under the mats in an entry, in the way as the duke went to his bedchamber; the cipher it self was found in the tiles of the house. This plainly declares how the duke in dealing with the Scottish Queen and the Pope, pursued his purpose of advancing the Scottish Queen to the crown of England: that the Scottish Queen was in practice for it with the Pope and referred the dispatch of Rudolph to the duke; and the receipt of those letters is confessed by Hickford and by the duke himself.

Here was read the letter of the Scottish Queen to the Bishop of Ross.

Attorney. By this letter appeared how the Scottish Queen has set out the whole plot of the treason: a message should be sent for aid from foreign parts; Rudolph the fittest man to be the messenger; and that Rudolph should be dispatched to go about it when the Duke of Norfolk would. The device was to move King Philip for aid, upon a consideration of her state here, to enter into deliberation of the time and opportunities to set her friends to field, and to seize themselves of her. This is confessed by Hickford; and this letter is also confessed by the duke himself, that he received it about January was twelve month, and it was hid under the mats.

Duke. I bid that the letter should be burnt.

Attorney. God would not have it so; but that it should remain for disclosing the matter.

Duke. As touching Rudolph, what manner of man he was, is no matter to me. I know of no more, nor am to be charged with no more than I myself am privy to. I never dealt with him about any cause of mine. I received no such letter, but that which Barker said came from him which was not that January that you speak of about two years ago; and as for instructions and letters about that January was twelve month, I received none.

Burleigh. Here the Lord Burleigh said to Mr. Attorney, you may mistake it was this time twelve month, for now we are in January. And so Mr. Attorney remembering this present month to be January, referred the letter to January now a year past; and said this letter that I now charged you with, came to your hands at this January was twelve-month. It came first to the Scottish Queen's hand; she took occasion upon considering her own case here in England, in France, and in her own country, that it was best for her to cleave to Spain. She wrote to the Bishop of Ross her discourse to that end: she counted Rudolph the fittest messenger; matter was devised for his instructions; she referred the dispatch wholly to the Duke of Norfolk; the duke dealt in it, his message appears. And thus it continued till March; and then according to the plot before laid, Rudolph was dispatched, and went over indeed.

Duke. What was delivered to Barker, I know not; that is nothing me. I am sure they will not say they delivered it me, nor that I received any such letters or instructions. This I say the bishop sent me a letter of the Scottish Queen's together with a letter of his own in her letter she complained of her own subjects, and faith, she will seek other means for her relief. This letter was deciphered; I disliked the device and had that the letter should be burned; so the letter in cipher was burned, and the alphabet was saved. I sent word that I disliked all the Bishop of Ross and Rudolph about the matter, and the Scottish Queen's willingness to have him sent about the matter. Thus it proceeded it was agreed that Rudolph should have his message in writing; and at the same conference, Barker being also among them, it was agreed and set down in his instructions that his message should be this, he should go to the Pope and the King of Spain in the name of the Scottish Queen and of the Duke of Norfolk, to require of them money and men for the Enterprise. Rudolph required to speak with the duke. Barker brought him to the those devices, and I advised the Scottish Queen to the duke at Howard-House; there they talked together, depend only upon the Queen's majesty, or else if she would take any other cause, both I, and all other her friends in England would give her over; and thereupon it was that I said that the Queen if she fell to such practices, would publish her letters and doings to her infamy. Upon which my words, the Bishop of Ross excused himself and said all this matter, of this new device to Beyton and Rewley. It is not true that Barker made me privy to any such message or instructions as has been alleged. Also he is not to be allowed for a witness against me, for he has confessed treason against himself; and persons outlawed, or attainted of treason, are no sufficient witnesses.

Catlin. My lord, there is none of those witnesses that have declared matter against you, outlawed, or attainted of treason, or yet indicted.

Duke. They are worse; for they have confessed treason.

Attorney. The Bishop of Ross at this time, was in custody and these men also that have confessed against you were also kept in custody, kept asunder in several places, and severally examined, agreed all in one and your own confessions agree with them, how can this be imagined and false? All these do testify it with one consent. The Bishop of Ross when he first came to the city was examined of these things, he denied all, he stood in it earnestly; when questions were asked him, he said he was an ambassador and not so to be dealt with, but to be referred to his own mistress the Scottish Queen. When he was committed to the Tower and there again examined, seeing things confessed already; and by the manner of the questions that were asked, perceiving some light that the truth was known; then he confessed also, and in his confessions does agree fully with Barker and the rest, which consent could not possibly be if the matter were not true; besides that, he has in his confession touched himself.

Duke. They have not agreed in confession against me that I told them any such thing; but one of them told another and so from hand to hand it went among them.

Attorney. Well, you see what is confessed and with what consent we are at issue; here is but your lordship's denial; I leave it to my lords here to consider of the proofs. If you had been a good subject, being then a prisoner in your own house, when such dangerous matter came to your understanding, you would have opened it, that the Queen's majesty and her council might have provided to withstand them, but you did it not. The Duke of Norfolk found flat treason intended; Rudolph was the messenger that procured it; the duke knew it; Rudolph was referred to the duke's dispatch upon the conference of the duke and Rudolph a whole hour till it was nine of the clock at night. After this talk, the duke delivered to Barker a paper saying that Rudolph left it with him; which paper contained the sum of the treason, and therein was also a paper of the names of divers noblemen, knights, and gentlemen in cipher, whom they counted that they would take the duke's part, but they counted without their host; so that there was for every name a cipher of the which 40 was for the duke and 30 for the Lord Lumley. Barker received it of the duke and delivered it again to Rudolph. Upon this cipher of 40, fell out the understanding of the treason.

Here was read Barker's deposition, 10 October, Interr. 8.

Item, Barker to the 22 Interr.

Attorney. In this bill the duke is proved to be 40, the duke himself has also confessed that 40 stands for his own name. Barker brought Rudolph to the duke, which the duke also confessed and that Barker brought him instructions for Rudolph's money.

Here Mr. Treasurer and Mr. Chancellor of the Exchequer sworn, did testify that Barker made all these confessions freely without compulsion.

Also Mr. Wilson, sworn, did testify the same; and that Barker was never offered torture, nor was once in the prison where the rack was but the duke said Barker saw where his fellow had been.

Attorney. Did not Barker bring Rudolph to you at nine of the clock at night? Did he not leave with you instructions in French?

Duke. I confess it.

Then was read Barker to the 16th.

Attorney. Rudolph came also the second time to the duke; after he was come from the duke, he said to Barker that the duke and he were agreed of his journey and that the duke prayed him to depart with speed.

This message was to procure men and money for the enterprise of the treason; and on this message the duke dispatched him.

Duke. Touching Rudolph's coming, I have indeed confessed that he came to me. I was in summer was twelve-month bound in recognizance for 1800£ to Rudolph for my Lord of Arundel and for my brother Lumley; the day was passed whereby I stood in danger of my recognizance. I sent to Rudolph to entreat him to cancel my recognizance and I offered to give him twenty yards of velvet; Rudolph would not persuaded, but desired to speak with me himself, which Barker reported to me. I was very loath that he should come to me, for he was in trouble at my last trouble and so I thought coming to me would be suspicious. Barker promised that he would bring him to me secretly, and at such a time as it should not be known to make any suspicion. So Rudolph came to me and I did what I could to entreat him about my recognizance, and I could not persuade him more than to promise that he would not sue me. He told me of his trouble and of his imprisonment at Mr. Walsingham's and what words Mr. Walsingham gave to him, also of the Scottish Queen; and that he should deal with the Duke of Alva for money for her to her own use and for necessaries as he had done before. He prayed also my letters in the Scottish Queen's favor to the Duke of Alva. I began to dislike him and was loath to write; I sought ways to shift me from him; I said I was not well at ease; I could not write, and it was late, and so I would not deal. As for the bill of names, I saw none such, nor understood of any such till the letter that came over from Rudolph about Easter. I delivered a writing to Barker. I confess it; but it was about that matter which I have confessed already for my recognizance; and so I dealt not with any such matter as is alleged against me, nor received any other instructions, but only as I have said about my own matters.

Attorney. My lord, this is but your own saying and it carried no likelihood: but Barker goes nearer to you; he tells you plainly what the instructions were, it was to King Philip for men, and to the Pope for money.

Duke. Barker has confessed himself a traitor, and therefore is no sufficient witness against me. I never knew of any such bill of names, nor such instruction in French.

Attorney. It is sufficiently proved. Now Rudolph came to you again a second time.

Duke. I deny it: he came no more to me.

Attorney. That is not so: for Barker tells plainly not only the time, but also the several ways by which he himself brought Rudolph to you.

Duke. There be ways enough, he might have deviled also a dozen ways more if he would, in that house.

Here was read Barker ad. 11.

Attorney. Lo! He tells you which way Rudolph came to you.

Duke. So he may devise more ways when he will.

Attorney. Now you shall also hear it confessed by the Bishop of Ross, who at the time of his confession was in prison, not knowing what Barker had said.

Here was read Ross's confession of that matter. Here was also read Ross, the sixth of November.

Attorney. Here you see how the duke agrees with Barker. And there was read Ross more, the sixth of November; how Rudolph made account of his time and of his return before the Parliament ended.

Then Mr. Attorney made a brief rehearsal of the matters contained in those confessions and showed the agreement of Ross and Barker and then was read Ross, Fol. 3. Touching Rudolph's account of his old soldier that he could bring against the English of the Duke of Medina's coming of 7000 Spaniards to be spared. Now the duke had satisfied Rudolph for his credit, and though the duke subscribed not yet if the duke were a Christian man, he was assured of him and so would assure foreign princes on the duke's part.

Then was read the confession of the Bishop of Ross, to the 18th.

Now shall you hear further: Rudolph, before his voyage, moved to have letters of credit that he might deal with foreign princes; whereupon three letters were devised to commend Rudolph to the Pope, the King of Spain, and the Duke of Alva, and to give him credit in his message that he might be able to procure aid for the Scottish Queen, and for the advancement of the Catholic faith.

The duke answered I am loath to write; for if I write, the Queen's majesty has great intelligence and so if my writing should come to light, all were marred; and so he would not write. Then the Bishop of Ross and Barker, travailed earnestly with him to subscribe the letters; but he would not. Then at length, it was advised and agreed among them that if the duke should send one to the Spanish ambassador to declare his assent to affirm the letters, it should satisfy Rudolph and the foreign princes, though he subscribed not: wherewith the duke was content and sent Barker with the Bishop of Ross, and Rudolph, to declare to the Spanish ambassador that the duke was content to affirm the letter, and to let it pass in his name. And so the Spanish ambassador recommended Rudolph's message in the duke's name, without the duke's subscription.

Here was read the Bishop of Ross, October ad. 20.

Also Barker was read of the same matter.

Attorney. Thus it is plainly proved and if they say true, as it cannot be that they can so agree, if it were not true; then can it not be denied that the duke is guilty of all this treason.

Duke. Here is too much at once for me to answer without book; my memory is not so good to run through everything as they do that have their books and their notes lying before them, therefore, I pray you if I forgot to answer to anything, remember me of it. It is said that there are two or three witnesses against me; all this two or three are but one witness: for Rudolph said it to the Bishop of Ross, and of his mouth the Bishop of Ross told it to Barker, and so from mouth to mouth; they are all but one witness. Besides that they have confessed themselves wholly in treason, and now they would bring me in with them too; and so are no sufficient witnesses against me. Note, I pray you, the advices and see how likely they are: ten thousand men must be landed, whereof three or four thousand must be horsemen; they must land at Harwich, and a port in my country; neither is Harwich a port in my country. And I am not of so little skill that I would have three or four thousand horsemen land in Essex, the unfittest place for horsemen to land in all England, a country best inhabited of noblemen, gentlemen, and other ability to resist them and who would land horsemen in Essex, a country all full of lanes, woods, ditches, and marshes? I would have chosen some other country rather if I had been so minded. Again, in respect of religion, I would not have landed them in Essex, that came to destroy religion, and so should have found but little assistance. And would I have brought in power joined with them to the overthrow of religion. It has lately been said by that side, that I could not be recovered from my religion. I would not be changed from my religion; I had rather be torn with wild horses. Besides that the county of Essex adjoining to the county of Suffolk, is most unfit for that purpose; no county in England more replenished with Protestants nor of better ability and none more likely to withstand Papists. As for moving of friends, I never dealt to move any person in the matter; I never made provision for it; I provided no amour, shot, powder, nor money; I made no friends privy to any such intent. Some presumption it is that if I had intended any such matter, I would have made some privy to it. I was no otherwise so destitute of friends, I would have provided armor, shot, and powder; I would have provided money; I am sure there was not much money found. For armor, I had not at my house here past eight armors which were of proof, and a hundred harquebusiers, and besides this, I bestowed not 10£ in armor these ten years: powder I have not two barrels; yea, not above a barrel in all. So see the likelihood of their devices; no conference of friends to take part; no provision of furniture; a country, both in religion and situation, unapt for the matter.

Where they say Rudolph told Barker, and Barker told me; and Barker came from Ross and from Rudolph to me, and from me to Ross, to declare that I was content to affirm the letters of credit, I deny it. As for my consent that the Spanish ambassador should affirm the letters in my name, how unlikely a thing it is that I was content to affirm them, but not to subscribe them; as if I knew not how small is the difference between subscribing and affirming; and as if I had such slender wit. Rudolph never came to me but once; indeed I heard that Rudolph would fain have came to me again the second time, but I would not; Barker earnestly urged it, but I refused. To please the curious Italian head of Rudolph, they devised it among them to deal with the Spanish ambassador. As for me, I never heard from the Spanish ambassador in the matter; I never saw him but once at my Lord Treasurer's. I was angry with Barker for going to him in my name, and he excused it, and said he could not otherwise contort the Bishop of Ross and Rudolph and so that affirming of the letters was Barker's own doing, and not mine. I would they might in our private examinations have been brought face to face with me. I could have put them in mind of things; they have confessed treason of themselves, and they would bring me in with them and lay it on my shoulders. I am hardly handled, I have been eighteen weeks committed, I can speak with no body; if I might have had them face to face, and been allowed to bring forth my proofs, I would have brought forth direct matter and proofs, and therewith made them remember themselves. Consider, I beseech you, what they be that accuse me; the presumptions be in all likelihood that I should not so do as they accuse me; and as for them, they be persons that have accused themselves of treason, and so be of no credit. As for mine own examinations, they wholly agree in such sort as I have here declared in mine answer.

Attorney. Your answer is nothing but bare denial; and here are three witnesses against you and all three severally examined, have agreed in one; and Barker has directly confessed; and if you doubt of impulsion, you shall hear how willingly and how freely he confessed it, because the same examination was taken before Sir Thomas Smith, and subscribed with his hand. Mr. Wilson upon his oath declared the same to be Sir Thomas Smith's hand.

Duke. Where it is said that I should bid them to write, or should affirm their writing, it is not true. Indeed Bannister spoke to me to write for money for the Scottish Queen and I refused to do it. If I should have dealt in any such matter, I would have trusted one Bannister afore fifteen Barkers. And as for your number of witnesses in this manner by hands one from another, twenty witnesses may prove but one witness.

Attorney. You shall hear your own confession agreeing with them; you were content Rudolph should use your name to the Duke of Alva, and that he should assure the duke you were a Catholic, and that he should assure tokens to prove it; for that you kept Papists in your house, and were a friend to Papists.

Here was read the duke's confession, 10 October, adinterr. 58.

Here his own hand confessed the matter.

Duke. I saw the instructions indeed, and this matter was in it. They sought to have it thought I was a Catholic, to serve their purpose, and did put it in of themselves; but I allowed it not, I would rather be torn with wild horses than forsake my religion.

Attorney. These instructions remained still in your custody: why did you not burn these as well as you say that you commanded the letter to be burned?

Duke. Because it was their writing, and not mine.

Wilbraham. You are content it should be extant; to what purpose was that if you disliked it?

Attorney. Your lordship shall yet see further a letter of the Bishop of Ross written to the Scottish Queen, wherein the whole plot and course of the treason is plainly set out at large, the letter came to the Scottish Queen's hands while my Lord Steward was there, which my Lord Steward affirmed. So the letter was read.

Duke. The Bishop of Ross is no sufficient witness against me, for the causes that I have declared.

Attorney. I leave his credit to my lords here to consider, let them weigh it as they see cause. Now come to consider your own doings; since your last imprisonment, letters have been conveyed to you, and you have sent letters abroad by many subtle and secret ways of conveyance. One letter you sent out, written with red-ochre, wherein plainly appears that you feared the matter, and that something was confessed, and that you were afraid of more; you willed the Bishop of Ross should take all upon him because he was an ambassador and that a bag of writings should be sought out and burned.

Here the letter written in red-ochre was read, which the duke confessed to be his own.

Attorney. This letter gave occasion to seek the bag, and so were the writings found under boards fast nailed, and thereby was understood that Quarante was the duke; and so by God's work broke out the whole practice of the treason. This letter was directed to nobody.

Duke. It was written to Bailey, and Bailey received it. I can answer this letter well enough. Here I am charged with two matters, for matter of my confessions and for burning the bags of letters. As for that which is there said, that I confessed nothing but what I saw confessed by others, the truth is, I received a letter, wherein I was charged that I had accused some falsely. I wrote to satisfy that I had not accused any of any matter of treason, nor could if I would; and this was the meaning of that part of my letter.

Attorney. Where is the letter whereby you were charged that you had accused falsely?

Duke. I kept it not; think you I would keep letters? Burned letters do no hurt. As for burning the writings in the bag, it makes nothing against me in this case; for they were nothing but private letters of the Scottish Queen's, written before, and when I was last in trouble, long before this matter. At Bannister's coming up at Easter last, he brought them to me, and I willed Barker to lay them up, what needs such searching for elder matters? I had them be made away, for they were but private matters between the Scottish Queen and me.

Attorney. There was the letter that disclosed you to be Quarante, whereby the treason was known: now here is also another letter of your own, which you secretly sent out of the Tower, which showed your guiltiness in the matter of the great treason with Rudolph.

Here the duke's other letter was read.

Duke. This was only as I have declared before, for my conference with Rudolph, for the matter of money, both touching mine own recognizance and procuring of money for the Scottish Queen, for her necessity.

Attorney. By the whole course of the matter that goes before, it is for the treason, and not for the money.

Here is also another letter of your own, which carried manifest presumptions of the treason, where among other things, you will Barker to confess no further if he love his life: besides other most manifest suspicious matters.

Duke. I wrote it not in respect of any fear that Barker could hurt me when I willed that Barker should confess no more as he loved his life, for indeed he might touch himself in treason, (as he has done) but not me, for I never consented to it.

Attorney. Now shall you see how the matter proceeded further: after the dispatch of Rudolph in Lent last as he had made show before, that he intended to go over sea, and was all this while practicing about this treason; at length being frightened with these messages, he came to sue to the Queen's majesty for a passport, which was granted him, and he carried over two geldings with him, which is evident proof that he went over. Now shall you see what effect it took and by the answer you shall discern the message and practice being beyond the sea and having done his message, he sent advertisement to the duke how he sped, and likewise from the Pope; which plainly disclosed the whole purpose and plot of the treason, as shall be declared to your Lordships.

Here began Mr. Solicitor.

Solicitor. For that the time is spent, and your Lordships, I think, are weary. I will not now make any collection what has been gathered of the attempt of marriage with the Scottish Queen, only I will deal with the matter of Rudolph's message and the effect thereof and the duke's adhering to the Queen's enemies and rebels shall be another part. In this matter of Rudolph, has been laid before you a plain plot for a rebellion and for invasion of the realm set forth in the Scottish Queen's letter, which was deciphered by

Hickford by the duke's commandment as has been said to you; the effect whereof was as has been declared.

And here he repeated the effect of that letter containing the device of putting men into the field and to seize the Scottish Queen. Now if the device were followed, and if the duke were a doer in it, if he were a contender to it, if Rudolph were practiced with for the journey, if he received his message to that end, if he went and pursued it, if he lent answer accordingly; then it must needs be that here is matter of high-treason, and the Duke of Norfolk guilty of it. It has been showed by the declaration of Barker, and of the Bishop of Ross, how Rudolph was the Pope's factor, was commended by the Scottish Queen for a fit messenger in this matter was conferred with about it, articles were devised, they were showed the duke, and the duke himself has confessed that he spoke with Rudolph and that he saw the instructions. Now is the question, how far the instructions extended, whether to matter of high treason, as has been alleged, or no? The duke said for his excuse, that the instructions were but for a private cause of money, and that when Rudolph required him to write his letters, the duke refused and cast him off. See how this accorded, if it were but a private cause, whereto served that refusal to write? As well he might by letters, as by instructions pursued in a private cause. What needs that secret coming in the night time about a private cause? The duke himself confessed that the instructions were showed him before Rudolph came to him; he confessed also that Rudolph was commended by the Scottish Queen the instructions have here been showed, containing the matter of his journey, and extending to the treason he came to confer with the duke. Now let your lordships judge why, and about what matters they conferred.

The Bishop of Ross and Barker do, of their own knowledge, declare how for furniture of this message, there were letters of credit devised in the name of the Scottish Queen and the Duke of Norfolk to the Pope, the Spanish King, and the Duke of Alva; the duke refused to subscribe them, for fear if he should deal too openly, the treason might perhaps to some appear, therefore a device was found out how to solve the matter, that he should by his servant, affirm the letters to the Spanish ambassador, and so they should by the Spanish ambassador's commendation, pass with as good credit as if they had been subscribed. This device was performed, his assent was witnessed and the letters of credit confirmed accordingly. Rudolph went over to the Duke of Alva and from there to the Pope; he returned answer of his message and gave advertisement to the duke. Did not he send his answer concerning the very instructions that have been alleged, and the matter of treason, and not of a private cause? And to whom? Sent he not answer to the duke, by the name of Quarante? Would Rudolph make answer and of a matter that he never sent him about? By this you may see the intent of the message. Now shall you see what answer was returned.

The Bishop of Ross, after this, sent over a servant of his, one Charles Bailey, to fetch certain books that were printed in those parts; books containing very seditious matter, whereof I have seen some, by permission, tending to these ends, first, therein is conveyed to the Scottish Queen a title to the crown of England, a descent above the conquest and so laboring to impair the interest of all our Kings that have reigned since the conquest. Then the judgment of the right of the crown of this realm is reduced to an universal law, which they call *Jus Gentium*, and the discerning thereof exempted from the laws of this realm. And of that universal law they establish one universal judge whom they insinuate to be the Pope, whose bulls you see have passed in prejudice of the Queen's majesty's undoubted right. This Charles Bailey being in those parts for this occasion of the books, met with Rudolph at Brussels, after that Rudolph had had his dispatch from the Duke of Alva, and was hasting to the Pope; and therefore having haste of his journey, and much to write and small leisure, he desired Charles Bailey to write for him two letters for two noblemen of this realm, both in cipher, but to whom the letters were directed, Charles himself could not tell; for Rudolph subscribed the letters himself, one to Quarante, the other to Trente. Charles Bailey bringing their books and letters; was taken at Dover, the books were brought to the Council, the packet of letters were conveyed away to the Bishop of Ross and daily more and more grew the suspicion by reason of the repair of the Bishop of Ross's servants to the Marshalsea, where Charles was. At length there were letters taken between the Bishop of Ross and Charles mentioning the recovery of Rudolph's packet. In this packet was the advertisement of the success of the voyage, from Rudolph to the duke by the name of 40. This letter of Rudolph's was sent to the duke from the Bishop of Ross by Barker; Barker delivered it to the duke, from whence it was sent back again to the Bishop of Ross by Gutbert, and by Gutbert it was deciphered and carried again to the duke by Barker, upon this occasion Gutbert was sought for the duke conveyed him away, and this conveying away of Gutbert, the duke has confessed. If this be thus, then must it needs be that Rudolph was sent by him and to such end as the letter brings answer of. In the letter, this was contained that Rudolph had spoken with the Duke of Alva; that he had very good and loving audience; that the Duke of Alva lovingly promised all the help that he could; and that he would commend the cause to the King of Spain his master and he advised Rudolph to go forward to the Pope and that he said he could not do further without more warrant, which he would seek to procure. Also certain questions were asked by the Duke of Alva; as what fort was between the Haven where they should land and London? How near London it was? So the nearness of London was respected, how incommodious so ever your Lordship said the place was for horsemen. These questions belike depended upon the matter propounded, which touch the plot of the treason, and not a private cause as your lordship pretends. The Duke of Norfolk confessed the receipt of these letters and the deciphering of them. So Charles Bailey, by Rudolph's request, wrote the two letters in ciphers; Rudolph himself directed them to 40 and 30. Charles being taken, and confessing the writing, and bringing of these letters, and the matter contained in them in April last, yet knew not who was 40 nor 30. This was strangely conveyed, treason known in matter, and yet the person not known to himself that wrote it.

Here was read Charles Bailey's letter.

These letters of Rudolph were conveyed to the Bishop of Ross to deliver to 30 and 40, referring the rest to his dispatch at Rome. And this falls out also very likely for the time; for Rudolph departed home about Easter before.

Here was read Charles Bailey's confession, ad 3.

Solicitor. Now you see to what end the effect of the message tended; you see what it was, and how it was done, you see how it was received, and the Duke of Alva's questions upon it: now you shall see the contents of the answer, by the examinations of the Bishop of Ross, and Barker; the receipt of the letters of answer the duke himself has confessed.

Duke. Where they say this message was sent by my privities, by reason that I was meant by 40, I deny it; I never wrote by Rudolph, I refused to do it, I knew not his letters were to me, but as Barker said, and it was not likely they should be to me; for it was a matter which I was not privy of and in a cipher which I had not; Rudolph left no cipher with me. As for the taking of the packet, I knew nothing of it; the letter I never saw in cipher; Barker brought me a decipher, telling me that 40 was for me and 30 for the Queen of Scots. When he told me first he had the cipher, I asked what I should do with it, and how I should read it, having no cipher? Barker answered that it was left with Gutbert; for Rudolph at his departure had told him that he would write answer of the money for the Scottish Queen, and that he would leave the cipher with Gutbert; and that he had so done, and in the letters deciphered did appear, that the Duke of Alva had promised aid of money for the Scottish Queen for her necessities; but he could not yet do it for want of commission, but as soon as he had commission he would. When I heard of this I disliked this dealing with the Duke of Alva, having before refused to write to him in the matter at Rudolph's request; and I threatened Barker if he so dealt any more with me. The letters might be to me, as Barker said, but I knew not so much.

Solicitor. This your answer is in all no more than a bare denying, and so be all your speeches, all upon your own credit only.

Here was read Barker's confession, ad 2, & 3, concerning Rudolph's letters in cipher, and the deciphering by Gutbert, and the port where the walloons should have landed, &c.

Then was read the Bishop of Ross's to the 12 and 13, to the same effect.

Then Mr. Solicitor recited again the effect of the letters, and the said confessions of Ross and Barker, and proceeded further thus:

You see all these agree in one concerning the contents of the letter; now the letter being deciphered by Gutbert, and Gutbert being able to discover the whole, this Gutbert, when he was sent to for by the council, was conveyed away by the duke's means as the duke himself has confessed.

Duke. It may be Barker received this letter as you spoke of, and that Gutbert deciphered it and that it contained the matters that you allege; it may be that they kept that letter still to themselves, and might bring me another letter containing only such matter as I was contented with containing the private cause.

Solicitor. An unlikely matter, but thus you see the duke confessed the receipt of the letter, he only denied that it was to this effect. It was confessed, that a letter to this effect was written to 40; he also confessed that 40 was for the duke himself.

The Duke of Alva's questions proved the form of the matter; the duke read that letter.

Duke. I read not that letter, but of another matter, and you bring but one witness to prove it.

Solicitor. There be two witnesses, Barker and the Bishop of Rose, severally examined, who agreed directly, expressing it. And Bailey also wrote the letter himself containing the treason and not knowing to whom the letter was directed, accorded with them.

Duke. Barker and Gutbert might make the letter themselves and put in and out what they list.

Solicitor. Why did Rudolph write you a letter at all?

Duke. I know not. Barker presented me the letters out of cipher, and I had not the cipher, nor saw any such letter as you allege.

Solicitor. It appears further, how after this dispatch with the Duke of Alva, Rudolph went forward on his message to the Pope; and having also good success there, he so advertised again. The Pope sent letters to the duke and the Scottish Queen to this effect that he liked well of their enterprises, &c.

Would Rudolph have gone to the Pope and procured letters if he had not had instructions accordingly? The duke himself has confessed such a letter, conceived there came letters both of one tenor; the one by the way of France, the other by the way of Flanders: the effect you have heard, and the receipt is confessed.

Duke. Barker indeed brought me about six or seven lines written in a Roman hand in Latin beginning thus, *Diletle fili salutem.* I asked what it was and Barker told me it was a letter from the Pope to me: wherewith I was offended, and said a letter to me from the Pope! What have I to do with him that is enemy to my religion and country? How comes this to pass? So I received it, and not otherwise: and Barker excused it, and said that Rudolph had procured it for his own credit.

Here was read Barker, ad 29.

Solicitor. Thus you see the effect of this letter and how this was directed to the duke from Rudolph, also by the name of 40, deciphered by Gutbert and delivered to the duke by Barker. The duke received it and read it, and said Rudolph has been at Rome, I perceive there will nothing be done this year. By this it appears that he reproved not Barker at all for bringing it to him, for Barker brought it him twice, would he have brought it him the second time if the duke had been angry with him for it at the first?

Duke. I knew not at the first time what it was, for it was in cipher.

Then was read Barker's confession to the 8th.

Duke. Barker is not of credit, he accuses me falsely.

Solicitor. He was your servant and of near place and credit about you; why should he accuse you wrongfully?

Duke. He was not of credit about me; for I used him not this fourteen years.

Solicitor. That is not so, as has well appeared. Besides this, the conveying away of Gutbert which was done by your means, and who deciphered this letter, and could have disclosed the matter, proves a great guiltiness in you.

Duke. He was conveyed away at his own request made, and not for my safety.

Solicitor. You caused him to be conveyed away, and were privy to his conveying.

Duke. Barker removed him: indeed I was not privy.

Solicitor. You moved Bowes to join with Barker to do it.

Then Mr. Solicitor said further to the peers, I have also my lords, one thing more to say to you from the Queen's majesty's own mouth; the lords that be here of the Privy Council do know it very well, not meet here in open presence to be uttered, because it touches others that are not here now to be named; but by her highness's order we pray that their lordships will impart it to you more particularly. In Flanders, by the ambassador of a foreign prince, there the whole plot of this treason was discovered and by a servant of his brought to her majesty's intelligence; the minister not meaning to conceal so foul and dishonorable a practice, gave intelligence hither by letters, and has therein disclosed the whole treason in such form as has here been proved to you: wherefore I refer the more particular declaration thereof to the peers of the Privy Council.

Then began Mr. Wilbraham, Attorney of the Wards, and said to this effect.

Wilbraham. There is yet something unspoken, it consists in two points, I will be short in both. The matters are plain and easy to understand. Let my lord answer and your lordships shall easily judge of them. Here have been set forth before you the imagining and practicing of the deprivation and death of the Queen's majesty, with bringing in of strangers into the realm to invade, and levy war, with the appurtenances both miserable and many. This request I am now to make that for proof of these treasons, that I will entreat you to have in memory what has before been said; for though the proofs of these treasons we divide to several parts for ease and shortness, as the seeking of the marriage, Rudolph's voyage, the success thereof, and the residence that remained, ought all to be compared together; any one appearing plainly true, gives credit to the rest. The Queen's majesty's proceeding in this trial is very honorable, mild and gracious; the confessions have been made by the parties freely, without torture or constraint. You shall see each of them, and each part so prove the other as the whole shall be clearly out of doubt; where the Earl of Northumberland and his wife, the Earl of Westmoreland, Richard Norton and others in the north parts raised rebellions and levied open war against the Queen's majesty within her realm; and being overthrown by the Queen's power, fled into Scotland, and there were received by the Duke of Chastelleroy, the Lord Harris, the Lord Hume, the Lord Buccleugh, and others, and by them were comforted and detained against the Queen's majesty, requiring to have them delivered. Her majesty being denied to have them restored, published and proclaimed open war against those detainees of her rebels, and appointed the Earl of Sussex her Lieutenant General, with an army to invade Scotland, and there to pursue those her enemies, sparing the rest. He entered into the land, made open war upon them, blew up their houses with powder, wasted their countries, and drove the rebels out of Scotland. The one matter now that I am to disclose, is that the Duke of Norfolk knowing all this, yet did adhere to, comforted and relieved the said rebels; he procured money to be distributed to the Earl of Westmoreland, the Countess of Northumberland, and other of them: and this is manifest treason. The other matter is that the Duke of Norfolk knowing all this to be true, adhered to, comforted and relieved the said Lords of Scotland, the Queen's enemies, receivers and detainees of her rebels and this is also treason. And first for the aiding of the rebels; after this rebellion, and their overthrow by the Queen's power, they fled into Scotland, (a very bare country) where they were driven to hard shifts, so were they enforced to sue to the Pope for help; they wrote to him, the Scottish Queen wrote in their favor to the Pope's Nuncio, the matter was pursued for them by one D. Morton this Morton was he that was the procurer of the bull that was sent over against the Queen's majesty: this Morton was he that reconciled the Earl of Northumberland to the Roman Church by a bull of absolution: he went to the Pope on their message, the Pope granted them relief, and wrote letters in the mean time to comfort them, which were directed thus; *Thomæ & Carolo Northumbriæ & Westmorlandiæ Comitibus, reliquifque Nobilibus Catholicis partium Borealium Regni Angliæ*: To Thomas and Charles, Earls of Northumberland and Westmoreland and other of the Catholic noblemen of the north parts of the realm of England. Belike so calling them noble in the fulfilling of D. Story's promise, that by their rebellious enterprise they were now of worshipful become honorable.

Here was read the effect of the Pope's letters to the rebels.

The letters hereof came to the Bishop of Ross the money was assigned in Flanders; the Bishop of Ross sent to the Duke of Norfolk for his advice, and for his help to convey the money to them. The bishop thought it best to have the money sent by the west borderers where the Lord Harris was, and with him Leonard Davis: the duke, for their special displeasures to Leonard Davis was not willing that Leonard Davis should have part of it, but had more mind to have his brother of Westmoreland relieved, and to that end he devised with Bannister for the sending of the money. In the mean time, behold how that course was interrupted. The Queen's majesty had a treaty with the Queen of Scots, wherein one special article was that the rebels should be delivered. This the Scottish Queen was loath and liked not to do; she asked the Duke of Norfolk's counsel in it, he advised that in no wise they should be delivered, for that were too much against her honor; nevertheless, for that he scared that the article concerning the delivery of the rebels might be some stay to such conclusion, as otherwise they might have liked of; he gave advice that the rebels should depart out of Scotland. Ross wrote to them to that end, and there with sent them the Pope's letters, and so they all departed out of Scotland into Flanders, except only Leonard Davis, who remained with the Lord Harris and the Earl of Northumberland, who would also fain have been gone if he might; and so by this occasion, and by Bannister's means, was this sending of the money into Scotland disappointed. Then was there another device taken to distribute it in Flanders; and because it should not all be suddenly wasted, it was agreed by the Bishop of Ross that it should be distributed monthly.

This order was opened to the Duke by Barker, the duke liked well of it, and willed it to be done accordingly. A man was sent over for this purpose, and the money distributed. The Countess of Northumberland wrote over to the Bishop of Ross a letter of thanks. Hereupon report was made to the duke, that it was done as he had appointed. Now the duke will ask us what proof we have hereof? We say the confessions of Ross and Barker. Against this he takes exception; his only answer is his bare denial, and his defacing of their credit. He said they are traitors and have confessed treason against themselves, and not to be received for sufficient witnesses against him. This has been well answered already by my Lords the Justices that by the law they this Morton was he that was the procurer of the are sufficient witnesses. You may not stand upon bull that was sent over against the Queen's majesty your honor and difference of degree, and there by limit how far they are to be credited. But now let us examine their credit, and their likeliness to tell truth, and how meet in this case they are to be believed. First, For the Bishop of Ross, he is a wise man, he is learned, he is a bishop, he is an ambassador, a great friend to the Duke of Norfolk; so far in credit with the Scottish Queen that he has been the principal doer of all her affairs; so the fittest man for this treason, the meekest man to be used in it since the Scottish Queen's title is the ground of the treason. Who then but such a man was fit to be used? Who meter to be heard in such a matter than he? A Scot, a wise man, well acquainted with the matters, well able to deal in them, ever at hand, and every way the meekest man. He was a Scot, say you; the more to blame the Duke of Norfolk to deal so with him against the express commandment of his sovereign upon his allegiance, and against his own faith, submission and promise, and so himself unworthy man to be believed than the Scottish witness. Why should the Bishop of Ross accuse him falsely? What should move him to it? He accuses you, he also proves it against you; he is the aptest man to know it, the aptest of all other to repeat it. And why will you say he is so oft produced for every matter against you? Surely great cause, great difference between him and all other; he knew all; he dealt in all, and where the rest had every one but his part to play, the Bishop of Ross continually kept the stage; he had a long part, he answered all men; when every man brought forth their tallies, he kept the stocks of all; he speaks of that he understands, he speaks credibly, he carries proof and consent of other. Speaks he of malice against the duke? That cannot be, the duke never offered him; the duke was ever his greatest friend and he the greatest friend to the duke, and the chief advancer of the marriage that the duke so earnestly sought as most beneficial he has in his confession touched his own mistress upon whom he depended to whom he ought no malice; he has disclosed the treacheries of the Pope, him he has offended, he gets no more benefices at his hand; he has offended the King of Spain and the Duke of Alva, he is fallen out with all his friends, he is fallen from all his commodious hopes by his confession. Besides that, how has he told it? Not at the first as of malice and desirous to do the duke a shrewd turn; but with leisure after other former confessions. He held off and disclosed nothing, till his face (though it were a face of brass) could no longer withstand apparent truth disclosed by others; except he had been mad and a stark fool as he is very wise, he would not have thrust himself into all those hardiness's to tell an untruth to his own so great loss and hindrance. Would he, being wise, for malice to the Duke of Norfolk, undo his own mistress the Scottish Queen; and bring upon himself the hatred of the Duke of Alva, the Spanish King, and the Pope; and so lose all his friends, and make them his foes, and in danger himself, and undo himself, with confessing treason against himself for only malice of the Duke of Norfolk? It cannot be true; I must needs believe him, because it is treason that he speaks of the man's own faculty: he is a credible traitor. If he had told us a matter of virtue, good life, and true religion, it had been a vanity to hear the Bishop of Ross speak; but speaking of treason, he is the skill fullest man, and meekest to be heard. As for Hickford and Bannister, they be both still in credit, the duke excepts not against them, and yet they accuse him deeply. For comparison of their values and credit, the duke is noble, and these are said not able to spend five marks. What then? Indeed their honor is less, but their understanding is great, and their credit sufficient. Barker is disliked, and counted by the duke not worthy to be believed. It is disliked that he is still brought forth; he is as the base instrument still played on. There is good cause why the duke so continually used him; you must understand that things must be done by means and instruments: the heads need the service of inferior members; the heads do devise, the hands and the feet do put in execution. If the Duke of Norfolk should, for every message and matter to be treated with the Bishop of Ross, Rudolph, and the Spanish ambassador, or other, have himself trotted through dirty Smithfield, and the streets of London to Thames-street, and other places, it must needs have been wondered at, and would not have been without notable suspicion. But Barker, a sly fellow, sufficient for skill, exercised in the matters, acquainted with the practices, might well go dreaming to all places without suspicion. Sometimes upon a robbery or a shrewd turn done, the length of a foot in die snow, or in the mire, has betrayed the doer; so the foot may sometimes accuse the head. Barker was one of the duke's secretaries, privy to his greatest affairs, the writer of his ciphers, the common carrier of ciphered and deciphered letters, the common conveyer and sender of his messages and letters between him and the Queen of Scots: the duke himself agreed with them in confessing of sundry circumstances of the matters which he called his errors and inferior faults; with these men he dealt in them himself, gave them credit, therefore it is no reason himself should take from them the credit of their confessions. But he said there are but two of them; the fault is in the Duke of Norfolk there are no more, for there are more if they were here, and by the duke's means they are absent; Liggons, Gutbert and Rudolph could tell it also. The one of them, Liggons, he has sent away, and finds him in France. Gutbert, as the duke himself has confessed, the duke has caused to be carried away. Rudolph is, by the duke himself, sent out of the realm on his message and not returned (it is no reason that their absence excuse him) for it is not reason that he should take advantage of his own wrong that has made them be absent; so their absence must stand for great testimony against him, and be judged to concur with them that are present, and have confessed.

Rudolph. The greatest testimony of all is in person withdrawn, but his letters speak lively. He has testified by his letters against the duke, and of a matter that himself well knew, not constrained, not examined, but with the tenor and course of the proceeding of the treason, advertising the duke of the answer of his message. You say he dealt for you in other private matters, not in the treason; if that were so, then the Pope had not given him charge to deal with the Scottish Queen and you; the Scottish Queen had not commended him to you; the instructions had not been so penned, the answer had not been so returned. But said the duke, it is true, Rudolph talked with me indeed, he required my letters to the Duke of Alva for the Scottish Queen; he moved me about these matters; but I was angry with him, I would not write by him, I departed from him in anger, and thus in anger away he went. And whither went he? Even straight to the Duke of Alva, and from thence to the Pope, even to the same places and persons to whom he should have gone for the duke, if the duke had been without anger, best pleased and contented with his journey. To what intent, and of what message went he thither? Even the same that the duke said he was angry to be moved of, and refused to write in. What effect has it? Gentle audience, great promises and agreement to the requests, as if he had travailed not for a man angry with the matter, but most desirous. What answer returned he? Even the same that accords with the instructions concerning the treason, the very plat and ground of his message. He reported questions asked by the Duke of Alva, agreeing only with the matter of the treason, and no private case. Would he have written answer to him that sent him not? Would he have written as to please him with good news of a good audience that sent him not? From whence departed he in anger? He writes of the course to be kept in execution of the treason, which he would not have done to him that was angry to hear of it. He bragged of his 10,000 walloons, old beaten soldiers. If the Duke of Norfolk had been a true man and angry with the matter as he now said and done his duty; though they had come, his walloons, his old beaten soldiers, might have been so new beaten of the old English fashion, as they were never so swinging in their lives.

This point Mr. Attorney spoke with such a grace, such cheerfulness of heart and voice as if he had been ready to be one at the doing of it; like a hearty true Englishman, a good Christian, a good subject, a man enough for his religion, prince and country.

If the duke says it was the Scottish Queen's message only, and not (for his advancement of her wrongful claim by force) he knowing this, why sought he to marry her against the Queen's majesty's will, and to pursue it by force? If he say it was Barker's single device to send these messages, to procure these treasons, and work all these mischief's of his own head; to what end I pray you should Barker do it but to advance the marriage of the duke his master, and the Scottish Queen? And was this without the duke's privy? Could Barker compel the duke to take a wise at his pleasure? Examine now all these witnesses, and weigh their credits together; consider them severally, their credits are great; join them all together, they be much greater; but severally examined, and all according in one, they be greatest of all, and not possible to be false. Add to that the duke's own confessions of circumstances concerning himself and their uttering of matters of treason against themselves; consider the difference of dangers in telling truly or falsely; for if they uttered it, and it were true, then stood they but in danger of their bodily life; if they should falsely accuse, yet that accusation suffering against themselves for treasons, they lost both body and soul, in falsely accusing others. The duke was their master, they his servants, and his true servants, and such as were to gain by his prosperity would they untruly accuse him the stay of their preferment? For though they be traitors, and howsoever they be otherwise without credit, yet against the Duke of Norfolk they are well to be believed.

Now on the other side, consider the duke's own credit which he has by his own doings impaired and made inferior to these of lower degree: you have heard of his oath especially taken for the commission at York to deal truly and sincerely; he kept it not, he so dealt as if an oath were of no great weight with him. His oath of a counselor he has broken, both in disclosing of secrets, and in giving advice to a foreign prince, and a competitor of the Queen's crown, against the Queen's majesty his sovereign lady. Now may it not be that these men of mean degree and value, against whom it is not alleged that they have been at any time perjured, may be produced and credited against him that has so little esteemed his oath? I have heard also that there was an oath willfully taken upon a bible in denying of things laid to his charge, and yet the matter found true, and by himself within a short space confessed: so that his oath, his hand, and his word, bear no sway with him.

He submitted himself, he subscribed his submission, and scaled it; he added solemn promises upon his faith and allegiance not to proceed in the marriage between the Scottish Queen and himself: but he kept no touch, he broke promise also, and yet he said his hand, mouth and heart go together. If they go together in the right way, it is well; but when they go together in untruth, it is evil and dangerous; therefore it is not for my Lord of Norfolk to stand so much upon the discrediting of the witnesses, and advancing of his own credit, which himself has so much decayed. Now I will go to the proof.

Duke. I shall hardly come, after so smooth a tale as Mr. Attorney of the wards can tell; yet one good proof I have to my comfort that they be as please your lordships to weigh them. If you would not have dealt thus untruly with me, I would not have taken exception against them, though I chiefly challenge none but Barker, in whom you may see what fear may do, besides that they have confessed themselves traitors, and so men of no conscience or credit. It is well known that Barker's stomach is nothing; he has been known well enough, fear has done much in him. The Bishop of Ross is also a fearful man. As touching Barker and the Bishop of Ross, Bratlon has a saying that witnesses must be freemen and not traitors, neither outlawed nor attainted.

Catlin. None of them be outlawed, attainted, or indicted.

Duke. I mean not that they were indicted, but they be in as ill case, for they have confessed themselves traitors. He said also they must be legal, lawful men, and so cannot strangers be as the Bishop of Ross and Rudolph; it is these strangers that charge me only, the other having dealt so disloyally, and confessed it against themselves, are not to be believed. As for Barker, I have not used him for my secretary these thirteen years: he entered with the Bishop of Ross, and dealt with him in these matters against my knowledge.

Catlin. Bratlon indeed is an old writer of our law, and by Bratlon he may be a witness; a stranger, a bondman may be a witness; ask you all the judges here. And the judges affirmed that he may.

Duke. If a stranger be to give evidence whereby lands should be recovered, you shall not recover upon that evidence given by a stranger.

Wilbraham. This were a strange device, that Scots might not be witnesses, for so, if a man would commit treason, and make none privy but Scots, the treason were unpunishable; and so were a kind of men found out, with whom a man might freely conspire treason.

Duke. You say my indictment is only upon the statute of 25 Edward III that statute stands upon three points, compassing the death of the prince's person, levying of war against the prince, and aiding of the prince's enemies; and all these must be proved overt fact. If by any way, by any overt fact, you can prove that I have directly touched the prince's person, or done any of the said things that the statute extended to, I will yield myself guilty. If anything be doubtful, the statute referred it to the judgment of the Parliament.

Catlin. Usage is the best expounder of the law, that is, the common use how the statute has been taken and expounded; and the same statute is but the declaration of the common law.

Duke. The preamble of the statute is to bring the laws of treason to a certainty, that men may certainly know what is treason.

Attorney-General. You complained of your close keeping, that you had no books to provide for your answer; it seems you have had books and counsel, you allege books, statutes, and Bratlon; I am sure the study of such books is not your profession.

Duke. I have been in trouble these two years; think you that in all this time I have not had cause to look for myself?

Attorney-General. But if you stand still upon proof, whether you have done anything to the destruction of the prince's person, if the lords upon the evidence already produced, do think the matters true in fact that are already alleged against you, surely the same must needs be construed a compassing of the Queen's death; for the law of treason has ever been largely construed for the prince's safety. Think you that practicing to levy war within the realm is not treason? Yes indeed is it, and a compassing of the prince's death. Sir William Stanley's case was this: he did but send Clifford over sea, to hearken and send him word what Perkin Warbeck was that if he thought Perkin was such a man as he was said to be, he would take his part. This was Stanley's case, and this was judged treason and a compassing of the King's death.

Here was read Barker's confession the 6th of November.

Duke. I never dealt with that money, nor heard of it; I dealt not at that time with Barker, nor heard anything of the rebels since they went in to Flanders.

Then was read the Bishop of Ross's confession of the same matter, 6 November, ad 5. And again Ross, 6 November, Fo. Also Ross 29, of 1700 Crowns sent by Moreton's means and what Moreton was.

Wilbraham. You hear how the money was procured; how it was distributed by the duke's order, and thanks written by the Countess of Northumberland for the receipt of it, which was also declared to the duke. You shall hear that after the practice of the marriage, it was a general rule between the Scottish Queen and the duke that the Bishop of Ross should never propone to the Queen's majesty's council, nor deal in any great matter, but by the advice and directions of the Duke of Norfolk.

Here was read, for the proof thereof, the Bishop of Ross.

Wilbraham. This is a plain course.

Duke. What does this make against me?

Wilbraham. That he followed his commission, that he kept his manner of conference continually and that according to that use, the money was distributed by your directions.

Duke. He dealt not with me in a great time, and I can tell when he broke off and dealt no more with me; I was never privy to the distribution of the money, nor I never spoke with Barker about it; I was in the Tower at that time.

Wilbraham. That was when you were not in the Tower; they lurked in Flanders a while in great necessity, without apparel, and suddenly with this money, they were waxed gay; and these men have confessed that it is distributed by your order and direction.

Duke. None accuse me but three, one absent, a stranger, and a traitor.

Wilbraham. And if every one that is privy to treason must be refused for witnesses, then should no treason be proved for none can tell it but they that be privy, and all such are guilty.

Now to the second point, that you adhered to, all and aided the Scottish Lords, the Queen's majesty's enemies, and maintainers of her rebels. The rebels, after their flying into Scotland, were there received by the Duke of Chastelleroy, the Lord Harris, the Lord Hume, the Lord of Buccleugh and others, and being there, they entered again of new into the realm and made new roads, and burned and wasted England with fire and sword. These Scots that thus assisted the rebels, the nobles of Scotland that remained in amity with the Queen's majesty, went about to suppress. The Queen's majesty proclaimed open war against them; she appointed my Lord of Sussex her lieutenant with a strong army to invade them and to pursue both the rebels and the said Scots that were her enemies. This my Lord of Sussex pursued, made open war upon them, burned their towns, houses, corn and goods, blew up their castles with powder, and kept good peace with the rest: so were they published the Queen's enemies, both by proclamation, which is here ready to be showed, and by open war itself, the best proclamation of all. The Queens power there tarried a great while, some came home, some remained still in Hume-Castle and other places. These thus known the Queen's enemies, and so published the Scots that were the Queen's friends did still pursue so far that the said Scottish Queen hearing thereof, complained to the Duke of Norfolk, *viz.* How she had no aid from France, and if none came at all, her friends in Scotland must of force be constrained to yield; she prayed the Duke of Norfolk's advice. The duke made answer, and Hickford wrote it to the Scottish Queen that she should procure the French ambassador's letters to them in Scotland to put them in some good hope, that they might hold out a while till aid come. The Scottish Queen accordingly wrote to the French ambassador Monsieur de la Mot; he by and by wrote six letters to the Lord Harris and other Lords of Scotland with fair aid comfortable promises. The packet of these letters were sent to the duke, he had it, he caused it to be sent with a letter to Bannister to convey it to Lowther upon the west borders of Scotland, and that Lowther should convey it over to the Lord Harris Hickford, the duke's secretary, delivered this French packet and the other letter to Henry the duke's footman, who carried it to Bannister, and Bannister sent it to Lowther by Colborn his servant: and to dissemble the cause of his servant's going, and to know some certainty whether it came to Lowther's hand or no. Hill feigned a privy token between him and Lowther about the gathering of the rent of the Lord Dacre's lands. Lowther sent over the packet and returned answer to Bannister that he had sent it to the Lord Harris, and willed Colborn to tell him which was their privy token, that though it were troublesome, yet he would gather up the rents for him.

Here was read Barker's confession, 14 September, that in July last he received the packet &c.

All Hickford's confession the same day, with a great protestation why he confessed not at the first, but tarried till Barker had disclosed; because he would not be counted a betrayer of his master.

Wilbraham. You hear how Barker betrayed it; you hear also how Hickford himself confessed it: and in what manner, I pray you, do they disclose it? They make no haste to accuse the duke, but by leisure; and Hickford makes it a matter of great conscience to utter it against his master. And here is a lesson meet to be learned of all servants. Many supposed it a treason and foul offence to utter their master's treasons; they must otherwise think it is a dangerous opinion.

Duke. I challenge not this man.

Then was read Hickford's examination, 11 October.

Also Bannister, 17 September 1.

The same Bannister, 29 November, pa.

Also Bannister, 28 and 29 September, ante 5 and 6.

Wilbraham. Thus it appears that those the Scottish Queen's friends in Scotland for whom she sorrowed and feared their yielding, were the Queen's majesty's enemies; and how to those the duke adhered, those he comforted, for those he procured the comfortable letters to be sent, as you have heard.

Duke. I confess it, that I caused the letters to be sent, but that I procured the letters to be written, I remember not; but therein I trust Bannister's memory.

Wilbraham. Now for sending money to relieve the Queen's majesty's enemies and touching the 6000£. The French ambassador had 14 hundred crowns ready to relieve them, which he sent to the Scottish Queen to know how it should be bestowed. She would have had the duke to make it up three thousand crowns, she sent one thousand more herself and referred the direction of all to the duke himself. The duke having the chief charge of all, willed two thousand crowns to be conveyed to the Queen's majesty's enemies in Scotland. The Bishop of Ross had devised that it should be sent sewed in Panton's doublet. The duke was made privy to it on the Sunday after Bartholomew-Day; because Panton was a Scot and like to be searched, this device was disliked so was the money delivered to Brown of Shrewsbury; and so he rehearsed the manner of the delivery to Brown and the letters in cipher, as it was afore rehearsed by Mr. Attorney-General.

Duke. I received the money at Tambour's hands; I was not by at the writing of the letter in cipher.

Wilbraham. I said not so.

Then was read the letter to Bannister: you shall receive a bag by this bearer, &c.

Duke. I do not deny the conveying of the money; but it never came to the Queen's enemies hands.

Wilbraham. It was out of our possession; Panton was sent before to receive the money.

Duke. Not of my knowledge. And as for Grange and Ledington, I have not heard they were the Queen's enemies.

Wilbraham. That is no matter; for the indictment is generally of the Queen's enemies and you know the money went to the Lord Harris.

Duke. Lord Harris was not appointed to have any part of it.

Wilbraham. This is no matter, it was a comfort to him, being the Queen's enemy, to be the factor and to have the countenance and distribution of it at his pleasure: beside that, you may be sure he would not let all pass without some share to himself.

Duke. May a subject be the Queen's majesty's enemy, while the prince is her friend and in amity with her?

Catlin. In some cases it may be so: as in France, if the Dukedom of Brittany should rebel against the French King and should (during the amity between the French and Queen's majesty) invade England, those Britons were the French King's subjects and the Queen's enemies, though the French King remained in amity; and so in your case.

Duke. Where was the proclamation made?

Wilbraham. The proclamation was made in England, and here it is to be showed, but the war itself is sufficient proclamation. The Queen's army was sent against him, and the Queen otherwise bound to proclaim.

Duke. I trust my lords the peers will have consideration of me, who they be that accuse me, the Bishop of Ross and strangers; and the rest over-reached in treason themselves.

The Lord Steward asked if they had aught else to say. The duke said I trust to God and my truth. Then the prisoner was withdrawn.

Then the sergeant made an 'O' yes, saying Lord Grace the Queen's commissioner, High Steward of England charged all men to keep silence upon peril of imprisonment.

Then the Lord Steward spoke to the lords willed them to go together.

Note, that the money was taken up by the way.

Then the lords withdrew themselves into a place prepared in the Chancery-Court for consolation, and the prisoner was withdrawn. The lords continued in consultation an hour and a quarter; the Lord Steward still remained in his seat. After an hour and a quarter, which was immediately after eight of the clock at night, the lords came again upon the scaffold and took their places as they were afore; and then the Lord Steward demanded of every of them severally, sitting in their places, beginning at the youngest baron in this manner:

My Lord De la Ware, what say you, is the prisoner guilty of these treasons or not? And they all severally answered in order and form following:

Lord De la Ware, Buckhurst, St. John of Bletshoe, North, Rich, St. John, Mordant, Burghe, Wentworth, Sandes, Mountjoy, Grey of Wilton, Burleigh, Howard, Hereford, Leicester, Hertford, Pembroke, Bedford, Warwick, Huntington, Sussex, Worchester, Kent: guilty.

Then the lieutenant was, by the sergeant commanded to bring again the prisoner to which he did.

Then the Lord Steward said thus; Thomas Duke of Norfolk, thou hast been heretofore indicted of high-treason and has been arraigned upon the same, and hast pleaded not guilty and has put thyself upon thy peers; the lords, thy peers have found thee guilty: what hast thou to say, why I may not proceed to judgment? The duke answered, the lord's will be done, God be judge between me and my false accusers. Then the axe was turned the edge towards him.

Then stood up Mr. Sergeant Barham and said; it appears that Thomas Duke of Norfolk has heretofore been indicted of high-treason, now has been arraigned upon the same, and has pleaded not guilty and has put himself upon his peers; now the lords his peers upon consideration of the evidence showed forth to prove the indictment, have found him guilty. I am most humbly to pray of your grace judgment against him for the Queen's majesty, according to the verdict.

Then said the Lord Steward; Thomas Duke of Norfolk, whereas thou hast heretofore been indicted of high-treason and has been arraigned upon the same, and has pleaded not guilty, and has put thy self upon thy peers, and the lords thy peers upon consideration of the evidence showed forth, have found thee guilty: wherefore thou shall be had from hence to the Tower of London, from there thou shall be drawn through the midst of the streets of London to Tyburn, the place of execution, there thou shall be hanged, and being alive thou shall be cut down quick, thy bowels shall be taken from thy body, and burnt before thy face, thy head shall be smitten off, thy body shall be divided into four parts or quarters; thy head and thy quarters to be set up where it shall please the Queen's majesty to appoint, and the Lord have mercy upon thee.

Then the duke said this is the judgment of a traitor, and I shall die as true a man to the Queen as any lived; knocking himself hard upon the breast, he said I will not desire any of you all to make any petition for my life; I will not desire to live, I am at a point. And my lords, seeing you have put me out of your company, I trust shortly to be in better company: only I beseech you my lords, to be humble suitors to the Queen's majesty for my poor orphan children, that it will please her majesty to be good to my poor orphan children and to take order for the payment of my debts, and some consideration of my poor servants; for I am at a point. God does know how true a heart I bear to her majesty, and how true a heart to my country, whatsoever this day has been falsely objected against me. Farewell, my lords.

Then the lieutenant was commanded to avoid his prisoner; which thing was done.

Then the sergeant made an 'O' yes, and proclaims thus; my lord's grace, the Queen's Commissioner, High Steward of England, charged all persons to depart in God's peace and the Queen's and has dissolved his commission.

And therewith the Lord Steward standing up afore his chair, broke his rod in the midst, and the people cried God save the Queen. Amen.

On the 2nd of June 1572, about eight in the morning, the duke was brought to a scaffold erected on Tower-Hill, attended by Alexander Nowel, Dean of St. Paul's, who having desired the people to keep silence, the duke said:

It is not rare, good people, to see a man come to die; although thanks be to God, since the beginning of the Queen's majesty's reign in this place has not been any such has been, and is the mercifulness of her majesty, whom God long preserve. But since it is my fortune to be the first, I pray God I may be the last. You know I have been long looked for in this present case of mine, divers times in this place; but by her majesty's clemency prolonged hitherto. It is not common to see a man of my vocation to be a speaker; nevertheless I will be brief, and gladly show you the estate of those offences which my conscience does burden me for. I have been by my peers found worthy of death, whereof I do acquit them; for I come not hither to justify myself, neither yet to charge my peers with injustice, but rather submit myself to this which God has prepared for me. And thus considering the weakness of my flesh and blood, that at such a time a man's senses will partly fail, I do mind to divide my speeches into three parts, desiring you to take it full and whole, and not to tear it in pieces.

And first, in dealing in matters temporal towards the Queen of Scots, I dealt not as a good subject, for that I made not the Queen's majesty privy thereto, which indeed I confess I ought to have done; for this offence I was committed to this house (pointing to the Tower) and upon my humble submission, delivered; then making promise to the Queen's majesty (whom I pray God long to prosper) never to deal in those matters again; but contrary to my submission and promise made to the Queen's majesty, abusing her clemency towards me; which has and does grieve me more than any one thing has done; I dealt in this matter again, perfectly for saving my life, and other causes which I could allege.

[Here Mr. Sheriff Branch, standing by the duke, desired him very courteously to make an end as short as might be, for the time did spend]

Then the duke beginning again, said it has been bruited, that I took my oath, and received the sacrament, that I should never deal in those matters again; which is untrue and yet the oath too much.

[Now Mr. Christopher, one of the officers, hearing these words, desired the duke to be short, we are come here, said he, to see you put to execution, and we must not delay while these speeches pass from you, for in this we hazard our lives.]

Then the duke said, I do not excuse myself, but I come to discharge my conscience, and to acquit my peers, and not to complain of any injustice, for

I have deserved this, and more a great deal in that I have abused the Queen's majesty's mercy towards me; whom once again, with hands lifted up, I pray God long to preserve and reign over you and that my death may be an end of all troubles. And to augment my fault, it is said I had familiarity with evil dealers; indeed I will confess and tell you, that I never saw, nor never had conference, but once with one Rudolph and yet never against the Queen's majesty, God is my judge; although many lend offers and motions were made to me; for it is well known I had to do with him by reason I was bound to him by recognizance for a great sum of money. And as for the two letters that came from the Pope, I confess I did see them, the one ciphered, the other deciphered; I never consented to them, neither was I consenting to the late rebellion in the north, notwithstanding I come not hither as un-guilty.

To the second part, I know I have not only been thought to be a Papist, but a favorer of Papists, and a maintainer of them. God is my judge, before whom I stand (lifting up his eyes) I thank God I was never a Papist since I knew what religion meant; but I did always detest Papistry, and all the vain toys thereof, embracing ever, from the bottom of my heart the true religion of Jesus Christ, trusting, by the assurance of faith in his blood, that he is my only redeemer and savior: indeed I must confess that I had servants and friends that were Papists; but if thereby I have offended God's church, or any Protestant, I desire God and them to forgive me.

Well now to the third point, wherein I am to show how much I am bound to the Queen's majesty for her mercifulness towards me, in that her majesty has promised to be good and gracious to my poor children. I remember good Father Latimer making a sermon in a more honorable place than this is out of the pulpit (neither do I compare myself to him) he said that God did oftentimes take away a good and gracious prince, for the sins and disobedience of his subjects; which God grant not to be in these days, but that it will please God to continue and increase her majesty's years; yea, until the world's end, if it be his blessed will and pleasure. You have a most gracious Queen, as I must needs confess, and also godly religion, therefore look that your livings and conversations be answerable to the religion of Christ that proves you; that God may prosper the prince, overthrow the Pope, and maintain your wealth and quietness. Let not my person, good people, make my speech worse; they that have factions (I speak not particularly, but generally) let them beware they be given over betimes; seek not to brevity God's doings, lest God prevent yours.

And then the sheriff hastening him, he turned to the people, and embracing Sir Henry Lee, said I have and always have had as true a heart to my prince as ever any subject has had. And so Sir Henry Lee staying him by the left arm, he kneeled down and asked the Queen's majesty for forgiveness; and rising again, he embraced Mr. Dean of Paul's with a cheerful countenance; and after wards for the most part shaking those that were on the scaffold by the hands, and desiring them to pray for him; amongst the rest, the executioner did on his knees desire forgiveness of his death, who did very courteously forgive him and put into the hand of the executioner four sovereigns of gold and eighteen shillings and six pence of silver. This done, the duke kneeling down and the Dean of Paul's with him, he made his prayers to God, and read the 51st psalm, saying on to the last verse save one, *viz.* build up the walls of Jerusalem; he paused and said the walls of England, good Lord. That psalm finished, he began to read another; and at the seventh verse of the psalm, he paused and said I had almost forgotten, but not too late; I ask all the world forgiveness and I forgive all the world. The psalm finished, and other prayers; he said, *In manus tuas Domine commendo Spiritum meum*, Lord into thy hands I commend my spirit. Then he rose up and pulled off his velvet gown, his black satin doublet, and his velvet night-cap, and gave them to the executioner; and being in a white fustian waistcoat, he said to Mr. Dean of Paul's this is the white satin doublet I made to die in, which the preacher did speak of; and so kneeling at the block, he laid down himself, and rose again, and laid the straw and other things in such sort as he might in a more convenient manner yield himself for the speedier execution. This done, his eyes and hands lifted up, Mr. Dean desired the peoples silence, and said now all together with one voice, pray for him, saying Lord Jesus receive thy soul. The duke yielding himself to the block, refusing to have any handkerchief before his eyes, his head was at one chop cut off, and showed to all the people; and afterwards his corpse was put into a coffin appertaining to Barkin Church, with the head also and the burial-cloth laid over him, and so was carried by four of the lieutenant's men, and was buried in the Chapel of the Tower by the Dean of St. Paul's.

[*Cobbett's Complete Collection of State Trials*, V-1. 82-117]

Robert Hickford

Though a couple sources have recorded variants of Robert Hickford's trial, history has not recorded personal information about the man or his life other than his service to the Duke of Norfolk.

The trial of Mr. Robert Hickford, (servant of the Duke of Norfolk), at the Queen's Bench, for high treason: 14 Eliz. February 9, A.D. 1571- [MS. Brit. Mus. 1427.]

After the reading of the indictment, being asked by the Clerk of the Crown if he were guilty or not guilty? He answered to this effect; being admonished to speak higher, whereto he excused himself by the lowness of his voice:

Hickford. I am here indicted of divers points of high treason, part whereof I deny, for that I was never privy to the same; my fact, such as it is, I am ready to confess and declare as I have already confessed it. I am not learned in the law. I know not in what form to answer to it. This only I require to be heard to declare the truth, so far as the matter touches me. I here protest before your honors, and in the presence of God, that I bring a conscience touched with any intent of hurt, ever conceived by me against the Queen's majesty's person or my country; I never meant any such thing in my heart. I know the law has not intent to the conscience, or intent of men; but is to judge only of the mind according to the appearing of outward facts; so the law cannot accept my intent for my purgation. Therefore I shall declare the truth of my doing, and upon that further open to you at large my dealing in the matters contained in the indictment. First, for the matter of moving of sedition, I did never know that any such thing was meant by my lord, or any other; and whatsoever was by him, or any other intended, I was not privy to it. I do confess indeed that the articles mentioned in the indictment were sent to my lord, my late master, which by his commandment I deciphered, for they were brought in cipher. Then my lord read them and folded them up, and put them in the pocket of his hose, and said the Bishop of Ross will never be quiet, and then he went to supper; and from that time I never saw that writing till it was showed me in the Tower. What answer my lord made to them, or whether he answered them or no, I know not.

C.J. Catlin. Hickford, you seem to be a man of knowledge and learning, you have been indicted, and are now arraigned according to order of law; you must follow order, you must answer to the indictment, confess or deny it, you shall be heard after to say your mind. You must plead to it guilty or not guilty.

Hickford. I do confess the law has not respect to man's intent, but judges according to his fact. I confess I saw these articles and deciphered them, I showed them to my lord; I revoked them not as in duty I ought to have done, and therefore I think myself guilty.

Catlin. The indictment contains divers clauses of treason, therefore answer if you be guilty to any special matters contained in the indictment, or that you will confess yourself guilty of the whole.

Hickford. I may not confess of myself that whereof my conscience does not accuse me, some parts I am not privy to; the first point concerning stirring of sedition, I do not know that ever any such thing was meant by my lord. What intention he had, God and his own conscience knows it. As touching the matter of Rudolph's going over to the King of Spain, to the Pope, and the Duke of Alva, and the instructions of that voyage contained in the thing, that by my lord's commandment I deciphered; I answer as I have before said that I never knew of any proceeding, nor dealt therein afterwards; and my lord, when he read it deciphered, he answered as I said before, The Bishop of Ross will never be quiet. I thought he had burnt that paper as a thing that he liked not; but what he did with it, or in the matter afterward, I cannot tell.

Catlin. You must answer more roundly and directly to the matter; for these circumstances and points, you shall be heard afterward. In the menu time answer plainly, if you be guilty or not guilty.

Southcote. Mr. Southcote spoke to the same effect, and told him that if he pleaded not guilty, these his declarations should be heard at large upon the evidence.

Hickford. To part of the indictment I confess myself guilty, which concerns the deciphering of the letters by my lord's procurement and commandment; after which time I never dealt in it.

Southcote. You were best to plead not guilty to the whole indictment; and for such matters and parts of the indictment as you can clear yourself, the jury may find you not guilty, and find you guilty for the rest.

The Lord Chief Justice and Mr. Attorney advised to the same effect.

Hickford. I am guilty. I know under how merciful a Queen I live; I submit myself wholly to her majesty's mercy. I will not stand long upon that whereof mine own conscience condemn me.

Catlin. Confess you guilty to the whole indictment?

Hickford. Yea.

Attorney. (Mr. Gilbert Gerrard.) Are you guilty of adhering to and comforting the Queen's enemies and the conveying of the French packet and money that was sent to relieve them?

Hickford. I confess myself guilty.

Sergeant. Then, after time pause, Mr. Sergeant Barham spoke to this effect: forasmuch as Robert Hickford has been indicted of high treason, and, among other things, that he has adhered to and comforted the Queen's enemies, and the same indictment has been read to him and he has confessed the treasons; I am to pray your lordships on the Queen's majesty's behalf that his confession may be entered, and judgment given for the Queen against him, according to the law.

Hickford. May I now declare to what points I am not guilty?

Attorney. There are two points in the indictment that concern yourself; the dealing in the matter about Rudolph's voyage, and the instruction for the same; and the adhering to and comforting of the Queen's enemies: are you not guilty of these?

Hickford. I am guilty.

Catlin. If you will yet wave and forsake your confession, we are content to admit you to do so, and you may yet plead not guilty and you shall have your trial.

Hickford. No, I will submit me wholly to her majesty's mercy. I know under how merciful a prince I live, though my deserts be far unworthy, by my master's means and procurement. I know I bring, as I said, a conscience touched with any intent or meaning of hurt to her majesty's person, or to my country. And this I say before God and in the presence and witness of you all; howbeit the law accepts not, nor judges by secret intents, for so might every man clear himself.

Catlin. Hickford, thou hast heard the indictment read, where by the oaths of a jury thou art found and presented guilty of divers high-treasons; thou has been arraigned thereof, and confessed thyself guilty and submitted thyself to her majesty's mercy. The Queen's majesty's sergeant has on her behalf, required confession to be entered, and judgment to be given against thee, according to the order of the laws; so nothing rests now but judgment to be given against thee, and that thou hear thy judgment. A few words for good admonition shall serve. Thou art a gentleman, wise, and well learned, I would to God there had been in thee as much loyalty and truth as there is learning, and other good qualities and gifts of God, then had thou not fallen into this great fault and misery. But there have been evil enticers, evil school-masters, evil seeds men, as one called them here last day; they have brought thee from truth and good estate, to untruth, treason, and wretchedness; where before thou and others were of good name and fame, they have brought you to infamy; of loyal, good, and true subjects, they brought you to the name and state of disloyal traitors. A great blot to be a traitor, and the greatest infamy that can be. It is the chief point of the duty of every natural and reasonable man, which by the gift of reason differs from a beast to know his prince and head, to be true to his head and prince. All the members are bound to obey the head; every man is bound to repair life, to lay out and expend goods, lands, and possessions, to forsake father, mother, kindred, wife, and children, in respect of preserving the prince; for in defending the prince, they preserve father, mother, kindred, wife, children, and all. It was well and wisely spoken here the last day by one that stood at the bar, that was learned and as wise as you are, upon his confessing of himself guilty of treason against his prince; I would he had had as much truth and loyalty as he had of learning and understanding, in few words, he comprehended a great help of matter concerning the duty of the subject to the prince. All the duties said he, to father, mother, friends, kindred, children, yea to a man's wife, that is his own flesh are all inferior to the duty that a subject owes to his prince, for this duty comprehended them all. In respect of duty to the prince, and preserving the prince, neither wife, parent, nor other are to be regarded, they must all stand behind. If in any case, any respect shall allure a man from loyalty and truth to his prince, they must be forsaken, they must come behind; it must be said, *Vade post me, Satana.* We must first look to God the high prince of all princes and then to the Queen's majesty the second prince, and God's deputy, and our sovereign prince on earth. In these few words he comprehended much matter, he satisfied the hearers for their duty to the Queen's majesty. You are wise and learned as he was, and for knowledge of duty and understanding as much bound to God as he; but the evil seeds men, the evil enticers and seducers have wrought evil effect in you both, the great good seeds man has sowed in you good gifts, learning, knowledge, and good quality, to serve him, your prince and your country with as it is said in the gospel, *Bonus seminator seminavit semen bonum;* but *supervenit iuimicus et seminavit zizania:* the good seeds man sowed good seed; but there came the enemy, the evil seeds man, and he sowed darnel, cockle, and noisome weeds. Such wicked seeds men have been in England; if they had sown the right seed for their own use, the seed of hemp, and felt of it, they had received according to their deserving. God has sown in you good gifts and qualities, meet to have served any prince in Christendom; but *supervenit inimkus,* the Devil and his ministers, wicked seeds men, sowed in you darnel and cockle, treason and disloyalty; they have made you forget your duty to your natural prince and country. If these had be handled as they have deserved, they should long ago have had of their own due seed, hemp bestowed upon them, meet seed for such seeds men; such mischievous seeds men they be, that corrupt men otherwise well endued, that sow treason so abundantly in this realm. O strange matter! That such treasons should be, and so ripe in this realm; a common slander to this realm of England, the treasons of England are every where talked of among strange nations: for proof of it they refer us to our histories of H. 2. Ed. 2. Ric. 2. Ed. 3. and so prove the practices in this realm to murder and depose our princes to the great infamy and slander of our country. The very regard of our country's fame, that this great slander of treason should not by your fault have been renewed and increased against us, if nothing else would, it should have staid you from so foul dealing in treason. But is this sowing of treason, lawful for any? May ambassadors be such seeds men? Be these the parts of ambassadors? They have their articles in law, by which they are bound, let them do as law will let them. If they will transgress these and fall to treason, and procure the danger of princes, let them feel as law will. I can show you a precedent and history for it within memory, about 37 or 38 years ago, about the 25th Hen. 8. It was done by the Duke of Milan. The French King, that then was, Francis, grandfather to the French King that now is sent one M. de Marseilles to the Duke of Milan as his ambassador; this M. de Marseilles, the French King's ambassador, conspired treason against the state and the Duke of Milan; the duke understood it, he caused him to be arraigned after the order of their law, and being found guilty, he beheaded him: and this *jure gentium* was lawfully done. May messengers conspire treason against princes to whom they be sent? Treason to princes is not their message, it is no lawful cause of their sending; if of their own heads they presume it, they must by law be touched and taught to keep them within their duties. As for them that seek fame by treason, and by procuring the destruction of princes, where shall sound that fame? Shall the golden trump of fame and good report, that Chaucer spoke of? No; but the black trump of shame shall blow out their infamy for ever. Again, these that follow such heinous treasons, that bring forth the fruit of such seeds as such wicked seeds men have sown, are in foul fault, and justly to be condemned, and worthy extremely to feel it. For that you are in misery, men may have pity and compassion of your misery, and so forbear to grieve you with due rehearsal, else men might aggravate your offence with setting out the particulars of it at length, and as they should have fallen out, if you had stood in trial; but you have confessed it, and yielded yourself guilty, and submitted yourself to the Queen's majesty's mercy. Therefore I will leave to aggravate your faults, and will proceed as the order of law required, to judgment. I pray God to give you grace to make a good end. I need not give you long exhortation, I am no doctor of divinity; you are learned yourself, your knowledge is great I would your loyalty and truth had been as great. But because we are to do with law, we must follow the order of law, one must speak for all, and so I, for all the rest, shall proceed to judgment.

Then my Lord Chief Justice pronounced the judgment usual in treason, concluding it in these words; God be merciful to you, and give you grace to make a good end.

Then Hickford answered to this effect; I humbly thank your lordship for your good admonition; I know and confess that I ought to the Queen's majesty a much greater and higher duty than to my master. And as it is said of your lordships to have been wisely spoken, so was it truly said that the duty of all subjects to the prince is a much greater duty than a man owes to his master, or to any other; yea, or to those that bare him into the world. I unless I have neglected that duty to my prince, howbeit I did it by my lord, my late master's procurement and commandment, and for good intent as my master bare me in hand and persuaded me, whereof I pray your lordships I may declare the truth. When first my lord made choice of me to wait on him in the Tower, as I would to God he had rather made choice of any other, within short time he received a letter from the Scottish Queen in cipher. He made me privy to it, and willed me to acquaint myself with that cipher, for the deciphering of the like hereafter. At that first time I said little to it; within three weeks after there came another letter to him from the Scottish Queen, and then I began to dislike the matter. Then my lord walking on the leads, (having so much liberty granted him) Sir Henry Neville and Mr. Lieutenant being present upon the leads, add departing a little aside, my lord called me to him, and after other matters entered into talk of the Scottish Queen. I said to him I would ask a question of you, if I might without offending you. He asked me what? I said I would show him, so that he would not he offended, for otherwise I durst not. After he had assured me he would not be offended, I said to him. My lord, I marvel much at your doings; you are here, as you know, committed upon high displeasure of the Queen's majesty for dealing with the Scottish Queen without the Queen's majesty's consent.

Now in proceeding further by letters between you, the contrivance of this dealing must much aggravate her highness's displeasure against you. He answered me, thus fool, thou art a fool, thou understand not the matter. I answered I presumed to say this to you upon your assurance that you would not be offended, and that makes me ask, why you continue this dealing with the Scottish Queen? He answered me again, thou art a fool, thou sees not my case; I hold a wolf by the ears, I can neither let go without danger, nor hold without peril. Unhappy man I was when I was first committed; for if I could then have come to the speech of the prince, I would have laid it all at her feet, and I trust I should have found grace to have obtained favor: but now, on the one side, I am entered into my prince's high displeasure; on the other side, if I should pull the Scottish Queen, and all her friends upon me, and make them mine enemies, then were I in worse case than ever I was. If I could once recover my prince's favor, then would I soon shake off all dealing with the Scottish Queen. In the mean time, till her majesty's favor may be recovered, I am driven to this hardness that you see. I answered him again, you are yourself much wiser than I am; but, in my poor opinion, the sooner you rid yourself of this dealing the better. Then because I was persuaded that he trusted to recover the Queen's majesty's favor, I was in the mean time contented to decipher the letters from time to time, as they passed between them. Shortly after he had so much favor and liberty, that his men had recourse to him freely into the Tower; whereupon we conceived hope of his short delivery, but it fell contrary, mid so continued till midsummer. Then was he advised to make submission to the Queen's majesty, and promised that if he would submit himself, and renounce all dealing with the Scottish Queen, there was hope that the Queen's majesty would receive him to grace. Whereupon he wrote a submission, he sent it, it was delivered, and as we heard, it was very well liked of. Within a fortnight after he laid the liberty of the Tower, and comfortable letters came. I looked and had hope that he should have been delivered presently; it came not so to pass, the cause God knows.

Here the Lord Chief Justice offered to interrupt and end this course of speech as impertinent, when he yet proceeded further, and said:

Hickford. I beseech you, my lord, let me use a few words to declare the course of my doing. My lord was not then delivered: shortly after it happened, that by occasion of a sickness, and being sick of the plague in the lower, my lord was removed to his own house at the Charter-House; then we had great hope that we should shortly be received into her majesty's favor, and come to the court again, and so continued till the cipher came from the Bishop of Ross, before which time and since I was never privy to that matter. The cause why I was never afterward made privy was this; my lord being at home at his house at Charter-House, I told him, I liked not his doing, it would not have good end.

Attorney. Why did you then still follow? Why left you him not?

Hickford. He answered me, thou art a fool, thou understands not.

Catlin. He told you truth that you were a fool, for you played the fool indeed.

Hickford. I would then have gone from him, and I sought to depart; he would never give me leave, as Mr. Bannister well knows.

Catlin. Why? He was not your prince, you were not so bound that he could compel you to tarry with him.

Hickford. Otherwise I dealt not with the Bishop of Ross.

Catlin. In following him, the hurt was yours; if you had been a good subject, and had regard of your duty, you might and should have taken other course; but you had higher hope to have seen your master in higher state to advance you; you had more respect to your master than to your mistress. But this is nothing to the matter.

So his purposed longer speech was cut off, and then he said shortly thus:

Hickford. I humbly thank your lordship again for your good admonition; and as your lordship has rehearsed the history of the French ambassador to the Duke of Milan, so I would and pray God that he that has brought my lord to this, may have the like success. I humbly submit myself to the Queen's majesty's mercy. I know I have lived under a most gracious and merciful Queen. I wish God long to preserve her majesty, and this little time that I have left I will spend in prayer for her preservation; and I beseech God have mercy upon me.

Whereto the court, and all that were present, said amen; and some said secretly, he had then showed himself a wiser man than his master. And so the lieutenant was commanded to avoid the prisoner. God save Queen Elizabeth.

[Emlyn, Sollom. *A Complete Collection of State Trials and Proceedings*, 117-212]

John Story

Some early historians often paint a disturbing portrait of John Story as a cruel man. An early narrative describes an episode when he ran his sword through an unarmed man and left him for dead over an insignificant matter shortly after graduating from Oxford around 1538. He was imprisoned, but soon released because the man did not die.

Story's troubles began after Edward VI ascended the throne. Story vehemently opposed Edward's religious beliefs and by doing so, he declared himself a traitor and fled England. When Mary ascended the throne, Story returned to England and relentlessly prosecuted all that opposed the new Queen's beliefs. History recounts the pitiless cruelty he exhibited in using the rack, stocks, whipping and burning of innocents without respect of age, virtue or education: 'All was fish that came into the net. That the burning of heretics was too gentle a death,' he said.

When Elizabeth ascended the throne, Story refused to change his views and candidly spoke against her during a session of Parliament. By publicly declaring his opinion, he declared himself a traitor possibly without consideration of the ramifications. He attempted to flee, but was captured in the west wearing clothes disguised as a servingman. He was escorted to London on the charge of treason but he escaped, possibly with the assistance of friends, to Flanders where he continued his slanderous talk against the Queen with such vehemence, that England declared him an enemy of the realm. He was tricked into boarding a ship with a promise of great rewards, but was captured and returned to London. He was committed to Lollardes Tower and then moved to the Tower of London where he remained until 26 May 1571 to stand trial in Westminster Hall.

Arraignment, judgment, and execution of John Story, for treason: 14 Elizabeth A.D. 1571.

After the death of Queen Mary, so soon as our most dear sovereign lady came to the possession of the crown and that she had called a Parliament, chiefly for the restitution of God's blessed word, and the true administration of the sacraments to God's high honor, and also for the amendment of the decayed state of this realm; John Story, being of the Parliament House, who was an enemy to all godly reformations did with great vehemence speak against the bill that was there exhibited for the restitution of the book of Common-Prayer, and said these words. I did often-times, in Queen Mary's time, say to the bishops, that they were too busy with *Pecora campi* (for so it pleased him to term the poor commons of England) chopping at twigs, but I wished to have chopped at the root; which if they had done, this gear had not come now in question: and herein most traitorously he meant the destruction of our dear and sovereign lady Queen Elizabeth. For which words spoken, in such an audience and in such vehement manner, there was no honest nor true heart that heard him but did utterly abhor him.

And soon after that he had declared his traitorous heart to the Queen's highness, and his conscience accusing him, he tied and lurked about to sundry corners as did Cain when he had murdered his brother Abel. But at the last he was taken in the West Country, riding before a mail in a frieze coat like a serving man, and was apprehended in the highway by one Mr. Ayleworth, a gentleman, one of the Queen's servants, and brought before the council, and after sent to prison to the Queen's-Bench (for more than suspicion of treason) in the first year of her highness's reign.

And after the said Story had remained there a while, he espying his time and by the help of his friends (as commonly such lewd Papists lack none) he broke the said prison and fled again beyond the seas, namely into Flanders, and there not only practiced divers wicked and traitorous enterprises towards our sovereign lady the Queen's majesty and the state of' this realm, by sundry conferences that he had with such as have of late rebelled and conspired the destruction of the same; but also he became an open and common enemy to every good subject of this realm of England, and obtained in Flanders, of the Duke of Alva, a commission and authority to practice his old cruelty and to arrest and apprehend all such Englishmen's goods as should arrive in those countries, or who did traffic out of England into those parts, or from there into England, and to confiscate the same by reason of which authority he used there such extremity, that he was the spoiler and undoer of divers merchants, and of more would have been if he had longer continued; wherefore the said merchants were enforced to study and devise some remedy, and to practice some way or means how to remove this cumbersome man from them.

And among other devices, they having experience of him to be a greedy and ravenous wolf, put into his head (by such as he suspected not) that there was a prey for him of English goods in a ship that lay in a certain place which was named to him, where he should find such a treasure of goods to be confiscated, as would be sufficient for him during his life. The wolf being hungry and desirous of this great prey set forward and came into a ship that promised to bring him to the place where the prey was. But, to be short, as soon as he was entered the ship, the same brought him clear away out of Flanders into England and landed him at Harwich in the month of August last past.

And soon after, knowledge being given to the Queen's honorable council of his landing, he was brought to London, and there he was committed to prison to the Lollards Tower, in Powles, where he continued a while that he might well peruse that place wherein he had most cruelly tormented many a good Christian. But he lacked there one thing which was the monstrous and huge stocks that he and Bonner, his old faithful friend, had used to turmoil and persecute the poor and innocent Christians in hanging some therein by the heels so high, that only their heads lay on the ground; some were stocked in both feet and arms; some also were stocked by both their feet and by both their thumbs, and so did hang in the stocks; and some also were stocked by both their feet and chained by the neck with collars of iron made fast behind them to a post in the wall, and such other devilish and tyrannous engines and devises by him practiced. These at his being in the Lollards Tower he missed, and great pity it was that he had not tasted of them: but alack, the good Bishop Grindel, late Bishop of London, had burned and consumed them with fire.

But to return where I left, after that Story had continued a certain of time in Lollards Tower and had been divers times examined, he was from there removed to the Tower of London where he remained until the 26th of May 1571. And then was he brought from thence into Westminster-Hall before the judges of the Queen's Bench, and there arraigned: and after the indictment had been read to him, the effect whereof was that whereas, Richard Norton, Thomas Markenfield, Christopher Nevill, Francis Norton and Thomas Jenny, alias Jennings, with other traitors, after their offences committed in the North, and being thereof indicted in the 12th year of the Queen's highness's reign, before the right honorable Thomas Earl of Sussex, Lord President of the Queen's Council in the North parts, John Lord Darcy, &c. they after their indictment did the 23rd of June in the year aforesaid, embark themselves in sundry ships and fled this realm to Antwerp in Brabant, which is under the government of King Philip, and there, contrary to their allegiance, did lead their lives; and the aforesaid John Story, D. W. P. and J. P. being born in England and the Queen's subjects, did with them conspire, compass, and imagine the Queen's death, and her highness to depose and deprive.

And by diver's persuasions and letters did also procure strangers to invade this realm of England, did receive comfort and help them at Antwerp aforesaid, against their allegiance, &c.

And after the indictment read, he being called upon by the court to answer to the same, pleaded that he was not the Queen's subject, nor had not been these seven years, but was the subject of the most Catholic and mighty prince King Philip, King of Spain, to whom he was sworn, and had in fee of him one hundred pounds by the year; therefore, said he I am not bound to answer to that indictment, neither will I answer to it.

And here he used many pretty taunts, as well to the judges as also pleasing himself with giving of pretty nips and girds. And very stoutly he maintains his former plea, affirming also that they were not his lawful judges, neither that they had law to proceed against him, being none of the Queen's subjects.

And then, being demanded where he was born? He answered, In England.

Then, said they, it followed that you are subject to the laws of this realm and should be so to our Queen.

Whereto he replied, and said, that God commanded Abraham to go forth from the land and country where he was born, from his friends and kinsfolk into another country; and so he following his example, for conscience sake in religion did forsake his country and the laws of this realm and the prince also, and had wholly given himself to the service of a foreign governor, King Philip, King of Spain.

And hereupon he stood very stoutly, but to small purpose.

Then when he perceived that they would proceed in judgment against him, he said they had no law so to do. And with that he turned him about to the people and said, good people I trust you see how violently I am used; and how unjustly, and contrary to all justice and equity they use me. And he added that he had good hope, that he was not destitute of some friends there who would give notice and knowledge to the most Catholic prince his master, how cruelly they dealt with him. And then again, being called upon to answer, one said to him, Master Story, because you think it violence that is showed to you instead of law and justice; you shall know that we do nothing but that we may do, both by law and equity.

And then one of the judges said, this is Scarborough's case. Nay, said Story, my case is not Scarborough's case, but indeed I had Scarborough's warning to come to this arraignment; for I knew nothing thereof until seven of the clock in the morning.

Then there was a book delivered him to read, wherein he might see what they might do by law; and after he had read it, the judge demanded of him how he liked it? And he answered God have mercy upon me. Then the Lord Chief Justice gave him judgment, to be drawn, hanged, and quartered; and so was he again sent to the Tower. And as he went by the way, certain persons in several places met with him, and one said, O Story, Story! Thou art a strange Story; remember Master Bradford, that godly man; his blood asked vengeance on you, Story; repent in time. Another cried on him and said, Story, call to mind the rigor you showed upon Master Read, a gentleman whom you did utterly destroy; ask God's forgiveness, Story, for that wicked deed.

Another cried to him and said, blessed be God, Story, who has made you partaker of such bread as you want wont to deal to the innocent members of Jesus Christ.

Another also cried out upon him and said, Story, Story, the abominable cup of fornication and filthiness that you have given others to drink, be heaped up topful, that your plagues may be the greater at the terrible day of God's wrath and vengeance unless thou ask mercy for your filthy, corrupt and stinking life. And yet again, another cried out to him and said, I pray God that your heart be not hardened, as was Pharaoh's, and made harder than the adamant stone, or the steel; that when he would he could not repent and call for grace.

And among all the rest, one came to him, at London Stone, and saluted him with this meter, saying;

Master Doctor Story,

For you they are right sorry,
The court of Lovaine and Rome:
Your holy father, the Pope,
Cannot save you from rope,
The hangman must have your gown.

To whom he answered not one word.

The 1st day of June, the said Mr. Story was drawn upon a hurdle from the Tower of London to Tyburn where was prepared for him a new pair of gallows made in triangle manner. And by the way, as he went, many people spoke to him and called to him to repent his tyranny and wickedness; and willed him to call upon God for mercy; but he lay as though he had been asleep, and would not speak to any person.

And when he was taken from the hurdle and set in a cart, he made there a solemn protestation, and said:

I am come hither to die: and truly, if this death were ten times more fierce and sharp than it is, I have deserved it. I have lived the space of threescore and seven years; and now my body must abide this temporal pain and punishment provided for me here in this life by means whereof, my days shall be cut off. But, where at the first I stood in fear of death, I thank God this night passed; I have been so comforted with God and godly men that the fear of death is taken from my sight. And now I appeal to God the father, trusting in the passion of his son Jesus Christ, and hoping by the shedding of his blood only to be saved. And although of a long time I could not apply the virtue of his passion and death to the use and benefit of my soul, because of my long hovering in fear; yet now, I thank God, I know how to apply this medicine; as for example.

An apothecary may have a medicine in his shop seven years that may help a sick or diseased man by the counsel of a physician; but if this medicine be not applied to the patient, but still remains in the apothecary's shop, it profited nothing. No more, said he, could the benefit of Christ's death help me; because, though I knew the medicine good, I did not apply it to my soul's health: but now it has pleased almighty God to call me to account of my 67 years which now must have an end, and this corrupt body must feel a temporal punishment, for my sins have deserved it (as I said before) I am now come to the proof of this medicine. David, when he had committed adultery with Bathsheba, the wife of Uriah, (whose husband also he caused to be put into the front of the battle, and so was murdered) he for that trespass felt a temporal punishment by the loss of his son, which he loved tenderly. Also, when he numbered his people, he greatly displeased God: and for his offence and transgression, he felt a temporal pain and choice was given to him from above to chose one of these three temporal and bodily punishments: that is to say; three days pestilence: the sword; that is to say, bloody battle seven years; or famine seven years. And he thought to choose the least; and he chose three days pestilence, but this scourge took away an infinite number of his subjects. So now as my sins deserve a temporal pain, which here have an end, even in this flesh; I am of the same mind that the prophet David was, and with him I agree, saying, *Invoco it Domine, &c.* Lord, I call upon you in this day of my trouble, hear me, O Lord, out of thy dwelling place, &c.

But now to speak a little of my arraignment: when I was at Westminster, I alleged in my plea that I was no subject of this realm; as I did likewise before the Queen's commissioners, Sir Thomas Wroth, Mr. Thomas Wilbraham, late Recorder of London, Mr. Peter Osborne, Mr. Marsh, and Mr. Dr. Wattes; where the Recorder of London made the like demand as was demanded of me at Westminster: and that was, whether I was born in England, or no? Whereto I answered I was. Then said he, it followed that you are, and ought to continue the Queen's faithful subject. Whereto I replied then as I do now, saying; I am sworn to the noble King, defender of the ancient Catholic faith, King Philip of Spain, and he is sworn again by a solemn and corporal oath to maintain and defend the University of Lovaine, whereof I am a member; and therefore no subject of this realm, nor yet subject to any laws thereof. For it is well known that I departed this realm being freely licensed thereto by the Queen, who accounted me an abject and cast away; and I came not hither again of my own accord, but I was betrayed. And although I had an inkling given me before of such a thing pretended towards me, yet I could not shun nor escape it, for sure it was God who made dim my understanding, and blinded my eyes so that I could not perceive it. But Holy Writ commanded me to love my enemies; and here I forgive them freely with all my heart; beseeching God that they take no harm for me in another country; I would be right sorry they should, although they betrayed me.

I traveled with them from ship to ship, by the space of eight days, and mistrusted no peril to be at hand until I was clapped fast under the hatches. But sure, sure, it was God who wrought it, yea, and although I was accounted a poller of the Englishmen of your country, I stand now here before God and by the death I shall die, I had never out of any ship more than two pieces of gold, and forty dollars that were laid in my hand. But once again to my arraignment; where there were certain fitters laid to my charge, wherein I should go about to provoke the Norton's, the Neville's and others to rebel; I never meant it, yet will I discharge my conscience freely and frankly and tell you truth. There was a commission for like matter sent into Scotland, which I wrote with mine own hand, but it contained a proviso wherein the Queen of England and her dominions were excepted. There are yet two things that I purpose to talk of; namely, for that there are here present a great number of youth; and I would to God I might say or speak that which might bring all men to the unity of the church; for there is but one church, one flock, and one shepherd, if I could this do, I would think myself to have wrought a good work.

The first point touched my cruelty, wherewith I am sore burdened; and the second concerned my religion. As touching the first: there were three in commission, of which I was one who might do least, for I was the last of the three. And though I might, by persuasion, assay to cause them to revoke the articles which they had maintained and to confess the presence, wherein I stand, you now that he who chided, is not worthy to be condemned for fighting; no more am I worthy to be counted cruel for chiding. It was the bishop who pronounced the sentence (*Excommunicanus*) and against that I could not do, for I was one of the laity. Yet oftentimes the bishop, to whom I was a servant, was bold with me when he had so many prisoners that he could not well bestow them. For at one lime the Lord Kitche sent him out of Essex 28, and at another time 16, and 14, and some of them were sent to me, whom I kept in my house with such fare as I had provided for myself and my family at mine own cost and charge. And to prove that I was not so cruel as I am reported to be, let this one tale suffice; there were at one time 28 condemned to the fire, and I moved the Dean of Paul's to tender their state, who after was Abbot of Westminster a very pitiful minded man, I think most of you know him; it is Master Feckman, and we went by and persuaded with them, and we found them very tractable; and Master Feckman and I labored to the Lord Cardinal Poole showing that they were *nescientes quid fecerunt*.

The cardinal and we did sue together to the Queen, and laid both the swords together, and so we obtained pardon for them all, saving an old woman who dwelt about Paul's church yard; she would not convert and therefore she was burned. The rest of them received absolution and that with all reverence. Search the register and you shall find it. Yea and it was my procurement that there should be no more burned in London; for I saw well that it would not prevail, and therefore we sent them into odd corners into the country. Wherefore, I pray you, name me not cruel; I would be loath to have any such slander run on me: but since I die in charity, I pray you all of charity to pray for me that God may strengthen me with patience, to suffer my death: to the which I yield most willingly. And here I make a petition to you my friends, who would have bestowed anything on me. I beseech you, for charity sake, bestow it yearly on my wife who has four small children, and God has now taken me away who was her staff and stay, and now my daughter Weston and her three children are gone over to her, and I know not how they shall do for food unless they go a begging from door to door for it, although indeed no English persons do beg but of English, being helped by the Lady Dorm, and Sir Francisco. I have good hope that you will be good to her, for she is the most faithful wife. The most loving and most constant that ever man had and twice we have lost all that ever we had, and now she has lost me, to her great grief, I know.

The second point that I thought to speak of is concerning my religion, for that I know many are desirous to know what faith I will die in; the which I will briefly touch. I say with St. Jerome, that ancient father and pillar of the old ancient Catholic and apostolic church, grounded upon the patriarchs, prophets and apostles, that in the same faith that was born in, I purpose to die in. And as the ark that Noah and his family did possess, figured the ship of Christ's Church, out of which slip whosoever is cannot be saved, in that ship am I; example, a ship that is tossed on the floods is often in danger of loss on the sands, and sometimes on the rocks, but when the men who are in the ship espy present peril at hand, there is a cockboat at the tail of the ship, whereto they fly for succor, so likewise I being in the ship of Christ, once fell out of the same ship and was in present peril and great danger: but then I, following the example of a good mariner, took the cockboat thinking for to land; and at the last, being in the boat, I espied three oars, that is to wit, contrition, confession, and absolution; and I held all these fast, and ever since I have continued in the ship of Christ, of which the Apostle Peter is the guide and principal and in the faith Catholic of my king I die.

Then said the Earl of Bedford; are you not the Queen's subject? No, said Story, yet I do not exclude the Queen, but I pray for her, her council, and the nobility of this realm long to continue.

Then said the Lord Hunsdon, are you not the Queen's subject? You were born in England. Then said Story, every man is free born and he has the whole face of the earth before him to dwell and abide in where he likes best; and if he cannot live here, he may go elsewhere. Then was there (as I think) one of the ministers hearing him to make so light of our noble Queen and country, demanded of him whether she were not next, and immediately under God, supreme head of the Churches of England and Ireland? Whereto he answered, I come not hither to dispute, but if she be, she is. My nay will not prevail to prove it otherwise.

And then they cried, 'Away with the cart.' And so he was hanged according to his judgment.

[*Harleian Miscellany*, VI. 411-418]

An early narrative survives, recounting his execution. He was cut down from the gallows too soon and when the executioner began to quarter him, he stood up and punched the executioner in the ear. The executioner then proceeded to dismember him.

John Leslie, Bishop of Ross

John Leslie, Bishop of Ross, was born 29 September, 1527 in Scotland into the ancient noble house of Leslie of Balqhain, but early historians suggest he was illegitimate. Nevertheless, he received an education at Aberdeen University and then in France at Poitiers, Toulouse and Paris, graduating as doctor of law. About 1554, he taught canon law at King's College, Aberdeen and ordained in 1558.

Leslie held a judicial office in 1561 when Mary Stuart returned to the Scottish throne. She named him her adviser and a member of her Privy Council circa 1565. He remained faithful to Mary even through the investigation regarding her participation in the murder of her husband. In 1569, he was implicated in an unsuccessful revolt in the north, but was fully acquitted of all charges. Leslie then joined Ridolfi in his rebellion, was captured and imprisoned, then released in 1573.

He was unable to regain support from Mary and banished from the country where he traveled to various courts. James VI later restored him to bishop and his former entitlements, but he never returned to Scotland. He died on 31 May, 1596 near Brussels.

The case of the Bishop of Ross, resident of the Queen of Scots; who was seized and committed to the Tower by Queen Elizabeth, for traitorous practices, and endeavoring to raise a rebellion against her. (1571)

Ridolph the Florentine, who was sent to solicit the Queen of Scots affairs beyond sea, had communicated to Charles Bailiff, a Netherlander, the Queen of Scots servant, all his transactions with the Duke d'Alva; and had given him letters written in ciphers for her, the Spanish ambassador, the Duke of Norfolk, Ross, and the Baron of Lumley, made up in one packet; which Bailiff brought over himself though Ross had ordered him to leave them with the Governor of Calais to be conveyed over.

But, as soon as Bailiff was arrived at Dover, he was apprehended and imprisoned, and the packet sent to the Lord Cobham, Governor of the Cinque-ports. Ross was the first that had notice of it, who managed his business so industriously and cunningly with the Lord Cobham that the packet was delivered to him, and another packet made up of other obsolete letters delivered to the council; and this Bailiff was acquainted with. But however, being put to the rack, he confessed some things, and amongst the rest that a packet of letters was come to Ross's hands. Nor was Ross ignorant of this, who presently sent away Cuthbert his secretary and left his ciphers and what else might do him any prejudice among his friends; so that when Sussex, Burleigh, Mildmay, and Sadler made a careful search in his house, they found nothing, nor could they get anything out of him by questions, who stiffly maintained that an ambassador was not to be accountable to any but his prince, however, the third day after he was committed to the custody of the Bishop of Ely, and a while after conveyed to the Isle of Ely.

But since by the confession of all, even of the Duke of Norfolk himself, the Bishop of Ross was charged as principal contriver of the business, they entered into a serious consultation what should be done with him, being an ambassador. For, whilst he, after the manner of other ambassadors, thought he might lawfully promote the interest of his prince by any methods, and that by the sacred and inviolable privilege of ambassadors, he was not to be accountable to another's jurisdiction; he had already committed many irregularities by raising rebellion, and holding nocturnal cabals with the Earl of Southampton and others; and now lately with the English fugitives in the Netherlands, the Duke d'Alva the Spaniard, and the Pope, for invading of England. It was therefore proposed to Daniel Lewis, Valentine Dale, William Drury, William Aubrey, and Henry Jones, learned civilians.

First, whether an ambassador that raises rebellion against the prince to whom he is sent should enjoy the privileges of an ambassador, and not rather be liable to punishment as an enemy?

They answered: that such an ambassador by the law of nations and the civil law of the Romans, has forfeited the privileges of an ambassador, and is liable to punishment.

Secondly, whether the minister or agent of a prince deposed from his public authority, and in whose stead another is substituted, may enjoy the privileges of an ambassador?

They answered: if such a prince be lawfully deposed, his agent cannot challenge the privileges of an ambassador, since none but absolute princes and such as enjoy a royal prerogative, can constitute ambassadors.

Thirdly, whether a prince, which comes into another prince's Kingdom and is there kept prisoner, can have his agent; and whether that agent can be reputed an ambassador?

They answered: if such a prince have not forfeited his principality, he may have an agent; but, whether that agent may be reputed an ambassador, depended upon the authority of his commission.

Fourthly, whether, if a prince declare to such an agent, and his prince in custody, that he shall be no longer reputed an ambassador, that agent may, by law, challenge the privilege of an ambassador?

They answered; that the prince may forbid the ambassador entrance into his Kingdom and may command him to leave the Kingdom if he keep himself not within the bounds prescribed to an ambassador; yet in the mean time he may enjoy the privileges of an ambassador according to the authority deputed to him.

According to these answers of the civilians, Ross being called up from the Isle of Ely and receiving a sharp reprimand, it was declared by the council that he should be no longer reputed an ambassador, but be severely punished, according to his demerits.

He answered; that he was the ambassador of an absolute Queen that was unjustly deposed, and had, according to his duty, carefully endeavored the delivery of his princess and the safety of both Kingdoms; that he came into England with the full authority of an ambassador under public warrants which he had produced and that the sacred privileges of ambassadors are by no means to be infringed.

Burleigh most gravely informed him, that neither the privileges of an ambassador, nor letters of public warrants could protect ambassadors that offended against the public majesty of a prince, but that they are liable to be punished for the same; else wicked ambassadors might plot against the life of princes without any punishment.

On the other hand, he stiffly maintained that the privileges of ambassadors had never been violated (to use his own words) *via Juris*, but *via Facti*; and he pleasantly wished them not to show him fouler play than the English ambassadors Throckmorton in France, and Randolph and Tamworth in Scotland had found; who had raised rebellions and openly fomented them; and yet suffered no greater punishment than the being commanded to depart within such a time.

When they began to urge him with testimonies of Englishmen, he gently desired them not to do it, since by a common received custom, which (as he said) was grown into a law, the testimony of an Englishman against a Scotchman, or of a Scotchman against an Englishman, was not to be allowed.

After some debates whether this would hold good unless between the borders of both Kingdoms, and that in cases relating to the frontiers; and whether the English ambassadors had raised rebellions; Ross was committed to the Tower of London; where being kept close prisoner within a while he answered to all questions with this *proviso*, that his answers should not be prejudicial to any: he excused the Queen of Scots, for that she being a prisoner in the flower of her age, could not but use her utmost endeavors to regain her freedom, since Queen Elizabeth denied her access to her presence, debarred her from all hope of her liberty, and openly relieved her enemies. The Duke of Norfolk he excused, in that he had done nothing as to the marriage with the Queen of Scots, but with the consent of many of the Queen's council; nor could he forsake her, though he had promised to do so under his hand and seal since there was before a mutual engagement of marriage betwixt them. Lastly, he excused himself, for that since he was an ambassador and a servant, he could not without a sin depart from his duty and abandon his princess in her distress. But that he proposed the design of seizing on the Queen with no other intent than to try whether the duke had courage to undertake such an attempt. The crimes of the other conspirators he cunningly extenuated, but could by no means be brought to tell the names of the gentlemen who had devoted their service to the duke in seizing the Queen. But he confessed, that by the Queen of Scots orders, he had, by servants employed between them, treated with the duke, Arundel, Lumley, and Throckmorton, and with the Lord Viscount Montacute by Lumley about putting the castles in Scotland, the hostages and the King of Scots into Englishmen's hands, about renouncing the title and giving up the English rebels. Thus far of these transactions for this year, extracted wholly out of the Duke of Norfolk's confession, and Ross's own account under his own hand to the Queen of Scots.

[*Harleian Miscellany*, VI. 405-408]

Commission on the Use of Torture

Instigations of the use of torture to persuade prisoners to confess their crimes prompted the formation of a commission by Queen Elizabeth to address the concerns. Although the following is not a trial, it has a place in this edition.

A declaration of the favorable dealing of her majesties commissioners appointed for the examination of certain traitors, and of tortures virtuously reported to be done upon them for matters of religion. 1583. In black letter, quarto, containing six pages.

To the reader.

Good reader, although her majesties most mild and gracious government be sufficient to defend itself against those most slanderous reports of heathenish and unnatural tyrannies and cruel tortures, pretended to have been executed upon certain traitors who lately suffered for their treason, and others; as well spread abroad by runagate Jesuits and seminary men in their seditious books, letters, and libels, in foreign countries and princes courts, as also insinuated into the hearts of some of our own country men and her majesties subjects: yet, for your better satisfaction, I have conferred with a very honest gentleman whom I know to have good and sufficient means to deliver the truth against such forgers of lies and shameless slanders in that behalf which he and other that do know, and have affirmed the same will at all times justify; and for my further assurance and satisfaction herein, he has set down to the view of all men these notes following.

Touching the rack and torments, used to such traitors as pretended themselves to be Catholics upon whom the same have been exercised, it is affirmed for truth and is offered upon due examination so to be proved to be as follows; first, that the forms of torture in their severity or rigor of execution, have not been such and in such manner performed as the slanderers and seditious libelers have slanderously and maliciously published; and that even the principal offender, Campion himself who was sent and came from Rome and continued here in sundry corners of the realm having secretly wandered in the greatest part of the shires of England in a disguised sort to the intent to make special preparation of treasons; and to that end, and for the furtherance of those his labors, sent over for more help and assistance and cunningly and traitorously at Rome before he came from there procured toleration for such prepared rebels to keep themselves covert, under pretence of temporary and permissive obedience to her majesty, the state standing as it does; but, so soon as there were sufficient force whereby the bull of her majesties deprivation might be publicly executed they should then join altogether with that force upon penne of curse and damnation; that very Campion, I say before the conference had with him by learned men in the Tower, wherein he was charitably used was never so racked, but that he was presently able to walk and to write and did presently write and subscribe all his confessions as by the originals thereof may appear. A horrible matter is also made of the starving of one Alexander Bryant; how he should eat clay out of the walls, gathered water to drink from the droppings of houses with such other false ostentations of inhumanity where the truth is this; that whatsoever Bryant suffered in want of food he suffered the same willfully and of extreme impudent obstinacy against the mind and liking of those that dealt with him. For certain traitorous writings being found about him, it was thought convenient by conference of hands to understand whose writing they were; and thereupon, he being in her majesties name commanded to write which he could very well do, and being permitted to him to write what he would himself in these terms; that if he liked not to write one thing he might write another or what he listed (which to do being charged in her majesties name, was his duty and to refuse was disloyal and undutiful) yet the man would by no means be induced to write anything at all. Then was it commanded to his keeper to give to him such meat, drink, and other convenient necessaries as he would write for; and to forbear to give him anything for which he would not write. But Bryant being thereof advertised, and oft moved to write persisting so in his curst heart by almost two days and two nights, made choice rather to lack food then to write for the sustenance which he might readily have had for writing, and which he had indeed, readily and plentifully so soon as he wrote. And, as it is said of these two so is it to be truly said of other with this that there was a perpetual care had and the Queen's servants the wardens whose office and act it is to handle the rack, were ever by those that attended the examinations specially charged to use it in as charitable manner as such a thing might be.

Secondly, it is said and likewise offered to be justified that never any of these seminaries, or such other pretended Catholics which at any time in her majesties reign have been put to the rack were upon the rack or in other torture, demanded any question of their supposed conscience; as what they believed in any point of doctrine or faith, as the mass, transubstantiation or such like; but only with what persons at home or abroad and touching what plots, practices and conferences they had dealt, about attempts against her majesties estate or person? Or to alter the laws of the realm for matters of religion by treason or by force? And how they were persuaded themselves and did persuade other touching the Popes bull and pretense of authority to depose Kings and princes; and namely, for deprivation of her majesty and to discharge subjects from their allegiance expressing herein always the Kingly powers and estates and the subjects allegiance civilly without mentioning or meaning therein any right that the Queen as in right of the crown has over persons ecclesiastical being her subjects. In all which cases, Campion and the rest never answered plainly but sophistically, deceitfully and traitorously; restraining their confession of allegiance only to the permissive form of the Popes toleration as for example, if they were asked whether they did acknowledge themselves the Queen's subjects and would obey her? They would say, yea; for so they had leave for a time to do. But, adding more to the question and they being asked if they would so acknowledge and obey her any longer than the Pope would so permit them or not withstanding such commandment as the Pope would or might give to the contrary? Then they either refused so to obey or denied to answer or said that they could not answer to those questions without danger; which very answer without more saying, was a plain answer to all reasonable understanding that they would no longer be subjects nor persuade other to be subjects than the Pope gave license. And, at their very arraignment when they labored to leave in the minds of the people and standers by, an opinion that they were to die not for treason, but for matter of faith and conscience in doctrine touching the service of God, without any attempt or purpose against her majesty, they cried out that they were true subjects and did, and would obey and serve her majesty. Immediately to prove whether that hypocritical and sophistical speech extended to a perpetuity of their obedience or to so long time as the Pope so permitted or no, they were openly in place of judgment asked by the Queen's learned counsel whether they would so obey and be true subjects if the Pope commanded the contrary. They plainly disclosed themselves in answer saying by the mouth of Campion, this place (meaning the court of her majesties bench) has no power to enquire or judge of the holy father's authority and other answer they would not make.

Thirdly, that none of them have been put to the rack or torture, no not for the matters of treason or partnership of treason or such like, but where it was first known and evidently probable by former detections, confessions, and otherwise that the party so racked, or tortured, was guilty and did know, and could deliver truth of the things wherewith he was charged; so as it was first assured that no innocent was at any time tormented; and the rack was never used to wring out confessions at adventure upon uncertainties in which doing it might be possible that an innocent in that case might have been racked.

Fourthly, that none of them had been racked, or tortured unless he had first said expressly or amounting to as much, that he will not tell the truth though the Queen command him. And, if any of them being examined did say he could not tell, or did not remember if he would so affirm in such manner as Christians among Christians are believed such his answer was accepted if there were not apparent evidence to prove that he willfully said untruly. But, if he said that his answer in delivering truth should hurt a Catholic and so be an offence against charity which they said to be sin and that the Queen could not command them to sin, and therefore howsoever the Queen commanded they would not tell the truth which they were known to know or to such effect, they were then put to the torture, or else not.

Fifthly, that the proceeding to torture was always so slowly, so unwillingly and with so many preparations of persuasions to spare themselves and so many means to let them know that the truth was by them to be uttered both in duty to her majesty and in wisdom for themselves as whosoever was present at those actions must needs acknowledge in her majesties ministers, a full purpose to follow the example of her own roost gracious disposition; whom God long preserve.

Thus it appeared that albeit by the more general laws of nations, torture has been and is lawfully judged to be used in lesser cases and in sharper manner for inquisition of truth in crimes not so near extending to public danger as these ungracious persons have committed whose conspiracies and the particularities thereof, it did so much import and behoove to have disclosed yet, even in that necessary use of such proceeding enforced by the offenders notorious obstinacy, is nevertheless to be acknowledged the sweet temperature of her majesties mild and gracious clemency; and their slanderous lewdness to be the more condemned that have in favor of heinous malefactors and stubborn traitors, spread untrue rumors and slanders to make her merciful government disliked under false pretense and rumors of sharpness and cruelty to those against whom nothing can be cruel and yet upon whom nothing has been done but gentle and merciful.

[*Harleian Miscellany*, 514-517]

William Parry

William Parry was born to Henry Parry, a gentleman of a well established family of Northop, Flintshire, and Margaret, daughter of Archdeacon of St. Asaph. At an early age Parry served an apprenticeship to Mr. Fisher of Chester who was reputed as having a small knowledge of law. A colorful story survives of his frequent attempts to escape his master while attending grammar school and having finally succeeded, he traveled to London.

He married a widow, daughter of Sir William Thomas, resulting in his attachment to the household of William Herbert, first Earl of Pembroke, whom he served until the Earl's death in 1570. Parry received a small appointment in the Queen's service then married Catherine, although it is not clear what happened to his first marriage. Through that marriage, he possessed several manors, but nevertheless was forced into litigation in 1571. He had squandered money and accepted a position as a spy, possibly to avoid his creditors. This continued for several years as he visited numerous European cities. He returned to England infrequently, again possibly to avoid his creditors. In 1580, he returned to England and assaulted a chief creditor. Though the offence was not a felony, he was charged with burglary and sentenced to death but received a pardon.

In 1582, he fled as he felt his position in England was fragile and became influenced by Jesuits who, as he interpreted their words, suggested the 'lawfulness of assassinating Elizabeth.' He continued to travel seeking approval for the plan, but was unable to accumulate the support he wanted. Upon his return to England, he disclosed a plan he heard to murder the Queen and to free Mary Stuart and place her on the throne. Parliament met and passed a bill against 'Jesuits, seminary priests, and other such-like-disobedient persons' with a unanimous approval. During the third reading of the bill, Parry denounced it as 'a measure savoring of treasons, full of blood, danger, and despair to English subjects, and pregnant with fines and forfeitures which would go to enrich not the Queen, but private individuals.' Parry was committed to the sergeant-at-arms and required to justify his words, but released the following day. Shortly after, a co-conspirator had stated that Parry would murder the Queen while she was driving in the park. He was arrested and placed in the Tower on a charge of treason. On 18 February, 1585, he stood trial.

The trial of Dr. William Parry at Westminster, for high treason: 26 Elizabeth, February 25, 1584.

The commissioners were, Henry Lord Hunsdon, Governor of Berwick; Sir Francis Knolles, Knight, Treasurer of the Queen's majesty's household; Sir James Croft, Knight, Comptroller of the same household; Sir Christopher Hatton, Knight, Vice Chamberlain to her majesty; Sir Christopher Wray, Knight, Chief Justice of England; Sir Gilbert Gerrard, Knight, Master of the Rolls; Sir Edmund Anderson, Knight, Chief Justice of the Common

Pleas; Sir Roger Manwood, Knight, Chief Baron of the Exchequer; and Sir Thomas Hennage, Knight, Treasurer of the Chamber.

The court being sat; first, three proclamations for silence were made according to the usual course in such cases. Then the lieutenant was commanded to return his precept; which he did, and brought the prisoner to the bar; to whom Miles Sandes Esq. Clerk of the Crown, said, William Parry, hold up your hand: and he did so. Then said the Clerk of the Crown, you are here indicted by the oaths of twelve good and lawful men of the county of Middlesex, before Sir Christopher Wray, Knight, and others, who took the indictment by the name of William Parry, late of London, gentleman, otherwise called William Parry, late of London, doctor of the law; for that you, as a false traitor against the most noble and Christian princess Queen Elizabeth, your most gracious sovereign and liege lady, not having the fear of God before your eyes, nor regarding your due allegiance, but being seduced by the instigation of the devil, and intending to withdraw and extinguish the hearty love and due obedience which true and faithful subjects should bear to the same our sovereign lady, did at Westminster, in the county of Middlesex, on the first day of February, in the 26th year of her highness's reign, and at divers other times and places in the same county, did maliciously and traitorously conspire and compass, not only to deprive and depose the same our sovereign lady of her royal estate, title and dignity, but also to bring her highness to death, and final destruction, and sedition in the realm to make, and the government thereof to subvert, and the sincere religion of God established in her highness's dominions to alter and subvert. And that whereas you William Parry, by the letters sent to Gregory Bishop of Rome, did signify to the same bishop your purposes and intentions aforesaid, and thereby did pray and require the same bishop to give you absolution; that you afterwards, that is to say, the last day of March in the 26th year aforesaid, did traitorously receive letters from one called Cardinal de Como, directed to you William Parry, whereby the same cardinal did signify to you that the Bishop of Rome had perused your letters and allowed of your intent; and that to that end he had absolved you of all your sins, and by the same letter did animate and stir you to proceed with your enterprise; and that thereupon you the last day of August, in the 26th year aforesaid, at St. Giles in the Fields, in the same county of Middlesex, did traitorously confer with one Edmund Nevil, Esquire, uttering to him all your wicked and traitorous devices, and then and there did move him to assist you therein, and to join with you in those wicked treasons aforesaid, against the peace of our said sovereign lady the Queen, her crown and dignity. What say you, William Parry, are you guilty of these treasons whereof you stand here indicted, or not guilty?

Then Parry said, before I plead not guilty, or confess myself guilty, I pray you give me leave to speak a few words; and with humbling himself, began in this manner: God save Queen Elizabeth, and God send me grace to discharge my duty to her and to send you home in charity. But touching the matters that I am indicted of, some were in one place, and some in another, and done so secretly as none can see into them, except that they had eyes like to God; wherefore I will not lay my blood upon the jury, but do mind to confess the indictment. Contained it but the parts that have been openly read, I pray you tell me? Whereto it was answered that the indictment contained the parts he had heard read, and no other. Whereupon the Clerk of the Crown said to Parry, Parry, you must answer directly to the indictment, whether thou be guilty or not.

Then said Parry, I do confess that I am guilty of all that is therein contained; and further too, I desire not life, but desire to die. To which the Clerk of the Crown said, If you confess it, you must confess it in manner and form as it is comprised in the indictment. Whereto he said, I do confess it in manner and form as the same is set down and all the circumstances thereof. Then the confession being recorded, the Queen's learned counsel being ready to pray judgment upon the same confession, Mr. Vice Chamberlain said, these matters contained in this indictment and confessed by this man, are of great importance; they touch the person of the Queen's most excellent majesty in the highest degree, the very state and well-being of the whole commonwealth, and the truth of God's word established in these her majesty's dominions and the open demonstration of that capital envy of the man of Rome, that has set himself against God and godliness, all good princes and good government, and against good men. Wherefore, I pray you, for the satisfaction of this great multitude, let the whole matter appear, that every one may see that the matter of itself is as bad as the indictment purported, and as he has confessed. Whereto in respect that the justice of the realm has been of late very impudently slandered, all yielded as a thing necessary to satisfy the world in particular of that which was but summarily comprised in the indictment, though in the law his confession served sufficiently to have proceeded thereupon to judgment. Whereupon the lords and others the commissioners, her majesty's learned counsel, and Parry himself agreed, that Parry's confession taken the 11th and 13th of February 1584, before the Lord of Hunsdon, Master Vice Chamberlain, and Master Secretary, and Cardinal de Como's letters, and Parry's letters to the Lord Treasurer and Lord Steward, should be openly read.

And Parry, for the better satisfying of the people and standers-by, offered to read them himself; but being told that the order was the Clerk of the Crown should read them, it was so resolved of all parts. And then Master Vice Chamberlain caused to be showed to Parry his said confession, the cardinal's letter, and his own letter aforesaid; which after he had particularly viewed every leaf thereof, he confessed, and said openly they were the same.

Then said Master Vice Chamberlain; before we proceed to show what he has confessed, what say you, said he to Parry, is that which you have confessed here true? And did you confess it freely and willingly of yourself, or was there any extort means used to draw it from you? Surely, said Parry, I made that confession freely without any constraint, and that is all true, and more too; for there is no treason that has been since the first year of the Queen, any way touching religion saving receipt of *Agnus Dei's*, and persuading of others, wherein I have not much dealt, but I have offended in it.

And I have also delivered my opinion in writing, who ought to be successor to the crown, which is said to be treason also.

Then his confession of the 11th and 13th of February, all of his own hand writing, and hereafter particularly set down, was openly and distinctly read by the Clerk of the Crown.

The voluntary confession of William Parry, doctor of the law (now prisoner in the Tower), and accused of treason by Edmund Nevil, Esq. promised by him (with all faith and humility) to the Queen's majesty in discharge of his conscience, and duty towards God and her; before the Lord Hunsdon, Lord Governor of Berwick; Sir Christopher Hatton, Knight, Vice-Chamberlain; Sir Francis Walsingham, Knight, principal secretary; the 13th of February 1581.

In the year 1570, I was sworn her majesty's servant from which time until the year 1580, I served, honored, and loved her with as great readiness, devotion and assurance as any poor subject in England. In the end of that year and until midsummer 1582, I had some trouble for the hurting of a gentleman of the temple. In which action I was so disgraced and oppressed by two great men (to whom I have of late been beholden) that I never had contented thought since. There began my misfortune, and here followed my woeful fall.

In July after, I labored for license to travel for 3 years, which (upon some consideration) was easily obtained. And so in August, I went over with doubtful mind of return; for that being suspected in religion, and not having received the communion in 22 years, I began to mistrust my advancement in England. In September I came to Paris, where I was reconciled to the church and advised to live without scandal; the rather, for that it was mistrusted by the English Catholics that I had intelligence with the greatest counselor of England. I staid not long there, but removed to Lyons (a place of great traffic) where, because it was the ordinary passage of our nation to and fro, between Paris and Rome, I was also suspected.

To put all men out of doubt of me, and for some other cause, I went to Milan, from where, as a place of some danger, (though I found favor there) after I had cleared my conscience, and justified myself in religion before the inquisitor, I went to Venice. There I came acquainted with father Benedicto Palmio, a grave and learned Jesuit. By conference with him of the hard state of the Catholics in England and by reading of the book *'De Persecutione Anglicann,'* and other discourses of like argument.

1. I conceived a possible mean to relieve the afflicted state of our Catholics, if the same might be well warranted in religion and conscience by the Pope, or some learned divines. I asked his opinion; he made it clear, commended my devotion, comforted me in it, and after a while made me known to the Nuncio Campeggio, resident there for his holiness. By his means I wrote to the Pope, presented my service and sued for a passport to go to Rome, and to return safely into France. Answer came from Cardinal Como, that I might come, and should be welcome. I disliked the warrant, sued for a

better which I was promised: but it came not before my departure to Lyons, where I promised to stay some time for it. And being indeed desirous to go to Rome and loathe to go without countenance, I desired Christophero de Salazar, secretary to the Catholic King in Venice, who had some understanding by conference of my devotion to the afflicted Catholics at home and abroad, to commend me to the Duke de Nova Terra, governor of Milan, and to the count of Olivaris Embi, then resident for the King his master in Rome; which he promised to do effectually for the one, and did for the other. And so I took my journey towards Lyons, whither came for me an ample passport (but somewhat too late) that I might come and go, in *verbo Pontificiis per omnes-Jurisdictiones Ecclesiasticas, absque impedimenta.* I acquainted some good fathers there of my necessity to depart towards Paris by promise, and prayed their advices upon divers points; wherein I was well satisfied. And so assuring them that his holiness should hear from me shortly, it was undertaken that I should be excused for that time. In October I came to Paris, where (upon better opinion conceived of me amongst my Catholic countrymen) I found my credit well settled and such as mistrusted me before, ready to trust and embrace me. And being one day at the chamber of Thomas Morgan a Catholic gentleman (greatly beloved and trusted on that side) amongst other gentlemen, talking (but in very good sort) of England, I was desired by Morgan to go up with him to another chamber; where he broke with me and told me that it was hoped and looked for that I should do some service for God and his church. I answered him, I would do it, if it were to kill the greatest subject in England; whom I named, and in truth then hated. No, no, said he, let him live to his greater fall and ruin of his house.

2. It is the Queen I mean. I had him as I wished, and told him it were soon done if it might be lawfully done and warranted in the opinion of some learned divines. And so the doubt once resolved, (though as you have heard I was before reasonably well satisfied) I vowed to undertake the enterprise, for the restitution of England to the ancient obedience of the See Apostolic. Divers divines were named; Dr. Allen, I desired, Parsons I refused; and by chance came Master Watts a learned priest, with whom I conferred, and was over-ruled.

3. For he plainly pronounced (the case only altered in name) that it was utterly unlawful; with whom many English priests did agree, as I have heard, if it be not altered since the book made in answer to the "Execution of the English Justice" was published, which I must confess has taken hard hold in me, and (I fear me) will do in others, if it be not prevented by more gracious handling of the quiet obedient Catholic subjects, whereof there is good and greater store in England, than this age will extinguish. Well, notwithstanding all these doubts, I was gone so far by letters and conference in Italy that I could not go back, but promised faithfully to perform the enterprise, if his holiness upon my offer and letters would allow it, and grant me full remission of my sins.

4. I wrote my letters the 1st of January 1584, by their computation; took advice upon them in confession of Father Anibal a Codreto, a learned Jesuit

in Paris; was lovingly embraced, commended, confessed, and communicated at the Jesuit's at one altar with the Cardinals of Vandosmi and Narbone, whereof I prayed certificate, and enclosed the same in my letter to his holiness to lead him the rather to absolve me; which I required by my letters, in consideration of so great an enterprise undertaken without promise or reward.

5. I went with Morgan to the Nuncio Ragazzoui, to whom I read the letter and certificate enclosed, sealed it, and left it with him to send to Rome; he promised great care of it and to procure answer; and so lovingly embraced me, wished me good speed and promised that I should be remembered at the altar.

6. After this I desired Morgan, that some special man might be made privy to this matter, lest he dying, and I miscarrying in the execution, and my intent never truly discovered, it might stick for an everlasting spot in my race. Divers were named, but none agreed upon, for fear of betraying.

7. This being done, Morgan assured me, that shortly after my departure, that I Lord Fernehurst (then in Paris) should go into Scotland and be ready upon the first news of the Queen's fall to enter into England with 20,000 or 30,000 men to defend the Queen of Scotland (whom, and the King her son, I do in my conscience acquit of any privet, liking, or consent to this, or any other bad action for anything that I ever did know.) I shortly departed for England and arrived at Rye in January 1583 from where I wrote to the court, advertised some that I had a special service to discover to the Queen's majesty.

8. Which I did more to prepare access and credit than for any care I had of her person, though I were fully resolved never to touch her (notwithstanding any warrant) if by any device, persuasion, or policy she might be wrought to deal more graciously with the Catholics than she does or, by our manner of proceeding in Parliament means to do, or anything yet seen. I came to the court (then at Whitehall) prayed audience, had it at large and very privately discovered to her majesty this conspiracy, much to this effect, though covered with all the skill I had. She took it doubtfully, I departed with fear. And amongst other things, I cannot forget her majesty's gracious speech then uttered touching the Catholics, which of late after a sort I avowed in Parliament; she said to me that never a Catholic should be troubled for religion or supremacy, so long as they lived like good subjects, whereby I mistrusted that her majesty is born in hand, that none is troubled for the one or the other. It may be truly said that it is better than it has been, though it be not yet as it should be. In March last, while I was at Greenwich (as I remember) suing for St. Catharine's, came letters to me from Cardinal Como, dated at Rome the last of January before; whereby I found the enterprise commended and allowed, and myself absolved in his holiness's name, of all my sins, and willed to go forward in the name of God. That letter I showed to some in court, who imparted it to the Queen; what it wrought; or may work in her majesty, God knows; only this I know.

9. That it confirmed my resolution to kill her, and made it clear in my conscience, that it was lawful and meritorious. And yet was I determined never to do it, if either policy, practice, persuasion, or motion in Parliament could prevail. I feared to be tempted, and therefore always when I came near her I left my dagger at home.

10. When I looked upon her majesty and remembered her many excellencies, I was greatly troubled: and yet I saw no remedy, for my vows were in heaven, my letters and promises in earth; and the case of the Catholic recusants, and other little bettered. Sometimes I said to myself why should I care for her? What has she done for me? Have I not spent 10,000 marks since I knew her service, and never had penny by her; it may be said, she gave me my life, but I say (as my case stood) it had been tyranny to take it; and I fear me it is little less yet. If it please her graciously to look into my discontentment's, I would to Jesus Christ she had it for I am weary of it. And now to come to an end of this tragical discourse; in July I left the court, utterly dejected, discontented, and as her majesty might perceive by my passionate letters, careless of myself. I came to London; Dr. Allen's book was sent me out of France.

11. It redoubled my former conceits; every word in it was a warrant to a prepared mind: it taught that Kings may be excommunicated, deprived, and violently handled; it proved that all wars civil or foreign undertaken for religion, are honorable. Her majesty may do well to read it, and to be out of doubt (if things be not amended) that it is a warning, and a doctrine full dangerous. This is the book I showed, in some places read, and lent it to my cousin Nevil (the accuser) who came often to my house, put his finger in my dish, his hand in my purse; and the night wherein he accused me, was wrapped in my gown, six months at least after we had entered into this conspiracy; in which space her majesty and ten princes in several provinces, might have been killed. God bless her majesty from him; for before Almighty God, I joy and am glad in my soul, that it was his hap to discover me in time, though there were no danger near. And now to the manner of our meetings. He came to me in the beginning of August, and spoke to me in this or like sort. Cousin, let us do somewhat, since we can have nothing. I offered to join with him, and gladly heard him, hoping because I knew him to be a Catholic, that he would hit upon that I had in my head; but it fell not out so. He thought the delivery of the Queen of Scotland easy, presuming upon his credit and kindred in the north; I thought it dangerous to her, and impossible to men of our fortunes: he fell from that to the taking of Berwick. I spoke of Quinborough and the navy, rather to entertain him with discourse, than that I cared for those motions, my head being full of a greater matter.

12. I told him that I had another matter of enterprise, more honorable and profitable to us and the Catholic's commonwealth, than all these, if he would join in it with me, as he presently vowed to do; he pressed to know it; I willed him to sleep upon the motion, he did so, and (belike overtaken) came to me the next morning to my lodging in London, offered to join with me, and took his oath upon a bible to conceal and constantly to pursue the

enterprise for the advancement of religion; which I also did, and meant to perform the killing of the Queen was the matter. The manner and place, to be on horseback with eight or ten horses when she should ride abroad about St. James's, or some other like place. It was once thought fit in a garden, and that the escape would be easiest by water into Sheppy, or some other part; but we resolved upon the first. This continued as agreed upon many months, until he heard of the death of Westmoreland, whose land and dignity (whereof he assured himself) bred belike this conscience in him to discover a treason in February contrived and agreed upon in August. If it cost him not an ambitious head at last, let him never trust me. He brought a tall gentleman (whom he commended for an excellent pistolier) to me to Chanon-Row, to make one in the match: but I refused to deal with him, being loathe to lay my head upon so many hands. Master Nevil had (I think) forgotten, that he did swear to me at divers times, that all the advancement she could give, should serve but for her scourge, it every time and occasion should serve; and that though he would not lay hand upon her in a corner, his heart served him to strike off her head in the field. Now leaving him to himself, this much (to make an end) I must confess of myself, I did mean to try what might be done in Parliament to do my best to hinder all hard courses to have prayed hearing of the Queen's majesty to move her (if I could) to take compassion upon her Catholic subjects, and when all had failed, to do as I intended. If her majesty by this course would have eased them, though she had never preferred me, I had with all comfort and patience borne it.

13. But if she had preferred me without ease or care of them, the enterprise had held. Parry. God preserve the Queen, and incline her merciful heart to forgive me this desperate purpose; and to take my head (with all my heart) for her better satisfaction.

These matters being read openly, for manifestation of the matter, Parry prayed leave to speak, whereto Mr. Vice Chamberlain said if you will say anything for the better opening to the world of those your foul and horrible facts, speak on; but if you mean to make any excuse of that which you have confessed, which else would have been and do stand proved against you, for my part, I will not sit to hear you.

Then her majesty's Attorney General Popham stood up and said, it appears before you my lords, that this man has been indicted and arraigned of several heinous and most horrible treasons and has confessed them, which is before you of record; wherefore there rests no more to be done, but for the court to give judgment accordingly, which here I require in the behalf of the Queen's majesty.

Then said Parry, I pray you hear me for discharging of my conscience. I will not go about to excuse myself, nor to seek to save my life, I care not for it; you have my confession of record, that is enough for my life. And I mean to utter more, for which I were worthy to die. And said, I pray you hear me in that I am to speak to discharge my conscience.

Then said Mr. Vice Chamberlain, Parry, then do thy duty according to conscience, and utter all that you can say concerning those your most wicked facts.

Then said Parry, my cause is rare, singular, and unnatural, conceived at Venice, presented in general words to the Pope, undertaken at Pans, commended and allowed of by his holiness and was to have been executed in England, if it had not been prevented. Yea, I have committed many treasons, for I have committed treason in being reconciled, and treason in taking absolution. There has been no treason since the first year of the Queen's reign touching religion, but that I am guilty of, (except for receiving of *Agnus Dei's*, and persuading, as I have said, and yet never intending to kill Queen Elizabeth) I appeal to her own knowledge and to my Lord Treasurer's, and Master Secretary's.

Then said my Lord Hunsdon, have you acknowledged it so often and so plainly in writing under your hand, and here of record; and now, when thou should have your judgment according to that which you have confessed thyself guilty of, do you go back again and deny the effect of all? How can we believe that you now say?

Then said Master Vice-Chamberlain, this is absurd; you have not only confessed generally that you are guilty according to the indictment, which summarily, and yet in express words, does contain that you have traitorously compassed and intended the death and destruction of her majesty; but you also said particularly, that you were guilty of every of the treasons contained therein, whereof the same was one, in plain and express letter set down, and read to you. Yea, you said that you were guilty of more treasons too besides these. And did you not upon your examination voluntarily confess how you were moved first thereto by dislike of your state after your departure out of the realm and that you did dislike her majesty, for that she had done nothing for you; how by wicked Papists and Popish books you were persuaded that it was lawful to kill her majesty; how you were by reconciliation become one of that wicked sort that held her majesty for neither lawful Queen nor Christian, and that it was meritorious to kill her? And did you not signify that thy purpose to the Pope by letters, and received letters from the cardinal, how he allowed of your intent, and excited you to perform it, and thereupon did receive absolution? And did you not conceive it, promise it, vow it, swear it, and receive the sacrament that you would do it? And did not you thereupon affirm that your vows were in heaven, and your letters and promises on earth to bind you to do it? And that whatsoever her majesty would have done for you, could not have removed you from that intention or purpose, unless she would have desisted from dealing as she had done with the Catholics, as you called them? All this you have plainly confessed; and I protest before this great assembly, you have confessed it more plainly and in better sort than my memory will serve me to utter: and say you now, that you never meant it?

Ah, said Parry, your honors know how my confession upon my examination was extorted.

Then both the Lord Hunsdon and Master Vice-Chamberlain affirmed that there was no torture or threatening words offered him. But Parry then said, that they told him, that if he would not confess willingly, he should have torture: whereto their honors answered, that they used not any speech or word of torture to him. You said, said Parry, that you would proceed with rigor against me, if I would not confess it of myself. But their honors expressly affirmed that they used no such words. But I will tell you, said Master Vice-Chamberlain, what we said. I spoke these words; If you will willingly utter the truth of yourself, it may do you good, I wish you to do so; if you will not, we must then proceed in ordinary course to take your examination. Whereto you answered, that you would tell the truth of yourself. Was not this true?

Which then he yielded to.

And hereto her majesty's Attorney-General put Parry in remembrance what speeches he used to the Lieutenant of the Tower, the Queen's majesty's Sergeant at Law Master Gawdie, and the same attorney, on Saturday the 20th of February last, at the Tower, upon what he was by them then examined by order from the lords; which was, that he acknowledged he was most mildly and favorably dealt with in all his examinations: which he also at the bar then acknowledged to be true.

Then Mr. Vice-Chamberlain said, that it was a wonder to see the magnanimity of her majesty, which, after that you had opened those traitorous practices in sort as you had laid it down in your confession, was nevertheless such, and so far from all fear, as that she would not so much as acquaint any one of her highness's Privy Council with it, to his knowledge, no not until after this your enterprise discovered and made manifest. And besides that which you had set down under your own hand, you did confess that you had prepared two Scottish daggers fit for such a purpose; and those being disposed away by you, you did say that another would serve your turn. And withal, Parry, did you not also confess before us how wonderfully you were appalled and perplexed upon a sudden, at the presence of her majesty at Hampton-Court this last summer, saying, that you did think you then saw in her the very likeness and image of King Henry 8? And that therewith and upon some speeches used by her majesty, you did turn about and weep bitterly to thyself? And yet did still call to mind that your vows were in heaven, your letters and promises on earth; and that therefore you did say with thyself, that there was no remedy but to do it? Did you not confess this? The which he acknowledged.

Then said the Lord Hunsdon, say you now that you did never mean to kill the Queen? Did you not confess that when you did utter this practice of treachery to her majesty, that you did cover it with all the skill thou had, and that it was done by you, rather to get credit and access thereby, than for any regard you had of her person. But in truth you did it, that thereby you might have better opportunity to perform your wicked enterprise. And would you have run into such fear as you did confess that you were in when you did utter it, if you had never meant it? What reason can you show for thyself?

With that he cried out in a furious manner, I never meant to kill her; I will lay my blood upon Queen Elizabeth and you, before God and the world. And thereupon fell into a rage and evil words with the Queen's majesty's Attorney-General.

Then said the Lord Hunsdon, this is but your popish pride and ostentation which you would have to be told to your fellows of that faction to make them believe that you die for Popery, when you die for most horrible and dangerous treasons against her majesty, and your whole country. For your laying of thy blood, it must lie on your own head as a just reward of your wickedness. The laws of the realm most justly condemn you to die, out of your own mouth, for the conspiring the destruction both of her majesty and of us all: therefore your blood be upon you; neither her majesty nor we at any time sought it, thyself has spilt it.

Then he was asked, what he could say, why judgment of death ought not to be awarded against him? Whereto he said, he did see that he must die because he was not settled.

What mean you by that? Said Mr. Vice-Chamberlain. Said he, look into your study and into your new books, and you shall find what I mean. I protest, (said his honor) I know not what you mean; you do not well to use such dark speeches, unless you would plainly utter what you mean thereby. But he said, he cared not for death, and that he would lay his blood amongst them.

Then spoke the Lord Chief Justice of England, being required to give the judgment, and said: Parry, you have been much heard, and what you mean by being settled, I know not; but I see you are so settled in Popery that you cannot settle yourself to be a good subject. But touching that you should say to stay judgment from being given against you, your speeches must be of one of these kinds, either to prove the indictment (which you have confessed to be true) to be insufficient in law: or else to plead somewhat touching her majesty's mercy, why justice should not be done of you. All other speeches wherein you have used great liberty, is more than by law you can ask. These be the matters you must look to, what say you to them? Whereto he said nothing.

Then said the Lord Chief Justice; Parry, you have been before this time indicted of divers most horrible and hateful treasons committed against your most gracious sovereign and native country. The matter most detestable, the manner most subtle and dangerous, and the occasions and means that led you thereto most ungodly and villainous. That you did intend it, it is most evident by thyself. The matter was the destruction of a most sacred and an anointed Queen, your sovereign and mistress, who has showed you such favor, as some your betters have not obtained; yea, the overthrow of your country wherein you where born, and of a most happy commonwealth whereof you are a member, and of such a Queen, as has bestowed on you the benefit of all benefits in this world, that is, your life, heretofore granted you by her mercy when you had lost it by justice and desert. Yet you her servant, sworn to defend her, mean with your bloody hand, to have taken away her life, that mercifully gave you yours, when it was yielded into her hands: this is the matter wherein you have offended. The manner was most subtle and dangerous, beyond all that before you have committed any wickedness against her majesty; for you making show as if you would simply have uttered for her safety the evil that others had contrived, did but seek thereby credit and access, that you might take the apt opportunity for her destruction. And for the occasions and means that drew you on, they were most ungodly and villainous, as the persuasions of the Pope, of Papists, and popish books. The Pope pretended that he is a pastor, when as in truth he is far from feeding of the flock of Christ, but rather as a wolf, seeking but to feed on, and to suck out the blood of true Christians, and as it were thirsty after the blood of our most gracious and Christian Queen. And these Papists and Popish books, while they pretend to set forth divinity, they do indeed most ungodly teach and persuade that which is quite contrary both to God and his word; for the word teaches obedience of subjects towards princes, and forbids any private man to kill; but they teach subjects to disobey princes, and that a private wicked person may kill; yea, and whom? A most godly Queen, and their own natural and most gracious sovereign. Let all men therefore take heed how they receive anything from him, hear or read any of their books, and how they confer with any Papists. God grant her majesty, that she may know by you, however she trust such like to come so near her person. But see the end, and why you did it, and it will appear to be a most miserable, fearful, and foolish thing; for you did imagine that it was to relieve those that you call Catholics, who were most likely amongst all others to have felt the worst of it, if your devilish practice had taken effect. But since you have been indicted of the treasons comprised in the indictment, and thereupon arraigned, and have confessed yourself guilty of them, the court does award that you shall be had from here to the place where you did come, and so drawn through the open city of Loudon upon an hurdle to the place of execution, and there to be hanged and let down alive, and your privy parts cut off, and your entrails taken out and burnt in your sight; then your head to be cut off, and your body to be divided in four parts, and to be disposed of at her majesty's pleasure: and God have mercy on thy soul.

Parry (persisting still in his rage and passion) said, I here summon Queen Elizabeth to answer for my blood before God.

Whereupon the Lieutenant of the Tower was commanded to take him from the bar, and so he did: and as he was going away the people cried out, 'Away with the traitor, away with him', whereupon he was conveyed in a barge to the Tower again by water. Upon the 2d of March ensuing he was delivered by the Lieutenant of the Tower early in the morning to the sheriffs of London and Middlesex, who received him at Tower-Hill; and according to the judgment caused him to be forthwith set on an hurdle, on the which he was drawn through the midst of the city of London to the place for his execution in Palace Yard Westminster, where having long time of stay permitted him before his execution, he impudently denied that he was ever guilty of any intention to kill Queen Elizabeth; and so (without any request to the people to pray for him, or using any outward prayer himself) he was turned off, and executed according to the Sentence.

[Emlyn, Sollom. *A Complete Collection of State Trials and Proceedings*, 121-128]

Anthony Babington and others

Several attempts were made to free Mary Queen of Scots from imprisonment and remove Elizabeth from the throne. Perhaps the most noteworthy was the Babington plot named after Anthony Babington who conspired with other Catholics including Philip II of Spain.

Anthony Babington exchanged correspondence in cipher with Mary describing how they would free her and of a promise by Philip II to supply troops after Elizabeth was assassinated. In another letter, Babington had requested Mary's permission to assassinate Elizabeth. After Babington was named in the plot, he and the co-conspirators were quickly arrested and stood trial. Elizabeth was aware of the plots and the contents of the intercepted letters.

Proceedings against Anthony Babington, Chidiock Titchbourne, Thomas Salisbury, Robert Barnewell, John Savage, Henry Donn, and John Ballard, at Westminster, for high treason: 28 Elizabeth the 13th and 14th of September, A.D. 1586.

The commission of Oyer and determiner of all manner of treasons, rebellions, felonies, offences, routs, riots, &c. was directed to William Lord Cobham, Lord Warden of the Cinque-Ports; Thomas Lord Buckhurst; Sir Francis Knowles; Sir James Croft; Sir Christopher Hatton; Sir Francis Walsingham; Sir Christopher Wray, Lord Chief Justice of England; Sir Edmund Anderson, Lord Chief Justice of the Common-Pleas; Sir Roger Manwood, Lord Chief Baron of the Exchequer; Mr. Dr. Dale; Mr. Rugby, Master of the Requests; Sergeant Fleetwood, Recorder of London; Mr. Brograve, Attorney of the Duchy; Mr. Randall; Mr. Cook; Mr. Wrathe. By force whereof was a precept directed to the Lieutenant of the Tower, commanding him to have the bodies of Anthony Babington, Esq. Chidiock Titchbourne, Esq. Thomas Salisbury, Esq. Robert Barnewell, gent. John Savage, gent. Henry Dunn, gent, and John Ballard, clerk, before the said commissioners, the day and year aforesaid. At which day, before the commissioners above said, (excepting Sir Francis Knowles, Sir Francis Walsingham, and Sir Christopher Wray) Sir Owen Hopton, Lieutenant of the Tower, returned his precept in effect, that the said prisoners were committed to his custody by commandment of the Privy Council, there to be safely kept. Whereupon Mr. vice-chamberlain demanded of the Queen's learned counsel what order they would take in arraigning the prisoners; and answer was by them given, that they would proceed to the arraignment of Savage first, forasmuch as he meddled first in these matters.

Savage's arraignment, indictment and confession.

Then Savage being brought to the bar, and the other prisoners removed, the Clerk of the Crown said:

Sands, Clerk of the Crown. John Savage, gent, hold up thy hand. You have been before this time indicted by virtue of commission, directed to Sir Edmund Anderson Knight, &c. (and so read his indictment) which in effect was, that William Gilford, D.D. maliciously moved him at Rhemes in the country of Champaigne, traitorously and wickedly to kill and murder the Queen's most excellent majesty, his liege sovereign and natural prince; affirming to the said Savage that the killing of her majesty was an action lawful, honorable and meritorious: and that thereupon the said John Savage did traitorously agree, conspire and swear to murder the Queen's most excellent majesty, his own natural prince. And afterwards, that is to say the first day of April 1586, at St. Giles's in the fields in the county of Middlesex, did falsely conspire to murder her said majesty, to disinherit her of her Kingdom, to stir up sedition in the realm, and to subvert the true Christian religion, and that to perform this malicious practice, devised with John Hallard how to bring the same to pass, and afterwards, the last day of May, did receive letters from Morgan, William Gifford, and Gilbert Gilford, whereby they did persuade and provoke the said Savage to execute and fulfill his said purpose and determination. How say you, Savage, are you guilty, or not guilty?

Savage. For conspiring at St. Giles's, I am guilty; that I received letters, whereby they did provoke me to kill her majesty; I am guilty; that I did assent to kill her majesty, I am not guilty.

C. J. Anderson. Whether you did conspire at St. Giles's, or not, is not the substance of the indictment; but, whether you did conspire or no, is the matter and the rest is but circumstance, moreover you must say either that you art guilty or not guilty, for so has the law ordained everyone to answer; and if you answer not so, thou refused to be tried by the law, and so shall be causer of thy own death.

C. B. Manwood. Whosoever refused to answer directly, the law pronounces grievous punishment to such, and they are murderers of themselves, which is abominable before God.

Hatton. To say that you art guilty to that, and not to this, is no plea; for you must either confess it generally, or deny it generally. Wherefore delay not the time, but say either guilty, or not; and if you say guilty, then shall you hear further; if not guilty, her majesty's learned counsel is ready to give evidence against thee.

Savage. Then, sir, I am guilty.

Then her majesty's counsel said albeit there were nothing now further to be done, but to proceed to judgment upon his own confession; yet forasmuch as they desired that the hearers should be satisfied, and all the world know how justly he was to be condemned, they crave license to give such evidence an would sufficiently and fully prove the indictment. Which being granted, the Clerk of the Crown did read Savage's own confession taken before the Lord Chancellor, Lord Treasurer, Mr. Vice-Chamberlain, and Mr. Secretary; which particularly in substance was:

That the said John Savage served in the camp of the Prince of Parma, and from there he departed towards Rhemes, where falling acquainted with one Hodgson, and talking with him about exploits of services, it chanced Dr. Gilford over heard them, and coining to them, said, 'but a better service could I tell you than all this' (moving the murder of the Queen of England), but Savage seemed to object how dangerous and difficult it was. So they went to supper, and after supper ended Gilford declaring to them how necessary, how just and meritorious the committing of the murder should be, said, that peradventure he slicked to do the fact, forasmuch as he, precise, was not resolved whether the killing of a prince were lawful or not. Whereupon he desired him to advise himself, and to ask opinions of others; and Savage having heard others affirm, that the murder was lawful, forasmuch as in their pretence she was a heretic, an enemy to true religion, and a schismatic person. At last, after three weeks, wherein he had not seen Gilford, he answered that he was contented to do anything for his country's good. Then said Gilford, assure yourself you cannot do a greater good to your country, nor whereby the country should be more beholden, especially all the Throckmorton's and Gilford's. At last Savage, overcome with their persuasion, gave his assent and oath that he would put the same in practice when he had given his oath to murder her, Gilford declared to him, how, and in what place her majesty might be slain, and therefore Gilford charged him to forbear no time nor place, but to murder her; and therefore, as her majesty should go into her chapel to hear divine service, Savage might lurk in the gallery, and stall her with his dagger. Or if her majesty should walk into her garden, he might then shoot her through with his dagger; or if her majesty did walk abroad to take the air, as she would often do, rather (as Gilford said) accompanied with women than men, and those few men but with slender weapon, Savage might then assault her with his arming sword, and so make sure work; albeit in all these cases Savage should be in extreme hazard of his own life, forasmuch as the thing itself was so lawful, honorable and meritorious, and he sure to gain heaven thereby. Thereupon came Savage over into England with this intent and purpose, for to kill the Queen, but not doing the same as soon as was looked for, he received letters from Morgan and Gilford from beyond the seas, persuading him to execute the same. But then he fell acquainted with the most notorious conspiracy of Babington, whereby was another plot devised that there should be six which should kill the Queen. Savage would not assent thereto, forasmuch as he thought, except he did it himself, his conscience could not be satisfied, because he had promised and vowed to do that himself. But Babington told him, he should be one. In the mean season was Ballard the priest apprehended, the 4th of August last. Then came Babington to Savage, saying, Ballard is taken, all will be betrayed, what remedy now? Then said Savage, no remedy now, but to kill her presently. Very well, said Babington; then go you to the court tomorrow and there execute the fact. Nay, said Savage, I cannot go tomorrow, for my apparel is not ready, and in this apparel shall

I never come near the Queen. Go to, quote Babington, here is my ring, and all the money I have, get the apparel and dispatch it. But the same night, Babington fearing lest Savage alone should fail to do it, continued his other plot, that six should ride to the court and do it, but the next day, Babington suspecting somewhat, fled, and all was discovered. And also it appeared by Savage's own confession, how, between Midsummer and Alhallon tide, 1585, he was solicited by Gilford to kill the Queen and the Earl of Leicester. Furthermore divers other proofs were showed forth by confession of other, all agreeing to Savage's confession.

Attorney. (Sir John Popham) Now I hope, is Savage's indictment sufficiently and fully proved.

Hatton. Savage, I must ask thee one question. Was not all this willingly and voluntarily confessed by thyself, without menacing, without torture, or without offer of any torture?

Savage. Yes.

Then spoke her majesty's learned counsel, desiring to adjourn the court until the morrow.

Hutton. Forasmuch as if we should now proceed with the other prisoners which be here put, I would ask time till three of the clock in the morning, and the day is already far spent; also her majesty's counsel having prayed that Savage's judgment be deferred till tomorrow by seven of the clock; therefore it is necessary that the court should be adjourned. Whereupon the crier made an O yes, that all should keep their day tomorrow morning by seven of the clock, and so the court arose.

Wednesday, 14 September, 1586.

The next day being Wednesday, the same prisoners were brought to the bar and the commissioners being set, the crier commanded every man to hold his peace and keep silence; and then spoke Sandes the Clerk of the Crown, in sort ensuing.

Clerk of the Crown. John Ballard, Anthony Babington, John Savage, Robert Barnewell, Chidiock Titchbourne, Thomas Salisbury, and Henry Donn, hold up your hands; which being done, he said, before this time you were indicted before Sir Edmund Anderson, Knight and others, &c. by virtue of her majesty's commission, &c. That whereas Bernardino de Mendoza, a Spaniard, and Charles Paget, the 26th day of April, 1586, at Paris in France, did maliciously and wickedly devise by what ways and means this realm of England might be invaded, and by what ways and means Mary Queen of Scots might be delivered, it was concluded then, that you the said John Ballard should go into this realm of England to understand and know what ports and landings might be procured and provided for the enemies invasion, and for to learn by what means and ways the said Mary Queen of Scots might be delivered from the custody wherein she was. And that you the said John Ballard, coining into this realm of England; you the said Anthony Babington, John Savage, Robert Barnewell, Chidiock Titchbourne, Thomas Salisbury, and Henry Donn, as false traitors against the crown, and the Queen's most excellent majesty, your true and natural sovereign; intending to put away the love of her majesty's most loving subjects, the 5th day of June, in the 28th year of the reign of our sovereign Lady Queen Elizabeth, by the grace of God, &c. at St. Giles's in the Fields, within the county of Middlesex did falsely, horribly, traitorously and devilishly, conspire, conclude and agree, the Queen's most excellent majesty not only from her royal crown and dignity to depose, but also her to kill and slay; and sedition, insurrection and rebellion to stir up and procure, and the government of this realm, and the true and Christian religion therein planted to subvert, and the whole state thereof for to destroy; and for to raise and levy war within the realm. And you the said John Ballard, the 17th day of June, in the 28th year aforesaid, at St. Giles's aforesaid in the county of Middlesex aforesaid, did go to have speech and confer with thee the said Anthony Babington by what means and ways your false traitorous imagined practices might be brought to pass. And that you the said John Ballard didst oftentimes declare of an army of the Pope, and the King of Spain, for to invade this realm; and didst also declare that Paget and Mendoza required them the said Babington, Savage, &c. to procure means how this realm of England might he invaded. And that there you the said Anthony Babington did say the same could not be brought to pass, without the murder of the Queen's most excellent majesty, and afterwards, that is to say, the 7th day of June, at St. Giles's aforesaid, in the county of Middlesex aforesaid, you the said Anthony Babington did falsely, horribly, traitorously, and devilishly conspire to kill the Queen's most excellent majesty, and for to deliver the said Mary Queen of Scots out of the custody wherein she was, and how to bring foreign enemies for to invade this realm. And that you Thomas Salisbury went to St. Giles's aforesaid, in the county of Middlesex aforesaid, traitorously to confer by what means and ways your traitorous imagined practices might be brought to pass; and that you did there conclude falsely and traitorously to go into thy country in the county of Denbigh, thereto move and stir up sedition and rebellion; and for to persuade the subjects to conjoin with you, for the delivery of the said Mary Queen of Scots from the custody wherein she was, and for to aid and assist the foreign enemies which should invade the realm. And afterwards the 9th day of June, that you the said Anthony Babington and John Savage, went to St. Giles's aforesaid, in the county of Middlesex aforesaid, traitorously to confer how and by what means your traitorous imagined practices might be brought to pass, and afterwards, the 10th of June, you the said Anthony Babington, and John Savage, maliciously between yourselves, did appoint and conclude that you the said John Savage traitorously the Queen's most excellent majesty should kill and slay and her to final destruction for to bring. And that you the said Babington and Savage should join and assist the foreign enemies which should invade this realm. And that you the said Anthony Babington, Chidiock Titchbourne, and Robert Barnewell, afterwards, that is to say, the 11th day of June, in the year aforesaid, went to St. Giles's aforesaid, in the county of Middlesex aforesaid, to confer by what ways and means your treasons might be fulfilled and brought to pass. And thereupon the 12th day of June, you the said Babington, Titchbourne, and Barnewell, with divers other false traitors, most horribly, devilishly, wickedly and traitorously did conclude and agree that you the said Robert Barnewell, Chidiock Titchbourne, with divers other horrible traitors, the Queen's most excellent majesty would kill and slay and the foreign invaders would aid and assist. And furthermore, that you the said Thomas Salisbury, together with Edward Jones, Esq. and other false traitors, to bring to pass your traitorous imagined practices, the 13th day of June, in the year aforesaid, did go to St. Giles's Fields aforesaid, in the county of Middlesex aforesaid, to confer how your treasons might be brought to pass. And the same 13th day did confer, and had speech by what means your traitorous compassed imaginations might he performed. And afterwards, that is to say, the 15th of June, at St. Giles's Fields aforesaid, in the county of Middlesex aforesaid, you the said Thomas Salisbury and the said Edward Jones, did conclude and agree that the said Edward Jones should conjoin with you for the delivery of the said Mary Queen of Scots and for to aid and assist the foreign enemies which should invade this realm. And furthermore, that John Travels, gent, another false traitor in this conspiracy, went to Clerkenwell in the county of Middlesex aforesaid, traitorously to confer with thee the said Thomas Salisbury how your traitorous compassed imagination might be brought to pass. And the same 15th day of June, at Clerkenwell aforesaid, in the county of Middlesex aforesaid, the said John Travers did traitorously conspire and agree for the delivery of Mary Queen of Scots, and to assist the foreign invaders of this realm. And furthermore, that you the said Henry Donn, for the compassing of thy traitorous practices, the 22nd of June, in the year aforesaid, traitorously did repair, and go to have speech and confer with the said Anthony Babington and John Ballard, how your traitorous compassed imaginations might be brought to pass. And the same 22nd of June, as well in St. Giles's aforesaid, as in other places, didst confer, and had speech how your treasons might be brought to pass. And that you the said Henry Donn, the 24th day of June at St. Giles's-Fields aforesaid, did conclude and agree with the said Ballard and Babington to perform the best they could for the compassing of your treasons. And furthermore, that you the said Anthony Babington, the 8th day of July, in the year aforesaid, received letters dated the 25th of June, from Mary Queen of Scots by which she signified to you, that she would not be unmindful of thy affection towards her; and required you to send her letters from friends in France and Scotland. And the same day, you the said Anthony Babington did write to the said Mary Queen of Scots declaring the plot of thy treasons and requiring from her as from thy sovereign and prince, authority and commission to proceed in your practices; and the 25th of July received letters of answer, by which the said Mary Queen of Scots willingly allowed of these treasons; and also by her said letters did animate, comfort and provoke thee to fulfill the same effectually. And furthermore, that Sir Thomas Gerrard, another false traitor, and you the said John Ballard, as false traitors, not having the fear of God before your eyes, the 27th of July, in the 28th year aforesaid, at St. Giles's aforesaid, in the county aforesaid, did conspire traitorously to deprive and depose the Queen's most excellent majesty from her royal crown and dignity, and her to final death and destruction for to bring and sedition and rebellion to stir up and procure, and to alter the government of the realm, and the true religion to subvert. And that you the said Anthony Babington, and the said Sir Thomas Gerrard, the 29th of July in the year aforesaid, went to St. Giles's aforesaid in the county aforesaid, traitorously to conspire how and by what menus your traitorous compassed imaginations might be brought to pass. And thereupon the last day of July, at St. Giles's aforesaid, in the county aforesaid, you the said Anthony Babington and the said Sir Thomas Gerrard, did agree that you the said Sir Thomas Gerrard would join with you the said Anthony Babington for the delivery of the said Mary Queen of Scots from the custody wherein she was, and for the aiding and assisting of the foreign enemies which should invade this realm. And furthermore, that you the said John Ballard did traitorously go to Southampton House in Holborne within the county of Middlesex, traitorously to confer with John Charnock, gent, and other false traitors in this conspiracy, how your traitorous compassed imaginations might be brought to pass; and there did confer and had speech by what means your treasons might be performed and afterwards the 2nd day of August at Southampton House aforesaid, the said John Charnock did traitorously assent to perform the best he could in fulfilling of your treasons, contrary to your allegiances you owe to the Queen's most excellent majesty, her crown and dignity, and contrary to divers statutes in such case provided.

Sandes. How say you John Ballard, art you guilty of these treasons whereof you stand indicted, or not?

Ballard. That I practiced the delivery of the Queen of Scots, I am guilty; and that I went about to alter the religion, I am guilty; but that I intended to slay her majesty, I am not guilty.

Sandes. Answer directly art you guilty according to the purport of the indictment?

Ballard. I answer as my case is.

C. J. Anderson. Either deny the indictment generally, or confess it generally.

Hatton. Ballard, under your own hand are all things confessed; therefore now it is much vanity to stand vain gloriously in denying it.

Ballard. Then, sir, I confess I am guilty.

Sandes. How say you Anthony Babington, are you guilty of the treasons contained in the indictment?

Babington. Then began Babington with a mild countenance, a sober gesture and a wonderful good grace to declare the beginnings and proceedings of his treasons, which was according as he was indicted, and according to Savage's confession, and Ballard's indictment. In the end he laid all the blame upon Ballard for bringing him to his destruction.

Hatton. A very fit author for so bad a fact!

Babington. Very true, sir, for from so bad a ground never proceeds any better fruits; he was he that persuaded me to kill the Queen, and to commit the other treasons, whereof now I confess myself guilty.

Sandes. How say you, John Savage, are you guilty of the treasons contained in the indictment?

Savage. I am guilty.

Sandes. How say you, Robert Barnewell, are you guilty?

Barnewell. I never intended harm to her majesty's person, but I confess I knew thereof, and I held it not lawful to kill the Queen, howbeit, for my other actions, forasmuch as I know I am within the danger of the law, I plead guilty.

Sandes. How say you, Chidiock Titchbourne, are you guilty?

Titchbourne. That I knew of these treasons and concealed them, I must confess that I am guilty; but to the rest, I am not guilty.

Sandes. You must either answer guilty, or not guilty.

Titchbourne. What I am guilty of, I plead guilty, and I will confess no more.

Hatton. Then you may plead not guilty.

Titchbourne. Then, sir, I say, that I am not guilty.

Hatton. Very well, stay then till we have asked as much of Salisbury and Donn, and then you shall be tried.

Sandes. How say you, Henry Donn, art you guilty?

Donn. When I was moved and made privy to these treasons, I always said that I prayed to God that that might be done which was to his honor and glory.

Hatton. Then it was thus, that they said the Queen should be killed, and you said, God's will be done.

Donn. Yea, sir.

Hatton. O wretch, wretch! My conscience and own confession show that you are guilty.

Donn. Well, sir, then I confess I am guilty.

Sandes. How say you, Thomas Salisbury, are you guilty?

Salisbury. For killing of the Queen's majesty, I protest I always said I would not do it for a Kingdom.

Sandes. You are indicted, that you practiced the delivery of the Queen of Scots, the invasion of this land with foreign forces and of stirring up rebellion and sedition in this realm; are you guilty of that?

Salisbury. Then I am guilty of that I stand indicted of.

Sandes. Chidiock Titchbourne, you have pleaded not guilty, how will you be tried?

Titchbourne. I beseech you my lords, give me leave to speak.

Hatton. Say what you will.

Titchbourne. I thank your honors. My good lords, in the beginning of this broil I had sent for my horses to ride into the country; and the occasion of my longer abode in London, was for that I had a lame leg. Then what probability may it be, that I went to kill the Queen here hard by London; when, had it not been for my lame leg, I had been in Hampshire.

C. J. Anderson. Well then, if you plead not guilty, we will proceed to your trial.

Sandes. How say you, are you guilty, or not guilty?

Titchbourne. I will confess a truth, and then I must confess that I am guilty.

Then albeit nothing were to be done but judgment to be given; yet for satisfying all the people, her majesty's learned council gave in such evidence, as would sufficiently prove the indictment; first Savage's own confession according to his former arraignment, how that Gilford hearing them talk of services at Rhemes, said I know not what service you mean. But what say you to such a service, meaning the cutting of the throat of the Queen of England, and of the Earl of Leicester? Saying he should never do more good than kill an excommunicate[d] person, and that to do the same were a far better service than to study divinity. And Gifford said moreover that if Savage failed to do it, others should do it. And how that Ballard going over into France at Lent last, did meet with one Grateley, who brought him to Charles Paget, who told him that the Pope would reform the state here in England; and how that Bernardino de Mendoza said the King of Spain his master would invade this realm. And that thereupon Ballard should be sent into England to know what friends they could make, and thereupon Ballard took an oath to perform the same; and how that he had in mind to move Babington in that behalf before he came, and that he came over about Whitsuntide last. And breaking the same with Babington, who thereupon said that the invasion would never come to effect during her majesty's life; whereupon Ballard said that would easily be removed and then made him privy to Savage's practice, and that thereupon Ballard sent to Savage to speak with him on Lambeth side, and there told Savage of Babington's practice, and brought him to Babington, who was not friends with Savage before. Then Ballard went into the North to solicit the people, and at his coming up said he had made five hundred sure more than he knew of before. Furthermore, it was declared that during Ballard's abode in the North, Babington did write letters to the Queen of Scots, a true copy of which letters written with Babington's own hand were read in the court. Wherein he began, most high and mighty princess, his true and sovereign liege, to whom alone he owes fidelity; declaring how he was her servant and that he studied to devise her one good day's service; and how himself with ten gentlemen, and one hundred horse would work her delivery from the custody wherein she was, being in the guard of a Puritan knight, a mere Leicestrian. And how that he had appointed six noble gentlemen for dispatch of the wicked competitor, declaring also at large the remainder of his treasons and what means he had invented to compass the lame. And then Ballard returned from the North; and before it was determined that Savage should have gone to the North, but he could not go, because he had sworn to kill the Queen. And therefore when Babington had devised that six should kill the Queen, Savage would not agree, except himself were one and how in the mean season, Ballard on Thursday the 4th of August, about 11 of the clock, was apprehended. Then Babington went to Titchbourne's lodging, where not finding him, he went to a barber's without Bishops gate, where were his own, Titchbourne and Savage's pictures; and on Babington's picture was written, *Hi mihi sunt Comitcs, quos ipsa pericula jungunt.* But then disliking that, was written; *Quorsum lute alio properantibus.* Then Babington went to Smithfield, and there walked with Titchbourne, and there said to him I had rather than 500£ thy leg were whole, for then this matter should be dispatched. Also Salisbury confessed how Babington, Titchbourne, and he had communication as concerning the sacking of the city of London. Also it was proved by their confession how that to provide themselves of money for this practice, they had devised to rob all the richest men in England and to set fire on the ships (although Babington disliked to fire the ships), and to cloy all the great ordnance. And all the indictment was sufficiently and most plainly proved by their confessions, accordingly as they were intended.

Sandes. John Ballard, you have been indicted of high treason, and thereupon arraigned, and last pleaded guilty; what has you to say for thyself, wherefore judgment and execution of death should not be given against thee?

Ballard. Spoke something, but not to any effect.

Sandes. Demanded of Babington in like manner.

Babington. Who said he was guilty of the treasons, according to his confession, for killing of the Queen, and the rest, by Ballard's persuasion.

Hatton. O Ballard, Ballard, what have you done? A sort of brave youths otherwise endued with good gifts, by your inducement have you brought to their utter destruction and confusion.

Babington. Yea, I protest before I met with this Ballard, I never meant nor intended for to kill the Queen; but by his persuasions I was induced to believe that she was excommunicate, and therefore lawful to murder her.

Ballard. Yea, Mr. Babington, lay all the blame upon me, but I wish the shedding of my blood might be the saving of your life: howbeit, say what you will, I will say no more.

Hatton. Nay, Ballard, you must say more and shall say more, for you must not commit high treason and then huddle them up; but is this thy *Religio Catholica?* Nay rather, it is *Diabolica.*

Sandes. John Savage, you have been indicted of high treason.

Savage answered nothing, neither did Titchbourne, being demanded in like sort also.

So Sandes demanded of Hubert Barnwell in like manner.

Barnewell. Forasmuch as I have offended against the law, I am contented to suffer punishment according to the law; howbeit, I here protest what I have done, was only for my conscience sake, neither did I ever intend violence to her majesty's person.

Hatton. O Barnewell, Barnewell, did not you come to Richmond, and when her majesty walked abroad, did not you there view her and all her company, what weapons they had, how she walked alone? And did traverse the ground, and thereupon coming back to London, did make relation to Babington, how it was a most easy matter to kill her majesty, and what you had seen and done at the court? Yes, I know you did so, how can you then say, that you never did intend to lay violent hands on her majesty? Nay, I can assure you moreover, and it is most true which I say, that her majesty did know that you did come to that end, and she did see and mark you how you did view her and her company; but had it been known to some there, as well as to her, you had never brought news to Babington. Such is the magnanimity of our sovereign, which God grant be not over much, in not fearing such traitors as you are.

Barnewell. What I did was only for my conscience sake, and not for any malice, or hatred to her majesty's person.

Hatton. Then would you have killed the Queen for conscience. Fie on such a conscience!

Sandes. Henry Donn, you have been indicted of high-treason, &c. *ut supra* to Ballard; what can you say for yourself wherefore judgment and execution of death should not be pronounced against thee?

Donn. What I have done herein, was for my religion and conscience sake; and since it is counted treason, I must abide the punishment, and therefore *Viut voluntas Dei.*

Sandes. Salisbury, what can you say wherefore judgment?

Salisbury. I beseech her majesty's most merciful pardon for my offence.

Then Mr. Attorney began to declare at large the sum of their treasons, how they had conspired her majesty's death, and to make the Queen of Scots Queen of England; and if peradventure she miscarried in these hurly burly's as to be slain, then would they set up the King of Scots, if he were a Catholic; if he were not a Catholic, then would they enforce the King of Spain to take the crown and set it on his head, and derive him a title from the House of Clarence. But because that title would be but slender, the Pope should dispense, and so make it clear without question. Furthermore he declared, how priests continually had been the beginning of all the treasons committed against her majesty; he began at the rebellion in the North, and so proceeded till the treasons of Throckmorton and Parry, and so ended.

Then began Sir Christopher Hatton, and made an excellent good speech in opening and setting forth their treasons, and how they all proceeded from the wicked priests the ministers of the Pope. And first he showed how these wicked and devilish youths had conspired to murder the Queen's most excellent majesty; secondly, to bring in foreign invasion; thirdly, to deliver the Queen of Scots and make her Queen; fourthly, to sack the city of London; fifthly, to rob and destroy all the wealthy subjects of this realm; sixthly, to kill divers of the Privy Council, as the Earl of Leicester, the Lord Treasurer, Mr. Secretary, Sir Ralph Sadler, Sir Amias Paulett. Seventhly, to set fire on all the Queen's ships; eighthly, to cloy all the great ordnance; ninthly and lastly, to subvert religion and the whole state of government. The inventors and beginners whereof were these devilish priests and seminaries, against whom he doubted the Parliament had not yet sufficiently provided, who, now-a-days, do not go about to seduce the ancient and discreet men, for they (as the priests say) be too cold; but they assail, with their persuasions, the younger sort, and of those, the most ripe wits, whose high hearts and ambitious minds do carry them headlong to all wickedness. In the end, he concluded with remorse for the youth of some of these unhappy men, and with detestation of the facts of Ballard; and also showed forth a notable proof of the falsehood of these lying Papists, which was a book printed at Rome, and made by the Papists, wherein they affirm, that the English Catholics which suffer for religion, be lapped in bear-skins and bated to death with dogs; a most monstrous lie, and manifest falsehood.

Then spoke my Lord Anderson to the like effect, almost in every point, in abhorring the abomination of the Jesuits and Seminaries; and in the end concluded with an exhortation for the health of their souls; and last of all pronounced the sentence of their condemnation.

[*Cobbett's Complete Collection of State Trials, Vol. 1.* 1128-1140]

Edward Abington and others

The following trial concerned additional members of the Babington plot.

The trial of Edward Abington, Charles Tilney, Edward Jones, John Thavers, John Charnock, Jerome Bellamy, and Robert Gage, at Westminster, for high treason: 28 Elizabeth, 15th of September, A.D. 1586.

On Thursday the 15th of September, the commissioners came and the crier commanded silence and the Lieutenant of the Tower was commanded to bring forth the prisoners, which were Edward Abington, Charles Tilney, and Edward Jones, Esquires; John Travers, John Charnock, Jerome Bellamy and Robert Gage, gentlemen; and Elizabeth Bellamy, widow. All which the Lieutenant of the Tower had ready at the bar and there informed the court the woman's name was Catharine and not Elizabeth; whereupon the lieutenant was commanded to take her from the bar, and bring her to some other place. Whereupon Sandes, Clerk of the Crown, began in sort ensuing; Edward Abington, Charles Tilney, Edward Jones, John Travers, John Charnock, Jerome Bellamy and Robert Gage, hold up your hands: which being done, he proceeded:

Clerk of the Crown. Before this time you were indicted, that where Bernardyne de Mendoza, a Spaniard, Charles Paget and John Ballard, the 2nd day of

April in the 28th year of the reign of our sovereign lady the Queen's majesty, that now is at Paris in France, did confer in what place this realm of England most aptly might be invaded, and what aid and assistance might be procured for the same, and how and try what ways and means Mary Queen of Scots might be delivered from the custody wherein she was. And that thereupon it was resolved by the counsel of Morgan, a most notorious traitor, that the said Ballard should pass into this realm of England to understand what help might be procured, and to prepare ports to land the enemies, for to invade the realm and to prepare ways and means how Mary Queen of Scots might be delivered; and thereupon the said John Ballard coming into England, you the said Edward Abington, Charles Tilney, Edward Jones and John Travers, together with Anthony Babington, John Ballard, John Savage, Henry Donn, Thomas Salisbury, Chidiock Titchbourne and Robert Barnewell, as false traitors, the 8th day of June in the 28th year of the reign of our sovereign lady the Queen's majesty that now is at St. Giles's in the Fields, in the county of Middlesex, did conspire the Queen's most excellent majesty, not only from her crown and dignity to depose, but also her to kill and slay, and to stir up sedition and rebellion in the realm, and slaughter among the subjects for to make and the government and religion to subvert, and the whole estate for to destroy, and divers strangers, her majesty's enemies, to invade the realm, did procure and stir up. And afterwards, the twelfth day of June, in the year aforesaid, thou the said Charles Tilney and Anthony Babington, Robert Barnewell, and Chidiock Titchbourne, went to St. Giles's aforesaid, to confer by what ways and means your traitorous compassed imaginations might be brought to pass; and there, the same day had speech and did confer how your treasons might be performed, and on the said 12th day of June, in the year aforesaid, at St. Giles's aforesaid, did conclude that thou the said Charles Tilney, and Robert Barnewell, and Chidiock Titchbourne, would kill the Queen and aid the foreign enemies that should invade the realm; and that thou Edward Jones, with Thomas Salisbury, to perform your traitorous imaginations, the 13th day of June in the 28th year aforesaid, went to St. Giles's aforesaid, to confer how your traitorous compassed imaginations might be brought to pass. And thereupon thou the said Edward Jones, with the said Thomas Salisbury, the 15th day of June, in the year aforesaid, at St. Giles's aforesaid, did conclude and agree traitorously to join with the said Thomas Salisbury, for the delivery of the said Mary Queen of Scots, and for to aid and assist the foreign enemies which should invade this realm, and that thou the said John Travers, to fulfill thy traitorous compassed imaginations, the 15th day of June in the 28th year aforesaid, traitorously did go to Clerkenwell within the county of Middlesex, to confer by what means your treasons might be brought to pass; and the same 15th day of June, at Clerkenwell aforesaid, in the county aforesaid, had speech and did confer how your traitorous compassed imaginations might be brought to pass. And the 16th of June at Clerkenwell aforesaid, in the county aforesaid did appoint and conclude with the said Thomas Salisbury, to join with him for the delivery of Mary Queen of Scots, and in aiding and assisting the foreign enemies which should invade this realm. And further, that thou John Charnock, with Thomas Gerrard Knight, John Ballard and Anthony

Babington, the 27th of July, at St. Giles's aforesaid in the county aforesaid, did conspire the Queen's most excellent majesty not only from her crown and dignity to depose, but also her to murder and slay, and to make sedition and rebellion, and slaughter of her majesty's subjects, and the true and Christian religion to subvert, and the whole estate and government to alter. And that thou John Charnock traitorously didst go to Southampton House in Holborne, within the said county of Middlesex, the last day of July; and the same last day didst confer there with John Ballard how your traitorous compassed imaginations might be brought to pass; and thereupon, the 2nd day of August at Southampton House in Holborne aforesaid, did conclude and agree to do the best thou could for performance of the treasons aforesaid. And that thou Jerome Bellamy and Robert Gage, knowing that the said Anthony Babington, Robert Barnewell and Henry Doan, had committed high-treason at Harrow on the Hill in the county of Middlesex, did receive and aid them, contrary to your allegiance you owe to our sovereign lady the Queen, her crown and dignity, and contrary to divers statutes in such case provided. How says thou, Edward Abington, art thou guilty of the treasons whereof thou stands indicted, or not guilty?

Abington. Not guilty.

Sandes. How wilt thou be tried?

Abington. By God and my good country.

Sandes. Thou must say, by God and my country.

Abington. Yea sir, by God and my country.

Sandes. How says thou, Charles Tilney, art thou guilty, &c.?

Tilney. In no sort guilty, no more guilty than you are.

Sandes. Answer me directly, art thou guilty or not guilty?

Tilney. No Sir, I am not guilty; and that I am ready to answer and prove.

Sandes. How wilt thou be tried?

Tilney. By God and honest men.

Hatton. What answers are these? Abington says, by God and my good country; and thou says, by God and honest men. Thou must say, by God and my country.

Tilney. Yea sir, so I say.

In like manner, Jones, Travers, Charnock, Bellamy, and Gage pleaded not guilty.

Thereupon was an inquest of Middlesex called, who appeared at the bar and their names were, Rd. Martin, Win. Fleetwood, Jasper Cholmeley, Wm. Keinpton, Robert Loshe and John Barnes, Esqs, John Hill, Rob. Wood, Tho. Hargrave, Tho. Clark, John Chawkellett and John Draper, gentlemen.

Then said Sandes to the prisoners, have you any challenge?

Tilney. No, not I; for I know them not.

Anderson. Lieutenant of the Tower take away Gage and Bellamy to some other place out of the hearing of the court.

So the Lieutenant did.

Abington's Trial.

Then said Abington, I beseech your honors I may have a pair of writing tables to set down what is alleged against me, that I may yield a sufficient answer thereto.

Sandes. It was never the course here.

Hatton. When you hear anything you are desirous to answer, you shall speak an answer at lull, which is better than a pair of tables.

Sergeant Puckering. Well sir, then will we give evidence. And first, because it falls out that Abington and Tilney were acquainted with Savage's conspiracy, we will show a little that which yesterday was opened at full, and therefore, by Ballard's confession, this summer was twelvemonth, Ballard went into Scotland to understand of the willingness of the people, and Tilney offered to go with him.

Tilney. Yea sir, so I did. What can you prove by that?

Puckering. Soft, I will tell you when I come to give evidence against you. After Christmas, Ballard went into the north, and afterwards had speech with Tilney to go over beyond the seas and Tilney agreed and was contented. Ballard went over and sent letters to Tilney, desiring to stay till Ballard came over back, and he would tell him more. When Ballard came over, Tilney was acquainted with Savage's purpose, and Abington too. But then Ballard fell acquainted with Babington, and so came a greater conspiracy. And Abington put forth a proposition to surprise the Queen, and Tilney was privy. And it is under Babington's hand that Tilney, Titchbourne, Barnewell and Savage undertook to kill the Queen. Jones, at London, talked with Salisbury and stayed for him and was privy to a writing that was sent for Salisbury's apprehension. And Jones repaired to Salisbury at midnight, being in Jones's house, and told him that he had undone them all, and lent him his own horse and his man's cloak. Charnock, the same day that Ballard was taken, was moved by Babington to be one of the six to kill the Queen; and he assented, and afterwards lent Babington apparel to fly in. Whereupon was Ballard's confession read, which was that he confessed that he conferred with Paget about the state of our country; and that Ballard said, it is now more easy to invade the realm than before, because the Earl of Leicester with the best of our captains, were in Flanders and that the two talked with Mendoza; who asked them what armed men they could make, and what ports they could yield to the invaders for to land in; and Mendoza told them his master had a greater preparation than ever he had by sea, but he knew not for what matter; but he said he cared not whether they have any help of them or no, but said if you will not assist us herein, we will be as conquerors when we come, and use him also like enemies. For when it came to the brunt, they always shrunk, only he had a great care for the delivery of the Queen of Scots, and so sent Ballard into England; and said his master the King of Spain had vowed to lose his crown, and the Pope his life, but they would convert England and deliver the Queen of Scots. After Ballard arrived, he talked with Babington and he seemed willing; also he confessed the killing of the Queen.

Attorney. (Sir John Popham). Edward Abington, upon his examination, denied he knew Ballard; which we will prove to be false, therefore read first his denial, which was that he denied the surprising of her majesty; he denied the knowledge of Ballard, Fortescue, or Brown; he denied the delivery of the Queen of Scots; and being told that the Frenchmen would invade this land, he said he would spend his life in her majesty's defense, he confessed that on Sunday was seven night, he and his brother lay on a haymow.

Solicitor. (Sir Thomas Egerton). Who so is guiltless will speak truly and directly, but the counterfeit must speak untruths. Thereupon was another examination of his read, which was that Ballard being brought to his face, said that Ballard was not with him since Whitsuntide; but he confessed he knew him some years ago at Chertsey, Abington's brother confessed that Ballard was twice at Edward Abington's lodging at Charring-Cross; and at one of the times his brother Ballard talked secretly in one end of the chamber and Ballard was first acquainted with Thomas Abington at Rheims; and Ballard said that he made Edward Babington acquainted with these treasons, and he gave his consent. And Babington said that Abington moved first the surprise of the Queen. Then was read the confession of Babington, which was that Edward Abington moved first the surprise of the Queen to some strong place, and there to move her for reformation or toleration of religion. Tilney confessed that at the Three Tuns in Newgate-market, Babington moved a proposition for removing of the Lord-Treasurer and Mr. Secretary; and that Abington spoke broad speeches concerning that matter; and that Tilney did reprove him for the same.

Tilney. I deny it, I never said so.

Puckering. Here is your own hand, and read it.

Tilney. It is mine own hand, but what did I mean? When I said concerning that matter, I must interpret mine own meaning. I meant to speak broad words concerning religion.

Attorney. Then belike you reproved Abington for religion?

Tilney. Yea, I reproved him for speaking broad words concerning religion.

Attorney. What matter did you talk of then but Treason? It is well the jury does hear your answers.

C. B. Manwood. Tilney, you are too hot, this evidence is against Abington, you shall answer yourself when it comes to you.

Solicitor. Tilney confessed that there was speech between him and Abington concerning a surprise of the Queen; and that Abington said he would ride to Thomas Salisbury in to the country.

Then said the Queen's attorney to the jury, you perceive now that Abington is found false for his acquaintance with Ballard. Then was read Babington's confession, that Abington and Tilney were disposed to kill the Queen.

Attorney. Salisbury confessed that Abington desired him to make haste to his country; and said he understood by Babington of certain matters, and that he would come to Salisbury's country for things to be done shortly.

Solicitor. He confessed himself, that he was privy to it, and concealed it.

Then was read Babington's confession before the lords, which was that when certain seminaries in Rome came to take leave of the Pope, and to kiss his foot, the Pope asked what they were; and it was told him that they were Englishmen, which went to spend their lives for reformation of religion in their country. The Pope said it was a good slow way; but said that he would make a bridge over that ditch into England ere it were long. Also he confessed that he and Babington heard Edward Abington use speech to the same effect.

So you hear how Babington sets down Abington to be one of the six to kill the Queen. Also here is Ballard's own hand, that Babington appointed six to kill the Queen, Abington, Titchbourne, Tilney, and others.

Abington. It is very well, if I be at Babington's commandment; I protest I never knew thereof.

Solicitor. Here is Babington's letter to the Queen of Scots which proves you to be one.

The letter was read; among other this sentence was in there be six noble gentlemen which have undertaken the tragical execution, meaning the murdering of the Queen of England, only it rests that their attempt be honorably rewarded.

Abington. I protest before heaven and earth, as I am a true Christian, I never knew thereof.

The letter went further and contained this; all the actors have vowed either to die, or else to perform their purpose.

Abington. This is Babington's brag, to get credit with the Queen of Scots.

Attorney. We will prove, Abington, that you did provide amour of proof too for your brother and yourself, and one for another person.

Then was Foster's examination, an armorer in Holborne read, which proved so much directly.

Attorney, to Hatton. Mr. Vice-Chamberlain, you desired Abington to set down the truth of these things, thereupon he set down a great deal in writing, and yesterday he tore it in a hundred pieces; and here Mr. Lieutenant of the Tower has given me the pieces and here they be.

Hatton. Abington, you be very obstinate and seem indurate in these treasons.

Abington. I will answer what is laid against me. My first acquaintance was with Savage by reason that my brother and he were both of Bernard's-Inn, and by him came I acquainted with Savage, who talking with me, he told me of a book written at Rhemes which inveighed against the Earl of Northumberland, Throckmorton and Parry, for that they intended violence against her majesty's person which book I liked; yea, but, said Savage, it may be but for a color. Then he told me that it was written but for to blind the counselors in England, and make them secure and careless, when in very deed they at Rhemes desire nothing more than the murder of the Queen of England. Then I answered, he that allows of Parry's actions, savor not of divinity. And this I protest is true. For Ballard's acquaintance, true it is, he came to my chamber, and I knew him not; and then he told me he had seen me four years ago at Chertsey. So then I asked what news? And he told me of an invasion intended against this country. Whereto I gave such cold answers and such cold entertainment as I never saw him since. For my doings with Babington, his lodging was right in my way to go from Charring Cross through the fields to London; and true it is, he made me privy to his treasons and that I concealed them, and when he told me strangers would invade this realm to reform religion. I protested to Babington I had rather be drawn to Tyburn by the heels for my religion than to have it reformed by strangers. And for Babington's accusation, what force can it be of? For he having committed and confessed treason in the most high degree, there was no hope for him but to accuse.

Hatton. For Babington's hope thereof, I am persuaded he has no hope at all; and my lords here can assure there is no hope at all of his life, but he confessed what he knew for discharge of his conscience and what he did, he did it willingly and voluntarily for had not Babington voluntarily named Abington, who could have named Abington? And had he not also willingly accused Tilney, who could have accused Tilney?

Abington, Well then Sir, to you my lords the judges I do now speak, there is a statute in the first and thirteenth of this Queen made that who shall conspire, &c. it shall be treason, &c. Provided that he shall have two lawful witnesses, face to face, to avow it, &c. Now may it please your honors to have two lawful witnesses to testify against me. As for Babington, what witness can he be, a condemned man, Savage a condemned man also and Ballard a condemned man likewise? So then there is no witness against me; but I stand not upon this point, I stand upon mine own not guiltiness. Furthermore, it is not proved that Babington and I would be one to kill the Queen, but that he had appointed me to be one; and it is not proved that I knew thereof and that I said to Salisbury I would come into the country to understand of things to be done, I protest I remember not; for what needed any coming into the country to understand when as Salisbury and Babington did ride to St. Albans in Babington's coach?

C. B. Manwood. You answer by arguments, and not by answers.

Abington. If it be true that they rode together, as it is most true, what needed those speeches?

C. B. Manwood. That only answers that Babington might confer; but it does not answer that you needed not to go into the country to understand of things to be done, for you rode not in the coach with them.

Abington, I protest before God, I remember not that ever I said so.

C. B. Manwood. Let the jury consider of this answer.

Anderson. For answer to you, Abington, for the point of the statute, true it is, had you been indicted on the statute of the 1st and 13th of this Queen, two witnesses ought to have been produced; but you stand indicted by the common law, and the statute of 25 Edward 3, which is, who shall intend the death of the King, &c. and in that statute is not contained any such proof.

Tilney. The statute of 25 Edward 3 is, who shall compass or imagine, &c.

Anderson. Very well, and not contained to prove by witnesses, as you would have it.

Solicitor. See how they would acquit themselves for want of witness; and if it should be as they would have it, then could never any treason be sufficiently proved. The statute of 1 Elizabeth is so, the overt-act must be proved by two witnesses; but the statute of 25 Edward 3 is who shall imagine how then can that be proved by honest men, being a secret cogitation which lies in the minds of traitors? And such traitors will never reveal their cogitations to honest men, but undo such as themselves, and they I hope be no honest men; so then they would have their treasons never revealed.

Abington. For answer that I lay in a haymow, it is most true I was in Herefordshire when my house in Worcestershire was in searching, and there I heard how my house was searched; and coming to Worcestershire the country hearing of the horribleness of the things wherewith I was charged I knew none would receive me nor entertain me; and so I was constrained to lie in a haymow. And for preparing mine armour, I protest I had the same in Shoe-Lane, and would have had it ready against the going over of the Earl of Leicester; and hearing him in Holborn to be commended for the most singular man in England in his trade, I sent to him to have it finished.

Then said the attorney to the jury, you have heard how Babington confessed. Abington would be one to kill the Queen, and you have heard his answer thereto.

Abington. If Babington ever moved it to me, let me die for it.

Attorney. It is Babington's own confession, that six whereof Abington was one were disposed to kill the Queen.

Abington. If ever I imagined, or any part thought of the indictment which you have alleged, I beseech God I sink as I stand in this place.

Anderson. You had a seminary priest in your house.

Abington. He was only with me, but not in mine house.

Hatton. Before Babington was taken, Ballard did voluntarily declare that you two, Abington and Tilney, were disposed to kill the Queen.

Anderson. The jury has heard the indictment and your answers, let them consider thereof in their consciences.

Tilney's Trial.

First was read his confession, wherein he denied Ballard's acquaintance, and he denied that ever he heard Ballard say we should have it new world shortly. Then was read Ballard's confession, which was that before Christmas last, Ballard did confess Gage and Tilney at a house in Holborn.

Tilney. I denied Ballard's acquaintance, because by the last statute, he is a traitor and not for my guilt or crime. And for that I was confessed by him, it was no otherwise than all the subjects of the realm of England were confessed in the days of King Henry 7.

Solicitor. But now is the estate of this realm quite other than it was in the days of Henry 7. For now the Pope is the greatest enemy her majesty has, but it was not so then.

Tilney. How know I the Pope is her greatest enemy?

Hatton. Know not you how he invaded the realm of Ireland?

Attorney. Know not you how he induced Mary?

Tilney. No sir, in my conscience wherein I shall die, I never conspired any treason.

C. B. Manwood. Were not you sworn when you were made a pensioner? How far different is it to these actions to be confessed, and to conceal traitors?

Tilney. Yea sir, but I was not then a Catholic, but now I am; for which I thank God most heartily.

Puckering. Did not you say, if her majesty would forgive you this, you would never deal more with any seminary priest; but if there were any old priest in England, you would have him if he were to be gotten for money?

Tilney. But what is this? This only concerns my religion, which I was promised I should not be charged withal.

Attorney. No more you are for lands nor goods; this is only an introduction to the treason.

Then was read Tilney's own confession wherein he confessed (which also was given in evidence against Abington) that Abington said, why might not her majesty be as well surprised as the Queen of Scots? Which words he spoke at the Three Tuns in Newgate market. He confessed Ballard came to his chambers in Westminster in his withdrawing chamber (as it was termed), where Ballard told him he had provided a pension for Windsor in France and would do so for him; and told him of an invasion intended against this realm. He confessed he would have gone to Scotland to have lived there among the Catholics when Billiard went there and said that Windsor made him acquainted with Bullard.

Tilney. These things I confess, but yet it is no treason to hear treason talked of by

others; as for myself, what presumptions may there be if I should be guilty being her majesty's sworn servant, (whose highness God grant long to reign) a young roan of small ability, neither in lands nor goods able to make any power at all? For religion, I confess I am a Catholic, which I thank God for it, but that I am not now to be charged withal. As for Ballard's coming to me, I do confess it; but it was in such public manner as no man in the world could judge his coming for any such intent as treason, for he came openly in the day time, not in the night, and never came disguised.

Solicitor. Tilney, you say true; he came not disguised, but I will tell you how he came; being a Popish priest, he came in a gray cloak laid on with gold lace, in velvet hose, a cut satin doublet, a fair hat of the newest fashion, the band being set with silver buttons; a man and a boy after him, and his name Captain Fortescue.

Tilney. All this concerns my religion only.

Solicitor. You confess that you were privy to these treasons; then we will prove directly that you did assent thereto.

Then was read Ballard's confession, wherein Ballard thinks that Tilney did assent to kill the Queen, for he saw him not dissent when he told him these treasons, likewise Tilney requested him for some pension in France when he came over.

Tilney. I stand upon the assent.

Solicitor. Ballard affirms it; Babington said that you Tilney were one of the six.

Tilney. Babington told him so! That proves that Babington forsooth will be a statesman, when God knows he is a man of no gravity.

Solicitor. Abington's confession is that Tilney and Abington were disposed to kill the Queen.

Puckering. Babington said yesterday at the bar that Tilney would have had her majesty set upon in her coach.

Tilney. No, I said not so; only at the Three Tuns in Newgate-market, I said it might be her majesty might be set upon in her coach, and I said no more. But that proves not I did consent.

Attorney. You have said enough, if we had no other evidence against you.

Tilney. How so?

Attorney. Because you have confessed high treason.

Tilney. I tell you no, there is no such matter intended in my words.

C. B. Manwood. Your censure was your assent, and your censure was to kill the Queen in her coach.

Hutton. Your words prove that you were concluded upon the matter and were devising in the manner.

Attorney. Babington and Ballard reckoned Tilney for one of the six to kill the Queen as by their confession appears.

Tilney. The first time that I knew Babington was that he came to my chamber in Westminster to crave mine acquaintance; I used him courteously, as appertained to a gentleman. The second time was at the Three Tuns in Newgate-market. And the third time was in the fields, and I never saw him else, that I should trust him in so high a matter for three times acquaintance is altogether improbable. As for Babington himself, albeit he be very wise, yet is he altogether vain.

Hatton. Babington declared all this voluntarily for who could accuse Tilney before Babington named Tilney?

Tilney. I will tell you how I meant my words in Newgate-market. If a servant which is faithful, knowing where his master's money is, do say. If I would be a thief, I could rob my master, for in such a place his money is; this proves not that he would rob his master. Albeit he used such words. And so, although I said she might be set upon in her coach, it proves not that I assented to the same; for I protest before God, I never intended any treason in my life.

Anderson. But if a servant, knowing where his master's money is among thieves which are devising to take away the master's money, do say, this way my master's money may be taken, and be in view when it is taken; I say that he is accessory. And you Tilney, being amongst traitors that were devising how to kill her majesty to show by what means her majesty might be slain, it manifestly proves your assent. Therefore let the jury consider of their evidence.

Then said Tilney to the jury. My very good friends and countrymen of the jury, forasmuch as I am charged highly to have offended against the law, I am now to be tried according to the law by you. And therefore if you shall find this evidence sufficient to prove my guilt, you ought to find me guilty; but if you see in your consciences that I have answered fully each objection laid to my charge, I charge you to find me not guilty, as you will answer me at the dreadful day of judgment.

The trial of Jones.

First was read his confession. That he said to John Travers at Jones's house in Denbighshire, Salisbury has brought us all to destruction. What remedy? Said Travers, it is then time for us to be packing. But Jones lent Salisbury his horse to ride away with. Salisbury confessed he acquainted Jones with the foreign invasion and delivery of the Queen of Scots desiring his aid, which he promised him in Lincolns-Inn-Fields; and how that Salisbury fled upon Jones's relation of Babington's apprehension. Also Salisbury confessed that he caused Jones to protest he would not discover him. Jones said in his examination that Salisbury never asked his assent because he always thought himself assured of him. Also Jones said to Salisbury what have you done? You have undone us all. This was the effect of the evidence, which was given against him.

Jones. For concealing of the treason, I put me to her Majesty's mercy; I confess I hastened Salisbury away.

C. B. Manwood. Then you deny not but that you horsed him away?

Then said Jones to the jury, I confess this and put me to her majesty's mercy, my case was hard and lamentable, either to betray my dearest friend whom I loved as my own self; and to discover Thomas Salisbury, the best man in my country of whom I only made choice; or else to break my allegiance to my sovereign and so undo myself and my posterity for ever. And this was my case.

Travers's arraignment.

Salisbury confessed he acquainted John Travers with his treasons and that he consented to him. And Travers said to him he would go beyond the seas with him. Salisbury confessed he exacted no oath of Jones and Travers when he acquainted them but that they protested they would not discover him. Also it was proved that when Jones intended to have gone to Ireland, now lately when it was to have been inhabited by the Englishmen, Travers asked him what he meant to go now when his presence was necessary; and said if Mr. Salisbury came home, he would surely stay him.

Then was read Culey's confession, that Travers and Salisbury fled and Travers called his own name Lacon, and Salisbury called his name Johnson, and that Culey would not change his name, because he had changed it before.

Travers. I fled and changed my name because I was a Catholic, and doubted to be troubled for my religion and conscience.

Solicitor. Nay Travers, thou did fly for treason; for when Jones told you Salisbury had undone you all, thou said what remedy and that it was time to be packing; and you had your chaplain with you, Culey I mean.

Travers. If he be a priest, I honor him for his priesthood. And he said little else as one that seemed not to care what evidence came against him, but was resolute to be hanged.

He confessed nothing in his examination; he denied he had any speech with Babington, saving salutations. He confessed he served in the Spanish camp and there was acquainted with Savage; and it was proved against him that he said Savage's sudden bravery would betray all their matters.

Charnock's trial.

Charnock. I confess that Ballard did make me acquainted with the invasion of the realm and the other treasons and thereupon I sounded Savage, who answered he was not his own man but said there was one in the court who should have done that long since, and that he was a Morganist.

Then was read Babington's confession, that Charnock promised him to be at his commandment and Babington told him the Queen of Scots liked of their actions. And Ballard's confession was read. That he told Charnock at large, and Charnock liked very well and said he would do the best he could herein. And Savage's confession was read, which was what Babington moved Charnock to be one of the six and Charnock told Savage that Babington moved him also.

Charnock. That I said to Babington I would be at his commandment, it is very true; for Babington was my good friend in divers respects and therefore I thought it pertained to courtesy to say I remained at his commandment.

Solicitor. Nay, thou didst offer to be at Babington's commandment in this action of treason.

Then was Babington's confession read, which was that he talking in Paul's with Charnock of the Queen's death, Charnock promised to be disposed by him in this action and that he offered to spend his life wherein Babington should direct him. Then was read Charnock's own confession wherein he confessed he lent apparel to Savage to ally in and that he fled into the woods himself.

Charnock. Savage and I were acquainted when he was of Barnard's-Inn, and I of Furnivals-Inn and we both served in the Spanish camp together and Savage brought me acquainted with Ballard. As for Savage, because I knew he was an excellent soldier, a man skilful in languages and learned besides, when I met him here in England I was glad to renew old acquaintance with him. That I should consent to Ballard the 2d day of August, see (if you please) what probability there is to the contrary. For on the 4th of August, Ballard was apprehended, and before his apprehension Ballard sent a letter to Mr. Secretary offering to discover all; myself was the bearer of the letter and delivered it to one of Mr. Secretary's men, what likelihood is it then that I knowing of this letter after that Ballard was taken would consent to Babington to kill the Queen, or that I consented to Ballard the 4th of August; Ballard being apprehended the 4th of August and before that time had written to Mr. Secretary, and myself was the messenger?

Hatton. Savage confronted thee to thy face and avouched these things to thy face.

Charnock. For flying away with my friend, I fulfilled the part of a friend therein.

Hatton. To perform thy friendship, thou did break thy allegiance to thy sovereign.

Charnock. Therein have I offended.

Anderson. You of the jury, you have now heard their several answers at large; go together and consider thereof in your consciences.

Then the jury, upon this evidence and their answers went up to a home to agree upon their verdict; and these five prisoners were sent away from the bar.

Then Bellamy and Gage were called to the bar, and a new inquest was called and appeared at the bar and evidence was given against the two prisoners in sort ensuing.

The trial of Gage.

First, was given in evidence that Gage knew Ballard to be a priest and was reconciled, and gave lodging to Ballard, and attended Ballard as his man when he went into the north to provoke the people to rebellion. Also when all the matter was discovered, he lent Savage a horse to fly to Corydon and directed him to one of Savage's father's men who should help him away, also he lent Babington his apparel to fly in. Then was showed forth his own confession which was that Ballard told him we should have a new world shortly, and that he lodged Ballard for his safety, also he confessed that during his flight he lodged in a barn. Also he confessed that he was reconciled by Ballard. Also Charnock's confession was read that Gage borrowed apparel of him to fly in.

Then Gage was asked by the Lord Chief Baron Manwood wherefore he fled into the woods?

Gage stoutly and fiercely answered, for company.

Bellamy's trial.

He confessed that the noise of the country was that they (that is to say Babington, Barnwell and Donn) had conspired the Queen's death, and how that after that he brought them meat into the woods and lodged them in his house. Also evidence was given that one coming to Bellamy's house to seek for the traitors, telling him they conspired the Queen's death, he denied he knew whom they were; whereas at the same time he had them in his house. Bellamy spoke very little for himself, only he seemed to be a very clownish, blunt, willful and obstinate papist.

Then this other jury went up to a house to agree upon their verdict and by that time was the first jury agreed, which came to the bar and Alderman Martin being their foreman spoke for them and said that they found all the live prisoners guilty, and further that they knew not what lands, tenements, goods or chattels the prisoners had, &c. So the Clerk of the Crown set down the verdict and discharged the inquest of that service.

Forthwith was the other inquest agreed of their verdict and found Gage and Bellamy also guilty of the treasons they were indicted of.

Puckering. Then Puckering, the Queen's Sergeant, craved judgment of death against the prisoners.

Sandes. Then said Sandes, the Clerk of the Crown, Edward Abington, thou hast been indicted of high treason and there upon arraigned, and has pleaded not guilty, thy country has found thee guilty; what has thou to say for thyself, wherefore judgment and execution of death should not be given against thee?

Abington. My good lords, since I have been tried by the law and am found guilty of offence against the law, I am contented to abide the punishment due to my guilt. The inquest I cannot accuse, forasmuch as they thought in their consciences the evidence sufficient to condemn me; howbeit, that brainless youth Babington, whose proud stomach and ambitious mind incensing him to commit most abominable treasons, hath been the cause to shed the blood of others guiltless in his actions. But I cry not vengeance against him, for I am contented to die, being condemned to die. Only this one petition to you, my good lords, I make, I have one sister, whose preferment also has miscarried; wherefore if it might please her majesty with the revenues of my lands in some sort to provide for her. If I live, I will endeavor to be thankful; and if I die, I will pray for her.

Then the Clerk of the Crown demanded the like of Tilney; who said:

Tilney. And I, my good lords, am able to say nothing in deterring of my judgment. This humble suit must I make to your honors; I owe in London about two or three hundred Pounds, and I beseech your honors to procure my friends to pay it for discharge of my conscience.

Then the Clerk of the Crown demanded the like of Jones; who said.

Jones. I beseech your honors to be a means to her majesty for mercy, for I desiring to be counted a faithful friend, am now condemned for a false traitor. The love of Thomas Salisbury has made me hate myself, but God knows how far I was from intending any treason. But if mercy be not to be had, I beseech your honors this; I owe some sums of money, but not very much, and I have more owing me. I beseech that my debts may be paid with that which is owing me. Moreover, my good lords, the lands I have, which I had by descent from my father at the marriage of a gentlewoman which is now my wife, were entailed to me and the heirs male of my body; I beseech you some consideration may be had of my posterity.

Hatton. Jones, did not you tell me that your lands were fee simple for an argument of your innocence?

Jones. Yea sir, so my lands are; but at the time of my marriage they were entailed as I tell you.

Sandes. Then the Clerk of the Crown demanded the like of Travers; who said,

Travers I never committed any treason, but for my religion, I will die in it; only I owe 4£ or such a matter, I beseech you it may be paid out of the profits of my lands.

Then the Clerk of the Crown demanded the like of Charnock; who said.

Charnock. I beseech your honor Mr. Vice Chamberlain, to get her majesty to pardon me.

Hatton. Charnock, thy offence is too high for me to be an obtainer of thy pardon, but I am sorry for thee; if thou had applied thyself the best way, thou might have done thy country good service.

Charnock. I beseech you then that six angels, which such a one has of mine, may be delivered to my brother to pay my debts.

Hatton. How much is thy debts?

Charnock. The same six angels would discharge it.

Hatton. Then I promise thee it shall be paid.

Then the Clerk of the Crown demanded the like of the rest, who answered little: whereupon they all received judgment of death, according to their demerits.

On the 20th of the same month, John Ballard, Anthony Babington, John Savage, Robert Barnewell, Chidiock Titchbourne, Charles Tilney and Edward Abington, were drawn on hurdles from the Tower to their execution to St. Giles's Fields, being the place where they used to meet; where was erected a scaffold, and thereupon a gallows.

John Ballard the priest, the principal conspirator, confessed that he was guilty of those things for which he was condemned but protested they were never enterprised by him upon any hope of preferment, but only as he said, for the advancement of true religion. He craved pardon and forgiveness of all persons to whom his doings had been any scandal, and so made an end; making his prayers to himself in Latin, not asking her majesty forgiveness otherwise than if he had offended.

Anthony Babington also confessed that he was come to die, as he had deserved; howbeit he (as Ballard before) protested that he was not led into those actions upon hope of preferment, or for any temporal respect; nor had ever attempted them, but that he was persuaded by reasons alleged to this effect, that it was a deed lawful and meritorious. He craved forgiveness of all whom he had any way offended; he would gladly also have been resolved whether his lands should have been confiscated to her majesty, or whether they should descend to his brother; but howsoever, his request was to the lords and others of the commissioners there present, that consideration might be had of one whose money he had received for lands, which he had passed no fine for, for which the conveyance was void in law. He requested also, that consideration might be had of a certain servant of his, whom he had seat for certain merchandize into the east countries, who by his means as greatly impoverished. For his wife he said she had good friends, to whose consideration he would leave her. And thus live finished, asking her majesty forgiveness, and making his prayers in Latin.

John Savage confessed his guilt, and said (as the other two before) that he did attempt it, for that in conscience he thought it a deed meritorious, and a common good to the weal public, and for no private preferment.

Robert Barnwell confessed that he was made acquainted with their drifts, but denied that ever he consented, or could be in conscience persuaded that it was a deed lawful. And being urged that he came to the court to spy opportunities for the achieving of their purposes, and that being there, her majesty observing his prying looks acquainted before with their intents, she prayed God that all were well. Try this he answered, that it was not unknown to divers of the council, that he had matters which he solicited, which was the cause of his being there at that time; but I confess, said he, at my return, Babington asked me what news; to whom I told that her majesty had been abroad that day with all the circumstance that I saw there;

and if I have offended her majesty, I crave forgiveness; and assuredly, if the sacrifice of my body might establish her majesty in the true religion, I would most willingly offer it up. Then he prayed to himself in Latin.

Chidiock Titchbourne began to speak as follows, viz. Countrymen and my dear friends, you expect I should speak something; I am a bad orator, and my text is worse. It were in vain to enter into the discourse of the whole matter for which I am brought hither, for that it has been revealed heretofore, and is well known to the most of this company. Let me be a warning to all young gentlemen, especially *generosa adolescentulis*. I had a friend, and a dear friend, of whom I made no small account, whose friendship has brought me to this he told me the whole matter, I cannot deny, as they had laid it down to be done; but I always thought it impious, and denied to be a denier in it; but the regard of my friend caused me to be a man in whom the old proverb was verified, I was silent, and so consented. Before this thing chanced, we lived together in most flourishing estate. Of whom went report in the Strand, Fleet-street, and elsewhere about London, but of Babington and Titchboume? No threshold was of force to brave our entry. Thus we lived, and wanted nothing we could wish for and God knows what less in my head than matters of state? Now give me leave to declare the miseries I sustained after I was acquainted with the action, wherein I may justly compare my estate to that of Adam's, who could not abstain one thing forbidden to enjoy all other things the world could afford; the terror of conscience awaited me. After I considered the dangers wherein to I was fallen, I went to Sir John Peters in Essex and appointed my horses should meet me at London, intending to go down into the country. I came to London, and there heard that all was betrayed; whereupon, like Adam, we fled into the woods to hide ourselves, and there were apprehended. My dear countrymen, my sorrows may be your joy, yet mix your smiles with tears and pity my case; I am descended from a house, from two hundred years before the conquest, never stained till this my misfortune. I have a wife and one child; my wife Agnes, my dear wife, and there is my grief, and six sisters left on my hand, my poor servants, I know their master being taken; were dispersed, for all which I do most heartily grieve. I expected some favor though I deserved nothing less, that the remainder of my years might in some sort have recompensed my former guilt, which seeing I have missed let me now meditate upon the joys I hope to enjoy. This done, he prayed first in Latin, and then in English, asking her majesty and all the world, heartily, forgiveness and that he hoped steadfastly now at this his last hour his faith would not fall.

Charles Tilney said, I am a Catholic and believe in Jesus Christ, and by his passion I hope to be saved; and I confess I can do nothing without him which opinion all Catholics firmly hold and whereas they are thought to hold the contrary, they are in that, as in all other things, greatly abused. To Dr. White seeming to school him in points of religion differing from those which he held, he spoke in anger. I came hither to die doctor, and not to argue. He prayed in Latin for himself, and after he prayed for Queen Elizabeth that she might live long; and warned all young gentlemen of what degree or calling so ever to take warning by him.

Edward Abington said I come hither to die holding all points firmly that the Catholic Church does; and for the matters whereof I am condemned, I confess all, saving the death of her majesty, to which I never consented. He feared as he said, great bloodshed in England before it was long. Sheriff Ratcliff said, Abington, see thou all these people whose blood shall be demanded at thy hands, if thou dying, conceal that which may turn to their peril; therefore tell why, or which way such blood should be shed he said all that I know you have of record; and at last said he, this country is hated of all countries for her iniquity, and God loves it not. And being urged by Dr. White to be of a lively faith; he answered he believed steadfastly in the Catholic faith. The doctor asked him how he meant for I fear me said he, thou deceives thyself; he answered that faith and religion which is held almost in all Christendom, except here in England. Thus done, he willed them not to trouble him any longer with any more questions, but made his prayers to himself in Latin.

Ballard was first executed. He was cut down and bowelled with great cruelty while he was alive. Babington beheld Ballard's execution without being in the least daunted, whilst the rest turned away their faces and fell to prayers upon their knees. Babington being taken down from the gallows alive too and ready to be cut up, he cried aloud several times in Latin *parce mihi domine Jesu*! Spare me, O Lord Jesus! Savage broke the rope, and fell down from the gallows, and was presently seized on by the executioner, his privies cut off and his bowels taken out while he was alive. Barnwell, Titchbourne, Tilney and Abington were executed with equal cruelty.

On the next day Thomas Salisbury, Henry Donn, Edward Jones, John Charnock, John Travers, Robert Gage, Jerome Bellamy were drawn to the place of execution.

Thomas Salisbury said, since it has pleased God to appoint this place for my end, I thank his infinite goodness for the same; I confess that I have deserved death and that I have offended her majesty, whom to forgive me I heartily beseech with all others whom I have any way offended. I desire all true Catholics to pray for me; and I desire them as I beseech God they may to endure with patience whatsoever shall be laid upon them and never to enter into any action of violence for remedy. Then he said his prayers, looking earnestly with his eyes to heaven and prayed in Latin a long while. When he had thus done, he cried in English and Latin, Father, forgive me!

Henry Donn said, do the people expect I should say anything? I was acquainted, I confess, with their practices, but I never did intend to be a dealer in them. Babington oftentimes requested me to be one and said for that he loved me well, he would bestow me in one of the best actions; which should have been the delivery of the Queen of Scots to which I could not for a long time agree; at length, by many urgent persuasions he won me, so as I told him I would do my best. And being asked as he was ascending the ladder, whether he thought it lawful to kill her majesty? He answered. No, no; for I take her to be my lawful and natural prince. And (as Salisbury) he desired all Catholics to endure with patience and never to attempt anything against her majesty, under whose government he had lived quietly until within these ten weeks, that those things were first imparted to him and whereas he was indebted to divers, and divers in like manner to him, he forgave all that was owing to him and craved forgiveness of what he owed. He desired God to forgive Babington, the only cause of his fall and death; and was right sorry for a gentlewoman, one Mrs. Bellamy, at whose house he with the rest were relieved after they fled; he prayed God whom he had chiefly offended, next her majesty and last of all the people, forgiveness; saying no soul was more sorrowful than his, nor none more sinful; and prayed for her majesty wishing she might live in all happiness and alter this life be eternized in everlasting bliss; and so he prayed in Latin and English.

Edward Jones said, I come hither to die, but how rightfully God knows; for thus stands my case. At Trinity term last, Mr. Salisbury made me acquainted with their purposes; and for that he knew me to be well horsed, he thought me as fit as any to attempt the delivery of the Queen of Scots and requested me to be one; which I utterly denied, altogether disliking their practices and persuading him by what means I might from it, and told him this was the haughty and ambitious mind of Anthony Babington, which would be the destruction of himself and friends; whose company I wished him to refrain; and for that I would have him out of his company. I have divers times lent him money and pawned my chain and jewels to buy him necessaries to go into the country. And whereas I had made conveyance of my lands to divers uses with some annuities, and placed my wife with my friends, and given over housekeeping and by reason of my conscience thought to live at ease. I called my servants together again and began to keep house more freshly than ever I did, only because I was weary to see Salisbury's straggling, and for that I was willing to keep him about home and never consented to any of his treasons. But always advised him to beware; for though I was and am a Catholic, yet I took it to be a most wicked act to offer violence to my natural prince. I did intend to go into Ireland with Mr. Edward Fitton, and there to have served until at length very shortly after this, my determinate mind being not settled, I received a note of their names, amongst whom was the name of my dear friend then I began to fear what has happened. I heard that night he would be at my house and indeed he came there about twelve o'clock and the door being opened to him as he was very familiar with me, he came running up to my bedside with a candle in his hand, which he took from one of my men, saluting me with these words; Ned Jones, how dost thou? Ah! Tom said, I art thou one of them that should have killed the Queen? Yea, said he, what means thou by that? See and read this, said I, giving him the note wherein his name was; he seeing, turned about and said, there be many Catholics in England as far in this act as we are the more the worse, quote I. Here is the sum of my fault, in which I know I have offended her majesty; first, because I did conceal it at London, and lastly, because I did not apprehend my dear friend Tom, being in my house, for which fault I am heartily sorry, and do ask her majesty's forgiveness. There is one thing wherein I am to move you concerning my debts: I have set them down so near as I could what they are. Good Sir Francis Knowles, I shall entreat you to be a means to her majesty that there may be some care had of my creditors and debtors.

The debts which I owe do amount in the whole, to 980£.

The debts which are owing me are 1600£.

But who shall look into my compting-house shall find many of 100£, 200£, or 300£. Whereof all is discharged except some of 50£ and some 40£ and such like, without any defeasance, and lie only in my credit so that unless some man of conscience enter into the action of my compting-house, it is like to be the utter undoing of a number; but God knows my mind and I hope it shall not be laid to my charge. And so concluded with his prayers, first, in Latin, and then in English, that the people might better understand what he prayed.

John Charnock and John Travels having their minds wholly fixed on prayer, recommended themselves to God and the saints. Gage extolled the Queen's great grace and bounty to his father and detested his own perfidious ingratitude towards his princess. And Jerome Bellamy with confusion and deep silence, suffered last.

The Queen being informed of the severity used in the executions the day before, and detesting such cruelty, gave express orders that these should be used more favorably; and accordingly they were permitted to hang till they were quite dead, before they were cut down and bowelled.

[Sollom, *A Complete Collection of State Trials and Proceedings*, 134-142]

Mary, Queen of Scots

Mary Queen of Scots is a popular character of Tudor history and there is nothing I am able to add to the plethora of biographies available other than her trial, which is often overlooked or omitted from biographies.

Proceedings against Mary Queen of Scots, Fotheringay-Castle, the 12th of October, 1586. For being concerned in a conspiracy against Queen Elizabeth; with some things previous thereto, and necessary to introduce and explain those proceedings.

The subjects of England finding the Kingdom in danger of an invasion from abroad and the life of the Queen attempted by various plots at home, carried on by the Papists, in prospect of a popish successor; voluntarily entered into an association for the Queen's safety, solemnly engaging and obliging themselves to each other to revenge her death on those who should be the occasion of it which association was as follows.

Forasmuch as almighty God has ordained Kings, Queens, and princes to have dominion and rule over all their subjects, and to preserve them in the possession and observation of the true Christian religion, according to his holy word and commandment; and in like sort, that all subjects should love, fear and obey their sovereign princes, being Kings or Queens to the utmost of their power; at all times to withstand, pursue, and suppress all manner of persons; that shall by any means intend and attempt anything dangerous or hurtful to the honor, state, or persons of their sovereigns.

Therefore we whose names are or shall be subscribed to this writing, being natural born subjects of this realm of England; and having so gracious a lady, our sovereign Elizabeth, by the ordinance of God, our most rightful Queen, reigning over us these many years with great felicity, to our inestimable comfort. And finding lately by divers depositions, confessions, and sundry advertisements out of foreign parts, from credible persons well known to her majesty's council, and to divers others, that for the furtherance and advancement of some pretended title to the crown, it has been manifested that the life of our gracious sovereign Queen Elizabeth has been most dangerously designed against to the peril of her person, if almighty God, her perpetual defender of his mercy had not revealed and withstood the same; by whose life, we and all other her majesty's true and loyal subjects do enjoy all inestimable benefit of peace in this land do for these reasons and causes before alleged, not only acknowledge ourselves most justly bound with our lives and goods for her defense, and in her safety to prosecute, suppress and withstand all such intenders, and all other her enemies, of what nation, condition or degree so ever they shall be, or by what counsel or title they shall pretend to be her enemies, or to attempt any harm upon her person; but do further think it our bounden duties for the great benefit of peace, wealth, and godly government, we have more plentifully received these many years under her majesty's government, than any of our forefathers have done in any longer time of any of her progenitors, Kings of this realm; to declare, and by this writing make manifest our bounden duties to our sovereign lady for her safety.

And to that end, we and every of us, first calling to witness the name of almighty God do voluntarily and most willingly bind ourselves, every one of us to the other, jointly and severally in the band of one firm and loyal society; and do hereby vow and promise by the majesty of almighty God, that with our whole powers, bodies, lives and goods, and with our children and servants, we and every of us will faithfully serve and humbly obey our said sovereign Lady Queen Elizabeth against all states dignities and earthly powers whatsoever; and will as well with our joint and particular forces during our lives withstand pursue and offend, as well by force of arms, as by all other means of revenge, all manner of persons, of whatsoever state they shall be, and their abettors that shall attempt any act, or counsel, or consent to anything that shall tend to the harm of her majesty's royal person, and will never desist from all manner of forcible pursuit against such persons to the utter extermination of them, their counselors, aiders and abettors. And if any such wicked attempt against her most royal person shall be taken in hand, or procured, whereby any that have, may or shall pretend title to come to this crown by the untimely death of her majesty so wickedly procured (which God of his mercy forbid) that the same may be avenged) we do not only bind ourselves both jointly and severally never to allow, accept or favor any such pretended successor, by whom, or for whom any such detestable act shall be attempted or committed, as unworthy of all government in any Christian realm or civil state.

But do also further vow and protest, as we are most bound, and that in the presence of the eternal and everlasting God, to prosecute such person or persons to death with our joint and particular forces and to act the utmost revenge upon them that by any means we or any of us can devise and do, or cause to be devised and done for their utter overthrow and extirpation.

And to the better corroboration of this our loyal band and association, we do also testify by this writing that we do confirm the contents hereof by our oaths corporally taken upon the holy evangelist with this express condition, that no one of us shall for any respect of person or causes, or for fear or reward, separate ourselves from this association, or fail in the prosecution thereof during our lives upon pain of being by the rest of us prosecuted and suppress as perjured persons, and as public enemies to God, our Queen, and to our native country; to which punishment and pains we do voluntarily submit ourselves, and every of us, without benefit of any color and pretence.

In witness of all which premises to be inviolably kept, we do to this writing put our hands and seals; and shall be most ready to accept and admit any others hereafter to this society and association.

This association, although entered into voluntarily by persons in their private capacities was confirmed and established by a statute made 27 Elizabeth 1585, entitled an act for the security of the Queen's royal person, and the continuance of the realm in peace; and is as follows:

Forasmuch as the good felicity and comfort of the whole estate of this realm consists only (next under God) in the surety and preservation of the Queen's most excellent majesty; and for that it has manifestly appeared that sundry wicked plots and means have of late been devised and laid, as well in foreign parts beyond the seas, as also within this realm, to the great endangering of her highness's most royal person and to the utter ruin of the whole commonweal, if by God's merciful providence the same had not been revealed, therefore for the preventing of such great perils as might hereafter otherwise grow by the like detestable and devilish practices, at the humble suit and earnest petition of the lords spiritual and temporal, and the commons in this Parliament assembled, and by the authority of the same Parliament, be it enacted and ordained, if at any time after the end of this present session of Parliament, any open invasion or rebellion shall be had or made into or within any of her majesty's realms or dominions, or any act attempted, tending to the hurt of her majesty's most royal person, by or for any person that shall or may pretend title to the crown of this realm after her majesty's decease; or if anything be compassed or imagined, tending to the hurt of her majesty's royal person, by any person, or with the privacy of any person that shall or may pretend title to the crown of this realm, that then by her majesty's commission under her great seal, the lords and other of her highness's Privy Council, and such other lords of Parliament to be named by her majesty as with the said Privy Council shall come up to the number of four and twenty at the least, having with them for their assistance in that behalf such of the judges of the courts of record at Westminster, as her highness shall for that purpose assign and appoint, or the more part of the same council, lords and judges, shall by virtue of this act, have authority to examine all and every the offences aforesaid, and all circumstances thereof, and thereupon to give sentence or judgment, as upon good proof the matter shall appear to them. And that after such sentence or judgment given, and declaration thereof made and published by her majesty's proclamation under the great seal of England, all persons against whom such sentence or judgment shall be so given and published, shall be executed and disabled for ever to have or claim, or to pretend to have or claim the crown of this realm, or of any her majesty's dominions any former law, or statute whatsoever to the contrary in any wise notwithstanding. And that thereupon all her highness's subjects shall and may lawfully by virtue of this act, and her majesty's direction in that behalf, by all forcible and possible means pursue to death every such wicked person, by whom or by whole means, assent, or privacy, any such invasion or rebellion shall be in form aforesaid denounced to have been made, or such wicked act attempted, or other thing compassed or imagined against her majesty's person, and all their aiders, comforters and abettors.

And if any such detestable act shall be executed against her highness's most royal person, whereby her majesty's life shall be taken away (which God of his great mercy forbid) that then every such person, by or for whom any such act shall be executed, and their issues being any wise assenting or privy to the same, shall by virtue of this act be excluded and disabled forever to have or claim, or pretend to have or claim the said crown of this realm, or any other her highness's dominions, any former law or statute to the contrary in any wise notwithstanding. And that all the subjects of this realm, and all other her majesty's dominions shall and may lawfully by virtue of this act, by all forcible and possible means pursue to the death every such wicked person, by whom or by whose means any such detestable fact shall be in form hereafter expressed, denounced to have been committed, and also their issues being any wise assenting or privy to the same, and all their aiders, comforters and abettors in that behalf.

And to the end that the intention of this law may be effectually executed, if her majesty's life be taken away by any violent or unnatural means, (which God defend); be it further enacted by the authority aforesaid, that the lords and others, which shall be of her majesty's Privy Council at the time of such her decease, or the more part of the same council, joining to them for their assistance five other earls, and seven other lords of Parliament at the least (foreseeing, that none of the said earls, lords or council be known to be persons that may make any title to the crown) those persons which were chief justices of either bench, master of the rolls, and chief baron of the exchequer at the time of her majesty's death, or in default of the said justices, master of the rolls, and chief baron, some other of those which were justices of some of the courts of records at Westminster at the time of her highness's decease, to supply their places; or any four and twenty, or more of them, whereof eight to be lords of the Parliament, not being of the Privy Council, shall to the uttermost of their power and skill examine the cause and manner of such her majesty's death, and what persons shall be any way guilty thereof, and all circumstances concerning the same, according to the true meaning of this act; and thereupon shall by open proclamation publish the same, and without any delay by all forcible and possible means, prosecute to death all their aiders and abettors; and for the doing thereof, and the withstanding and suppressing all such power and force, as shall be any way levied or stirred in disturbance of the due execution of this law, they shall by virtue of this act, have power and authority, not only to raise and use such forces as shall in that behalf be needful and convenient but also to use all other means and things possible and necessary for the maintenance of the same forces, and prosecution of the said offenders. And if any such power and force shall be levied and stirred in disturbance of the due execution of this law, by any person that shall, or may pretend any title to the crown of this realm, whereby this law may not in all things be fully executed, according to the effect and true meaning of the same; that then every such person shall by virtue of this act be therefore excluded and disabled for ever to have, or claim, or pretend to have or claim the crown of this realm, or of any other her highness's dominions, any former law or statute whatsoever to the contrary notwithstanding.

And be it further enacted by the authority aforesaid, that all and every the subjects of all her majesty's realms and dominions, shall to the uttermost of their power aid and assist the said council and all other the lords and other persons, to be adjoined to them for assistance, as is aforesaid, in all things to be done and executed according to the effect and intention of this law; and that no subject of this realm shall in any wise be impeached in body, land or goods, at any time hereafter, for anything to be done or executed according to the tenor hereof, any law or statute heretofore made to the contrary in any wise notwithstanding.

And whereas of late many of her majesty's good and faithful subjects have in the name of God, and with the testimonies of good consciences, by one uniform manner of writing under their hands and seals, and by their several oaths voluntarily taken, joined themselves together in one bond and association, to withstand and revenge to the uttermost all such malicious actions and attempts against her majesty's most royal person; now for the full explaining of all such ambiguities and questions, as otherwise might happen to grow by reason of any sinister or wrong construction or interpretation to be made or inferred of, or upon the words or meaning thereof; be it declared and enacted by the authority of this present Parliament, that the same association, and every article and sentence therein contained, as well concerning the disallowing, excluding, or disabling any person that may, or shall pretend any title to come to the crown of this realm, as also for the pursuing, and taking revenge of any such wicked act or attempt as is mentioned in the same association, shall, and ought to be in all things expounded and adjudged according to the true intent and meaning of this act and not otherwise, or against any ether person or person.

The following year, 1586, Babington and others being convicted of a conspiracy to assassinate Queen Elizabeth; and the Queen of Scots being charged with countenancing and encouraging that conspiracy, a commission was issued out, founded upon the above said statute for the examination the trial of the said Queen of Scots, to the effect following.

Elizabeth, by the grace of God, of England, France, and Ireland, Queen, defender of the faith, &c. To the most reverend father in Christ, John Archbishop of Canterbury, primate and metropolitan of all England, and one of our Privy Council; and to our trusty and well beloved Sir Thomas Bromley Kt. Chancellor of England, and one of our Privy Council; and also to our trusty well beloved William Lord Burghley, Lord Treasurer of England, another of our Privy Council; and also to our most dear cousin William Lord Marquis of Winchester, one of the lords of the Parliament; to our most dear cousin Edward Earl of Oxford, Great Chamberlain of England, another of the lords of the Parliament; and also to our most dear cousin George Earl of Shrewsbury, Earl Marshal of England, another of our Privy Council; and to our most dear cousin Henry Earl of Kent, another of the lords of the Parliament; and also to our most dear cousin Henry Earl of Derby another of our Privy Council; and to our most dear cousin William Earl of Worcester, another of the lords of the Parliament, and also to our most dear cousin Edward Earl of Rutland, another of the lords of the Parliament; and to our most dear cousin Ambrose Earl of Warwick, Master of our Ordnance, another of our Privy Council; and to our most dear cousin Henry Earl of Pembroke, another of the lords of the Parliament and also to our most dear cousin Robert Earl of Leicester, Master of our Horse, another of our Privy Council; and to our most dear cousin Henry Earl of Lincoln, another of the lords of the Parliament; and also to our most dear cousin Anthony Viscount Montague, another of the lords of the Parliament; and to our trusty and well beloved Charles Lord Howard, our Great Admiral of England, another of our Privy Council; and to our trusty and well beloved Henry Lord of Hudson, our Lord Chamberlain, another of our Privy Council; and also to our trusty and well beloved Henry Lord Abergavenny, another of the lords of the Parliament; and to our trusty and well beloved Edward Lord Zouch, another of the lords of the Parliament; and also to our trusty and well beloved Edward Lord Morley, another of the lords of the Parliament; and to our trusty and well beloved William Lord Cobham, Lord Warden of our Cinque-Ports, another of our Privy Council; and also to our trusty well beloved Edward Lord Stafford, another of the lords of the Parliament; and also to our trusty and well beloved Arthur Lord Grey of Wilton, another of the lords of the Parliament; and also to our trusty and well beloved John Lord Lumley, another of the lords of the Parliament; and also to our trusty and well beloved John Lord Sturton, another of the lords of the Parliament; and to our trusty and well beloved William Lord Sandes, another of the lords of the Parliament; and also to our trusty and well beloved Henry Lord Wentworth, another of the lords of the Parliament; to our trusty and well beloved Lewis Lord Mordant, another of the lords of the Parliament, and to our trusty and well beloved John Lord St. John of Bolitho, another of the lords of the Parliament; and also to our trusty and well beloved Thomas Lord Burkhurst, another of our Privy Council; and to our trusty and well beloved Henry Lord Compton, another of the lords of the Parliament, and also to our trusty and well beloved Henry Lord Cheney, another of the lords of the Parliament; to our trusty and beloved Sir Francis Knolles Kt. Treasurer of our Household, another of our Privy Council; and also to our trusty and well beloved Sir James Crofts Kt. Comptroller of our said Household, another of our Privy Council, and to our trusty and beloved Sir Christopher Hatton Kt. our Vice-Chamberlain, another of our Privy Council; and also to our trusty and beloved Sir Francis Walsingham Kt. one of our principal secretaries, another of our Privy Council; and also to our trusty and beloved William Davison Esq.; another of our principal secretaries and of our Privy Council; and to our trusty and beloved Sir Ralph Sadler Kt. Chancellor of our Duchy of Lancaster, another of our Privy Council; and also to our trusty and beloved Sir Walter Mildmay Kt. Chancellor of our Exchequer, another of our Privy Council; and to our trusty and beloved Sir Amias Powlet Kt. Captain of our isle of Jersey, another of our Privy Council; and to our trusty and beloved John Wolley Esq.; our Secretary for the Latin tongue, another of our Privy Council; and also to our trusty and beloved Sir Christopher Wray Kt. Chief Justice assigned for the pleas to be held before us; and to our trusty and beloved Sir Edmund Anderson Kt. our Chief Justice of the Bench; Sir Roger Manwood Kt. our Chief Baron of our Exchequer; Sir Thomas Gawdy Kt. one of our justices assigned for the pleas to be held before us; and William Periam one of our justices of the bench, greeting, &c.

Whereas since the end of the session of Parliament, namely, since the first day of June in the 27th year of our reign, divers matters have been compassed and imagined, tending to the hurt of our royal person, as well by Mary daughter and heir of James V. King of Scots and commonly called Queen of Scots and dowager of France, pretending title to the crown of this realm or England; as by divers other persons, *cum ſcientia*, in English, with the privy of the same Mary, as we are given to understand. And whereas we do intend and determine that the act aforesaid be in all and every part thereof, duly and effectually executed according to the tenor of the same, and that all offences above said in the act above said mentioned, as aforesaid and the circumstances of the same be examined and sentence or judgment thereupon given, according to the tenor and effect of the said act to you, and the greater part of you we do give full and absolute power, faculty and authority according to the tenor of the said act to examine all and singular matters compassed and imagined, tending to the hurt of our royal person as well by the aforesaid Mary as by any other person or persons whatsoever, *cum ſeientia*, in English, with the privy of the same Mary, and all circumstances of the same and all other offences above said in the act above said (as aforesaid) mentioned whatsoever and all circumstances of the same and of every of them. And thereupon according to the tenor of the act aforesaid to give sentence or judgment as upon good proof matter shall appear to you. And therefore we do command you that you do at certain days and places, which you or the greater part of you, shall thereto fore-appoint, diligently proceed upon the premises in form aforesaid.

The most part of these commissioners came the 11th of October to Fotheringay-Castle in the county of Northampton, seated upon the bank of the river Nen where the Queen of Scots was then kept. The next day the commissioners sent to her Sir Walter Mildmay, Poivlet, and Edward Barker a public notary; who delivered into her hands Queen Elizabeth's letter which when she had read, she, with a countenance composed to royal dignity and with a mind untroubled, said it grieved me that the Queen, my most dear sister, is misinformed of me; and that I having been of many years straightly kept in prison and grown lame of my limbs, have lien neglected after I have offered so many reasonable conditions for my liberty. Though I have thoroughly forewarned her of many dangers, yet has no credit been given to me, but I have been always contemned, though most nearly allied to her in blood. When the association was entered into and the act of Parliament thereupon made, I foresaw that whatsoever danger should happen either from foreign princes abroad, or from ill disposed people at home or for religion's sake, I must bear the whole blame having many mortal enemies in the court. Certainly I might take it hardly and not without cause that a confederacy has been made with my son without my knowledge but such matters I omit. As for this letter it seems strange to me that the Queen should command me as a subject to appear personally in judgment. I am an absolute Queen, and will do nothing which may prejudice either mine own royal majesty, or other princes of my place and rank, or my son. My mind is not yet dejected, neither will I sink under my calamity. I refer myself to those things, which I have protested before Bromley, now chancellor, and the Lord La-Ware. The laws and statutes of England are to me most unknown; I am destitute of counselors, and who shall be my peers I am utterly ignorant. My papers and notes are taken from me, and no man dares step forth to be my advocate. I am clear from all crime against the Queen, I have excited no man against her, and I am not to be charged but by mine own word or writing, which cannot be produced against me. Yet can I not deny but I have commended myself and my cause to foreign princes.

The next day there returned to her in the name of the commissioners, Powlet and Barker who showed to her this answer drawn in writing and asked her whether she would persist in the same. When she had heard it distinctly read, she commended it as rightly and truly conceived and said she would persist therein. But this, said she, I have forgotten which I would have to be added thereto whereas the Queen has written that I am subject to the laws of England and to be judged by them because I have lived under the protection of them; I answer that I came into England to crave aid and ever since have been detained in prison and could not enjoy the protection or benefit of the laws of England; nay, I could never yet understand from any man what manner of laws those were.

In the afternoon came to her certain selected persons from amongst the commissioners with men learned in the civil and canon-law. But the lord chancellor and the lord treasurer declared their authority by patent, and showed that neither her imprisonment nor her prerogative of royal majesty could exempt her from answering in this Kingdom with fair words advising her to hear what matters were to be objected against her, otherwise they threatened that by authority of law, they both could and would proceed against her, though she were absent. She answered that she was no subject and rather would she die a thousand deaths than acknowledge herself a subject, considering that by such an acknowledgment, she should both prejudice the height of regal majesty and withal confess herself to be bound by all the laws of England even in matter of religion, nevertheless she was there ready to answer to all things in a free and full Parliament for that she knew not whether this meeting and assembly were appointed against her being already condemned by fore-judging to give some show and color of a just and legal proceeding. She warned them therefore to look to their consciences, and to remember that the theatre of the whole world is much wider than the Kingdom of England. She began then to complain of injuries done to her and the lord treasurer interrupting her began to reckon up Queen Elizabeth's kindnesses towards her, namely that she had punished some which impugned the claim she laid to England, and had been a means to keep her from being condemned by the estates of the realm, for the marriage sought with the Duke of Norfolk, for the rebellion in the north and for other matters. All which when she seemed little to esteem, they returned back.

Within a few hours after they delivered to her, by the hands of Powlet and the solicitor the chief points of their commission and the names of the commissioners, that she might see that they were to proceed according to equity and right and not by any cunning point of law and extraordinary course. She took no exceptions against commissioners, but most sharply excepted against the late law upon which the authority of their commission wholly depended it as that it was unjust, devised of purpose against her that it was without example and such whereto she would never subject herself. She asked by what law they would proceed, if by the civil or canon-law, then said she interpreters are to be fetched from Pavia or Poicliers, and other foreign universities; for in England none are to be found that are meet. She added also that it was manifest by plain words in the Queen's letters, that she was already fore-judged to be guilty of crime though unheard; and therefore there was no reason why she should appear before them and she required to be satisfied touching some scruples in the said letters which she had for herself noted confusedly and by snatches, severally by themselves but would not deliver them written out; for it stood not said she, with her royal dignity to play the scrivener.

Touching this matter, the said selected commissioners went to her again to whom she signified that she did not well understand what those words meant seeing she is under the Queen's protection. The lord chancellor answered that this was plain to every one of understanding, yet was it not for subjects to interpret what the Queen's meaning was neither were they made commissioners for that end. Then she required to have her protestation showed and allowed which she had formerly made. It was answered that it never had been, nor now was to be allowed for that it was prejudicial to the crown of England. She asked by what authority they would proceed? It was answered by authority of their commission and by the common law of England.

But, said she, ye make laws at your pleasure, whereto I have no reason to submit myself considering that the English in times past refused to submit themselves to the law salique of France and if they would proceed by the common law of England, they should produce precedents and cases forasmuch as that law consisted much of cases, and custom and if by the canon law none else ought to interpret the same, but the makers. It was answered that they would proceed neither by the civil nor canon law, but by the common law of England that it might nevertheless be proved by the civil and canon law that she ought to appear before them if she would not refuse to hear it. And indeed she refused not to hear it, but as she said by way of locution, not judicially.

From hence she fell into other speeches that she had intended nothing to the destruction of the Queen; that she had been incensed with injuries and indignities; that she should be a stone of offence to others, if she were so unworthily handled that by law she had offered her best means for revoking the Bishop of Rome's bull; that she would have defended her innocence by letters but it was not allowed her; and finally that all the offices of kindness which she had tendered these twenty years, were rejected. Thus while she wandered far in these digressions, they called her back again and prayed her to speak plainly whether she would answer before the commissioners. She replied that the authority of their delegation was founded upon a late law made to entrap her, that she could not away with the Queen's laws which she had good reason to suspect; that she was still full of good courage and would not offend against her progenitors, the Kings of Scots by acknowledging herself a subject to the crown of England for this were no thing else but to profess them openly to have been rebels and traitors. Yet she refused not to answer, so as she might not be reduced to the rank of a subject but she had rather perish utterly than to answer as a criminal person.

Whereto Hatton, Vice-Chamberlain to Queen Elizabeth answered, you are accused (but not condemned) to have conspired the destruction of our lady and Queen anointed. You say you are a Queen; be it so. But in such a crime the royal dignity is not exempted from answering neither by the civil nor canon law nor by the law of nations nor of nature. For if such kind of offences might be committed without punishment all justice would stagger, yea, fall to the ground if you be innocent you wrong your reputation in avoiding a trial. You protest yourself to be innocent, but Queen Elizabeth thinks other wise and that neither without grief and sorrow for the same. To examine therefore your innocence she has appointed for commissioners most honorable prudent and upright men who are ready to hear you according to equity with favor, and will rejoice with all their hearts if you shall clear yourself of this crime. Believe me the Queen herself will be much affected with joy who affirmed to me at my coming from her that never anything befell her more grievous than that you were charged with such a crime. Wherefore lay aside the bootless privilege of royal dignity which now can be of no use to you, appear in judgment and show your innocence lest by avoiding trial you draw upon yourself suspicion and lay upon your reputation an eternal blot and aspersion.

I refuse not (said she) to answer in a full Parliament before the estates of the realm lawfully assembled so as I may be declared the next to the succession; yea, before the Queen and council, so as my protestation may be admitted and I may be acknowledged the next of kin to the Queen. To the judgment of mine adversaries, amongst whom I know all defense of mine innocence will be barred, flatly I will not submit myself.

The lord chancellor asked her whether she would answer if her protestation were admitted? I will never (said she) submit myself to the late law mentioned in the commission.

Hereupon the lord treasurer answered; we, notwithstanding will proceed tomorrow in the cause though you be absent and continue contumax.

Search (said she) your consciences, look to your honor, God reward you and yours for your judgment against me.

On the morrow which was the 14th of the month, she sent for certain of the commissioners and prayed them that her protestation might be admitted and allowed. The lord treasurer asked her whether she would appear to her trial if her protestation were only received and put in writing without allowance. She yielded at length, yet with much ado and with an ill will, lest she should seem (as she said) to derogate from her predecessors or successors; but was very desirous to purge herself of the crime objected against her being persuaded by Hatton's reasons which she had weighed with advisement.

Soon after the commissioners which were present assembled themselves in the presence-chamber. At the upper end of the chamber was placed a chair of estate for the Queen of England under a cloth of estate. Over against it, below and more remote, near the transom or beam that ran cross the room stood a chair for the Queen of Scots. At the walls on both sides were placed benches, upon which sat on the one side the Lord Chancellor of England, Lord Treasurer of England, the Earls of Oxford, Kent, Derby, Worcester, Rutland, Cumberland, Warwick, Pembroke, Lincoln, and the Lord Viscount Montacute; on the other side, the Barons of Abergavenny, Zeuch, Morley, Stafford, Grey, Lumley, Sturton, Sandes, Wentworth, Mordant, St. John of Bolitho, Compton, and Cheney. Nigh to these sat the Knights of the Privy Council, Sir James Crofts, Sir Christopher Hatton, Sir Francis Walsingham, Sir Ralph Sadler, Sir Walter Mildmay and Sir Amias Powlet. Forward before the earls, sat the two chief justices, and the chief baron of the exchequer; and on the other side two barons, the other justices, Dale and Ford, doctors of the civil law; and at a little table in the midst sat Pelham the Queen's attorney, Egerton the Solicitor, Gaudy the Queen's Sergeant at Law, the Clerk of the Crown, and two writers.

When she was come and had settled herself in her seat after silence proclaimed, Bromley Lord Chancellor turning to her, spoke briefly to this effect; the most high and mighty Queen Elizabeth being not without great grief of mind advertised that you have conspired the destruction of her and of England and the subversion of religion, has out of her office and duty lest she might seem to have neglected God, herself and her people and out of no malice at all appointed these commissioners to hear the matters which shall be objected to you and how you can clear yourself of them, and make known your innocence.

She rising up, said that she came into England to crave aid which had been promised her and yet was she detained ever since in prison. She protested that she was no subject of the Queen's but had been and was a free and absolute Queen, and not to be constrained to appear before commissioners or any other judge whatsoever, for any cause whatsoever save before God alone the highest judge, lest she should prejudice her own royal majesty, the King of Scots her son, her successors, or other absolute princes. But, that she now appeared personally to the end to refute the crimes objected against her. And hereof she prayed her own attendants to bear witness.

The lord chancellor not acknowledging that any aid had been promised her, answered that this protestation was in vain, for that whosoever (of what place and degree so ever he were) should offend against the laws of England, in England, was subject to the same laws and by the late act might be examined and tried, the said protestation therefore made in prejudice of the laws and Queen of England was not to be admitted. The commissioners nevertheless commanded that as well her protestation as the lord chancellor's answer, should be recorded.

Then after the commission was openly read, which was grounded upon the act already often mentioned, she stoutly opposed her protestation against the same act as enacted directly and purposely against her and herein she appealed to their consciences.

When answer was made by the lord treasurer that every person in this Kingdom was bound even by the latest laws and that she ought not to speak against the laws; and that the commissioners would judge according to that law what protestations or appellations so ever she interposed, she said at length that she was ready to hear and answer touching any fact whatsoever against the Queen of England.

Gawdy now opened the law from point to point, affirming that she had offended against the same; and hereupon he made an historical discourse of Babington's conspiracy and concluded that she knew of it, approved it, assented to it, promised her assistance and showed the way and means.

She answered with stout courage that she knew not Babington, that she never received any letters from him, nor wrote any to him; that she never plotted the destruction of the Queen and that to prove the same, her subscription under her own hand was to be produced; that for her part she never so much as heard speak thereof; that she knew not Ballard, nor ever relieved him; but she understood from some that the Catholics in England took many things very hardly and hereof she herself had advertised the Queen by letters; and besought her to take pity on them; that many also which were to her utterly unknown, had offered her their help and assistance, yet had she excited no man to commit any offence; and being shut up in prison, she could neither know nor hinder what they attempted.

Hereupon it was urged out of Babington's confession that there had been intercourse by letters between her and Babington. She confessed that here had passed conference by letters between her and many men yet could it not thereby be gathered that she was privy to all their wicked counsels. She required that her own subscription under her hand, might be produced; and asked what hurt it were if she remanded the letters which had been kept from her almost a whole year? Then were read the copies of letters between her and Babington, wherein the whole conspiracy was set down.

The Scottish Queen's letter to Anthony Babington.

My very good friend, albeit it be long since you heard from me, not more than I have done from you, it is against my will; yet would I not you should think I have in the mean while, nor ever will be unmindful of the effectual affection you have showed heretofore towards all that concerns me. I have understood, that upon the renewing of your intelligence, there were addressed to you, both from France and Scotland, some packets for me; I pray you, if any be come to your hands, and be yet in place to deliver them to the bearer hereof who will safely convey them to me, and I will pray to God for your preservation. Your assured good friend, Mary Regina.

Anthony Babington's letter to the Scottish Queen.

Most mighty, most excellent, my dread sovereign lady and Queen, to whom I owe all fidelity and obedience; may it please your gracious majesty to admit excuse of my long silence, and discontinuance from those dutiful offices, intercepted upon the removal of your royal person from the ancient place of your abode to the custody of a wicked puritan, and mere Leicestrian a mortal enemy both by faith and faction to your majesty and to the Catholic estate: I held the hope of our country's as weal depending (next under God) upon the life of your majesty to be desperate, and thereupon resolved to depart the realm determining to spend the remnant of my life in such solitary sort as the miserable and wretched estate of my country does require; only expecting according to the just judgment of God, the present confusion thereof, which God for his mercy sake, prevent. The which my purpose being in execution, and standing upon my departure, there was addressed to me from the parts beyond the seas, one Ballard a man of virtue and learning and of singular zeal to the Catholic cause and your majesty's service. The man informed me of great preparations by the Christian prince's allies for the deliverance of our country from the extreme and miserable estate wherein for a long time it has remained. Which when I understood, my especial desire was to advise by what means I might with the hazard of my life, and all my friends in general do your sacred majesty one day's good service. Whereupon most dread sovereign, according to the great care which those princes have of the preservation and safe deliverance of your majesty's sacred person, I advised of means and considered of circumstances accordingly to and with so many of the wisest and most trusty, as with safety I might commend the secrecy thereof to I do find by the assistance of the Lord Jesus, askance of good effect, and desired fruit of for travel. These things are first to be advised in this great and honorable action; upon issue of which depends not only the life of your most excellent majesty, which God long preserve to our inestimable comfort and to the salvation of English souls and the lives of all us actors therein; but also the honor and weal of our country, far more dear than our lives to us and the last hope ever to recover the faith of our forefathers, and to redeem ourselves from the servitude and bondage which hereby heretofore has been imposed upon us with the loss of many thousand souls. Firsts for the assuring of invasions, sufficient strength on the invaders parts to arrive is appointed with a strong party at everyplace, to join with them and warrant their landing, the deliverance of your majesty the dispatch of the usurping competitor. For the effecting of all may it please your majesty to rely upon my service, I protest before the almighty who has long miraculously preserved your royal person, no doubt to some universal good that what I have said shall be performed, or all our lives happily lost in the execution thereof. Which vow all the chief actors have taken solemnly; and are upon assurance by your majesty to me, to receive the blessed sacrament thereupon either to prevail in the church's behalf and your majesty's, or fortunately to die for so honorable a cause. Now forasmuch as delays are extreme dangerous, it might please your most excellent majesty by your wisdom to direct us, and by your princely authority to enable us and such as may advance the affairs, foreseeing there is not any of the nobility at liberty, assured to your majesty in this desperate service except unknown to us; and seeing that it is very necessary that some there should be to become heads to lead the multitude who are disposed by nature in this land to fellow nobility considering withal, it does not only make the commons and country to follow without contradiction or contention which is ever found in equality, but also does add great courage to the leaders. For which necessary regards I would recommend some to your majesty are fittest, in my knowledge, to be your lieutenants in the west parts, in the north parts, south Wales, and north Wales, the countries of Lancaster, Derby, and Stafford. In all which countries, parties being already made and fidelity taken in your majesty's name, I hold them as most assured, and of undoubted fidelity. Myself; with ten gentlemen of quality and a hundred followers, will undertake the delivery of your person from the hands of your enemies and for the dispatch of the usurper, from obedience of whom; by the excommunication of her, we are made free, there be six noble gentlemen all my private friends, who, for the zeal they bear to the Catholic cause and your majesty's and your majesty's service will undertake the tragical execution. It rests, that according to their infinite deserts and your majesty's bounty, their heretical attempts may be honorably rewarded in them if they escape with life or in their posterity; and that so much by your majesty's authority I may be able to assure them. Now it remains only in your majesty's wisdom that it be reduced into method that your happy deliverance be first for that thereupon depends the only good, and that the other circumstances concur; that the untimely end of the one do not overthrow the rest. All which your majesty's wonderful experience and wisdom will dispose in so good manner as, I doubt not, through God's good assistance shall take deserved effect for the obtaining of which every one of us shall think his life most happily spent. Upon the twelfth day of this month, I will be at Litchfield expecting your majesty's answers and letters to execute what by them shall be commanded.

Your majesty's faithful subject, and sworn servant, Anthony Babington.

As for these letters (said she) it may be that Babington wrote them, but let it be proved that I received them. If Babington or any others affirm it, I say they lie openly; other men's crimes are not to be cast upon me. A packet of letters which had been kept from me almost a whole year, came to my hands about that time, but by whom it was sent, I know not.

To prove that she had received Babington's letters, there were read out of Babington's confession the chief heads of certain letters which he had voluntarily confessed that she wrote back to him wherein when mention was made of the Earl of Arundel and his brethren and the Earl of Northumberland, the tears burst forth and she said, alas! what has that noble house of the Howard's endured for my sake? And shortly after having wiped away the tears she answered that Babington might confess what he list, but it was an open lie, that she had devised such means to escape that her adversaries might easily get the ciphers which she had used to others and with the same write many things falsely that it was not likely she should use Arundel's help, whom she knew to be shut up in prison; or Northumberland's, who was very young and to her unknown.

There were read also certain points picked out of Savage's and Bollard's confessions who had confessed that Babington imparted to them certain letters which he had received from the Queen of Scots.

She affirmed that Babington received none from her, yea that she was angry with some which had secretly suggested counsels to her for invading of England, and had warned them to beware.

Now was there a letter brought forth wherein Babington's plot was commended and approved.

The answer of the Scottish Queen to a letter written by Anthony Babington, 12 July, 1586.

Trusty and well beloved, according to the zeal and entire affection which I have known in you towards the common cause of religion, and mine, having always made account of you as a principal and right worthy member to be employed both in the one, and in the other; it has been no less consolation to me to know your estate, as I have done by your last letter and to have further means to renew my intelligence with you than I have felt grief's all this while past to be without the same. I pray you therefore to write to me hereafter so often as you can, of all concurrents which you may judge in any sort importunate to the good of mine affairs, wherein I shall not fail to correspond with all the care and diligence that shall be by possibility. For divers great and importunate considerations, which were here too long to be deducted, I cannot but greatly praise and commend your common desire to prevent, in time, the design of our enemies, for the extirpation of our religion out of this realm with the ruin of us all for I have long ago showed to the foreign Catholic princes what they have done against the King of Spain and in the time the Catholics here remaining, exposed to all persecutions and cruelty, do daily diminish in number, forces, means and power, so as if remedy be not thereto speedily provided. I fear not a little but that they shall become altogether unable for ever to rise again to receive any aid at all when so ever it is offered. Then for my own part, I pray you assure our principal friends, that albeit I had no particular interest in this case, that all that I may pretend to being of no consideration to me in respect of the public good of the state, I shall be always ready and most willing to employ therein my life, and all that I have, or may look for in this world. Now to ground substantially this enterprise, and to bring it to good success, you must examine duly:

First, what forces, as well on foot as on horse, you may raise among you all; and what captains you shall appoint for them in every shire, in case a general cannot be had.

Secondly, which towns, ports and havens you may assure yourselves, as well on the north, west and south, to receive succors, as well from the low-countries, Spain and France, as from other parts.

Thirdly, what place you esteem fittest, and of most advantage to assemble the principal company of your forces at the same time, which would be compassed conform to the proportion of your own.

Fourthly, for how long pay and munitions, and what ports are fittest for their landing in this realm, from the foresaid three foreign countries.

Fifthly, what provision of monies and armor, in case you should want, you would ask.

Sixthly, by what means do the six gentlemen deliberate to proceed.

Seventhly, The manner of my getting forth of this hold.

Which points having taken amongst you who are the principal actors, and also as few in number as you can; the best resolution in my device is that you impart the same with all diligence to Bernardino de Mendoza, Ambassador Lieger for the King of Spain in France, who besides the experience he has of the estate on this side, I may assure you will employ himself most willing. I shall not fail to write to him of the matter with all the recommendations I can, as also I shall do in any wise that shall be needful. But you must take choice men for the managing of the affairs with the said Mendoza, and others out of the realm of some faithful and very secret, both in wisdom and personage, to whom only you must commit yourselves; to the end things may be kept the more secret, which for your own security I commend to yourself. If your messenger brings you back again sure promise and sufficient assurance of the succors which you demand, then thereafter (but not sooner, for that it were in vain) take diligent order that all those on your part make secretly as they can, provision of armor, fit horses, and ready money, wherewith to hold themselves in a readiness to march so soon as shall be signified to you by the chief and principal of every shire and for the better coloring of the matter, reserving to the principals the knowledge of the ground of the enterprise, it shall be enough at the beginning to give it out to the rest that the said provisions are made only for the fortifying of yourselves in case of need against the puritans of this realm, the principal whereof having the chief forces thereof in the low countries as you may let the bruit go disguised, do seek the ruin and overthrow at their return home of the Catholics and to usurp the crown not only against me and all other lawful pretenders thereto, but against their own Queen that now is, if she will not altogether submit herself to their government.

These pretexts may serve to found and establish among all associations or confederations general, as done only for your preservation and defense, as well in religion as lands, lives and goods, against the oppression and attempts of the said puritans; without directly writing, or giving out anything against the Queen, but rather showing yourselves willing to maintain her and her lawful heirs after her, not naming me. The affairs being thus prepared and forces in readiness, both without and within the realm, then shall it be time to set the six gentlemen on work, taking good order upon the accomplishment of their discharges, I may be suddenly transported out of this place and meet without tarrying for the arrival of the foreign aid which then must be hastened with all diligence. Now for that there can be no certain day appointed for the accomplishment of the said gentlemen's design, to the end others may be in a readiness to take me from hence, I would that the said gentlemen had always about them, or at least at court, divers and sundry scout men, furnished with good and speedy horses, so soon as the design shall be executed to come with all diligence to advertise me thereof, and those that shall be appointed for my transporting to the end, that immediately after they may be at the place of mine abode, before my keeper can have advertisement of the execution of the said design or at the least before he can fortify himself within the house, or carry me out of the same. It were necessary to dispatch two or three of the said advertisers by divers ways, to the end, if one be staid, the other may come through at the same instant it were needful also to assay to cut off the posts ordinary ways. This is the plot that I think best for this enterprise and the order whereby we shall conduct the same for our common security for stirring on this side before you be sure of sufficient foreign forces, that were for nothing but to put ourselves in danger of following the miserable fortune of such as have here to fore traveled in the like actions; and if you take me out of this place, be well assured to set me in the midst of a good army, or some very good strength, where I may safely stay till the assembly of your forces and arrival of the said foreign succors. It were sufficient cause given to the Queen, in catching me again, to enclose me in some hold out of the which I should never escape if she did use me no worse; and to pursue with all extremity those that assisted me, which would grieve me more than all the unhappiness might fall upon myself. Earnestly as you can, look and take heed most carefully and vigilantly to compass and assure all so well that shall be necessary for the effecting of the said enterprise, as with the grace of God you may bring the same to happy end remitting to the judgment of your principal friends on this side, with whom you have to deal, therein to ordain and conclude upon these points, which may serve you for an overture of such propositions as you shall amongst you find best and to yourself in particular, I refer the gentlemen aforementioned, to be assured of all that should be requisite for the entire execution of their good wills. I leave their common resolution to advice; in case the design do not take hold, as may happen whether they will or no, do not pursue my transport, and the execution of the rest of the enterprise. But if the mishap should fall out, that you might not come by me, being set in the Tower of London, or in any other strength, with strong guard; yet notwithstanding, leave not for God's sake to proceed in the enterprise for I shall at any time die most contentedly, understanding of your delivery out of the servitude wherein you are holder as slaves, I shall assay, that at the same time that the work shall be in hand at that present to make the Catholics of Scotland to arise and put my son into their hands to the effect, that from thence our enemies here may not prevail by any succor. I would also that some stirring were in Ireland, and that it were labored to begin some time before anything be done here, and then that the alarm might begin thereby on the flat contrary side that the stroke may come from your designs, to have some general, or chief head, are very pertinent; and therefore were it good to send obscurely for the purpose to the Earl of Arundel, or some of his brethren, and likewise to seek to the young Earl of Northumberland, if he be at liberty from over the sea; the Earl of Westmoreland may be had, whose hand and name, you know may do much in the north parts also the Lord Paget of good ability in some shires thereabouts both the one and the other may be had amongst whom secretly some more principal banished, may return, if the enterprise be once resolute. The said Lord Paget is now in Spain and may treat of all that (by his brother Charles or directly by himself) you will commit to him touching the affairs. Beware that none of your messengers that you send forth of the realm, carry any letters upon themselves; but make their dispatches, and fend them either after or before them by some others. Take heed of spies and false brethren that are amongst you, especially of some priests, already practiced upon by your enemies for your discovery and in any case keep never a paper about you, that may in any sort do harm for from like errors have come the condemnation of all such as have suffered heretofore, against whom otherwise nothing could justly have been proved. Discover as little as you can, your names and intentions to the French ambassador, now Lieger at London; for although as I understand, he is a very honest gentleman, yet I fear his master entertains a course far contrary to our design which may move him to discover us, if he had any particular knowledge thereof. All this while I have sued to change and remove from this house; and for answer, the Castle of Dudley only has been named to serve the turn; so as by appearance about the end of this summer, I may go thither, therefore advise so soon as I shall be there, what provision may be had about that part for my escape from thence. If I stay here, there is but one of these three ways or means to be looked for.

The first, that at a certain day appointed for my going abroad on horseback on the mores between this and Stafford, where ordinarily, you know, but few people do pass, let fifty or threescore horsemen, well mounted and armed, come to take me away as they may easily; my keeper having with him but eighteen or twenty horses, with only dogs.

The second means, to come at midnight or soon after, and set fire on the barns and stables which you know are near the house; and whilst my guardian servants shall come forth to the fire, your company having duly on a mark, whereby they may be known one from another, some of you may surprise the house, where I hope with the few servants I have about me, I shall be able to give you correspondent aid.

And the third is, some there be that bring carts hither early in the morning, three carts may be so prepared that being in the midst of the great gate, the carts might fall down, or overthrow; that thereupon you might come suddenly and make yourselves masters of the house, and carry me suddenly away so you might easily do before any number of soldiers, who lodge in sundry places forth of this place, some half a mile, and some a whole mile, could come to relieve. Whatsoever issue the matter takes, I do, and shall think myself obliged, so long as I live, towards you, for the offers you make to hazard yourself as you do for my deliverance; and by any means that ever I may have, I shall do my endeavor to recognize by effects your deserts therein I have commanded a more ample alphabet to be made for you, which herewith you shall receive. God almighty have you in his protection. Your assured friend for ever, Mary Regina.

Fail not to burn this privately and quickly.

Of this letter she required a copy, and affirmed that it proceeded not from her, but haply from her alphabet of ciphers in France that she had done her best endeavor for the recovery of her liberty, which nature it self allowed, and had solicited her friends to deliver her; yet to some, whom she listed not to name, when they offered her their help to deliver her, she answered not a word. Nevertheless, she much desired to divert the storm of persecution from the Catholics, and for this she had made earnest suit to the Queen for her part, she would not purchase the Kingdom with the death of the meanest man of the common people, much less of the Queen that there were many which attempted dangerous designs without her knowledge; and by a very late letter, which she had received pardon was asked of her by some if they should enterprise anything without her privities that it was an easy matter to counterfeit the ciphers and characters of others, as a young man did very lately in France, which had vaunted himself to be her son's base brother that she feared also lest this were done now by Walsingham to bring her to her death, who (as she heard) had practiced against her life and her son's. She protested that she not so much as thought the destruction of the Queen; that she had rather most gladly spend her own life, than for her sake the Catholics should be so afflicted in hatred of her, and drawn to cruel death. And withal she shed plenty of tears.

But (said the lord treasurer) no man which has showed himself a good subject, was ever put to death for religion; but some have been for treason, while they maintained the Pope's bull and authority against the Queen.

Yet I (said she) have heard otherwise, and have read it also in books set forth in print.

The authors (replied he) of such books, do write also that the Queen has forfeited her royal dignity.

Walsingham, who had found himself taxed even now by her words, took opportunity, and rising up, protested that his mind was free from all malice. I call God (said he) to record that as a private person I have done nothing unbecoming an honest man; nor as I bear the place of a public person, have I done anything unworthy my place. I confess, that being very careful for the safety of the Queen and realm, I have curiously searched out the practices against the same. If Ballard had offered me his help, I should not have refused it; yea, I would have recompensed the pains he had taken. If I have practiced anything with him, why did he not utter it to save his life?

With this answer, she said she was satisfied: she prayed him he would not be angry that she had spoken freely what she had heard reported; and that he would give no more credit to those that slandered her than she did to such who accused him that spies were men of doubtful credit, which dissemble one thing, and speak another; and that he would in no sort believe that she had consented to the Queen's destruction. And now again, she burst forth into tears; I would never (said she) make shipwreck of my soul, by conspiring the destruction of my dearest sister.

It was answered by the lawyers that this should soon be disproved by testimony. Thus far in the forenoon.

In the afternoon, to disprove this, was produced the copy of a letter which Charles Paget had written; and Curie, one of her secretaries, had witnessed that she had received; touching a conference between Mendoza and Ballard about the design for invading of England, and setting her at liberty.

This (answered she) was nothing to the purpose, and proved not that she had consented to the destruction of the Queen.

The lawyers proceeded further to prove that she was both privy to the conspiracy, and conspired also the destruction of the Queen by Babington's confession, and letters also that had passed between her and him wherein he called her his most dread and sovereign lady and Queen and by the way, they mentioned that a plot was said for conveying the Kingdom of England to the Spaniard she confessed that a priest came to her and said that if she would not intermeddle, she and her son both should be excluded from the inheritance, but the priest's name she would not tell. She added, that the

Spaniard did lay claim to the Kingdom of England and would not give place to any but to her.

Then pressed they her with the testimonies of her secretaries Naw and Curie, out of Babington's confession, and the letters sent to and fro between her and Babington, and the whole credit of their proofs rested upon their testimony; yet were not they produced before her face to face. Curie she acknowledged an honest man, but not a meet witness to be against her. As for Naw, he had been sometimes a secretary (said she) to the Cardinal of Lorain, and commended to her by the French King, and might easily be drawn either by reward, or hope, or fear, to bear false witness, as one that had sundry times rashly bound himself by oath, and had Curie so pliable to him that at his beck he would write what he bade him. It might be that these two might insert into her letters, such things as she had not dictated to them. It might be also that such letters came to their hands, which notwithstanding she never saw; and so she broke forth into such words as these, the majesty and safety of all princes falls to the ground, if they depend upon the writings and testimony of secretaries I delivered nothing to them but what nature delivered to me, that I might at length recover my liberty, and I am not to be convicted but by mine own word or writing. If they have written anything which may be hurtful to the Queen my sister, they have written all altogether without my knowledge; and let them bear the punishment of their inconsiderate boldness. Sure I am, if they were here present, they would clear me of all blame in this cause. And I, if my notes were at hand, could answer particularly to these things.

Amongst these speeches, the lord treasurer objected to her that she had purposed to send her son into Spain, and to convey her title she claimed in the Kingdom of England, to the Spaniard.

To whom she answered, that she had no Kingdom which she could convey, yet was it lawful for her to give those things which were hers, at her pleasure, and not to be accountable for the same to any.

When her alphabets of ciphers sent over to Babington, the Lord Lodouic and Fernihurst, were objected to her out of Curie's testimony; she denied not, but she had written out many; and amongst others, that for the Lord Lodouic when she had commended him and another to the dignity of a cardinal; and that without offence, (she trusted) for that it was as lawful for her to have intercourse of letters, and to negotiate her matters with men of her religion, as for the Queen with the professors of another religion.

Then pressed they her hard with the consenting testimonies of Naw and Curie reiterated, and she reiterated her answers, or else repelled their testimonies by a flat denial; protesting again, that she neither knew Babington nor Ballard.

Amongst these speeches, when the lord treasurer had mentioned that she knew Morgan well, which had sent Parry with privy to murder the Queen, and that she had assigned him a yearly pension. That she knew not whether Morgan had done so, but she knew that Morgan had lost all for her sake, and therefore it concerned her in honor to relieve him; and she was not bound to revenge an injury done the Queen by a friend, that had deserved well at her hands; yet had she terrified the man from such wicked attempts, but contrariwise (said she) pensions have been assigned out of England to Patrick Gray, and to the Scots my adversaries, as also to my son.

The lord treasurer answered, when the revenues of Scotland were by the negligence of the regents much diminished, the Queen bestowed somewhat in bounty upon your son the King, her near kinsman.

Afterwards were produced the chief points of certain letters sent to England, and the Lord Paget and to Bernardino de Mendoza about foreign aid. But when she had answered that these things made not to the destruction of the Queen; and if foreigners labored to set her at liberty, it was not to be laid to her charge; and that she had sundry times openly signified to the Queen, that she would seek her own liberty, the matter was prorogued till the next day following.

The next day she returned her former protestation, and required to have it recorded and a copy thereof delivered to her lamenting that the most reasonable conditions, which she had many times propounded to the Queen, were always rejected, even when she promised to deliver her son and the Duke of Guise's son for hostages that the Queen or Kingdom of England should receive no detriment by her so as she saw herself already quite barred from all hope of her liberty. But now she was most unworthily dealt withal whose honor and reputation was called in question before foreign lawyers, which by wretched conclusions drew every circumstance into a consequence, whereas princes anointed and consecrate are not subject to the same laws that private men are. Moreover, whereas authority was granted to the commissioners to examine matters tending to the hurt of the Queen's person; yet was the cause so handled, and letters wrested that the religion which she professed, the immunity and majesty of foreign princes and the private intercourse betwixt princes were called in question, and she herself made to descend beneath her royal dignity, and to appear as a party guilty before a tribunal seat and all to no other purpose but that she might be quite excluded out of the Queen's favor, and her own right to the succession whereas she appeared voluntarily to clear herself of the matters objected against her, lest she might seem to have neglected the defense of her own honor and innocence. She called also to remembrance how Queen Elizabeth herself had been drawn in question about Wyatt's conspiracy, whereas notwithstanding she was most innocent, religiously affirming that though she wished the safety of the Catholics might be provided for; yet would she not that it should be effected with the death and blood of any one. For her part, she had rather play Hester than Judith; make intercession to God for the people, than deprive the meanest of the people of life. She expostulated, that her enemies had divulged abroad that she was irreligious; but the time was (said she) when I would have been instructed in the Protestant religion, but they would not suffer me to be so, as if they cared not what became of my soul. And now concluding, when ye have done all ye can (said she) against me, and have excluded me from my right, you may chance fail of your cause and hope. And withal making her appeal to God and to the princes her kinsmen, and renewing her Protestation, she prayed that there might be another meeting about this matter, and that an advocate might be granted to her to plead her cause; and that seeing she was a princess, she might be believed in the word of a princess for it were extreme folly to stand to their judgment, whom she saw most plainly to be armed with prejudice against her.

To these things the lord treasurer said, whereas I bear a double person, one of a commissioner, another of a counselor, receive first a few words from me as a commissioner. Your protestation is recorded, and a copy thereof shall be delivered to you. To us our authority is granted under the Queen's hand, and the great seal of England, from which there is no appeal; neither do we come with prejudice, but to judge according to the exact rule of justice. The Queen's learned counsel do level at nothing else but that the truth may come to light, how far you have offended against the Queen's person. To us full power is given to hear and examine the matter, even in your absence; yet were we desirous you should be present, lest we might seem to have derogated from your honor, we purposed not to object anything to you, but what you were privy to, or have attempted against the Queen's person. The letters have been read to no other purpose, but to discover your offence against the Queen's person, and the matters to it belonging, which are so interlaced with other matters, that they cannot be severed. The whole letters therefore, and not parcels picked out here and there have been openly read for that the circumstances do give assurance, what matters you dealt with Babington about.

She interrupting him, said the circumstances may be proved, but never the fact her integrity depended not upon the credit and memory of her secretaries, though she knew them to be honest and sincere men. Yet if they have confessed anything out of fear of torments, or hope of reward and impunity, it was not to be admitted, for just causes, which she would allege elsewhere. Men's minds (said she) are diversely carried about with affections and they would never have confessed such matters against her, but for their own advantage and hope. Letters may be directed to others, than those to whom they are written and many things have been often inserted which she never dictated. If her papers had not been taken away, and she had her secretary, she could better confute the things objected against her.

But nothing (said the lord treasurer) shall be objected, but since the 19th day of June; neither will your papers avail you, seeing your secretaries and Babington himself being never put to the rack, have affirmed that you sent those letters to Babington which though you deny, yet whether more credit is to be given to an affirmation than to a negation, let the commissioners judge. But to return to the matter; this which follows, I tell you as a counselor many things you have propounded time after time concerning your liberty; that they have failed of success, it is long of you, or of the Scots, and not of the Queen. For the lords of Scotland flatly refused to deliver the King in hostage. And when the last treaty was held concerning your liberty, Parry was sent privately by Morgan a dependant of yours to murder the Queen.

Ah (said she) you are my adversary. Yea (said he) I am adversary to Queen Elizabeth's adversaries. But hereof enough, let us now proceed to proofs. Which when she refused to hear; yet we (said she) will hear them and I also (said she) will hear them in another place, and defend myself.

Now were read again her letters to Charles Paget, wherein she showed him that there was no other way for the Spaniard to reduce the Netherlands to obedience, but by setting up a prince in England that might be of use to him; and to the Lord Paget to hasten his auxiliary forces to invade England, and Cardinal Allen's letter, wherein he called her his most dread sovereign lady, and signified that the matter was commended to the Prince of Parma's care.

As these letters were in reading, she interposed these speeches; that Babington and her secretaries had accused her to excuse themselves; that she never heard of the six executioners, and that the rest made nothing to the purpose. As for Allen, she held him for a reverend prelate, and she acknowledged no other head of the church, but the Bishop of Rome. In what rank and place she was esteemed by him and foreign princes, she knew not; neither could she hinder it, if in their letters they called her Queen of England. As for her secretaries, seeing they had done contrary to their duty and allegiance sworn to her, they deserved no credit. They which have once forsworn themselves though they swear again with never so great oaths and protestations, are not to be credited. Neither did these men think themselves bounden by any oath whatsoever in court of conscience, forasmuch as they had sworn their fidelity and secrecy to her before, and were no subjects of England. That Naw had many times written otherwise than she had dictated to him, and Curie wrote whatsoever Naw bade him. But for her part she was willing to bear the burden of their fault in all things, but what might lay a blot upon her honor. And haply also they confessed these things to save themselves; supposing that they could not hurt her by confessing, who they thought should be more favorably dealt withal as being a Queen. As for Bollard, she never heard of any such, but of one Hallard, which had offered her his help; which notwithstanding, she had refused, for that she had heard that the same man had also vowed his service to Walsingham.

Afterwards were read certain brief notes of her letters to Mendoza, which Curie had confessed he had written in privy cipher.

I find myself greatly troubled what course to take a new, for the affairs on this side the sea. Charles Paget has a charge from me to impart to you certain overtures in my behalf; whereupon I pray you deliver him freely, what you think may be obtained thereof from the King your master.

There is another point depending thereof, which I have reserved to write to your own self, for to be by you sent to the King your master on my behalf, no man else, if it be possible, being privy thereto; that is, that considering my son's great obstinacy in heresy and foreseeing hereupon the imminent danger and harm like to ensue to the Catholic church, he coming to the succession of this realm, I have resolved with myself in case my said son do not reduce himself before my death to the Catholic religion, (as I must tell you plainly, I have small hope so long as he shall remain in Scotland) to give and grant my right to the said King your master in the succession of this crown, by my last will and testament; praying him in consideration hereof from this time forward to take me wholly into his protection, likewise the state and affairs of this country the which for discharge of my conscience, I cannot think I can put into the hands of a prince more zealous of our religion and able in all respects to reestablish the same on this side, as it imports all the rest of Christendom. Let this be kept secret, forasmuch as if it come to be revealed, it should be in France the loss of my dower in Scotland a clear breach with my son, and in this country my total ruin and destruction.

Thank on my behalf the said King your master, for the favor and liberality extended to the Lord Paget and his brother, which I pray him most earnestly to continue, and to gratify for my sake with some pension poor Morgan, who has so much endured not only for me, but for the common cause.

I recommend likewise to you Fulsambe (whom you know) to help him to some supply, above the entertainment that I have allotted him, according to the small means I have.

Out of these she was pressed as if she had purposed to convey her right in the Kingdom to the Spaniard and that Allen and Parsons lay now at Rome for that cause. She complaining that her secretaries had broken their allegiance bound by oath, answered, when being prisoner I languished in cares without hope of liberty, and was without all hope to effect those things which very many expected at my hands, declining now through age and sickness, it seemed good to some, that the succession of the crown of England should be established in the Spaniard, or some English Catholic. And a book was sent to me to avow the Spaniards title; which when it was not allowed by me, I incurred displeasure among some: but now all my hope in England being desperate, I am fully resolved not to reject foreign aid.

The solicitor put the commissioners in mind what would become of them, their honors, estates and posterities if the Kingdom were so conveyed. But the lord treasurer showed that the Kingdom of England could not be conveyed, but was to descend by right of succession according to the laws; and asked her, if she would any more.

She required that she might be heard in a full Parliament, or that she might in person speak with the Queen, who would (she hoped) have regard of a Queen and with the council. And now rising up with great confidence of countenance, she had some conference with the Lord Treasurer Hatton, Walsingham, and the Earl of Warwick by themselves apart.

These things being done, the assembly was prorogued to the 25th of October at the Star Chamber at Westminster. Thus far touching this matter out of the commentaries of Edward Barker; Principal Register to the

Queen's majesty; Thomas Wheeler Pubic Notary, Register of the Audience of Canterbury; and other credible persons which were present.

The said 25th day of October, all the commissioners met saving the Earls of Shrewsbury and Warwick, which were both of them sick at that time and after Naw and Curie had by oath, *viva voce*, voluntarily without hope of reward, before them avowedly affirmed and confirmed all and every the letters, and copies of letters, before produced to be most true; sentence was pronounced against the Queen of Scots and confirmed with the seals and subscriptions of the commissioners and recorded in these words; by their joint assent and consent they do pronounce and deliver their sentence and judgment at the day and place last recited; and say, that after the end of the aforesaid session of Parliament, in the commission aforesaid specified, namely master the aforesaid 1st day of June, in the 27th year above said, and before the date of the same commission, divers matters have been compassed and imagined within this realm of England, by Anthony Babington and others, *cum scientia*, in English, with the privacy of the said Mary, pretending title to the crown of this realm of England, tending to the hurt, death and destruction of the royal person of our said lady the Queen. And namely that after the aforesaid 1st day of June in the 27th year above said, and before the date of the commission aforesaid, the aforesaid Mary pretending title to the crown of this realm of England, has compassed and imagined within this realm of England, divers matters tending to the hurt, death and destruction of the royal person of our sovereign lady the Queen, contrary to the form of the statute in the commission aforesaid specified.

Concerning this sentence which depended wholly upon the credit of the secretaries and they not brought forth face to face, according to the first act of the 13th year of Queen Elizabeth, much talk there was, and divers speeches ran abroad; while some thought them credible persons and some unworthy to be credited. I have seen Naw's apology to King James, written in the year 1605, wherein laboriously protesting, he excused himself, that he was neither author nor persuader, nor the first revealer of the plot that was undertaken, nor failed of his duty through negligence, or want of foresight; yea, that this day he stoutly impugned the chief points of accusation against his lady and mistress which notwithstanding appears not by records. But the same day was there a declaration made by the commissioners and judges of the land, that the said sentence did derogate nothing from James King of Scots, in title or honor, but that he was in the same place, degree and right, as if the same sentence had never been pronounced.

Some few days after, a Parliament was held at Westminster, begun by virtue of a certain power of vice-gerency, granted by the Queen to the Archbishop of Canterbury, the lord treasurer, and the Earl of Derby and that not without precedent in which Parliament the proscription of the Lord Paget, Charles Paget, Sir Francis Englefield, Francis Throckmorton, Anthony Babington, Thomas Salisbury, Edward Jones, Chidiock Titchbourne, Charles Tilney, and the rest of the conspirators, was confirmed and their goods and possessions confiscated. The estates also of the realm, which had by their voices approved and confirmed the sentence given against the Queen of Scots, did with joint assent put up a supplication to the Queen by the hands of the Lord Chancellor, as follows:

May it please your most excellent majesty, our most gracious sovereign, we your humble, loving and faithful subjects, the lords and commons in this present Parliament assembled having of long time to our intolerable grief excellent majesty the universal state of your whole seen by how manifold most dangerous and execrable practices, Mary the daughter and heir of James V. late King of Scots, dowager of France, and commonly called Queen of Scots, has come passed the destruction of your majesty's sacred and most royal person, in whose safety (next under God) our chief and only felicity doth consist; and thereby not only to bereave us of the sincere and true religion of almighty God, bringing us and this noble crown back again into the thralldom of the Roman tyranny, but also utterly to ruin and overthrow the happy state and commonweal of this most noble realm; which being from time to time by the great mercy and providence of God, and your highness's singular wisdom, foreseen and prevented, your majesty of your exceeding great clemency and princely magnanimity has either most graciously passed over, or with singular favor tolerated, although often and instantly moved by your most loving and faithful subjects to the contrary, in times of your Parliaments, and at many other times; and has also protected and defended the said Scottish Queen from those great dangers which her own people, for certain detestable crimes and offences to her imputed, had determined against her. All which notwithstanding, the same Queen was nothing moved with these and many other your majesty's most gracious favors towards her, but rather obdurate in malice, and by hope of continual impunity emboldened to prosecute her cruel and mischievous determination by some speedy and violent course and now lately a very dangerous plot being conceived and set down by Anthony Babington and others, that six desperate and wicked persons would undertake that wicked and most horrible enterprise to take away your majesty's life, whom God of his infinite mercy long preserves me did not only give her advice and direction upon every point, and all circumstances concerning the same, make earnest request to have it performed with all diligence, but did also promise assurance of large reward and recompense to the doers thereof which being informed to your majesty, it pleased your highness, upon the earnest suit of such as tendered the safety of your royal person and the good and quiet state of this realm to direct your commission under the great seal of England to the lords and others of your highness's Privy Council, and certain other lords of Parliament of the greatest and most ancient degree, with some of your principal judges, to examine, hear and determine the same cause, and thereupon to give sentence or judgment according to a statute in that behalf, made in the 27th year of your most gracious reign by virtue whereof, the more part of the same commissioners, being in number thirty six, having at sundry times fully heard what was alleged and proved against the said Scottish Queen in her own presence, touching the said crimes and offences, and what she could say for her defense and excuse therein, did after long deliberation give their sentence and judgment with one consent, that the death and destruction of your royal person was imagined and compassed by the said Anthony Babington with the privy of the same Scottish Queen and that she herself did also compass and imagine the death and destruction of your most royal person. Now for as much as we your majesty's most humble, loyal and faithful subjects, representing to your most excellent majesty the universal state of your people of all degrees in this your realm, do well perceive, and are fully satisfied, that the same sentence and judgment is in all things most honorable, just and lawful; and having carefully and effectually, according to our most bounden duties, weighed and considered upon what ground and cause so many traitorous complots, and dangerous practices against your most royal person and estate and for the invading of this realm, have for the space of many years past grown and proceeded, do certainly find, and are undoubtedly persuaded that all the same have been from time to time attempted and practiced by and from the Scottish Queen, and by her confederates, ministers and favorers, who conceive an assured hope to achieve speedily by your majesty's untimely death that which they have long expected, and whereof during your life (which God long preserve to our inestimable comfort) they despair; to wit, to place her the said Scottish Queen in the imperial and Kingly seat of this realm, and by her to banish and destroy the professors and professing of the true religion of Jesus Christ, and the ancient nobility of this land, and to bring this whole state and commonweal to foreign subjection, and utter ruin and confusion which their malicious and traitorous purpose they will never cease to prosecute by all possible means they can, so long as they may have their eyes and imaginations fixed upon that lady, the only ground of their treasonable hope and conceits, and the only seed plot of all dangerous and traitorous devices and practices against your sacred person. And seeing also what insolent boldness is grown in the heart of the same Queen, through your majesty's former exceeding favors and clemencies towards her; and thereupon weighing with heavy and sorrowful hearts, in what continual peril of such like desperate conspiracies and practices your majesty's most royal and sacred person and life (more dear to us than our own) is and shall be still without any possible means to prevent it, so long as the said Scottish Queen shall be suffered to continue and shall not receive that due punishment which by justice, and the laws of this your realm, she has so often and so many ways for her most wicked and detestable offences deserved, therefore, and for that we find, that if the said lady should now escape the due and deserved punishment of death for these her most execrable treasons and offences, your highness's royal person shall be exposed to many more and those more secret and dangerous conspiracies than before, and such as shall not or cannot before foreseen or discovered, as these her late attempts have been; and shall not hereafter be so well able to remove or take away the ground and occasion of the same, as now by justice may or ought to be done, we do most humbly beseech your most excellent majesty, that as well in respect of the continuance of the true religion now professed amongst us and of the safety of your most royal person and estate, as in regard of the preservation and defense of us your most loving, dutiful and faithful subjects, and the whole commonweal of this realm it may please your highness to take speedy order, that declaration of the same sentence and judgment be made and published by proclamation, and that thereupon direction be given for further proceedings against the said Scottish Queen according to the effect and true meaning of the said statute, because upon advised and great consultation, we cannot find that there is any possible means to provide for your majesty's safety, but by the just and speedy execution of the said Queen, the neglecting whereof may procure the heavy displeasure and punishment of almighty God, as by sundry severe examples of his great justice in that behalf left us in the sacred scriptures does appear. And if the same be not put in present execution, we your most loving and dutiful subjects shall thereby (so far as man's reason can reach) be brought into utter despair of the continuance amongst us of the true religion of almighty God, and of your majesty's life, and the safety of all your faithful subjects, and the good estate of this most flourishing commonweal.

The Queen with great majesty of countenance and voice, answered to this purpose. So many and so great are the bottomless graces, and immeasurable benefits bestowed upon me by the almighty, that I must not only most humbly acknowledge them as benefits, but admire them as miracles, being in no sort able to express them. And though there lived not any that may more justly acknowledge himself bound to God than I, whose life he has miraculously preserved from so many dangers, yet am I not more deeply bound to give him thanks for any one thing than for this which I will now tell you, and which I account as a miracle, namely, that as I came to the crown with the most hearty goodwill of all my subjects, so now after 28 years reign, I perceive in them the same, if not greater goodwill towards me; which if I once lose, well might I breathe, but never think I lived. And now though my life has been dangerously shot at, yet I protest there is nothing has more grieved me, than that one not differing from me in sex, of like rank and degree, of the same stock, and most nearly allied to me in blood, has fallen into so great a crime. And so far have I been from bearing her any ill will, that upon the discovery of certain treasonable practices against me, I wrote to her secretly that if she would confess them by a private letter to myself, they should be wrapped up in silence. Neither did I write thus in mind to entrap her, for I knew then as much as she could confess. And even yet, though the matter be come thus far, if she would truly repent and no man would undertake her cause against me, and if my life alone depended hereupon, and not the safety and welfare of my whole people, I would (I protest unfeigned) most willingly pardon her. Nay if England might by my death attain a more flourishing estate, and a better prince, I would most gladly lay down my life, for your sake it is, and for my people's, that I desire to live. As for me, I see no such great cause why I should either be fond to live, or fear to die. I have had good experience of this world, and I know what it is to be a subject, and what to be a sovereign. Good neighbors I have had, and I have met with bad; and in trust I have found treason. I have bestowed benefits upon ill deservers; and where I have done well, have been ill requited.

While I call to mind these things past, behold things present, and expect things to come; I hold them happiest that go hence soonest. Nevertheless against such mischief's as these, I put on a better courage than is common to my sex, so as whatsoever befall me, death shall not take me unprepared; and as touching these treasons; I will not so prejudice myself, or the laws of my Kingdom; as not but to think that she having been the contriver of the same treasons, was bound and liable to the ancient laws, though the late act had never been made; which notwithstanding was no ways made to prejudice her. So far was it from being made to entrap her that it was rather intended to forewarn and terrify her from attempting anything against it. But seeing it was now in force of law, I thought good to proceed against her according to the same. But your lawyers are so curious in scanning the nice points of the law, and following of precedents and form, rather than expounding the laws themselves, that by exact observing of your form, she must have been indicted in Staffordshire, and have held up her hand at the bar, and have been tried by a jury of twelve men. A proper course forsooth of trial against a princess! To avoid therefore such absurdities, I thought it better to refer the examination of so weighty a cause, to a good number of the noblest personages of the land, and the judges of the realm and all little enough. For we princes are set as it were upon stages, in the sight and view of all the world. The least spot is soon spied our garments, a blemish quickly noted in our doings. It behooves us therefore to be careful that our proceedings be just and honorable. But I must tell you one thing, that by this last act of Parliament you have brought me to a narrow straight, that I must give order for her death, which is a princess most nearly allied to me in blood, and whose practices against me have stricken me into so great grief, that I have been glad to absent myself from this Parliament, lest I should increase my sorrow by hearing it spoken of, and not out of fear of any danger, as some think. But yet I will now tell you a secret (though it is well known that I have the property to keep counsel) it is not long since these eyes of mine saw and read an oath, wherein some bound themselves so kill me within a month, hereby I see your danger in me, which I will be very careful to avoid.

Your association for my safety I have not forgotten, which I never so much as thought of till a great number of hands, with many obligations, were showed me; which as I do acknowledge as a strong argument of your true hearts, and great zeal to my safety, so shall my bond be stronger tied to a greater care for your good. But forasmuch as this matter now in hand is very rare, and of greatest consequence, I hope you do not look for any present resolution, for my manner is, in matters of less moment than this to deliberate long upon that which is once to be resolved. In the mean time I beseech almighty God to illuminate my mind that I may foresee that which may serve for the good of his church, the prosperity of the commonwealth, and your safety. And that delay may not breed danger we will signify our resolution with all convenience. And whatever the best subjects may expect at the hands of the best princes that expect from me to be performed to the full.

The twelfth day after, when she had thoroughly weighed the matter in her mind, being distracted with doubtful care and thought, and as it were in some conflict with herself what to do in so important a business, she sent the lord chancellor to the higher house, and Puckering to the rest in the lower house; praying them to enter into a new consideration upon so weighty a matter, and to devise some better remedy, whereby both the Queen of Scots life might be soared, and her own security provided for.

After much and long deliberation, they judging that both the welfare and hurt of the prince belongs to all, concurred again with one voice in the same opinion, and that for these causes; for that the Queen's safety could not be secured as long as the Queen of Scots lived unless the either seriously repented and acknowledged her offence, or were kept with a more straight guard, good assurance being given by bond and oath for her good demeanor, or delivered hostages, or else departed the realm. As for her repentance, they were out of all hope of it, considering that she had ill requited the Queen which had saved her life, and did not yet acknowledge her fault. As for a sorer guard, straighter custody, bonds, oath, and hostages, they held them all as nothing, for that the Queen's life being once taken away, these would presently vanish. And if she should depart the realm, they feared lest they would presently take arms to invade the same.

These reasons the lord chancellor, and Puckering, Speaker of the Lower House, opened more at large, in the manner following:

Unless execution of this just sentence be done,

I. Your majesty's person cannot any while be safe.

II. The religion cannot long continue among us.

III. The most flourishing present state of this realm must shortly receive a woeful fall.

IV. And consequently, in sparing her, your majesty shall not only give courage and hardiness to the enemies of God, of your majesty's self and of your Kingdom, but shall discomfort and daunt with despair the hearts of your loving people; and so deservedly provoke the heavy hand and wrath of God.

And that summarily for the reasons ensuing:

I. For as much as concerns the danger of your majesty; both she and her favorers think she has right, not the succeed, but to enjoy your crown in possession; and therefore as she is a most impatient competitor, (acquainted with blood) so will she not spare any means that may take you from us, being the only Lett, that she enjoys not her desire.

She is hardened in malice against your royal person, notwithstanding that you have done her all favor, mercy and kindness; as well in preserving her Kingdom, as saving her life and honor.

And therefore there is no place for mercy, where there is no hope of amendment, or that she will desist from most wicked attempts.

The rather, for that her malice appears such as that she makes, as it were, her testament of the same to be executed after her death, and appointed her executors to perform the same.

She affirms it lawful to move invasion, therefore, as of invasion victory may ensue and of victory the death of the vanquished, so does she not obscurely profess it lawful to destroy you.

She holds it not only lawful, but honorable also and meritorious to take your life, &c. being deprived of your crown by her Holy Father, and therefore me will (as she has continually done) seek it by all means whatsoever.

She is greedy of your death, and preferred it before her own life, for in her late direction to some of her accomplices so willed, whatsoever became of her, the tragical execution should be performed on you. There is by so much the more danger to your person since the sentence than before, by how much it behooved them, that would preserve her or advance her, to hasten your death now or never before execution done upon her; as knowing that you, and none else, can give direction for her death, and that by your death the sentence would lose the force of execution, and otherwise they should come too late if they take not the present opportunity to help her.

Her friends hold invasion unprofitable while you live, and therefore in their opinion your death is first and principally to be sought, as the most compendious way to ruin the realm by invasion.

Some of the eldest and wisest Papists set it down for a special good drift to occupy you with conceit, that the preservation of her life is the safety of your own; and therefore you may be assured that they verily think that her life will be your death and destruction.

II. For as much as concerns religion:

It is most perilous to spare her, who has continually breathed the overthrow and suppression of the same being poisoned with Popery from her tender youth, and at her age joining in that false termed holy-league, and ever since and now a professed enemy of the truth.

She rested wholly upon popish hopes to be delivered and advanced, and so devoted and doted in that possession, that she will (as well for satisfaction of others, as feeding her own humor) supplant the gospel, where and when so ever she may. Which evil is so much the greater, and the more to be avoided, as that it slayed the soul, and will spread itself not only over England and Scotland, but also into all parts beyond the seas, where the gospel of God is maintained, the which cannot but be exceedingly weakened, if defection should be in these two most valiant Kingdoms.

III. For as much as concerns the happy estate of this realm:

The Lydian's say, *Unum Regem agnoscunt Lydii, duos autem tolerare nonpofiunt*: so we say, *Unam Reginam Elizabethan agnoscunt Angli, duas autem tolerare nonpoffunt*. And therefore, since she said that she is Queen here, and we neither can nor will acknowledge any other but you to be our Queen; it will follow if she prevail, the will rather make us slaves than take us for her children; and therefore the realm sighed and groaned under fear of such a step mother.

She has already provided us a foster-father and a nurse, the Pope and the King of Spain, into whose hands if it should misshapen us to fall, what can we else look for, but ruin, destruction, and utter extirpation of goods, lands, lives, honor and all?

Whilst she shall live, the enemies of the state will hope and gape after your death. By your death they trust to make invasion profitable for them; which cannot be but the same should be most lamentable for us and therefore it is meet to cut off the head of that hope.

As she has already by her poisoned baits, brought to destruction more noblemen and their houses and a great multitude of subjects during her being here, than she would have done if she had been in possession of her own country and armed in the field against us; so will she still be continually cause of the like spoil to the greater loss and peril of this estate and therefore this realm neither can nor may endure her.

Her secretaries do write and print that we be at our wits end, worlds end, if she over live your majesty; meaning thereby that the end of our world is the beginning of theirs and therefore, take her away and their world will be at an end before it begin.

Since the sparing of her in the 1st year of your reign, popish traitors and recusants have multiplied exceedingly, and if you spare her now again, they will grow both innumerable and invincible also.

IV. And therefore now in the fourth place mercy in this case would in the end prove cruelty against all. *Nam est quedam crudelis Mijericordia.* And therefore to spare her is to spill us.

She is only a cousin to you in a remote degree, but we be the sons and children of this land; whereof you be not only the natural mother, but also the wedded spouse. And therefore much more is due from you to us all, than alone to her. It would exceedingly grieve and wound the hearts of your loving subjects, if they should see so horrible vice not condignly punished. If any be wavering, it will win them to the worse part and many will seek to make their own peace. Wherefore as well for the comfort of the one as stay of the other and retaining of all, it is most needful that justice be done upon her.

Thousands of your loving subjects of all degrees, which have for special zeal of your safety made oath before God, to pursue to death by all forcible and possible means, such as she is, by just sentence, found to be cannot save their oaths if you keep her alive for then either we must take her life from her without direction which will be to our extreme danger by the offence of your law, or else we must suffer her to live against our express oath which will be to the uttermost peril of our own souls; wherewith no act of Parliament, nor power of man whatsoever, can in any wise dispense. And therefore, seeing it rest in you by a most worthy and just execution of this sentence to keep us upright and free us in both, we most humbly and earnestly beseech you that speedy justice be done upon her, whereby yourself maybe safe, the state of your realm preserved, and we not only delivered from this trouble of conscience but also reconfirmed to venture ourselves and all ours, into whatsoever other peril for the preservation and safety of you.

Lastly, God's vengeance against Saul for sparing Agag against Ahab for sparing the life of Benbadad is apparent; for they were both by the just judgment of God deprived of their Kingdom for sparing those wicked princes whom God had delivered into their hands of purpose to be put to death by them as by the ministers of his eternal and divine justice.

How much those magistrates were commended, that put to death those mischievous and wicked Queens, Jezebel and Anthelia!

How wisely proceeded Solomon to punishment, in putting to death his own natural and elder brother Adonis for the only intention of a marriage which gave suspicion of treason! Whereas there is no more desired of your majesty than the very Pope, (now your sworn enemy) some of these late conspirators and this wicked lady herself have thought fitting to fall upon her. He in like case gave sentence, *Vita Conradini, mors Carolo; mors Conradini, vita Carolo*. They in their best minds and remorse of conscience setting down the best means of your safety, said he that has no arms cannot fight and be that has no legs cannot run away, but be that hath no head can do no harm. *Pisces primum a capite fatent.* She by her voluntary subscribing to the late association, &c. gave this sentence against herself.

And after in her letters of these treasons to Babington, wrote that if she were discovered, it would give sufficient cause to you to keep her in continual close prison. By which words she could mean nothing else but pains of death.

Therefore we seeing on the one side how you have to the offence of mighty princes advanced religion, with what tender care, and more than motherly piety you have always cherished us the children of this land with what honor and renown you have restored the ancient rights of the crown, with what peace and justice you have governed and with what store and plenty you have reigned over us.

On the other side, seeing that this enemy of our felicity seeks to undermine our religion, to supplant us, and plant strangers in the place, to transfer the rights of the crown to that Italian priest, and the crown to herself, or to some other, from you; and therefore lies in continual wait for to take away your life.

Therefore we pray you, for the cause of God, his church, this realm, ourselves and yourself; that you will no longer be careless of your life, or sovereign safety; nor longer suffer religion to be threatened, the realm to stand in danger, nor us to dwell in fear, but as justice has given rightful sentence, so you will grant execution that as her life threaten your death, so her death may, by God's favor prolong your life; and that this evil being taken away from the earth, we may praise God for our deliverance and pray him for our continuance and with the psalmist say, *Domi ms fecit Judicium*, and, the ungodly is trapped in the works of her own hand.

And so pray God to incline your heart to our just desires, &c.

They concluded that as it were injustice to deny execution of law to any one of her subjects that should demand it, so much more to her whole people of England with one voice and mind making humble and instant suit for the same. The Queen then spoke in this manner:

Full grievous is that way, whose going on, and end yield nothing but cumber for the hire of a laborious journey. I have this day been in greater conflict with myself, than ever in all my life, whether I should speak, or hold my peace. If I speak, and not complain, I shall dissemble. And if I should be silent, your labor taken were all in vain. If I should complain, it might seem strange and rare; yet I confess that my most hear to desire was that some other means might have been devised to work your security and my safety, than this which is now propounded. So as I can not but complain, though not of you, yet to you; that I perceive by your petitions, that my safety depends wholly upon the death of another. If there be any that think I have prolonged the time purpose to make a counterfeit show of clemency, they do me the most undeserved wrong, as he knows, which is the searcher of the most secret thoughts of the heart. Or if there be any that be persuaded that the commissioners durst not pronounce other sentence, as fearing thereby to displease me, or to seem to fail of their care for my safety, they but heap upon me most injurious conceits. For either those whom I have put in trust, have failed of their duties, or else they signified to the commissioners in my name, that my will and pleasure was that every one should deal freely according to his conscience and what they would not openly declare that they should reveal to me in private. It was of my most favorable mind towards her that I desired some other means might be found out to prevent this mischief. But since now it is resolved that my surety is most desperate without her death, I have a most inward feeling of sorrow, that I, which have in my time pardoned so many rebels, winked at so many treasons or neglected them with silence, must now seem to show cruelty upon so great a princess.

I have since I came to the crown of this realm, seen many defamatory books and pamphlets against me accusing me to be a tyrant, well fare the writers hearts, I believe their meaning was to tell me news; and news indeed it was to me to be branded with the note of tyranny. I would it were as great news to hear of their impiety, but what is it which they will not write now, when they shall hear that I have given consent that the executioner's hands shall be imbrued in the blood of my nearest kinswoman? But so far am I from cruelty, that to save mine own life, I would not offer her violence; neither have I been so careful how to prolong mine own life, as how to preserve both which that it is now impossible, I grieve exceedingly. I am not so void of judgment as not to see mine own perils before mine eyes, nor so mad to sharpen a sword to cut mine own throat; nor so careless as not to provide for the safety of mine own life. But this I consider with myself, that many a man would put his own life in danger to save a princess's life. I do not say, so will I yet have I many times thought upon it. But seeing so many have both written and spoken against me, give me leave, I pray you, to say somewhat in mine own defense, that you may see what manner of woman I am, for whose safety you have passed such careful thoughts; wherein as I do with most thankful heart consider your vigilant care, so am I sure I shall never requite it, had I as many lives as you all.

When first I took the scepter, I was not unmindful of God the giver and therefore began my reign with his service, and the religion I had been both born in, bred in, and I trust shall die in. And though I was not ignorant how many perils I should be beset withal at home for altering religion, and how many great princes abroad of a contrary profession would attempt all hostility against me; yet was I no whit dismayed, knowing that God, whom only I respected, would defend both me and my cause. Hence it is, that so many treacheries and conspiracies have been attempted against me that I rather marvel that I am, than muse that I should not be, were it not that God's holy hand has protected me beyond all expectation. Then to the end I might make of the better progress in the art of swaying the scepter, I entered into long and serious cogitation what things were worthy and fitting for Kings to do and I found it most necessary that they should be abundantly furnished with those special virtues, justice, temperance, prudence, and magnanimity. As for the two latter, I will not boast myself, my sex does not permit it, but for the two former, I dare say, (and that with out ostentation) I never made a difference of persons, where right was one; I never preferred for favor, whom I thought not fit for worth; I never bent my ear to credit a tale that was first told, nor was so rash to corrupt my judgment with prejudice, before I heard the cause. I will not say but many reports might haply be brought me in too much favor of the one side or the other; for we princes cannot hear all ourselves, yet this I dare say boldly, my judgment went ever with the truth according to my understanding. And as full well Alcibiades wished his friend, not to give any answer till he had run over the letters of the alphabet; so have I not used rash and sudden resolutions in anything,

And therefore as touching your counsels and consultations, I acknowledge them to be so careful, provident and profitable for the preservation of my life, and to proceed from minds so sincere and some most devoted, that I shall endeavor myself all I can to give you cause to think your pains not ill-bestowed, and strive to make myself worthy of such subjects.

And now for your petition, I pray you for this present to content yourselves with an answer without answer. Your judgment I condemn not, neither do I mistake your reasons, but pray you to accept my thankfulness, excuse my doubtfulness, and take in good part my answer answerless. If I should say, I would not do what you request, I might say perhaps more than I think and if I should say I would do it, I might plunge myself into peril, whom you labor to preserve; which in your wisdoms and discretions you would not that I should, if you consider the circumstances of place, time, and the manners and conditions of men.

After this, the assembly of the estates was prorogued.

About that time were Lord Buckhurst and Beale sent to the Queen of Scots, to signify to her that sentence was pronounced against her; that the same was approved and confirmed by act of Parliament, as most just and the execution thereof instantly sued for by the estates out of a due regard of justice, security and necessity and therefore to persuade her to acknowledge her offences against God and the Queen, and to expiate them before her death by repentance letting her understand, that as long as she lived, the received religion in England could not subsist. Here as she seemed with a certain unwonted alacrity to triumph, giving God thanks, and rejoicing in her heart that she was held to be an instrument for the re-establishing of religion in this island. And earnestly she prayed that she might have a Catholic priest to direct her conscience, and minister the sacraments to her. A bishop and a dean whom they commended to her for this use, she utterly rejected, and sharply taxed the English nation saying often that the English had many times slaughtered their Kings, no marvel therefore if they now also show their cruelty upon me, that am issued from the blood of their Kings.

The publication of the sentence was stayed a while by the intercession of L'Aubespine the French Ambassador, but in the month of December, through the earnest instance of some courtiers, it was publicly proclaimed all over the city of London, the lord mayor, the aldermen, and principal officers and citizens being present, and afterward throughout the whole realm. In the proclamation the Queen seriously protested that this publication was extorted from her not without exceeding grief of mind, out of a certain necessity, and the most vehement prayers and ostentations of the estates of the realm; though there were, which thought this to proceed of women's cunning, who though they much desire a thing, yet will always seem rather to be constrained to it. Afterwards on February the 1st, a commission passed the great seal for her execution, which was as follows:

Elizabeth, by the grace of God, Queen of England, France and Ireland, &c. to our trusty and well beloved cousins, George Earl of Shrewsbury, Earl Marshal of England; Henry Earl of Kent, Henry Earl of Derby; George Earl of Cumberland; and Henry Earl of Pembroke, greeting, &c. Whereas since the sentence given by you, and others of our council, nobility and judges against the Queen of Scots, by the name of Mary, the daughter of James V. late King of Scots, commonly called the Queen of Scots, and Dowager of France, as to you is well known; all the states in the last Parliament assembled did not only deliberately by great advice, allow and approve the same sentence as just and honorable, but also with all humbleness and earnestness possible, at sundry times require, solicit, and press us to direct such further execution against her person as they did adjudge her to have daily deserved; adding thereto, that the forbearing thereof was, and would be daily certain and undoubted danger, not only to our own life, but also to themselves, their posterity, and the public estate of this realm, as well for the cause of the gospel, and true religion of Christ, as for the peace of the whole realm whereupon we did, although the same were with some delay of time, publish the same sentence by our proclamation, yet hitherto have forborne to give direction for the further satisfaction of the aforesaid most earnest requests made by our said states of our Parliament, whereby we do daily understand, by all sorts of our loving subjects, both of our nobility and council, and also of the wisest, greatest, and best devoted of all subjects of inferior degrees, how greatly and deeply from the bottom of their hearts, they are grieved and afflicted with daily, yea hourly, fears of our life and thereby consequently with a dreadful doubt and expectation of the ruin of the present happy and godly estate of this realm, if we should forbear the further final execution, as it is deserved and neglect their general and continual requests, prayers, counsels and advices. And thereupon contrary to our natural disposition in such case, being overcome with the evident weight of their counsels and their daily intercessions, importing such a necessity as appears directly tending to the safety not only of our self, but also to the weal of our whole realm, we have condescended to suffer justice to take place; and for the execution thereof, upon the special trusty experience and confidence which we have of your loyalties, faithfulness and love, both toward our person and the safety thereof, and also to your native countries, whereof you are most noble and principal members; we do will and by warrant hereof do authorize you as soon as you shall have time convenient, to repair to our Castle of Fotheringay where the said Queen of Scots is in custody of our right trusty and faithful servant and counselor, Sir Amias Powlet Kt. and then taking her into your charge, to cause by your commandment execution to be done upon her person in the presence of yourselves, and the aforesaid Sir Amias Powlet, and of such other officers of justice as you shall command to attend upon you for that purpose; and the same to be done in such manner and form, and at such time and place, and by such persons, as to five, four or three of you, shall be thought by your discretions convenient, notwithstanding any law, statute or ordinance to the contrary. And these our letters patent sealed with our great seal of England, shall be to you and every of you, and to all persons that shall be present, or that shall be by you, commanded to do anything appertaining to the aforesaid execution, a full sufficient warrant and discharge for ever. And further we are also pleased and contented, and hereby we do will command and authorize our chancellor of England, at the requests of you all, and every of you that the duplicate of our letters patent be to all purposes made, dated and sealed with our great seal of England, as these presents now are in witness whereof, we have caused these our letters to be made patent. Given at our manor of Greenwich, the 1st day of February, in the 29th year of our reign.

Queen Elizabeth's letter directed to Sir Amias Powlet Kt. Keeper of the Queen of Scots, at the Castle of Fotheringay.

Amias, my most faithful servant, God reward thee treble fold in the double of thy most troublesome charge so well discharged if you knew, my Amias how kindly, besides dutifully my grateful heart accepts your double labors and faithful actions, your wise orders and safe regards, performed in so dangerous a charge it would ease your travel, and rejoice your heart in that I cannot balance in any weight of my judgment the value that I prize you at, and suppose no treasure to countervail such faith; and shall condemn myself in that thought I never committed, if I reward not such deserts;

yea, let me lack when I most need if I acknowledge not such a merit with a reward, not *omnibus datum*, but let your wicked murderess know how with hearty sorrow her vile deserts compel these orders; and bid her from me, ask God forgiveness for her treacherous dealing against my life many years to the intolerable peril of her own; and yet not content with so many forgiveness's but must fall again so horribly, far passing a woman's thought, much less a princess's; instead of excusing whereof, not one can serve it being so plainly confessed by the author of my guiltless death. Let reperitance take place and let not the fiend possess her so that the better part be lost, which I pray, with hands lifted up to him, that can both save and spill with my most loving adieu and prayer for thy long life, your assured and loving sovereign, as heart, by good desert, endured, Elizabeth Regina.

In pursuance of this commission, she was executed the 8th day of February following in which Queen Elizabeth afterwards pretended she was surprised; the manner whereof is thus related by Camden.

Queen Elizabeth, after some hesitation, having delivered a writing to Davison, one of her secretaries, signed with her own hand commanding a warrant under the great seal of England to be drawn up for the execution, which was to lie in readiness in case of any dangerous attempt upon Queen Elizabeth, commanded him to acquaint no man therewith; the next day the Queen changed her mind and commanded Davison by Killigrew that the warrant should not be drawn. Davison came presently to the Queen and told her that it was drawn and under seal already; at which she was somewhat moved and blamed him for making such haste. He notwithstanding acquainted the council both with the warrant and the whole matter and easily persuaded them, who were apt to believe what they desired that the Queen had commanded it should be executed. Hereupon without any delay, Beale who in respect of religion was the Queen of Scots most bitter adversary was sent down with one or two executioners, and a warrant, wherein authority was given to the Earls of Shrewsbury, Kent, Derby, Cumberland, and others, to see execution done according to law; and this without the Queen's knowledge. And though she at that very time told Davison, that she would take another course, yet did not he for all that call Beale back.

As soon as the earls were come to Fotheringay, they, together with Sir Amias Powlet, and Sir Drue Drury, to whose custody the Queen of Scots was committed, came to her and told her the cause of their coming, reading the warrant and in few words admonished her to prepare herself for death, for she was to die the next day. She undauntedly and with a composed spirit, made this answer: I did not think the Queen, my sister, would have consented to my death, who am not subject to your law and jurisdiction, but seeing her pleasure is so, death shall be to me most welcome; neither is that soul worthy of the high and everlasting joys above, whose body cannot endure one stroke of the executioner.

She desired she might have conference with her almoner, her confessor, and Melvin, the master of her household for her confessor it was flatly denied that he should come at her; and the earls recommended to her the bishop, or the Dean of Peterborough to comfort her; whom she refusing, the Earl of Kent in a hot burning zeal to religion broke forth into these words among other speeches, your life will be the death of our religion as contrariwise your death will be the life thereof. Mention being made of Babington, she constantly denied his conspiracy to have been at all known to her, and the revenge of her wrong she left to God. Then enquiring what was become of Naw and Curie; she asked whether it were ever heard of before, that servants were suborned and accepted as witnesses against their master's life.

When the earls were departed, she commanded supper to be hastened, that she might the better dispose of her concerns. She supped temperately as her manner was; and seeing her servants, both men and women weeping and lamenting as she sat at supper, she comforted them with great courage and magnanimity, had them leave mourning and rather rejoice that she was now to depart out of a world of miseries. Turning to Burgoin her physician, she asked him whether he did not now find the force of truth to be great, they say (quote she) that I must die because I have plotted against the Queen's life, yet the Earl of Kent tells me there is no other cause of my death, but that they are afraid for their religion because of me; neither has my offence against the Queen, but their fear because of me, drawn this end upon me, while some, under the color of religion and the public good, aim at their own private respects and advantages.

Towards the end of supper she drank to all her servants who pledged her in order upon their knees, mingling tears with the wine and begging pardon for their neglect of their duty as she also in like manner did of them.

After supper she perused her will read over the inventory of her goods and jewels, and wrote down the names of those to whom she bequeathed every particular. To some she distributed money with her own hand. To her confessor she wrote a letter, that he would make intercession for her to God in his prayers. She wrote also letters of recommendation for her servants to the French King and the Duke of Guise. At her wonted time she went to bed, slept some hours; and then waking spent the rest of the night in prayer.

The fatal day being come which was the 8th of February, she dressed herself as gorgeously as she was wont to do upon festival days and calling her servants together, commanded her will to be read; prayed them to take their legacies in good part for her ability would not extend to giving them any greater matters.

Then fixing her mind wholly upon God in her oratory or ordinary place of prayer, with sighs and groans and prayers, she begged his divine grace and favor till such time as Thomas Andrews, sheriff of the county, acquainted her that she must now come forth and forth she came with state, countenance and presence majestically composed; a cheerful look, and a matron like and modest habit; her head covered with a linen veil and that hanging down to the ground, her prayer beads hanging at her girdle, and carrying a crucifix of ivory in her hands.

In the porch she was received by the earls and other noblemen where Melvin her servant, falling upon his knees and pouring forth tears, bewailed his hard hap, that he was to carry into Scotland the woeful tidings of the unhappy fate of his lady and mistress, she thus comforted him, lament not but rather rejoice, thou shall by-and-by see Mary Stuart freed from all her cares. Tell them that I die constant in my religion, and firm in my fidelity and affection towards Scotland and France. God forgive them, who have thirsted after my blood as hearts do after the fountain, thou, O God, I who art truth itself and perfectly and truly understand the inward thoughts of my heart, knows how greatly I have desired that the Kingdoms of England and Scotland might be united into one. Commend me to my son and assure him that I have done nothing which may be prejudicial to the Kingdom of Scotland; admonish him to hold in amity and friendship with the Queen of England; and see thou do him faithful service.

And now the tears trickling down, she bid Melvin several times farewell who wept as fast as she. Then turning to the earls, she prayed them that her servants might be civilly dealt withal, that they might enjoy their legacies, that they might stand by her at her death and might be sent back into their own country with letters of safe conduct. The former request they granted, but that they should stand by her at her death, the Earl of Kent showed himself somewhat unwilling fearing some superstition. Fear it not (said she) these harmless souls desire only to take their last farewell of me. I know my sister Elizabeth would not have denied me so small a matter that my women should be then present, were it but for the honor of the female sex. I am her near kinswoman descended from Henry VII. Queen Dowager of France, and anointed Queen of Scots.

When she had said this and turned herself aside, it was at last granted that such of her servants as she should name should be present. She named Melvin, Burgoin her physician, her apothecary, her surgeon, two waiting women, and others of whom Melvin bore up her train. So the gentlemen, two earls and the sheriff going before her, she came to the scaffold which was built at the upper end of the hall on which was placed a chair, a cushion, and a block, all covered with black cloth. As soon as she was set down and silence commanded, Beale read the warrant, she heard it attentively, yet as if her thoughts were taken up with somewhat else. Then Fletcher, Dean of Peterborough began a long speech to her touching the condition of her life past, present, and to come. She interrupted him once or twice as he was speaking, prayed him not to trouble himself protesting that she was firmly fixed and resolved in the ancient Catholic Roman religion and for it was ready to shed her last blood. When he earnestly persuaded her to true repentance and to put her whole trust in Christ by an assured faith; she answered that in that religion she was both born and bred and now ready to die. The earls said they would pray with her, to whom she said that she would give them hearty thanks if they would pray for her; but to join, said she, in prayer with you, who are of another profession would be in me a heinous sin. Then they appointed the dean to pray with whom while the multitude that stood round about were praying, she fell down upon her knees and holding the crucifix before her in her hands prayed in Latin, with her servants out of the office of the blessed virgin Mary.

After the Dean had made an end of praying, she in English recommended the church, her son, and Queen Elizabeth to God, beseeching him to turn away his wrath from this island and professing that she reposed her hope of salvation in the blood of Christ, lifting up the crucifix she called on the celestial choir of saints to make intercession to him for her, she forgave all her enemies and kissing the crucifix and signing herself with the cross, she said as thy arms, O Christ! Were spread out upon the cross, so receive me with the stretched out arms of thy mercy and forgive my sins. Then the executioners asked her forgiveness, which she granted them. And when her women had taken off her upper garments (which she was eager and hasty to have done) wailing and lamenting the while, she kissed them; and signing them with the cross with a cheerful countenance bid them forbear their womanish lamentations, for now she should rest from all her sorrows. In like manner turning to her men-servants, who also wept, she signed them with the cross, and smiling bid them farewell. And now having covered her face with a linen handkerchief, and laying herself down to the block, she recited the psalm, *in thee o' lord! Do I put my trust, let me never confounded.* Then stretching forth her body and repeating many times, into thy hands o' lord! I commend my spirit, her head was taken off at two strokes; the dean crying out so let Queen Elizabeth's enemies perish; the Earl of Kent answering amen and the multitude sighing and sorrowing. Her body was embalmed and ordered with due and usual rites and afterwards interned with a royal funeral in the Cathedral Church of Peterborough. A pompous obsequy was also performed for her at Paris, by procurement of the Guises.

[*A Complete Collection of State Trials.* V1, 143-164]

Sir Richard Knightley

Sir Richard Knightley was born in 1533 to Sir Valentine Knightley and Anne, a well-established branch of the Staffordshire family in Northamptonshire who possessed numerous estates and wealth. History records that Richard had a happy childhood and the family leaned toward the reformed religion, but he later became a rigid Puritan. Richard married Mary in 1556, and together had three sons and three daughters. Through his second marriage to Elizabeth, they had seven sons and two daughters. Richard was knighted in 1566 at Fotheringay. He was appointed sheriff of Northamptonshire several times and was appointed a member of Parliament.

In 1588, Richard was involved with individuals protesting episcopacy by printing material for distribution. The traveling printing press was concealed in his home at Fawsley where several pieces of material were printed. The press was moved to his home at Norton after Christmas and finally confiscated in February 1588, resulting in several arrests, including Richard, but he was eventually released.

The arraignment of Sir Richard Knightly and others in the Star-Chamber for maintaining seditious persons, books and libels: 31 Elizabeth Feb. 31, A.D. 1588.

On Friday, the 13th of February, were brought as prisoners to the bar before the lords in the high court of Star-Chamber, Sir Richard Knightly, Mr. Hales, Sir Wickstone and his wife, whose offences hereafter follow. And first:

Mr. Attorney-General Popham began, that the prosperous and happy state of her majesty was not unknown to them all that were present and so dilated thereon, &c. until two enemies had chosen to disturb this quietness, viz. the Papists abroad, who by foreign arms, &c. and the seditious sectaries at home, whereof there are lewd people; next the Brownists and their fellows, but justice had been done on these men, and the law executed. But there is another sort of sectary that are of no settled state, but seek to transform and subvert all. These men would have government in every several congregations, severally in each province, in every diocese, yea, in every parish; whereupon would ensue more mischief than any man by tongue can utter; they themselves cannot agree among themselves, but are full of envy and emulation; for what greater emulation than to fall to contention, and from contention proceed to violence? But they stay not here, nor contented with railing against the church and the state thereof, but proceed to court and the commonweal, that all things might contribute to preserve unity among the brethren; no law, no order left, all propriety of things taken away and confounded. But of what sort of people are these sectaries? Of the very vilest and basest sort, and these must make confusion of all state, and so advance themselves in their congregations, this their course and this their purpose; so the heel should govern the head, and not the head the heel, if these men be allowed, her majesty in her great wisdom duly considered the great danger of these inconveniences, took order that no pamphlets or treatises should be put in print, but such us should be first seen and allowed; and farther, lest that were not sufficient, she ordained that no printing should be used any where but in London, Oxford, and Cambridge. Notwithstanding all this served not, but they would print in corners, and spread abroad things imprinted; wherefore her majesty set forth a proclamation in anno 25, that all Brownists books, and such other seditious books should be suppressed and burnt. Afterwards, when their new, seditious, and infamous libels were spread abroad, her majesty in February last set forth another proclamation that all her subjects might take warning but because no reformation is had, she now holds it necessary to proceed injustice and therefore these men now prisoners at the bar, but answer to their offences, and receive according to their demerits and first for their faults. Sir Richard Knightly being a great man in his country, a deputy-lieutenant, who had the government thereof, a seditious and lewd rebel came to him to have place and entertainment with him and there Sir Richard received him to print. Sir Richard does confess that Penry told him he would set forth such a like book as he had beforetime set forth for the government of Wales. That book contains sedition and slander most opprobrious; and yet Sir Richard was contented such a like book should be printed.

But farther, Sir Richard sent his man a ring for a token to receive the press into his house, who did so and there they printed the Epitome, Walgrave himself being the printer; this is a most seditious and libelous pamphlet, fit for a vice in a play, and no other but then the parson of the parish having found out the printing, told Sir Richard that it was very dangerous; whereupon Sir Richard caused him to take it down; but neither disliked nor discovered it, but kept it secret, and read the books himself. Again, when it was told him that his house would be searched for the press, he said he would course them that come to search his house; beside, at his recommendation Walgrave was commended to Mr. Hales and there had entertainment, and there 'The Supplication to the Parliament,' was printed by Walgrave and published by Newman, Sir Richard's man; and another book, viz. 'Have you any Work for the Cooper?' was there printed likewise. Therein the sectaries themselves confess that inconvenience would ensue of this government which they so sought to establish; but yet it must be brought in because they were so determined. And from Mr. Hale's house in Coventry, these books and this press must be conveyed to Sir Wickstone's, where Martin senior and Martin junior were both printed; wherein these libelers say that all laws that any way impugn this doctrine of theirs are not to be obeyed in any cause then if this be suffered, confusion and disorder must needs ensue. But farther, in those books they affirm that the time does idler them a great opportunity, as though all things would be suffered in this so troublesome a time, rather than they should any way be disquieted. And for Sir Wickstone, albeit he knew the press was in his house, yet he kept secret and would never discover it, but came many times and did visit there at the press; and his wife by whose procurement and persuasions with her husband, they were first received into his house, did often relieve them with meat and drink and gave them money in their purses. This is the substance and sum of their offence which if they will deny, uncontestable and manifest proofs shall be produced against them. And so he concluded.

Hereupon Sir Richard Knightly began to answer and most humbly besought their lordships to consider of his simple wit, and weak capacity, not able to speak in such a place, and before so honorable an assembly and said that these mishaps which were now so aggravated against them were a punishment imposed by God, to put him in mind of other his grievous crimes committed against the majesty of the most highest. He affirmed constantly that he was no sectary, but of that religion, that self-same religion which he hoped all they which were then present were of, and so he trusted were all other her majesty's loving subjects. And if he should speak anything amiss, he desired them not to impute it to his ill disposition, but to his wants which were many and the more by reason of his late imprisonment and said he was right glad that their honors were ordained by God, and appointed by her majesty to be his judges at whose hands he was sure to receive nothing but justice; wherefore he besought them to be an intercessor and mediator to her majesty in his behalf, against whom, for any offence committed, or against the state to his knowledge, he was as clear as any present and as good a subject as ever came to that bar. He utterly disclaimed the books, and denied to have any familiarity to his knowledge with those that were the writers of them; and showed that the press was brought into his house upon this reason there was a book that before time was printed in Oxford, which to his knowledge was never called in; this book was written by one Mr. Penry, who requested Sir Richard that this book might be printed again in his house, and in respect of the want of learning which he knew to be in the ministry, he did the rather incline an ear to. For although he must needs confess there were in the ministry some good, yet to his thinking for one good, there were forty bad; yea, so bad, as he thought them not worthy to sweep the church; and therefore his zeal for the furtherance of God's glory caused him to allow of this book. This as he said, was about St. James tide was twelve-month and he had heard nothing thereof again until All-Hallow-tide following; and said that the press was never in his own house, but in a house at the further end of the town. And he said at Christmas following Walgrave came to him and desired the press and said that Mr. Cartwright had wrote a book against the Jesuits which he hoped to print. This is the truth, said he. He wrote to Mr. Hales to defend a house for a poor man all this was done before the proclamation, since which time he never meddled therein, as he said; for my Lord Chancellor most honorably gave him warning to look to that, which he had accomplished like a good subject to her majesty to whom he confessed himself most bounden as he thinks all the world is beside; and now had learned of David, not so much as to touch the hem of the lord's anointed. He hoped her majesty will likewise forgive him as she had forgiven greater offences and besought them all to be good to him, and he for his part would say with Moses and Paul that he would rather desire to be wiped out of the book of life than not perform his duty to her majesty. And so he concluded.

Mr. Hales began that albeit it were a great grief to him to be convented before their lordships, yet in this he joyed that they were his judges, that were the governors and judges of the land which could and would do him nothing else but justice; he confessed the blessing of God to be exceeding great to the commonwealth for placing her majesty over the same by whose means we enjoy that peace which other nations want, and were happy that lived under her he disclaimed the hooks; but he had great reason as he thought to gratify Sir Richard Knightly in anything, to whom he owed much reverence, as him that had married his aunt. Sir Richard desired him to lend his house for a poor man, to the which he condescended; but he knew not the man nor his intent; he met with Penry in Coventry, at a sermon, who desired him to direct him to his house, there he had 'The Supplication to the Parliament' that was printed at Oxford; he told him he would print Mr. Cartwright's book 'against the Romish Testament' he was privy that there was a press there, but nothing else. It was an easy matter for a wiser man than himself to be thus overtaken; Penry himself was not indicted nor impeached. And he hoped if a man ignorantly did receive a traitor or Jesuit, that it was not treason, unless himself knew of it.

Attorney. You acknowledge you had a book of him?

Hales. I do.

Attorney. And you came to the maker of it?

Hales. It was before the proclamation.

Attorney. It was after.

Hales. It was after the first, and before the second proclamation. Hereupon was read the first proclamation made in 27 Elizabeth against schismatically and seditious libels, Dr. Brown, and such others.

Hales. But Mr. Penry's was no libel, for he subscribed his name.

Attorney. There is no doubt but it is a libel, though it be subscribed whereto

Hales said nothing. And then was read the Oilier proclamation in 31 Elizabeth. And the order in the Star Chamber made in 28 Elizabeth whereby printing was allowed only in London, Oxford and Cambridge.

Wickstone said he was an ignorant man and craved he might answer by counsel, which might direct him whereto the Lord Chancellor answered, that this was matter of tact which lay most properly within his own knowledge and that he must provide to answer for himself, and that he needed no counsel. Whereupon Wickstone confessed that his wife desired him to permit them a home in his house, which he consented to, knowing the purpose of them, and that was all.

Lady Wickstone confessed that the zeal of reformation in the church caused her to give them entertainment in her house, and she was the cause that they came thither, not thinking that it had been any way hurtful or dangerous to the state; and she humbly besought that what fault so ever she had committed, her husband might not be punished therefore since he was not privy, but only by her means and request.

Hereupon Mr. Puckering the Queen's Sergeant, began to lay open the enormities of those books which they had in court, and diver's clauses of them were read. First, he affirmed they tended to the ruin of the whole state, next to the abolishing of all ecclesiastical government, to the removing of all manner of service, the overthrow of laws; and yet, say they all laws which resist these men are no more to be allowed than those which maintain stews. But Penry will never give that over, he says, though the Spaniards were overthrown and discomfited by famine and by hunger, yet the lord will raise them up again and make a weak and feeble generation to overthrow us. So here was read a great part of the epitome.

Puckering. This is most scornful and seditious; but what is their conclusion? They conclude our Parliament and councils be assembled where no truth bear sway which is most false and scandalous but if this their government be not received, those of the Parliament House nor their seed shall never prosper, nor they ever bear any more rule in England. And I Penry will never leave till either this be performed, or that the Lord in vengeance and blood do plague and punish us. For the other book 'Have you any work for the Cooper?' therein is affirmed that our church government is utterly unlawful. And albeit this form of theirs would be inconvenient in many points, yet every Christian is bound to receive pastors, doctors, elders and deacons. For Martin junior, he affirms, that it is unlawful to have any other government, that all human laws maintaining any Oilier form are ungodly and not to be obeyed that the warrant that bishops have to maintain their authority is no better than that which did maintain the stews; that antichrist is the head of their doctrine, and they part of his body. For Martin senior, he loudly termed the book of common service, the book at Lambeth, that 100,000 hands would sign to their positions and government which they seek. And further, that they are the strength of the land that it were no policy to reject their suit at such a time when the land was invaded.

After which they read Sir Richard's examination wherein he confessed that Penry came to him as before; but when Sharp the minister told him the books were lewd and dangerous, he caused them to be pulled down and that he knew of no book but 'The Epitome.' He sent a ring to his man Jackson by Penry to receive a load of stuff into his house which was the press and other necessaries for printing. Newman the cobbler wore his livery, and Wastal his man helped Walgrave away from his house, to Mr. Hales at Coventry. Fox his schoolmaster and Wastal his man, would commonly read the books in Sir Richard's house, and scoff and scorn at John of Canterbury.

Sharp said that Sir Richard conferred with Walgrave as Newman told him the 'Epitome' was printed there that when it was told Sir Richard his house would be searched, he answered the knaves did not search his house; and if they did, he would have coursed them.

The printer's man said, that the 'Mind All's', were printed there but Sir Richard answered he never knew so much before. 'Have you any work for the Cooper?' went in hand there, but they went away then to Coventry. The printer's man would have submitted himself long before, but Sir Richard advised him not to do so in any case, for the lords were so incensed, as he should be hanged if he were caught. For Hales, 'Have you any work for the Cooper' was printed at his house, he came once to the press as they were printing it. Mrs. Wickstone confessed Martin junior and Martin senior were printed in her house, she gave them entertainment and placed them in a parlor; her husband knew it not till it was done; she told him it was works of embroidering and willed him to will his servants not to peep or pry into the parlor, since it pertained not to them. Hodgskins and two more printed them all. Hodgskins was desired to print more, but he refused. Hodgskins confessed that he printed them two; and from Mr. Wickstone's they were conveyed to Warrington in Lancashire. She gave them 2*s*. 6*d* at their departure, and her husband 2*s*.

Upon this Mr. Solicitor Egerton began to declare the danger of these books, that they tended to confusion of all states, to take away her majesty's prerogative royal, to the diminution of her yearly revenue where she at this time was forced to sell her revenues for maintenance of her realm and people, to the dispersion of a great number of their patronages and avows and appropriations, to the abrogating of the common law and the civil law in many points, whereupon he desired their lordships to proceed to sentence.

All the lords agreed that the books were most lewd, dangerous and seditious, and pernicious to the state, most scandalous in respect to our adversaries the Papists who took occasion of our disagreement, that they were slanderous to her majesty in accusing her for not maintaining religion. Whereas she for defense of religion only had scared all the enemies of the state; that the sword of war had been drawn out against her for that cause; nay, the sword of death had compassed her chair in her own chamber [Mr. Parrie and Mr. Barnewell]; notwithstanding she, nothing dismayed, being of princely magnanimity and fortitude, had not feared any of these dangers only for religion sake. That they took away her majesty's regal power, disinherited noblemen and gentlemen, took away all properly, abolished the reverend estate and calling of bishops which are one of the three ancient estates of this land; and so they meant to pick out one stone after another till they pulled the whole house on their heads. That the faults of them there present were gross and grievous; Sir Richard, a man highly favored of the Queen and much bounded mare than ordinarily any of his state.

Yet notwithstanding said Mr. Vice-Chamberlain, you be beloved of all of us, yet justice must be done without affection or compassion; for *puniantur hi, ne tu runioris*; let the magistrate punish offenders, lest himself be punished. And again, St. Augustine said, *pereat unus ne pereat unitas*; let the offender rather be punished, than the unity of the church be confounded. That their ignorance was no excuse, that ignorance which was willful and malicious only to escape the punishment of law, which is as high an offence as any privities. That it was a sillier answer of Mr. Wickstone to say his wife desired him, a great folly to be ruled by her, and she passed the modesty of her sex to rule him. And Sir John Parrot said expressly he thought him worthy of the greater punishment for giving such a foolish answer as that he did it at his wife's desire.

The Lord Chancellor gave the assembly that stood by to note that these prisoners were not the devisers and makers of these books; for if they had, another place had been fit for them, and not this that the county of Northampton did swarm with these sectaries, and in one place there was a presbytery planted among them till at length one of the brethren had offended, wherefore the other would have punished him; but he, when he should be punished, fled and complained to justice of peace and so their power surceases, and all revealed; whereby he noted the vanity of their government, yea, said he, it is proceeded so far in that country that the people were offal contention and in some places had risen in arms about that quarrel; whereby he concluded it was necessary to prevent such mischief and to make example of it, and desired the judges to notify his action herein in their circuits abroad, to the end the whole realm might have knowledge of it and the people no more seduced with these lewd libelers. For punishment, they all agreed that Sir Richard should be fined 2,000£; Mr. Hales,

1000 marks; Mr. Wickstone for obeying his wife and not discovering it, 500 marks; Mrs. Wickstone a 1000£; and all of them imprisonment at her majesty's pleasure.

[*Cobbett's Complete Collection of State Trials*. 1264-1272]

Richard did not stop printing material and over a period of several years, he continued to print and distribute material. He was arrested several times with one incident resulting in a fine of 10,000£. Richard died 1 September 1615.

Philip Howard

Philip Howard was born 28 June, 1557 in Strand London, to Thomas Howard, 4th Duke of Norfolk and Lady Mary Fitzalan. He was baptized at Whitehall Palace and named after King Philip II of Spain, who was his godfather.

At about the age of fourteen, he married his stepsister Anne Dacre. In 1574, he graduated St. John's College, Cambridge. His time at Cambridge and court was described by early historians as frivolous. Toward the end of 1581, Philip Howard was present at the disputations of Edmund Camron in the Tower of London. This is believed to be the initial step in his conversion. As the Catholic revival increased in popularity, Philip Howard found himself out of favor with Queen Elizabeth. This was exasperated with the conversion of his wife. By 1584, he reconciled with his wife and converted to Catholic. Sensing the danger in his conversion, he attempted to flee England, but was captured at sea. The following is the trial.

The trial of Philip Howard, Earl of Arundel, before the lords for high treason: 31 Elizabeth 18th of April, A.D. 1589.

From the outward bar in the King's bench, there was a court made of 30 foot square within which was a table of 12 foot square covered with green cloth; and in the same court where benches to sit upon covered with green say. In the midst of the same court at the upper end, was placed a cloth of state with a chair and cushion for the Lord Steward, from the midst of the same court to the midst of the hall was built a gallery for the prisoner to come upon to the court, in length 110 foot, and in breadth 15 foot, and in height from the ground 6 foot, railed round about and going down with seven steps. Between eight and nine of the clock in the morning the Earl of Derby, Lord Steward his grace, entered the hall attended by diver's noblemen and officers, four sergeants at arms with their maces waiting before him; next before his grace the Earl of Oxford, Lord Great Chamberlain of England. My Lord of Derby's grace being seated in his chair of state, every nobleman was placed in his degree, by Garter King of Heralds. At his grace's feet did sit Mr. Winckefield, one of her majesty's gentlemen ushers holding a long white wand in his hand, being accompanied with Mr. Norris, Sergeant of the Garter. Before them did sit Mr. Sandes the Clerk of the Crown of the King's-Bench.

Opposite against my lord's grace did sit the Queen's learned counsel, viz. 1. Sergeant Puckering. 2. Sergeant Shettleworth. 3. Mr. Popham the Queen's Attorney-General. 4. Mr. Egerton, the Queen's Solicitor.

The names of the commissioners on the right-hand sitting upon a lower bench, under the lords of the jury. 1. Sir Francis Knowlet, Kt. Treasurer of the Household. 2. Sir James Crofts Kt. Comptroller of the Household. 3. Sir John Parrat, one of her majesty's most honorable Privy Council. 4. Mr. Wolley, Secretary of the Latin tongue, of the Privy Council. 5. John Fortescue, Master of the Wardrobe and of the Privy Council. 6. Dr. Dale, one of the Masters of Request to her majesty. 7. W. Fleetwood, Sergeant at Law and Recorder of London. 8. Mr. Huckby, Master of Requests and Master of St. Catherine's.

The names of the commissioners on the left-hand. 9. The Lord Chief Justice of England, Sir Christopher Wray. 10. The Master of the Rolls, Sir Gilbert Gerrard. 11. The Lord Chief Justice of the Common-Pleas, Edmund Anderson. 12. The Lord Chief Baron of the Exchequer, Roger Manwood. 13. Justice of the Common-Pleas, William Periam. 14. Justice Gawdy, of the King's-Bench. The Sergeant at Arms, usually attending on the Lord Chancellor, named Roger Wood, was commanded to make an O Yes three times. Then Mr. Sandes, Clerk of the Crown, read the commission. And Sir Francis Knowles, Kt. gave up the verdict of the great assize. Then was called Matthew Spencer, Sergeant at Arms, to return his precept; which was returned and read.

After that the noblemen and peers of the jury for his trial were severally called by their names, as followed: 1. William Lord Burleigh, Lord Treasurer of England. 2. Edward Earl of Oxford, Lord Great Chamberlain of England. 3. William Lord Marquis of Winchester. 4. Henry Earl of Kent. 5. Henry Earl of Sussex. 6. Henry Earl of Pembroke. 7. Edward Earl of Hereford. 8. Henry Earl of Lincoln. 9. Henry Lord Hunsdon, Lord Chamberlain of her majesty's Household. 10. Peregrine Lord Willoughby of Eresby. 11. Lord Morley. 12. Lord Cobham. 13. Arthur Lord Grey. 14. Lord Darcy, of the North. 15. Lord Sandes. 16. Lord Wentworth. 17. Lord Willoughby of Parham. 18. Lord North. 19. Lord Rich. 20. Lord St. John of Bletsho. 21. Lord Buckhurst. 22. Lord de la Ware. 23. Lord Norris.

Then the Lieutenant of the Tower was called to return his precept and to bring forth his prisoner Philip Earl of Arundel. The Earl came into the hall being in a wrought velvet gown, furred about with martins, laid about with gold lace and buttoned with gold buttons, a black satin doublet, a pair of velvet hose and a long high black hat on his head; a very tall man looking somewhat swath-colored. Then was the Earl brought to the bar, with the axe carried before him by Mr. Shelton, gent, Porter of the Tower, being accompanied with Sir Owen Hopton, Kt. Lieutenant of the Tower, Sir Drew Drury, Constable of the Tower for the time, Mr. Henry Bronkard, and others. At my Lord of Arundel's coming to the bar he made two obeisances to the state and to the nobles, and others there present. Then did Mr. Sandes, Clerk of the Crown say he was indicted of several treasons and said to him, Philip Howard Earl of Arundel, late of Arundel in the county of Sussex, hold up thy hand. He held up his hand very high saying here is as true a man's heart and hand, as ever came into this hall.

Mr. Sandes then read the indictment. That whereas divers traitorous persons in the parts beyond the seas, being natural Englishmen, viz. Dr. Allen, Parsons, Champion, Mott, and divers others have heretofore, divers and sundry times, with sundry persons as well Englishmen as of other countries, practiced to accomplish and bring to pass several dangerous and unilateral treasons against the Queen's majesty, her royal person, crown and dignity, viz. to subvert the state, invade the realm, to set up Catholic religion, to raise insurrections, &c. among which number of unnatural traitors the Earl of Arundel was well acquainted with that notorious traitor Dr. Allen by means of Bridges, Weston, Ithill, amid other popish priests with whom divers times since the 20th year of her majesty's reign, he has had private and secret conference and communication of several treasons; insomuch that the Earl of Arundel did presently dispatch his several letters by Bridges aforesaid to Dr. Allen to wish him at any hand to do something concerning the cause Catholic; wherein he promised to perform anything that Dr. Allen should think fit for him to do. And whereas, the 24th day of April in the 27th year of the Queen's reign, he was flying by sea to Dr. Allen that arch-traitor; and that the Bishop of Rome and the King of Spain were thereupon solicited by Allen aforesaid, to raise war against this realm. And whereas also the Earl of Arundel had understanding of a bull, that Sextus the fifth, Pope of that name, had sent into England for the excommunication of her majesty, and for the invading of the realm, &c. And that at the Tower, the 21st of July, in the 30th year of her majesty's reign, he did imagine with other traitorous persons that the Queen was an heretic and not worthy to govern the realm; and that he did move and procure one William Bennett, a seminary priest to say mass for the happy success of the Spanish fleet; whereupon he had mass and did help to say mass himself, to that purpose and having news of the conflict at sea between the Spanish fleet and the English, he procured Sir Thomas Gerrard and divers others then prisoners in the Tower, to say mass with him for the fortunate success of Spain and that he made a prayer specially for that purpose to daily use and exercised amongst them.

Hereupon Mr. Sandes asked the Earl of Arundel if he were guilty or not guilty of the several treasons comprised in the said indictment? To this the Earl answered he would fain know whether the several points in the indictment contained were but one indictment, yea or no. The judges satisfied him, it was but one indictment and a matter he need not stand upon.

He desired to know if they could proceed against him for the treasons in the statute of 13 Elizabeth after the six months were expired; to this he was answered, that they did not proceed against him on that statute, but on the 25th Edw. 3. After this being called upon to plead, he pleaded not guilty; and said he was well contented to he tried by his peers and liked the trial well, that he should he tried by such good noblemen there present that knew his life, he said, he had been prisoner four years, and twenty-five weeks close prisoner and that he had been sick and weak, whereby his memory might fail him; and therefore humbly desired my Lord Steward's grace, making these several obeisance's on both knees, that he might be heard to make answer to every particular point.

My Lord Steward answered that there was no other meaning nor intent, and that he should be heard deliberately.

Then did Mr. Sergeant Puckering deliver to the lords of the jury the effect of the indictment and other evidence at large as follows:

First, that my lord had private and secret conference with Bridges aforesaid, and divers other traitors and seminary priests; and that he had written his letters to Dr. Allen to find which way he might further the cause Catholic. That he did fast twenty-four hours and prayed for the happy success of the Spanish fleet. That Allen and others being arrant traitors, had taken order that in the 22nd year of her majesty's reign, there should be 50 men in privy coats and pocket-daggers to kill the Queen; and that one Pain, and one Elliot, were put in trust to perform the same. That my lord was a Catholic, and favored their proceedings.

My lord answered, he was no Catholic in the 22nd year of the Queen's reign.

That he secretly was flying out of the realm to Dr. Allen being an arch-traitor; which did argue my lord to be no good subject. That Throckmorton practicing his treasons by sounding the ports, he did set down in his catalogue that a south-west wind would serve from Spain to Arundel-castle in Sussex and an easterly wind from the Low-Countries. That in Throckmorton's catalogue of all the names of all the noblemen and gentlemen of every shire that affected the Catholics; he began in Sussex and set down the Earl of Arundel's name the first. That further, one Mott a priest informed Throckmorton that he was come over to sound the intents of the Earls of Arundel and Northumberland, and others.

My Lord answered when Mott was in Sussex, he never came there but always attended at court.

Mr. Puckering said the traitors have a good conceit of my Lord of Arundel in knowing him to be affected to the Catholic cause. It was defined that the Catholic cause was mere treason. Petro Paulo Rosetto came over to sound noblemen and gentlemen in England.

Then said my lord how prove you me to be a traitor in these points?

Because, said Mr. Popham, you have confederated with traitors by desiring Dr. Allen in your letters to employ you anyway that concerned the cause Catholic, because you have been reconciled to the Pope; and there was a law made in the 22nd year of this Queen that whosoever was reconciled to the Pope from the obedience of the Queen's majesty was in case of treason.

My lord confessed that Bridges did confess him, but not reconcile him in any such sort, but only for absolution of his sins.

Sir Popham charged him that he did once submit himself, but since fell from his submission and therefore practiced new treasons.

He confessed he was acquainted with the priests, and by two of them had been absolved and confessed.

Since which time, said Mr. Popham, he came to the church and full to the Catholic cause again which he cannot do by their order, unless he be reconciled.

My lord denied that ever he came to the church after that time.

There was a letter sent to the Queen of Scots by Morgan of France in commendation of two priests, wherein he said one of them had reconciled the Earl of Arundel.

Edmonds, a priest, upon examination said that reconciliation was odious.

My lord said these be but allegations and circumstances, and that they ought to be proved by two witnesses.

It was justified, he said, once in the Star Chamber amongst the lords there assembled concerning a libel there in question, that whosoever was a priest or papist was an arrant traitor.

Mr. Popham said it was a discontentment made my lord a Catholic, and not religion; and that he did disguise himself in shadow of religion.

There was a picture showed that was found in my lord's trunk, wherein was painted a hand bitten with a serpent shaking the serpent into the fire, about which was written this poesy, *Quit contra nos?* On the other side was painted a lion rampant, with his chops all bloody, with this poesy, *Tamen Leo*. My lord said one Walgrave's man gave him the same with a pair of hangers for a new-year's gift. One Jonas Meredith being examined about his communication with a town's man who commended my Lord of Arundel for his forwardness, in that he had often observed my lord at Paul's Cross, this Jonas answered that he knew he had often been at Paul's Cross in the forenoon and had heard a mass with him at the Charter-House in the afternoon. To this my lord said nothing, but seemed to deny it. My lord being examined in the Tower of his sudden going away to sea, he answered to serve the prince of Parma, or whither Dr. Allen should direct him for the cause Catholic. My lord said also he was going away for fear some statute should be made in the 22nd of this Queen's reign against the Catholics in that Parliament; and that Dr. Allen advised him that he should not go over if he could tarry here in any safety because he might be the better able to make a party in England when they came. Before my lord's going to sea, he wrote a letter to be given to the Queen after he was gone, wherein he found fault with her hard dealing in giving countenance to his adversaries, and in disgracing him; and that he was discontented with the injustice of the realm towards his great grandfather, his grandfather, and his father. My lord, said Holinshed, was faulty for setting forth in his chronicle that his grandfather was attainted by act of Parliament, but showed no cause wherefore. He said in his letter his grandfather was condemned for such trifles that the people standing by were amazed at it, he found fault also with the proceedings against his father. Whereby it is apparent, said Mr. Popham, it was discontentment moved my lord and not religion and fearing lest his friends should think amiss of him, he left a copy of his letter with Bridges a traitor to be dispersed, to make the Catholics to think well of him; for, said Mr. Popham, being discontented he became a Catholic, and being so great a man he became a captain of the Catholics, which is as much as to be a captain over traitors. A counterfeit letter was made 22 days before his going to sea, directed to one Baker at Lynn, there being no such man abiding; wherein was signified that my lord was very hardly dealt withal by some of the council and that he was gone into Sussex, and a farther voyage, and that he would come home by Norfolk. This was a counterfeit letter said Mr. Attorney, appointed by my lord to be dispersed, to make it known be was discontented. Also Allen sent a letter to the Queen of Scots in ciphers, showing a great party in England. Allen sent my lord word if he did come over he must take a greater title than that of Earl upon him, and therefore addressed my lord in this style, 'To Philip Duke of Norfolk, Earl of Arundel.' Babington in his examination said the Queen of Scots sent him word that the Earl of Arundel was a fit man to be a chief head for the Catholics. Allen sent word to Rome that the bull which was last sent over into England, was at the intercession of a Trent man in England. My lord (said Mr. Popham) was one of the principals and acquainted thus far with Allen; ergo my Lord of Arundel, that great man. Dr. Allen made a most villainous and slanderous book which was very hard to be got, in which was contained that the Earl of Arundel was a procurer of the last bull and the procurer of the invasion also. The bull itself was some part read, and the book was part read also. My lord being charged on his confession, being examined why he would be ruled thus by Dr. Allen, he excused it by saying that he said he would be ruled by Allen in all things, saving in that did concern her majesty and the state; and thereupon appealed to my Lord Chancellor, and Sir Walter Mildmay, who were not present. The book aforesaid intended that my lord was a practicer with Allen about the invasion. Then said my lord, be would serve the Queen against all princes, Pope, or potentates whatsoever.

The Queen's solicitor stood upon these points; and because it was proved that the Earl of Arundel would be ruled by Allen in anything that should concern the Catholic cause and for that Dr. Allen had since that time practiced divers monstrous treasons, and continually had built upon the help of some chief man in England, there is none yet known of his degree that had anything to do with Allen; and therefore my lord must needs be capable of all the treasons Allen had practiced and procured in flying to Allen to serve the Prince of Parma, *ut antea*.

My lord was charged with relieving of divers traitors as priests; and that he did converse, and was confederate, with divers and sundry traitors attainted, indicted and suspected being prisoners in the Tower and that he had mass in the Tower; and that if the Spaniards should surprise the Tower, Sir Owen Hopton should he put to the rack-house. He was also charged that divers Papists, seminaries, and such like, being prisoners in Newgate, and other prisoners, reported that they hoped to see the Earl of Arundel King of England, and that Cardinal Allen should direct the crown of England. Before the coming of the Spaniard's fleet, when our commissioners were in the Low Countries, news was brought to the Tower that we should have peace between Spain and England; then would my Lord of Arundel be pensive. When the Spanish fleet was upon our coast, and news was brought to the Tower that the Spaniards sped well, then the earl would be merry. Then when news came, the English fleet sped well, the earl would be sorry. When news came, the Spanish fleet was come upon the coast of Kent, my lord said, it is a great wood and a puissant fleet, we shall have lusty play shortly, I hope we shall plague them that have plagued us. My lord said he would not fight against any that came to fight for the Catholic faith. He said when the Spanish fleet was at sea, he would have three masses a day for the happy success of Spain. He said also he would have continual prayer without ceasing for a time for the good success of Spain, viz. he would have every twenty-four hours five priests to pray two hours a piece for the defect of laymen, and fourteen laymen to pray every one an hour a piece for the happy and fortunate success of Spain. He made himself a special prayer for that purpose and caused copies in haste thereof to be made. Mr. Shelley, then prisoner in the Tower, told my lord that to exercise that prayer were dangerous, and wished my lord to let it alone, therefore my lord called for the copy of the prayer again, and would not have it copied. He was charged that he did conjure Sir Thomas Gerrard, Knt. to keep counsel in all these matters before set down, who promised him he would. Rennet also promised to keep his counsel, and divers others. Then were Sir Thomas Gerrard, Mr. Shelley, Rennet the priest, and divers others removed from the Tower to several other prisons, and upon examination confessed all as aforesaid.

My lord hearing all these matters laid hard against him by Mr. Solicitor, grew into some agony and called for his accusers face to face; which the learned counsel did not yet yield to.

He was likewise charged that he came once merrily to Rennet the priest in the Tower saying, 'Come, Mr. Rennet, let us pray that the Spaniards may beat down London-bridge' and promised to give him a damask gown shortly, and that he hoped to make him Dean of Paul's ere it were long that the time of their delivery was at hand and willed him in any wise to be secret, for if he should reveal these things, he would deny them to his face.

When news came to the Tower that the Spanish fleet was driven away, my lord said we are all undone; there is no hope for us this year, and the King of Spain cannot provide such a power again these five or six years, some of us may be dead and rotten ere that time.

There were then brought into the court, *viva voce*, upon their several oaths, Anthony Hull and Richard Young a justice of the peace, who aimed something by hearsay to the proof of the former matter. Also Sir Thomas Gerrard, William Rennet, Tuchnon, Snoden, and Ithel, and divers others were closely kept in a place over the King's-Bench, closed in with arras and were thereupon severally called into the court, *viva voce*, upon their several oaths to affirm that which is specified before since Mr. Solicitor began to speak, how this Mark Rennet the priest was charged with a letter written to my lord wherein he should be sorry for the opening of these matters as aforesaid against my lord. One Randal had writ this letter in Rennet's name, by advice of my Lord of Arundel to blind his practices. Rennet openly denied the writing of that letter; whereupon my Lord Grey and my Lord Norris asked Rennet, if he knew of the letter, yea, or no? For the better evidence, Bennet confessed he had been moved to such a matter, but he did it not. Against Sir Thomas Gerrard, my lord stood very stoutly in denial of what he witnessed willing him to look him in the face, and charging him as he would answer before God, in whose presence he spoke to tell nothing of him but truth. In answer whereof, Sir Thomas referred himself to his depositions before read to which he said he was sworn; yea, twice sworn.

There were called into the court two witnesses more, viz. one Walton and one Church, who justified letters were brought from England to Rhemes where they both were; which letters were sent by one Hill, one of my lord's faction, that the Earl of Arundel should be general of the Catholics when the Tower should be surprised. To Walton, my lord took exception affirming that he was a naughty lewd fellow who had sold that little land he had to three several men and of the other witnesses he said, that some were attainted, some indicted bad men and prisoners and that their words were worth little credit.

Then said Mr. Popham, they were never tortured but confessed all this willingly, and they are such as you have accompanied.

Here ended every man's speech and the noblemen and peers of the jury went together.

My Lord humbly having submitted himself to the consideration of his peers, with protestation of loyalty; the lieutenant brought him from the bar to a seat near to the court of Common-Pleas where the Warders attended upon him.

My Lord Steward likewise withdrew himself a little while as it seemed to take some refreshment; having all the day for the time of his business, forborne to eat anything; and presently returned to his seat of state.

Within one hour after the noblemen of the jury came every one back, and were again placed by Garter King at Arms. Then Mr. Sandes asked every man of the jury, severally, beginning at my Lord Norris, the youngest baron and proceeding to my Lord Treasurer the foreman, whether the prisoner were guilty, yea, or no? Which every one of them, laying their hands upon their hearts, did protest in their consciences, and upon their honors, that he was guilty.

Then was the lieutenant called to bring his prisoner to the bar, who was brought accordingly, attended as before. Then said Mr. Sandes to him that he had been indicted of several treasons, and that he had put himself upon the trial of his peers, who had found him guilty; and therefore asked why judgment should not be given against him.

Whereupon my lord making three very low obeysances upon his knees, did humbly submit himself to my Lord Steward's Grace and the favors of the rest of the nobles and peers there present, and sought them to be mediators for him that he might obtain at her majesty's hands, to have order taken for his debts and to have conference with his officers and to talk with his wife and to see his infant, born after his imprisonment, whom he had never seen.

Then my lord's grace pronounced judgment, viz. that he should be conveyed to the place from whence he came, and from there to the place of execution and there to be hanged until he were half dead, his members to be cut off, his bowels to be cast into the fire, his head to be cut off, his quarters to be divided into four several parts, and to be bestowed in four several places and so (said my Lord Steward) the Lord have mercy on your soul!

To this the Earl of Arundel said as it were softly to himself, *Fiat voluntas Dei*. And so having made a low obeisance to the state, the lieutenant took him away; Mr. Shelton going before him with the edge of the axe towards him. Then there was an O yes made by the Sergeant at Arms and the court, together with my Lord Steward's commission, dissolved which done, my Lord of Derby took the white wand out of Mr. Winkfield's hand and broke the same in pieces; and every man cried, 'God save the Queen.'

Whereupon the Earl of Arundel was carried back to the Tower, where after several reprieves he died a natural death, October 19, 1595, having been prisoner there ten years and six months; four years whereof passed before he was brought to his trial.

[Emlyn, Sollom. *A Complete Collection of State Trials and Proceedings. V. 6.* 164-168]

Philip was left in prison to die. His last request was to visit with his wife and child, who was born after his imprisonment, but this was denied. If he had consented to attend a Protestant service, not only would he have been allowed to visit with his family, but he would have gained his freedom and been restored to his family honors. He died in the Tower never seeing his family on 19 October, 1595, and became recognized as a Catholic martyr.

John Udall

John Udall or Uvedale, was the fourth and youngest son of Sir William Uvedale, although there is speculation that he was related to the Uvedale families of Wickham in Hampshire. He enrolled at Christ's College, Cambridge in 1577 then transferred to Trinity College and graduated in 1581 with a B.A., and then a M.A. in 1584.

A passionate student of theology, he developed an interest in Puritanism and Hebrew. Over the following years, he continued to establish himself as a Puritan. In 1586, he was summoned by the Bishop of Winchester and the Dean of Windsor to appear before the Court of High Commission. In 1588, Udall persuaded a Puritan printer in London to print an anonymous pamphlet denouncing the Church of England from a puritan view point. He was immediately deemed seditious. The press was shut down and confiscated, although without ties to Udall.

The printing press was again secretly set up and additional pamphlets were printed denouncing the officials of the Church of England and although there was no conclusive evidence that Udall was behind the printings, he nevertheless offended the High Commission. After a short period, he published a non-controversial publication but officials were still seeking the source of the previous pamphlets. In 1589, Udall was summoned to London to be examined by the Privy Council, but refused to admit that he was the author of the controversial material. In July 1590, a second examination by the council yielded the same results. Less than ten days later, he stood trial at Croydon, Assizes for the felony of publishing 'scandalous, and seditious libel.' The following is the record of the trial as recorded by Udall himself.

The Trial of Mr. John Udall, a puritan minister, at Croydon Assizes, for felony: 32 Elizabeth 24th July, A.D. 1590.

[Wrote by Himself.]

On Tuesday the 13th of January, 1589, I appeared at my Lord Cobham's house in the Blackfriers before my Lord Cobham, my Lord Buckhurst, my Lord Anderson, the Bishop of Rochester, Mr. Fortescue, Mr. Egerton, the Queen's Solicitor, Dr. Aubery, and Dr. Lewen. Then was I called in before them; whereupon my Lord Anderson said to me.

Anderson. How long have you been at Newcastle?

Udall. About a year, if it please your lordship.

Anderson. Why went you from Kingston upon Thames?

Udall. Because I was silenced there, and was called to Newcastle.

Rochester. What calling had you there?

Udall. The people made means to my Lord of Huntingdon, who sent me there.

Rochester. Had you the allowance of the bishop of that diocese?

Udall. There was none at that time.

Rochester. Then you should have gone to the archbishop.

Udall. There was no Archbishop of York neither.

Anderson. You are called here to answer concerning certain books which are thought to be of your making.

Udall. If it be for any of Martin's books (according as my Lord Chamberlain's letters that fetched me, import) I have already answered, and am ready so to do again.

Anderson. Where have you answered and in what manner?

Udall. At Lambeth, a year and a half ago. I cleared myself not to be the author, nor to know who he was.

Anderson. Is this true, Mr., Beadle?

Beadle. I have heard that there was such a thing, but I was not there at it, if it please your lordship.

Aubery, Lewen. There was such a thing, as my lord's grace told us.

Udall. I am the hardier dealt withal, to be fetched up so far at this time of the year. I have had a journey I would not wish to my enemy.

Rochester. You may thank your own dealing in matters that you should not have meddled withal.

Anderson. It is more than I heard, that ever you were called to answer; but you are to answer concerning other books.

Udall. I hope your lordships will not urge me to any others, seeing I was sent for about those.

Anderson. You must answer to others also what say you to those books? A demonstration or a dialogue, did not you make them?

Udall. I cannot answer thereto.

Anderson. Why would you clear yourself of Martin, and not of these, but that you are guilty herein?

Udall. Not so, my lord; I have reason to answer in the one, and not in the other.

Anderson. I pray you let us hear what reason, for I cannot conceive of it, seeing they are all written concerning one matter.

Udall. This is the matter, my lord I hold the matter proposed in them all to be one, but I would not be thought to handle it in that manner which the former books do; and because I think otherwise of the latter, I care not though they should be fathered upon me.

Buckhurst. But I pray you tell me, know you not Penry?

Udall. Yes, my lord, that I do.

Buckhurst. And do you not know him to be Martin?

Udall. No, surely, neither do I think him to be Martin.

Buckhurst. What is your reason?

Udall. This, my lord; when first it came out, he understanding that some gave out that he was thought to be the author; wrote a letter to a friend in London, wherein he did deny it, with such terms as declare him to be ignorant and clear in it.

Buckhurst. Where is that letter?

Udall. Indeed I cannot now show you, for I have forgotten to whom it was written.

Buckhurst. You will not tell where it is.

Udall. Why, my lord, it tends to the clearing of one, and the accusing of none.

Buckhurst. Can you tell where Penry is?

Udall. No, surely, my lord.

Buckhurst. When did you see him?

Udall. About a quarter of a year ago.

Buckhurst. Where did you see him?

Udall. He called at my door, and saluted me.

Buckhurst. Nay, he remained belike with you?

Udall. No, indeed; he neither came in my house, neither did he so much as drink with me.

Buckhurst. How came you acquainted with him?

Udall. I think at Cambridge, but I have been often been in his company.

Buckhurst. Where?

Udall. At divers places, and namely in mine own house while I dwelt at Kingston.

Buckhurst. What cause had you to be so often in his company?

Udall. He being a scholar and student in divinity, and one whom I always thought to be an honest man, your lordship may easily conceive the cause. Here was much to this same effect spoken about Mr. Penry, and my being at Mrs. Crane's house at Moulsey, and with her, &c which I always answered, as in the like case concerning Mr. Horton of Richmond before the archbishop. Thru Dr. Lewen reading my answers to those questions, that had been by the archbishop propounded to me concerning my papers in my study, and namely the notes of my several conferences with the bishops and their officers; I was asked, as I remember, by Mr. Fortescue.

Fortescue. Why did you pen such things and keep them?

Rochester. Because he and such like might apishly imitate the martyrs of firmer times and account themselves persecuted by us, as those were by the popish bishops.

Udall. The cause is this, for that in the quickness of wit and readiness of memory in youth, those things may be spoken that in age will be more easily made use of in writing than otherwise the memory of man not being infinite.

Anderson. What say you, did you make these books, or know you who made them?

Udall. I cannot answer to that question, my lord.

Anderson. You had as good say you were the author.

Udall. That will not follow; but if you think so, I cannot do withal.

Cobham. Mr. Udall, if you be not the author, say so, and if you be, confess it; you may find favor.

Udall. My lord, I think the author for anything I know, did well and I know that he is enquired after to be punished; and therefore I think it my duty to hinder the finding of him out, which I cannot do better than thus.

Anderson. And why so, I pray you?

Udall. Because if everyone that is suspected do deny it, the author at the length must needs be found out.

Anderson. Why dare you not confess it, if you be the author of it? Dare you not stand to your own doings?

Udall. I professed before that I liked of the books and the matter handled in them, but whether I made them or no, I will not answer; neither of any other book of that argument, whatsoever goes without name, if you should ask me for the reason alleged before, besides that if I were the author, I think that by law I need not answer.

Anderson. That is true, if it concerned the loss of your life.

Udall. I pray your lordship, does not the law say generally no man shall be put to answer without presentment before justices, or things of record, or by due process, or writ original? &c. Anno 42 Edw. 3. cap. 5.

Anderson. That is law, and it is not law.

Udall. I understand you not my lord; it is a statute which is in force, if it be not repealed.

Anderson. I tell you, by law you ought to answer in this case.

Udall. Good my lord, show me this favor to tell me in what book of the law I shall find it; for I profess to understand the Latin, French and English tongues, wherein all the laws be written.

Furies. You are very cunning in the law; I pray you by what law did you preach at Newcastle being forbidden at Kingston?

Udall. I know no law against it, seeing it was the official Dr. Hone who did silence me; whose authority reached not out of his archdeaconry.

Fortescue. What was the cause for which you were silenced?

Udall. Surely I cannot tell, nor yet imagine, saving the secret suggestions of Mr. Harvie.

Fortes. To be ignorant of that, is *crassa et supina ignorantia.*

Udall. No sir, the action was *crassa et supina injuria.*

Anderson. Well, what say you to those books? Who made them, and where were they printed?

Udall. Though I could tell your lordship, yet dare I not for the reasons before alleged.

Rochester. I pray you let me ask you a question or two concerning your book.

Udall. It is not yet proved to be mine; but I will answer to anything concerning the matter of the book, so far as I know.

Rochester. You call it a demonstration; I pray you what is a demonstration? I believe you now not what it is.

Udall. If you had asked me that question when I was a boy in Cambridge of a year's standing, it had been a note of ignorance in me to have been unable to answer you.

Rochester. Surely it seems by the frame of the syllogisms and reasons in it that you know it not if you be the author of that book. I read none of it late, but in the Parliament time sitting in a morning in the house, I read some of it; and it seemed to me in many things not to conclude probably, much less demonstratively.

Udall. I will show you, as I take it, why the author called it a demonstration; because the reason which is usually brought to prove the conclusions is commonly drawn from a place of scripture which has more force in it to manifest the conclusion [unable to translate], than any of Aristotle's proofs drawn, as they say, *ex primis, veris, necessariis, cl immediatis causis.*

Rochester. Indeed that which is proved by the scriptures is proved most demonstratively; but the proofs in that book are far from any such.

Udall. Let that be the question, and try it in someone.

Anderson. My Lord of Rochester, I pray you let us make short work with him, offer him a book; will you swear to answer to such things as shall be demanded of you in the behalf of our sovereign lady the Queen?

Udall. I will take an oath of allegiance to her majesty, wherein I will acknowledge her supremacy according to statute and promise my obedience as becomes a subject; but to swear to accuse myself or others, I think you have no law for it.

Anderson. Mr. Solicitor, I pray you tell him the law in this point.

Then Mr. Solicitor (who had sat all the while very soberly) noting what passed (and if a man's mind may be known by his countenance, seeming to dislike the course held against me) upon my Lord Anderson's commandment, stood up, and putting off his hat to me, said.

Egerton. Mr. Udall, I am sorry that you will not answer, nor take an oath, which by law you ought to do. I can assure you your answers are like the seminary priests answers; for they say there is no law to compel them to take an oath to accuse themselves.

Udall. Sir, if it be a liberty by law, there is no reason why they should not challenge it; for (though they be very bad ones) they are subjects, and until they be condemned by law, may require all the benefits of subjects; neither is that any reason, that their answering so should make the claim of less value for me, seeing that herein we are subjects alike, though otherwise of a most contrary disposition.

Buckhurst. My lord, it is no standing with him thus what say you, will you take the oath?

Udall. My lord, I have said as much thereto as I can.

They then commanded me to go forth, and they consulted a little space and called me again at which time almost every one of them used many words to persuade me to confess a truth; saying the Queen was merciful, and that otherwise it would go hardly with me to whom I said, my lords, I know not that I have offended her majesty; when it is proved that I have, I hope her mercy will not then be too late howsoever it be, I dare not take this oath.

Aubery, Lewen. You have heretofore taken it, and why will you not take it now?

Udall. Indeed you call to remembrance a good reason to refuse it; I was called to answer to certain articles upon my oath heretofore, which I voluntarily did, and freely confessed that against myself concerning my judgment and preaching of the points of discipline which could never have been proved; and when my friends labored to have me restored to my place, the archbishop answered that there was sufficient matter against me by mine own confession, why I should not be restored whereupon I covenanted with my own heart, never to be mine own tormentor in that sort again.

Anderson. Whatsoever be the issue of it you must do your duty and deal plainly with the magistrate.

Udall. I take my duty to be in this case not to answer, nor the magistrate's to require it of me; seeing the apostle said 'Receive not an accusation against an elder, under two or three witnesses' which Semanca the Spanish inquisitor alleged to the same purpose.

Buckhurst. What, you are an elder, are you?

Udall. My lord, howsoever the word elder be taken, whether so largely as I and my brethren that desire the discipline do take it, or only for a minister of the word, as our adversaries understand it, I am an elder.

Rochester. It is true, my lord, that an elder in that place contains all such as he is, but none else.

Buckhurst. Yea, but they would have other elders to govern the church; which desire of theirs when it comes to pass I will give over my barony, and become an elder.

Udall. If your lordship understood what great pains and small worldly recompense belongs to that office, you would never say so.

Rochester. The day is past, and we must make an end, will you take the oath?

Udall. I dare not take it.

Rochester. Then you must go to prison and it will go hard with you, for you must remain there until you be glad to take it.

Udall. God's will be done! I had rather go to prison with a good conscience, than to be at liberty with an ill one.

Rochester. Your sentence for this time is to go to the Gate-House close prisoner, and you are beholden to my lords here, that they have heard you so long.

Udall. I acknowledge it, and do humbly thank their honors for it.

And when they were all gone, my Lord Cobham stayed me to speak to me, who told me that it might be he and others wished things to be amended as well as I but the time served not, and therefore he wished me not to stand in it and I praying his lordship's good favor, he promised to do for me what he could; for which I humbly thanked him and so was carried to the Gate-House by a messenger, who delivered me with a warrant to be kept close prisoner and not to be suffered to have pen, ink, or paper, or anybody to speak with me. Thus I remained there half a year, in all which time my wife could not get leave to come to me; saving only that in the hearing of the keeper she might speak to me, and I to her, of such things as she should think meet, notwithstanding that she made suit to the commissioners, yea to the body of the council, for some more liberty all which time my chamber fellows were seminary priests, traitors, and professed Papists. At the end of half a year, I was removed to the White Lion in Southwark, and so carried to the assizes at Croydon; where what was done, I will not mention seeing there were present such as were both able, and I think willing to set down to whose report I refer those that would know the same.

At the Assizes at Croydon, the 11th July, 1590.

Mr. Udall was called and commanded to hold up his hand at the bar; who held up his hand accordingly. Then was his indictment read, being thus: John Udall, late of Loudon, clerk, you are indicted, &c. The form of which indictment was as against murderers namely, that he not having the fear of God before his eyes, but being stirred up by the instigation and motion of the devil, did maliciously publish a slanderous and infamous libel against the Queen's majesty, her crown and dignity. And being asked whether he were guilty, or not guilty, he answered thus:

Udall. My lords, may it please you to hear me a word or two?

Judge Clarke. Answer first to the indictment, and then you shall be heard.

Udall. My lords, I beseech you hear me first a word or twain.

Judge. Say on.

Udall. My case is rare, and such as has not been heard of heretofore, and consists upon divers points of law; I humbly crave of your lordship to grant me to answer by counsel if it may be.

Judge Clarke. You cannot have it, and therefore answer to your indictment.

Udall. Then I answer (my lord), that I am not guilty.

Judge Clarke. How will you be tried?

Udall. I do desire to be tried by an inquest of learned men; but seeing I shall not, I am contented to be tried by the ordinary course as men before me are, that is, as you use to say by God and the country.

Then the Clerk of the Assizes said to the parties arraigned after he had read the names of the jury before them, these men whose names you have heard are to go upon your lives and your deaths; look upon them when they are called to be sworn, and if you know any cause, take exception against them. Then the rest of the felons having nothing to say, Mr. Udall said, my lords I am ignorant of the law in this point; I pray you therefore show me the manner of challenging the jury; how many I may challenge and whether I may render a reason for the same.

Judge. I think you will know a cause in your conscience before you challenge any of them.

Udall. Then I pray you my lord, how many am I by law permitted to challenge?

Judge. Nay, I am not to tell you that; I sit to judge and not to give you counsel.

Then Mr. Udall keeping silence, proclamation was made according to the manner. That if any man could give in evidence against John Udall prisoner at the bar, that they should come into the court and be heard. Then Mr. Daulton stood up and in the mean while Mr. Udall said to the judges thus; my lords I beseech you answer me to one question before Mr. Daulton begin to speak.

Judge. Say on.

Udall. Is it permitted me by law to answer to those things in particular, which are brought to prove this indictment?

Judge. It is permitted.

Udall. Then I humbly crave of your lordships to grant me two petitions, which I think will greatly further both him in speaking, me in answering, and also be a more ready help to the memory of the jury, that they may be able to bear the matter away.

Judge. What are your petitions?

Udall. The first is, that when Mr. Daulton had spoken to one point what he can, I may answer to that before he proceed any further, lest my memory being overwhelmed with multitude of matter, I should forget to answer to some points of importance, and the jury made less able to discern of the particulars. The second is that it might please you to grant me to answer without interruption.

Judge. You shall have them both granted.

Daulton. Then Mr. Daulton said, Mr. Udall you have these petitions granted you, I desire the same of you. And then he desiring leave of the judges, before he should prove the indictment to say something touching this that this man, and such as he is, do maintain, &c. After leave given him, he used a very long speech to the great disgrace and slander of the cause and those men that professed the same, especially of Mr. Udall: and making mention in the same his speech of five several books of common-prayer, made by such as desire reformation; he affirmed that in one of the said books there was horrible blasphemy in these words of the consecration of the Lord's supper, take, eat, this is my body; drink, this is my blood. Then he cried out, saying, 'Oh horrible blasphemy!' And taking occasion upon the variety of these books he affirmed that there was no constancy in these men. And whereas one of the books does allow that over every congregation there should be a faithful pastor; that is, quote he, a shepherd whereby they may take the government out of her majesty's hand, and so bring her majesty to be one of their sheep; no, quote he, her majesty is no sheep under any shepherd in the world, except Christ and for the government that these men do seek for, I am assured there is nonesuch to be found in the word of God.

Udall. Mr. Daulton had used a very large speech which does nothing concern to prove the indictment, or me in particular; and therefore seeing I am not called here to dispute, as if I would, I should not be permitted, I will not answer it; only thus much will I say if it please your lordships, that seeing Mr. Daulton is by profession a lawyer and the cause is yet in question among the learned divines, methinks it had been more modesty for Mr. Daulton to have suspended his judgment until the controversy had been determined amongst them to whose profession it belonged especially seeing Mr. Daulton knows in his conscience that he had heretofore carried some show of liking to the cause, which now he speaks against.

Judge. Sirrah, Sirrah, answer to the matter that Mr. Daulton has against you; Mr. Daulton, proceed to the proof of the points of the indictment.

Daulton. My masters, you of the jury, &c. I will prove, first, that he had a malicious intent in making of this book. Secondly, that he is the author of it and thirdly, that these matters contained in the indictment are felony by the Statute, 23 Elizabeth cap. 2.

Then was Mr. Beadle the register called, who was sworn that these examinations following were as the parties themselves confessed the same and to prove the first, the clerk of the assizes caused Stephen Chatfield to be called into the court to give in evidence against John Udall; but he appeared not at all, for which the judges were offended; and Sergeant Puckering said there was a warrant sent for him whereupon some standing by affirmed that the warrant came after his departure from home.

Then Mr. Daulton said that he went out of the way of purpose; and Judge Clarke said Mr. Udall, you are glad of that. Mr. Udall answered.

Udall. My lords, I wish heartily he had been here; for as I am sure he never could say anything against me to prove this point, so I have heard and am able to prove it to be true that he is very sorry that ever he made any complaint against me confessing he did it in his anger when Martin came first out; and by their suggestions, whom he had proved since by experience to be very bad men.

Daulton. It is no great matter whether he be here or no, for we have his articles against you and your own confession to prove this point sufficiently.

Then were Mr. Chatfield's articles (that he brought to the archbishop against Mr. Udall) read by the clerk containing a report of certain written papers; tending as he supposed to the making of such a book as this is and thereupon asked Mr. Udall whose writing they were; who answered they are a friend's of mine whereto Chatfield replied, wishing him to take heed of them and to rid his hands of them and to return them to his friend from whom he had them, for he doubted they concerned the state. These papers he saw in Mr. Udall's study at Kingston. Also he further said that at another time, he having conferred with Mr. Udall in a certain field by Kingston, called Little-field, about this putting to silence; he said, that the said Mr. Udall uttered these words that if they put him to silence, he would give the bishops such a blow as they never had.

Udall. May it please your lordships that I may answer these things in particular?

Judge. Say on, let us hear your answer.

Udall. I was accused this time two years upon the words of Chatfield that these papers that he did see in my study, should be the mutter of 'Martin-Mar-Prelate' and because I cleared myself of that, it is now brought to prove another matter but it proves nothing unless it were set down in particular what they were.

Daulton. It proves this, that you had a purpose to write this book; and those things were collections from your friends, and preparations thereto.

Udall. Let the jury consider how that point is proved by it. Besides, it may be proved that this book was extant in men's hands before the conference between Chatfield and me; therefore how can it be proved that this is the book that should give them such a blow?

Daulton. But you cannot deny the second point, that you had a pretended malice, for it is extant in your own confession read his answer to those articles of Mr. Chatfield. Then the clerk read his answer to this effect, that if the bishops put him to silence, they would give him occasion and leisure to be employed in writing against them. Then said Mr. Daulton, is not this most evident, what can be plainer than it is?

Udall. I pray your lordships give me leave to explain these things.

Judge. Say on, and be brief.

Udall. Mr. Chatfield told me that he was commanded to come to Kingston and be resident there, of purpose that I might be put to silence and that there might not appear any want of a preacher, I being put down; whereupon I said in effect as is above rehearsed. I pray you hear in what sense these words were uttered.

Judge. The matter is clear, and we see what you can say to it well enough, proceed Mr. Daulton to the proof of the second point.

Daulton. And that you be the author of this slanderous and infamous libel, it shall be proved clearly to the jury before your face. Then said he to the clerk read the answer of Nicholas Thompkins, which was made upon his oath before her majesty's high-commissioners. Then was read to this verdict that Thompkins knew that Mr. Udall was the author of that book called 'The Demonstration,' for he said that Mr. Udall himself told him so. Also that he saw either in Mr. Udall's house, or in some other place in Kingston, a catalogue of all the books that Mr. Udall had made amongst which the demonstration was one.

Judge. You see here that this is clear and a sufficient testimony.

Udall. It carried some show, but it is nothing.

Judge. Do you call the testimony of one being an honest man, and upon his oath, before the high-commissioners to be nothing? Can you answer it?

Udall. My lords, I answer it thus, denying it to be his testimony; for if it be, why is he not present to verify it face to face, according to the law?

Judge Puckering. It is verified to be his true answer, under the hands of Dr. Anberie and Dr. Lewen, the latter whereof confirmed it before me upon his corporal oath.

Daulton. You can take no exceptions against that, and will you say he is not an honest man?

Udall. I am persuaded he was amazed and answered he knew not what for he had reported it so diversely, that it seems he remembered not what he said.

Judge. But the oath of Thompkins is to be preferred before his bare report.

Udall. My lords, I answer I protest to you, (and will verify it upon my oath, if it please you) that he told me the day before I was committed at his master's house that he could not say, neither would he for a thousand pounds affirm any more than this, that he heard me say I would not doubt but set my name to that book if I might have indifferent judges. And further (if it please you, my lords) here are some witnesses that upon their oaths will testify how diversely he had reported of his confession to this thing, if it please your lordships to accept them. And the witnesses offering themselves to be heard, were answered that because their witness was against the Queen's majesty they could not be heard. And after other speeches passing, Mr. Udall said.

Udall. My lords the speech of the catalogue is most vain, and has no sense in it; for can I have made so many books, as that I need make a catalogue of them? It may be my lords, he saw a catalogue of the books in my study, wherein if that were one, it is rather an argument that I made it not; for men use not to put their own works in the catalogue of those that they have in their study.

Daulton. You of the jury consider this, that Thompkins was Mrs. Crane's man, and one that was privy to all the printing that was at her house; and Mr. Udall used to go often there.

Udall. All that is nothing to me, what if I used to go there, she is of my acquaintance, I know her to be an honest gentlewoman; what can you gather by any of these things? Why isn't Thompkins here to declare his testimony and to say what he can?

Daulton. He is beyond the seas about Merchandizes, sent away by Mr. Gore who married Mrs. Crane's daughter.

Udall. How does that appear? He is no merchant, but a serving-man; and if he were, what is that to me? But it cannot be proved that Mr. Core did send him, so that here is nothing but bare papers to show for evidence against me.

Then there was much said to prove that the testimony of a man absent was sufficient if it were proved to be his upon the oaths of others. And then the judge said:

Judge. What say you? Did you make the book, Udall, yea, or no! What say you to it, will you be sworn? Will you take your oath that you made it not? We will offer you that favor which never any indicted of felony had before; take your oath and swear you did it not, and it shall suffice.

Udall. My lords, I pray you hear me to this. If I would have done so before the lords of her majesty's Privy Council that committed me, I had not come here; but I neither then might, nor may do so now, whereof I pray you let me show a reason to the jury. I and many more do think the book to be good for anything we can find in it, and to be written in defense of a cause which we take to be most true. Now the author is sought for, that he may be punished for some speeches that may be wrested in the book; therefore lest he should he found (if one after another that are suspected do deny it) it is thought best every one neither to confess nor to deny, yea though we suffer some punishment, rather than the author, being found out, should suffer extremity.

Judge. Nay, this is but a shift, I will go further with you; will you but say upon your honesty that you made it not and you shall see what shall be said to you?

Udall. My lords, it is all one, I make a conscience of my word as of my oath, for I must give account for both. This is no direct course in this place.

Judge. You of the jury consider this. This argument that if he were not guilty, he would clear himself, and consider well of it. And then speaking to Mr. Udall he said, do not stand in it, but confess it, and submit yourself to the Queen's mercy before the jury find you guilty.

Udall. My Lord, I answer, that according to my indictment I am not guilty, every point whereof must be proved, or else the whole is false. And I beseech your lordships give me leave, and I will be very brief, my conscience does not accuse me that I have so much as offended her majesty, her council, or the meanest of her people in anything I have done concerning this cause, for if I should of all either I deserved the least favor, being one that professed to teach others loyalty to her majesty and love to one another and would you have me to confess a fault where there is none? No, I cannot do it, neither will I; wherefore proceed in your course begun.

Daulton. We have yet more proof than this, though yet this were sufficient of itself; wherefore read the other examinations. Then was read the confession of Henry Sharpe of Northampton who upon his oath before my Lord Chancellor had said that he heard Mr. Penry say that Mr. Udall was the author of 'The Demonstration.'

Udall. Sharpe and I were never above once in company together (to my remembrance), neither knew he ever any of my dealings. This is nothing to prove me the author of the book, reports be uncertain; and if reports be true, the archbishop himself told me that Mr. Penry made it; which is more forcible for me than any of Sharpe's reports can be against me.

Daulton. You mistake the matter; the force of the point rests in Mr. Penry's report who was one of your great acquaintance and familiars; and you and Walgrave and he were at Mrs. Crane's house.

Udall. Here is one man's saying that another said so; let the jury consider of what force this proof is; if you have any more, let it appear.

Judge Clarke. You of the jury have not to enquire whether he be guilty of the felony, but whether he be the author of the book; for it is already set down by the judgment of all the judges in the land that whosoever was author of that book, was guilty by the statute of felony, and this is declared above half a year a gone.

Udall. Though it be so determined already, yet I pray your lordships give me leave to show that which I have to say, and I will be very brief; and it is to prove that though I were found to be the author, yet it cannot be within the compass of that statute, Anno 23 Elizabeth cap. 2. Whereupon the indictment is framed.

Judge. You shall be heard to say for yourself what you can, therefore say on.

Udall. Though I be not by profession a lawyer, yet I think I can show it clearly by these reasons following: 1. The intent of the lawmakers (which always is to be regarded in these cases) is to be considered, which appears in the preface of the statute in these words, 'To frustrate the malice of those that be evil affected to her highness.' Now I pray you consider this how can it be? Or how is it possible that a preacher of the same religion which her majesty professed and maintained who is known continually to pray to God for her highness's prosperity and happiness, both of soul and body; how is it possible, I say, that such a one should be maliciously affected towards her? Therefore it is evident that the statute was made against the Papists who use to slander her highness with the terms of heretic &c. and no way against us; for I dare boldly say of myself and in the name of all my brethren, cursed is he of God, and he deserves doubtless to be hated of men that does imagine the least hurt against her highness. 2. The matter that makes a man a felon by that statute must proceed from a malicious intent against her highness, which I or any such as I can no way justly be charged with; partly for that which is said before, and partly for that my course of teaching and living in this country these nine years (saving this last year, wherein I have been absent) is known to have tended to no other end than the provoking and persuading of the people to like of and yield obedience to her majesty, and the religion received in her dominions for the proof whereof I refer myself to the consciences of all men in the country that have known me. And further, is it likely that I who have been trained up in the universities under her majesty's protection, and have always bended my studies to the advancement of the sincerity of the gospel; so that those small crumbs of learning which I have gathered, I do acknowledge to have received by her majesty's means, these things considered, how can it be that I should be evil-affected towards her highness, whom I protest I unfeigned reverence? And therefore the worst that the author can be charged withal is his overheat and too much vehemence by reason of his zeal against the abuses, and not any malice against her majesty or the meanest of her subjects. Again, the matter to bring it within the compass of the statute must be false but this book is written in the behalf of a most true cause. Lastly, the end of it must be either to the defamation of the Queen's majesty or stirring up of insurrection, sedition or rebellion for the former, I trust that the whole course of our behavior, both in our ministry and conversation declares itself to be so far from seeking to defame her highness, as it tends, to the uttermost of our powers to the advancement of her honor. For I am persuaded that there is none of us that would refuse to undergo any pain whereby her majesty might anyway be the better honored; yea, we would not refuse if need so required, to lay down our lives for redeeming of the least asking of her majesty's little finger, wherewith she might be grieved. Now for the second end which is the moving or stirring up of rebellion, &c. I pray your lordships and you of the jury to consider this there have been since the first day of her majesty's reign learned men that have desired the advancement of this cause and many of the people that affected it, and yet has it never appeared that by occasion hereof there has in all this time been any in any place that have raised any insurrection or sedition yea this book, which is now in question, has been extant these two years; yet I trust neither your lordships, nor any here present can show that any people in any corner of the land, nay it cannot be justly proved that any one person has taken any occasion hereby to enterprise any such matter and therefore the making of this book cannot be felony. Besides all this if there had been any such tiling meant by the author, or received by the people, as the indictment charges me withal, (which is the defamation of her highness's government) yet as I take it, it should not be felony by that statute; for the whole course of it declares that it is only meant of them that defame her highness's person, and not her government, as it is manifest by the last proviso; wherein it is showed that the whole statue does determine an end with her majesty's life. And we may not think their wisdoms that made the law to be so unadvised as to make a law for the preservation of the prince's government, which is continual to last no longer than the life of one prince, which is temporary therefore, it seems that the statute has no further regard than this, that her highness's person might be preserved in that honor and dignity, which becomes her royal dignity and estate. And I do beseech your lordships to answer me, for I appeal to your consciences as you will answer to God for my life; and I pray you tell the jury whether you do think the intent of the statute were in any sort meant against us, and not rather against the Papists.

Judge Puckering. You do not well to charge us so with our consciences, which God only is to know. I answer you, the intent of the statute is against all, for so the words are.

Udall. The words, my lord, I confess are so; but is the principal intent so?

Judge. Yea, it is so.

Judge Clarke. We have heard you speak for yourself to this point at large which is nothing to excuse you; for you cannot excuse yourself to have done it with a malicious intent against the bishops, and that exercising their government which the Queen has appointed them, and so it is by consequence against the Queen.

Udall. My lords, I am persuaded that the author did it not of any malice against them; and for myself I protest I wish them as much good as I do to my own soul, and will pray to God to give them repentance. But the cause why the author did so earnestly inveigh against them was this as it seems because he perceived them not only to execute an authority which he takes to be unlawful by the word of God, but also for that they do not the tenth part of that good (even in those corrupt callings) which by law they might do; and I am persuaded that your lordships know in your own consciences, that they do not the tenth part of that they are bound to do.

Judge Clarke. That is true, they do not the good that they might do; but yet that does not excuse you for it is plain in your book that you write not against them only, but you write against the state; for is it not against the state when you say that it is easier to live in England a papist, than a baptist of the family of love, and what not? Yea, you say, I could live so in a bishop's house, it may be these twenty years and never he much molested for it. What is this but a plain slandering of the state? And mark the words, for you say you could live so in England. And does her majesty's laws allow of Papists? This makes evidently against you, and it is so plain that you cannot deny it.

Udall. My lords, if it might please you to hear me a word or two, I will show the meaning of the author of the book; I beseech you to hear me, and I will be very brief; I know the laws of England do not allow of any such as are mentioned in that book, for there are godly laws made for the punishing of them if they were put in execution. But this I take to be the author's meaning that it is not spoken in respect of her majesty's government and laws but in respect of the bishops, whom your lordships know to be wholly employed in finding us out and punishing of us, not regarding (in a manner) the punishing any sin else.

Judge. What, Sirrah, will you not confess any fault to be in the book? You seek to excuse all.

Udall. My lords, I do acknowledge that there was never any work of man so perfect, but there have been imperfections in the same and therefore there may be some fault in the manner, but surely none in the matter for the bishops themselves will confess that they may fail in their actions, and be partial (as they are men) in the manner of handling anything. So also the author of this book being assured that the matter is without reproof, may err in the manner in being over-zealous in the handling of it; and this fault I will easily confess to be in the book, my lord but I am sure the author never had any malicious intent against her highness, or any of her subjects.

Judge Clarke. This book has made you to come within the compass of the statute though your intent were not so for I am sure there was Mr. Stubbs, well known to divers here to be a good subject and an honest man; yet taking upon him to write a book against her majesty touching Mounseir, he thereby came within the compass of law, which he intended not in making of the book; and I am persuaded that he did it of a good affection towards her majesty; and yet if this law had been made then, which was made since, he had died for it, so you though you intended not to come within the compass of the statute, yet the law reaches to your fact, as that did to his.

Udall. My lords, this case and mine is not alike, for his book concerned her highness's person; but the author of this book touches only the corruptions of the bishops, and therefore not the person of her majesty.

Judge. But I will prove this book to be against her majesty's person; for her majesty being the supreme governor of all persons and causes in these her dominions, has established this kind of government in the hands of the bishops which you and your fellows so strive against and they being set in authority for the exercising of this government by her majesty, you have not strive against them, but her majesty's person, seeing they cannot alter the government which the Queen has laid upon then.

Udall. My lords, we are not ignorant of this, that her majesty has a care that all things might be well; and in that respect has given them often in charge, (upon the considerations of these controversies) to see to it that nothing be amiss; and because she had a good opinion of them for their gravity and learning, she believes them when they say all is well and in good case whereas, if they had the grace to look into these things and to make them known as they be, indeed her majesty and the state, I doubt not would quickly redress them; and therefore was it that the author did so charge them.

Then the judge proceeding farther in the book to prove him to have offended; he took occasion by the same to speak against railing against magistrates; and speaking to Mr. Udall, he said in effect thus:

Judge Clarke. Sirrah, you that should have been a teacher of her majesty's people, you should have taught yourself not to have rallied upon the rulers of the people; for do you not know what is written in the 23rd of Exodus, thou shall not rally upon the ruler of the people for whosoever does so shall die the death. And do you not know what is written in the 23rd of acts, where the Apostle Paul being before the high-priest called him a 'Painted Wall' and being smitten by one of the high-priest's servants if was said to him, 'revile you the lord's high-priest?' To which Paul answered, 'I knew not brethren that he was the high-priest.' Lo! thus did he acknowledge his fault. Do you know these things, Sirrah?

Udall. My lord, you know that we hold it not lawful for a minister to be a civil magistrate and there are at least 500 in this land, amongst whom I am the most unworthy that are of the same judgment in this point.

Judge. But how if the Queen does give it them?

Udall. They ought not to take it. And, my lord (if it please you), I will answer to your proofs, though I came not here to dispute. But in my answering my purpose is not to give any liberty to any man to rally upon any that are in authority. Now to your proofs; I say my lords, that the place out of Exodus 23, does rather concern your lordships and such as are under her majesty for judges than any way to concern the bishops and touching the second place out of Acts 23 where the Apostle said 'Brethren I will not that it was the high priest' the meaning of that place is as if he should say I thought there had not been any high-priest now, seeing Christ being come, the high priesthood was to cease; so that the Apostle does not acknowledge any fault in that his speech for there was no lawful high priest of that time, neither did he acknowledge any, seeing they did end in Christ. And thus do the best divines expound the place.

Then after some farther sketches of this exposition, the judge returned to the matter of the book again saying that the book did concern the state, and said:

Judge. But Sirrah, you can not so excuse yourself as though it touched not the Queen and the state; for is it not written in your book that this saying will not serve their turns the Queen and council will have it so? Where by it is plain that you did speak against the Queen and the state.

Udall. My lord, the author only means this, that when we are called before the bishops, they were often driven to use this argument (when they had nothing else to say for themselves), that they could be content many things were amended; but it must be so, for the Queen and council will have it so and surely herein methinks they slander her highness; and we tell them that however they bear it out here before men, yet before God that excuse will not serve their turn.

Judge. You can not carry it away so does not you plainly say, that they are not safe, though they have human authority on their side; but he that is on our side is mightier than they? Whereby you both abase her majesty and also do threaten them with some force and violence.

Udall. It is true that whosoever does unjustly is not safe in it, though all the princes in the world should defend him in it; and that is the meaning of the author. But to say that force and violence is threatened them, is farthest doubtless from his meaning; for it is known to all the world that we desire by all good means to commend this holy cause of reformation to her majesty and the state and do not look for neither, that ever it should by any force prevail, but that it would please God to honor her highness with the advancement of the same.

Judge. No, no, these are but excuses; these malicious speeches proceeded from you and were the ground work of all these libels that have been dispersed since and you are known to be the ring leader of this faction.

Udall. There is no reason to charge me with other men's doings, every man must answer for himself; but as for me (alas!), I am nobody, there are five hundred ministers in this land of my judgment in these things, the meanest of which I acknowledge to be far better learned than I am. But by the way, my lords, I pray your lordships give me leave to say one thing which I being about to speak of before, was interrupted; and therefore seeing now it comes into my memory, I pray you to hear me, though it be out of time concerning the felony whereof I am accused; it makes greatly for me.

Judge. What is it? Let us hear what you can say.

Udall. When I was before the lords of her majesty's council at the time of my commitment amongst other things that I alleged against the taking of an oath to accuse myself, I said that the thing was accounted criminal and therefore by law I was not to answer, my Lord Anderson said that I said true if the case had concerned either the loss of life or limb; whereby it is manifest, that then my case was not esteemed felony.

Judge. Though the judges had not then concluded it, yet it was law before, or else it could not so be determined after; the violent course of others since, has caused your case to be more narrowly sifted.

Then the judge (having spoken to the like effect also) said to the jury that they should not need to trouble themselves to find him guilty of the felony, but only it was sufficient if they found him guilty to be the author of the book, for quote he, it is already determined by all the judges of the land that the author of that book was in the compass of the statute of felony; and this, quote he, was concluded before we came here therefore you being ignorant of the law, and we being sworn as well as you are, you are to hear us and to take our exposition of the law. And after many other speeches, the judges said go your way, we will hear you no longer, get you here; and shaking his hand, he called for the other felons to hear their causes.

Then the jury said, what can we find?

Judge. Find him author of the book, and leave the felony to us.

And after some other speeches, Mr. Fuller said to the jury, you are to find him author of the book and also guilty of a malicious intent in making it.

Whereat Mr. Daulton said, what have you to do with the matter Mr. Fuller, to speak to the jury?

Then there being some noise at the bar, Mr. Udall could not any more be heard: yet as he was ready to depart, he said to the jury, you of the jury, consider this, that you have not to consult about the life of a seminary and popish priest, but of a minister of the gospel. Then Judge Clarke showed the reasons to the jury, why they must find him guilty; saying the evidences are manifest for the first point, that he is the author of the book and the second is a point in law agreed upon by all the judges as I have said.

So the jury after they had heard the evidences of the other felons at the bar, departed to consult about them; in which time of their consultation, there came two several messages exhorting him to submit himself and to yield to the judges before the jury had given up their verdict.

To whom Mr. Udall replied, willing them not to trouble him with any such matter; for he was clear in his conscience and therefore he was not to accuse himself. In which time also the jury divers times sent and received messages from the judges and at last, the foreman of the jury went himself to them. Thus having debated of the evidences of the rest of the felons with Mr. Udall after the judges had dined, the jury brought in their verdict that he was guilty of felony.

After that Baron Clarke had finished all other matters of law, and that the juries had given their verdicts on the felons, finding some guilty, and some not guilty, the judge commanded all the prisoners to stand forth and to answer to their names who did so. And first, Mr. Udall was called, who stood forth at the bar; but the judge commanded him for that time to stand aside saying that he would deal with him anon. Then some of the prisoners which were saved by their books, were burnt in their hands; and for that night there was nothing more done. Then the judge commanding the jailor to bring the prisoners betimes in the morning, commanded them to depart and so for that time every man departed to his place.

The next morning, being the 25th of July, about four of the clock, the prisoners were brought to the bar who stayed till the coming of the judges who came there by six of the clock, or thereabouts, and called the prisoners by their names to receive sentence of death and first, they began with Mr. Udall; who, after he was called was commanded to stand aside till anon. And then were seven felons that received sentence of death; who being taken aside, Mr. Udall was called the second time; and the Clerk of the Assizes said, 'John Udall, hold up your hand, what can you allege for yourself, why you should not receive judgment to die?'

Udall. My Lords, notwithstanding my earnest pleading and protesting of mine innocence yesterday, which I could and would have done more clearly, but that I was so much interrupted; yet it has pleased the jury upon their consciences to find me guilty of that which, I thank God, never entered into my heart now therefore must I plead another plea and therefore I crave of your lordships to grant me the benefit of the pardon granted the last Parliament.

Judge. I think you can have no benefit by it, for I am deceived if it be not excepted. Then said he to the clerk, or some other, reach me the statute-book and while he looked in the same.

Mr. Udall said, I pray your lordships consider the ground of my plea, albeit indeed it seems to be excepted your lordships confessed yesterday, and I showed it by my Lord Anderson's speeches to me that it was not thought felony till of late and therefore the things that be excepted, be such as be uninquired and punishable in the ecclesiastical courts.

Judge. That is nothing; for if the lesser be excepted, much rather is the greater.

Udall. My lords, I refer it to your consciences and favorable considerations the words are these in the pardon which he repeated and they finding it to be as he had said, the judge said, here is no help for you. And after other speeches between them of the meaning of the words of the pardon, the judge said, Mr. Udall, your counsel has deceived you.

Udall. My lords, I have not received any counsel herein, for I have been close prisoner this half year and therefore could not attain to have any counsel but thus much have I gathered, which is my judgment out of the book.

Judge. What can you allege more for yourself? For this helps you not.

Udall. Nothing but my own innocence, but that your lordships may proceed.

Judge. What say you? Are you contented to submit yourself to the Queen.

Udall. Yea, or else I were not worthy to live in her highness's dominions.

Judge. But will you acknowledge yourself to have offended her majesty in making this book? She is gracious and full of mercy; it may be, that we, reporting your submission to her majesty may procure her pardon for you.

Udall. May it please your lordships to hear me; the cause for which I am called in question I cannot forsake in any sort, for I hold it to be the undoubted truth of God but, &c. And then he was interrupted by Judge Puckering, who said:

Judge. Nay, stay there you cannot go away with that speech unanswered, to buzz into the people's ears such a conceit, that it is an undoubted truth that you hold; for I hold it to be an undoubted falsehood. And then he proceeded further in a large set speech the effect whereof was that this land having been governed by sundry nation has yet kept her ancient laws, which (he affirmed) would be overthrown if this government that these men seek for, should be established and then be further showed what inconveniencies (as he thought) would come by the same, viz. that we having laws and judges appointed to decide all controversies, this presbytery which these men seek for, would overthrow all and bring to their censure and government all men's causes, or else they would excommunicate them from their churches, yea, and they are so hot for this government that they will not stay for the magistrate; and if the magistrate will nor, they will reform themselves and one of them writing in a letter to a friend of his said let us number our hot brethren, that we may know who will stand to it, for it is high time. So that it is plain that if they cannot have it with her majesty's consent, they will have it though it make our hearts to ache as you say in your book. And whereas her majesty has revenue belonging to her crown out of the church livings and cathedral churches, these men would have her majesty give to them those revenues for the maintenance of their presbytery, and they would allow her a stipend at their discretions; so that they would bring the Queen and the crown under their girdles. And some of these men have gone so far that they say plainly we have no church, no sacrament, no ministers, nor any worship of God amongst us. If these things be not looked to in time, what confusion shall we have in this land shortly? Many other things he spoke against the cause of reformation which I cannot particularly lay down; but this is in effect the substance of it, concluding he said thus much, Mr. Udall, have your speeches enforced me to speak, lest the people here present (being deceived) should be carried away by it. To which Mr. Udall answered briefly:

Udall. My lords, it is bootless for me to enter disputation with you in this place touching this matter; only this I could wish you to leave it to be first decided by the learned divines to whose calling it belongs. And although some weak men wanting judgment have been headily carried in seeking the furtherance of this cause and so for want of this government have run into some errors, yet it is no reason to charge us with them; for your lordships know that we have been the men that have taken the greatest pains to reclaim them to the joining of themselves with the church from which they have separated themselves.

Judge Clarke. You are deceived; it is not a matter of divinity only, but it is a matter of state and within the compass of our profession; and it is not so greatly in controversy as you would have us to believe it is.

Udall. It is diversely debated (my lords), and the greatest number of learned men in Christendom do maintain the same.

Judge. How do you know that? Have you been beyond the seas to know the greatest number of learned men to be of this judgment?

Udall. Your lordships know that all the churches of France, the Low Countries, and of Scotland do maintain the same, besides many hundred of learned men in this land.

Judge. Have you been in all these churches that you can tell so much?

Udall. I know it to be true (my lords), for their practice does show them to be of this judgment.

Judge. Well, if you can allege no more, neither will submit yourself to the Queen's mercy, then hear your judgment.

Udall. My lords, I was beginning to speak, but you interrupted me; I pray you hear me what I will say, and then do as God shall move you.

Judge. Let us hear what you will say.

Udall. As I said before, so I say now, I believe the cause to be the undoubted truth of God; and therefore in the matter I cannot by any means yield yet seeing by your order of law I am found to be guilty, neither can I (for the reverence I bear to her majesty's laws) take any exceptions against you nor the jury; but that which you have done, I acknowledge to be done in all equity and right. Seeing, I say you have found me to be guilty, whereby I cannot live without her majesty's gracious and special favor, I acknowledge that whatsoever I have done to the advancement of the cause, I may offend in the manner; in which respect (if I have offended) seeing it has pleased your lordships and the jury to find me guilty, I do willingly submit myself and heartily crave her majesty's pardon.

Judge. But are you sorry that you have offended the Queen's majesty?

Udall. I am sorry that the course of the law has found me to have offended.

Judge. So is every thief that is condemned sorry that his offence is found out, but not for the feet. This a plain fallacy.

Udall. My lord, indeed if it were so as your lordship does understand it, it were a plain fallacy but I say farther if in the manner of handling so good a cause there be found in me any offence against her majesty's laws, I acknowledge that in the manner of handling it, her majesty may be justly offended, for which I am sorry. And I protest that I have never gone about to advance it by any other means than by manifesting it to all men and tendering it to them in authority; and that by such means as might not be contrary to the laws of this land that so it might he received by her majesty and the state and this is the care of us all, howsoever we be charged with factions.

Judge. You say, if there be found any offence; whereby you call in question the equity of dealing in this court against you.

Udall. My lords, I do not, neither will I let it be looked into by you and the rest whom it concerns, I hope you would not deal otherwise than lawfully against me.

Judge Puckering. You say you seek no unlawful means, what can be meant but unlawful means in the words of your book? If it come in by that means that will make all your hearts to ache, blame yourselves. What good means can be meant by these words?

Udall. My lords, yesterday I showed you what I took to be the meaning of the author in some places of the book alleged against me in the indictment; and then I would have spoken to all, but you cut me off. I pray you therefore let me show you the meaning of the author in those words now.

Judge. Let us hear you how you expound it.

Udall. My lords, your lordships must understand that the author takes it for granted that the cause is God's, and must prevail and therefore, seeing God has used all the means of his mercy to bring it in, in giving us a gracious prince long peace, and abundance, and of stirring up some to exhibit supplications to the Parliament; these things not prevailing in his mercy, he will bring it in by some judgment as plague or famine or some such like punishment and this is always the manner of God's dealing.

Judge. You cannot expound it so; for the words import another thing.

Udall. My lord, the author himself expounds it so in the words following; where he said that it must prevail, for such a judgment will overtake this land, as shall make the ears of all that hear thereof to tingle so that he means nothing but this that God will bring it in by his own hand by judgment, if by mercy he cannot prevail.

Judge. No, no; your meaning was that it should be brought in by force and violence.

Udall. God forbid! Far be it from us to conceive any such imagination. The author of that book does plainly show that he meant no such thing; and the words following in the end of the epistle do declare the same; for there he shows by whom it is to be brought in, namely by her majesty and her honorable counselors, that they may see it and establish the same.

Judge. Nay, the meaning is that if the Queen will not yet you say it shall come in; for so the words are that it must prevail, maugre the heads of all that stand against it.

Udall. Nay, my lords, the words are maugre the malice of all that stand against it. For there are many heads that are not maliciously bent against it, there is great difference between malice and heads; for some are against the cause through ignorance.

Judge. It is all one in effect.

Udall. Nay my lords, there is great difference.

Judge Puckering. Well Mr. Udall, you were best to submit yourself to the Queen's mercy and leave these courses; for I tell you that your book is most seditious and slanderous against her majesty and the state; and yet I assure you that your book had been passed over if there had not come forth presently after it such a number of slanderous libels, as 'Martin Mar-Prelate,' 'Martin's Epitome,' 'Martin Jun.' or '*Theses Martiniana*?' 'Martin Sen.' and other such like; of which your book was judged to be the ring leader.

Udall. My lords, those that are learned and do maintain this cause, do judge this book to be written very indifferently, howsoever it be hardly construed. But for 'Martin,' and the rest of those books that you have named, they were never approved by the Godly learned and I am fully persuaded that those books were not done by any minister; and I think there is never a minister in this land that does know who 'Martin' is. And I for my part have been inquisitive, but I could never learn who he is.

Judge Clarke. You will not acknowledge yourself faulty in anything, and therefore it is in vain to stand any longer with you.

Udall. I will easily confess that in manner the author has offended for no man can handle a cause so well, but there will fault appear ill it as appears by Job who having a good cause handled it weakly, it is easier to handle an ill cause cunningly than a good one well.

Judge. Nay, but you have maliciously offended in publishing this book, which tends to the overthrowing of the state and the moving of rebellion.

Udall. My lords, that be far from me; for we teach that reforming things amiss if the prince will not consent the weapons that subjects are to fight withal are repentance and prayers patience and tears.

Judge. Yea, you had done well if you had used these weapons rather than to have made this book.

Udall. God forbid but that we should give to her majesty that honor which justly is due to her! For we have not taught the people to reform the state without the prince, and our practice has proved the same; for we never taught any of her subjects to go before her but to leave that honor as belongs to her majesty.

Judge. Well, will you submit yourself or not? For else I must proceed to judgment and I have no authority to favor you, neither will I stay sentence of death according to my office what my brother has I know not, and therefore shortly submit yourself, or else I am to pronounce sentence of death.

Udall. And I am ready to receive it, for I protest before God (not knowing that I am to live an hour) that the cause is good, and I am contented to receive sentence, so that I may leave it to posterity how I have suffered for the cause. But, my lords the cause excepted, I will submit myself in anything.

Judge. Let the cause alone and tell us no more of it, but acknowledge yourself to have offended the Queen's majesty.

Udall. I may not in any case yield in the cause; I have almost ever since I was a preacher of the gospel professed it, and therefore I cannot be at this time changed.

Judge. Let (I say) the cause alone, say what you will do.

Udall. I must needs profess it and mention it, lest it should be thought that I have started from it; but for anything that I have done in the manner against law, I am heartily sorry for it more than this I cannot say, do with me what you will.

Judge. But are you sorry for offending her majesty and her laws, and be you contented to amend and to live in obedience as becomes a good subject?

Udall. I am content to seek the advancement of this cause by no other means than that which may stand with the laws of this land and the duty of a good subject.

Judge. I come not here to entreat you to submit yourself, but you shall do it willingly upon your knees and crave her majesties mercy.

Udall. Then Mr. Udall kneeling down, said I refuse not any kind of submission to her majesty and I entreat your lordships to be a means to her majesty for me; and if I were worthy that my poor papers might come to her majesty or to her honorable council, I would write thus much to them.

Judge. Nay, will you write thus much to us, that we may first see it and commend it to her majesty?

Udall. I willingly do it.

Thus they dismissed him.

And this is the sum of that which I with the help of others could remember, having not any intent to leave out or enlarge anything further than the meaning of the speakers did intend notwithstanding many more things were said on both sides, especially the set speeches of both the judges, and of Mr. Daulton, to the disgrace of the desired reformation which could not well be expressed in particular, and therefore I have left them. Also many other things Mr. Udall proposed and begun to say which they stopped, so that they could not be perceived.

The assizes being thus ended, Mr. Udall was returned to the prison of the White-Lion again where he continued till the sessions in Southwark beginning the 18th Feb. 1590; during which time he wrote a supplication or submission to the Queen's majesty as follows:

Mr. Udall's supplication to her majesty.

Most gracious and dread sovereign, the present and lamentable estate wherein I stand, being found guilty by verdict to be author of a book entitled, 'A Demonstration of Discipline,' and being without your gracious pardon to die for the same; I humbly prostrate myself at your majesty's feet submitting myself in most humble manner as becomes a dutiful subject to such order as it shall please your highness to appoint, to whom God has given so high and sovereign a power as is able both to kill and to quicken, to bring to the gates of death, and to cause to return to the comfort of life again before whom standing thus convict, I am not to plead my innocence; yet I most humbly desire it may not offend your excellent majesty that I protest (of the truth whereof I call God to witness who knows all secrets and will judge both the quick and the dead) that I had never any thought or imagination to publish, write, or do anything maliciously, or tending to the dishonor or slander of your majesty's royal person or princely estate, under whose gracious government I have attained so many benefits and blessings; amongst which I most highly esteem the true knowledge and fear of God; in regard whereof I have been always ready even to adventure my life, for the preservation of your most royal person and defense of your princely estate and the same have also taught to others as a thing specially commanded by God notwithstanding fearing the severity of justice to death, I fly for life to your majesty's most gracious mercy, most humbly desiring your highness of your merciful compassion for relief of my poor and miserable estate, to grant me your gracious and comfortable pardon, whereby I may be discharged both of the offence and punishment, which the law has laid upon me. Other hope than this have I none, but the trust I have in God, (according to his promises) that your majesty by a special gift of God is gracious and merciful and have vouchsafed to show mercy even to such as were not only by imputation of law, but indeed malicious and mortal enemies to your highness; and therefore I hope that the same goodness of so princely a nature may be moved, and will show forth itself in like gracious compassion on my behalf. Which gracious pardon on my knees I most humbly crave your excellent majesty to grant to me by which special favor being raised as it were from the dead, I promise and vow to lead the rest of my life in all humble and dutiful obedience to your majesty; praying continually for the preservation of your highness's precious life and happy government to the honor of almighty God, and the comfort of all obedient and dutiful subjects.

Further proceedings against Mr. Udall at the Assizes in Southwark: 33 Elizabeth, February 18, 19, 20, A. D, 1590.

Being called the first day of the Assizes in the afternoon, Sergeant Puckering said. We do not mean now to deal with you, only I must put you in mind that you have made a petition wherein you promise to submit yourself to such order as her majesty shall appoint; consider of it and look that you do it, for I can tell you it is looked for at your hands.

Udall. I know not, my lord, what you mean; I made a petition to her majesty and will willingly perform anything promised therein.

Puckering. Well, advise well with yourself and look that you do it, I tell you forehand.

Udall. Unless you mean that, I know not your meaning.

Justice Fenner dwelling in Surry, sat on the bench, and said: Mr. Udall, I must needs say something to you; I have heard much good of you and that you are learned; it were pity you should do otherwise than well; I pray you take heed that those good things which are in you be not marred for want of humility. I tell you humility is a special virtue in a man of your calling, the want whereof marred all in them that want it; I pray you stand not in your own opinion too much. I have heard that you have done much good, let not humility be wanting.

Udall. My lord, I acknowledge that humility is a virtue generally required in a man of my calling without which all other gifts are nothing; for God resists the proud, and gives wisdom to the simple and I desire that the same virtue may be found in me. But I trust your meaning is not thereby to persuade me to deny the truth which I trust the lord will keep me from, whatsoever befall me.

Justice Fenner. I speak to you of good will, I would not have you stiff in your own conceit.

Puckering. Remember what I said to you.

And so I was carried into a chamber to be conferred with by some of the bench, &c. And when that promise which the judge so much spoke of came to be examined, it was nothing but a sentence in my submission to her highness, the meaning whereof is (as the words going before it, and immediately following it, do declare) that I professed myself willing to live or die according as that power which God has given to her majesty shall appoint. I having been dealt withal to this effect the first day of the Assizes (by certain of the bench in private) as also the second day by some of them to this effect, that I would make such a submission as would condemn the book in question and justify the hierarchy; and perceiving that I was not to be heard till the last day, I entreated Sir William Moore and Mr. Bowyer to be a mean to the judges for me; that forasmuch as my case was rare, and I had (as I was persuaded) sufficient to allege why (notwithstanding the verdict again it me) judgment ought to be stayed, I might be heard over night that so (according to that good counsel given by them to me to advise with myself and to consider what I would do) also they might have a night to think of what I had to say and the next day to do with me as God should move them.

Hereupon I was fetched forth before the judges in private, immediately after dinner; who using many persuasions to draw me to relent (which being in private, I will not express) told me that they sent for me, for that they understood I desired to be heard over-night, which they were willing then and there to do. I answered, my lords, my meaning was not to desire private, but public hearing seeing I have nothing to say, but such as would prevent myself and disappoint my public speech if I should utter it in private, yet because they told me their other affairs would not permit them to have any time with me till the latter end of the assizes, I was rather willing that I should be prevented than they should be constrained to determine on a sudden upon so weighty a matter whereupon I did draw out a paper for each of them containing these reasons following:

I humbly pray your lordships to consider whether these reasons ought not in conscience to move you to stay the sentence notwithstanding the verdict against me and to be means of my release.

1. It seems that my case is not esteemed felony by the judges of the land, seeing they do usually sit in the high commission court where the printing and dispersing of the same, and such like books are usually enquired after as transgressions of another nature.

2. No judgment in law ought to be given in case of felony but upon a party first found guilty thereof by a verdict of twelve men; but I am not so for proof whereof I pray you it may be remembered that your lordship gave the jury in issue only for the trial of the fact, whether I were author of such a book and freed them from enquiring the intent without which there is no felony.

3. I humbly pray you call to mind by what means the jury was drawn to give that verdict they did, whether they were left wholly to their own consciences or were wrong to it partly by promise, assuring it should be no further danger to me, but tend to my good; and partly by fear, as appears in that it has been an occasion of great grief to some of them ever since. And then I pray you to consider whether upon such a verdict so drawn from twelve simple men, Christian judges in a good conscience, may proceed to sentence of death?

4. In case the verdict was never so free, yet your lordships being men of wisdom and knowledge are to consider whether the statute whereupon I am indicted do agree to my case in the truth and meaning of it there being nothing in that book spoken of her majesty's person, but in duty and honor; and whether the drawing of it from her majesty to the bishops (as being a part of her body politic) be not a violent depraving and wresting of the statute which if it be, you being Christian judges cannot in a good

conscience upon such a ground proceed to sentence contrary to your own knowledge. 5. But if the statute be to be taken so as it is urged, it ought to be considered that without a malicious intent against her majesty's person, the statute itself makes no act forbidden by it to be felonious; wherein I appeal first to God and then to all men that have seen the whole course of my life and to your lordships own consciences, wherein I pray you to examine yourselves in the sight of God, whether either by yourselves, or the just report of any other, you can find me guilty of any act in all my life that savored of any malice or malicious intent against her majesty, or of any other behavior than stands with the allegiance and duty of a most dutiful and Christian subject. Of which malice, or malicious intent against her majesty, if your consciences clear me before God, the act wherewith I am charged being not felony without such an intent; I hope you will consider that you cannot with a good conscience proceed to judgment.

6. Yet if the statute and intent were such as it is said in case of life the evidences ought to be pregnant and full living witnesses (I am sure by the word of God, and I trust also by the laws of this land) were to have been produced face to face to charge me. But I have none such against me, neither any other thing, saving only papers and reports of depositions taken by ecclesiastical commissioners and others; which kind of proof the judges of the land cast away in case of lands and by no means allow to be sufficient and therefore are much less to be allowed in a case of life which being so, your lordships ought to have a conscience, that upon so weak evidences sentence of death be not pronounced.

7. But if the same that has been given in for evidence in writing, had been testified by men living, standing out in the presence of the court and of me the accused; I trust your lordships will consider that no one of the evidences do directly prove me to be the author of the book in question; which as it was, has little force in it, as appears by this that the author of the chief testimony is so grieved, that he is ashamed to come where he is known. Whereupon, howsoever the jury have not discerned thereof, yet you being men of skill and understanding are to have regard of it, and not upon so weak and impertinent proofs, to proceed to judgment of death.

8. If all these things were such as they ought to be yet your lordships are to consider (supposing me to be the author of the book in question) that the said book for the substance of it contains nothing but that which is taught and believed to be a part of the gospel of Christ by all the best reformed churches in Europe; where in nothing being diverse from them, I cannot be condemned without condemning in me all such nations and churches as hold the same doctrine. In which (if there be no error in them) the offence commonly being in form, circumstance and manner of writing, which some men may think worthy an admonition, some more severe worthy correction and imbruement, the sharpest cannot judge it to deserve more than some short time of imprisonment. But death for an error of such a kind in terms and words not altogether dutiful of certain bishops, cannot be but extreme cruelty. Which seeing it ought to be far from any Christian man that has the

bowels of Christ in him, surely Christian judges professing the gospel for a service of the gospel (saving some oversight in words and terms) ought not to proceed against me (who have endeavored to show myself a dutiful subject and faithful minister of the gospel) to give sentence of death.

9. My offence not being aggravated but remaining as it was the last Assizes when my submission was accepted and judgment thereupon staid; I trust your favor will be the same towards me now also seeing I am ready to do the like. If all this prevail not, yet my redeemer lives to whom I commend myself and say as sometimes Jeremy said in a case not much unlike; 'Behold I am in your hands, do with me what seems good to you but know you this, that if you put me to death, you shall bring innocent blood upon your own heads and upon the land.' As the blood of Abel, so the blood of Udall will cry to God with a loud voice and the righteous judge of the world will require it at the hands of all those that shall be guilty of it.

This is the sum of that which I delivered to the judges.

The Assizes being almost finished and the other prisoners that were called to the bar to have sentence of death standing forth to hear the same; I was at the last called and demanded what I could say for myself why I should not have judgment to die. Hereupon I humbly craving audience, began to this effect:

Udall. My lords, I do acknowledge that I have been here proceeded against by due course of law and that a verdict was given in against me the last Assizes as guilty of felony, &c. But I do not only as heretofore, protest my innocence but also think that I have sufficient to allege why (notwithstanding the verdict) judgment ought not to be given; wherefore I entreat to be heard.

Judge Puckering. I pray you stay, you seem in the beginning to speak contraries; for first you acknowledge the course of law to be due and afterwards stand upon it that you are innocent. How can a due course of law condemn the innocent?

Udall. These things agree well enough as I will show if it shall please you to give me leave. It is by due course of law that I have been indicted, arraigned, have had a jury impaneled upon me been accused, heard speak for myself, and testimony produced against me, but in that the proof by witness was insufficient and the jury either in judgment or affection misled; thereupon it has come to pass that (notwithstanding the due course of law) guiltiness is laid upon a guiltless person. But I pray you let me proceed to the reasons that I have to allege for myself.

Then I left the first reason of purpose seeing I did rather wish that they only should understand it (which they did by my papers overnight) than to blaze it to the world; so that I did begin to speak according to the second reason mentioned before whereupon Sergeant Puckering prayed Baron Clarke to speak seeing it did most concern him.

Judge Clarke. I must needs tell you, you do us and the seat of justice great wrong. Indeed I told the jury what was the law in the opinion of all the judges of the land; for it was not my private opinion, as I said also at that time.

Udall. It is not material my lord in this case what the judges think; for though all the judges in the world thought so, our laws thought no man a felon or capable of sentence as a felon till he be convicted by the verdict of twelve men.

Clarke. You are so convicted, as the record will testify.

Udall. I acknowledge the record against me, but I appeal to your lordship's conscience, whether you delivered not to them speeches to this effect. As for the felony you are not so much to enquire, but only whether he made the book, leaving the felony to us.

Clarke. You do me great wrong, I only told them the law.

Udall. Well, I leave it to your lordship's favorable consideration; you perceive my reason.

Then I spoke to the third reason, whereupon it was said:

Puckering. All that you say tends to the disgracing of the court of justice held against you heretofore the jury were left to their own consciences, and did as they saw meet to do.

Udall. No my lords, I speak not anything to disgrace the court of justice; for I acknowledge both this course and all others of the like nature to be God's holy ordinance which I ought to reference; neither do I speak to defame the jury but only to give your lordships occasion why you may not proceed to sentence thereupon for if the jury did well, why should it grieve any of them? If they did ill your lordships may not proceed to sentence thereupon.

Puckering. We cannot remember the particular circumstances that then passed, neither are we to call in question the verdict; but it is your office to give sentence according to it.

Udall. I pray your lordships tell me one thing, must the judges always give sentence according to the verdict, or may there not be cause to stay it?

Clarke. Yes, there may be cause to stay the verdict, such may the case be.

Udall. And I desire no other, but that my reasons may be well weighed, whether my case be such or no.

Then I prayed for so much as they had the substance of that in writing a forehand which I meant to say it would please them to give me leave to say at once what I could lest my memory (being so much weakened and dulled by imprisonment) should fail me, and so I leave some material thing unspoken. Then I spoke according to the fourth and fifth reasons, whereto little was replied saying such things as were mentioned at my arraignment only Baron Clarke used a very long speech wherein he compared Mr. Stubb's cause and mine together; and after the end of his speech, judge Puckering said:

Puckering. Who taught you such law? I tell you, you are much deceived and abused in it; one may be within the compass of felony though he do not directly mean any such thing.

Udall. Your lordship knows I pleaded these points the last assizes when I came from close imprisonment to the bar. I understand English, which is the language wherein the statute was written and I profess myself a scholar; and therefore to have (through God's mercy) some understanding of the sense of that I read. It seems to me the most direct and no otherwise to be taken than I understand it.

Then I spoke according to the sixth and seventh reasons, whereto it was replied thus:

Puckering. You are deceived in that you think the witnesses against you the less lawful because the parties were not present. It is an ordinary thing to have witnesses examined in the chancery and other such like courts which do remain there of as sufficient credit for ever, as they were when the party's oath was taken upon the same.

Udall. Then would I have answered that the case was not alike seeing the high-commission is no court of record; but I was not then suffered to speak, for that it was said by the other judge:

Clarke. Where do you find that there must needs (by the word of God) be two witnesses face to face?

Udall. It is so clear, as the witnesses were also to have the first hand in executing the punishment upon the party offending.

Puckering. That was according to Moses's law which we are not tied to.

Udall. It is the word of God which has a perpetual equity in it; for the life of man is so precious in the sight of God as he would not have it taken away without most evident and manifest proof, such as in his law is set down.

Clarke. We are not now to call in question the proofs seeing the jury did think them sufficient this speech of yours tends to prove the jury perjured.

Udall. Not so, my lord; I think of them that they did according to their consciences; but being men unlearned, and the case being strange to them they may have done their best; and yet you being men of more knowledge and judgment are to look further into the matter.

Puckering. Whereas you say that none of the witnesses did directly prove you the author of the fact that was not necessary; for if all laid together and the circumstances considered do prove it, it is as good a proof as if every witness were direct.

Udall. But the law of God, from which I trust but laws disagree not, would that every proof be direct.

Puckering. And do you think indeed that the laws of this land are agreeable to the word of God?

Udall. I do not profess to know them; but surely I have so reverent an opinion of them that I trust the grounds of them are according to the word of God however in some particulars the proceedings may miss thereof.

Puckering. Then the government by archbishops and lord bishops is according to the word of God seeing the laws of the land do allow them.

Udall. I pray you, my lord, take me not so general; for that will not follow upon my speeches.

Puckering. Well, you may not now disgrace the witnesses; you should have done it at your arraignment.

Udall. I neither meant then, nor purpose now to disgrace the witnesses, but to show the insufficiency of their testimony in this case that your lordships may thereby see some reason to stay the sentence. The first testimony that was alleged was that of Mr. Chatfield who affirmed that it was not given in against me upon his oath; but only in his anger he set his hand to, but is now sorry for it.

Puckering. You should have alleged this before; it is now too late.

Udall. It is alleged too late to prevent the verdict. But if there be any force in it, it ought to be considered to stay the sentence. I could allege it no sooner because I knew it not till after the verdict.

Puckering. We may not suffer you to proceed so to disgrace that which is passed already if you have any other thing to say speak on; otherwise we must do our office.

Udall. It is not my meaning howsoever you take it to disgrace anything passed heretofore; only I pray you further to consider that Thompkins, whose testimony only carried some show, protested before my commitment that he would not for all the world affirm me to be the author of the book.

Puckering. Why did you not plead these things to the jury?

Udall. I did so, and offered to produce sufficient proof for it; but your lordships answered that no witnesses might be heard in my behalf, seeing it was against the Queen which seems strange to me; for me thinks it should be for the Queen to hear all things on both sides especially when the life of any of her subjects is in question.

Puckering. The witnesses were then thought by the jury sufficient to prove the matter which we may not now call in doubt; therefore say on, if you have any more.

Udall. Then I spoke according to the eighth reason; whereupon it was said.

Clarke. I tell you, you are not called in question for the cause (as you call it) nor for the body of the book; but only for slanderous things in the preface against her majesty's government and therefore you may let the cause alone.

Udall. But it is for the hatred borne to the cause that I am thus entreated; for had not it been handled in the book such matter as is now made of the preface had never been objected against me, or any other.

Puckering. Well, it is best for you to leave off all other pleas and submit yourself to the Queen's majesty's mercy.

Udall. I will do so with all my heart.

Puckering. But will you do it as you did the last Assizes?

Udall. Yea, that I will. And so I spoke according to the last reason; whereupon it was said.

Puckering. You confessed that you were justly condemned.

Udall. I am not yet condemned.

Puckering. I mean convicted by the jury. Then you acknowledged that you had offended her majesty; that you were sorry for it and promised that you would never do the like again.

Udall. My lord, it is not for me to oppose my word and credit (which is nothing) against yours; I refer it to them that heard it only I pray you give me leave to speak of it as I take it that it was. First, I did avow (and so I do now, and will do whilst I live) that the cause handled in that book is an undoubted truth.

Clarke. How often shall we bid you leave the cause and tell you that you are not troubled for it?

Udall. But it is the cause that is sought to be defaced in my person and therefore I must and will still profess it and justify it whatsoever disgrace I receive by it to myself. I pray you let me proceed. Secondly, I did protest that I never had any purpose in deface, but ever to seek to honor her majesty and her government. Thirdly, I professed that the course of law against me was due; whereby what I have meant, you have heard. Fourthly, I said that I never had any purpose to do anything to the advancement of this cause but keeping myself to the uttermost of my power within the compass of the law. Lastly, I never confessed myself to be the author of the book. Then my submission was this, that if I had done anything to the advancement of so holy a cause which had brought me within compass of the law, or might justly offend her majesty, I was heartily sorry for it. If this be not it, let me have any other drawn wherein the former points are justified, and I will set my hand to it.

Puckering. But all this is nothing to your book in particular; what say you to it?

Udall. I say this, that though I hold the matter in it to be a most manifest truth; yet I confess the manner of handling in some part to be such as might justly provoke her majesty's indignation.

Puckering. Because you stand so much upon the cause as you call it you provoke me so, as I must needs say somewhat of it lest the audience should think some matter in it, more than is.

Udall. My lord, you understand my judgment therein. I beseech you speak not against it unless you will give me leave to reply to you.

Puckering. I may not do so, you provoke me to it; your discipline that you stand upon whereupon is it grounded? Forsooth upon the saying of Christ tell the church which never was expounded these 1500 years as you do within these few years.

Udall. My Lord, he did abuse you that told you so? Chrysostom expounded it, 'Tell the Church,' that is the governors of the church.

Puckering. He meant the governors of the Jewish synagogue.

Udall. How can that be, when he lived above 400 years after Christ?

Puckering. Was there never any that could find it out before now if it were a truth?

Udall. Yes; it has testimony sufficient, if it might be received.

Puckering. And lest men should think that your matter were as good as you pretend, I will tell you what I know; as it is written in one of your books that without an eldership there is no salvation.

Udall. I am persuaded that cannot be showed.

Puckering. Yes, it is in 'Theses Martiniana'. One writ that it is time to number our hot brethren; another, Mr. Snape of Northampton by name wrote that the bishops should be put down all in one day.

These things he did discourse of at large in an invective speech, most bitter, tending to persuade the people that we meant to rebel and set up the discipline and pull down the bishops by strong hand; and went about to impair the Queen's prerogative and patrimony. After which with much ado, I got audience to this effect.

Udall. My lord, I protest in the presence of God and hearing of all this people, that neither I nor any of my brethren that ever I was acquainted with to my knowledge did so much as ever purpose or speak of any such means as your lordship mentioned to bring in the discipline; but only by prayer to God, supplication to her majesty, and such other peaceable means this is my answer to your large invective. And whereas, my lord you seem to be so hardly carried against the cause, I would not doubt but if I might privately confer with you with the blessing of God to persuade you to be a friend to it.

And after some other speeches of other books and the aforesaid speeches in the books mentioned already, Judge Puckering said:

Puckering. Nay, I tell you there are as foul things in your own book for do you not say that the church is committed to the mistress of the Stews and ruled by the laws of a brothel house?

Udall. It is spoken of the Popish canon-law; which is as unlit to rule the church of Christ, as the laws of a brothel-house to govern an honest woman.

Puckering. And those laws are established by her majesty's laws.

Udall. It would trouble the learned lawyer in England to prove that.

Then Baron Clarke began a voice tending again to compare my case to that of Mr. Stubbs and to persuade me to submit myself telling me what good I might do; but because he spoke low and I said I did not well hear him, he gave over and prayed the other to speak who told me his meaning and then said:

Puckering. We shall make short work with you will you here acknowledge all the laws ecclesiastical and temporal of this land to be agreeable to the word of God?

Udall. My Lord, I have disgrace enough upon me already you may easily perceive what I think of the present ecclesiastical government. I pray you press me not with these things; I can yield no further than you have heard.

Puckering. Then we must do our office, and pronounce sentence on you.

Udall. God's will be done.

Puckering. Yea, God's will be done on you indeed.

Then he gave sentence upon me and the rest. After which I did purpose to speak according to the last sentence after the reasons; but the clamors of the other prisoners calling to the judges to be good to them, disappointed me thereof. Thus was I returned to prison; what will be the issue, I know not. The Lord turn it to his glory, the good of his church and shame of his foes; and then welcome life or death.

I being reprieved (as the sheriff said by her majesty's own commandment), Dr. Bond, one of the Queen's chaplains came to me as from the Queen herself and from the council with the submission that was tendered to me to confer with me in general but especially to persuade me to yield thereto, or to take the reasons of my refusal. After two days conference, we agreed upon a form of submission, as follows:

The form of that submission which was offered to me, and I refused.

I, John Udall have been hitherto by due course of law, convicted of felony for penning and setting forth a certain book called 'A Demonstration of Discipline'; wherein false, slanderous and seditious matters are contained against her majesty's prerogative royal, her crown and dignity and against the laws and government ecclesiastical and temporal established by law under her highness and tending to the erecting of a new form of government contrary to her said laws all which points I do now by the grace of God perceive to be very dangerous to the peace of this realm and church, seditious in the common wealth and justly offensive to the Queen's most excellent majesty; so as thereby I now seeing the grievousness of this my offence, do most humbly on my knees before God and this presence submit myself to the mercy of her highness; being most sorry, that so deeply and worthily I have incurred her majesty's indignation against me promising if it shall please God to move her royal heart to have compassion on me, a most sorrowful convicted person that I will for ever hereafter forsake all such undutiful and dangerous courses and demean myself dutifully and peaceably to all authorities both civil and ecclesiastical, established in this realm; for I do acknowledge them to be both lawful and godly and to be obeyed of every faithful subject.

The form of that submission whereto I did consent and set my hand.

With these three protestations I do submit myself in manner as follows:

1. I hold the cause of discipline debated in that book to be an undoubted truth.

2. I never imagined any evil against her majesty's person or estate; but have sought to honor them both.

3. I never proposed to do or persuade anything whereby the discipline might be advanced but by peaceable means; endeavoring to keep within the compass of law.

I, John Udall have been by due course of law convicted and condemned of felony, for penning and publishing a certain book called 'The Demonstration of Discipline' in the preface whereof some matter as also, the manner of writing, I confess to be in some part so bitter and undutiful as deserves justly to be censured and punished and justly offensive to the Queen's most excellent majesty wherefore the trial of the law imputing to me all such defaults as are in that book and laying the punishment of the same in most grievous manner upon me; and I seeing the grievousness of this offence, do most humbly on my knees as in the presence of God submit myself to the mercy of her highness being most sorry that to deep and just occasions should be given to procure her majesty's displeasure against me; promising that if it shall please God to move her royal heart to have compassion on me a most sorrowful condemned person, that I will forever here after forsake all undutiful and dangerous courses and demean myself dutifully and peaceably as becomes a minister of the gospel and as a loyal subject to the Queen's most excellent majesty.

At the same time that Dr. Bond was with me, I received a letter from a friend of mine that did solicit Sir Walter Raleigh for me; wherein were these words:

Sir Walter Raleigh willed me to let you understand that her majesty is informed of you that you hold that the church of England is no church, and the sacraments of the same no sacraments; and that all her ecclesiastical laws are against the word of God and so her government; and that all ecclesiastical matters ought to be governed by a presbytery and she herself to be subject to the censures thereof and that for these things and such like, you are not worthy to live. But if you will write half a dozen lines under your hand to Sir Walter concerning these opinions that he may show it to her majesty, he hopes to obtain your life. I know it is an easy thing for you to answer all these things; and therefore do it with speed and in your writing to Sir Walter take knowledge that he has sent you such word.

Hereupon I wrote a letter to Sir Walter Raleigh and what I hold in these points, as follows:

To the right honorable Sir Walter Raleigh, Kt. Lord Warden of the Stannary: My duty being remembered to your lordship, I humbly thank your honor for your great and honorable care over me and for my good; whereof I trust you shall never be ashamed most humbly beseeching your good lordship to be a means to appease her majesty's indignation conceived against me by means of some accusations untruly suggested. For God is my witness,

I have never had any earthly thing in so precious account as to honor her highness; and to draw her subjects to acknowledge with all thankfulness the exceeding blessings that God bestowed upon them by her majesty's happy government, whereof I trust my adversaries will be witnesses when I am dead. I have sent to your lordship (as in perplexity I could upon the sudden) what I hold concerning certain points declared to me as from your lordship; praying that it would please you to make known the truth thereof to her highness and if neither my submission heretofore delivered, nor these things now set down will be accepted to draw her highness of her gracious compassion to pardon me that vet it would please her majesty (that the land may not be charged with my blood) to change my punishment from death to banishment. Thus trusting your lordship will vouchsafe me this favor and that it will please her majesty thereupon graciously to consider of me I humbly take my leave, from the White-Lion, Feb. 52, 1590. Your lordship's to command, John Udall, prisoner.

1. I do believe and have often preached that the church of England is a part of the true visible church of Christ; and that the preaching of the word and administration of the sacraments therein are the holy ordinances of God, profitable and comfortable to every one that rightly partakes thereof in which regard I have been and do yet desire to be a preacher in the same church and have communicated in the sacraments and prayers therein for the space of seven years at Kingston, and about a year at Newcastle upon Tine immediately before mine imprisonment. And therefore I do from my heart utterly renounce the schism where into the Brownists have fallen in condemning the churches of England and separating themselves from communicating in the public ministry thereof.

2. I know no other but that the statute laws of this land do maintain the holy ministry of the word and sacraments in such manner as any Christian may with a safe conscience, both administer therein and communicate therewithal also that the law which requires a subscription to the articles of religion so far as they contain the doctrine of faith and sacraments is agreeable to the word of God.

3. I do believe that by the word of God her majesty has and ought to have a supreme authority over all persons in all causes, both ecclesiastical and civil, to enforce every man to do his duty and to be obedient in everything that is not contrary to the word of God. And if the prince should command anything contrary to God's word it is not lawful for the subjects to rebel or resist, nor not so much as in thought but with patience and humility to bear all the punishments laid upon them; seeking only by prayer to God and supplication to authority and such like peaceable means to have faults amended.

4. I do believe that by the word of God, the churches rightly reformed ought to be governed ecclesiastically by the ministers assisted with elders; and this is not my private judgment but such as I have learned out of the word of God, been confirmed in by the writings of the most learned and godly men of ancient and latter times and have seen practiced with much

peace and comfort in the best reformed churches in Europe and even by those exiles which her majesty to her great honor has hitherto protected.

5. I do believe that the censures of the church ought merely to concern the soul and may not impeach any subject much less any prince in the liberty of body, dominion, goods or any earthly privilege whatsoever; and that therefore the papal excommunication that deposed princes and freed their subjects from their allegiance or any part of Christian obedience to civil authority is blasphemous against God, injurious to all men and directly contrary to God's word, neither do I believe that a Christian prince ought otherwise to be subject to the censures of the church, than our gracious Queen professes herself to be to the preaching of the word and administration of the sacraments according to the doctrine of our church in Mr. Nowell's Catechism, and the Homilies of the right use of the church at this day appointed publicly to be read. If I understand of any other thing that I am charged to hold as a strange and private opinion, I would be willing to show my mind freely in it; for my desire is that her highness might truly be informed of every thing that I hold; so should I be sure to obtain her gracious favor without which I do not desire to live.

These things thus passed, I remained as before without any great hope of liberty or fear of extremity until the next Assizes drew near at last there came Mr. Nowell Dean of Paul's and Mr. Dr. Andrews with a new submission yet containing nothing (one clause excepted) which was not in the former which I condescended to notwithstanding I refused presently to set my hand to it (though they promised in the name of the council that in yielding to it I should obtain pardon and liberty) because I would do nothing without good advice and consideration.

The copy of the submission given me by Mr. Dean of Paul's with his name to it as follows:

I, John Udall have been heretofore by due course of law, convicted and condemned of felony for penning and publishing a certain book called 'The Demonstration of Discipline'; in the preface whereof some matter as also the manner of handling of it I confess in some parts to be so bitter and undutiful as deserves justly to be censured and punished according to the laws of this realm established under her highness and justly offensive to the Queen's most excellent majesty wherefore I now seeing the grievousness of this offence do most humbly on my knees and in the presence of God, submit myself to the mercy of her highness being most sorry that so deep and just occasion should be given to procure her majesty's displeasure against me; promising that if it shall please God to move her majesty's royal heart to have compassion on me a most sorrowful condemned person I will ever hereafter forsake all undutiful, seditious and dangerous courses, and demean myself dutifully and peaceably as become a minister of the gospel and a loyal subject of the Queen's most excellent majesty.

This is the true copy of the submission sent to me from her majesty's most honorable Privy Council, Alexander Nowell.

When I had weighed with myself that the clause which is added may admit a good interpretation and the omitting of that which is left out of my former submission, causes no ill tense of that which is set down I condescended (being also advised thereto by my good and godly friends) to set my hand to it; and thereupon wrote a letter to Mr. Nowell as follows:

Right worshipful Mr. Dean, I praise God with all my heart that authority has so good remembrance of my lamentable estate and yet more that by the same I am for my form of submission to deal with a man of that piety and wisdom that you have been worthily in the church long gone esteemed to be of and so have continued to this reverend age that you are come to. It may please you sir, to understand that I have considered of the form of submission that your worship brought to me and find nothing in it but that in a good conscience I can yield to; for it required not of me any denial or disallowance of the cause of discipline debated in the book for which I am in question; the substance of which doctrine I believe to be the undoubted truth of God and therefore ought never to deny or disallow it notwithstanding with my persuasion I take God to witness that I never purposed to do or persuade anything whereby it might be advanced but by peaceable means endeavoring to keep within the compass of law. Further also the said form of submission charges me not with any malice against her majesty from which likewise I acknowledge as in the presence of our savior Christ that is ready to come to judge the quick and the dead that I have been always free and have carried a Christian loving and dutiful affection to her majesty's royal person and estate as I know by the word of God I ought to do; which being so, I have resolved to satisfy the authority from which you brought me the said form of submission and at your good pleasure without further limitation simply to subscribe it. Good Mr. Dean, in the bowels of Christ have compassion of my estate, more ways lamentable than I can in a few or many word's express, or (as I think) any other but only the spirit that is taught to pray with groans that cannot be uttered and in such Christian compassion by your favorable and earnest mediation to the authority that may relieve me procure my pardon and free discharge of the dangers and troubles wherein I am; that I may say with the prophet I shall not die, but live, and declare the works of the Lord. So shall not only my poor wife and children but I hope many others praise God for you in that respect and myself its beholden to you in a case of life, continually pray for your good estate to the lord of life blessed for ever. Amen.

After I had thus set my hand hereto I advised also to write to certain of the council and other honorable persons besides; partly to let them understand in what sense I had yielded hereto and partly to entreat their favor and furthermore for my liberty, the copy of which letter (for it was the same word for word to everyone, the title of their several estates excepted) here ensues.

Right honorable, my present lamentable condition enforces me in most humble manner to crave so much leisure of your lordships from the weighty affairs of the state as to consider of these few lines. The reverend Mr. Nowell,

Dean of Paul's and Mr. Dr. Andrews, a few days ago brought me a form of submission (as they said) from authority with hope of favor for my life if I would yield to it. Whereof having considered and finding nothing in it but which I had heretofore yielded to when Mr. Dr. Bond was with me, one clause excepted to wit that the faults do deserve to be punished according to the laws of the land which yet has no such words but may bear so good a sense as I think I may in such form submit myself without either condemning the suit for a further reformation or myself as justly deserving by the laws to die; I cannot discern sufficient cause to refuse it for by the hardest word that I have by due course of law been convicted and condemned; I understand the form of proceeding by indictment, arraignment, jury, witnesses and such like as also by that clause that the manner of writing is in some part such, as deserves justly to be censured and punished by the laws of this land. I mean of such censures as the good laws of this land administered with justice do ordain for punishing of such offences in the manner of writing; which cannot be of death without malice against her majesty; from which (I take almighty God to witness) I have been always free. In regard whereof I feared lest I might be thought to stand too contentiously and undutiful with authority and to be too careless of mine own estate if I should not yield to such a form of submission as they brought to me. Wherein having yielded as far as in conscience I may and as authority by their means requires of me; my most humble suit to your lordships is that in your Christian and honorable compassion of my most lamentable estate that it may please your lordships by your favorable mediation to her excellent majesty to further my most humble suit for my pardon and free discharge of these my grievous troubles. So shall I be bound yet more heartily to praise God for your honors and to pray to God for your prosperous estate long to endure to the glory of almighty God, and to your own everlasting comfort.

Within four or five days after, Mr. Dr. Andrews returned to me signifying that all that was done was mistaken for that was not the submission that was meant of me, but another. Which when I had perused I found it the same (only the last clause left out) which was offered me by the judges at the Assizes. And he said, the clerk to whom the making of the letter to Mr. Nowell was committed put in one for another. And because I utterly refused to consult of it as having yielded before to so much as I might he prayed me to understand what I took exception against and for what reasons. So we entered into many discourses; as first, how the discipline could be said to be against the Queen's prerogative royal seeing it was (as I said I did believe) expressed in the scriptures whereby all lawful privileges of princes are warranted. Then we debated whether the supremacy of a Christian prince be the same with an heathen or diverse from it. After that whether the authority of princes in making church laws be *de jure*, or *de facto* only and lastly of the most points of discipline. Thus we continued five or six hours and at last he would have no answer of me then but he prayed me to advise of it for he would come again. I answered that the oftener he came the welcome he should be, but I told him I would not accept of it; yet he came twice after and took my reasons of my refusal to yield thereto; and promising me all the favor he could procure me, he departed.

After this the Assizes approaching and the general report being that it would go hard with me; I being desirous to use any good means, did not only solicit the Earl of Essex and Sir Walter Raleigh who had heretofore dealt for me; but also I was advised to write again to Mr. Nowell earnestly charging him to take my cause to heart seeing he had promised to procure me favor whereupon I wrote to him this letter following:

Right worshipful Mr. Nowell. As I did rejoice when I perceived that you

were employed to deal with me about my submission because of that reverend estimation that you have been so long among the worthies in the church of God; hoping that I should have found thereby some comfortable means of mediation to authority for my release so I am now occasioned to fear that all that credit which you are of shall be used as an instrument to further and hasten extremity upon me. For so much time being passed since I voluntarily yielded to that submission which you brought to me and no liberty appearing from my place, but rather that being given out that my submission shall be a special means to hasten my death and no way to procure my liberty; I am constrained to write to you to let you understand that as I look for that end the next week at the Assizes at Kingston where I have been a preacher which has so long been threatened but (to the doubling of my torments) deferred; whereto I doubt not the lord will strengthen me as graciously be has here done so I pray you as you will answer to God for my blood which I am persuaded your credit being employed to the uttermost (as in the word and faith of a Christian you promised) might have preserved that you would so take my case to heart as it may in force you to leave no stone unturned which may either further my liberty or at least clear your conscience from being any way accessory to my death. For it will one day be a heavy thing to your heart to think that you should be set on work and the account that is worthily made of you employed under pretence, yea, and as it were with assurance of life and liberty to draw that from a preacher and professor of the gospel which afterward shall be used to hasten his end and you will say it had been better that you had never been of any reckoning than to be made an instrument to further such an action. This I write to you, not in any troubled affection with the fear of death, for I thank God I am willing to end my days and (if it please the Lord), even in this manner; and hope that my death shall further the cause for which I suffer more than my life but lest I should neglect any means which might seem to be a furtherance to prevent the same, or leave that duty unperformed to you, which I take myself in conscience bound to discharge. The Lord make us willing and able to discharge every good duty that he enjoins us to his glory, the good of his church and our own comfort whether by life or death.

About the same time came a letter from the King of Scotland to a Scottish merchant one Mr. Johnson lying in London to be delivered to her majesty (as was said), being written in my behalf as he had done once before when I was close prisoner; this letter did the merchant deliver to her majesty and the dean of Paul's upon my letter went to the council; whereby whatsoever was wrought as soon as the judges heard that I was brought to Kingston where the Assizes were then kept, I was immediately returned to the White-Lion in the evening before the first day thereof. Afterward Mr. Johnson had the copy of the King's letter sent to him which then appeared to be written not for me alone, but also for the rest of my brethren the ministers in prison for the same cause of discipline; the tenor of which letter here follows:

The just copy of the King's letter sent to her majesty.

Right excellent, high and mighty princess, our dearest sister and cousin in our heartiest manner we recommend us to you hearing of the apprehension of Mr. Udall, and Mr. Cartwright and certain other ministers of the evangel within your realm of whose good erudition and fruitful travels in the church we hear a very credible commendation; howsoever that their diversity from the bishops and others of your clergy in matters touching them in conscience has been a mean by their dilation to work them your disliking; at this present we cannot (weighing the duty which we owe to such as are afflicted for their conscience in that profession) but by our most infectious and earnest letter interpose us at your hands to any harder usage of them for that cause requesting you most earnestly that for our cause and intercession it may please you to let them to be relieved of their present strait, and whatsoever further accusations or pursuit depending on that ground, respecting both their former merit in setting forth of the evangel the simplicity of their conscience in this defense, which cannot well be their Lett by compulsion and the great slander which could not fail to full out upon their further striating for any such occasion which we assure us your zeal for religion besides the expectation we have of your good will to pleasure us will willingly accord to our request having such proofs from time to time of our like disposition to you in any matters which you recommend to us. And thus right excellent, right high and mighty princess, our dear sister and cousin, we commit you to God's good protection. From Edinburgh the 12th day of June, 1591.

Presently upon these things fell out that wretched matter of that lewd fellow Racket whereby the adversary did take occasion so to slander the truth and to disgrace the professors of the same to her majesty that I thought it bootless to sue. And so I did little till the Lord Chancellor was dead and forgotten by such as were sorry for it; so that about Easter term following, I sued for liberty to go to church which was denied me being a condemned man but by the lord treasurer's means I got a copy of my indictment, which before I could not obtain.

Hereupon I getting a pardon framed according to the indictment sent it with a petition by my wife to the council who referred me to the archbishop to whom I both had sent divers petitions and dutiful letters and also got many of my friends both honorable personages and others to sue him, yet could not his good will be gotten. At last the Turkey merchants having my consent to go for a time into Guinea to teach their people that abide in that place if they could procure my liberty, sent to him for his consent who promised his good will, so that they would be bound that I should go indeed when I had my liberty. But when two of the ancients of the company went to him for his hand thereto, he would not yield it unless they would be bound not only that I should go (which they were willing to) but also that I should tarry there till I had her majesty's license to come there. This condition they could not yield to for that I denied to go upon any such ground; so was their suit and my hope of liberty at an end; saving that one Mr. Cavell who had been the first beginner of it and being to go into Turkey did most affect it moved the Dean of Paul's in it who thereupon wrote to my lord keeper persuading him of the convenience of that journey for me and my fitness thereto. Which letter when he received, he did so deal with the archbishop as they both promised at their next meeting at court to deal with her majesty to sign my pardon that so I might have liberty to go the voyage. But her majesty never did sign the pardon and the Turkey ships going away without him, Udall died in the Marshalsea prison about the end of the year 1592, quite heart-broken with sorrow and grief.

[Emlyn, Sollom. *Complete Collection of State-Trials and Proceedings.* 168-188]

Robert of Essex

Robert Devereux, the Earl of Essex, and Henry Wriothesley, the Earl of Southampton, were involved in what has been referred to as the Essex Rebellion. Essex attracted the attention of Queen Elizabeth and advanced at court. He gained further recognition as a soldier in several successful campaigns. As he continued rising in popularity, he found a certain opposition that resulted in rivalries. His ego increased along with his confidence, often conflicting with Elizabeth's interests. A well-recorded event describes when Elizabeth boxed his ears over such a conflict.

In 1599, Essex and Southampton were sent to Ireland to stop a rebellion led by Hugh O'Neill. Southampton was recalled by the Queen to London but the rebellion failed for several contested reasons. Essex left his post in Ireland and disobeyed orders to return to London. Elizabeth reproached him sternly and placed him under house arrest, where he remained for almost a year. Following his release, he sought like-minded individuals to plot against the English government. He gathered several hundred supporters but was watched too closely to be able to launch the rebellion effectively.

Essex and Southampton sponsored a performance of *Richard III* by Shakespeare in early February 1601. Southampton is perhaps best known as the patron of Shakespeare, who dedicated the poems *Venus and Adonis* and *The Rape of Lucrece* to him. It is believed that many of his sonnets were addressed to him. *Richard III* is a play that describes the life of King Richard III, who lost his throne and life by following ill advice. Assumptions suggested that the play was based on Elizabeth's fate. The Queen quickly responded by seeking their arrest and, after a short skirmish at Essex house, Sussex was forced to surrender. Southampton would eventually gain his freedom but Essex was not as fortunate. The following is the trial.

The trial of Robert Earl of Essex, and Henry Earl of Southampton before the lords at Westminster for high treason: 43 Eliz. Feb. 19, 1600.

A spacious court was made in Westminster-Hall where the Lord Treasurer Buckhurst sat as High Steward of England under a canopy of state; where sat also about the table, the earls, barons, and judges of the land, according to their degrees. The judges were these; the L. C. J. Popham, and the L. C. J. Anderson. The L. C. B. Sir William Periam. Justices Gawdie, Fenner, Walmesley, Warburton, Kingsmill, and Mr. Baron Clarke.

These sat all in the court next to the bar before the High Steward, seven Sergeants at Arms came in with maces before the High Steward and laid them down before him in the court. The King at Arms stood on the one side of the High Steward by his chair of estate and one of her majesty's gentlemen ushers with his white rod in his hand on the other side. The Clerk of the Crown and his assistant sat before him to read the common indictments and examinations. The Captain of the Guard (Sir Walter Raleigh) and forty of the Queen's guard were there to attend the service. Then the Sergeant at Arms made three 'O-yes!' and proclamation that the Lord High Steward of England commanded silence and to hear the commission read upon pain of imprisonment. Then the Clerk of the Crown read the commission whereto the Earl of Essex was very attentive. Another proclamation was made that the Lord High Steward of England commanded all justices to whom any writs had been directed for this service to bring them in and certify the same. Another proclamation was made by a Sergeant at Arms that the Lieutenant of the Tower of London should return his precept and bring forth his prisoners, Robert Earl of Essex and Henry Earl of Southampton.

Then the Lord High Constable of the Tower, the Lieutenant of the Tower, and the gentleman porter who carried the axe before the prisoners came first in, and the prisoners followed and made their appearance at the bar, the gentleman porter with the axe standing before them with the axe's edge from them; and so the lieutenant delivered his precept into the court. The two earls (which were prisoners) kissed one another's hands and embraced each other. Another proclamation was made that the Sergeant at Arms to the Queen's majesty do return his precept of the names of all the peers of Robert Earl of Essex, and Henry Earl of Southampton, the which he delivered into the court accordingly. Another proclamation was made that all earls, viscounts, and barons, of the realm of England, which were peers of Robert Earl of Essex, and Henry Earl of Southampton, and summoned to appear this day, do make answer to their names, upon pain and peril that will fall thereon.

Then the lords were called and answered and appeared as follows: Edward Earl of Oxford, Gilbert Earl of Shrewsbury, William Earl of Derby, Edward Earl of Worcester, George Earl of Cumberland, Robert Earl of Sussex, Edward Earl of Hertford, Henry Earl of Lincoln, Charles Earl of Nottingham, Thomas Viscount Bindon, Thomas Lord De la Ware, Edward Lord Morley, Henry Lord Cobham, Henry Lord Stafford, Thomas Lord Grey, Thomas Lord Lumley, Henry Lord Windson, William Lord Chandous, Robert Lord Rich, Thomas Lord Darcy, George Lord Hunsdon, Oliver Lord St. John of Bletso, Thomas Lord Burleigh, William Lord Compton, Thomas Lord Howard, Baron of Walden.

Then the Earl of Essex desired to know of my Lord Chief Justice, whether he might challenge any of the peers or no; and Mr. Attorney General alleged a case in Henry 8's time of my Lord Darcy. Whereupon the earl had them go on. When the Lord Grey was called the Earl of Essex laughed upon the Earl of Southampton and jogged him by his sleeve.

Then they were called to hold up their hands at the bar, which they did. And then the Clerk of the Crown read the indictments. That being done, they were bid to hold up their hands again, which they did, and another indictment was read where to the Earl of Essex was attentive. After which, the Clerk of the Crown asked them whether they were guilty, or not guilty; they pleaded not guilty and for their trials they put themselves upon God and their peers. They spoke this severally. Then my Lord High Steward in a few words gave the peers a charge requiring them to have a due regard of their consciences.

Then Sergeant Yelverton opened the evidence, showed the effect of the indictment, held it in his hand, and said as follows:

May it please your grace (speaking to the High Steward), about the 8th of February last, my Lord of Essex (there prisoner at the bar) went about with armed men very rebelliously to disinherit the Queen of her crown and dignity; which when it came to her majesty's ear, she of her abounding mercy sent to see if it were possible to stop rebellion and who did she send? She sent (my lord) no worse persons than my Lord Keeper, my L. C. Justice of England, the Earl of Worcester, and Sir William Knowles; all which went in her majesty's name and commanded the earls and their adherents very strictly to dissolve their assemblies and to lay down their arms. But he knowing it, very treacherously imprisoned the said lords and counselors by her majesty so sent and altogether refused her majesty's authority and divers of their confederates erred out, kill them, kill them! Thereby putting her majesty's council in fear of their lives; and withal, left them with Sir John Davis to keep safe, lest they themselves should miscarry in the city. But, my lord, I must tell you this by the way that my Lord of Essex can no way excuse nor shadow this his rebellious purpose nor turn his actions to any other intent for the sending of Temple his secretary into London the night before, manifested his determination without scruple or question; for by that means he was in hopes to have had the help of the citizens, her majesty's most loyal and loving subjects and he used not only his best endeavors to strengthen himself abroad, but also fortified his house at home with strong defense and ammunition; all which were tokens of his inclinations to a sudden and unexpected rebellion and were confirmed in the opinion of all the world when he withstood divers of her majesty's subjects standing in her highness's right, and defense of her peace, against him and his confederates. Good my lord, I beseech your grace, and you my lords that are the peers to understand that if any man do but intend the death of the King, it is death by the law for he is the head of the commonwealth and all his subjects as members ought to obey and stand with him. But as for this rebellion being duly considered it contains in it many branches of treason which are and will be directly proved which being found to be so, my lords, who are their peers are to find them guilty. Hereof need to be made no doubt for it is more manifest than the sedition of Catiline to the city of Rome and consequently England is in no less danger; for as Catiline entertained the most seditious persons about all Rome to join with him in his conspiracy, so the Earl of Essex had none but Papists, recusants, and Atheists for his abductors and abettors in their capital rebellion against the whole estate of England. My lord, I much wonder that his heart could forget all the princely advancements given him by her majesty, and be so suddenly be flinted as to turn them all to rebellious ends; but it seems this overweighing a man's own conceit and an aspiring mind to wished honor is like the crocodile which is ever growing as long as he lives. Your lordships know in what sort they went into the city with amour and weapons and how they returned to Essex-House again as you my Lord Admiral, and my Lord of Cumberland with others of their honorable peers do know; which makes me wonder they do not blush to be so forward to stand upon their trials without confession when their intended treasons are in all men's judgments palpable. For my part, my lord, I can conjecture nothing hereby; and it will not easily out of my own conceit, but that there is some further matter in it than as to you appears; but my hope is that God of his mercy, that has revealed their treasons will not suffer the rest of his or any others to the hurt of the state or prejudice to her majesty's most royal person, whom I pray God long to preserve from the hands of her enemies. Amen, cried the Earl of Essex and the Earl of Southampton and God confound their souls that ever wished otherwise to her sacred person.

Attorney General, (Sir Edward Coke) may it please your grace, the Lords Chief Judges which are the fathers of the law, do know that the thought of treason to the prince, by the law is death; and he that is guilty of rebellion is guilty of an intent (by the laws of the land) to seek the destruction of the prince, and so adjudged treason and I will prove this to your lordships by two several cases. First, he that raised power and strength in a settled government the law will not suffer it, but it is construed as in cases of high treason; he that does usurp upon it the law does intend that he had purposed the destruction of the prince; he that does assemble power, if the King does command him upon his allegiance to dissolve his company, and he continue it without any question it is high treason. He that does levy forces to take any town in the prince's dominions, it is so likewise. But my Lord of Essex has levied power to take the Tower of London, and to surprise the Queen's own court; then this must needs be higher than the highest; and he that does fortify himself against the prince's power must needs be within the compass of treason. And by your favor my Lord of Essex, I will now speak a word to you, for I know you can speak as well as any man; that whereas you say the law of nature compelled you to do this which in judgment you have though most treacherously attempted I will in a word disprove your own judgment admitting you must make that freely your argument. 1st, I will open the quality of your rebellion; 2nd, the manner of it; 3rd, I will touch the circumstances; and lastly, I will observe the person. The quality has high treason; for which I think I shall not need to say anymore. For the manner of it I hold it an unnatural act for a natural subject to commit treason against his natural sovereign; and methinks it cannot be by any probability denied, but that this high treason is and must be both against the law of God, nature, and reason. And under your grace's favor my lord, the manner of it being of so high a nature as it is, must needs be high treason which was not only carried in their hearts, but for a continual remembrance kept in a black purse which my Lord of Essex wore on his breast next to his skin. Let me note to you my good lord that they being both born under the government of this princess, and so highly advanced by her majesty's favor should have trembled once to think of such a rebellion as they have enterprise. Does not my Lord of Essex now enjoy his Earldom of Essex by the gift of Henry 8th to his father? Was not he made Master of her Majesty's Horse at 22 years of age? One of her majesty's council? To be Earl Marshal of England? General of her majesty's forces in Ireland? And lastly, has he not received divers gifts and sums of money to his own use of her majesty's gracious and princely bounty to the value of 30,000£? Yet all these were as cleverly forgotten as if they had never been. Now shall I show you the person whom this concerns even her majesty's sacred person against whom their attempts have been only for the undertaking of God's cause and exercising of justice with admirable mercy; and though I cannot speak without reverent commendations of her majesty's most honorable justice yet I think her overmuch clemency to some turned to over much cruelty for herself for though the rebellious attempts were so exceedingly heinous, yet out of her princely mercy no man was racked, tortured, or pressed to speak anything farther than of their own accord and willing minds for discharge of their consciences they uttered; and then to see the mercy of God that will have the truth known it is admirable beyond the conceit of man's capacity for they being severally examined, notwithstanding all agree directly without varying. But when her majesty sent a counselor of state to have the earl come before her when she heard of his rebellion for no other end or purpose but for his admonishment, he refused to come; and having a guilty conscience and suspecting his treasons were laid open, took consultation to surprise the court and the Tower of London all at one instant and for this purpose had appointed Blunt the custody of the gates, Sir Joseph Davis of the hall, Sir Charles Davers of the presence, and himself of her majesty's person. Whereupon Blunt said, Ah! What humor shall we find them in at the court? This was not all; for the earl he must call a Parliament and he would decide matters not making for his purpose but now in God's most just judgment he of his earldom shall be Robert the last that of the Kingdom thought to be Robert the first. And my lord did not any whit amuse himself to give order that if he and his accomplices should miscarry in London then the counselors which he caused to be imprisoned in his house should be slain. It was plain treason in him to stand out being by them charged to dissolve his company upon his allegiance. What shall I need to stand upon further proofs? It is so evident and my lord himself will not deny, but that he had a schedule containing in it divers of his friends names; which as I conjecture must needs contain some other matter for he does not let it come to light, but burnt it and as for Owen, Salisbury, Davis and Tresltam they must have the guard of the lords of the council to use them at their pleasure.

Essex. Will your lordships give us our turns to speak, for he plays the orator and abuses your lordships ears and us with slanders; but they are but fashions of orators in corrupt states. Considering some privileges which we might challenge, equal answers and equal hearing were indifferent; for unless it will please your lordships that we might answer to every particular, we shall soon confound our own memories and give liberty and advantage to our enemies whereupon to lay hold, for lack of precise answer to each particular objection. And seeing now, my lord, you have undertaken the place of a judge; I beseech you as you prove against us we for ourselves may answer what may fall out to be fit.

Here the Lord of Essex was interrupted and not allowed to speak until Henry Witherington's examination was read which imported thus much:

Witherington's Examination. That upon the Sunday morning he was sent for to Essex-House, where he found the place guarded with many gentlemen in arms who told his uncle that came in his company that he feared they were come into an ill action; my Lord of Essex bid them very welcome and entreated him to go with him, for he feared hurt of some private enemies. And when Mr. Witherington perceived the council was staved, he feared danger to them; for he heard some bid, stab them and others, let us make an end of them we shall have the fewer to deal withal. And he proves further that order was left that if the earl should miscarry in London then the Lord Keeper and the L. C. Justice should be killed, and also when the council had commanded him upon his allegiance to dissolve his forces he answered nothing. He likewise saw my Lord of Bedford brought in that morning; and Mr. Witherington fearing he might be drawn on to his destruction, prayed him only to follow him for when opportunity served in London they would leave the troop and that they followed the earl into London, and on a sudden lost him.

Essex. I will not, I protest to God, speak to save my life; for those that prosecute it against me shall do me a good turn to rid me of my misery and themselves out of fear. As for Mr. Witherington, he does much disparage himself if he said so, for I protest to God upon my salvation, I never heard such words as 'Kill him, kill him' and Mr. Witherington came voluntarily to my house, unsent for, and in the forenoon did come into our company and took to heart as much as we did whatever we went about and these are but reports, for he that is the witness is now sent into the country about some employments. But if it had been a secret, Mr. Witherington being privy thereto, might have been a good witness but being so openly spoken, (as you say) a hundred more might have testified it, yet none spoke it besides. And as for locking up the council, I protest to God it was done in charity, and without disloyalty, but intending only to save them lest they should take hurt; considering the people abroad in the streets with a great and sudden outcry said, 'We shall be slain.' At which time we thought our enemies had been come to beset the house for my intent was no otherwise than loyal to her majesty and them.

The Lord Keeper, the Earl of Worcester and the L. C. Justice Popham, proved in court upon their honors that they heard the words 'Kill them, kill them:' but they would not charge my Lord of Essex that they were spoken either by his privy or command.

The declaration of the Lord Keeper, the Earl of Worcester, and the Lord Chief' Justice of England.

Upon Sunday, being the 8th of February last past, about ten of the clock in the forenoon, the Lord Keeper of the Great Seal, the Earl of Worcester, Sir Win. Knollis Comptroller of her majesty's household, and the L. C. Justice of England being commanded by direction from the Queen's majesty did repair to the late Earl of Essex's house and finding the gate shut against them, alter a little stay they were let in at the wicket. And as soon as they were within the gate, the wicket was shut upon them and all their servants kept out. At their coming there they found the court full of men assembled together in a very tumultuous sort. The Earls of Essex, Rutland and Southampton, and the Lord Sandys; Master Parker commonly called Lord Mounteagle, Sir Christopher Blunt, Sir Charles Davers, and many other knights and gentlemen and other persons unknown which flocked together about the Lord Keeper, &c. And thereupon the Lord Keeper told the Earl of Essex that they were sent from her majesty to understand the cause of this their assembly and to let them know that if they had any particular cause of grief against any persons whatsoever it should be heard and they should have justice. Hereupon the Earl of Essex with a very loud voice declared that his life was sought and that he should have been murdered in his bed; that he had been perfidiously dealt with; that his hand had been counterfeited and letters written in his name; and that therefore they were assembled there together to defend their lives with much other speech to like effect. Hereupon the L. C. Justice said to the earl that if they had any such matter of grief, or if any such matter were attempted or purposed against him he willed the earl to declare it; assuring him that it should be truly related to her majesty and that it should be indifferently heard and justice should be done, whomsoever it concerned. To this the Earl of Southampton objected the assault made upon him by the Lord Gray. Whereto the L. C. Justice said that in his case justice had been done and the party imprisoned for it. And hereupon the Lord Keeper did eftsoons will the Earl of Essex that whatsoever private matter or offence he had against any person whatsoever, if he would deliver it to them they would faithfully and honestly deliver it to the Queen's majesty and doubted not to procure him honorable and equal justice, whomsoever it concerned requiring him that if he would not declare it openly that he would impart it to them privately and doubted not but they would satisfy him in it. Upon this there was a great clamor raised among the multitude, crying, 'Away, my Lord, they abuse you, they betray you, they undo you, you lose time.' Whereupon the Lord Keeper put on his hat and said with a loud voice, my lord, let us speak with you privately and understand your grief's and I command you all upon your allegiance to lay down your weapons and to depart which you ought all to do being thus commanded if you be good subjects and one that duly to the Queen's majesty which you profess. Whereupon they all broke out into an exceeding loud shout and cry, crying, 'All, all, all.' And whilst the Lord Keeper was speaking and commanding them upon their allegiance, as is before declared the Earl of Essex and the most part of that company did put on their hats; and so the Earl of Essex went into the house, and the Lord Keeper, &c. followed him thinking that his purpose had been to speak with them privately as they had required. And as they were going some of that disordered company cried, 'Kill them.' And as they were going into the great chamber, some cried, 'Cast the Great Seal out of the window.' Some other cried there, 'Kill them;' and some other said, 'Nay, let us shop them up.' The Lord Keeper did often call on the Earl of Essex to speak with them privately thinking still that his meaning had been so until the earl brought them into his back chamber and there gave order to have the farther door of that chamber shut fast. And at his going forth out of that chamber, the Lord Keeper pressing again to have spoken with the Earl of Essex, the earl said, 'My lords, be patient a while, and stay here, and I will go into London and take order with the mayor and sheriffs for the city and will be here again within this half hour.' And so departed from the Lord Keeper, &c. leaving the Lord Keeper, etc. and divers of the gentlemen pensioners in that chamber guarded by Sir John Davis, Francis, Tresham, and Owen Salisbury, with musket shot where they continued until Sir Ferdinando Gorges came and delivered them about four of the clock in the afternoon. In the mean time we did often require Sir John Davis and Francis Tresham to suffer us to depart, or at the least to suffer some one of us to go to the Queen's majesty to inform her where and in what sort we were kept. But they answered, 'That my lord (meaning the Earl of Essex) had commanded that we should not depart before his return, which (they said) would be very shortly. Thomas Egerton. C. S. Edward Worcester. John Popham.

All which the Lord Chief Justice Popham attested, *viva voce.*

Attorney General. Yea, my lord, you had 300 men in arms in your house; why did you not dissolve them, being commanded upon your allegiance from the Queen to do it?

Essex. They hearing rumors of men about my house against them put them into such a fear and ecstasy that it was not in my power suddenly to dissolve them or to quench their passions and the rather for that Sir Walter Raleigh desired Sir Ferdinando Gorges to leave their company or else they would be all lost so that they stood amazed, and knew not what to do.

Southampton. Mr. Attorney, you speak all this as if it were as true as the gospel.

Essex. Good my lord, let me entreat you to mark the circumstances, word was brought that men were sent for into the country to take us in our own houses; then we conceiving the thirsty appetite of our private enemies took ourselves to our arms and were glad to stand upon our guard for our own defense. But as for the lords of the council that came to my house, we being before advertised that we should be beset, thought it the securest way for those of the council to keep them there not knowing what mischief would ensue.

Attorney General. My lord, your grace sees that this is without color or question for my L. C. Justice had proved it plain that they would not dissolve their company that was up in arms being charged upon their allegiance so to do.

Essex. Good my lord, know whether it were in my Lord of Southampton's power or in mine to withhold their purposes so suddenly for, not long before Sir Walter Raleigh had sent to my house to have Sir F. Gorges to come to him to Durham-house; and we tearing him to be a private enemy would not suffer Sir F. to go there but returned answer that he would meet him on the water upon equal terms where Sir Walter Raleigh used the former speeches to Sir Ferdinando Gorges wishing him to leave our company or else he would be undone. And whereas we are charged to have dealt with Papists, I assure your lordship and it is most true that Papists have been hired and suborned to witness against me; as by the means of one Sudall who was a seminary priest and sent into Ireland to deal with Sir Christopher Blunt whom he thought to be inward with me, to touch my honor and reputation. Then Bales, the Scrivener in the Old Bailey, has confessed under his hand to forge and counterfeit my hand in at least two letters and these two honest gentlemen can witness it.

Attorney General. Ay, by my truth this is true, but it was by the procurement of one of your own men.

Essex. Thou swears it, but it is not on a book; that man thou says I procured to do it, his name is John Daniel an errant thief, one that broke a standard of mine and stole a casket of my wife's and many other things. It is very probable that I should trust him so far that had before betrayed me, is it not? But it is well known who set him at work to attempt against me so much as he has done to procure my hand to be counterfeited; and yet this man by your judgment must be a practicer in such matters by my own consent. Well, Mr. Attorney, I thank God you are not my judge this day, you are so uncharitable.

Attorney General. Well, my lord, we shall prove you anon what you are, which your pride of heart and aspiring mind has brought you to.

Essex. Ah! Mr. Attorney, lay your hand upon your heart and pray to God to forgive us both.

Raleigh. That Sir Ferdinando Gorges told me upon the water that my Lord of Essex had put himself into a strong guard at Essex-House and this is like to be the bloodiest day's work that ever was wishing him to go to court with speed for prevention thereof then Sir Walter wished Sir Ferdinando Gorges to refuse their company, else he would be undone. To this Sir Walter was sworn.

Essex. Whatsoever Sir Walter had said differed altogether from that which Sir Ferdinando told us at Essex-House upon his return from the water.

Attorney General. Well, my lord, what can you devise to say for Sir John Davis another of your adherents, that Papist? For he has confessed that he is a Papist and a Catholic and drawn in by Sir Christopher Blunt, one of your chief counsel and that he called for a seminary priest upon his conversion to absolve him.

Essex. If Sir John Davis were such a man, it cannot be but strange to me to bear it; although I cannot search into the secrets of his heart to accuse him inwardly, yet I have seen him dutifully come to prayers, and to the service of God in my own house with me and behaved himself very godlily and of this I can be witness. And as for Blunt (God is my witness) I have been so far from Popery as I have so earnestly dealt with him to reform himself insomuch that he has told me I have been very passionate. But whereas you say we have committed treason, first prove that true.

Sergeant Yelvert. Why, my lord, if you deny the raising the power, why should so many men come to your house that day?

Southampton. By your favor, Mr. Sergeant Yelverton, a word I hope; for my coming there it was not strange news; and when I came that same morning to Essex-House, I protest I had not above 10 or 12 men attending me which was but my usual company therefore far from purposing to raise a tumult.

Attorney General. Why, the reason of that was for that you thought all London would have risen with you; but good my lord, I beseech your grace to hear the oath of Sir Ferdinando Gorges whose evidence was read and himself there in person did justify the same.

Sir Ferdinando Gorges his confession.

He deposed that in January last the Earl of Essex wrote to him a letter, wherein he complained grievously of his misfortunes and the miserable estate he stood in, whereof he purposed shortly to free himself and therefore prayed Sir Ferdinando Gorges to come up to London to him who coming accordingly, the earl told him how mightily he was crossed and discredited by his private enemies, which he could not endure; for, said he, I have 120 earls, barons, and gentlemen, that participate in my discontented humor, and will join with me and I desire your help and counsel therein.

One special friend I have in the court, whereby I have intelligence from time to time and I hold ourselves indifferently affected by the citizens of London and hope to have a good party in Wales. He confessed also that they had two several meetings at Drury-house to consult of these matters; and the projects were, whether it were better first to surprise the court, or to take the Tower of London, or to stir in the city. But most agreed first to surprise the court. And then and there Sir John Davis took pen, ink and paper, and set down that some should keep the hall, some the court-gates, some the guard-chamber and some the presence chamber; saying, many of the guard had been the Earl of Essex's servants and were preferred to the Queen by him and will be more indifferent to deal with than others; and so my lord shall have a way through his own guards to come to the privy chamber and the presence of the Queen. And Sir Ferdinando Gorges said to the Earl of Essex, Alas! my lord, what is so small a number of men able to do in so worthy an action? And so dissuaded the earl from surprising the court and rather bade him submit himself to the Queen's mercy than proceed any further. And that the Earl of Southampton said at Essex House, is it not three months since this plot began and shall we resolve on nothing? Then upon a sudden they all agreed first to stir in London where they assured themselves of great favor and after the counsel was locked up this deponent followed the troops into London; and after some advice the Earl of Essex sent him back again with a token to deliver to the Lord Chief Justice only by color of which token he set at liberty the Lord Keeper and the rest. Lastly, he confirmed that he told Sir Walter Raleigh first, upon the Thames, of my Lord of Essex's making his house a guard and putting his friends into arms as it is delivered by Sir Walter Raleigh.

Sir Charles Davers's Examination.

He confessed that before Christmas last the Earl of Essex entered into consideration how he might secure himself to have access to the Queen's presence without resistance; and that the resolution was agreeable to certain articles written with the Earl of Essex's own hand and sent to the Earl of Southampton to surprise the court; and that there were divers consultations about it and the points were these first, to take the Tower for it would command London, then to surprise the court; and after the court being taken and possessed, to have assembled the rest of their friends and to have presented themselves to the Queen and that being done, and the guards secured, Sir Christopher Blunt should keep the outward gates of the court, Sir John Davis the hall and water gate, Sir Charles Davers (this deponent) should keep the presence and guard chamber and seize upon the halberds and pensioners battle axes. The intent was to surprise the captain of the guard at the court or at his own house and some others; and then to surprise the Tower of London and that the Earl of Essex resolved (these things being accomplished) immediately to have called a Parliament to reform disorders and private grievances. That this deponent utterly disliked of these courses; and after the alarm was given at court, he persuaded the earl rather to flee into Wales, or other parts beyond the seas for his security and avoiding the imminent danger he was fallen into than to trust to the city. And lastly, he protested for his own part what he had done in the business was merely for the love he bore to the Earl of Southampton, and not for any malice or private discontent otherwise.

Sir John Davis's examination.

He said that the earl's purpose was to possess himself of the court and to take the Tower of London; and that they had several meetings of consultation together with the Earl of Southampton, Sir Ferdinando Gorges, John Littleton, Sir Christopher Blunt, Sir Charles Davers and this deponent. And these matters (he confessed) the Earl of Essex set down all with his own hand, viz. Sir Christopher Blunt to keep the outward gate of the court himself, this deponent the hall and water-gate and Sir Charles Davers the presence and guard-chamber; then my Lord of Essex and his forces would have come by land and so have possessed the presence of the Queen. The question was asked the Earl of Essex (as this deponent said), how he would deal with offenders and such as resisted him after he should be possessed of these things? He resolved them by way of answer that he meant to admit them all to an honorable trial.

Sir Christopher Blunt's examination.

He confessed that the Earl of Essex sent Wiseman about the 20th of January to visit his wife with letters of compliment and to require him to come up to him to London to settle his estate according as he had written to him before some few days. Being demanded to what end they went to the city to join with such strength as they hoped for there; he confessed it was to secure the Earl of Essex's life against such forces as should be sent against him. And being asked what against the Queen's forces? He answered that must have been judged afterwards. But being further asked whether he did advise to come to the court over night? He said no; for Sir Ferdinando Gorges did assure that the alarm was taken of it at the court and the guards doubled. Being asked whether he thought any prince could have endured to have any subject make the city his mediator? Or to gather force to speak for him? He said he is not read in stories of former times; but he does not know, but that in former times subjects have used force for their mediation. Being asked what should have been done by any of the persons that should have been removed from the Queen? He answered that he never found my lord disposed to shed blood; but that any that should have been found, should have had indifferent trial. Being asked upon his conscience whether the Earl of Essex did not give him comfort that if he came to authority there should be a toleration for religion? He confessed he should have been to blame to have denied it.

Sir Christopher Blunt's second examination

He said that four or five days before the insurrection in London the Earl of Essex set down divers articles with his own hand with petitions to the Earl of Southampton, Sir Charles Davers, Sir John Davis, Sir Ferdinando Gorges, John Littleton and this deponent; which were to the effect before remembered. And further this deponent remembers that the Earl of Essex's purpose was (after these things should be over passed and settled) to alter the state of government and further this deponent confessed himself to be reconciled to the Pope and moreover said that the Earl of Essex said he looked not that any should be troubled for religion and liberty of conscience;

that he received letters from the Earl of Essex the 20th of January to come to London, whereupon he came.

The Earl of Rutland's examination.

He said that being in London with the Earl of Essex, he heard him cry out in the streets, 'England is bought and sold to the Spaniard' and confessed when they had been possessed of London their purpose was to have taken the Lord Keeper with them to the court with the Earl of Essex's company; and that the Earl of Southampton and Sir John Davis were in special confederacy and trust with the Earl of Essex in these causes. Lastly, that the Earl of Essex said he was sure of Sheriff Smith and this deponent specially noted the Earl of Southampton was very much discontented.

Lord Cromwell's examination.

He said he never heard of the matter till the same Sunday morning when the Earl of Essex coming through Fleet street where this deponent lay, and being sent for by a man of my lord's, he came in to the street to him; where my lord and divers of his followers took him by the hand and bid him welcome, praying him to go along with him and the Earl of Essex cried it is for the good of the Queen and of you all my masters. First, he went to the mayor's house, and then to Sheriff Smith's house; and being in Grace Church Street, and hearing of the proclamation, the Earl of Essex said, where is the Sheriff? Let him bring muskets and pistols; for I am credibly informed out of Ireland that the Kingdom of England is sold to the Spaniard. And so upon the proclamation the deponent left him and his company.

Lord Sandes's Examination.

He said he was sent for on Sunday morning, the same day by the Earl of Essex; and coming to Essex house, he found then but a few there: but in a short time after, came the Earl of Southampton with the rest. This deponent agreed in divers other circumstances with former examinations he confessed he went with the earl into London and came back with him to Ludgate; and there being repulsed, he heard my Lord of Essex cry, Charge, charge! and call for his horse. And he said that Sheriff Smith was as far in the matter as the best of them.

Mr. Attorney here urged that there was a combination; and one Pashell affirmed the burning of a black purse by the Earl of Essex which my lord confessed; but said that there was nothing in it but a key of an iron chest which he took out and burnt a paper in the same purse which did not contain above five or six lines of secret matter and, for that he would not have so much as their names drawn into question which were altogether ignorant of these occurrences did throw the purse and paper into the fire. And also Pashell confessed further that when the Earl of Essex came out of London to his house, he told them that he was beloved in the city.

Lord Monteagle's Examination.

He said he had no foreknowledge of these matters; but confessed he followed the Earl of Essex down Fleet-Street intending to go to the mayor and so to his house in Seething-Lane. And this deponent being with the Earl of Essex in Grace Church-Street, confessed he did hear the earl (when the Lord Burleigh came with the herald at arms) command some of his followers to bid the herald stay for he would not hear him abuse the Queen's name. He said also he went back with the Earl to Ludgate and they were repulsed.

Mr. Attorney. Now, my lord, I beseech your grace and you my lords, that be the peers let the due consideration of these several examinations and depositions enter into your hearts; and do but note they have all agreed and jumped together in each particular point notwithstanding they were all severally examined; but I must needs think it the just judgment of God in his mercy towards our sovereign to have the truth so marvelously revealed; coming from them of their own accords without rack or torture to any of them.

Essex. Mr. Attorney, I answer then this for that point; the self same fear and the self same examiner may make these several examinations agree all in one were they never so far distant; but good my lord let me entreat your lordship to consider who they be that testify this against me my lord they are men within the danger of the law and such as speak with a desire to live; but I think they have much to answer for between God and their souls and me. I see they charge me with the surprising of the Tower; but upon what ground do they speak? They had only some particular notes of my friends names but ever very scornfully dashed at me for when my friends persuaded me to any course, this was my purpose to have come with eight or nine honorable persons who had just cause of discontentment (though not equal with mine) to her majesty and so by petition prostrating ourselves at her majesty's feet to have put ourselves to her mercy. And the effect of our desires should have been that she would have been pleased to have severed some from her majesty, who by reason of their potency with her, abused her majesty's ears with false information; and they were Cobham, Cecil and Raleigh for we thought my Lord Cobham carried himself in such factious and dangerous courses as he told her majesty many untruths which was a principal cause (as I think) of withdrawing her favor from us. And to that intent to remove such from her highness (I confess; was the only desire we had to present ourselves in all humility before her majesty but without any purpose of hurt to her highness for I protest before God I do carry as reverent and loyal duty to her majesty as any man in the world. But now my lord, seeing that I have heard the testimony of Sir Ferdinando Gorges and himself here in court to testify it, I will say no more, but that if it please her majesty to be merciful to him, I will be glad and pray for it; yet whatsoever he has said let my life and his dealing testify the truth and Sir Ferdinando speak nothing to touch thyself and speak what you will to me; for I see you desire to live, yet speak like a man.

Lord Admiral. I desire, for the better satisfaction of myself and fellow peers that Gorges might unfold openly what other secrets have passed between him and my Lord of Essex, touching the state.

Essex. Ah! My Lord Admiral, assure yourself in faith, no treason but yet I pray you good Sir Ferdinando speak openly whatsoever you do remember; and with all my heart I desire thee to speak freely.

Gorges. All that I can remember I have delivered in my examination; and further I cannot say.

Essex. Yes, Ferdinando if ever you knew any other matter which contained any thought of treason or disloyalty, speak it; for they are things not to be forgotten.

Southampton. Good Sir Ferdinando satisfy the court what was intended among all our conferences and talk of our enemies, and discontentment's and consultations and what was our best course for our defense against them.

Gorges. Some delivered their minds one way, some another; but by the oath I have taken I did never know or hear any thought or purpose of hurt or disloyalty intended to her majesty's person by my Lord of Essex.

Lord Admiral. I desire to know for the better satisfaction of my conscience whether my Lord of Essex did at any time deliver out any articles in writing under his hand therein laying open the projects of his purpose for surprising the court and Tower.

Southampton. It was a foolish action, I must needs confess the going through the town and that was suddenly passed over but my lord's purpose to have men planted at the court was in regard he feared hindrance by private enemies that would have stopped his passage to the Queen; which I protest he intended to no other end, but to prostrate himself at her majesty's feet and submit to her mercy as you have formerly heard.

Cobham. My Lord of Essex, let me know I entreat you why you lay such imputations upon me, as you have delivered.

Essex. My lord, I have forgiven all the world and therefore you shall not need to insist upon these circumstances; for I lay not my cause upon aught that shall do your lordship any harm for my sake for I protest my heart bears you no malice, but what I spoke was freely and in God's presence hoping her majesty would have heard us and our complaints being but true. And I do further assure your lordship that I never spoke it out of fear of death, or desire of life.

Bacon. My Lord, may it please your grace, whatsoever my Lord of Essex has here denied in my conceit it seems to be small. I speak not to any ordinary jury, but to prudent, grave and wise peers and this I must needs say, it is evident that you my Lord of Essex had planted a pretence in your heart against the government and now, under color of excuse you must lay the cause upon particular enemies. You put me in remembrance of one Pisistratus, that was come into a city and doting upon the affections of the citizens to him, he having a purpose to procure the subversion of a Kingdom and wanting aid for the accomplishing his humor, thought it the surest means for the winning of the hearts of the citizens to him and so in that hope entered the city and cut his body over thwart to the end they might conjecture he had been in danger and so by this means held the same conceit as you and your accomplices did; entering the city of London persuading yourselves if they had undertaken your cause, all would have gone well on your side. And now my lord, all you have said or can say in answer to these matters, are but shadows; and therefore methinks it were your best course to confess, and not to justify.

Essex. May it please your lordship, I must produce Mr. Bacon for a witness; for when the course of private persecution was in hand, and most assailed me, then Mr. Bacon was the man that proffered means to the Queen and drew a letter in my name and his brother Sir Nicholas Bacon's name; which letter he purposed to show the Queen, and Gosnal was the man that brought them to me wherein I did see Mr. Bacon's hand pleaded as orderly and appointed them out that were my enemies, as directly as might be. Which letters I know Mr. Secretary Cecil has seen and by him it will appear what conceit he held of me and no I otherwise than be here colored and pleaded the contrary.

Bacon. My Lord, I spent more hours to make you a good subject than upon any man in the world besides, but since you have stirred up this point my lord, I dare warrant you this letter will not blush for I did but perform the art of an honest man and ever labored to have done you good, if it might have been and to no other end; for what I intended for your good was wished from the heart without touch of any man's honor.

Essex. Well my Lord, I do here protest before the living God, that an honorable, grave, and wise counselor has lamented and grieved at the courses he has seen taken and therewith has wished himself often dead; and this I speak upon credible and honorable information but I can prove thus much from Sir Robert Cecil's own mouth; that he speaking to one of his fellow counselors should say that none in the world but the infants of Spain had right to the crown of England.

Here Sir Robert Cecil stepped forth into the court having kept himself private till then and humbly desired leave to speak to Essex.

Sir Robert Cecil. The difference between you and me is great; for I speak in the person of an honest man, and you my lord in the person of a traitor so well I know you have wit at will. The pre-eminence has been yours, but I have innocence, truth of conscience and honesty to defend me against the scandal of slanderous tongues and aspiring hearts; and I protest before God I have loved your person and justified your virtues and I appeal to God and the Queen that I told her majesty your afflictions would make you a fit servant for her. And had not I seen your ambitious affections inclined to usurpation, I could have gone on my knees to her majesty to have done you good; but you have a sheep's garment in show and in appearance are humble and religious but God be thanked we know you for indeed your religion appears by Blunt, Davis and Tresham, your chief counselors for the present and by promising liberty of conscience hereafter. I stand for loyalty, which I never lost; you stand for treachery wherewith your heart is possessed and you charge me with high things, wherein I defy you to the uttermost. You, my good lords, counselors of state, have had many conferences, and I do confess I have said the King of Scots is a competitor, and the King of Spain a competitor and you I have said are a competitor you would depose the Queen, you would be King of England and call a Parliament. Ah, my lord, were it but your own case, the loss had been the less; but you have drawn a number of noble persons and gentlemen of birth and quality into your net of rebellion and their bloods will cry vengeance against you. For my part, I vow to God I wish my soul was in heaven and my body at rest so this had never been.

Essex. Ah Mr. Secretary, I thank God for my humbling; that you in the rust of your bravery came to make your oration against me here this day.

Cecil. My lord, I humbly thank God that you did not take me for a fit companion for you and your humors; for if you had, you would have drawn me to betray my sovereign as you have done but I would have you name the counselor you speak of; name him, name him, name him if you dare, if you dare, I defy you; name him if you dare.

Essex. Here stands an honorable person (meaning the Earl of Southampton) that knows I speak no fables; he heard it as well as I.

Cecil. Then, my Lord of Southampton, I adjure you by the duty you owe to God, loyalty and allegiance you owe to your sovereign by all tokens of true Christianity and by the ancient friendship and acquaintance once between us that you name the counselor.

Southampton. Mr. Secretary if you will needs have me name the counselor, it was Mr. Comptroller.

Whereupon the secretary falling down upon his knees said, I thank God for this day; and upon his knee desired the Lord High Steward that a gentleman of the privy chamber (or one that might have access to the Queen) might go and humbly entreat her highness to command Mr. Comptroller to come before his grace.

Hereupon the Lord High Steward calling Mr. Knevet (a gentleman of her majesty's privy-chamber) said to him go Mr. Knevet to her majesty and let her understand Mr. Secretary's demand.

Cecil. Mr. Knevet you shall have free access to her majesty; tell her that I vow before the God of heaven that if she refuse to send Mr. Comptroller whereby I may clear myself of these open scandals I will rather die at her foot, (as her subject and vassal) than live to do her any more service in this honorable degree wherein her highness employs me. And withal, let me adjure you Mr. Knevet that you do not acquaint Mr. Comptroller with the cause why you come for him.

Mr. Knevet went and not long after returned with Mr. Comptroller to whom the Lord High Steward repeated the cause why he was sent for and desired him to satisfy the lords whether Mr. Secretary did use any such speech in his hearing or to his knowledge.

Mr. Comptroller. I remember that once in Mr. Secretary's company there was a book read that treated of such matters; but I never did hear Mr. Secretary use any such words, or to that effect.

Whereupon Mr. Secretary thanked God that though the earl stood there as a traitor, yet he was found an honest man and a faithful subject withal saying I beseech God to forgive you for this open wrong done to me as I do openly pronounce I forgive you from the bottom of my heart.

Essex. And I Mr. Secretary do clearly and freely forgive you with all my soul; because I mean to die in charity.

Bacon. My lord you may how perceive that my Lord of Essex went about to procure matter and to give over on the instant.

Southampton. Well I beseech your lordship let me satisfy your lordship and the rest thus much that for my own part I did never know the laws. Now to show the causes that made me adventure so far as I did the first occasion that made me adventure into these courses was the affinity betwixt my Lord of Essex and me, I being of his blood and marrying his kinswoman; so that for his sake I should have hazarded my life, but what I have by my forwardness offended in act I am altogether ignorant, but in thought I am assured never. And if through my ignorance in the law I have offended yet I humbly submit myself to her majesty and from the bottom of my heart do beg her gracious pardon if it please her and I hope that neither your lordship nor any of the peers will hold any of the former resolutions spoken of by these orators for any certainty which depends no otherwise than one upon another. For if any foolish speeches have passed, I protest as I shall be saved that they were never purposed by me, nor understood to be so purposed by me to the hurt of her majesty's person.

Essex. I beseech your lordship to understand me and assure yourself that what I now speak is not with any desire (I protest) to spare one drop of my blood; and because some honorable persons are interested in the cause I would (under favor) signify, because the point has been so much urged by Mr. Attorney that at our being in London when we were past Paul's, word was brought me that the chain was drawn at Ludgate and that my Lord of Cumberland was there which when I heard I was right glad; for if there had been cause, I would have been glad to put myself into so honorable a person's hands as his but it was a false report for my lord was not then come there. After which I went to Sheriff Smith's house and after my coming thither I sent the sheriff and Mr. Alderman Watts to my Lord Mayor desiring him to come to us; if he would not to send four of his aldermen to see if we demeaned ourselves loyally with intent to put ourselves into their hands to use as they would or to put us into any prison; yet in regard of our private enemies and the fear of their treachery we desired them to shut their gates and this was the end for which we went into the city.

Attorney. My lord if you had no other purpose, why did you go into Gracechurch Street, and Fenchurch Street crying out all the way you went England is bought and sold to the Spaniard!

Southampton. Mr. Attorney I protest (as I hope to have mercy in heaven) I never heard my lord speak any such word, neither did I hear of the proclamation you speak of made by my Lord Burleigh and the herald at arms; neither did I see them and I deny (my soul and conscience bearing me witness) that I never knew of any intent and meaning, or did ever mean or intend any treason, rebellion, or other action against my sovereign or the state; but only what I did was to assist my Lord of Essex in his private quarrel; and therefore Mr. Attorney you have urged the matter very far and you wrong me therein my blood be upon your head. As for my Lord of Rutland, whereas he inferred against me to be a persuader and inviter of my Lord of Essex to these actions, he wronged me exceedingly for he was never the man that saw me once discontented and therefore had small ground or reason so to say. And you Mr. Attorney, whereas you charge me for a papist, I protest most unfeigned, I was never conversant with any of that sort; I only knew one White, a priest that went up and down the town yet did I never converse with him in all my life.

Essex. My lord and you that be our peers, I beseech you give me bearing thus far; not that I will speak it for the safeguard of my life, but with this my desire I charge the souls of all them that be our censurers or tries because out of a form and custom of speaking these orators would make them more odious that come to the bar that I may not be thought to have done this upon revenge for within these few days I purposed to have received the communion to be a testimony that I was far from bearing of malice to any, not so much as to my private enemies. But the failing out between the Earl of Southampton and the Lord Grey happening on a Sunday hindered my intent; for so soon as I knew of it I found my affections to stir on it exceedingly: yet I have since that time labored and by my prayers to God earnestly desired, that I might be armed with patience to endure all afflictions. And here I protest before the ever living God as he may have mercy on me, that my conscience is clear from any disloyalty thought or harm to her majesty; and my desire ever has been to be free from bloodshed, as Mr. Dove can witness. But if in all my thoughts and purposes I did not ever desire the good estate of my sovereign and country as of my own soul, I beseech the Lord then show some mark upon me and my soul in this place for a just vengeance of my untruths to all the world. And God, which knows the secrets of all hearts, knows that I never sought the crown of England nor ever wished to be a higher degree than a subject. I greatly endeavored to have brought my conscience to peace, only by seeking to secure my access to the presence of the Queen that I might speedily have unfolded my grief's to her majesty against my private enemies; but not to have shed one drop of their blood and this my lord, I speak to the end I might put off all imputation of being an hypocrite, or an atheist; for I was never papist, neither did I ever favor any sectary (as my Lord of Canterbury knows and can testify) for my religion, it is sound and as I live, I mean to die in it.

Bacon. Well my lord, may it please your grace you may see how weakly he has shadowed his purpose and how slender he has answered the objections against him. But my lord, doubting that too much variety of matter may minister occasion of forgetfulness; I will only trouble your lordship's remembrance with this only point, rightly comparing this rebellion of my Lord of Essex to the Duke of Guise's that came upon the Barricadoes at Paris in his doublet and hose attended upon with 8 men, but his confidence in the city was such (even as my lord's was), that when he had delivered himself so far and that the shallowness of his own conceit could not accomplish what he expected, the King for his defense taking arms against him, he was glad to yield himself thinking to color his pretexts, turned his practices and alleged the occasion thereof to be a private quarrel.

Essex. My lord I must confess it was my fault to stand out and to maintain my house with defense and resisting; but I will not deny but that my Lord of Southampton and Sir Charles Davers did persuade me to parley with my Lord General which I hope your lordship will remember I did yield upon some indifferent terms and conditions; which were; 1. That I might have an honorable trial. 2. That I might deliver my grief's myself to the Queen. 3. That I might go in safety. 4. That I might have my minister with me. And, lastly, (Which I chiefly beg of her majesty,) that she would be pleased to redeem some that were with me in the house and guiltless for knowledge intent or action of what was by me purposed. All which I thought good to remember and so humbly submit the same to her majesty's gracious pleasure.

Sergeant at Arms. Then proclamation was made, Lieutenant of the Tower withdraw your prisoners from the bar. They being removed, the lords and peers went together into a private place made of purpose behind the canopy and chair of estate; then the two Chief Judges and the L. C. Baron were sent for in to them to deliver their opinions in law which they did upon two points; the one that in case where a subject attempted to put himself into such strength as the King shall not be able to resist him and to force and compel the King to govern otherwise than according to his own royal authority and direction, it is manifest rebellion. 'The other,' that in every rebellion the law intended as a consequent the compassing the death and deprivation of the King as foreseeing that the rebel will never suffer that King to live or reign, who might punish or take revenge of his treason and rebellion. After half an hour they came all out again and each man took his place; which being done, the Sergeant at Arms begun at the puisne lord and called Thomas Lord Howard, who stood up bare headed.

L. Steward. My Lord Thomas Howard whether is Robert Earl of Essex guilty of this treason whereupon he has been indicted as you take it upon your honor or no?

L. Thomas Howard. Whereupon the Lord Thomas Howard made answer bending his body and laying his left hand upon his right side, said, 'Guilty, my lord, of high-treason.' After which manner all the peers found him guilty one after another from the puisne to the highest and so delivered in like sort upon their honors. Being called over a new, they found Henry Earl of Southampton guilty of high treason also.

Then the Sergeant at Arms commanded the Lieutenant of the Tower to bring his prisoners to the bar again. Then the Clerk of the Crown speaking first to the Earl of Essex, said; Robert Earl of Essex you have been arraigned and indicted of high-treason; you bare pleaded not guilty and for your trial you have put yourself upon God and your peers; the peers here (who have heard the evidence and your answer in your defense) have found you guilty now what can you say for yourself, why you should not have judgment of death?

Essex. I only say this. That since I have committed that which has brought me within the compass of the law, I may be counted the law's traitor in offending the law for which I am willing to die, and will as willingly go thereto as ever did any but I beseech your lordship and the rest of the lords here to have consideration of what I have formerly spoken and do me the right as to think me a Christian and that I have a soul to save and that I know it is no time to jest lying and counterfeiting my soul abhorrent; for I am not desperate nor void of grace, now to speak falsely. I do not speak to save my life for that I see were vain. I owe God a death which shall be welcome how soon so ever it pleases her majesty. And to satisfy the opinion of the world that my conscience is free from Atheism and Popery, howsoever I have been in this action misled to transgress the points of the law in the course and defense of private matters and whatsoever through the weakness of my wit, and dullness of memory or through violent courses (if there be any violent that seek either life or death); or if I have omitted or may have uttered anything otherwise; yet I will live and die in the faith and true religion which here I have professed.

Then the Clerk of the Crown demanded of Henry Earl of Southampton what he could say for himself, why judgment of death should not he pronounced against him?

Southampton. My lords I must say for my part, as I have said before that since the ignorance of the law has made me incur the danger of the law, I humbly submit myself to her majesty's mercy; and therefore, my Lord High Steward, and my Lord Admiral, I beg you both that seeing you are witnesses I am condemned by the letter of the law, it would please you to let the Queen know that I crave her mercy. I know I have offended her, yet if it please her to be merciful to me, I may live and by my service deserve my life. I have been brought up under her majesty, I have spent the best part of my patrimony in her majesty's service with danger of my life as your lordships know; if there were any that could challenge me that I have ever heretofore committed or intended treason or any other thing prejudicial to her majesty or estate, God let me never inherit his Kingdom, neither would I desire mercy, but since the law has cast me, I do submit myself to death and yet I will not despair of her majesty's mercy; for that I know she is merciful and if she please to extend it, I shall with all humility receive it.

L. Steward. My Lord of Essex the Queen's majesty has bestowed many favors on your predecessors and yourself; I would wish therefore that you likewise would submit yourself to her majesty's mercy acknowledging your offences and reconciling yourself inwardly to her majesty by laying open all matters that were intended to prejudice her majesty and the actors thereof; and thereby no doubt you shall find her majesty merciful.

Essex. My lord, you have made an honorable motion; do but send to me at the time of my death and you shall see how penitent and humble I will be towards her majesty both in acknowledging her exceeding favors to my ancestors and to myself whereby I doubt not but the penitent suffering of my death and sprinkling of my blood will quench the evil conceited thoughts of her majesty against me. And I do most humbly desire her majesty that my death may put a period to my offences committed and be no more remembered by her highness. If I had ever perceived any of my followers to have harbored an evil thought against her majesty, I would have been the first that should have punished the same in being his executioner; and therefore I beseech you my good lord, mistake me not, nor think me so proud that I will not crave her majesty's mercy for I protest (kneeling upon the very knee of my heart) I do crave her majesty's mercy with all humility yet I had rather die than live in misery.

Then the Lord High Steward, after a few exhortations to the earls to prepare themselves for God, told them seeing the law had found them guilty it followed of course that he must proceed to judgment.

The Earl of Essex replied very cheerfully, and said; yea, my lord with a very good will I pray you go on.

Then the Lord High Steward gave judgment as follows: you must go to the place from where you came and there remain during her majesty's pleasure; from there to be drawn on a hurdle through London streets and so to the place of execution where you shall be hanged, bowelled and quartered; your head and quarters to be disposed of at her majesty's pleasure, and so God have mercy on your soul.

Essex. My lord I am not a whit dismayed to receive this sentence for I protest death is as welcome to me as life; and I shall die as cheerful a death upon such a testimony as ever did man. And I think it fit my poor quarters that have done her majesty true service in divers parts of the world should be sacrificed and disposed of at her majesty's pleasure; whereto with all willingness of heart I have submitted myself. But one thing I beg of you my lords, that have free access to her majesty's person, humbly to beseech her majesty to grant me that (during the short time I shall live) I may have the same preacher to comfort me that has been with me since my troubles began; for as he that has been long sick is most desirous of the physician which has been and is best acquainted with the constitution of his body; so do I most wish to have the comfort and spiritual physic from the preacher which has been and is acquainted with the inward grief's and secret affections of my soul. And my last request shall be only this; that it will please her highness that my Lord Thomas Howard and the Lieutenant of the Tower may be partakers with me in receiving the sacrament and be a witness of it in token of what I have protested to be true in this life for my loyalty, religion, and peace of conscience and then when so ever it shall please her majesty to call me I shall be ready to seal the same with my blood.

The lords promised they would move the Queen for his requests.

Essex. I humbly thank your lordships.

Then the Sergeant at Arms stood up with the mace on his shoulder and after proclamation was made said thus: all peers that were summoned to be here this day may now take their ease; and all other persons attending here this service may depart in her majesty's peace, for my Lord High Steward is pleased to dissolve this commission.

As the lords were rising, the Earl of Essex said my Lord De la Ware and my Lord Morley, I beseech your lordships to pardon me for your two sons that are in trouble for my sake. I protest upon my soul they knew not of anything that was or should have been done, but came to me in the morning and I desired them to stay and they knew not wherefore. And so farewell, my lords.

The Earl of Southampton obtained a reprieve, but the Earl of Essex was ordered for execution.

On the 25th of February 1601, which was the day appointed for his execution, Thomas Mountford and William Barlow doctors of divinity, with Ashton the minister of the church in the Tower were sent to him early in the morning to administer Christian consolation to his soul. In presence of these men he gave thanks to almighty God from the bottom of his heart that his designs, which were so dangerous to the state, succeeded not. He told them he had now looked thoroughly and seriously into his sin and was heartily sorry he had so obstinately defended an unjust cause at the bar. He thanked the Queen she had granted he should not be publicly executed, lest his mind which was now settled and composed, might be disturbed by the acclamations of the people protesting that he had now learned how vain a thing the blast of popular favor and applause was. He acknowledged how worthy he was to be sped out (these were his words) by the common wealth for the wickedness of his enterprise which he likened to a leprosy spread far and near and that had infected many.

The Queen in the mean time wavered in her mind. One while relenting, she sent her commands by Sir Edward Carey that he should not be executed, but then remembering his perverse obstinacy that he scorned to ask her pardon and had declared openly that his life would be the Queen's destruction, she soon after sent a fresh command by Darcy that he should be put to death.

Then he was brought forth between the divines to a scaffold erected within the courtyard of the Tower near which sat the Earls of Cumberland and Hertford, Viscount Howard of Bindon, the Lord Howard of Walden, the Lord Darcy of Chiche, and the Lord Compton. There were present also some of the aldermen of London and Sir Walter Raleigh who if we may believe himself, came with an intent to make answer if anything should be objected against him by the earl at his death; but others thought he came to feed his eyes with a sight of the earl's suffering and to satiate his hatred with his blood. But being admonished not to press upon the earl at his death, which is the part rather of ignoble brutes, he withdrew himself further off and beheld his execution out of the armory. The earl as soon as he was come upon the scaffold, uncovered his head and lifting up his eyes to heaven acknowledged that many and great had been the sins of his youth, for which with most fervent prayer (he begged pardon of the eternal majesty of God through Christ his mediator; especially for this last sin which he termed a bloody, crying and contagious sin wherewith so many had been seduced to sin against God their prince and country. He besought the Queen and her ministers to forgive him praying for her long life and prosperous estate, protesting withal that he never intended to lay violent hands on her person. He gave God thanks that he had never been Atheist, or Papist, but had placed all his hope and confidence in the merits of Christ. He prayed God to strengthen his mind against the terrors of death; desiring the standers by to join with him in a short prayer which with broken sighs and fervent affection of inward devotion, he presently uttered. Afterwards the executioner asking forgiveness he forgave him; he recited the apostles creed and then laying himself down, placed his neck upon the block; and having repeated the first verses of the 51st psalm, he said, 'In humility and obedience I prostrate myself to my deserved punishment: Thou, O God! Have mercy on thy prostrate servant, into your hands, O Lord! I commend my spirit.' His head was taken off at the third stroke, but the first took away all sense and motion.

[*Cobbett's Complete Collection of State Trials.* 1334-1360]

Captain Thomas Lee

Thomas Lee was born circa 1551 to Benedict Lee and Margaret Pakington. He is often described as spending most of his career in Ireland and estimated to have arrived there about 1575. In 1578, he married Elizabeth Peppard, gaining several pieces of property through the union. In 1580, he was arrested on the charge of highway robbery in Oxfordshire and returned to Ireland after his release.

In 1581, he was arrested and charged with 'wrong doings' and 'cattle theft'. It was determined that he could better serve the crown to prevent a rebellion then to be placed in prison, so the charges were dismissed. Lee was involved in another campaign in 1585 in Kilkenny where he was out numbered 5 to 1, but he captured the sheriff and killed several men.

In late 1587, Lee was imprisoned in Dublin castle for eight weeks, partially for non-payment of services. He separated from his wife about the same time, though it appears he maintained some interactions with her over the subsequent years. In 1591, his primary residence suffered a great fire resulting in a loss of many of his personal items.

Over the following years, Lee gained additional recognition in a couple successful campaigns. In 1595, he married Kinborough Valentine and returned to Ireland to kill Kedagh Macphelim Peagh in what was described as a 'cruel murder' and the 'sore wounding' of his brother that resulted in his imprisonment in Dublin Castle, but was released before March of the following year. He then served within a garrison that captured Clogham Castle. When they refused to relinquish the castle or evacuate the women, Lee set the buildings on fire, resulting in the deaths of forty-six people. Additional people died as a result of being thrown over the walls by Lee's soldiers.

In August 1598, Lee was arrested on a charge of treason after attempting to place a rebel leader as president of Ulster following the Battle of Yellow Ford. The trial was short and he gained his freedom after apologizing. In October, he found himself in prison again after making false accusations following a suppression of a rebellion in Munster. It is unclear how long he remained in prison, but he found himself again involved in a controversial matter in 1599 and was placed under house arrest. He gained his freedom in the early 1600's. In early 1601, he was accompanied by several other gentlemen who plotted seizing the Queen in her chamber and holding her until she released Robert of Essex. The plot failed because of a leak and Lee was arrested as he was watching the Queen's chamber door.

Following is his trial.

The arraignment and judgment of Captain Thomas Lee, at the Sessions-House near Newgate, for high treason: 43 Eliz. A.D. 1600.

That he plotted and compassed to raise sedition and rebellion to the Queen's majesty's person, to deprive her of her crown and dignity, take away her life, commit her people to slaughter, alter the form of government and religion; and upon this wicked resolution, on the 12th day of Feb. 1600, in the afternoon about the hours of four and five, he the said Captain Lee repaired to the chamber of one Sir Robert Crosse, Knight in the parish of St. Giles in the Fields, of purpose to discover his plot to him, and to persuade the said Sir Robert Crosse to consent to join with him; namely to go to the royal palace of our sovereign lady, being then at Westminster, and then and there to lay violent hands on her sacred person, and to take her prisoner; thinking by that means to set at liberty the Earls of Essex and Southampton, and other traitors now in prison. But the said Sir Robert Crosse not consenting to that traitorous practice; this Thomas Lee himself repaired to the said royal palace between the hours of 3 and 9 in the same night and pressed into the presence, even to the Privy-Chamber door with purpose to have taken the person of our said sovereign lady and performed his other traitorous designs. But there in that manner was apprehended, and examined, and so committed to prison.

To this being asked whether he were guilty, or not? He answered, not guilty in manner and form as there set down. And by whom he would be tried? Said, by God and the country if he might see his jury, he said farther, (protesting he was not guilty of any ill intent) that my Lord Admiral had long sought his life, and now he was like to have it.

The jury called, he took exception to one, saying he liked not his face but urged to show other reasons, he challenged him peremptorily. But that, the judges told him, could not be allowed in that case.

Captain Lee. Then I am contented; proceed as you will.

My L. C. Justice. At the end of the calling and impaneling, advertised the jury what treason was; namely to intend to lay violent hands upon her majesty, or to take away her life; to raise rebellion even the intent was treason, if it could be discovered by any overt act.

Attorney General. That he would prove him that stood at the bar, guilty of many foul treasons.

Captain Lee. Nay for all your wit and learning, you shall never do that. I care not what you can say. I have lost a great deal of blood in her majesty's service, and done good service in Ireland.

Attorney General. That we shall see anon; and proceeded upon the indictment where he showed how in the late rebellion of that arch-traitor Essex. For, said he, all the nobility draw their honor and dignity of the Queen, as the stars take the light from the sun; and so when they enter into any rebellions and traitorous practices against her majesty, they deprive themselves of the light, as it were, of that glory and honor which before time they received from her, the chief and fountain of all their light and so he doubted not to call those persons traitors, who, whilst they stood, were noblemen; and now, failing of their allegiance, lost their titles. In the late rebellion of this traitor Essex, this Lee came *flagrante crimine*, and offered his service to the Lord Admiral, and Mr. Secretary, as he pretended to kill the earl which he said he could do, as being well acquainted and loved of the earl but they refusing, he would needs have offered so much to the Queen's majesty; but with what mind, his practice will discover.

Captain Lee. It is true, I would have been the first man should have gone against him whilst I thought him a traitor, and so would have adventured against any, to have defended the Queen.

Attorney General. How you meant it that will be plain anon. After this he came to Sir Henry Nevil, a gentleman of noble blood and uttered his mind to him concerning the practice in the indictment; and after that came to Sir Robert Cross, as you shall hear and opened his vile purpose at large to persuade him. That these worthy men deserving all honor for their loyalty, refused, and revealed his vile plot in good time. And thus much he had confessed under his hand.

Captain Lee, What I have set my hand to, I cannot tell; but I am sure I had never such intent as you would persuade the jury I had.

Attorney General. That is to be proved by Sir Robert Crosse, what you meant when you went about to persuade him.

Captain Lee. I persuaded him not; and he will not say so.

Attorney General. Well; he shall speak it before your face.

Then Sir Robert Crosse was sworn and set in sight of the prisoner; and began to tell that upon Thursday about 5 at night, Captain Lee came to his lodging, he being ready to go abroad, and told him he should not go out, yet he must speak with him; and so taking him aside, he spoke to him of these matters of treason, and said that half a dozen resolute men, &c.

Captain Lee here interrupted him; saying nay good Robin Crosse, speak all the truth.

Mr. Attorney willed Lee to give him leave to speak upon his oath.

Captain Lee replied, I would nothing but put him in mind of the circumstance; and said Good Robin, remember how I began.

Sir Robert said he would. Thus then you spoke to me. I marvel what will become of these matters; a man might do a brave act to set those lords at liberty. Why how? Quote I, merry Sir Walter Raleigh might get him eternal honor and love more than ever he can otherwise if he would procure her majesty's warrant to free them, which he might compass by undertaking her person. I answered, you may be sure he will not do it. Then Lee replied, if half a dozen resolute men such as might have access to the presence, would step to the Queen and kneel before her and never rise till she had signed a warrant and then send it by the Lord Admiral, and never stir till the Earls of Essex and Southampton were brought to the Queen's presence, they might do it. And then he named Sir Henry Nevil, Sir Jarvis Clifton, Sir George Gifford, Sir R. Weston, and themselves. I objected how if some should offer to come upon us and remove us from her majesty, he answered we might keep anybody out by shutting the door and telling them that offered to come in, that if any harm came to the Queen, if she should do otherwise than well, be it at their peril; and this was all. To which Sir Robert answered, he would sleep upon it.

Captain Lee. But I did persuade you Sir Robert with protestation, saying I never meant to be an actor myself or persuade any other to it. And what a wretch am I to be thought a villain for that I never meant? For my Lord Essex, indeed I loved and honored him so long as I thought him an honest man and a good subject. I spoke these words with an if; if such a thing could be done.

Attorney General. Why pressed you to the Privy Chamber door at such a time, where you were not wont to come?

And then was showed the examination of William Poynes, (who was himself in the Fleet) to this purpose that he saw Captain Lee press towards the Privy Chamber door and stand very near, and mistrusting the worst, drew towards him. When he came near he marked his color that was pale, his countenance stern, and his face having great drops of sweat standing on it. When he came near to him, Captain Lee leaned hard on him and said it was one of the wonders of God that I was not in this action with the Earl of Essex. Why? Said Mr. Poynes. I was so well acquainted, and so much with my Lord of Essex, answered he. Then they paused. And Captain Lee asked whether the Queen were at supper? Mr. Poynes answered, no.

Attorney General. Mark, all the rest was but to bring in this.

Mr. Poynes told Lee further perhaps he might do good service if he were so well acquainted with the earl; it was likely he knew somewhat of the plot. Not I, answered Lee; but you shall hear more villainies and knaveries yet.

Attorney General. Mark what meant he by that speech?

To this Captain Lee could not deny but he spoke it; but said how was I there? Had I any company? Had I any dagger or anything about me that might show I meant to do the Queen any harm? No, I had not, neither did I mean any such thing; and for my being at the Privy Chamber door, I had been there 500 times, and never was noted. And what reason had I for my Lord of Essex to adventure any such thing. I have spent my blood in her majesty's service, and so would again.

Attorney General. You mark there was love between him and the traitor Essex. And then Mr. Attorney caused a letter to be read which was written in the behalf of Lee to the now deputy by the Earl of Essex: "That he knew it was for one in place to do what he would; and farther, what an unreasonable thing it was for any to require that at his friends hands, that were out of time. He desired his lordship to take notice of the bearer Captain Lee, one near allied to him, and that suffered for him; one that did as good service as any, when himself was in Ireland, and one that was as well seated for service as any; thus, whatsoever he did for the bearer, he would acknowledge as for himself: and so he concluded."

Then likewise was read the confession of Captain Lee this purpose that he loved and honored the Earl of Essex as much as any man in England, saving Sir Henry Lee.

Attorney General. This being but the prologue to an ensuing tragedy, he would give a taste of the practices and treasons of the Earl of Essex and his accomplices.

Captain Lee. He doubted the treason would light on some of them that held the earl a traitor.

Whereat a confused noise there was, that he was a villain to defend a traitor.

Mr. Attorney proceeded to show the Queen's great grace in sending to him the said earl and the contempt and indignities offered to those honorable persons and counselors sent to call him to his allegiance.

The *L. C. Justice* spoke to this point confirming of his own knowledge what the attorney said, much after the manner it was delivered at the earl's arraignment. The attorney continued he would of his own knowledge affirm that all the associates and accomplices of the earl in this practice were of these three sorts either Atheists, Papists, or men of broken estates: for he had looked into them all particularly. Then named he Sir Christopher Blunt and Sir John Davis, known Papists: Catesby and Tresham likewise; the last of which he said was a stock, that was *genere minax Dei*, and was he that abused the lord-keeper in Essex house; Salisbury also be named to be a notable villain and these seven years together laid out for by the Lord Chief Justice, and so of the rest he said he could speak.

Mr. Attorney. Besides in Ireland, it is plain to be proved how he held intelligence with seminaries and priests entertaining them to deal with the King of Spain and the Pope, to make himself King of England.

Captain Lee. Who! My Lord of Essex deal with seminaries and priests? Nay, it is well known he too much disliked those paternoster fellows to call them to a reckoning in any such matter.

Mr. Attorney said further it is well known that the Earl of Essex used this Captain Lee as a messenger to Tyrone; and Tyrone made him his bedfellow, and Captain Lee brought a message back to the Earl of Essex, as he had confessed. Then there was some mention of a letter between them; but I could not well hear what. Then was read Captain Lee's confession to that point how Sir Christopher Blunt being marshal, sent him to Tyrone and when he came, he found him very peremptory, using insolent speeches and condemning our nation as a base people and said the Earl of Essex was sent to kill him, but he should not compass it; any of his slaves might easily kill the earl, but he would not take the life of any. And further, if he would (meaning the Earl of Essex) follow his plot, he would make him the greatest in England. Captain Lee had them read out all they left out much matter that should be known.

Mr. Attorney would not have any further thing read, and pressed further the circumstances that Lee had confessed that made him think the Earl of Essex know of his going; namely for that the marshal was well known not to do such things of far less consequence, without the earl's privet and consent. Again, the Earl of Essex made a private sudden journey to the then house of the said Lee where the said Sir Christopher Blunt lay sick and within a day after, Sir Christopher sent him to Tyrone.

To these confessions read, Captain Lee answered nothing as not belonging to the matter of his indictment.

Mr. Attorney urged that it was very likely that this man had been made acquainted with these late practices; which Lee with protestation denied.

Mr. Attorney. Nay, it could not be but he must have an ill meaning that he should offer, as he did to kill the Earl of Essex, *flagrante crimine*, in that sort and after enter into this plot and practice. Mark, said the attorney, he said they might 'force' her majesty to do it: mark this word, 'force,' (which as I remember, was in some part of his own confession). 'Go in unto her and never leave her till she had done it.'

Captain Lee. Why I did say with an if; and then I am not a fool, but I know they must have been of a resolution that should have undertaken such a thing and such as would not fear to displease her majesty for half an hour, to please her all her life after but I never meant to have been an actor myself.

The court affirmed it was treason to undertake to 'force' her majesty to do anything against her will.

Captain Lee. I never undertook it.

Mr. Attorney urged his words to Sir Robert Mansfield riding in his coach after he was apprehended that showed himself guilty, and so willed Sir Robert should be sworn.

Sir Robert Mansfield affirmed that Captain Lee should say that he had humbly sued to her majesty this twelvemonth that he might be employed in some service, wherein he might have some throats cut and now he thought he had done somewhat to bring him to his end. Captain Lee seemed to take some exceptions against Sir Robert Mansfield.

Sir Robert protested he would neither wrong him, nor any man; and but for this cause, he had no reason to think otherwise than well of Captain Lee.

Captain Lee confessed he had lived in misery and cared not to live, his enemies were so many and so great.

Mr. Attorney urged her majesty's pardon to him heretofore; for he said he was a man many ways having passed the danger of the law, being full of cruelty and blood.

Captain Lee answered it was the worst thing her majesty did for him, to pardon him.

Mr. Attorney. Hark, how ungrateful he is!

Captain Lee. Nay, I humbly thank her majesty for that her grace; but it had been better for me I had died then. I have lost a great deal of blood since, and now am like to end worse and for that it is said I am a bloody man and cruel; I protest I have been in her majesty's service forward, and indeed in fair sight I would do the worst against her majesty's enemies but when they submitted to my mercy, I ever used them but as became a soldier and a gentleman, as merciful as any.

My Lord of London told him he knew it was a common thing in Ireland, they would not believe a man was dead till his head were off; and so you would not have anybody persuaded that you were a traitor, unless her majesty (God bless her) were dead.

Captain Lee. No, my lord, I never meant any such thing. You know my lord, it was never my fault to be loose and lavish of my tongue; and that was my fault now, and I am like to pay for it.

Then the jury were put together who quickly found him guilty.

Upon verdict given, Mr. Attorney said now Captain Lee, you may do well to confess this matter, what you know, and who set you on.

Captain Lee. What? I am not a fool to be set on like a dog upon a bear; nobody set me on, for I endeavored nothing.

Mr. Recorder with a very grave admonition to him, to make him see his fault and fly to God's mercy for pardon, pronounced judgment; which he took patiently.

They asked him, what he had to say, he answered nothing; but desired my lord of London that he might have one sent to him, fit for a man in his case.

Lord of London. What? You would not have a Jesuit or a priest?

Captain Lee. No, I am a Protestant. I never liked those Paternoster fellows; but I desire a minister and to receive the Sacrament: and further I desire my Lord Chief Justice that my son may have no wrong, and that he may have that little that he had got together and should leave behind him; for it was his by right and his son might prove an honest man and do his country good service one day.

L. C. Justice. He should have his right; nobody should be wronged. So the court broke up. Captain Lee still protesting he never intended any such thing against the Queen as was laid to his charge; which he continued to affirm afterwards to Mr. Pasfield to whom he confessed his other sins very freely even taking his death upon it. He died the next day at Tyburn very Christianly confessing his other vices, but still denying this.

[*Cobbett's Complete Collection of State Trials.* 1403-1410]

Bibliography

Primary Sources:

Cobbet's Complete Collection of State Trials. V1. London, 1809.

Emlyn, Sollom. *Complete Collection of State-Trials and Proceedings for High-Treason and other Crimes and Misdemeanours. V1.* London, 1742.

Friedman, Paul. *Anne Boleyn, a Chapter of English History.* London, 1884.

Harleian Miscellany, or a Collection of Scarce, Curious, and Entertaining Pamphlets and Tracts. Vol.1. London, 1808.

Holinshed, Raphael. *The First and Second Volumes of Chronicles, Comprising, The Description and History of England, Ireland and Scotland.* London England: Henry Denham at Aldersgate Street, 1587.

Howell, Thomas. *A Complete Collection of State Trials. V-1.* London, 1816.

Stephen, James. *A History of The Criminal Law of England.* 3 volumes. London, 1883.

Strype, John. *Historical Memorials, Ecclesiastical and Civil, of Events under the Reign of Queen Mary I.* London, 1721.

The Life of Thomas Cranmer Archbishop of Canterbury. London, 1856.

Trumbull, Jonathan H. *The True-Blue Laws of Connecticut and New Haven and the False Blue-Laws.* Hartford, Conn. 1876.

Willis-Bund, J. W. *A Selection of Cases from the State Trials. V-1.* Cambridge, 1879.

Secondary Sources:

Acts of the Privy Council of England. Vol. I., A.D. 1542–1547.

Bacon, Francis. *The History of the Reigns of Henry the Seventh, Henry the Eighth, Edward the Sixth and Queen Mary.* London, 1676.

Bayley, John Esq. F.S.A. *The History and Antiquities of the Tower of London.* In two volumes. London: T. Cadell, 1821-25.

Benger, Elizabeth and Aikin, Lucy. *Memoirs of the Life of Anne Boleyn, Queen of Henry VIII.* London, 1827.

Blackstone, Sir William. *Commentaries on the Laws of England.* Dublin, 1796. 4 volumes reviewed.

Blaxland, George. *Codex Legum Anglicanarum; or, A Digest of Principles of English Law.* London, 1939.

Bouvier, John. *Bouvier's Law Dictionary.* Boston, 1897.

Bowyer, George. *Commentaries on the Constitutional Law of England.* London, 1846.

Bright, J. Franck. *A History of England-Period II.* New York, 1878.

Calendar of State Papers, Domestic Series, of the Reigns of Edward VI, Mary, Elizabeth, 1547-1580. London, 1856.

Calendar of State Papers, Domestic Series, of the Reign of Elizabeth, 1601–1601, with Addenda, 1547-1565. London, 1870.

Calendar of State Papers, Foreign Series, of the Reign of Elizabeth, 1559–1560. London, 1865.

Calendar of State Papers, Foreign Series, of the Reign of Mary, 1553–1558. London, 1861.

Calendar of State Papers, Relating to Scotland. Vol. II The Scottish Series of the Reign of Queen Elizabeth, 1589–1603. London, 1858.

Chalmers, George. *The Life of Mary, Queen of Scots; Drawn from the State Papers.* 2 volumes. London, 1818.

Churton, Edward. *The Early English Church.* London, 1840.

Crabb, George. *A History of English Law; or Attempt to Trace the Rise, Progress and Successive Changes of Common Law.* Burlington, 1831.

Dasent, John Roche. *Acts of the Privy Council of England.* London, 1890.

Douglas, David. *Life of James Hepburn, Earl of Bothwell.* Edinburgh, 1880.

Encyclopedia Britannica, The. Volume IV. Cambridge, England. 1910.

England in the Sixteenth Century. London, The Religious Tract Society, 1841.

Edward VI. *Writings of Edward the Sixth, William Hugh, Queen Catherine Parr, Anne Askew, Lady Jane Grey, Hamilton, and Balnaves.* London, 1831.

Godwin, Francis. *Annals of England: Containing the Reigns of Henry the Eighth, Edward the Sixth, Queen Mary.* London England: by W.G. for T. Basset, 1675.

Hamilton, William Douglas. *A Chronicle of England, During the Reigns of the Tudors, from A.D. 1485 to 1559. By Charles Wriothesley, Windsor Herald.* London, 1877.

Hargrave, Francis. *A Complete Collection of State Trials and Proceedings. V-1.* London, 1776.

Heylyn, Peter. *Ecclesia Restaurata, or The History of the Reformation of the Church of England.* London England: H. Twyford, 1661.

Holdsworth, W. S. *A History of English Law.* London, 1903.

Hume, David. *The History of England, Under the House of Tudor.* Two volumes. London, 1759.

Hyland, George K. *A Century of Persecution.* London, 1920.

Jardine, David. *Criminal Trials. The Library of Entertaining Knowledge, Volume I.* London, 1832.

General Index to the Collection of State Trials. London, 1828.

Lee, Sidney. *Dictionary of National Biography. Vol. XLIII.* (Biographical information on William Parry). New York, 1895.

Life and Reign of that Excellent Princess Queen Elizabeth, from her Birth to her Death. London, 1748.

Lloyd, Charles Edward. *State Trials of Mary, Queen of Scots, Sir Walter Raleigh and Captain William Kidd.* Chicago, 1899.

Lolme, John. *The Rise and Progress of the English Constitution.* Two volumes. London, 1835.

Millar, John. *An Historical View of the English Government from the Settlement of the Saxons in Britain to the Accession of the House of Stewart.* London, 1790.

Morgan, J. *Phoenix Britannicus; Being a Miscellaneous Collection of Scarce and Curious Tracts.* London, 1732.

Nichols, John Gough. *The Chronicle of Queen Jane and of Two Years of Queen Mary and Especially of the Rebellion of Sir Thomas Wyatt.* Camden Society, 1850.

——, *The Legend of Sir Nicholas Throckmorton.* London, 1874.

Pitcairn, Robert. Esq. *Criminal Trials in Scotland, from 1488 to 1624.* Edinburgh, 1833.

Popham, Sir John. *Reports and Cases, Collected and Learned Sr. John Popham Kt., Late Lord Chief Justice of England.* London, 1682.

Raven, John. *The Parliamentary History of England from the Earliest Period to the Year 1803.* London, 1806.

Reeves, John. *History of the English Law, from the time of the Saxons to the end of the Reign of Philip and Mary.* Four volumes. London, 1787.

Ruddiman, Thomas. *Collections Relating to the History of Mary Queen of Scotland. Vol. III.* Edinburgh, 1724.

Salmon, Thomas. *A Critical Review of the State Trials.* London, 1735.

Scott, Walter. *A Collection of Scarce and Valuable Tracts. V.1.* (Biographical information of John Story) London, 1809.

Smith, Philip A. *A History of Education for the English Bar.* London, 1860.

Stowe, John. *The Abridgement of the English Chronicle, First Collected by M. Iohn Stow.* London 1611.

The Annales of England, Faithfully collected out of the most autenticall authors, records and other monuments of antiquitie. London 1605.

Street, Thomas A. *The Foundations of Legal Liability.* New York, 1906.

Strype, John. *Ecclesiastical Memorials: relating chiefly to religion, and its reformation, under the reigns of King Henry VIII. King Edward VI. And Queen Mary the First: with the appendixes containing the original papers, records, etc.* London, 1816.

——, *Ecclesiastical memorials, relating chiefly to religion, and the reformation of it, and the emergencies of the Church of England, under King Henry VIII. King Edward VI. and Queen Mary I.* London, 1822.

Stuart, Gilbert. *Lectures on the Constitution and Laws of England with a Commentary on Magna Charta.* Portland, 1805.

Taylor, Hannis. *The Origin and Growth of the English Constitution.* Boston, 1900.

Whitaker, John. *Mary Queen of Scots Vindicated. Vol. I.* London, 1790.
Williams, C. H. *The Rebellion of Humphrey Stafford in 1486.* Published in *The English Historical Review*, Vol. 43, No. 170 (April, 1928) pages 181-189. The Oxford University Press.
Whishaw, James. *A Synopsis of the Members of the English Bar.* London, 1835.
Wotton, Thomas. *The English Baronetage: Containing a Genealogical and Historical Account of all the English Baronets.* London, 1741.
Wright, Thomas. *Queen Elizabeth and Her Times.* Two volumes. London, 1838.

Made in United States
Orlando, FL
04 November 2026

90200862R10286